Lecture Notes in Compı   34

Commenced Publication in 1973
Founding and Former Series Editors:
Gerhard Goos, Juris Hartmanis, and Jan v.   ..uwen

Jürgen Münch Matias Vierimaa (Eds.)

Product-Focused Software Process Improvement

7th International Conference, PROFES 2006
Amsterdam, The Netherlands, June 12-14, 2006
Proceedings

Volume Editors

Jürgen Münch
Fraunhofer Institute for Experimental Software Engineering
Fraunhofer-Platz, 67663 Kaiserslautern, Germany
E-mail: Juergen.Muench@iese.fraunhofer.de

Matias Vierimaa
VTT Electronics
Kaitovayla 1,90570 Oulu, Finland
E-mail: Matias.Vierimaa@vtt.fi

Library of Congress Control Number: 2006926730

CR Subject Classification (1998): D.2, K.6, K.4.2, J.1

LNCS Sublibrary: SL 2 – Programming and Software Engineering

ISSN 0302-9743
ISBN-10 3-540-34682-1 Springer Berlin Heidelberg New York
ISBN-13 978-3-540-34682-1 Springer Berlin Heidelberg New York

Springer is a part of Springer Science+Business Media

springer.com

Printed in Germany

Typesetting: Camera-ready by author, data conversion by Scientific Publishing Services, Chennai, India
Printed on acid-free paper SPIN: 11767718 06/3142 5 4 3 2 1 0

Preface

The 7th International Conference on Product Focused Software Process Improvement (PROFES 2006) brought together researchers and industrial practitioners for reporting new research results and exchanging experiences and findings in the area of process and product improvement. The focus of the conference was on understanding, evaluating, controlling, and improving the relationship between process improvement activities (such as the deployment of innovative defect detection processes) and their effects on products (such as improved product reliability and safety). Consequently, major topics of the conference included the evaluation of existing software process improvement (SPI) approaches in different contexts, the presentation of new or modified SPI approaches, and the relation between SPI and new development techniques or emerging application domains.

The need for SPI is being widely recognized. Current trends in software intensive systems such as increased distribution of software development and growing dependability on software-intensive systems in everyday life emphasize this need. This implies the establishment of advanced process improvement capabilities and an adequate understanding of the impact of the processes on the generated products, services, and business value in different situations. Recent trends enforce the establishment of such capabilities: more and more products are being developed in distributed, global environments with many customer-supplier relations in the development chain. Outsourcing, off-shoring, near-shoring, and in-sourcing aggravate this trend. In addition, systems are being built from multiple disciplines (such as electronics, mechanics, and software). Supporting such distributed and multi-disciplinary development requires well-understood and accurately implemented development process interfaces, process synchronization, and process evolution. In addition, more and more organizations are forced to adhere to regulatory constraints that require the existence of explicit processes and the demonstration of adherence to those processes. Examples are the IEC 61508 standard for safety-related systems, the tailoring of ECSS (European Cooperation for Space Standardization) software engineering standards for ground segments in ESA (European Space Agency), or the German national standard V-Model XT for systems used by public authorities. Adhering to those standards requires systematic evolution of the existing processes. Finally, market dynamics force organizations to adapt better and faster to changes in the development environment and to enforce innovations (e.g., increase of reliability levels). These process changes impose risk challenges for SPI approaches. Advanced SPI is required to support the assessment of the impact of process changes and the flexible adaptation of processes. Due to the fact that software development processes are human-based and depend on the development context (including domain characteristics, workforce capabilities, and organizational maturity), changes to these processes typically cause significant costs and should be considered carefully. Alternative improvement options need to be evaluated with respect to their implementation cost and their potential impact on business goals.

Currently, two types of SPI approaches are mainly used in practice: a) continuous SPI approaches (also referred to as problem-oriented approaches) and b) model-based SPI approaches (also referred to as solution-oriented approaches).

Continuous SPI approaches (such as the Quality Improvement Paradigm, PDCA, or Profes) focus on selected problems of a software development organization and usually involve improvement cycles based on an initial baseline. One important advantage of continuous approaches is that they focus on solving specific problems by analyzing the problem at hand, implementing and observing problem-focused improvement actions, and measuring the effects of the actions. The interpretation of the measurement data is used as input for further optimization of the solution. In addition, solving one problem typically reveals further improvement potential in related areas. Continuous approaches are focused and, therefore, it is difficult to create an overall awareness for quality issues in a very large software organization with thousands of employees.

Model-based SPI approaches (such as ISO/IEC 15504, CMMI, or BOOTSTRAP) compare the current processes and practices of a development organization against a reference model or a benchmark. They provide so-called capability maturity levels with different sets of processes and practices. These levels define an improvement roadmap. The advantage of such models is that they can be easily used to enforce an awareness for quality issues in large organizations because many developers are involved in the improvement of the maturity level. From the management point of view, reaching a specific capability level can be defined as a clear and assessable goal. One important disadvantage is that model-based SPI approaches typically do not assess the impact of processes on product characteristics and therefore cannot be used to analytically identify and tackle process problems that cause concrete product deficiencies. Typically, it is checked whether a process or practice is in place, but its impact on a business goal or its value for the organization is not evaluated. The practices of the reference models are usually of a generic type and based on hypothesis. Having a high maturity level does not mean that the organization is successful in fulfilling its business goals (such as an appropriate trade-off between time-to-market and product quality).

Continuous and model-based SPI approaches can be seen as being complementary: model-based approaches can be used to identify problem areas and potential improvement options, and continuous approaches can be used to implement and optimize solutions. Although continuous approaches can be successfully applied without having a high maturity level, model-based approaches usually require continuous improvement at a certain maturity level.

In practice, the typical question is no longer whether process improvement is necessary, but how to define and implement a strategy for introducing advanced process improvement step by step and how to evaluate its success. Along with this, many research questions need to be solved.

The technical program was selected by a committee of leading experts in software process modeling and software process improvement research. This year, 55 papers from 26 nations were submitted, with each paper receiving at least three reviews. The Program Committee met in Amsterdam for one full day in February 2006. The Program Committee finally selected 26 technical full papers. The topics indicate that software process improvement remains a vibrant research discipline of high interest for industry. Emerging technologies and application domains, a paradigm shift from software to system engineering in many domains (such as automotive or space), and the need for better decision support for software process improvement is reflected in these papers.

The technical program consisted of tracks-decision support, embedded software and system development, measurement, industrial experiences, process improvement, agile development practices, and product line engineering. In addition, a track with 12 selected short paper presentations was added in order to demonstrate the variety of approaches, to support the discussions, and to exchange experience. We were proud to have four keynote speakers, Jan Bosch, Jan Jaap Cannegieter, Michiel van Gnuchten, and Barbara Kitchenham, as well as interesting tutorials and co-located workshops.

We are thankful for the opportunity to serve as program co-chairs for this conference. The Program Committee members and reviewers provided excellent support in reviewing the papers. We are also grateful to the authors, presenters, and session chairs for their time and effort to make PROFES 2006 a success. The General Chair, Rini van Solingen, and the Steering Committee provided excellent guidance. We wish to thank the Fraunhofer Institute for Experimental Software Engineering (IESE), the Centrum for Wiskunde en Informatika (CWI), VTT, the University of Oulu, Drenthe University, and Eindhoven University of Technology for supporting the conference. We would like to thank the Organizing Committee and all the other supporters for making the event possible. Last but not least, many thanks to Timo Klein at IESE for copyediting this volume.

April 2006

Jürgen Münch
Matias Vierimaa

Conference Organization

General Chair

Rini van Solingen, Drenthe University (The Netherlands)

Program Co-chairs

Jürgen Münch, Fraunhofer IESE (Germany)
Matias Vierimaa, VTT Electronics (Finland)

Organizing Chair

Mark van den Brand, Hogeschool van Amsterdam and CWI (The Netherlands)

Tutorial Chair

Dirk Hamann, Fraunhofer IESE (Germany)

Industry Chair

Carol Dekkers, Quality Plus Technologies, Inc.

PR Chair

Pasi Kuvaja, University of Oulu (Finland)

Publicity Chairs

Central Europe:	Michael Ochs, Fraunhofer IESE (Germany)
Southern Europe:	Gerardo Canfora, University of Sannio at Benevento (Italy)
USA:	Ioana Rus, Fraunhofer Center-Maryland (USA)
Canada:	Dietmar Pfahl, University of Calgary (Canada)
Japan:	Kenichi Matumoto, NAIST (Japan)
Korea:	Ho-Won Jung, Korea University (Korea)
Finland:	Tua Huomo, VTT Electronics (Finland)
Scandinavia:	Tora Dyba, Chief Scientist, SINTEF (Norway)
Benelux:	Ko Doorns, Philips
France:	Pierre-Etienne Moreau, INRIA/LORIA Nancy (France)
Oceania:	Bernard Wong, University of Technology, Sydney (Australia)
South America:	Christiane Gresse van Wangenheim (Brazil)

Program Committee

Pekka Abrahamsson, VTT Electronics, Finland
Andreas Birk, SD&M, Germany
Mark van den Brand, HvA & CWI, The Netherlands
Gerardo Canfora, University of Sannio at Benevento, Italy
Reidar Conradi, NTNU, Norway
Paolo Donzelli, University of Maryland - College Park, USA
Tore Dybå, SINTEF, Norway
Martin Höst, Lund University, Sweden
Frank Houdek, DaimlerChrysler, Germany
Tua Huomo, VTT Electronics, Finland
Hajimu Iida, Nara Institute of Science & Technology, Japan
Katsuro Inoue, Osaka University, Japan
Yasushi Ishigai, IPA, Japan
Janne Järvinen, Solid Information Technology, Finland
Erik Johansson, Q-Labs, Sweden
Philip Johnson, University of Hawaii, USA
Natalia Juristo, Universidad Politecnica de Madrid, Spain
Haruhiko Kaiya, Shinshu University, Japan
Kari Känsälä, Nokia Research Center, Finland
Masafumi Katahira, JAXA, Japan
Pasi Kuvaja, University of Oulu, Finland
Makoto Matsushita, Osaka University, Japan
Kenichi Matsumoto, NAIST, Japan
Pierre-Etienne Moreau, INRIA/LORIA, France
Maurizio Morisio, University of Turin, Italy
Jürgen Münch, Fraunhofer IESE, Germany
Paolo Nesi, University of Florence, Italy
Risto Nevalainen, STTF, Finland
Mahmood Niazi, Keele University, UK
Michael Ochs, Fraunhofer IESE, Germany
Hideto Ogasawara, Toshiba, Japan
Dietmar Pfahl, University of Calgary, Canada
Teade Punter, LAQUSO, The Netherlands
Karl Reed, La Tobe University, Australia
Günther Ruhe, University of Calgary, Canada
Ioana Rus, Fraunhofer Center - Maryland, USA
Kurt Schneider, University of Hannover, Germany
Carolyn Seaman, UMBC, Baltimore, USA
Veikko Seppäen, Elektrobit Ltd., Finland
Dag Sjöberg, University of Oslo, Norway
Matias Vierimaa, VTT Electronics, Finland
Otto Vinter, DELTA, Denmark
Giuseppe Visaggio, University of Bari, Italy
Hironori Washizaki, National Institute of Informatics, Japan
Isabella Wieczorek, Federal Ministery of Research and Education, Germany

Claes Wohlin, Blekinge Institute of Technology, Sweden
Bernard Wong, University of Technology Sydney, Australia

External Reviewers

Silvia Acuña, University of Madrid, Spain
Fabio Bella, Fraunhofer IESE, Germany
Jens Heidrich, Fraunhofer IESE, Germany
Sira Vegas, University of Madrid, Spain
Stein Grimstad, University of Oslo, Norway

Table of Contents

Keynote Addresses

Decision Support

Embedded Software and System Development

Measurement

Industrial Experiences

Process Improvement

Agile Development Practices

Product Line Engineering

Short Papers

Workshops

Tutorials

Processes and the Software Business

Michiel van Genuchten

General Manager, Philips HDSoftware

The amount of software in many electronic products is growing rapidly. Two examples: the amount of software in a mobile phone is expected to increase from 2 million today to 20 million in 2010. The amount of software in a car in 2010 is expected to be 100 million lines of source code (Charrette, 2005). Many companies see their business change from a hardware business to a software business. The impact on companies goes far beyond development and development processes. Adoption of proper software sales and legal processes is as important. The presentation is based on research into the software business and 10 years of experience in managing software companies.

J. Münch and M. Vierimaa (Eds.): PROFES 2006, LNCS 4034, p. 1, 2006.

Controlling the Chaos of the CMMI Continuous Representation

Jan Jaap Cannegieter

Director of SYSQA

In 2000, the Software Engineering Institute introduced the continuous representation of the CMMI. In the following years, many organizations based their process improvement effort on this representation. Despite the advantages of this model, several of these organizations found it hard to make a choice of which process areas to implement first. To help organizations make these decisions, three improvement paths are recognized: Project, Process and Product. This so-called PPP concept of continuous and the improvement paths will be addressed in this keynote presentation.

J. Münch and M. Vierimaa (Eds.): PROFES 2006, LNCS 4034, p. 2, 2006.

Evidence-Based Software Engineering and Systematic Literature Reviews

Barbara Kitchenham

Professor of Quantitative Software Engineering at Keele University

This keynote addresses the evidence-based paradigm currently being adopted in many practical sciences (e.g., medicine, education, social policy) and discusses whether it is applicable to software engineering. In the presentation, the view is taken that although Evidence-based Software Engineering may be unproven, one aspect of the evidence-based paradigm is hard to ignore, that is: Systematic literature reviews. Systematic literature reviews aim to summarize research studies related to a specific research question in a way that is fair, rigorous, and auditable. The keynote presentation will outline the potential benefit of systematic literature reviews and describe in detail the process of performing such a systematic literature review.

J. Münch and M. Vierimaa (Eds.): PROFES 2006, LNCS 4034, p. 3, 2006.

Expanding the Scope of Software Product Families: Problems and Alternative Approaches

Jan Bosch

Vice President of Research, Nokia Research

Software product families have found broad adoption in Nokia, the telecom industry, and the embedded systems industry as a whole. Product family thinking has been prevalent in this context for mechanics and hardware, and adopting the same for software has been viewed as a logical approach. During recent years, however, the trends of convergence, end-to-end solutions, shortened innovation and R&D cycles and differentiation through software engineering capabilities have led to a development where organizations are stretching the scope of their product families far beyond the initial design. Failing to adjust the product family approach, including the architectural and process dimensions, when the business strategy is changing is leading to several challenging problems that can be viewed as symptoms of this approach. The presentation discusses the key symptoms, the underlying causes for these symptoms as well as solutions for realigning the product family approach with the business strategy. The presentation uses examples from Nokia to illustrate the solutions and approaches that will be discussed.

J. Münch and M. Vierimaa (Eds.): PROFES 2006, LNCS 4034, p. 4, 2006.

Defining the Process for Making Software System Modernization Decisions

Jarmo J. Ahonen[1,*], Henna Sivula[2], Jussi Koskinen[2], Heikki Lintinen[2], Tero Tilus[2], Irja Kankaanpää[2], and Päivi Juutilainen[2]

[1] Department of Computer Science,
University of Kuopio, P.O. Box 1627, FI-70211 Kuopio, Finland
jarmo.ahonen@uku.fi

[2] Information Technology Research Institute,
P.O. Box 35 (Agora) FI-40014 University of Jyväskylä, Finland
{henna.sivula, jussi.koskinen, heikki.lintinen, tero.tilus, irja.kankaanpaa, paivi.juutilainen}@titu.jyu.fi

Abstract. This paper outlines a process for software system modernization decisions. The rationale of the process is explained and the process is defined in a way that allows its adaptation for other organizations and situations. The process is a light-weight one and is based on the use of objective data. The procedures for collecting the data are explained. The process has been used to solve a real industrial decision making situation in which the process was successful.

1 Introduction

Many large software systems, whether tailored or not, are nearing or have reached an age which makes it necessary to decide what to do with them. The alternatives are normally to do nothing really new — to continue with normal maintenance as before — reengineer the system, modernize the system, or replace the system. For large software-oriented service provider or user organizations those decisions may be so common that the process of making such decisions should be documented and guidelines for decisions should be provided. The making of those decisions should be implemented as a well-thought part of the collection of software engineering processes of the organization.

The reason why those decisions should be seriously considered is that the decision whether to modernize an old system is a remarkable one in the case of a business critical system. Major modernizations create several risks to the user organization. Those risks include the possible bugginess, potential misunderstandings of the previously implemented business-critical knowledge, delays, and many other issues that may have negative impacts to the business of the user organization. Therefore the economic impacts of the decisions can be remarkably higher than the actual software engineering costs caused by the decision. In the case of information technology infrastructure outsourcing or major long-time agreements those economic impacts should be taken into account by the service provider organizations' software engineering process.

* Corresponding author.

J. Münch and M. Vierimaa (Eds.): PROFES 2006, LNCS 4034, pp. 5–18, 2006.

One of the issues that should be taken into account is the fact that the life-cycle costs of an information system tend to have 50–70 % of maintenance costs [1] — those costs may be even higher [2][3]. That level of costs is not a surprise considering the remarkable amount of effort already invested into an old legacy system. It is, however, the case that an information system has to evolve in order to maintain its usability in the changing world and that as a consequence of the evolution the system becomes more and more complex and difficult to manage [4]. For every system there will be a day when the user organization and the service provider organization have to decide what to do with the system.

The cost of the modernization effort depends greatly on the complexity of the system [5]. Although complexity and potential costs are major factors in the modernization and replacement decisions [6], the actual need for the change should be considered. The systems' ability to perform its assigned task is one of the most important decision factors. The suitability of the system for the processes can be estimated by analyzing the business value of the system and the exceptions and other types of problems encountered in the normal use of the system. Exceptions are real-world cases which have be handled in order to perform the business process but which cannot be handled by using the system in question [7].

The most common software process improvement frameworks do not provide required answers for an organization that wants to improve its decision processes regarding old software systems. At least CMMI [8] and ISO [9] reference models do not include necessary information. There are some decision frameworks proposed. The most promising ones are the planning framework for reengineering proposed by Sneed [10] and the decisional framework for legacy system management proposed by De Lucia, Fasolino and Pompella [11]. Both of those frameworks stress that the business value of the existing software system should be evaluated and the ability of that system to serve the business should be analyzed.

Neither of those frameworks do, however, provide a sufficiently detailed description of the actual decision making process. Therefore an organization faced with such decisions has to develop and define a process of its own. In this article such a process is defined and tested with a real case. The structure of this article is: the rationale and the requirements set for the process and the definition of the process in Section 2 and outline of the industrial setting in which the process has been used for a test-run in Section 3, an overview of the data collected during the test-run (Section 4), a brief analysis of the process and its applicability in the real-world (Section 5), and discussion on the results and on the general importance of performing studies like the reported one (Section 6).

2 Defining the Process for Making Software System Modernization Decisions

The available models for the modernization decision process include the sub-process of finding out the business value of the analyzed system. Sneed's model [10] proposes the use of a business value evaluation table and De Lucia et al [11] propose a fairly similar approach to be used. Both of those approaches assume that the business value of the system should be analyzed, especially the utility value of the system [11] should be understood as well as the potential obsolescence of the system [10]. The utility value evaluation of the system includes understanding the business function coverage rate, actual usage frequency and user satisfaction of the system. The obsolescence is a factor of the deviation between the functions the software fulfills and what functions it is required to fulfill.

Using the proposed frameworks it is not easy to calculate the business value of a system or the obsolescence of a system. The difficulty it at least due to the fact that the actual process that should be used to calculate the business value of the system or the obsolescence of the system are not defined. Defined and controllably repeatable process of defining the business value of the system and the components of that business value are, however, required in order to create a stable and documented process for legacy system evaluation and management. A detailed work breakdown structure and documented processes are required already at the CMMI level 1 [12]. There is a clear need for a more detailed definition of the process and the techniques to be used if a company wants to improve its operations by using a reference model like CMMI.

The process should be easy to understand and based on unambiguous metrics. In order to be understandable the process should be very straightforward and the number of phases should be limited. During the early outlining of the requirements for the process it was decided that the process should concentrate on three main issues:

- the business value of the analyzed system;
- the obsolescence of the system; and
- the cost efficiency of the system.

The main criteria for deciding the business value of an information system were decided to be:

- the actual usability and usefulness of the system; and
- the amount of problems found in the system.

The usability and usefulness of the system were considered to be a combination of user satisfaction and usage metrics. The amount of problems was considered to be the sum of failures still present in the system and exceptions encountered in the real use of the system. In the vocabulary used in this article an exception denotes a situation which cannot be handled by an information system that should be able to handle the situation. In that sense the term exception is used in practically the same meaning as it has been used in [7].

The obsolescence of the system is not easy to measure. A part of the actual obsolescence is included in the problems — especially the exceptions — encountered in the normal use of a system. That measure was not, however, deemed sufficient because the number of exceptions do not tell anything about long-time trends without enough data over time. Therefore the problems data was decided to be accompanied with asking the users whether they think that the system is successful in everyday use and has the successfulness of the system increased or decreased. That query would reveal a metric that could be called the perceived obsolescence.

The cost efficiency was decided to be divided into:

- the cost of continuing maintenance as is;
- the cost of reengineering and its estimated business benefits;
- the cost of modernizing the system partially or as a whole and the estimated business benefits of the modernization; and
- the cost of replacement and its business benefits.

The calculation of the estimated business benefits is not, however, easy. There are no easily applicable methods for that purpose although some of existing ones can be used with proper modifications [13].

During the development of the process it was decided that the process should be as light to perform as possible. The process should not require large amount of effort from neither the software services provider nor the user organization. Therefore phases of the process should be light to perform and the used metrics should be unambiguous, easy to understand and easy to collect. The phases of the developed modernization/replacement need measurement process are:

P1 Create the timetable for the analysis in cooperation with the user organization (and the software services provider if necessary) and get the management to approve it.
P2 Get familiar with the system through documentation and interviews.
P3 Divide the use of the system into main functionalities which cover the most important parts of the system.
P4 Decide the trigger levels for the user satisfaction. See the definition of the phase P7 for different types of user satisfaction.
P5 Decide the trigger levels for the perceived obsolescence.
P6 Decide the trigger levels for the amount of working hours lost due to problems (including exceptions).
P7 Collect the user satisfaction data. Divide the user satisfaction into:
  P7.1 General user satisfaction (the whole system).
  P7.2 Perceived obsolescence, i.e. do the users think that the system is now better/worse than before. Perform this query for every main functionality.
  P7.3 Use of documentation and support.
P8 Collect data on exceptions and other problems during a suitable period of time. The data should include:
  P8.1 Data on different types of problems: frequencies and working hours lost.
  P8.2 Data on problems per main functionality.
P9 Analyze the results of the user-satisfaction query and the data on encountered problems and their economical impact.
P10 Decide whether any of the triggers fire. If a trigger fires, then the process used to perform the detailed analysis for the modernization/replacement decision should be started. In the other case the process stops here.

The pre-set level of required user-satisfaction is required in order to achieve honest decisions. That makes it sure that the interpretation of the query will be more objective and the level of user satisfaction will not be interpreted in a creative way. Setting the required levels will also help in describing and setting up the rationale for the decision.

The importance of setting the required or critical levels is even more important in the case of the working hours lost due to problems. The bugs are a sign of a bad program and the exceptions are a sign which tells that the system does not support the business process as well as it should. Both bugs and exceptions tell a clear story about the actual usefulness of the system.

3 Applying the Process in an Industrial Setting

The software services provider for which the process model was developed had delivered the first version of a complex system at the late 1980's. The provider and the user organization decided that the system in its current state would provide a suitable real-world setting for testing the process. The system will be denoted by the acronym WTB and its main functions were work tracking and customer billing. The problem with WTB was that there were many users who constantly complained that the user interface of WTB was bad and that the system was practically out of date. Therefore the management of the user organization had discussed the modernization needs of WTB and even the possibility of a complete replacement.

One of the reasons why that particular case was decided to be used was that the timing of the user organization's needs was suitable for the testing of the process. In addition to that, the user organization wanted to find out whether they should perform a more detailed analysis of the system from the evolution perspective and use methods like the ones reported in [14], [15], and [16]. Those methods were not, however, well known to the practitioners and the effort required by those methods was considered a way too expensive as the first level analysis. Therefore the developed light and business-value oriented process was very suitable for the user organization.

In order to provide sound answers to the outlined problem the guidelines of empirical research have been followed as well as possible in the field.. In [17] an extensive set of guidelines for empirical research has been provided. Also [18] and [19] have discussed these issues. Additional guidelines are provided in [17].

The process development was performed by academic researchers — the authors of this article — in close cooperation with the software services provider and the testing of the process in the real context was performed by the researchers. The whole work, including process development and real-world testing required about 80 effective working days from the researches. The amount of work invested by the software services provider or the user organization was not measured in any exact way. That work was estimated to be 9 days for the software services provider and 14 days for the user organization. Those amounts of work were in accordance to the required lightness of the process.

The duration of the project, i.e. applying the process in the real setting, was from May to March. The reasons for the long duration were the tight and limited resources available from both the software services provider and the user organization. Especially the available resources of the user organization were important in order to get the results meaningful. Another reason was that the process development was partly performed in parallel with the project. The phases of the project were:

- Determining the objectives of the project (May);
- Getting familiar with the system (June–August);
- Planning of the project (August–October);
- Planning of the user satisfaction query (October);
- Performing the query (November);
- Gathering and analyzing the results of the query (December–January);
- Planning the problem mapping procedure (January);
- Performing the problem mapping (February);
- Gathering and analyzing the results of problem mapping (March); and
- General analysis and reporting of the results (March).

The general objectives of the project was to finish the definition of the process for making software system modernization decisions and test the usefulness of the process with a real case. The final set of the objectives was set in cooperation with both the software services supplier and the user organization.

The second phase of the project was getting familiar with the system. That was performed by analyzing the functionality and structure of the system with the representatives of the software services provider and the user organization. During the visit to the user organization several members of the staff of the user organization were interviewed and several meetings held.

During the analysis of the system it turned out that the system was thought in terms that were related to the functionality provided by the system. That was a positive surprise since dividing the system into a group of functionalities, each of which consists of several individual functions, made it easier to measure the obsolescence of the system and to understand the relation between encountered problems and functionalities.

During that time it was decided that the internal functionality or system management oriented functionality or maintenance oriented functionality was excluded from the analysis. With the help from the users and the staff of the software services provider it was possible to distinguish 18 main functionalities — as defined in the process phase P3.

The user satisfaction query was performed by using a WWW-based system. The system presented questions using Likert-scale:

1. Nonexistent (N)
2. Bad (B)
3. Medium (M)
4. Good (G)
5. Excellent (E)

It was decided that answers N and B would be interpreted as negative or does not like. Answer G and E would be interpreted as does like, i.e. positive. Answer M was decided to be interpreted as neutral. In addition to that, each of the functionalities was divided into four subquestions which measured the following criteria:

1. Successfulness, in the beginning of the use;
2. Successfulness, current;
3. Usability; and

4. Performance and availability.

It was understood during the creation of the query that all of the users would not be able to answer every question. That was due to the fact that many of the frequent users used only a few of the main functions of the system. In addition to those specific questions the users were asked the general satisfaction by using the following scale:

1. Very rarely (N)
2. Less than half of the time (B)
3. Half of the time (M)
4. Over half of the time (G)
5. Practically all the time (E)

The results of the user satisfaction query are presented in Section 4.1.

The step following the user satisfaction query was the collection of problem data. Although in many cases the organization responsible for running and managing the information systems of the user organization collects very precise problem data it was decided that the decision making process should not assume that data to be available. The data may be unavailable for various reasons, one of them being the fact that the organization that manages the information systems may not be the actual user organization nor the software service provider which has created the system. A problem is either an exception in the sense of [7] or a bug inside the system. An exception is a situation that cannot be handled by using the system. The data was collected by using the on-line form shown in Figure 1. One of the basic ideas of the form was to collect data in a way that would allow us to associate a specific problem with a specific main function.

New problem situation

Classification of the problem

System's functionality related to the problem *

Description of the problem *

Date 6.10.2005 *

Time 12:12 *

Person who detected the problem

Cause of the problem

Time you spent to solve the problem hours *

Your actions to solve the problem

Other details

* required information

Save Clear

Fig. 1. The form used for collecting problem data

In this section the industrial setting has been described and in the next section the collected data will be presented and briefly analyzed.

4 The Data and a Brief Analysis

In this section the data collected by applying the decision making process is described and some immediate analysis is provided. There were 30 users participating the data collection phases of the project.

4.1 User Satisfaction

The employees of the user organization who answered the query were from three main staff groups. Those groups were assistants (18), low-level management (3), and mid-level management (7). There were also two answers from people who did not belong to any of those groups.

The general satisfaction was higher than expected. Before the query it was assumed that most of the users would be unsatisfied with the system. The user satisfaction can be seen from Table 1. Only a few evaluated criteria got less than 50 % of positive evaluations. An interesting issue is that all users were fairly satisfied with the information provided by the system and the up-to-date nature of that information. During further discussions with the representatives of the user organization it was clarified that some users used almost all of the functionalities and the others used only a few functionalities. The users who used only a few functionalities used mainly reporting and other similarly oriented functionalities. In those cases the business value of the provided information was realized and possible difficulties with the system endured. That analysis is supported by the realization that those people were especially unsatisfied with the user interface and usability of the system but were happier with the information provided by the system than the other users.

Table 1. The level of general user satisfaction

Issue	N	B	M	G	E	Likes
General satisfaction with the system	-	1	4	17	8	83 %
Satisfaction with the UI	3	5	8	10	4	47 %
Satisfaction with the help-functionality	2	5	10	10	3	43 %
Commands are easy to remember	1	7	5	11	6	57 %
Easiness of learning the system	1	3	7	11	8	63 %
Satisfaction with the provided information	-	1	7	13	9	73 %
The system is bug-free	-	2	3	20	5	83 %
Clarity of the provided information	2	2	7	12	7	63 %
General easiness of use	3	2	9	12	4	53 %
Information is up-to-date	-	1	7	12	10	73 %

Table 2. Current successfulness of the main functionalities and the number and cost of problems per functionality

Functionality	N	B	M	G	E	Likes %	Problems	Hours
F1	-	-	2	11	9	91 %	1	0.25
F2	-	-	4	18	8	87 %	12	10.40
F3	-	-	8	18	3	72 %	0	0
F4	-	-	2	16	4	91 %	2	1.10
F5	-	1	11	7	1	40 %	1	0.01
F6	-	-	-	8	10	100 %	11	2.15
F7	-	-	-	7	4	100 %	4	2.35
F8	-	-	-	9	8	100 %	0	0
F9	-	-	-	6	3	100 %	0	0
F10	-	1	2	10	4	82 %	4	3.15
F11	-	-	1	11	5	94 %	1	1.00
F12	-	-	3	8	7	83 %	4	3.55
F13	-	-	-	8	9	100 %	1	0.10
F14	-	-	-	11	5	100 %	1	1.00
F15	-	-	-	4	4	100 %	0	0
F16	-	-	-	3	3	100 %	0	0
F17	-	1	1	7	4	85 %	5	6.60
F18	-	-	5	6	4	67 %	4	5.00
Total							50	36.66

In the beginning we got the impression that the users were not very satisfied with the functionality of the system. The analysis showed a different story. The results are shown in Table 2, which shows the number and cost of problems per main functionality also. There was only one functionality that was not deemed satisfactory by the majority of the users. In addition to the user satisfaction measured for the main functionalities, the users were asked whether they thought that the successfulness of the system had improved over the time. About 70 % of users thought that successfulness had improved, 27 % thought that it had stayed the same and only 3 % thought that the successfulness of the system had declined.

4.2 Documentation and Support

One of the analyzed issues was the level and use of documentation and technical support. In order to analyze that better we divided support into four types that were: documentation, training, technical support personnel and other users. The use of technical support could, in some cases, be collected from the files of the organization that manages the information systems of the user organization, but that information was decided to be collected separately due to the same reason why information on problems was decided to be separately collected.

Table 3. Use and availability of different types of support

Type of technical support	Not available	Do not use	Uses	Do not know
Documentation	1	8	20	1
Training	0	4	20	6
Technical support personnel	1	2	26	1
Other users	1	2	24	3

All users were asked what type of support they use. The answers are shown in Table 3. The users were also asked whether the technical support was adequate or not. Twenty users answered that the documentation, training and support were adequate, five users answered that the support was not adequate. Other users did not provide an answer to this question.

4.3 Encountered Problems

Because the use of the system was very closely related to a monthly cycle, the data was decided to be collected for a month. Due to the fact that the maintenance personnel and the users could see different problems, it was decided that problems from both groups would be collected.

In one month there were 50 problems. The distribution of problems between the users and the maintenance personnel is shown in Figure 2 and its adjacent table. Further

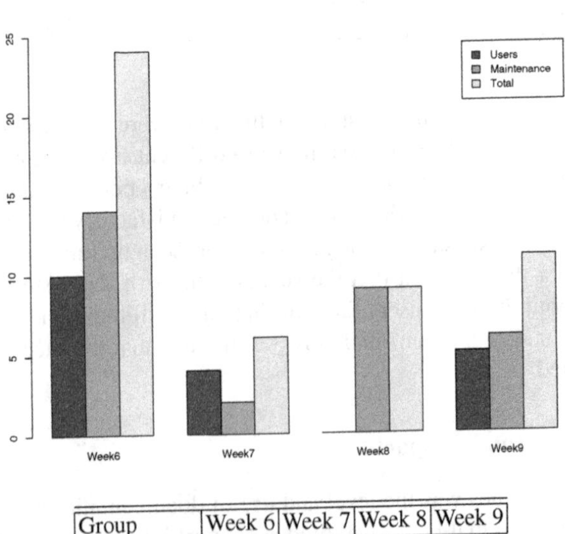

Group	Week 6	Week 7	Week 8	Week 9
Users	10	4	0	5
Maintenance	14	2	9	6
Total	24	6	9	11

Fig. 2. Encountered problems per week in one month

Table 4. Types, frequencies and costs of encountered problems

Type of problem	Users	Maintenance	Cost (min.)	Cost (h)
Error in WTB	7	3	132	2.23
WTB is slow	8	0	143	2.29
Wrong data, reason: user	1	9	558	9.30
Wrong data, reason: WTB	0	2	12	0.20
Wrong data, reason: other	0	3	132	2.2
User mistake	1	5	497	8.28
Missing functionality	2	2	198	3.30
Missing data	0	3	300	5.00
Data transfer	0	4	225	3.75
Total	19	31	2199	36.66

analysis of the collected problem data showed that there were nine different types of problems encountered by the maintenance personnel or the users. Four of those types were encountered only by the maintenance personnel and one type was encountered by the users only. The members of the maintenance group are not part of those 30 persons who participated the other types of data gathering. The types of encountered problems are shown in Table 4. The number of problems that could be identified as caused by WTB was 24/50 problems (error in WTB, WTB is slow, wrong data due to WTB, and missing functionality), which is about 50 % of the number of the problems.

One of the interesting issues is the amount of working hours lost due to the additional work caused by the problems. In Table 4 the cost of the problems is shown. The cost is not shown in money, it is shown as time. The total amount of the reported lost working time was less than 37 hours. The amount of lost ime is very small when compared to the amount of active working hours (1 743 hours/month) spent using the system. Therefore the lost working time was a bit over 2 % of the total time.

In addition to the total amount of lost working hours the number of problems for every main functionality was recorded. The distribution of lost work between the main functionalities is shown in Table 2. The number of corrected problems was 42, which is less than the number of encountered problems. It was not necessary to spend corrective work on every problem either because the problem was one-off and impossible to be corrected afterwards or because corrective action was deemed unnecessary.

5 An Analysis of the Process and the Data

The use of the decision making process was considered a success by both the software services provider and the user organization, although probably for different reasons. In this section the experiences of using the process and the results provided by the process are discussed.

The general aim of the process was reached. The process provided a documented way to perform a light-weight analysis of an information system. The effort required by both the software services supplier and the user organization was small enough to justify the use of the process in real cases in which the costs of the evaluation are a very significant factor. In addition to that, the collected measurements data was considered sufficiently objective in order to enable rational and justifiable decisions.

The costs imposed by using the process were clearly lower than the costs caused by even fairly minor reengineering, modernization or replacement decisions. The actual numbers are not available to the authors, but both the software services provider and the user organization were satisfied with the low costs and told the authors that the costs of using the process were significantly lower than the cheapest considered alternative. The difference in costs justified the costs caused by using the process.

The sufficient objectivity of the collected data was emphasized by the fact that the results of the data-gathering were a surprise to the representatives of both the software services provider and the user organization. Contrary to the original expectations the general user satisfaction was fairly high and the perceived obsolescence was low. The satisfaction with the information provided by the system was especially high, and that was the most important issue considering the use of the system. In addition to that, most of the users thought that WTB was more useful now than before, which was interpreted to mean that it was less obsolescent than before. That change was assumed to be a direct consequence of constant enhancive maintenance performed by the software services provider.

In addition to the perceived successfulness of the system, the measured number of problems and the working-time lost due to the problems were fairly small. Only 2% of working time spent using the system was lost due to the problems. That time would be only 2.4 hours in four weeks for an individual assuming that the effective working time is 120 hours in four weeks and the lost time is distributed uniformly (the individual amounts of lost time was not measured). That level was under the pre-set trigger-levels (unfortunately the exact values of the decided trigger-levels are not known to the authors).

The level of user satisfaction with the system, the level of the perceived obsolescence, and the measured number and cost of problems did not provide support for reengineering, modernization or replacement. In addition to that, those features of the system that were most unsatisfactory were related to the user interface of the system. The level of satisfaction with the user interface was related to the frequency of use. Frequent users were more satisfied with the interface than those who used the system less frequently. Even those users that were not satisfied with the user interface were satisfied with the information content and the functionality. Hence the most important target for improvements was the user interface of the system.

In general, the performed project revealed that the system was much more successful and problem-free than the management and decision makers of the user organization assumed before the project. Therefore the project, which was performed in a methodological and controlled way, provided results that were contrary to the expectations and that were able to provide necessary information for rational business decision making.The authors were later told that the results of applying the process had provided both the software services supplier and the user organization enough data for achieving an agreement on the modernization of WTB's user interface. For other part the decision was to continue as before with maintenance that includes enchantive aspects.

It is often possible and even likely that the perception of the modernization or replacement needs are different when viewed from the management level when compared to the need when viewed from the employee level or the level of the existing business processes. Major changes in the business processes and the organizational models are, of course, indisputable reasons for drastic decisions regarding the information systems used by the organization. That type of drivers for change cannot be neglected and may result in major modernizations or replacements in any case. One additional type of reasons for change that cannot be neglected are technological ones like the end of support for some types of technologies [6].

The fact that the management of the user organization did not expect results that did not support replacement or major modernization decisions makes it interesting to speculate on the possible percentage of unnecessary modernization or replacement decisions. Such unnecessary decisions may be based on false assumptions and the lack of hard data, i.e. bad process. The decision making process outlined in this article can provide necessary guidelines in order to perform fact-based decision making. The usefulness of the process was tested out by using it in a real industrial case which showed the process to be usable and reasonably light-weight in order to be applied in the case of strict economic constraints.

6 Discussion

The subprocess defined in this article and used in the outlined industrial case is just one of the processes that are required in order to define and document the whole spectrum of software engineering processes. Those processes must be defined, documented and tested in order to make the processes or an organization at least controlled. Actually this type of definition is required at the CMMI level 1 [12]. Other quality and reference models require the definition and documentation of the processes in any case.

A reference model like CMMI [8][12] requires the processes to be defined and documented. Those models do not provide process templates on which organizations could base their own process definitions and documentation, and it should be noted that providing such templates it not the the aim of those models. The models tell what is required from the processes, their definition and documentation.

There is, however, a clear need for well-thought process templates that could be adapted for the need of individual organizations. Such templates should be defined in a sufficiently detailed way and they should have been tested in real industrial settings before they are presented for a wider audience. The process presented in this paper can be used as such a template for defining the organization specific software system modernization decision making processes. Further development and testing of the process is, however, required before its general applicability can be asserted.

The authors of this article propose other researchers and organizations to document and distribute their process definitions in order to strengthen the general understanding of software engineering related processes and their aspects. The maturing of software engineering requires publicly available process models and other types of empirically asserted best-practices.

References

1. Lientz, B., Swanson, E.: Problems in application software maintenance. Communications of the ACM **24** (1981) 763–769
2. Erlikh, L.: Leveraging legacy system dollars for eBusiness. IT Pro (2000) 17–23
3. Seacord, R.C., Plakosh, D., Lewis, G.A.: Modernizing Legacy Systems. The SEI Series in Software Engineering. Addison-Wesley (2003)
4. Lehman, M.M., Perry, D.E., Ramil, J.F.: Implications of evolution metrics on software maintenance. In: Proceedings of the International Conference on Software Maintenance, IEEE Computer Society Press (1998) 208–217
5. Banker, R.D., Datar, S.M., Kemerer, C.F., Zweig, D.: Software complexity and maintenance costs. Communications of the ACM **36** (1993) 81–94
6. Koskinen, J., Ahonen, J.J., Sivula, H., Tilus, T., Lintinen, H.: Software modernization decision criteria: An empirical study. In: Proceedings of the 9th European Conference on Software Maintenance and Reengineering, CSMR'05, IEEE Computer Society (2005) 324–331
7. Saastamoinen, H.: On the Handling of Exceptions in Information Systems. Studies in computer science, economics and statistics, vol. 28, University of Jyväskylä (1995) PhD Thesis.
8. SEI: Capability Maturity Model Integration (CMMI), Version 1.1, Continuous Representation. Technical Report CMU/SEI-2002-TR-028, ESC-TR-2002-028, CMU/SEI (2002)
9. ISO: ISO/IEC TR2 15504, Part 1 – Part 9, Information Technology — Software Process Assessment. ISO, Geneva, Switzerland (1993)
10. Sneed, H.: Planning the reengineering of legacy systems. IEEE Software **12** (1995) 24–34
11. De Lucia, A., Fasolino, A.R., Pompella, E.: A decisional framework for legacy system management. In: Proceedings of the IEEE International Conference on Software Maintenance, ICSM 2001. (2001) 642–651
12. SEI: Capability Maturity Model Integration (CMMI), Version 1.1, Staged Representation. Technical Report CMU/SEI-2002-TE-029, ESC-TR-2002-029, CMU/SEI (2002)
13. Kankaanpää, I., Sivula, H., Ahonen, J.J., Tilus, T., Koskinen, J., Juutilainen, P.: ISEBA — a framework for IS evolution benefit assessment. In Remenyi, D., ed.: Proceedings of 12th European Conference on Information Technology Evaluation, Academic Conferences Limited (2005) 255–264
14. Sahin, I., Zahedi, F.: Policy analysis for warranty, maintenance and upgrade of software systems. Journal of Software Maintenance and Evolution: Research and Practice **13** (2001) 469–493
15. Visaggio, G.: Value-based decision model for renewal processes in software maintenance. Annals of Software Engineering **9** (2000) 215–233
16. Bennett, K., Ramage, M., Munro, M.: Decision model for legacy systems. IEE Proc. — Software **146** (1999) 153–159
17. Kitchenham, B.A., Pfleeger, S.L., Pickard, L.M., Jones, P.W., Hoaglin, D.C., Emam, K.E., Rosenberg, J.: Preliminary guidelines for empirical research in software engineering. IEEE Trans. Softw. Eng. **28** (2002) 721–734
18. Pickard, L.M., Kitchenham, B.A., Jones, P.: Combining empirical results in software engineering. Information and Software Technology **40** (1998) 811–821
19. Kitchenham, B.A., Travassos, G.H., von Mayrhauser, A., Niessink, F., Schneidewind, N.F., Singer, J., Takada, S., Vehvilainen, R., Yang, H.: Towards an ontology of software maintenance. Journal of Software Maintenance **11** (1999) 365–389

Introducing Tool Support for Retrospective Analysis of Release Planning Decisions

Lena Karlsson and Björn Regnell

Department of Communication Systems, Lund University,
Box 118, 221 00 Lund, Sweden
{lena.karlsson, bjorn.regnell}@telecom.lth.se

Abstract. The release planning activity in market-driven requirements engineering is crucial but difficult. The quality of the decisions on product content and release timing determines the market success, but as predictions of market value and development cost are uncertain, the decisions are not always optimal. This paper presents a prototype tool for retrospective analysis of release planning decisions based on tool requirements gathered in two previous empirical studies where retrospective analysis was done manually. The supported method enables representation of different views in the decision-making process. The results from an initial validation indicate that the retrospective analysis benefits from the supporting tool.

1 Introduction

The purpose of this paper is to describe a tool[1] that supports a method for retrospective analysis of release planning decisions. The method is called PARSEQ (Post-release Analysis of Requirements SElection Quality) and aims at finding process improvement proposals for the release planning activity. The retrospective analysis is acknowledged as an important means for software process improvement [9]. Release planning is regarded as one of the most critical activities in market-driven software development [2] as it can determine the success of the product. Generation of feasible assignments of requirements to increments in a changing environment is a very important but complex task [3]. The PARSEQ method has been successfully investigated in two prior case studies performed in industry. The experiences from the case studies provided the basis for developing the tool support and were used to elicit the PARSEQ tool requirements.

In [7], the method was applied at a company developing a software product for an open market. The company had regular releases and used a requirements management (RM) tool [13] when planning their releases. The PARSEQ analysis yielded a number of process improvements such as enhancing the overall picture of related requirements, increased attention to the elicitation of usability requirements and improved estimates of implementation costs. In the second case study [8], the method was applied using a different approach. The investigated project had an agile development procedure, inspired by the Extreme Programming (XP) [1]. The project

[1] Download at http://serg.telecom.lth.se/research/packages/ParseqTool/index.html

J. Münch and M. Vierimaa (Eds.): PROFES 2006, LNCS 4034, pp. 19 – 33, 2006.

was conducted in-house, i.e. both users and developers of the project were from within the company. Since the project used an agile approach to development, they had frequent iterations and regular releases when the system was put into operation. In each iteration the project used the Planning game [1] to prioritise the requirements and plan the next release. The requirements were elicited in the beginning of the project from internal stakeholders and documented in an excel sheet.

The experiences from the case studies have given input to the needed functionality of the PARSEQ tool support. We believe that tool support may improve the retrospective analysis in the following ways:

- Increase efficiency as more requirements may be analysed compared to the manual case
- Increase visualisation potential of release planning problems through charts and diagrams
- Decrease preparation and manual handling of requirements through import and export possibilities

The tool was validated in a retrospective analysis of the development of the PARSEQ tool itself. The analysis indicated that the tool is well functioning and we believe it will be helpful in future case studies.

The paper is structured as follows. Section 2 describes the PARSEQ method and Section 3 describes the PARSEQ tool that has been developed. Section 4 discusses some threats to validity and concludes the paper with suggestions for further work.

2 The PARSEQ Method

Retrospective evaluation is used for different purposes within software engineering. Some retrospective methods use metrics to evaluate a product from a certain perspective, such as maintainability or program structure, in order to improve software evolution [10]. Other methods aim at evaluating a conducted project in order to improve future projects [9]. Unlike these retrospective analysis methods, PARSEQ focuses on finding release planning process improvements through an analysis of earlier release planning decisions.

Release planning is used when developing products in an incremental manner, and provides the opportunity of releasing the most important functionality first instead of delivering a monolithic system after a long development time [3]. Release planning is used in incremental development and agile methods. Assigning requirements to increments is a complex task as many factors influence, such as different stakeholder needs, available resources, and technical precedence constraints. There are several techniques for release planning e.g. EVOLVE [3] and Planning game [1]. There are also a number of tools to support release planning e.g. ReleasePlanner [14] and VersionOne [15]. In contrast to these tools, the PARSEQ tool is not intended as a release planning tool, but as a tool for evaluating releases in retrospect. Thus, the aim is not to come up with a perfect release plan but to find process issues that need improvement in order to reach better release plans in the future.

The PARSEQ method is based on a systematic analysis of candidate requirements from previous releases. By identifying and analysing a set of root causes to suspected incorrect requirements selection decisions, it may be possible to find relevant improvements that are important when trying to increase the specific organisation's ability to plan successful software releases.

In order to perform the PARSEQ method the following is required:

- Multiple releases of the product and requirements from earlier releases saved in a repository.
- Data for each requirement stating which release it is implemented in, or if the requirement has been postponed or excluded.
- Methods for estimating each requirement's cost and value.
- Employees who have decision-making experience from prior releases.
- A facilitator with experience in performing retrospective analysis.

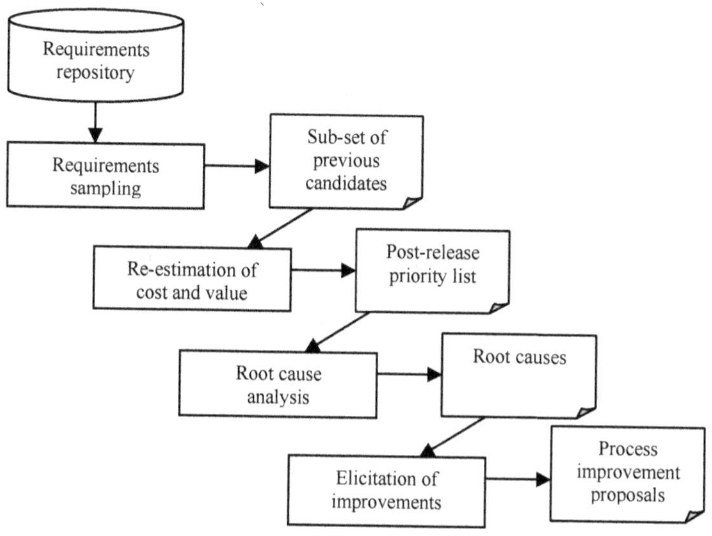

Fig. 1. An outline of the activities and products of the PARSEQ method

PARSEQ is divided into four steps: requirements sampling, re-estimation of cost and value, root cause analysis, and elicitation of improvements, as shown in Fig. 1. Each of the steps can be adapted to the particulars of a case study. For example, there are different approaches to requirements sampling that can be selected for the first step. There are also several different techniques for requirements prioritisation that can be used in the second step.

The method uses a requirements repository as input and assumes that information is available regarding when a requirement is issued and in which release a requirement is implemented. The output of the method is a list of prioritised process improvement proposals and a plan for improvement implementation. Each step in PARSEQ is subsequently described in more detail.

Step 1: Requirements sampling. The main input to the retrospective analysis is a list of requirements that were candidates for previous releases of the investigated product. The product should have been in operation long enough to allow for an assessment of the current user value of its implemented requirements.

The purpose of the sampling is to compose a reasonably small but representative sub-set of requirements, since the complete repository may be too large to investigate in the retrospective analysis. The sample should include requirements that were selected for implementation in one of the releases as well as postponed or rejected requirements. The requirement set is thereby useful for the analysis as it consists of typical examples of release planning decisions.

The requirements sampling can be performed with different focus, such as concentrating on a special market segment or on a difficult part of the product or on particularly difficult decisions. However, if the sample is to represent the whole product and its market, the sample should be as comprehensive as possible. If a random sample is used, some types of requirements may be excluded as they are not representative, e.g. very similar requirements, requirements dated several releases ago or dated recently, requirements estimated to have a very long or very short implementation time, etc.

The output from the requirements sampling is a reasonable number of requirements, large enough to be representative, yet small enough to allow the following steps of PARSEQ to be completed within a reasonable time.

Step 2: Re-estimation of cost and value. The requirement sample is input to the next step of PARSEQ, where a re-estimation of current market value and actual development cost is made in order to find suspected inappropriate decisions that can be further analysed. As the investigated product releases have been in operation for a while, a new assessment can be made, which applies the knowledge gained after the releases were launched. Presumably, this should result in more accurate priorities. The re-estimation determines how the organisation would have decided, i.e. which requirements would have been selected, if it knew then what it knows now. With today's knowledge, about market expectations and development costs, a different set of requirements may have been selected for implementation in the different releases. If this is not the case, either the organisation has not learned more about release planning since the releases were launched, or the situation on the market has not changed, or the organisation has been very successful with their estimations of cost and value during release planning.

The implemented requirements have a known development cost (assuming that actual implementation effort is measured for each requirement), but postponed or rejected requirements need to be re-estimated based on the eventual architectural decisions and the knowledge gained from the actual design of the subsequent releases.

By using, for example, a cost-value prioritisation approach, it is possible to see the trade-off between the value to the users and the cost of development in a so-called cost-value diagram [6], or in a bar chart [13]. These illustrations point out the requirements with high value and low cost (they should be implemented early), as well as the requirements with low value and high cost (they should be implemented late or perhaps not at all).

The purpose of the re-estimation is to apply the knowledge that has been gained since the product was released, to discover decisions that would be made differently today. The discrepancies between decisions made during release planning and during post-release prioritisation are noted and used in the root cause analysis. The output of this step is thus a number of requirements that were given a high post-release priority but were implemented late or not at all, as well as requirements that were given a low post-release priority but were implemented in an early release.

Step 3: Root cause analysis. The purpose of the root cause analysis is to understand on what grounds release-planning decisions were made. By discussing prior release planning decisions, and determining root causes of problematic ones, it may be possible to determine what went wrong and recommend how to do it better next time.

The output of the re-estimation, i.e. the discrepancies between the post-release prioritisation and what was actually selected for implementation in the different releases, is analysed in order to find root causes for suspected inappropriate decisions. This analysis is based on a discussion with persons involved in the requirements selection process. The following questions can be used to stimulate the discussion and provoke insights into the reasons behind the decisions:

- Why was the decision made? Based on what facts was the decision made?
- When was the decision made? What has changed since the decision was made?
- Was it a correct or incorrect decision?

Guided by these questions, categories of decision root causes are developed. Each requirement found to be implemented either too early or too late is mapped to one or several of these categories. This mapping of requirements to root cause categories is the main output of this step together with the insights gained from retrospective reflection.

Step 4: Elicitation of improvements. The outcome of the root cause analysis is used to facilitate the elicitation of improvement proposals. The objective of this step of PARSEQ is to arrive at a relevant list of high-priority areas of improvement. The intention is to base the discussion on strengths and weaknesses of the requirements selection process and to identify changes to current practice that can be realised. The following questions can assist to keep focus on improvement possibilities:

- How could we have improved the decision-making?
- What would have been needed to make a better decision?
- Which changes to the current practices can be made to improve requirements selection in the future?

In order to implement the most cost-effective and important ones first, it may be necessary to conduct a prioritisation among the suggested improvements. The prioritisation can be performed using a requirements prioritisation method, based on cost and value. Prioritisation of process improvements has been successfully conducted with a technique based on the Analytical Hierarchy Process (AHP), see [5]. The results of PARSEQ can be used in a process improvement programme where process changes are designed, introduced and evaluated. These activities are, however, beyond the scope of this paper.

2.1 Case Studies

Two consecutive case studies have been conducted to try the PARSEQ method in practice. These empirical studies were the foundation for developing tool support for the method, as some steps in the method could be more efficient and easier to manage if not performed manually. Each case study gave more information on the needed characteristics of the tool, as the characteristics of the involved companies were different. The organisational characteristics are described in Table 1.

Table 1. Comparison between the two studied cases

	Case A	**Case B**
Project type	Market-driven development	In-house
User base	Multiple, diverse views	Few, similar views
User location	Outside the organisation	Within the organisation
Development approach	Incremental	Agile
Organisation size	Small	Medium

The following sections briefly describe the two empirical cases.

Case A – The Market-Driven Software Development Company

The first case study [7] took place at a small-sized software product developer. The development followed an incremental approach with regular releases every 6 months. Users and customers were external as the product was sold on an open market. The releases were planned with a commercial requirements management (RM) tool [13]. The RM tool can be used to prioritise requirements according to an approach based on the AHP [12]. The RM tool was used in the second step of the method to re-prioritise the requirements. Several improvement suggestions for the release planning activity was found in the case study: enhance the overall picture of related requirements, increase attention to the elicitation of usability requirements, improve estimates of implementation costs, trim the division of large requirements into smaller increments, and improve estimations of market-value of features in competing products.

Case B – The In-House Project at an Embedded Systems Developer

The second case [8] was an in-house project at a medium-sized company developing embedded software products. The project used an agile development approach, inspired by Extreme Programming [1] and had frequent iterations and regular releases when the system was put into operation. They used the Planning game to prioritise requirements and plan each iteration. The requirements were elicited in the beginning of the project from internal stakeholders and documented in an excel sheet.

As we wanted to investigate a more agile alternative to the RM tool, the Planning Game was selected for the re-estimation of cost and value. The application of PARSEQ in an agile setting seems promising and the release planning activity in the investigated project was found successful. The participants concluded that this could be due to the iterative development, as requirements were prioritised continually and release plans were flexible enough to adapt to the project scope. It may also be explained by the project type; users of in-house projects have similar requirements, and users and developers can co-operate during development as they are located close by. The participants concluded that iterative development and prototyping were reasons for the success.

Tool Requirements from Case Studies
The main problems with performing the PARSEQ analysis manually include time-consumption and lack of visualisation. Commercial tools only support a few steps of the method (as in case study A) and performing the method manually is too time-consuming (as in case study B). It is also essential to be able to import requirements automatically, and to export the discovered process improvements. Performing import and export manually is very time-consuming. As different organisations are used to different prioritisation techniques, we also needed the possibility to select different requirements prioritisation techniques during the analysis.

3 The PARSEQ Tool Support

The experiences from conducting the two earlier PARSEQ case studies were used to develop a requirements specification for the PARSEQ tool. The tool handles all steps from the import of a sample of requirements to the export of process improvement proposals, which in turn can be prioritised in the tool.

The PARSEQ tool was developed by two students in collaboration with the researchers, who acted as customers. The students used ideas from Extreme Programming in the development, and each release was planned in collaboration with the customers.

3.1 Tool Description

The tool consists of a number of different windows guiding the user through the PARSEQ process. The main window is returned to after each step of the process and visualises the requirements at each step.

Step 1: Requirements sampling. The main window of the tool includes an Import button, which is selected for the import of the requirements. We chose to support import of requirements from MS Excel™, as a predefined Java library was found on the Internet. For this prototype, we chose not to include import possibilities from RM tools and other programs.

The tool requires the imported list of requirements to be in a certain format with columns representing requirement number, requirement description and release number, see Fig. 2. Therefore, the original requirements repository may need to be altered before importing it. The tool supports manual entering of requirements as well as editing of imported requirements. The tool cannot manage random sampling, only manual selection of requirements from the imported list. Therefore, it is more efficient to conduct the sampling prior to the PARSEQ session, so that manual selection does not have to be performed.

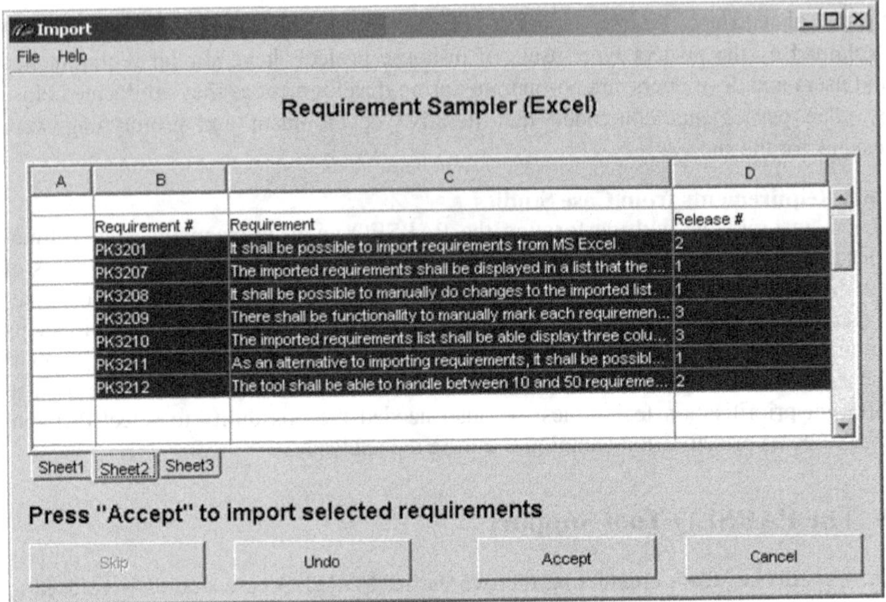

Fig. 2. Import window of the PARSEQ tool

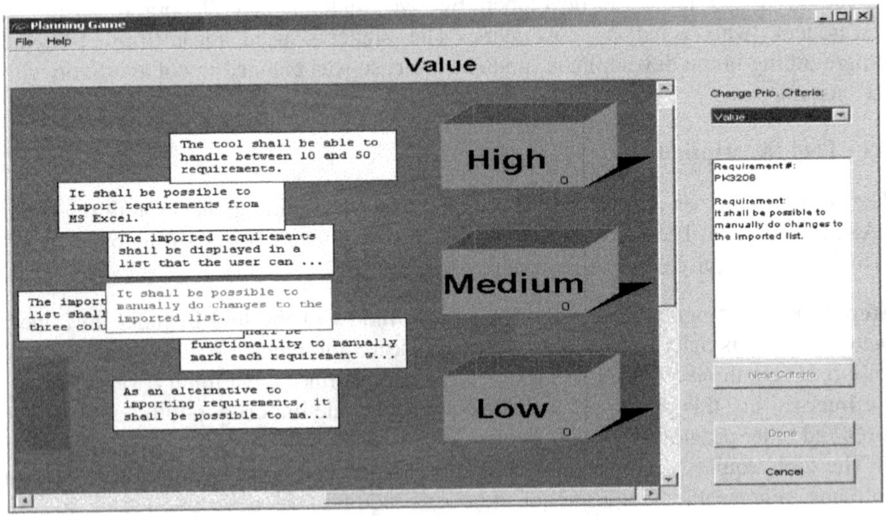

Fig. 3. The Planning Game prioritisation boxes

Step 2: Re-estimation of cost and value. When requirements have been imported into the tool along with each requirement's release number and description, the second step can be performed. The re-estimation of cost and value is performed by using one of the three available requirements prioritisation techniques. We chose to include the two techniques that were used effectively in the prior case studies, i.e. the AHP and the Planning game, and in addition we included the $100 technique, as it has been used successfully by the researchers before [11].

At this step it is also necessary to select the criteria to base the prioritisation on. Pre-defined criteria include cost, value, and risk. It is also possible to enter two criteria of your own choice. It is essential to choose one criteria to maximise, e.g. value, and one to minimise, e.g. cost.

The Planning Game helps the decision maker rank requirements by first assigning each requirement to the high, medium or low box, and then within each box to arrange them in falling order, see Fig. 3. This is performed for both selected criteria, for example cost and value before continuing. Within each box it is possible to use drag-and-drop to rearrange the order or requirements. The top requirement in each box has the highest rank for that criterion. If some requirement is discovered to be in the wrong box, the card can be sent back to the desk and be put in another box. In addition to the ranks, it is also possible to assign relative values to the requirements by using a modified $100-technique on the complete list of ranked requirements.

The AHP requires the user to perform pair-wise comparisons between all possible pairs of requirements. As the number of comparisons increases drastically with the number of requirements, this is very time-consuming for large amounts of requirements. However, there are different algorithms to reduce the number of comparisons, for example the Incomplete pair-wise comparisons (IPC) [4]. The implementation of the AHP prioritisation technique was inspired by the IPC. In the tool, it is possible to stop before all pairs are compared and receive an approximate value. This reduces the necessary comparison effort, but also the trustworthiness of the result. For each requirement pair, one of the radio buttons should be selected, see Fig. 4. The one in the middle represents equal weight, and the further to the left the more weight is given to the left requirement, and similarly for the requirement to the right. The same process is performed for both selected criteria.

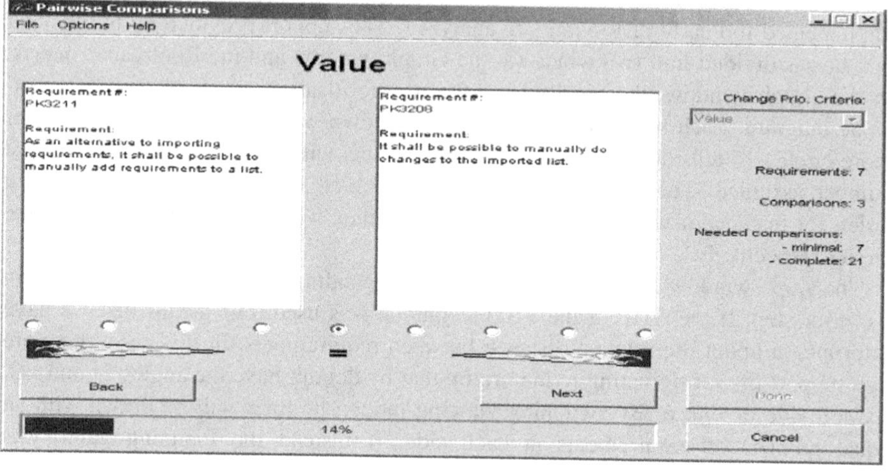

Fig. 4. Prioritisation with pair-wise comparisons, i.e. the AHP

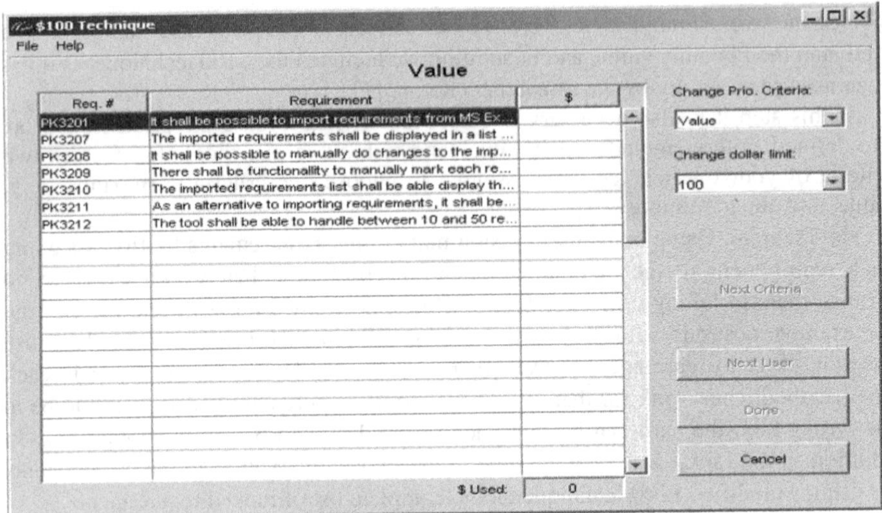

Fig. 5. The $100 technique window

The $100 technique prioritises the requirements by providing each requirement with a share of a total budget of 100 dollars. This gives each requirement a percentage of significance according to the currently used criteria. The cell at the bottom shows the total amount spent so far, see Fig. 5. If a large number of requirements is prioritised, the $100 limit can be extended to $1000 to make it easier to divide the fictive money. The same process is performed for both criteria before continuing. If the development costs of requirements are available, it is possible to use the $100-technique and re-scale the actual costs accordingly.

Step 3: Root cause analysis. In the root-cause analysis, the requirements identified as implemented too early or too late are analyzed. The support provided by the tool for this step is divided into two windows, the Graph window and the Root-cause matrix. In the Graph window, the results from the re-prioritisation are displayed in a cost-value diagram. Each requirement's position is shown with an icon: a "+" or one or more circles, to tell releases apart. The requirements with a "+"-sign have no release number assigned. The number of circles are decided in alphabetical or numerical order, for instance if we have releases 1, 2 and 3 they would have one, two and three circles respectively.

The graph window can take different shapes depending on the prioritisation used in the prior step. If the AHP or the $100 technique was used, this means that we have information about the relative distance between requirements. In this case, there are two support lines, originating in the origin, that by default have the angles *2x* and *x/2*, see left side of Fig. 6. By switching viewing mode, the lines will be drawn with an equal number of requirements at each side. If instead the Planning game was used, and requirements are ranked, the axes represent ranks. There are horizontal and vertical lines instead of diagonal ones, to distinguish the high, medium and low

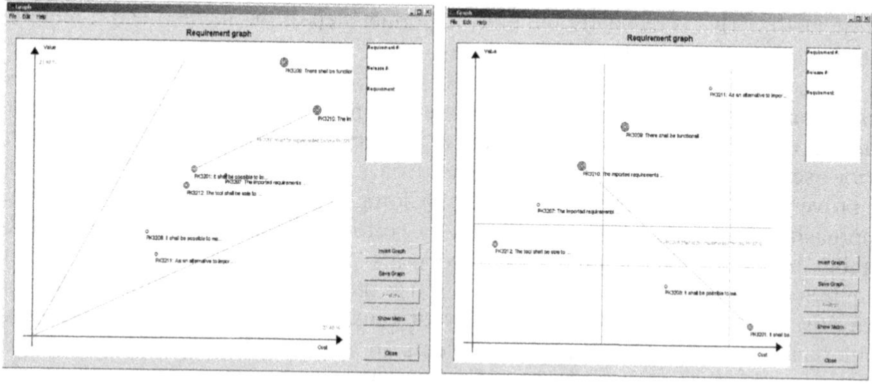

Fig. 6. Cost-value diagrams for the AHP or the $100 method (left), and the Planning game (right)

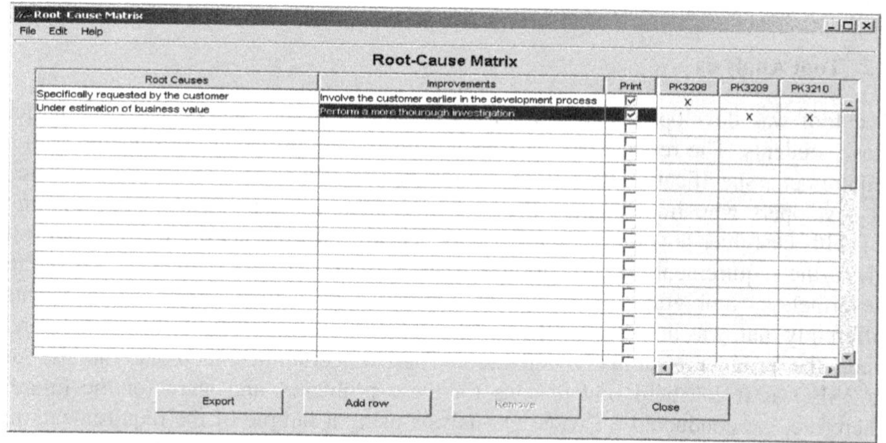

Fig. 7. The Root cause matrix with two root causes and improvements

groups, see right side of Fig. 6. It is also possible to visualize dependencies between requirements in the graph, which is indicated by the broken lines between requirements in Fig. 6.

After discussing the root causes of making incorrect release planning decisions for a certain requirement, the requirement can be added to the Root-cause matrix, see Fig. 7. In the matrix, selected requirements end up in columns and root causes can be entered at each row. By marking an "X" in the appropriate cell, it is possible to assign root causes to requirements.

Step 4: Elicitation of improvements. At this point it is desirable to discuss the root causes and reasons for making incorrect decisions. Possible improvements to manage the incorrect decisions in the future can be entered next to the root causes in the root cause matrix. This is evidently the most important step of the method and it requires intense discussion between decision makers.

When improvement proposals have been extracted, it is possible to export the results back to MS Excel™. Both the Root cause matrix and the cost-value diagrams can be exported and used for presentation purposes. Finally, it is possible to prioritise the improvement proposals based on e.g. the importance of putting the improvement into operation and the cost of doing so. In this manner the cost-value approach is used again. This is achieved by performing the first steps of PARSEQ again; importing the improvement proposals in the same manner as when requirements were imported, then re-prioritise the improvements using one of the prioritisation techniques. The resulting root cause diagram can indicate the most important, yet cost-effective, improvements to implement first. The root cause matrix can be used to enter reasons for implementing a certain improvement and plans on how this can be done. It would also be possible to add notes about dependencies between improvement proposals if, for example, conflicting proposals are found. The improvements, the root cause diagram and the root cause matrix can again be exported to MS Excel™.

3.2 Tool Analysis

The tool was developed in collaboration between the researchers and two master thesis students. The researchers acted as customers and provided the students with a requirements specification with all the known needs for the tool and the students acted as developers who implemented the tool in collaboration, using pair-programming [1]. This customer-developer situation is typical for the contract-driven development where the requirements specification acts as a contract of what shall be delivered. Nevertheless, ambiguity leaves room for developers to interpret requirements differently than was intended by the customer, and the customer may change his mind when the product is actually delivered. These uncertainties motivate the use of PARSEQ as it can help find reasons for these problems, and learn for the future. Therefore, we conducted a PARSEQ analysis using a sample of the requirements in the original specification to analyze which requirements that should have been implemented earlier, and which that should have been postponed. From the 52 product requirements, a sample of 20 randomly selected requirements were listed in an Excel sheet together with their release status, to be used for the evaluation. We decided to use the Planning game as prioritisation technique. First the customers sorted the cards by value, i.e. how important they found the specific feature. Then the developers sorted the cards by cost, i.e. the time it took to implement the feature or, if the feature had been excluded, an estimate of the time it would have taken. After the prioritisation, the cost/value graph was studied to find requirements implemented in a too early or too late release. What were sought for were in other words, requirements with high value and low cost that had been implemented in a late release and vice versa. When the identification of these requirements was done, they were added to the root-cause matrix. Then the PARSEQ evaluation was ended with completing the last steps in the method by eliciting root-causes, possible reasons for the deviations and possible improvements to, if possible, avoid the deviations in the future. The root causes and improvements are shown in Table 2.

Table 2. Root cause matrix resulting from the PARSEQ analysis of the PARSEQ tool development

Root causes (Requirements implemented later than optimal)	**Improvements**	**PK321**	**PK320**	**PK340**	**PK350**	**PK341**	**PK310**
Inadequate elicitation (the req was not in the original spec)	Earlier prototyping and more disc. of spec. with customer	X				X	
The prototype did not need it	Not an incorrect decision		X		X		
Was expected to be time-consuming before an existing library was found	Search for existing solutions before starting		X		X		
The requirement was changed	Write high-level reqs, not solutions			X			
Expected to be time-consuming and no good solution alternative	More discussion of spec. with customer					X	
Partly implemented	Not an incorrect decision						X

Note that all of the root causes regard requirements that were implemented later than optimal. Evidently, this could not have been completely prevented, as all features cannot be implemented at once. The conclusions were entered in the root-cause matrix and exported to an Excel file. The session was then completed by ranking the possible process improvements for importance. The improvement suggestions are (in order of importance):

1. More time should be spent on discussing and understanding the requirements and the specification in the beginning of the project
2. The customer should write higher level requirements instead of solution-oriented requirements
3. More time should be spent on looking for existing solutions to presented problems
4. Earlier prototyping should be made to get earlier feedback

Note that some of the root causes do not reveal an incorrect decision, as some requirements have to be implemented later than optimal due to e.g. architectural reasons.

As the PARSEQ tool was possible to use for a PARSEQ evaluation, the conclusion is that the tool works appropriately. It was also concluded that the tool usability is high enough for users familiar with the PARSEQ method. Some parts of the process, for example the automatically generated root cause graph, were found less time-consuming and more flexible than without the tool. It remains to evaluate the tool in an industrial case.

4 Discussion and Further Work

Earlier case studies [7, 8] have shown that the PARSEQ method is a valid means for finding improvements to the release planning process. The experiences from the case studies were used to design tool support for the method in order to make it more efficient and easier to use. The tool was developed in collaboration between the researchers and two masters students. At the end of development, the tool was evaluated and validated in a PARSEQ analysis of our own project. The input was the requirements specification and the analysis consisted of the four steps described earlier. The output was a number of possible improvements to the development of the tool. First of all, we can draw the conclusion that the tool worked satisfactory. It increased visualisation of release planning problems and time consumption was low compared to earlier studies since certain steps were automated. Secondly, several improvement proposals were extracted from the analysis, including more discussion of the requirements specification to decrease misinterpretations, higher level requirements in the specification instead of solution-oriented requirements, searching for existing solutions e.g. on the internet, and earlier prototyping.

The generalisability of these findings is important, as we would like to use the tool in future case studies in industry. The method itself has been satisfactory in prior case studies, and the tool is demonstrated as useable in the analysis of the development of the PARSEQ tool. Therefore, we believe that it will also work in an industrial case. The results from the analysis of the PARSEQ tool may have been affected by participant bias as the tool was developed in close collaboration between students and researchers. This could have affected the type of root causes and improvements that were found. However, as the improvements regard both suggestions for the researchers and for the students, we believe that all participants were honest and objective during the analysis and we do not regard this as a threat to validity.

Further work includes using the tool in an industrial case study to investigate release planning issues in a collaborative environment in industry. This situation has not been investigated before in a PARSEQ analysis and is therefore a complement to the previous case studies of the method. One example of a collaborative situation is when an organisation employs sub-contractors who produce separate parts to be integrated in the product. Cross-organisational collaboration increases the complexity of the release planning process and enhances the need for clarification of different viewpoints. Therefore, we believe that the retrospective method may give valuable insights to the collaboration regarding requirements engineering and release planning. Representatives from both organisations are intended to participate in PARSEQ workshops to extract retrospective priorities of requirements and to discuss different perspectives of release planning decision-making.

The four steps of the PARSEQ method can take the following form:

1. *Requirements sampling:* The focus of the analysis is on requirements that are collaborative, i.e. that are stated by the integrating partner and that should be negotiated between the parties.
2. *Re-estimation of cost and value:* This can be performed with any of the three implemented prioritisation techniques. However, if the organisations are used to e.g. some kind of numeral assignment or grouping, the Planning game may be appropriate. The developing organisation, e.g. a sub-contractor, re-estimates the development cost and the integrating organisation re-estimates the customer value as they probably have the best customer contacts.
3. *Root cause analysis:* The important issue for the third step is that both parties are present so that a discussion regarding release planning problems can be discussed

and dealt with. Decision makers need to explain how and why some release planning decisions were made. Different opinions about the importance of requirements can be highlighted and causes of late awareness of differences can be identified.

4. *Elicitation of improvements:* Decision makers can discuss how release planning problems can be prevented in the future. If several improvements are discovered, these can be imported into the tool again for prioritisation regarding their expected value to the collaborating organisations and the expected cost of implementation.

Acknowledgements

This work is supported by VINNOVA (Swedish Agency for Innovation Systems) within the ITEA project MERLIN. We would like to give special thanks to Dr. Martin Höst for careful reviewing and valuable comments. The authors would like to thank Mikael Jönsson and Per Klingnäs, for high-quality implementation of the PARSEQ prototype requirements.

References

1. Beck, K.: Extreme Programming Explained. Addison-Wesley (1999)
2. Carlshamre, P.: Release Planning in Market-Driven Software Product Development: Provoking an Understanding. Requirements Engineering, Vol. 7. (2002) 139–151
3. Greer, D., Ruhe, G.: Software Release Planning: an Evolutionary and Iterative Approach. Inf. and Software Techn., Vol. 46. (2004) 243–253
4. Harker, P. T.: Incomplete Pairwise Comparisons in the Analytical Hierarchy Process. Math. Modelling, Vol. 9. (1987) 837–848
5. Kanungo, S., Monga, I.S.: Prioritizing Process Change Requests (PCRs) in Software Process Improvement. Software Process Improvement and Practice, Vol. 10. (2005) 441–453
6. Karlsson, J., Ryan, K.: A Cost-Value Approach for Prioritizing Requirements. IEEE Software. Sept/Oct (1997) 67–74
7. Karlsson, L., Regnell, B., Karlsson, J., Olsson, S.: Post-Release Analysis of Requirements Selection Quality - An Industrial Case Study. Proc. of the 9th Int. Workshop on Requirements Engineering - Foundation for Software Quality (REFSQ'03), Velden Austria (2003) 47–56
8. Karlsson, L., Regnell, B., Thelin, T.: A Case Study in Retrospective Analysis of Release Planning in an Agile Project. Workshop on the Interplay of Requirements Engineering and Project Management in Software Projects (REProMan'05), Paris France (2005)
9. Kerth, N. L.: Project Retrospectives - A handbook for team reviews. Dorset House Publishing, New York (2001)
10. Mens, T., Demeyer, S.: Evolution Metrics. International Workshop on Principles of Software Evolution (IWPSE 2001), Vienna Austria (2001)
11. Regnell, B., Höst, M., Natt och Dag, J., Beremark, P., Hjelm, T.: An Industrial Case Study on Distributed Prioritisation in Market-driven Requirements Engineering for Packaged Software. Requirements Engineering, Vol. 6. Springer-Verlag (2001) 51–62
12. Saaty, T.L.: The Analytic Hierarchy Process. McGraw-Hill, New York (1980)
13. http://www.focalpointus.com (visited March 2006)
14. http://www.releaseplanner.com (visited March 2006)
15. http://www.versionone.net (visited March 2006)

A Qualitative Evaluation Method for Business Process Tools

Erika M. Nieto-Ariza[1], Guillermo Rodríguez-Ortiz[1,2], and Javier Ortiz-Hernández[1]

[1] Centro Nacional de Investigación y Desarrollo Tecnológico,
Interior internado Palmira s/n, Cuernavaca, Morelos, 62490 México
{erika, ortiz}@cenidet.edu.mx
[2] Instituto de Investigaciones Eléctricas, Reforma 113, 62490,
Cuernavaca, Morelos, México
gro@iie.org.mx

Abstract. The web plays a central role in such diverse application domains as business. As the use of web grows, organizations are increasingly choosing to use it to provide their services to their clients. Services are the systemization of the business processes in the organization. A bad definition and management of the services makes the systematization fail or not to have the expected success. The business process modeling is the first step in the systematization. Due to the great number of modeling tools in existence it is necessary to identify the information that they allow to specify. In this paper, a set of concepts is proposed to evaluate modeling tools for business process modeling using three levels of abstractions –organizational, conceptual and web. The evaluation compares the modeling capabilities supplied by the different techniques. This evaluation also allows determining what modeling tool is the most appropriate to model specific concepts of interest to a particular organization or problem.

1 Introduction

The development projects fail due to a bad administration of the requirement, lack of abilities of the responsible people and the incorrect use of the techniques to specify requirements. Additionally, organizations confront the problem of integration of different technology at their business process. They should decide how the technology systems support business and how incrementally the technology systems become an integral part of the business process [1, 2]. Models are commonly used to flexibility represent complex systems and to observe the performance in the business process when a technology system is integrated [3, 4, 5].

The documented knowledge about the organization and its business processes is a great help to define the requirements for an information system to be develop. To model a system that meets the organizational needs, must first understand both business organization and the requirements specific to the desired web system. This model must capture the domain without reference to a particular system implementation or technology [4]. Information in the models about the organization and business process allows to define the web system requirements. A business model must include information about the business processes and among other things, the rules that govern the business execution, the process goals, and the problems that

J. Münch and M. Vierimaa (Eds.): PROFES 2006, LNCS 4034, pp. 34–46, 2006.

might appear when trying to achieve these goals [4]. This information will support better decision making that result in a correct business performance with the right documentation to specify the web system requirements.

One of the problems in the process modeling is the great number of techniques to model and specify requirements, each ones has its own elements, it makes complex and laborious to compare the techniques. To select an incorrect technique makes that the model of the organization does not represent the organization needs.

Three modeling levels are proposed who integrate a set of concepts to build web application models (fig.1). Each level of abstraction describes the business process in a specific view and certain information concepts are integrated. The concepts are properties that structurally describe types of requirements in a specific level of abstraction [1, 2, 3, 4, 5]. Here, the concept of model is used to indicate a textual or graphical knowledge representation at any of the following levels of abstraction: a)Organizational, its goal is to describe how the organization works and the business process that are going to be systematized with a web information system; b)Conceptual, its goal is to describe the role of the software system and its integration with a particular organizational environment; c) Web, its goal is to describe the business process on the basis of the semantic of web application [6,7].

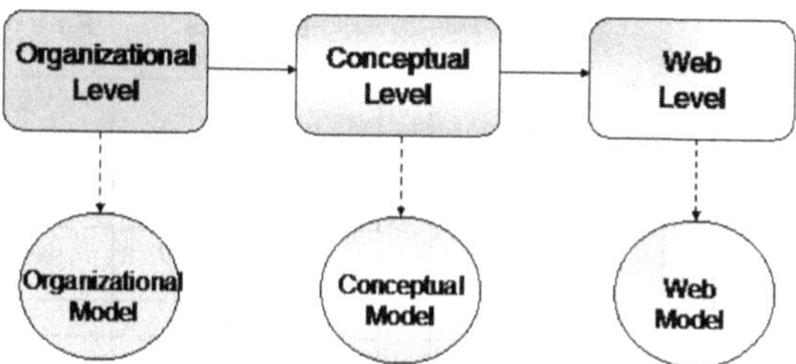

Fig. 1. Levels of abstraction

The basis of our contribution is in the detection and classification of a set of concepts which are used to evaluate modeling tools and to identify the capabilities that each tool has to model at the three levels of abstraction. There are some methods and methodologies to evaluate business process modeling, however, they do not evaluate capabilities but rather the functionality of the application or the modeling tools. Rosemman proposal an ontology to evaluate organizational modeling grammars identifying their strength and weaknesses [8]. Luis Olsina [9] and Devanshu Dhyani [10], their proposal is a methodology to evaluate the characteristics of a web application in operational phases. The evaluation method proposed in this paper is useful for the analyst, designer and evaluator; it allows knowing how many capacities the tools offers and how complex the models obtained are when the tools are used. It is a previous step in the selection of a business modeling tool, and it allows to select a tool by its capacities before to evaluate the functionality that it has.

The structure of this paper is as follows: in section 2 the modeling concepts that comprise our approach are presented, in section 3 the evaluation methodology for tools is presented, in section 4 the results of the evaluation are presented, in section 5 the evaluation methodology for products is presented, in section 6 the benefits of the methodology are presented, and last conclusions is discussed.

2 Concepts for a Business Process Modeling

Business processes model can be viewed at many levels of abstraction, and complementary model views can be combined to give a more intelligible, accurate view of a system to develop than a single model alone [3, 4, 5, 11]. For this reason, this approach establishes three levels of abstraction and each one includes certain modeling concepts of features as shown in table 1. Concepts in each one level of abstraction were selected based on the analysis of several techniques and tools for business process modeling [1, 3, 4, 6, 8, 9, 10, 11, 12, 13, 14, 15] at three levels of abstraction –organizational, conceptual and web. Concepts define the key elements in a business process.

Table 1. Modeling concepts at each level of abstraction

Organizational level	Conceptual level	Web level	
		Business process	Pure navigation
Actor	Actor	---	Navigation page - Relationship
		User profile (Rol)	User profile (Rol)
		Class (object)	---
Resource	Artifact	Artifact	Artifact
Goal	Goal	---	Goal
Task	Function	Service	Service
Activity	Event	Event	---
Business rule	Constraint	Precondition and postcondition	---
Quality	No functional requirement	No functional requirement	---

The concepts integrate the levels of abstraction, such that, starting with the organizational model, the elements of the web application are identified. Through the correspondence of an aspect in one level to its corresponding concept in the next level, the three levels are integrated in a complete view of the business process. For example, the task concept in the organizational level corresponds to the function concept at the conceptual level and later it will be correspond to a service concept at the Web level of abstraction (business process and pure navigation).

The **organizational** modeling concepts are as follows.

- *Actor.* It describes an entity (human, hardware, software or process activity) that has a specific goal, participates in the business process, or has relationships with other actors. An actor may have different roles.

- *Resource.* It describes an informational or physical entity that is transferred between actors as a result of a task executed by an actor.
- *Goal.* It describes a business process desired state that an organization imposes to itself, with a certain degree of priority; the goal must be quantified whenever possible.
- *Task.* It describes a series of activities oriented to reach a goal; it may indicate how should be accomplished.
- *Activity.* It describes a set of actions to carry out one task.
- *Business rule.* It describes the actions and criteria that govern the execution of the business process.
- *Quality.* It describes the desired characteristics in the business process as speed, effectiveness, etc.

The **conceptual** modeling concepts are as follows.

- *Actor.* It describes an entity (human, hardware, software or process activity) that interacts with the information system and that might play different roles.
- *Artifact.* It describes an abstract or physical entity that is transferred between an actor and the information system.
- *Goal.* It describes the information system purpose, limitations and responsibilities, from the business view point.
- *Function.* It describes a service that must be provided by the information system to the actors.
- *Event.* It describes a change in the business process in one instant specific of time.
- *Constraint.* It describes a condition for a service execution provide by the information system.
- *Non functional.* It describes the desired quality features or constraints for the information system as for example, response time, platform and interface requirements, etc.

The **Web** modeling concepts are as follows.

- *Navigation relationship.* It describes a global vision of the Web application according to a user profile with relation to the information to be presented and the desired page sequencing.
- *User profile.* It describes the user unique use of the Web application. A user can have many profiles for the same Web application.
- *Class.* It describes an object type to model the entities that integrate the application, and the information handling for the users to navigate. It is a set of objects that share a template.
- *Artifact.* It describes an abstract object to be transferred between the Web application and a user or vice versa as a result of an event execution.
- *Objective.* The purpose of the Web application, from a simple information pages displayer to a complex and sophisticated corporate portal.
- *Service.* It describes an activity or an action that the web application has.
- *Event.* It describes the trigger of an activity or action that might be carried out to obtain a result or artifact.

- *Pre and pos condition.* Describes the performance of an event execution where a precondition is a required object state before the event can be executed and a post condition is the required object state after the event execution.
- *Non functional.* Describes the desired quality features or constraints for the Web application, as for example, access security, data encryption, response time, interface requirements, etc.

Each concept is used as an evaluation parameter of one capability of an information modeling tool according to the following methodology. Each concept integrated the business process modeling and they are related to each other. In this paper we only present one of the three concepts relationships (fig.2).

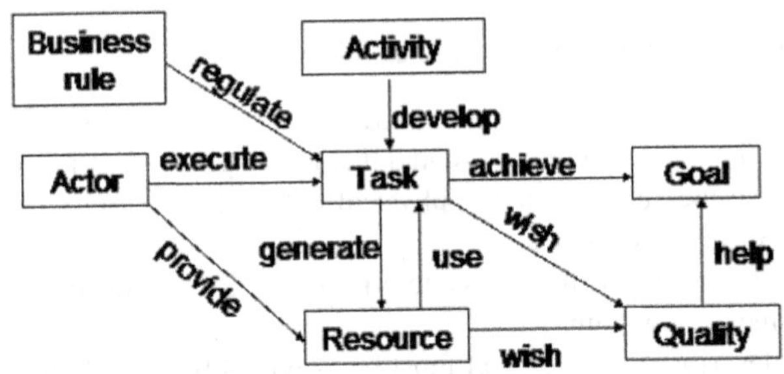

Fig. 2. Concepts relationship at organizational level

3 Evaluation Method of Tools

In this approach, we use qualitative variables with a nominal scale for the evaluation methodology tools. A nominal scale indicates assignments to groups or classes such as gender, geographic region, business type, etc. Numerical identification is chosen strictly for convenience [16]. The evaluation strategy first associates to each aspect a scale between 0 and 5 which is going to be used to evaluate one of the modeling capabilities. Then one information tool is evaluated for all the aspects in each level of abstraction. After the first modeling tool, a second one is evaluated, and so on until all selected tools are evaluated.

3.1 Concept Evaluation Scales

The definition of an evaluation scale for each aspect is a task that requires the analysis of different modeling tools. An evaluation scale is obtained by first taking a list of the capabilities of one tool, and then a list of capabilities from a second tool, from a third, etc., until, finally a total set of all the capabilities from all the tools analyzed is obtained. These capabilities are sorted by the concepts presented before and a scale is defined for each aspect using the capabilities related to the aspect. Also, a desired capability mentioned in the literature may be used in the definition of a scale.

Table 2. Evaluation scale for the actor concept at the organizational level of abstraction

The modeling tool has the capability to: Show actors in a general way. Indicate the type of an actor: a human, software, hardware or a subprocess. Indicate the role or roles of each one of the actors in the business process.
Grade: 0: No actors are supplied by the tool. 2: Describes actors in a general way. 3: Describes actors and their types. 3: Describes actors and their roles. 5: Describes actors, their types and their roles.

Table 3. Evaluation scale for the business rule concept at the organizational level of abstraction

The modeling tool has the capability to: Show the business rules. Indicate the type of a business rule: restriction, condition, law or action. Indicate who the origin of a business rule is. Indicate who the concept connected to the business rule is. Indicate the execution hierarchy.
Grade: 0: No business rules are supplied by the tool. 1: Describes business rules. 2: Describes business rules indicating which concept is connected to it. 3: Describes business rules indicating which concept is connected to it and one of the next characteristics: origin, type or execution hierarchy. 4: Describes business rules indicating which concept is connected to it and two the next characteristics: origin, type or execution hierarchy. 5: Describes business rules indicating which concept is connected to it, the origin, type and execution hierarchy.

The aspects evaluation scales facilitate the comparison of the different modeling tools capabilities. In this paper we only present two of the 23 evaluation scales (see Tables 2 and 3). The grade assigned to the properties of the concept is chosen strictly for convenience

The evaluation consists in assign a value in each concept of the tool. For example, the concept business rule at the organizational level of abstraction; if the method contains the business rule concept, the method should have 1 point. If the method in the business rule indicates which concept is connected to it; the method in this concept should have 2. If the method contains the concept of business rule and it indicates which concept is connected to it, and also one of the follows: the origin, type or execution hierarchy, the method should have 3 points. If the method contains the concept of business rule and it indicates which concept is connected to it, and also two of the follows: the origin, type or execution hierarchy; the method should have 4 points. The method should have 5 points if the method contains the concept of business rule, it indicates which concept is connected to it, who is the origin, type and execution hierarchy.

3.2 Evaluation of Tools

To perform an evaluation, the objective must be clear to the evaluators and the modeling tools to be evaluated are selected accordingly. The evaluators have to evaluate the three levels of abstraction –organizational, conceptual and Web- for a total of 23 parameters and for each parameter *pi* and for a modeling tool a corresponding evaluation e_i is obtained.

The results are displayed in a table for easy of comparison and a total score is obtained for each tool and for each level of abstraction as Σe_i. Here, the results are integrated comparing them to determine the grade of satisfaction of each tool at one level of abstraction. A tool that score better than other means that it has additional capabilities to model requirements at the corresponding level of abstraction.

3.3 Weighted Assessment

The methodology allows assigning weights to each of the 23 evaluations to reflect the interests of the enterprise or the modeling group, or the nature of a particular problem. A weight w_i is to be multiplied by the evaluation e_i to ponder the corresponding capacity with respect to the modeling capabilities necessary to build a particular requirements model.

The weight w_i can be seen as a relevance level of a modeling capability with respect to a specific modeling task. The weight w_i is a factor, for each evaluation e_i, defined by the representatives of the organization to characterize its interests, the final evaluation of a tool will be calculated as follows:

$$\Sigma\, w_i\, e_i \qquad \text{where} \qquad 0 < w_i < 2 \tag{1}$$

The weight w_i is given a value of 0, 1, or 2, where a 0 means that the enterprise does not have any interest in that modeling capacity. A value of 2 for weight w_i means that the corresponding modeling capability is very important for the model(s) to be built, and that if a tool does not have that modeling capacity, then the tool is not of use for a problem domain or the organization needs. Finally, 1 means that the capability is to be used for requirements modeling in the enterprise. In this way, the value of $\Sigma w_i\, e_i$ will be greater for those tools that have the desired modeling capabilities for a specific problem.

4 Results in the Evaluation Tools

To evaluate the scale some tools were evaluated. The following tools i*, Tropos, EKD, BPM-UML, OO-Method/OOWS, and OWS [6,8,4,9,10,11,12,13,14,15] were evaluated as shown in tables 4, 5, 6a and 6b. Three different studio cases were developed with each tool, they were used to observe the behavior of the tools and the concepts they model or not. Some comments are included below each table.

Table 4. Organizational level evaluation of the tools

Organizational level	Max. Value	I*	Tropos	EKD	BPM-UML
Actor	5	5	5	5	5
Resource	5	5	5	2	5
Goal	5	1	3	4	3
Task	5	2	4	3	2
Activity	5	0	2	0	4
Business rule	5	2	0	5	4
Quality	5	3	4	4	4
Total	**35**	18	23	23	27

The result shows the capacities of each tool. BPM-UML obtains good scores for this level, but i* has the lowest score. The tools were evaluated with respect to the parameters defined for the approach presented here. During the evaluation of tools, they show their own characteristics, in this level we only present for the concept actor:

- The modeling tool i* provide actors and a classification for them: agent, rol, and position. An agent can be a person, artificial agents, hardware or software.
- The modeling tool Tropos does not provide actors, but uses the concept agent with the same meaning in both concepts.
- The modeling tool EKD provides actors with the semantic of this approach.
- The modeling tool BPM-UML does not provide actors as such things, but uses resources provided or required by the business processes. However, BPM-UML allows describing person-resources that have the characteristics indicated above for actors.

Table 5. Conceptual level evaluation of the tools

Conceptual level	Max. Value	I*	Tropos	EKD	BPM-UML	OO-Method
Actor	5	5	5	5	5	1
Artifact	5	5	5	4	5	4
Goal	5	1	3	4	3	1
Function	5	2	2	5	5	2
Event	5	0	1	0	4	3
Constrain	5	2	0	5	4	5
No functional	5	3	4	4	4	0
Total	**35**	17	20	27	30	16

The result shows the capacities of each tool, for example, BPM-UML obtains good scores for this level, but OO-Method has the lowest score. During the evaluation of tools, they show their own characteristics, in this level we only present for the concept event:

- The modeling tools i* and EKD do not provide events.
- The modeling tool Tropos does not provide events as such things, but uses the concept sub-plan that has some characteristics indicated above for events.
- The modeling tools BPM-UML and OO-Method provide the concept event.

Table 6 (a). Web level evaluation of the tools (business process)

Web level	Max. Value	Tropos	OO-Method / OOWS	OOWS
User profile	5	3	4	4
Class	5	0	5	5
Artifact	5	4	4	4
Service	5	3	3	3
Event	5	1	3	2
Pre and post condition	5	2	5	3
No functional	5	3	0	0
Total	**35**	16	24	21

The result shows the capacities of each tool, for example, OO-Method/OOWS obtains good scores for this level, but Tropos has the lowest score. During the evaluation of tools, they show their own characteristics, in this level we only present for the concept precondition and postcondition:

- The modeling tools OO-Method/OOWS and OOWS provides the concept precondition and postcondition.
- The modeling tool Tropos does not provide the concept precondition and postcondition, but uses the concept of simples and complex action that have the some characteristics indicated above for precondition and postcondition.

Table 6 (b). Web level evaluation of the tools (pure navigation)

Web level	Max. Value	Tropos	OO-Method / OOWS	OOWS
Navegational page – relationship	5	1	5	5
User profile	5	3	4	4
Goal	5	3	0	0
Artifact	5	4	4	4
Service	5	3	3	3
Total	**25**	14	16	16

The result shows the capacities of each tool, for example, OO-Method/OOWS and OOWS obtain highest scores for this level, but Tropos has the lowest score. During the evaluation of tools, they show their own characteristics, in this level we only present for the concept goal:

- The modeling tools OO-Method/OOWS and OOWS does not provide the concept goal.
- The modeling tool Tropos provides the concept goal, but it provides the concept with the following characteristics: a) describe the goal, b) who provide the goal, and c) the service associated to it.

5 Evaluation Methodology of Products

The concepts allow to evaluate the products obtained when different tools are applied to a definition problem. The evaluation capability can be completed with the product evaluation. In this paper, we present a brief example of the product methodology.

Business process (at conceptual level): Sale registration. The product existence must be updating. A client selects a product and the system registers the sale. Also, the system registers the payment. The payment must be with cash or VISA card. When the sale is ended, the stock is updating, and then a receipt of sale is printed.

The model obtained with the i* tool is showed in the figure 3.

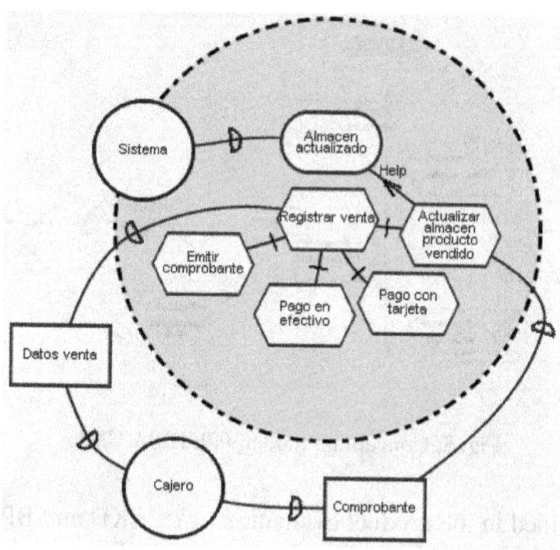

Fig. 3. Conceptual model with i*

The model obtained with the EKD tools is showed in the figure 4.

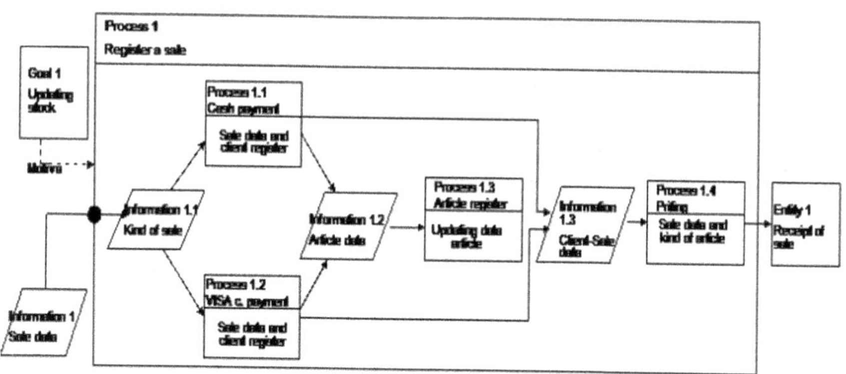

Fig. 4. Conceptual model with EKD

The model obtained with the BPM-UML tool is showed in the figure 5.

Some of the variables defined for the analysis and evaluation of the products are the following:

a) Work flow
b) Execution order in the function
c) Tree of decomposition
d) Organization.
e) Clear identification of the elements that the tools model

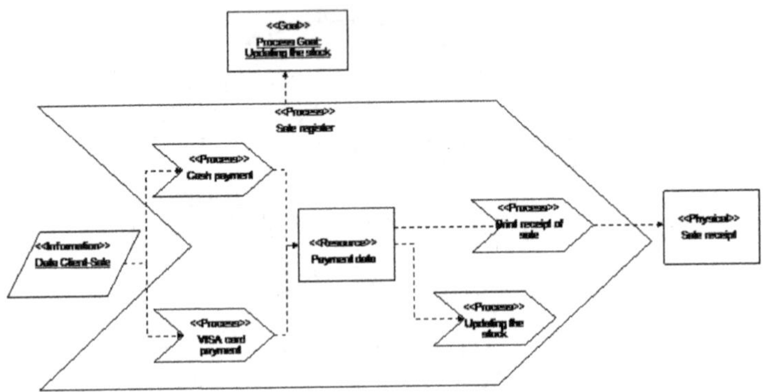

Fig. 5. Conceptual model with BPM-UML

The results obtained in the product evaluation of i*, EKD and BPM-UML tools are presented in the table 5. In this paper we present only three models evaluated. The results obtained in the product evaluation can be used with the results of the capability evaluation. The capability evaluation shows that BPM-UML obtains good score, but in the product evaluation EKD obtains the best score. A model in EKD presents the four variables defined in this evaluation methodology. The product evaluation is another reference to select a tool to model a specific problem or a business process (capability – product).

Table 5. Products evaluation

VARIABLES / TOOLS	Work flow	Execution order	Tree of decomposition	Organization	Identification of elements
I*	YES	NO	YES	NO	NO
EKD	YES	YES	YES	YES	YES
BPM-UML	YES	NO	YES	YES	YES

6 Benefits of the Methodologies

The approach has been used to evaluate e-learnig systems [17]. Additionally, it has been applied in the development of various study cases to evaluate tools and to clearly appreciate the concepts that the tools allow to model. The approach has also the advantage of the flexibility to use weights which allows evaluating tools with respect to the desired capacities for the organization.

There are many proposals to model the organizational, conceptual and web requirements and each one has its own elements. Some use the same concepts but the names are different, which makes it complex and laborious to compare the tools. The approach presented here unifies the various terminologies allowing establishing evaluation parameters for the tools modeling capacities and techniques. It is unimportant if the technique or tool are graphical or not, because the evaluation methodology gives the semantic assessments of the tools.

7 Conclusion

The approach presented allows to evaluate the modeling capacities offered by several tools and to establish comparisons between the corresponding tools techniques. This helps to select the tool that is more appropriate to the needs of the problem domain, since the methodology is quite flexible. On the other hand, the actual definition of the evaluation parameters can be changed, and on the other hand, the establishment of weights by the evaluator, is a powerful means to select the relevant aspects for a specific organization.

Additionally, the approach presented allows to evaluate the products or models obtained when different tools are applied to a requirements definition problem. In this evaluation a set of variables is proposed to evaluate the complexity of each model. This allows not only knowing how many capacities the tools offers, but also how complex the models obtained are when the tools are used. To continue with this project, one future work is also to use metrics on the products or models obtained when different tools are applied.

References

1. James Pasley, "How BPEKL and SOA are changing web services development", IEEE Internet Computing. May – June 2005.
2. Peter F. Green, Michael Rosemann y Marta Indulska, "Ontological Evaluation of Enterprisee systems Interoperability Using ebXML", IEEE Transactions on Knowledge and Data Engineering, Vol 17, No. 5, IEEE Computer Society, may 2005.
3. Mersevy T. and Fenstermacher K., "Transforming software development: and MDA road map", IEEE Computer Society, September 2005.
4. H. E. Eriksson and M. Penker, Bussiness, Modeling with UML, Chichester, UK, Wiley Editorial, 2000.
5. Thomas O. Meservy and Kurt D. Fenstermacher, Transforming software development: An MDA Road map, computer Society, IEEE, September 2005.
6. E. Yu, Modelling Strategic Relation for Process Reengineering, Universidad de Toronto, Canada, 1995. Thesis submitted for the degree of Doctor of Philosophy.
7. Ginige and S. Murugesan, "Web Engineering: An Introduction" IEEE Multimedia, pp 1-5, Jan-Mar 2001.
8. Peter F. Green, Michael Rosemann y Marta Indulska, "Ontological Evaluation of Enterprisee systems Interoperability Using ebXML", IEEE Transactions on Knowledge and Data Engineering, Vol 17, No. 5, IEEE Computer Society, may 2005.

9. Olsina, Luis A., Metodología cuantitativa para la evaluación y comparación de la calidad de sitios web. Tesis doctoral. Facultad de Ciencias Exactas, Universidad Nacional de La Plata, noviembre de 1999.
10. Devanshu Dhyani, Wee Keong Ng, and Sourav S. Bhowmick, A survey of web metrics, ACM computer survey, Vol 34, No. 4. December 2002, pp. 469-503.
11. Bubenko J., Brash D. y Stirna J. EKD User Guide, Royal Institute of technology (KTH) and Stockholm University, Stockholm, Sweden, Dept. of Computer and Systems Sciences, 1998.
12. E. Insfrán, O.Pastor y R. Wieringa, "Requirements Engineering-Based conceptual Modelling", Requirements Engineering Springer-Verlang, vol. 2, pp. 7:61-72, 2002.
13. J. Gómez, C. Cachero and O. Pastor, "Conceptual modeling of device-independent Web applications" IEEE Multimedia, vol. 8 issue: 2 , pp 26-39, April-June 2001.
14. L. Liu, E. Yu Intentional Modeling to support Identity Management 23rd Int. Conference on Conceptual Modeling (ER 2004). Shanghai, China, November, 2004. Springer. pp. 555-566.
15. J. Fons, O. Pastor, P. Valderas y M. Ruiz, OOWS: Un método de producción de software en ambientes web. 2005. http://oomethod.dsic.upv.es/anonimo/..%5Cfiles%5CBookChapter%5Cfons02b.pdf
16. William L. Carlson and Betty Thorne, Applied statistical methods economics, and the social sciences. Prentice may, 1997
17. Eduardo Islas P., Eric Zabre B. y Miguel Pérez R., "Evaluación de herramientas de software y hardware para el desarrollo de aplicaciones de realidad virtual", consultado en el 2005, http://www.iie.org.mx/boletin022004/tenden2.pdf

An Effective Source Code Review Process for Embedded Software

Masayuki Hirayama, Katsumi Ohno, Nao Kawai, Kichiro Tamaru, and Hiroshi Monden

Software Engineering Center, Information Technology Promotion Agency, 2-28-8, Honkomagome Bunkyo-ku, Tokyo, 113-6591, Japan
{m-hiraya, k-ohno, n-kawai, tamaru,h-monden}@ipa.go.jp

Abstract. This paper discusses about the improvement of source code review process for embedded software development project, and also proposes an effective approach to source code review for embedded software. As the start point of the discussion, this paper firstly discusses the results of a survey we conducted of about 290 embedded software development projects in Japan from the viewpoint of quality. Next, this paper discusses the problems of current source code review process and the way for improvement of the process. In the discussion, we focus on quality characteristics in ISO/IEC9126 and apply this to our improved review process. That is, we propose a new review process which is based on selection of review target portion in the target source code and selection of the review check items. As for the selection of review check items, using the characteristics viewpoints in ISO/IEC9126, review check items are selected according to the target software features.

1 Introduction

Recently, various embedded systems have come into widespread use in everyday life. An embedded system is composed of various hardware devices and their control software. According to the technical evolution of hardware devices, the functional size of software embedded in this hardware has been increased. At the same time, the code size or the code complexity of this software is also increasing. These trends tend to lead to the increased incidence of serious trouble concerning the behavior of embedded systems resulting in serious trouble concerning system behavior, which in turn causes serious inconvenience in everyday life.

So, the problems for embedded software quality are very serious problems and the suitable solutions are required. In this paper, we focus on quality perspective of source code for embedded software and propose a way to improve source code review process based on software quality characteristics in ISO/IEC9126[1] .

In this paper, section 2 discusses the features of embedded software development projects based on the results of a survey we conducted covering about 290 embedded software development project profiles in Japan. Following this discussion, section 3 summarizes problems concerning source code review process. In section 4, we propose a way to improve source code review process by Selective Review

J. Münch and M. Vierimaa (Eds.): PROFES 2006, LNCS 4034, pp. 47–60, 2006.

Tech-nique(SRT). We have been developing SRT in order to solve problems concerning code review process and also in order to improve source code quality. Section 5 briefly introduces an experimental trial and its results.

2 Feature for Embedded Software

In this section, we confirm the factors which deeply impact on source code quality for embedded software, and discuss the problems concerning embedded software development based on the results of the survey.

2.1 Outline of the Survey

We conducted survey of embedded software development projects. The survey was conducted by corporation between Information technology Promotion Agency Japan and Ministry of Economy, Trade and Industry (METI). The survey was aimed at making clear the current status of embedded software development and their features. Target area of the survey was ranged about 15 domain segments from embedded software in home appliances to industrial control system (Table 1). In the survey, we distributed questionnaire sheets to about 400 organizations in above domain areas via mail-survey style, and got 290 valid responses. In the survey, we mainly focused on software engineering viewpoint in embedded software development. The questionnaire sheet include following four main topics – project overview, quality perspective, process perspective and project management perspective. There are about fifty questions in the questionnaire sheet. In this paper, we mainly discuss the quality perspective of embedded software development by using the survey results.

Table 1. Target domain area of the survey

1	Audio Visual system	9	Transportation system
2	Home appliances	10	Factory automation
3	Personal information system	11	Business facirities
4	Education systems	12	Medical system
5	Office automation system	13	Mesearment facirities
6	Business system	14	Other application system
7	Communication systems	15	Software development environment
8	Communication infrastructure system		

2.2 Quality for Embedded Software

Figure1 and Figure2 show analysis results of embedded software trouble based on the results of our survey. Figure 1 indicates that about 50 % of embedded software trouble is related to the software implementation phase. Though the trouble related to upper phase – requirements or design phase –accounts for about 40% trouble in the implementation phase is notable. As for a poor quality of the implementation phase of embedded software development, following two factors can be considered.

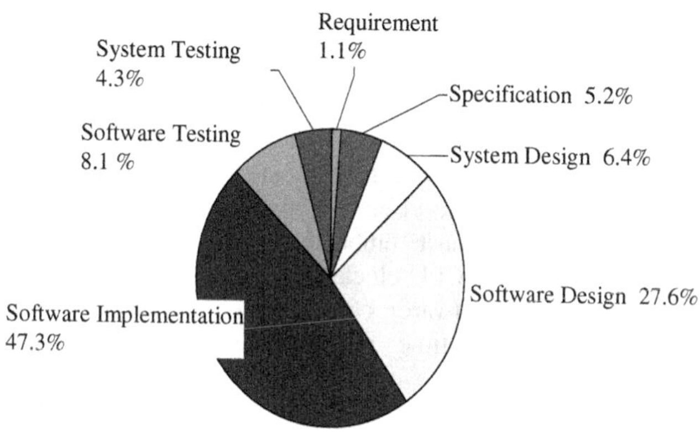

Fig. 1. Problem Occurring phase

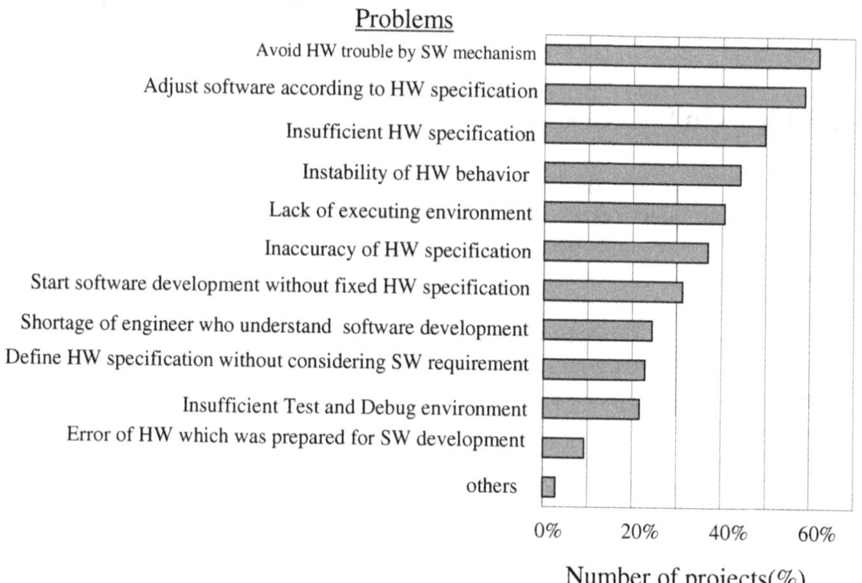

Fig. 2. Cause of trouble

(a) Programming Language effects and engineer's skill

From our survey, we confirmed that the most popular language for embedded software development is C language. That is, about 70 % of the projects are developed by using C language in the survey. C++ or Java, for which plenty of software components or libraries are prepared, is not always used sufficiently in embedded software development. C language has a powerful ability for expressing memory accesses which is a typical feature of embedded software. According to this feature, in many embedded software development, C language is widely used as usual. However, C language has considerable ambiguity of expression and tends to reflect the engineer's skill or experience concerning source code. So, source code in C language is often of uneven quality. As a result, relatively large number of troubles is occurred in implementation phase.

(b) Hardware constraints' effects
On the other hand, Figure 2 shows that most trouble in embedded software development is related to hardware effects. Typically, embedded software runs on microcomputers[2]. Therefore most embedded software is subject to various constraints such as memory size, CPU clock speed, or other execution timing, which are mainly depended on hardware constraints. Accordingly, severe system performance such as hard real-time response tends to required, and in the implementation phase, performance turning is inevitable. However, excessive performance turning causes complexity explosion in source code. As a result, various constraints related to hardware devices become major obstacles in the implementation of embedded software, causing various kinds of trouble in source code of embedded software. So the above mentioned survey results suggest that there are some pitfalls of quality perspective in the implementation phase of embedded software development.

3 Problems in Source Code Review

Conventionally, as for the quality perspective in embedded software implementation, precisely source code review process is said to be an effective solution for improvement of source code quality.

In enterprise system development, various code review or code inspection techniques and their processes have been proposed [3] [4][5][6]. However, since embedded software is subject to various constraints, it is not suitable to apply these conventional techniques to the source code review process of embedded software. In this section, problems concerning source code review process for embedded software are discussed.

3.1 Problems Concerning Code Size

In line with the explosive growth in the functionality of embedded software, source code has been increasing in size. Figure 3 shows the trend of source code size (LOC) for cellular phone control software developed by a certain company. As this figure shows, code size has been increasing rapidly. On the other hand, in actual development fields, the time available for software development (doted line) has been shortening. As a result, time for source code review has been limited. So, efficiency of source code review is an important issue.

3.2 Variety of Code Check Items

Generally, before conducting source code review, viewpoints and review check items for code review should be arranged. For example, in automotive control software, the MISRA-C coding standard has been proposed and review to check that the code

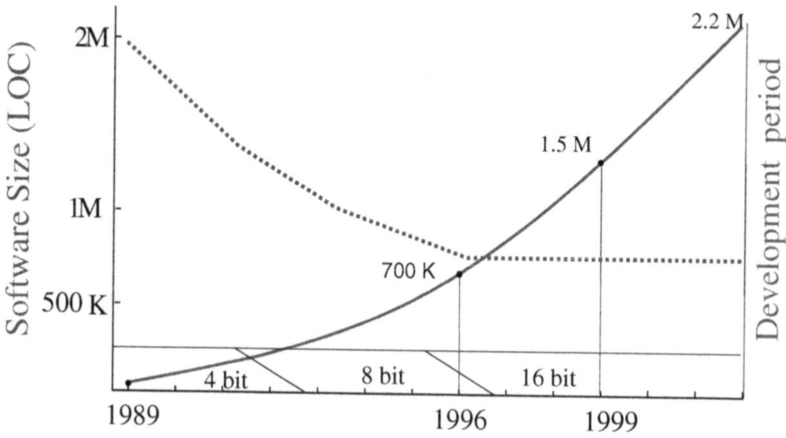

Fig. 3. Trend of software size in cellular phone

conforms to MISRA-C is recommended [7]. About 150 rules are defined in the MISRA-C standard. If we review the correctness of the code using MISRA-C, a large number of review check items are required. However, in an actual development project, it is difficult to conduct the code review by referring to the large number of review check items, because this type of rigorous review process requires a great effort and much time. Although the customization approach is also proposed in MISRA-C, the idea or standard for rule selection is largely depended on the reviewers' experiences.

3.3 Viewpoint for Source Code Review

Conventionally, most coding rules or standards are summarized according to the programming language's grammar or notations. However, coding rules of this type make it difficult to clarify the effects on software quality. As a result, engineers are sometimes insufficiently motivated to preserve the rules. Or, without suitable selection or consideration of the rules, engineers sometimes continue to utilize inefficient review processes by using unsuitable review items, with the result that the code review process is ineffective. So one of the most important factors in source code review processes are selection of review viewpoints.

4 Selective Review Process

4.1 Overview

In order to improve source code quality for embedded software, we have been discussing a more efficient source code review process. In our discussion, we concluded that the following two key requirements are essential for high efficient source code review process for embedded software.

1. Taking into consideration the target software's characteristics, viewpoints of the code review and target portion of the code review should be selected.
2. Moreover, effective review check items should also be selected from the pre-established review check items

In order to satisfy the above requirements for effective review process for embedded software, by applying Selective Review Technique, we work out an improved review process, SRP (Selective Review Process). Figure 4 shows an overview of the process. SRP consists of the following three steps, and the main features of the SRP are selection of the review target portion and selection of the review check items.

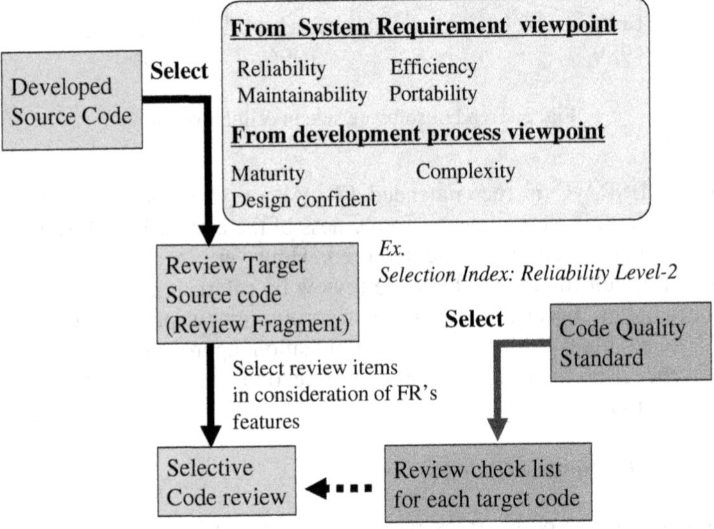

Fig. 4. Overview of the proposed process (SRP)

Step-1: Selection of the review target portion

Regarding a source code review in embedded software, problems related to the increase in source code size should be resolved. So, in order to solve this problem, the target source code is divided into small fragments taking into consideration the source code structures. Here, we call these fragments review fragments (RF)". For example, a typical RF in source code in C language is a programming module in C language. In our revised source code process, the necessity of code review for each RF is evaluated, and then RFs for which source code review is strongly required are selected. Taking the system quality requirement viewpoint and development process viewpoint into consideration, the characteristics of the RFs constituting the target software, are clearly identified and selected. We named this revised process "SRP (Selective Review Process)".

Step-2: Selection of review check items

In selection of review check items, the characteristic of the RFs are taken into consideration. That is, we select suitable review check items which matches the

RF's feature. In SRP, referring to the various coding rules already proposed or defined, a database for coding rules is prepared. And SRP also propose a selection strategy for review check items from this database. Using this strategy, suitable review check items matching RF characteristics are selected.

Step-3: Conducting source code review

According to the above steps, suitable RFs are selected and reviewed in accordance with suitable review check items reflecting RF's characteristics. Execution of this procedure within the framework of SRP ensures code reviews are conducted rigorously and efficiently. This approach to source code review is quite different from the conventional review process based on the engineer's experience.

4.2 Selection of the Review Target Fragment

Table 2 and Table 3 show strategies for RF selection. In order to select RFs, two viewpoints are considered: system quality requirement and system development process.

(a) System Quality Requirement Viewpoint

Conventionally, the ISO/IEC 9126 standard defines the software quality viewpoint as consisting of functionality, reliability, efficiency, maintainability, portability and usability[1]. These characteristics are mainly concern features of the software product's quality. On the contrary, as Figure 6 shows, from the source code implementation viewpoint, the following four characteristics are particularly importance: reliability, maintainability, portability and efficiency. Figure 6 shows review viewpoints which, according to the results of our survey, are significant in the review process of actual projects. In the development of actual products, these four viewpoints are considered to have the direct relations to the source code qualities. That is, if we intensively check or review source code by using these viewpoints, quality of the target source code can be improved. On the other hand, other viewpoints, usability and functionality, should mainly be considered in earlier phase – such as requirement or design phase. So, as for source code quality perspective, quality requirements for RFs are evaluated from these four viewpoints in SRP.

For example, if we want to evaluate the reliability viewpoint of a particular RF, the reliability level of the RF is evaluated according to a 4-level scale (Level 0 to Level 3) to determine whether the behavior of the overall system would be effected by trouble concerning the RF. In the evaluation, sub-characteristics of each characteristic in ISO/IEC9126 are taking into consideration and also hardware dependent affections are also evaluated.

(b) Development Process Viewpoint

At the same time, during the development of the target RFs, whether a suitable process is conducted is another important selection viewpoint for RFs. From the development process viewpoint, maturity, complexity and design confidence are important factors. Here, maturity represents the skill of the engineer who developed the fragment, and complexity means the extent of complexity in software design or implementation of the fragment. Design confidence represents whether a suitable design confirmation has been conducted. Regarding engineer's skill, whether an engineer has hardware related skill is evaluated. In addition, as for complexity, we also evaluate the complexity of interfaces between hardware and software. Generally, if the fragment is developed by an engineer with low skill or is developed without suitable design confirmation, the risk of quality troubles in software implementation is much greater. Thus, in SRP, development process factors are also evaluated in RF selection and RFs with poor development process are added to portions for review.

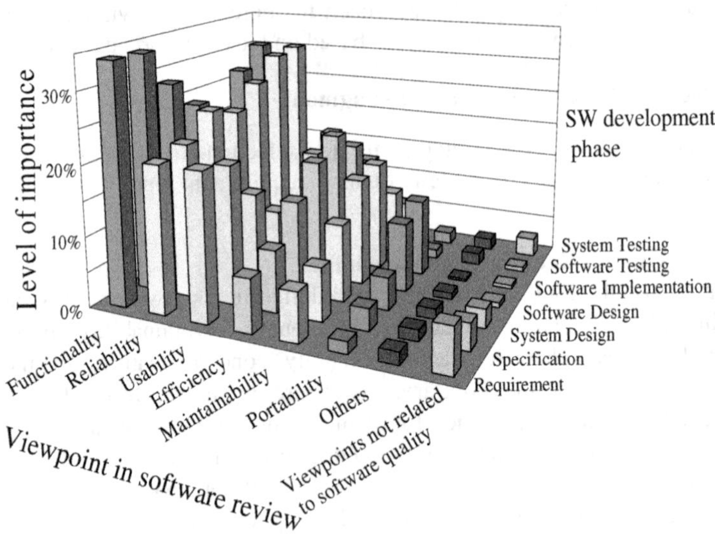

Fig. 5. Viewpoint in software review

Table 2. RF selection category

Selection Index *For the target portion of the software*

Reliability	Does the trouble of the portion gives large effects on overall system's behavior ?	L-3: Largely Yes L-2: Partially Yes L-1: No L-0: Not adapted
Efficiency	Is the portion deeply related to the system efficiency? -system behavior timing viewpoint -system's real time viewpoint -hardware resource efficiency viewpoint	L-3: Largely Yes L-2: Partially Yes L-1: No L-0: Not adapted
Maintainability	Does the portion have any plan for reuse? From the system evolution viewpoint Is the portion candidate of the system core asset ?	L-3: Largely Yes L-2: Partially Yes L-1: No L-0: Not adapted
Portability	Does the portion have any plan to execute on another execution environment?	L-3: Largely Yes L-2: Partially Yes L-1: No L-0: Not adapted

Table 3. RF selection category (Process view)

Selection Index (Process view) *For the target portion of the software*

Maturity	Does the portion developed by low skill engineers ?	L-3: Largely Yes L-2: Partially Yes L-1: No L-0: Not adapted
Complexity	Does the portion have large complexity in design or source code ?	L-3: Largely Yes L-2: Partially Yes L-1: No L-0: Not adapted
Design confident	Have the suitable review process for the target Portion been executed in design phase	L-3: Largely Yes L-2: Partially Yes L-1: No L-0: Not adapted

4.3 Review Check Item Selection

In SRP, considering the features of embedded source code, check items for code review are collected in the coding rule database. In the database, MISRA-C rules[7], Indian Hill coding rules[8][9], GNU coding style rules[10]and various other coding rules are used as references. In the coding rule database in SRP, as Figure 5 shows, four characteristics(reliability, efficiency, maintainability and portability) closely related to source code implementation are used as a framework for categorize rules. Moreover, in each characteristic category, a three-tire structure -rule/ instruction/ directive, is used. This three-tire structure makes it easy to select rules as review check items. For example, as Figure 6 shows, the maintainability category has the rule "1. Be conscious for reading by another engineer". Three instructions are associated with this rule: "Don't describe meaningless commands, sentences or calculation operations", "Remove any unused description", and "Avoid ambiguous declaration". Moreover, two directives are associated with the instruction "Avoid ambiguous declarations": "1.4 Declare one variable in one declaration description" and "Prepare one variable for one purpose". These directives for coding convention may be checked by source code grammatical check tools. The compliance level of each directive is clearly expressed: mandatory, recommend or informative. The meanings of the compliance level are as follows.

Mandatory :Check items with high priorities,
irrespective of the RF features
Recommend: Check item with medium priorities
Informal : Check item with low priorities

If the target RF requires high quality level, it is preferable for check items of this level to be adopted as review check items For the evaluation for each directive's level, real-time perspectives and reactive perspectives for embedded software are also taken into consideration.

Maintainability

Rule	Instruction	Directive	Level
1. Be conscious for reading by another engineers	Do not describe meaningless commands, sentences or calculation operations	1.1 Describe sentences which have suitable meanings.	R
		1.2 Do not declare modules, variables, and argument which will not be used in the system	M
	Remove any the unused description	1.3 Do not comment out for the source code description	
	Avoid ambiguous declarations	1.4 Declare one variable in one declaration description	R
		1.5 Prepare one variable for one purpose	R
2. Describe source code with consolidated manner	Define the description items and their order in the source files	2.1 Define the description item in the header files	M
		2.2 Define the items (declaration, definition etc.) in the source code	M
		2.3 Don't declare external variables or modules in the header files	M
	Set the coding style	2.5 Define indentation, space, Blanc and other rules for code description	
⋮	⋮	⋮	

Fig. 6. Coding Rule example in SRP

Table 4. Number of Coding rules in SRP

Catregory	Instructions	Num. of Directives
Reliability	1. Initialization for data areas – pay attention to their size and lifetime	9
	2. Pay attention to the data's scope, size and inner expression	18
	3. Pay attention to the illegal value of the data	11
Efficiency	4. Pay attention to timing, hardware resources	3
Maintainab	5. Be conscious for reading by the other engineers	28
	6. Describe code by the correct manner – without simple negligence	2
	7. Describe simple source code	6
	8. Describe source code with consolidated manner style	19
	9. Consider testability in source code	4
Portability	10. Do not use compiler dependent instruction set	15
	11. Localize the instruction set which have some problems in their portability	3

As shown in Figure 6, if the system requirement of a target RF requires Level 3 maintainability, all check directives categorized in mandatory, recommend and informative levels should be selected as the check items for this RF. On the other hand, if a target RF requires Level 1 maintainability, only check directives at the mandatory level should be selected. In the SRP database, about 120 rules are prepared as shown in Table 4. In SRP, since we can select suitable review check items from the database by referring to the system quality requirements, we can conduct a more efficient review of embedded software source code.

5 Case study

5.1 Target System of the Case Study

This section introduces an example of application case study of the SRP method for an actual embedded software development project. The target of the case study is a line tracer system which autonomously traces lines on the ground. Using a sensor, the system checks a line drawn on the ground and autonomously operates forward movement or backward movement with automatic handling according to the line's condition. The system contains the following typical features of embedded software.

1. Reactive perspective: the system should respond to outer contexts of the system
2. Real-time perspective: Running speed and handling times require rigid real-time behavior.
3. Hardware constraints perspective: this is closely related to embedded microcomputer characteristics.

5.2 Approaches

The purpose of the case study is to get an impression of adaptability of the SRP method. In the trial, which was conducted during the system development, source code the development team had finished developing was submitted to the SRP trial team. Then, the SRP trial team conducted a review of the submitted source code by using the SRP method, and comments and findings were summarized and analyzed. After that, the result of the review and its comments were fed back to the engineering team, and the effectiveness or adaptability of the method was confirmed. In addition, in this case study, each reviewer has a certain amount of experience of software development. However they do not have little experience for developing the target system.

5.3 Results

(a) Review fragment selection

The SRP trial team firstly divides a source code into fragments and evaluates each fragment's features and selects suitable RFs. Table 5 shows the results of RF selection. Since the source code of the target system is described in C language, we defined the program module in C language source code as a fragment for the code review. In the case study, we evaluate each fragment by referring to two viewpoints, namely, system quality requirements and development process, as shown in Table 2 and Table 3. The evaluation results are summarized in Table 5.

In this trial, as indicated in the Table 5, the quality requirements for fragments differ only slightly. On the other hand, since development team is relatively small, engineer's skill levels differ little. So, from the development process viewpoint, evaluation results related to maturity and design confidence are the same value for all fragments. From this fact, selection of RFs is mainly conducted from the system quality viewpoint in this trial (see Table 5). Some examples of RF selection are shown below.

Module "main" : Since high level are required for reliability and maintainability, we selected review check items which mainly focused on these characteristics.

Module "RunIniy" : Since this module is essential portion for the system behavior and high reliability is required, we select all review check items which belong in all classes (mandatory, recommend, informative) for this viewpoint. As for a maintainability and portability, since requirements for these viewpoints are slight, we select check items which are categorized in recommend level directives.

Table 5. RF selection result

Modeule name	Requirement viewpoint				Development Process viewpoint		
	Relaibility	Efficiency	Maintaina bility	Portability	Maturity	Complexit y	Design confident
main	3	1	3	1	1	1	2
RunInit	**3**	1	**2**	**2**	1	2	2
Run	3	3	2	1	1	3	2
RunStopRecover	3	3	3	1	1	3	2
RunWarp	**3**	**3**	1	1	1	**3**	2
DecideDrivePattern_OutEd	3	3	3	2	1	3	2
DecideDrivePattern_InEdg	3	3	3	2	1	3	2
DetectSteeringDirection	3	2	3	1	1	1	2
MoveForward	3	1	2	1	1	1	2
MoveBack	3	1	2	1	1	1	2
MoveBrake	3	2	2	2	1	1	2
LS_InitSensor	**3**	1	1	**2**	1	1	2
Steer	3	2	2	1	1	1	2
SteerStop	3	1	2	1	1	1	2
GetColor	3	2	2	2	1	1	2
CheckLineCenter	2	1	3	2	1	2	2
CheckStop	3	3	2	1	1	3	2
⋮	⋮	⋮	⋮	⋮	⋮	⋮	⋮
Mean value	2.65	1.81	1.88	1.27	1.00	1.62	2.00

Module "LS IniSensor" : This module is closely related to hardware devices. For reliability viewpoint, all check items are selected. And for the portability viewpoint, only recommend check items are selected. On the other hand, since this fragment requires relatively low maintainability or efficiency, so basic check items classified at the mandatory level are adopted.

(b) Discussion of the result

As the number o RFs is relatively small in the target system of the case study, here, we discuss the overall trends for all RFs. In this case study, evaluated mean values for the reliability, efficiency, maintainability, and portability characteristics are 2.65,1.81,1.88 and 1.27, respectively. From these values, review viewpoints in this case study are selected mainly by focusing on reliability and maintainability. In Table 6, review comments are summarized according to the review viewpoint categories. From this table there are found to be about 10 maintainability problems, which account for about 80% of all the problems pointed out in the SRP review process.

The conventional review process tends to focus on detecting illegal descriptions which may have serious impacts on system behavior. Consequently, the conventional review process tends to emphasize system reliability while neglecting other features of source code. On the other hand, in this case study, we focused on maintainability as well as reliability for the review check items. As a result, a relatively large number of items are pointed out in the source code concerning maintainability.

So the result of the case study clearly shows that the proposed review process can be improve source code review efficiency and it has an ability to improve source code quality in embedded software. By selecting code review viewpoints that take the target software's features into consideration, a code review matching the required quality level can be performed.

(c) Problems of dependencies and interrelations among the RFs
On the other hand, in the proposed review process, target source code is decomposed into small RFs and reviewer reviews these RFs. In the case study, some reviewers pointed out the difficulty for reviewing the dependencies and interrelations of each RFs. In order to review these perspectives, relation diagrams or relations maps for each RFs should be prepared.

Table 6. Number of directive violation detected in code review

Catregory	Instructions	Num. of directive violation
Reliability	1. Initialization for data areas – pay attention to their size and lifetime	0
	2. Pay attention to the data's scope, size and inner expression	1
	3. Pay attention to the illegal value of the data	0
Efficiency	4. Pay attention to timing, hardware resources	0
Maintainabili	5. Be conscious for reading by the other engineers	4
	6. Describe code by the correct manner – without simple negligence	2
	7. Describe simple source code	0
	8. Describe source code with consolidated manner style	3
	9. Consider testability in source code	1
Portability	10. Do not use compiler dependent instruction set	0
	11. Localize the instruction set which have some problems in their portability	1

6 Conclusion

This paper introduces the SRP method which can improve source code quality for embedded software. SRP is a method for reviewing source code efficiently and use of SRP in the review process can resolve the problems posed by the increasing size of source code.

In SRP, referring to the quality characteristics in ISO/IEC9126, four characteristics are adopted as evaluation viewpoints for source code fragments: reliability, efficiency, maintainability and portability. By using these four viewpoints, fragments in the target software are characterized. Then, review rules are selected based on a consideration of the required quality level for the system. Thus, by selecting review targets (review fragments or RFs) and review check items, a highly efficient source code review is realized. In the application trial of the SRP method for a line tracer system, we detected several pitfalls concerning maintainability by conducting a source code review focusing on maintainability.

In our future work, by applying our method to various system development projects, we intend to analyze more precise evaluation data for software features and set more precise criteria for check item selection. Additionally, through these activities, we will collect know-how concerning code review and reflect it in our method. Especially, we would like to establish a review method for dependency or interrelation among the Review Fragments.

References

1. ISO/IEC 9126-1,"Product Quality –Quality Model", http://www.iso.org/
2. Lee,E.A.:Embedded Software,Advances in computers, Vol.56,Academia Press(2002)
3. Poter,A..,H.Sity,C.A.Toman,"An experiment to assess the cost-benefits of code inspections in Large Scale software decelopment",Proc. Third ACM SIFSOFT Symposium on the Foundations of Software Engineering, 1996, ACM Press,pp.
4. Wheeler D.A., Brykczynski B.,Alexandria V.,"Software Peer Reviews," pp454-469 in R.Thayer, Software Engineering Project Management,IEEE Computer Society Press,1997
5. Tor Stalhane et.al, "Teaching the Process of Code Review",pp271-278,Proc, of ASWEC'04, 2004,IEEE.
6. Jason Remillard, "Source Code Review Systems", IEEE Software, vol.22, No.1,pp 74-77, January 2005.
7. MISRA-C:2004-Guidelines for the use of the C language in critical systems, http://www.misra.org.uk
8. L.W.Cannon et.al,"Recommend C style and coding standards",1990,http://www.csl.cornell.edu/courses/ece314/tutorials/cstyle.pdf
9. L.W. Cannon at. al. Recommended C Style and Coding Standards. Pocket reference guide. Specialized Systems Consultants, 1991. Updated version of ATT's Indian Hill coding guidelines R.Stallman et.al, GNU coding standards,2005,http://www.gnu.org/prep/standards

Troubleshooting Large-Scale New Product Development Embedded Software Projects

Petri Kettunen

Nokia Corporation
P.O. Box 301, 00045 NOKIA GROUP, Finland
petri.kettunen@nokia.com

Abstract. Many modern new product development (NPD) embedded software projects are required to be run under turbulent conditions. Both the business and the technological environments are often volatile. Uncertainty is then an inherent part of the project management. In such cases, traditional detailed up-front planning with supporting risk management is often inadequate, and more adaptive project management tools are needed. This industrial paper investigates the typical problem space of those embedded software projects. Based on a literature survey coupled with our practical experiences, we compose an extensive structured matrix of different potential project problem factors, and propose a method for assessing the project's problem profile with the matrix. The project manager can then utilize that information for problem-conscious project management. Some industrial case examples of telecommunications products embedded software development are illustrated.

1 Introduction

Most new electronic products contain embedded software in particular to enable more intelligent features and flexibility [1]. Thus, there will be more and more software projects developing embedded software for such new product development (NPD) markets.

Managing those modern industrial NPD projects successfully requires situation-aware control with the possible and oncoming troubles, taking the anticipated and even unexpected situational conditions into account [2]. Uncertainty is inherent [3, 4]. Project risk management is a traditional way of handling the obstacles, which may affect the project success adversely [5-7].

In this paper our premise is that in turbulent industrial business environments the product development projects must typically work under imperfect conditions. For example, it is hardly ever possible to avoid all external schedule pressures. In other words, the project management faces some problems all the time, and the project may be in some trouble even from the very beginning. This is sometimes referred to as project issue management [8]. In practice both proactive risk management as well as reactive problem (issue) management are needed [9].

The first step of problem-aware project management is to be able to recognize the current project problem factors. Project problems and uncertainties should be actively searched [10, 11]. There are no standard solutions, since the actual unique project context has to be taken into account.

J. Münch and M. Vierimaa (Eds.): PROFES 2006, LNCS 4034, pp. 61 – 78, 2006.

The purpose of this paper is to propose focused aids for identifying and evaluating the typical problem factors of large-scale NPD embedded software projects (such as telecommunications equipment). The rest of the paper is organized as follows. Chapter 2 explores the background and related work, and sets the exact research questions. Chapter 3 then describes our solution ideas, while Chapter 4 evaluates them. Finally, Chapter 5 makes some concluding remarks, and outlines further research ideas.

2 NPD Embedded Software Project Problems

2.1 Typical Software Project Problem Factors

Over the years, there have been numerous investigations about typical software project problems and failure factors. Table 1 lists some of the known ones (ordered by the year of publication). For more, see for example [6, 8, 12-19].

Table 1. A survey of software project problems, risks, and failure factors

Investigation	Distillation
Brooks [20]	Fundamental problems of software engineering management
Curtis, et al. [21]	Human and organizational factors affecting productivity and quality of large projects (including embedded systems)
Boehm [5]	Top 10 general software project risk items
McConnell [22]	36 "classic" software project mistakes; Common schedule risks
McConnell [23]	Software project "survival test"; Checklists
Royce [24]	Top 10 risks of "conventional" process
Brown [25]	Typical software project management malpractices and pitfalls
Ropponen, et al. [26]	Categories of software project risks and their influencing factors
Schmidt, et al. [27]	Systematic classification of empirically observed project risk factors
Smith [28]	40 root causes of software project failure
May, et al. [29]	Common characteristics of dysfunctional software projects
Fairley, et al. [30]	10 common software project problem areas and some antidotes

It is possible to categorize different project problem factors from various different points of view. For example the classic SEI taxonomy defines one way of categorizing common risk factors under project environment, product engineering, and program constraints [31]. Other alternatives are for example in [22, 26, 27, 32].

It is in addition important to understand that in complex (multi)project environments the project problems do not usually manifest themselves in isolation, but there are often multiple overlapping problems at the same time. Furthermore, there are often complex cause-effect relationships of the different problem factors, i.e., a single problem may have adverse additional consequences [32/Ch. 5, 33/Ch. 3].

2.2 Embedded Software Project Concerns

Compared to traditional software projects, embedded systems introduce certain additional intrinsic software development problems. There are both software engineering technical and management challenges [1, 21].

Figure 1 illustrates those many potential sources of problems. Notably many problems really stem from the software project external reasons and dependencies.

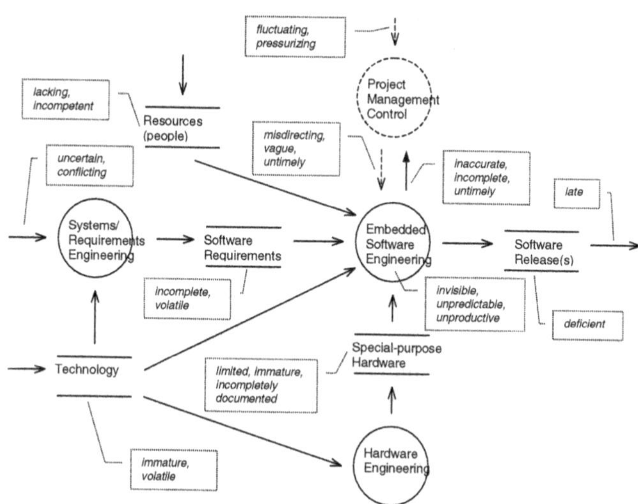

Fig. 1. Some embedded software project problem sources

Those special problem factors of embedded software projects have not been investigated especially widely in the literature. For some related studies, see for example [34-36]. Many embedded software project problems originate fundamentally from knowledge management issues [37].

2.3 NPD Software Project Characteristics

The development of new market-driven commercial products creates additional special characteristics of the software project environment. Figure 2 illustrates a typical NPD environment: The embedded software project team is an element of it. The NPD environment is not fundamentally different from other software development contexts. However, the emphasis on business drivers and product innovation management put considerable weight on certain problem areas in particular in large organizations.

The embedded software project teams working in such environments often face many sources of turbulence [4, 38]. The company, responding to emerging and fluctuating market needs, has to manage its product development portfolio (aggregate

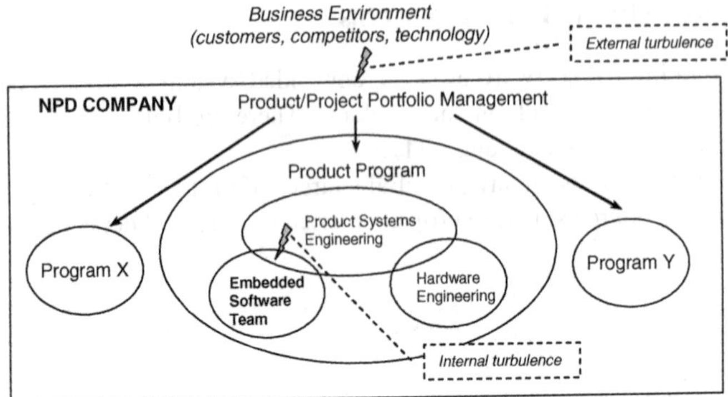

Fig. 2. Embedded software project team NPD context

project plan) accordingly [39/Ch. 2]. This may consecutively introduce various changes to the embedded software project teams (e.g., product features, releases schedules, project resource allocation). In addition, the other internal parts of the product development program (e.g., concurrent hardware engineering) may cause changes to the software part. It is important to understand the true nature of the project and the success criteria, and to incorporate the embedded software development as an integral part of the overall product system development [35, 40].

The problems of NPD projects have gained increasing research interests due to the current major transitions in many product development areas (e.g., telecommunications industry). A seminal survey of NPD literature is presented in [25]. An integrative model of different contributing product development project success factors is constructed. Ernst makes a critical summary of the NPD success factors empirical research results [41]. Notably there is no universal definition of "success". Recently for example Cooper, Edgett and Kleinschmidt survey the general success/failure factors [42]. In general, software new product development can be seen as a series of questions and problems to be solved [11].

2.4 Research Questions

Based on the background presented in Ch. 2.1-2.3, we now set the following specific research questions:

1. How to recognize the typical problems of large-scale NPD embedded software projects?
2. How to assess the feasibility and achievability ("health") of such projects?

Answering the former question brings insight to the latter one. By recognizing the particular alerting problem areas, the project manager can conduct and steer the project rationally, even under considerable trouble conditions.

The rest of this paper proposes pragmatic aids for answering those questions in a systematic way. The research method is constructive, based on the literature surveys coupled with our own practical experiences with large-scale embedded software development for new telecommunications products. Our primary scope is in breakthrough development projects, creating entirely new market-driven products for the organization. Note that project financial issues (such as budgeting, rewarding) are excluded.

3 Troubleshooting NPD Embedded Software Projects

3.1 Project Problem Profiler

Our proposition for recognizing and evaluating the project problem issues is a matrix of typical problem factors and their likely impacts. Table 2 illustrates the overall structure of the matrix (see Appendix for the complete table).

Table 2. Project problem profiler (Appendix) structure

Characteristic Project Problems, Risk Factors	Categorization (Nominal)	Typical NPD Embedded SW	Typical IMPACT	Project STATUS	Project index
Program/Project Management					
Ineffective project management	Company	-	Critical!	x_1	y_1
Inadequate planning and task identification	Project	-	Moderate	x_2	y_2
Inter-component or inter-group dependencies	Project	NPD special concern!	Major	x_3	y_3
Personnel Management					
...					

The matrix has two main sections. The static part is basically a directory of typical software project problem factors, with a special emphasis on NPD embedded software projects. It comprises the following read-only fields (see Appendix):

- *Characteristic Project Problems, Risk Factors*:
  This column is a list of potential problem factors. They are grouped under the main sections of Program/project Management, Personnel Management, Scheduling and Timing, Requirements Management, System Functionality, Resource Usage and Performance, and Subcontracting. Under these main headings there are two levels of subgroups (only level 1 shown in Table 2).

- *Categorization (Nominal)*
  The problem items are further categorized according to the scope (Business Milieu / Company / Project / Team / Individual), class (Development Environment / Product Engineering / Program Constraints), type (Business / Technical / Process / People / Organizational), and the project phase of most likely concern (Project Initialization / Scoping / Planning / Execution / Completion).
- *Typical NPD Embedded SW*
  This highlights those problem areas, which are typically of special significance in embedded software projects (see "NPD special concern!" in Table 2).
- *Typical IMPACT*
  This value indicates the typical seriousness (Critical-Major-Moderate) of the problem for the project success.

The latter part of the matrix is dynamic, intended to be filled in by the user (more about that in Ch. 3.2). It consists of the following two fields:

- *Project STATUS*
  This value is the current evaluation of the project status with respect to the problem items (No problem / Minor issue / Concern / Serious!).
- *Project INDEX*
  The project's profile is indicated as a numeric value for each problem item. It is calculated based on the fields *Typical IMPACT* and *Project STATUS* as defined below (Formula 1). This index can further be used to plot graphical profiles of the current project situation (Ch. 3.2).

The matrix has in principle been composed as follows. The reasoning is discussed further in Ch. 4.

We have distilled a wide range of typical project problem factors (*Characteristic Project Problems, Risk Factors*) based on the literature survey (Ch. 2), coupled with our own real-life product development project experiences, with a special focus on NPD embedded software project concerns. Currently our matrix contains some 500 problem items organized in three levels (23 / 121 / 334 items, respectively). For example the following references have been used as the sources: [4-6, 12-19, 22, 27, 29-32, 34-36, 39, 42-48].

Most of the problem items are straightforward statements (e.g., "Poor communication"), but some of them are in a form of questions (like "Does management work to ensure that all customer factions are represented in decisions regarding functionality and operation?"). We have normally used the exact wording of the respective sources, with only some minor editorial changes.

The main grouping of the problem items is initially based on the seminal Boehm's risk list, refined by Ropponen and Lyytinen [5, 26]. We have in addition augmented it with one more main group: program/project management (comprising overall planning and coordination).

The problem item categorization (*Categorization (Nominal)*) is only suggestive. The *Scope* field is based on [21] and the *Class* field follows [31].

We have then estimated the relevance and typical impact of each problem item for NPD embedded software projects (*Typical NPD Embedded SW, Typical IMPACT*).

This evaluation is based partially on the ranking of the respective sources (if any given), and partially on our own experiences.

Finally, the *Project INDEX* is calculated according to the following formula:

$$Project\ INDEX_i = Weight * Typical\ IMPACT_i * Project\ STATUS_i \tag{1}$$

where the scales are currently defined as follows:

Weight:	1 (constant)
Typical IMPACT:	0-3 (Critical = 3)
Project STATUS:	0-3 (Serious = 3)
Project INDEX:	0-9

This formula is influenced by the commonly used calculation rule of risk exposure (more in Ch. 4.3).

3.2 Using the Profiler

The profiler matrix (Appendix) is in principle intended to be used as follows:

- For each problem item (level 1, 23 items altogether):
  - Answer the following question:
    - *Is this currently a problem in our case?*
    - If so, how serious is it (Minor issue / Concern / Serious)?
  - Write your rating down to the corresponding cell of the matrix (x_i in Table 2).
  - The corresponding *Project INDEX* value can then be calculated (y_i in Table 2).
- Finally, the *Project INDEX* values can be plotted graphically like illustrated in Appendix (Profile Chart). This gives a visual profile of the project's problem situation. The results can now be utilized in various ways during the course of the project (see Ch. 3.3).

For helping the evaluation of each main level (1) problem items, the lower-level (2, 3) items of the matrix can be used as guidance of thinking. For example, under the problem heading "New market with uncertain needs", there are more detailed items as illustrated in Appendix (Problem Sheet). The user can first ponder these lower-level items (at least part of them), and then give the aggregate rating of the level 1 item accordingly.

Naturally one can utilize the matrix also partially for example in case some sections are irrelevant (e.g., Subcontracting). On the other hand, it is of course also possible to extend the matrix with new problem items.

We have implemented the matrix as a computerized spreadsheet, which makes it easy to browse the different levels of the problem items, and automate the *Project INDEX* calculations and plottings. The Search functions of the spreadsheet can be used for example to find all problem items with certain keywords (e.g., "NPD").

3.3 Application Possibilities

The profiler matrix (Appendix) is a versatile tool. There is no one right way of using it. However, our key idea is to utilize it as follows:

- The project manager can use the matrix to self-assess her project (even privately). This assessment can be done while preparing the initial project plan as well as periodically during the course of the project:
  - The initial evaluation gives early insight and warning.
  - During the course of the project, the project manager can use the problem profile to focus the management activities on the alarming areas and trends.
  - The problem matrix can also be used as a tool in project (or iteration) post-mortem reviews. What were the biggest problems? The profile data could then be utilized for future projects (or iterations) for reference purposes.
- The assessments can also be done as group exercises together with the project team. The project manager and the project team could compare their evaluations.
- A more objective assessment ("health check") could be done by an outsider expert (such as a Quality Manager). The program and even corporate management could further utilize such information for ranking the individual projects. This kind of a ranking of risky projects have been investigated in [49]. This may be sensitive.

Naturally it is not enough to just recognize the problems. The project manager has to use other means to link the current identified problems to consequent improvement actions. In some cases no immediate action may be needed, while in other areas alarming trends (e.g., constant flow of unreasonable requirements changes) may require improvements even external to the current project. Combined results of individual project assessments could also be used for larger-scale company process improvement purposes (e.g., portfolio management).

4 Evaluation and Discussion

4.1 Empirical Experiments

We have conducted some empirical experiments with the problem profiler matrix (Appendix) in certain industrial NPD project environments at a large company developing telecommunications products containing embedded software. The method was to let the project managers to assess their project status with the matrix. Based on the responses, we expected to be able to draw conclusions about how well the profiler captures real project problem situations.

The following project background information was first recorded:

- product type: terminal / network element / etc.
- project nature: new features / completely new product / platform development
- project size, length (order of magnitude)
- major dependencies (e.g., hardware development, system integration)
- current state: launch / active / ending / completed / canceled

The project managers were then asked to fill in the problem matrix like instructed in Ch. 3.2. The survey was conducted by e-mail.

Table 3 shows a quantitative summary of the responses provided by the project manager (or the project quality manager). For confidentiality reasons the actual problem profile values cannot be shown here. In these project cases 5 common problem items (out of 23, level 1) were identified. All respondents provided additional narrative description of their project's main issues. This data was not codified, however.

Table 3. NPD project case studies

	Project Case	# of Problem Items flagged (out of 23)	# of Problem Items assessed as 'Serious!'	# of 'NPD special concern' items (out of 6)
1	Terminal software platform subsystem, new features; Project ending.	8	2	2
2	Network element software, completely new product; Project completed.	17	5	6

We can see that the profiler matrix captured critical problem areas of the case study NPD projects. None of the project cases identified any such significant problems that were not covered by the matrix. It is not possible to say, if the matrix approach highlighted such problem areas which had not yet been seen by the project manager.

4.2 Answering the Research Questions

We have composed a structured directory of typical problems encountered in NPD embedded software projects. This matrix (Appendix) helps identifying the project problems by pointing out such key concern areas (Question 1 in Ch. 2.4). The matrix is certainly not an all-encompassing database of all possible problem items, but the idea is to guide the thinking like a checklist and a structured interview technique. The user is encouraged to consider further problem items.

There are many ways of using the matrix, as described in Ch. 3.3. It can thus be used to check the "health" of the embedded software projects either internally or independently by an outsider assessor (Question 2 in Ch. 2.4). Naturally such checking can only give partial suggestions of the status of the project, but if this assessment indicates even some problems, further focused investigations should be considered. On the other hand, if there seem to be only very few problems (even none at all), one should become equally suspicious.

The matrix (Appendix) is composed with a generic viewpoint of NPD projects. While utilizing it in actual projects, it is important to understand the overall positioning and the nature of the project. Two such major issues are the front-end activities done prior to starting the actual software development project, and the level of new technology development involved. In NPD projects it is equally important to consider both commercial as well as technical risks [42, 46/Ch. 12, 50].

4.3 Limitations

We acknowledge the following limiting factors and constraints of our propositions presented in Ch. 3:

- The prescribed problems items scoping and categorization of the problem matrix (Appendix) are inherent bias factors. That could possibly skew the project's problem space exploration (even subconsciously). In some cases the assessor has to make a subjective mental mapping between her actual problems and the ones written in the matrix – unless there is an exact match. Consequently, different projects could show somehow different profiles, although the underlying problems would really be the same. These are typical pitfalls with checklist-based approaches [7].
- It is not reasonable to attempt to compose a complete list of absolutely all the possible project problems. Our matrix (Appendix) should therefore not be taken as a universal answer to all questions but merely a framework of thought. The usefulness of the matrix depends much on the creativity, experience, and competence of the project manager.
- There are many ways of categorizing and grouping different problem items, and currently our matrix shows only one way of doing it. Some of the lowest-level problem items could have been consolidated, but we have chosen to keep them separate for reference purposes. However, it is important to realize, that many problem items could be grouped under multiple categories, and there are different levels of problems and cause-effect dependencies. Notably the computerized spreadsheet of the matrix (Appendix) makes it possible to reorganize the problem items and groupings quite easily.
- We have highlighted those problem areas, which are usually pivotal in industrial NPD environments (*Typical NPD Embedded SW*). However, this is to some extent relative to the actual project circumstances, and in some cases certain other areas could still be key concerns. There is no guarantee, that following the matrix will always reveal the most important project problems.
- We have given suggestive default values of the typical impacts of the different problems (*Typical IMPACT*). However, the actual severity may vary depending on the project situations. What is typically a "showstopper" in most cases may still be manageable in some projects – with extreme measures. In addition, the sum effect of different problem factors may amplify (or lessen) the actual impact. The *Typical IMPACT* values should thus – if necessary – be adjusted (calibrated) to ensure the fidelity of the calculated *Project INDEX*.
- The *Project INDEX* value is not an absolute measure of the project's status. It is merely a gauge of potential warning signals. In particular, it should not be used to rank different projects unless the same person has done the underlying evaluation according to equal criteria. The ultimate project success/failure cannot be determined based on this assessment alone (for example because of business factors).
- The suggested self-assessment method is obviously subjective. Healthy self-criticism is necessary in order to avoid delusion. Cross-checking with multiple assessors is therefore recommended like described in Ch. 3.3.

4.4 Discussion

The underlying theoretical foundation of our approach is in conventional project issue and risk management. What is said about risk identification is in general applicable here, too. However, we have taken a specific viewpoint of product development projects with embedded software concerns. While there is much related work published about typical software project risks and failure factors in general (see Ch. 2.1), not many investigations focus on embedded software projects, and only very few take the NPD context into account. We see problem-awareness an inherent part of intelligent project management practice in turbulent NPD environments.

Our problem matrix (Appendix) is in addition a survey of the related literature, showing what different problem areas have been acknowledged by different investigations over the years. Some common areas are identified by many studies, while some problems are less frequently advocated, depending on the scope and viewpoints of the investigations. Our special focus of NPD embedded software projects is not often published.

The question of how to group the project problem factor space has been addressed by many investigations over the years. Clearly, there is no one absolutely right universal categorization, but it depends on the selected viewpoints. A notably rigorous approach is presented in [27]. Traditional general-purpose categorizations are available in standards and other project management guides (e.g., PMBOK, ISO/IEC 15504). We have selectively adopted them. One newer alternative has been proposed in [51]. A life-cycle process area categorization aimed specifically for embedded products development is proposed in [34]. Product integration is one typical key problem area. Note, however, that with a computerized tool it is not necessarily binding to fix any one particular grouping, but the user could basically reorganize the problem item space from different points of views.

There is a profound underlying difference of our project problem assessments and those ones done following general-purpose frameworks, such as CMMI. While such generic models suggest a set of key activities expected to be performed for good software engineering and management, our problem matrix (Appendix) does not prescribe any particular activities. For example, while requirements management is one of the level 2 key process areas in the CMMI model, we simply ask the project manager to evaluate, whether it is a problem or not in her case. Such situational problem diagnosis has been applied to embedded software projects in [52].

A high-level project risk factor matrix is shown in [53]. It includes some basic technology, product acceptance, and project execution risks. A weighting scale is suggested for each risk area. This is basically similar to our problem matrix.

One recent, similar to our questionnaire-based approach of recognizing 'risky' software projects is proposed in [54]. Likewise, they compose their questionnaire (having the main categories of requirements, estimations, planning, team organization, and project management) following a literature survey and some industrial experiences of embedded software projects. However, more detailed embedded software and NPD problem items are not covered.

A general-purpose (not limited to IT) project risk rating method has been presented in [49]. It is similar to our method in the sense that the project manager rates a set of project risk factors (risk drivers, e.g., novelty), and the overall project risk level is then calculated accordingly.

A project uncertainty profile is proposed in [55]. Overall business, product, project, and organizational risk factors are rated according to their level of uncertainty. This is in principle similar to our problem profiling technique.

A project assessment method in terms of overall complexity and uncertainty is proposed in [56]. Both complexity and uncertainty are rated based on a few prescribed attributes (e.g., domain knowledge gaps, dependencies, project duration). Project complexity and uncertainty indices are then calculated. This is essentially a subset of our problem profile. However, in our case it is up to the project manager to evaluate whether the increased uncertainty caused for example by a long project duration is really a problem.

Some publicly available / commercial risk management software tools provide similar functionalities to our problem matrix. However, the purpose of our matrix is not to replace such tools.

5 Conclusions

We have constructed some pragmatic aids for understanding the various trouble spots of NPD embedded software projects. The outcome is not any particular solution for managing such projects, but it provides a holistic view over the problem space. A wise project manager can utilize this view for managing her particular project successfully even under unfavorable circumstances. After all, such cases are not so unusual in modern turbulent product development environments [48].

The problem matrix (Appendix) is certainly not a silver-bullet troubleshooter of every possible project problem case. However, the idea is to illuminate the overall picture of the project's problem space so that the major areas are revealed. Based on this guidance, the project manager can then focus on analyzing the problem indicators in more detail according to the project's actual contextual information. The usefulness of the matrix thus depends much on the experience of the project manager. For less experienced managers it shows the major areas to be considered to begin with. For a more experienced user, it serves merely as a structured checklist, giving hints and reminders of the typical trouble spots.

This paper leaves room for further study:

1. More empirical validation: At the time of the writing we are able to present only limited empirical case data about our propositions. More data should be collected by experimenting the matrix (Appendix) like described in Ch. 4.1. The empirical validation could follow the principles used in [54]. In particular, are there any significant problem areas that are currently not addressed in the matrix? How much does the prescribed categorization bias the problem assessments?
2. More rigorous categorization of the problem space.
3. As defined now, the calculated *Project INDEX* value is a simple measure with certain bias limitations (see Ch. 4.3). More advanced measures could possibly be developed for example by taking into account the basic nature of the project (e.g., high market uncertainty vs. high technological uncertainty). Can the overall project uncertainty and complexity be measured? Does the project type change it?
4. What can we say about projects based on their problem profiles (Appendix: Profile Chart)? Can we identify particularly risky (or "unhealthy") projects [49]? When should we cancel or not even start the project? How does the problem profile change over the project's life-cycle? A reference database of problem profiles of both successful and failed projects could be collected.

5. Problem-conscious project management: The problem matrix could be extended with suggestions of potential maneuvers for each problem item. We have already investigated elsewhere, how different software process models tackle certain project problems [57, 58]. Those results could be linked to the problem matrix.

Acknowledgements

The author would like to thank Maarit Laanti (Nokia Corporation) for her influence and critique. We are also grateful to the anonymous case study project managers.

References

1. Farbman White, S., Melhart, B.E., Lawson, H.W.: Engineering Computer-Based Systems: Meeting the Challenge. IEEE Computer **34**(11) (2001) 39-43
2. Iansiti, M.: Shooting the Rapids: Managing Product Development in Turbulent Environments. California Management Review **38**(1) (1995) 37-58
3. MacCormack, A., Verganti, R., Iansiti, M.: Developing Products on "Internet Time": The Anatomy of a Flexible Development Process. Management Science **47**(1) (2001) 133-150
4. Mullins, J.W., Sutherland, D.J. New Product Development in Rapidly Changing Markets: An Exploratory Study. Journal of Product Innovation Management **15** (1998) 224-236
5. Boehm, B.W.: Software Risk Management: Principles and Practices. IEEE Software **8**(1) (1991) 32-41
6. DeMarco, T., Lister, T.: Walzing with Bears: Managing Risks On Software Projects. Dorset House Publishing, New York (2003)
7. Kontio, J.: Software engineering risk management: a method, improvement framework, and empirical evaluation. Helsinki University of Technology (2001)
8. Glass, R.L.: Software Runaways. Prentice-Hall, Upper Saddle River (1998)
9. Pavlak, A.: Project Troubleshooting: Tiger Teams for Reactive Risk Management. Project Management Journal **35**(4) (2004) 5-14
10. Kwak, Y.H., Stoddard, J.: Project risk management: lessons learned from software development environment. Technovation **24** (2004) 915-920
11. Sheremata, W.A.: Finding and solving problems in software new product development. Journal of Product Innovation Management **19** (2002) 144-158
12. Conrow, E.H., Shishido, P.S.: Implementing Risk Management on Software Intensive Projects. IEEE Software **14**(3) (1997) 83-89
13. Evans, M.W., Abela, A.M., Belz, T. Seven Characteristics of Dysfunctional Software Projects. CrossTalk **15**(4) (2002) 16-20
14. Houston, D.: Results of Survey on Potential Effects of Major Software Development Risk Factors. http://www.eas.asu.edu/~sdm/dhouston/risksrvy.htm (1999) (accessed February 2005)
15. Jones, C.: Patterns of Software System Failure and Success. International Thompson Computer Press, Boston (1996)
16. May, L.J.: Major Causes of Software Project Failures. CrossTalk **11**(7) (1998) 9-12
17. Reel, J.S.: Critical Success Factors In Software Projects. IEEE Software **16**(3) (1999) 18-23
18. Reifer, D.: Ten Deadly Risks in Internet and Intranet Software Development. IEEE Software **19**(2) (2002) 12-14

19. Wiegers, K.E.: Know Your Enemy: Software Risk Management. http://www.processimpact.com/articles/risk_mgmt.pdf (1998) (accessed February 2005).
20. Brooks, F.P. Jr.: The Mythical Man-Month: Essays on Software Engineering (20th Anniversary Edition). Addison-Wesley (1995)
21. Curtis, B., Krasner, H., Iscoe, N.: A Field Study of the Software Design Process for Large Systems. Communications of the ACM **31**(11) (1988) 1268-1287
22. McConnell, S.: Rapid Development: Taming Wild Software Schedules. Microsoft Press, Redmond (1996)
23. McConnell, S.: Software Project Survival Guide. Microsoft Press, Redmond (1998)
24. Royce, W.: Software Project Management. Addison-Wesley (1998)
25. Brown, S.L., Eisenhardt, K.M.: Product Development: Past Research, Present Findings, and Future Directions. Academy of Management Review **20**(2) (1995) 343-378
26. Ropponen, J., Lyytinen, K.: Components of Software Development Risk: How to Address Them? A Project Manager Survey. IEEE Trans. Software Engineering **26**(2) (2000) 98-111
27. Schmidt, R., Lyytinen, K., Keil, M., Cule, P.: Identifying Software Project Risks: An International Delphi Study. Journal of Management Information Systems **17**(4) (2001) (Spring) 5-36
28. Smith, J.M.: Troubled IT Projects – prevention and turnaround. IEE (2001)
29. May, G., Ould, M.: Software project casualty. IEE Engineering Management Journal **12**(2) (2002) 83-90
30. Fairley, R.E., Willshire, M.J.: Why the Vasa Sank: 10 Problems and Some Antidotes for Software Projects. IEEE Software **20**(2) (2003) 18-25
31. Carr, M., Kondra, S., Monarch, I., Ulrich, F., Walker, C.: Taxonomy-Based Risk Identification (Technical Report CMU/SEI-93-TR-6). SEI (1993)
32. Brown, W.J., McCormick H.W. III, Thomas, S.W.: AntiPatterns in Project Management. John Wiley & Sons, New York (2000)
33. Ould, M.A.: Managing Software Quality and Business Risk. John Wiley & Sons, Chichester (1999)
34. Kuvaja, P., Maansaari, J., Seppänen, V., Taramaa, J.: Specific Requirements for Assessing Embedded Product Development. In: Proc. International Conference on Product Focused Software Process Improvement (PROFES) (1999) 68-85
35. Rauscher, T.G., Smith, P.G.: Time-Driven Development of Software in Manufactured Goods. Journal of Product Innovation Management **12** (1995) 186-199
36. Ronkainen, J., Abrahamsson, P.: Software development under stringent hardware constraints: Do agile methods have a chance? In: Proc. 4th Int'l Conf. Extreme Programming and Agile Processes in Software Engineering (2003) 73-79
37. Kettunen, P.: Managing embedded software project team knowledge. IEE Proc. – Software **150**(6) (2003) 359-366
38. Riek, R.F.: From experience: Capturing hard-won NPD lessons in checklists. Journal of Product Innovation Management **18** (2001) 301-313
39. Wheelwright, S.C., Clark, K.B.: Revolutionizing Product Development: Quantum Leaps in Speed, Efficiency, and Quality. The Free Press, New York (1992)
40. Song, X.M., Montoya-Weiss, M.M.: Critical Development Activities for Really New versus Incremental Products. Journal of Product Innovation Management **15** (1998) 124-135
41. Ernst, H.: Success factors of new product development: a review of the empirical literature. International Journal of Management Reviews **4**(1) (2002) 1-40
42. Cooper, R.G., Edgett, S.J., Kleinschmidt, E.J., Benchmarking Best NPD Practices – III. Research • Technology Management **47**(6) (2004) 43-55

43. Jones, C.: Minimizing the Risks of Software Development. Cutter IT Journal **11**(6) (1998) 13-21
44. Jones, C.: Software Assessments, Benchmarks, and Best Practices. Addison-Wesley (2000)
45. Rautiainen, K., Lassenius, C., Nihtilä, J., Sulonen, R.: Key Issues in New Product Development Controllability Improvement – Lessons Learned from European High-tech Industries. In: Proc. Portland Int'l Conf. Management of Engineering and Technology (PICMET) (1999)
46. Smith, P.G., Reinertsen, D.G.: Developing Products in Half the Time: New Rules, New Tools. John Wiley & Sons, New York (1998)
47. Ulrich, K.T., Eppinger, S.D.: Product Design and Development. McGraw-Hill, New York (2000)
48. Yourdon, E.: Death March – The Complete Software Developer's Guide to Surviving "Mission Impossible" Projects. Prentice-Hall, Upper Saddle River (1999)
49. Baccarini, D., Archer, R.: The risk ranking of projects: a methodology. International Journal of Project Management **19** (2001) 139-145
50. Holmes, M.F., Campbell R.B. Jr.: Product Development Processes: Three Vectors of Improvement. Research • Technology Management **47**(4) (2004) 47-55
51. Keil, M., Cule, P.E., Lyytinen, K., Schmidt, R.C.: A Framework for Identifying Software Project Risks. Communications of the ACM **41**(11) (1998) 76-83
52. Iversen, J., Nielsen, P.A., Nørbjerg, J.: Situated Assessment of Problems in Software Development. The DATA BASE for Advances in Information Systems **30**(2) (1999) (Spring) 66-81
53. Fitzgerald, D.: Principle-Centered Agile Project Portfolio Management. Agile Project Management Advisory Service Executive Report 6(5), http://www.cutter.com/project/fulltext/reports/2005/05/index.html (2005) (accessed June 2005)
54. Takagi, Y., Mizuno, O., Kikuno, T.: An Empirical Approach to Characterizing Risky Software Projects Based on Logistic Regression Analysis. Empirical Software Engineering **10** (2005) 495-515
55. DeCarlo, D.: Leading Extreme Projects to Success. Agile Project Management Advisory Service Executive Report 5(8), http://www.cutter.com/project/fulltext/reports/2004/08/index.html (2004) (accessed June 2005)
56. Little, T., Greene, F., Phillips, T., Pilger, R., Poldervaart, R.: Adaptive Agility. In: Proc. Agile Development Conference (ADC) (2004) 63-70
57. Kettunen, P., Laanti, M.: How to steer an embedded software project: tactics for selecting the software process model. Information and Software Technology **47**(9) (2005) 587-608
58. Kettunen, P., Laanti, M.: How to Steer an Embedded Software Project: Tactics for Selecting Agile Software Process Models. In: Proc. International Conference on Agility (ICAM) (2005) 241-257

Appendix. Project Problem Profiler Matrix

Problem Sheet: The following shows the complete level 1 table. The *Project STATUS* values put here do not represent any particular project case, but in our experience this kind of ratings could well be observed in typical NPD embedded software projects.

Characteristic Project Problems, Risk Factors	Categorization (Nominal) SCOPE	 CLASS	 TYPE	 PHASE	Typical NPD Embedded SW	Typical IMPACT	Project STATUS	Project INDEX
Program/Project Management								
Ineffective project management (multiple levels possible)	Company	Development Envi	Organizational	Project ALL	-	Critical!	No problem	0
Inadequate planning and task identification	Project	Development Envi	Process	Project Planning	-	Moderate	No problem	0
Inter-component or inter-group dependencies	Project	Development Envi	Process	Project Execution	NPD special concern!	Major	No problem	0
Personnel Management								
Personnel shortfalls (lack of qualified personnel and their	Company	Program Constrai	Organizational	Project ALL	-	Major	Minor issue	2
Inability to acquire resources with critical skills	Project	Development Envi	Organizational	Project Init	-	Critical!	No problem	0
Instability and lack of continuity in project staffing	Project	Program Constrai	Organizational	Project ALL	-	Major	Minor issue	2
Lack of staff commitment, low morale	Team	Development Envi	People	Project ALL	-	Major	No problem	0
Scheduling and Timing								
Unrealistic schedules, budgets (time and budget estimated	Company	Program Constrai	Business	Project Planning	NPD special concern!	Critical!	Minor issue	3
Inherent schedule flaw	Project	Development Envi	Process	Project Planning	-	Major	No problem	0
Inaccurate cost estimating	Project	Development Envi	Process	Project Planning	-	Moderate	No problem	0
Poor productivity	Project	Development Envi	Process	Project Execution	-	Major	No problem	0
Requirements Management								
New market with uncertain needs	Business Milieu	Program Constrai	Business	Project Scoping	NPD special concern!	Critical!	No problem	0
Gold plating (adding unnecessary features)	Project	Product Engineeri	Process	Project Scoping	-	Moderate	Minor issue	1
Continuing stream of requirements changes (uncontrolled	Project	Product Engineeri	Process	Project Scoping	-	Major	Concern	4
System Functionality								
Complex application	Company	Product Engineeri	Technical	Project Planning	-	Major	Minor issue	2
Developing wrong software functions (functions that are not	Project	Product Engineeri	Technical	Project Scoping	NPD special concern!	Critical!	No problem	0
Specification breakdown	Project	Product Engineeri	Process	Project Execution	-	Major	No problem	0
Developing wrong user interface (inadequate or difficult)	Project	Product Engineeri	Technical	Project Execution	-	Moderate	No problem	0
Resource Usage and Performance								
Real-time performance shortfalls	Team	Product Engineeri	Technical	Project Execution	NPD special concern!	Major	Serious!	6
Ineffective development technologies	Team	Development Envi	Process	Project Planning	-	Moderate	No problem	0
Straining computer science capabilities (lacking technical	Team	Product Engineeri	Technical	Project Execution	NPD special concern!	Critical!	No problem	0
Subcontracting								
Shortfalls of externally furnished components (poor quality)	Project	Program Constrai	Process	Project Execution	-	Moderate	No problem	0
Shortfalls of externally performed tasks (poor quality or	Project	Program Constrai	Process	Project Execution	-	Moderate	No problem	0

Problem Sheet: The following shows a section of the expanded level 2-3 table (c.f., above).

Characteristic Project Problems, Risk Factors	Categorization (Nominal) SCOPE	CLASS	TYPE	PHASE	Typical NPD Embedded SW	Typical IMPACT		Project STATUS	Project INDEX
Requirements Management									
New market with uncertain needs	Business Milieu	Program Constrair	Business	Project Scoping	NPD special concern!	Critical!		No problem	0
Lack of clear product vision					NPD special concern!	Critical!	No problem	↑	
New product strategy exists					NPD special concern!	Major	-	↑	
Misalignment with business goals					-	-	-	↑	
Business needs change.					-	-	-	↑	
What market segments should be considered in					-	-	-	↑	
Who is the target customer?					NPD special concern!	Critical!	-	↑	
Inadequate coverage of target markets with competitive					-	-	-	↑	
Is the concept chosen by the team best suited to the					NPD special concern!	Major	-	↑	
Focus on current customers and confusion about future					-	-	-	↑	
Is the product a winner?					NPD special concern!	Critical!	-	↑	
Product advantage: unique, superior					-	-	-	↑	
Lack of Product Distinctiveness (new product not as					-	-	-	↑	
Poor timing of market introductions of products					NPD special concern!	Major	No problem	↑	
Uncertainty associated with the inability of the customers to					NPD special concern!	Critical!	No problem	↑	
Sharp, early product definition (fact-based, e.g., the benefits					-	-	No problem	↑	
Failure to gain user commitment: Laying blame for "lack of					-	-	No problem	↑	
Customer-furnished items or information					-	-	No problem	↑	
Lack of client support					-	-	No problem	↑	
Lack of contact person's competence					-	-	No problem	↑	
Gold plating (adding unnecessary features)	Project	Product Engineerir	Process	Project Scoping	-	Moderate		Minor issue	1
Continuing stream of requirements changes (uncontrolled	Project	Product Engineerir	Process	Project Scoping	-	Major		Concern	4

Profile Chart: The following shows an example plot of the problem profile chart based on the sample Problem Sheet values above.

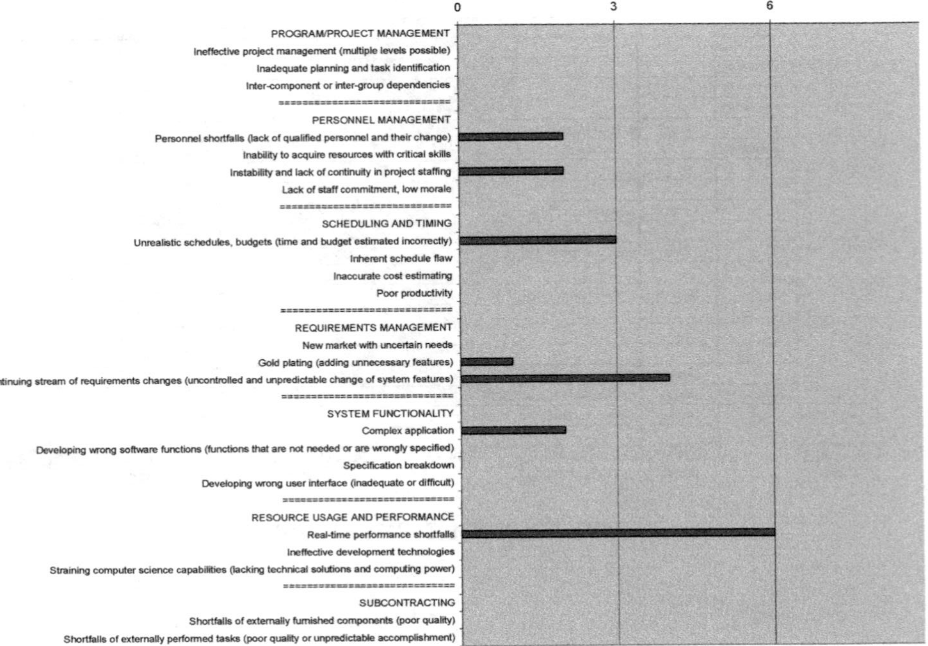

Software Process Improvement with Agile Practices in a Large Telecom Company

Jussi Auvinen[1], Rasmus Back[1], Jeanette Heidenberg[1], Piia Hirkman[2,3], and Luka Milovanov[2,4]

[1] Oy L M Ericsson Ab, Telecom R&D
Lemminkäisenkatu 14-18C, FIN-20520 Turku, Finland
Name.Surname@ericsson.com
[2] Turku Centre for Computer Science – TUCS, Åbo Akademi University
Lemminkäisenkatu 14 A, FIN-20520 Turku, Finland
Name.Surname@abo.fi
[3] Institute for Advanced Management Systems Research
[4] Department of Computer Science

Abstract. Besides the promise of rapid and efficient software development, agile methods are well-appreciated for boosting communication and motivation of development teams. However, they are not practical "as such" in large organizations, especially because of the well-established, rigid processes in the organizations. In this paper, we present a case study where a few agile practices were injected into the software process of a large organization in order to pilot pair programming and improve the motivation and competence build-up. The selected agile practices were pair programming, the planning game and collective code ownership. We show how we adjust these practices in order to integrate them into the existing software process of the company in the context of a real software project.

1 Introduction

Agile methods hold the promise of rapid and efficient software development. Reports from industry [1, 2, 3, 4], research [5, 6, 7] and educational [8, 9, 10] settings describe positive experiences of agile practices. While agile software development responds to the challenge of change, people is often stated to be one of its main focal points [11]. Also, issues related to individual agile practices, such as knowledge building [12], have been found alluring.

However, agile approaches also have their limitations and recommended application areas, as software development methods usually do. One of these issues is that many agile methods are best suited for small and medium projects [13]. For example, Extreme Programming does not easily scale for large projects [14]: all of the developers simply cannot work together in one big room.

Regardless of project size, the interest towards agile approaches rises to a great extent from the same needs, but the actual implementation is different. It requires much more tailoring in large companies than in smaller ones [15]. The challenge lies in fitting agile methods in existing processes where software development is only a small part

J. Münch and M. Vierimaa (Eds.): PROFES 2006, LNCS 4034, pp. 79–93, 2006.

of the product development process. The question is whether corporations with well established and rigid processes can use just a few agile methods and still see significant benefits. Beck's discussion of the 80/20 rule would suggest not, as implementing all of the principles and practices creates synergy benefits [14], but experiences in practice have tried to prove otherwise [15, 16]. This paper presents an account of how agile methods were assessed in a case study for a large organization.

The pilot project was conducted at Ericsson, the largest supplier of mobile systems in the world. Ericsson's customers include the world's 10 largest mobile operators and some 40% of all mobile calls are made through its systems. This international telecommunications company has been active worldwide since 1876 and is currently present in more than 140 countries. The pilot project was conducted at a design department at Ericsson Finland.

This paper proceeds as follows: Section 2 presents the background and drivers for the pilot. Section 3 states the goals for the pilot and describes the means to achieve these goals. In Section 4 we describe the agile practices selected for and implemented during the pilot, while in Section 5 we present the results of the pilot in the context of the goals stated in Section 3. We discuss open issues in Section 6 and present our conclusions in Section 7.

2 Background

In early spring 2004, the design department in question arranged a workshop where different improvement areas for the software design process were identified. This workshop was a part of the continuous Software Process Improvement (SPI) [17] activity performed at the company. One of the identified areas was the motivation of the employees, and an SPI team was assigned to come up with innovative improvement proposals for this area. The results of a survey conducted within the company indicated that job satisfaction could be enhanced by changing the way the work was assigned, arranged and carried out. The organization would benefit from increasing the employees' motivation by promoting shared responsibilities among the designers, and increasing their competence in different areas of the large software systems they are working with.

An investigation of potentially suitable methods was conducted. The SPI team found that pair programming, an agile software development practice, could promote learning and shared responsibility, and hence increase motivation. The SPI team also noted that the chosen methods would need to be easy to implement within the existing process and easy to learn. Furthermore, such methods should be flexible enough in order to be changed and adapted to the standard process of the company to keep its integrity and strict deadlines. The SPI team considered an agile approach to be well-suited for the purpose.

The SPI team presented its ideas and results to the management in the summer of 2004. Based on this proposal, the management decided to pilot pair programming together with a number of other agile practices at the design department. The pilot was to be done in a real, live project so that the experiences from the pilot would be directly applicable in the organization. Since agile practices were new to the department in question, the management team decided to cooperate with the Department of Computer Science at Åbo Akademi University where agile practices had been tried out and developed further in the Gaudí Software Factory for the last four years [5].

3 Goals and Settings

The pilot started in January 2005 with planning and start-up activities and the actual implementation was done from February to mid-April. The following sections describe the goals of the pilot, and the implementation settings, such as the team composition.

3.1 Goals

The pilot set out to investigate the possibility of using pair programming and an assortment of other agile practices in the analysis, design and early testing of the project. More specifically, the question was whether it would be possible to introduce pair programming into the standard way of working of a designer, and what changes should be made to the pair programming recommendations for them to suit the surrounding environment, including premises, IT infrastructure and project process.

The second goal, competence build-up, was set during the pilot preparation. When a new designer comes to work in a design team, he or she has at least basic skills in methods and tools, but lacks the knowledge about the specific parts of the system the team is working with. The newcomer is assigned a mentor and is assumed to be up to 70% less productive than a designer familiar with the subsystem. In this situation, the mentor's productivity is also assumed to drop by up to 20%. At the beginning of the pilot it was speculated that the mentoring of a newcomer could be effectively substituted with pair programming.

One of the most important goals of the pilot was to study the impact of pair work on the motivation of the designers. But while piloting pair programming as a means to improve the motivation of the designers and build up their competence, we wanted to keep up the efficiency of the existing way of working. Even though boosting the employee's motivation was the primary goal, the deadlines and the quality could not be sacrificed for increased motivation.

3.2 Project Scope and Selected Practices

The pilot was implemented in only two subsystems of a product called the Ericsson Media Gateway for Mobile Networks (M-MGw) [18]. The whole M-MGw application system consists of eight subsystems. The application runs on the CPP (Connectivity Packet Platform), Ericsson's 3G platform. The Media Gateway itself is a part of Ericssons' Mobile Core Network, a much larger system. The Media Gateway has an interface to several of the other nodes on the Core Network. Because of the hierarchical structure of the system, the testing of the M-MGw application is performed on many levels: from unit and subsystem tests up to call cases covering the whole network and interoperability tests with other telephony networks. The multitude of required test phases puts strict constraints on the delivery process. As a consequence, it is very difficult to have a truly agile process when developing the system. Consequently, a set of agile practices was selected for the pilot instead of trying to implement a completely agile process.

Pair programming was the first selected practice. It is supposed to be a "fun" way of doing implementation [14] and could therefore be expected to improve motivation. Furthermore, it offers a way of ensuring quality in an early phase, by having an extra pair of eyes checking the code as it is being written. In order for pair programming to be easily introduced in the company and to be efficient, a few supportive agile practices were considered necessary. The practices chosen to support pair programming were collective code ownership and the planning game. These practices are presented and discussed in more detail in Section 4. Originally, we also introduced a customer representative [19] to the pilot, but during the pilot it became clear that there was no need for this role in this project [20].

3.3 The Pilot Team and Room Arrangement

The design department where the pilot was conducted is one of the departments involved in creating the M-MGw product. More on M-MGw design projects can be found in [20]. There are two main roles in the design department, the designer and the subsystem tester. The designer mainly does design, implementation and unit testing, while the subsystem tester is responsible for testing on the subsystem level. The pilot was organized in such a way that only four designers involved in the actual implementation faced the pilot-induced changes in their work. In other words, the subsystem testers were only affected by the output produced by the designers. The system work was unaffected by the pilot.

Usually, each subsystem has its own team to handle all the implementation. However, the pilot team worked on two neighboring subsystems. This meant that the competence of the designers varied, allowing us to study the effect of pair programming on competence build-up. The features implemented during the pilot mostly impacted one of the subsystems, and only one of the designers had previous experience in that subsystem. Of the three other designers, two had worked with the other, less impacted subsystem. One of the designers was new to both of the subsystems. All designers were competent in the tools used as well as in the overall system principles and basic functionalities.

The room arrangements for the pilot required some attention. Since four designers were to participate in the pilot, two dedicated places for pair programming were needed. All the designers had responsibilities that required them to work alone as well, so they also needed personal work places. Furthermore, the needs for obstacle free communication and for work peace needed to be balanced. The detailled plan of the pilot's room can be found in [20]. Each of the designers had his own corner for solo work while the pair programming work places were located in the center of the room. A divider was placed between the pair programming places to give some work peace for the pairs, without completely isolating them from each other.

3.4 Pilot Steering

In addition to the actual pilot team, the project also had a management sponsor and a steering group. The pilot steering group was formed in order to follow the progress of the pilot and to make necessary adjustments to the pilot whenever refinement was necessary. The group included a researcher who was experienced in coaching and managing agile software projects in an academic setting and had participated in developing the process used in these projects. The task of the steering group was to monitor the adaptation of the selected agile practices into the existing process, propose changes in the practices based on this monitoring, and to collect the data needed to evaluate the achievement of the goals in the end of the pilot.

The pilot steering group and the designers held one hour long pilot steering meetings every Monday during the pilot project. The first part of each meeting was a regular team progress follow-up: what had been done, what features were currently under work and was the schedule kept. The team leader would later summarize this to the project manager. Before the pilot, this follow-up had been based on informal estimations, expressed as the designers' gut feelings, such as *"60% of the coding is done"*. This did not really provide a good sense of project progress to the managers.

During the second part of each meeting, the pilot steering group presented the results of the pilot monitoring. Typical data shown here included the distribution of the designers pair-solo work, and the accuracy of the designers' time estimation, to mention a few. The meetings proceeded with a discussion of the pilot practices both in the context of this data and the subjective opinions of the designers. These discussions aimed at finding any need for improvement and adapting the practices better into the existing process. The designers were also expected to give feedback at the end of the project. This feedback was provided in the form of questionnaires and interviews, but they also could propose ways to improve the process and the adaptation of the selected practices.

4 Agile Practices in Action

In this section, we go in detail through the agile practices selected for the pilot. We proceed with the practices one by one, first introducing the original definition of the practice and explaining the reason for selecting it. We then discuss how the practice was changed in order to be adapted to the existing process. Additionally, the sections embody some comments made by the designers during the pilot steering meetings.

4.1 Pair Programming

Pair programming is a programming technique in which two persons work together on one computer, one keyboard and one mouse [21]. Pair programming is broadly studied [22, 23, 24, 25, 26], and it is well appreciated for good quality of the code [22], promotion of communication and learning as well as for being a "fun" way of working. The productivity in pair programming follows Nosek's principle [27]: two programmers will implement two tasks in pair 60% slower than two programmers implementing the same tasks in parallel with solo programming.

According to the experiences with pair programming in the Gaudí Software Factory [28], pair programming should be enforced by the coach in order for it to dominate significantly over solo programming. When the choice between doing pair or solo work is left to the students working in the Gaudí Factory, they tend to distribute pair and solo work equally, though they all agreed that they enjoyed working in pairs more. In this pilot, it was considered that pair programming should be recommended instead of enforced. A recommendation gives room for the designers' own experience and rhythm, and allows for them to truly opt for pair programming.

4.2 The Planning Game

The planning game is the XP planning process. There are two types of planning in XP: planning by scope and planning by time [14]. The planning game practice was chosen in order to facilitate pair switching. We wanted the pairs to be switched approximately weekly, but the requirements analysis documents did not as such provide suitable slots for pair switching. Moving people around when they are in the middle of working on specific parts of the system would disturb the designers, would have negative influence on productivity and quality, and would not necessarily promote competence build-up. We needed to split the features into small (one week) units supporting the desired pair dynamics. The planning game seemed to be the answer.

In the pilot, the planning game was not directly based on user stories written by the customer as in XP. The XP approach is to split the user stories to tasks [29, 30]. The stories describe the required functionality from a user's point of view, whereas the tasks are written by the programmers and contain a lot of technical details [14]. The pilot planning game followed the principle of splitting requirements chunks into smaller entities. But in the pilot, the chunks corresponding to XP stories were derived from the requirements analysis document and they were called features. A task was defined as something which requires one to three days to implement, while a feature was composed of few tasks and was estimated as a week or maximum two weeks of work.

The features and tasks were identified during the planning game, which was held twice for this pilot: on the first day and in the middle of the pilot. During the first planning game, the designers selected the main pieces of the functionality from the requirements analysis document. Each of these features was then split into detailed tasks and the tasks were estimated. These estimations were in ideal programming hours and did not consider that the implementation would be done in pairs, thus no additional time for pair programming was reserved. The new estimations confirmed the original deadlines for the project. It was, however, unclear whether the pilot could follow the original deadlines since pair programming is considered to be less productive then solo programming. In a live project the deliveries have to be on schedule and if pair programming caused the schedule to slip the pilot would be cancelled.

The designers did not sign up for the tasks during the planning game. They formed pairs as needed during the development. Initially, the idea was that in order to promote competence build-up, a pair should consist of a person who is highly competent for the task, while his partner has little or no knowledge about the part of the system the task concerned. But by the time the second planning game was held, it had become clear that when defining the tasks, also the difficulty of the task should be specified and that should be used as one criterion when forming pairs and assigning tasks. Consequently, besides selecting features and splitting them to tasks, the tasks were assigned complexity (*High, Medium, Low*) and ordered during the second planning game. The division into categories was done from the most experienced designers' point of view.

After the second planning game, the distribution of tasks among pairs took both competence build-up and deadlines into consideration by using some guidelines where the level of difficulty of the task played a central role. These guidelines generally say that the simple tasks should be implemented as solo programming or in pairs where both of the designers are less familiar with the task at hand. Tasks of medium complexity should be done in pairs where the driver has less competence than the navigator. The most difficult tasks should be done in pairs where at least one of the designers has a good level of competence. These complex tasks should not be left to the end of an iteration. Additionally, both designers should be equally good when debugging in pairs.

In summary, the planning game used in the pilot was a customization of the original XP planning game. It was targeted towards the most efficient competence build-up while respecting the deadlines of the project. When implementing a task in pair, the more experienced designer taught his skills to his programming partner. This practice was highly appreciated by the designers and also by the testers. Furthermore, the designers found this type of planning game *"perhaps the most valuable practice introduced in this pilot"*. They even recommended this practice to higher management before the pilot steering group started working on the final evaluation of the pilot.

4.3 Collective Code Ownership

Collective code ownership in XP means that no one person owns the code and may become a bottleneck for changes. Instead, every team member is encouraged to contribute to all parts of the project. Every programmer improves any code anywhere in the system at any time if they see the opportunity [14, 31].

We chose to enforce collective code ownership in order to empower the pairs to change and update any part of the code when necessary. This concept of sharing the responsibility for the code was also necessary due to the competence build-up. By the end of the pilot, every designer should ideally have the same level of system competence. The different pairs were working with all parts of the system, designers with high competence in a particular part of the code were not the bottlenecks for changes and did not have more responsibility for these parts of the system than the rest of the design team.

Surprisingly, the design team commented this practice as *"something we already have been using, just did not know the right name for this practice"*. Nevertheless, the testers found positive changes with the introduction of shared code ownership: *"Whenever we had a question concerning some part of the code, any designer could answer us – this is something we have not seen before the pilot"*.

5 Results

Based on Nosek's principle [27], we expected pair programming to be less efficient than solo programming. Furthermore, other factors such as competence build-up and the overhead of introducing a new methodology led us to assume a best case scenario of a 100% increase in lead time. Nevertheless, the deliveries were made on schedule without deviations from the original man-hour estimates. This came as somewhat of a surprise, since the other teams not involved in the pilot had to work overtime to achieve their corresponding objectives on time.

Within the pilot, more than half of the work was done in pairs: 51% pair vs. 37% solo. The pair programming practice was not enforced in the pilot, it was only recommended. The designers decided on whether to work alone or in pair based on the estimated complexity of the task as described in Section 4.2. There were 37 tasks defined during the planning games and implemented during the pilot. Some of the tasks required upfront design, while others were straightforward programming tasks. Four tasks were implemented completely in pairs and five completely solo. For the rest of the tasks the average share of the pair work was dominating: 68% pair vs. 32% solo.

Due to the space limitation, we cannot present the metrics collected during the pilot project in this paper. The data concernig various activities of the designers and the detailled information about pair-solo work distribution can be found in [20]. In the following sections we present the results concerning software quality, competence build-up and motivation.

5.1 Software Quality

When the designers make the official release of the code, any faults found result in a trouble report (TR) being written. A TR describes the problem, the test which finds the fault and so forth. These TR's are the principal measure of code quality at the company. To assess the impact of the pilot on the code quality we compared the TR count from the pilot to the TR count from a previous delivery which is similar in size and complexity. The analysis showed a 5.5% decrease in TR's. In addition to the quantitative measure, a formal code review was conducted at the end of the pilot. The review found that the code produced during the pilot was of the same quality as code produced previously.

To assess the impact of the introduced agile practices on the subsystem testers, each of the testers was interviewed. The feedback provided by the testers was mainly positive. The first advantage of the pilot from the testers' point of view was that the planning game and the division of the system requirements into tasks. Usually, the testers start their work when the code is almost complete, but in the pilot, writing the tests could be started much earlier. This was mainly because the tasks produced by the designers in the planning game had enough information for the testers to start their work. Consequently, this evened out the testers workload.

Another positive impact of the pilot noticed by the testers was improved communication. Getting answers to questions about the code was easier: all the designers were sitting in the same room and thanks to pair programming there were always at least two designers who were familiar with the particular piece of code a tester was asking about. As for the non-positive impact, the testers found that the number of faults found remained on the same level as before. One could argue here that this was due to the testing which was more efficient in the pilot. Another observation concerned an increase in basic (beginner's) mistakes. This could be attributed to the learning process taking place at the same time.

5.2 Competence

A very important aspect of the pilot was to measure how pair programming can improve the competence level and knowledge sharing of the designers. The designers were asked to rate their competence improvement subjectively in a questionnaire (see Section 5.5 for more details). They also answered a short quiz on both subsystems before and after the pilot. The quiz was the same on both occasions and it contained questions covering both subsystems completely. The results of the quiz before the pilot and the quiz after the pilot were compared in an effort to assess any change in competence.

The result from the first quiz was subtracted from the maximum available points. This number represented how much room for improvement the designer had. The result from the first quiz was then subtracted from the results of the second quiz. This number showed how much the score had changed after the pilot. An improvement percentage was calculated from these two numbers according to the formula shown below:

$$Improvement\% = \frac{t_2 - t_1}{max - t_1} \cdot 100\%$$

where t_1 is the score from the first quiz, t_2 the score from the second quiz and *max* is the maximum score of the quiz.

If a designer received 40 points out of 50 available on the first quiz, the designer's room for improvement was 10 points. If the designer then scored 45 points on the second test, the actual improvement was 5 points. Dividing 5 by 10 gives a competence improvement percentage of 50. Table 1 shows the competence improvement of each designer during the pilot. The results show a clear improvement in competence – the whole team gained 47%. The largest overall competence improvement was 67%, while the smallest was 19%.

Table 1. Percentage of competence improvement

	Subsystem 1	Subsystem 2	Total
Designer 1	42	31	37
Designer 2	59	67	63
Designer 3	100	33	67
Designer 4	30	7	19
Team	58	35	47

5.3 Motivation

The results concerning motivation and job satisfaction are based on semi-structured interviews conducted before and after the pilot with each designer. At the beginning of each interview, the designers also answered a questionnaire, which included statements to be rated on a 5-point scale (agree – disagree) and some open-ended questions. As the sample was small, the results of the questionnaires were not analyzed using statistical methods; they were used as an additional basis for discussion. Each interview session was recorded and took approximately an hour.

The pre-pilot interviews and questionnaires concerned general issues in job satisfaction and motivation: work content, the results of work, management, communication and social environment. Before the change in work arrangements, the questionnaires and interviews indicated that the designers liked their jobs, were well aware of the goals and expectations of their work, and had a sense of responsibility of the results. They were also committed to their work and rather content with the social environment, besides some communication aspects between teams/projects. Overall, they were rather content with their jobs. When explicitly asked about their work motivation, the designers considered their motivation to be rather good; on a school grade scale from 4 to

10, most designers gave an eight. Things that they found motivating in work included salary, challenging problems, good team, varying assignments, and learning. That is, the designers seemed to have a pragmatic view on work and job satisfaction. This down-to-earth stance reflected also on their expectations concerning the pilot. They had a somewhat positive attitude, but they did not expect any miracles. One can also note that answering motivation-related questions had become somewhat of a routine.

The nature of the post-pilot interviews was slightly less general in nature, excluding issues which were in no way affected by the pilot, such as management. On the other hand, the post-pilot questions concerned also how the designers found specific features of the pilot, such as pair programming, and how they affected their work. Concerning motivation, the results of the analysis on general and pilot-specific issues differ from each other to some extent. Regarding general issues in job satisfaction, no significant changes could be seen compared to pre-pilot results. The designers did not explicitly acknowledge any change in the motivation level. The same general ingredients were still present: a pragmatic view on work, liking the job, the environment, and awareness and sense of responsibility over results. However, the pilot-specific answers reflected the actual changes in work in more detail.

The most noticeable pilot feature was pair programming. The designers found that it increases the sense of team work, slightly increases the sense of responsibility, smoothes out fluctuations in alertness, and facilitates learning. Pair programming also increases feedback from peers as discussions and answers immediately follow action. The most notable issue in pair programming was learning. The challenge of new things was regarded as motivating from the beginning and learning always motivating. At the same time, learning and enlarging one's area of experience also increases the meaningfulness of work. In addition to the positive effects, the designers also discussed the downsides of pair programming: shared pair programming schedule competes with other duties and pair work requires patience and humility. Additionally, some mentioned that pair programming was strenuous; the other side of keeping alert.

Another important pilot feature was the planning game. The designers liked the fact that the work was divided into smaller entities making it more systematic. But a mentioned drawback was that the pair wanted to get tasks done as fast as possible, a sense of completion frenzy. In summary, pair programming and planning game (task planning) induced a sense of learning, feedback, problem solving, responsibility, alertness, and improved structure of work.

Looking at the effects of the pilot practices from a job enrichment perspective, the detailed effects are also connected with motivation. According to Hackman and Oldham, as presented in [32], five core job characteristics form the basis for job outcomes. These characteristics include skill variety, task identity, task significance, autonomy, and feedback. Comparing these with the findings in the pilot, it can be seen that all of these characteristics were affected by the changes in work during the pilot. New challenges and learning give skill variety and possibility for variation at work. Better structured work content improves task identity. Task significance is increased as the knowledge on related tasks grows. Ongoing interaction with peers increased feedback. The autonomy of work is to some extent decreased by pair programming, but the effect on felt responsibility on the other hand compensated by the increase in alertness.

The core job characteristics, in turn, influence how work is experienced with regard to three aspects: meaningfulness of work (derives from skill variety, task identity, and task significance), knowledge of actual results (feedback), and responsibility for outcomes (autonomy). These three aspects, together with an individual's need for growth, lead to job outcomes, one of which is a high level of motivation and satisfaction.

6 Discussion

As we showed in the previous section, the piloted implementation process was a success. The selected agile practices were modified to suit the existing environment and three of them were followed throughout the pilot. In spite of the new arrangements, the deliveries were made on time. However, regarding the three main goals, the outcome of the pilot was slightly different than we had expected. While the focus before the pilot was mainly on motivation and software quality, the main benefit of the pilot seems to be competence build-up. This implies that this method of working should be used specifically when there is a need for efficient competence build-up. The next two sections present possible explanations for the goal-specific results and the experiences and improvements concerning the selected agile practices. The discussion continues with directions for future work.

6.1 Goal-Related Issues

The fact that the designers did not explicitly acknowledge any change in motivation level after the pilot can relate to three things. First, the pilot had both positive and negative effects, which were found to balance out each other. Second, the pilot was known to last only for a certain time and many aspects of work remained the same even during the pilot. The third possible reason is related to the already stated impression of a pragmatic attitude towards work, motivation, and also measuring motivation. The pilot was possibly regarded as a refreshing interlude which broke the daily routines, but the designers were aware of the provisional nature of the pilot arrangements. In addition, a number of factors which in theory have an influence on the motivation level were not affected by the pilot. A more long-running and stable work arrangement can weigh more than temporary changes.

The question of quality, in turn, is also open for discussion. The design team was not a representative sample of a normal design team at the company, mainly due to the focus on competence build-up, which was chosen as a goal. The competence areas concerned especially the application domain and the existing base implementation of the subsystems. This fact might be the one most dominant factor to give uncertainty if the work at hand can be carried out with good enough quality and in timely fashion. Nevertheless, the outcome of the implementation was working code delivered on time.

With regard to schedule, we saw that the lead time and used man hours did not grow because of the introduction of pair programming. There is no clear reason why this is the case. This might relate to the way the process was monitored. Usually the work hours are not monitored with half-an-hour precision, and the coffee breaks and lunches are just reported to effective hours. Since it now was possible to calculate the truly effective hours, the used effective man hours might have grown, but it is impossible to tell exactly how much. Also, the increased attention to the designers' work and the more accurate monitoring of work hours was likely to increase the efficiency.

6.2 Experiences on Agile Practices

The pilot provided useful experiences considering the selected agile practices. The first improvement of the pilot was project monitoring. When originally stating the goals, transparency was not an issue. However, this was the first thing mentioned at the first steering meeting of the pilot. Previously, the data about the status of the project was vague, but during the pilot the managers and the testers could get tangible deliverables, thanks to the planning game and smaller tasks.

From the four selected practices we saw that the planning game was the most beneficial. It gave clarity to the implementation work itself, and furthermore helped in tracking the timeliness of a process. On the other hand, the customer on site was not used at all as there was no need for that. The existing organization already gives the support needed for implementation phase. Furthermore, collective code ownership was implemented so that a pair does all the needed changes for a feature (or a task) in two subsystems. Normally there would be two different teams, one making changes only to one subsystem. This new approach seemed to help in work allocation and overall function understanding, for example.

A couple of improvements were made to the piloted process already while executing the pilot. Use case realizations in the form of sequence diagrams were seen as good documents to implement in pairs. Tasks that are easy to implement should not be done in pairs. The team also noticed that some functionality is easily left out of the original tasks as the task definitions were too specific. On the other hand, it was not always easy to see what should be done for a task. Thus, the designers chose to combine some of the tasks.

6.3 Future Work

One of the suggestions for future study that was identified after the pilot was task allocation and how it could be formalized to optimize different factors, such as competence build-up or lead time. The basic idea is that each task should be assigned a complexity level (*High, Medium, Low*) and an estimated completion time. Competence areas should be defined. Those areas can be based on functionality of the system or on architectural elements. Each task should belong to one competence area. Each designer should be assigned a competence level for every competence area (*High, Medium, Low*). The tasks should then be assigned based on the sum of the competence of the pair. E.g., a pair of *Low* + *Low* competence with respect to the competence area that the task belongs to, should only implement tasks of *Low* complexity, while a pair of *Low* + *High* competence should do tasks of *Medium* complexity or higher.

Using these classifications on tasks and designers, the tasks may be allocated to people in order to optimize different aspects of the development. For example, if the lead-time or more precisely the total amount of used man-hours, would be the object function, an optimization function could be of the form:

$$\sum_{i=0}^{n}[\frac{t_i^e t_i^c}{a}(2-\frac{c_i^x+c_i^y}{2})+t_i^e]$$

where t_i^e is the estimated amount of man-hours needed to implement the task i; $t_i^c \in [0..2]$ is the complexity of a task i; $c_i^x \in [1..3]$ are competence factors for a task i for designer x, and finally a is a parameter for adjusting competence impact on implementation time. We discuss more on this optimization function and give some examples of its application in [20].

This type of a task allocation can also affect job satisfaction. More time is left for learning whenever it is possible. By taking time, competence and complexity into consideration, we can decrease some of the downsides of pair programming, such as competence build-up at a time when project deadline is approaching fast. Another modification which can facilitate the use of agile practices as methods for job enrichment is having a limited, specific goal, such as job rotation, training new team members or task planning.

7 Conclusions

In this paper we presented a case study where a number of agile practices were introduced in the design department of a large company in the context of a real software project. We showed how we adjusted these practices in order to integrate them into the existing software process. The paper presented the background and goals for the pilot, the measures for the outcome of the pilot, and the actual results. The pilot concerned a small number of designers during a limited period of time.

The pilot plan originally included four agile practices, three of which were finally followed: collective code ownership, pair programming, and the planning game. While the first two provided a good experience by being helpful in overall function understanding and building competence, we found the planning game to be the most beneficial practice. The planning game with its tasks gives structure and clarity to the implementation work itself as well as increases the transparency of following the schedule. The planning game should be made an integral part of the design work as a method for work planning and progress status follow-up.

The goals of the case study were to pilot pair programming, improve the motivation and build up the competence of the designers. While two of the stated goals were reached clearly, pair programming was introduced and the increased competence was both felt and measured, the results concerning the original focus area, the motivation of employees, remained somewhat oblique and requires further study. This suggests that pair programming should be used specifically when there is a need for efficient competence build-up. The effects of learning on job satisfaction, again, can be argued for.

The value of this pilot lies ahead: the pilot gave guidelines on how to proceed with the development of the implementation process practices. Also, it seems to be beneficial to test the ideas on a wider scale, e.g. within system design or testing, and to take competence build-up and lead time into account in task allocation. On the whole we concluded that the pilot was a success. It demonstrated that is worthwhile to use pair programming, the planning game and collective code ownership in the design and implementation. Agile methods could be refined to suite the existing settings of a large company.

References

1. Ilieva, S., Ivanov, P., Stefanova, E.: Analyses of an Agile Methodology Implementation. In: Proceedings of the 30th EUROMICRO Conference, IEEE Computer Society (2004) 326–333
2. Jedlitschka, A., Hamann, D., Göhlert, T., Schröder, A.: Adapting PROFES for Use in an Agile Process: An Industry Experience Report. In: Proceedings of 6th International Conference on Product Focused Software Process Improvement – PROFES 2005. Lecture Notes in Computer Science, Springer (2005)
3. Murru, O., Deias, R., Mugheddu, G.: Assessing XP at a European Internet Company. IEEE Softw. **20** (2003) 37–43
4. Rumpe, B., Schröder, A.: Quantitative Survey on Extreme Programming Projects. In: Third International Conference on Extreme Programming and Flexible Processes in Software Engineering – XP2002, Alghero, Italy (2002) 95–100
5. Back, R.J., Milovanov, L., Porres, I.: Software Development and Experimentation in an Academic Environment: The Gaudi Experience. In: Proceedings of 6th International Conference on Product Focused Software Process Improvement – PROFES 2005. Lecture Notes in Computer Science, Oulu, Finland, Springer (2005)
6. Reifer, D.J.: How Good are Agile Methods? IEEE Software **19** (2002) 16–18
7. Salo, O., Abrahamsson, P.: Evaluation of Agile Software Development: The Controlled Case Study approach. In: Proceedings of the 5th International Conference on Product Focused Software Process Improvement PROFES 2004. Lecture Notes in Computer Science, Springer (2004)
8. Hedin, G., Bendix, L., Magnusson, B.: Teaching Extreme Programming to Large Groups of Students. J. Syst. Softw. **74** (2005) 133–146
9. Melnik, G., Maurer, F.: Introducing Agile Methods: Three Years of Experience. In: EUROMICRO, IEEE Computer Society (2004) 334–341
10. Melnik, G., Maurer, F.: A Cross-Program Investigation of Students' Perceptions of Agile Methods. In: 27th International Conference on Software Engineering, St. Louis, Missouri, USA, ACM (2005) 481–488
11. Highsmith, J., Cockburn, A.: Agile Software Development: The Business of Innovation. IEEE Computer **34** (2001) 120–122
12. Canfora, G., Cimitile, A., Visaggio, C.A.: Working in Pairs as a Means for Design Knowledge Building: An Empirical Study. In: Proceedings of the 12th International Workshop on Program Comprehension (IWPC2004), Bari, Italy (2004) 62–69
13. Boehm, B.: Get Ready for Agile Methods, with Care. IEEE Computer **35** (2002) 64–69
14. Beck, K.: Extreme Programming Explained: Embrace Change. Addison-Wesley (1999)
15. Lindvall, M., Muthig, D., Dagnino, A., Wallin, C., Stupperich, M., Kiefer, D., May, J., Kähkönen, T.: Agile Software Development in Large Organizations. IEEE Computer **37** (2004) 26–33
16. Spayd, M.K.: Evolving Agile in the Enterprise: Implementing XP on a Grand Scale. In: Agile Development Conference, Salt Lake City, UT, USA, IEEE Computer Society (2003) 60–70
17. Zahran, S.: Software Process Improvement: Practical Guidelines for Business Success. Addison-Wesley (1998)

18. : Softswitch in Mobile Networks. Ericsson AB. 284 23-3025 UEN Rev A (2005) White Paper.
19. Hirkman, P., Milovanov, L.: Introducing a Customer Representative to High Requirement Uncertainties. A Case Study. In: Proceedings of the International Conference on Agility – ICAM 2005, Otaniemi, Finland (2005)
20. Auvinen, J., Back, R., Heidenberg, J., Hirkman, P., Milovanov, L.: Improving the Engineering Process Area at Ericsson with Agile Practices. A Case Study. Technical Report 716, TUCS (2005)
21. Williams, L., Kessler, R.: Pair Programming Illuminated. Addison-Wesley Longman Publishing Co., Inc. (2002)
22. Cockburn, A., Williams, L.: The Costs and Benefits of Pair Programming. In: Proceedings of eXtreme Programming and Flexible Processes in Software Engineering – XP2000, Cagliari, Italy (2000)
23. Constantine, L.L.: Constantine on Peopleware. Englewood Cliffs: Prentice Hall (1995)
24. Johnson, D.H., Caristi, J.: Extreme Programming and the Software Design Course. In: Proceedings of XP Universe, Raleigh, NC, USA (2001)
25. Müller, M.M., Tichy, W.F.: Case Study: Extreme Programming in a University Environment. In: Proceedings of the 23rd International Conference on Software Engineering, Toronto, Ontario, Canada, IEEE Computer Society (2001) 537–544
26. Williams, L.A., Kessler, R.R.: Experimenting with Industry's Pair-Programming Model in the Computer Science Classroom. Journal on Software Engineering Education **10** (2000)
27. Nosek, J.: The Case for Collaborative Programming. Communications of the ACM **41** (1998) 105–108
28. Back, R.J., Milovanov, L., Porres, I.: Software Development and Experimentation in an Academic Environment: The Gaudi Experience. Technical Report 641, TUCS (2004)
29. Wells, D.: Extreme Programming: A gentle introduction website. (Online at: http://www.extremeprogramming.org/)
30. Jeffries, R., Anderson, A., Hendrickson, C.: Extreme Programming Installed. Addison-Wesley (2001)
31. Beck, K., Fowler, M.: Planning Extreme Programming. Addison-Wesley Longman Publishing Co., Inc., Boston, MA, USA (2000)
32. Mitchell, T.R., Jr., J.R.L.: People in Organizations: An Introduction to Organizational Behavior. McGraw-Hill (1987)

Assessing Software Product Maintainability Based on Class-Level Structural Measures

Hans Christian Benestad, Bente Anda, and Erik Arisholm

Simula Research Laboratory, P.O. Box 134, NO-1325 Lysaker, Norway
{benestad, bentea, erika}@simula.no
http://www.simula.no

Abstract. A number of structural measures have been suggested to support the assessment and prediction of software quality attributes. The aim of our study is to investigate how class-level measures of structural properties can be used to assess the maintainability of a software product as a whole. We survey, structure and discuss current practices on this topic, and apply alternative strategies on four functionally equivalent systems that were constructed as part of a multi-case study. In the absence of historical data needed to build statistically based prediction models, we apply elements of judgment in the assessment. We show how triangulation of alternative strategies as well as sensitivity analysis may increase the confidence in assessments that contain elements of judgment. This paper contributes to more systematic practices in the application of structural measures. Further research is needed to evaluate and improve the accuracy and precision of judgment-based strategies.

1 Introduction

Software engineering is a complex problem solving activity with conflicting quality goals [1]. Quality attributes that are difficult to measure may therefore receive little attention. A prime example of this is the quality attribute known as maintainability, defined as the capability of the software product to be modified [2]. Researchers have proposed a number of structural measures as indicators of maintainability. For example, the CBO (Coupling Between Objects) measure is defined as the count of classes to which a class is coupled. Two classes are coupled if one class uses methods or instance variables of the other. An increased CBO measure is hypothesized to indicate more difficult testing, maintenance and reuse [3]. Existing research on the application of structural measures have focused on analyzing historical data to build product specific prediction models that can identify error-prone classes or classes that will be difficult to maintain [4].

In some situations, the required focus of an assessment is on the software product as a whole, as opposed to on individual classes. For example, a software acquirer may want to assess the maintainability of a software system prior to acquisition, or a software provider may want to monitor the maintainability of a system during its construction. In this paper, we investigate the use of structural measures as indicators of quality attributes at the *system* level, focusing on maintainability in particular.

J. Münch and M. Vierimaa (Eds.): PROFES 2006, LNCS 4034, pp. 94 – 111, 2006.

Based on current practices reported in literature, alternative strategies for conducting system level maintainability assessment from structural measurements are identified and discussed. We explore possible strategies by applying them on four functionally equivalent software systems that were developed as part of a multi-case study conducted by our research group. In this study, we needed to rank the four systems with respect to likely future maintenance effort. The historical data required to build statistically based prediction models was not available; hence we had to use elements of judgment in our assessment. To increase the confidence in the assessment we cross examined results from applying alternative strategies, and from altering judgment based parameters. These techniques, called triangulation and sensitivity analysis are intuitive and straightforward; however our survey indicates that they are rarely put to use in practice. A possible explanation is that few guidelines exist for identifying and selecting alternative assessment strategies. The main contribution of this paper is to identify and structure possible assessment strategies, in order to support future measurement initiatives in their selection and combination of alternative strategies.

The remainder of this paper is structured as follows: Section 2 describes related work. Section 3 discusses alternative strategies for selecting and interpreting structural measures for system-level assessment of maintainability. Section 4 applies alternative strategies to our systems under study. Section 5 concludes.

2 Related Work

This section outlines related work, focusing on research that has used structural measures to assess software maintainability.

The *Goal/Question/Metric* paradigm [5] prescribes development of *measurement models* that links measurement goals to operational questions that can be answered by measuring aspects of products, processes or resources. The method is useful in order to ensure goal-driven and purposeful measurements, but must be combined with domain knowledge specific to the quality focus in question.

Hierarchical quality models, [2, 6, 7], relate external quality attributes (such as maintainability) to internal attributes and measures of internal attributes. These models provide a useful framework for designing measurement programs related to software quality, but still provide limited guidance in the specifics of selecting and interpreting structural measures.

Structural measures of software. Early structural measures included lines of code (LOC) and complexity measures by McCabe [8] and Halstead [9]. These measures are commonly adapted and used for object-oriented systems, with class-level interpretations such as "LOC per class". The Maintainability Index (denoted MI) is a polynomial based on these measures that was suggested and validated as an indicator of maintainability by Oman [10]. With the advent of object-orientation, additional measures for size, complexity, inheritance, coupling and cohesion were suggested. The set of measures by Chidamber & Kemerer [3] (denoted CK) is among the most popular. The CK measures were hypothesized to be indicators of maintainability aspects, such as analyzability and testability, and have been empirically validated and used in a number of contexts [11].

Application of structural measures. A number of studies have applied structural measures to assess system-level design properties. We conducted a survey with the goal of characterizing assessment strategies that were employed in the studies [3, 6, 12-22]. These strategies are discussed further in the next section, and we summarize to what extent the different strategies are used in the surveyed studies[1].

3 Strategies for System Assessment Based on Structural Measures

In order to facilitate the investigation of assessment strategies, we choose to subdivide an overall strategy into the categories of *selection, combination, aggregation and interpretation*. *Selection* is the process of selecting the structural measures that best fit the purpose of the measurement initiative. *Combination* is the process of providing a combined view of the values for the selected structural measures, at a given granularity level. *Aggregation* is the creation of a derived measure at the system level, based on class-level measures. *Interpretation* is the assignment of a meaning to the measurement values with respect to the quality attributes of interest. Table 1 summarizes options that were identified for each sub-strategy. The options are not mutually exclusive. Furthermore, sub-strategies can in principle be applied in any order. In particular, an important decision to be made is the order in which aggregation and combination are performed: Measures may be combined at the class level before this combined class-level measure is aggregated to the system level. Alternatively, each class-level measure may be aggregated to the system level before the system-level measures are combined.

Table 1. Sub-strategies and options for creating a system level assessment strategy

Selection	Aggregation	Combination	Interpretation
1. Tool-driven selection 2. Pre-defined set of measures 3. Evidence-based 4. Statistical analysis of structural measures 5. Univariate regression analysis	1. Summary statistics 2. Distribution analysis 3. Outlier analysis 4. Visualization: Histograms, box plots, pie charts, scatter plots	1. Inspection of measures related to common quality attribute. 2. Multi criteria decision aid techniques 3. Multivariate regression analysis 4. Visualization: Kiviat charts, Chernoff faces	1. Relative 2. Thresholds 3. Trend analysis 4. Prediction models 5. Visualization ; Pie charts, line charts

If n measures are collected for each of k classes, aggregation, combinations and interpretation can be expressed by:

[1] Details from the survey can be found at: http://www.simula.no/departments/engineering/projects/ooad/StudyData/StudyDataProfes2006/surveytable

m_{ij}	Measure value for measure *i*, class *j*.
$C_j=f_c(m_{1j}..m_{nj})$	Combined view of a class *j*.
$A_i=f_a(m_{i1}..fm_{ik})$	Aggregated view for a measure *i* to a higher level of granularity
$M_1=f_{m1}(C_1..C_k)$	Aggregation of combined views to the system level
$M_2=f_{m2}(A_1..A_n)$	Combination of aggregated views at the system level
$I=f_I(m_{ij} \vee C_j \vee A_i \vee M_1 \vee M_2)$	Interpretation of one or more measures or views

The following sections discuss the options summarized in Table 1 in further detail.

3.1 Selection

Tool-driven selection is probably a common practice when structural measures are selected. For example, we believe that part of the popularity of the LOC measure can be contributed to the wide availability of tools that can count lines in text files. More advanced tools, such as Borland Together [23], collect a wide selection of structural measures. The selected measures should support the goals and questions of the specific measurement initiative, regardless of the sophistication of the tools employed.

A number of *pre-defined sets of measures* have been suggested by researchers. These sets are hypothesized to be indicators of aspects of maintainability, and they have to a varying degree been empirically validated. Popular sets include the CK measures and the MOOD measures [24]. Most of the studies in our survey used a pre-defined set of measures.

With *evidence-based selection* practitioners search for empirical evidence on questions that are similar to their own, using the principles of evidence-based software engineering [25]. For example, the survey by Briand & Wüst [4] provides concrete recommendations on types of measures to consider as indicators of different quality attributes. Although the infrastructure and extent of empirical knowledge is not yet sufficient for wide adaptation of the evidence-based selection strategy [26], mature organizations may still gain from an evidence-based strategy because it better supports changing goals and questions, than do the use of a pre-defined set of measures.

Selection based on *statistical analysis of structural measures*, addresses the weakness of the former strategies where the selections are not based on the particularities of the systems under study. Such analysis can address the *discriminating power* and *orthogonality* of structural measures: If the interpretation of measure values is based on comparison with other versions or systems, we consider it advantageous to select measures that can discriminate between the designs in question. For example, if coupling by data abstraction (attribute has class as type) is a rare construct in the analyzed systems, this measure would be a non-optimal choice for measuring coupling. Simple summary statistics can be used to identify measures with low variance or with few non-zero observations. Interpretation is simplified if *orthogonal* measures are selected, meaning that the same design aspects are not measured more than once. *Principal component analysis* (PCA) [27] is a statistical method that addresses both the discriminating power and orthogonality.

If it is possible to collect historical data that are direct or indirect measures of the quality attribute of interest, a *univariate regression analysis* can be conducted.

The purpose of the analysis is to obtain historically based evidence on a relationship between a specific structural measure and a given quality attribute. This strategy is used in studies surveyed by Briand and Wüst [4].

In practice, a specific strategy for selecting structural measures may contain elements of several of the above described options. Availability of tools may impose limitations on which structural measures can be considered. The availability of tools may be limited e.g. due to lack of support for a given technological platform. Furthermore, a combined strategy is to use statistical analysis of structural measures to adjust a predefined set of measures to better be able to discriminate between systems. An example of a combined strategy is provided in Section 4.1.

3.2 Combination

Structural measures should ideally measure one and only one aspect of design. The complex concept of maintainability can be expected to be influenced by several aspects of design. For example, the effort required to comprehend a class may be influenced by size, complexity and coupling. A combined view must be created for these measures to support the assessment of the required comprehension effort. It is inherently difficult to merge largely unrelated measures into a derived measure that can serve as an indicator of a quality attribute of interest. However, some formal or informal combination is required if several structural measures influence on the quality attribute.

Some of the surveyed studies perform combination by inspecting measures that are believed to influence a common quality attribute, c.f., [15, 21]. If there is a consistent pattern of more desirable measure values for System A than for System B, the interpretation is that System A is more desirable than System B with respect to the chosen quality attribute (see Section 3.4 regarding interpretation).

Using the *weighted sum* of several structural measures is an alternative strategy. A weight is assigned to each measure to account for differences in measurement units and importance. Then the sum of the products of the weight and each measure value is computed. The complicating aspect of different measurement units are frequently resolved by converting the measure values to a common, ordinal scale with scores from e.g. 1 to 6. There are two main problems with this strategy: First, from a measurement theoretical point of view it can be questioned whether weighing and summing are legal operations. Second, the derived measure is difficult to interpret as a standalone measure. Third, the weighted sum method is *compensating*, meaning that low scores are compensated by high scores, making relative comparison between software artifacts difficult. Bansiya and Davis [6] use a weighted sum strategy as part of establishing a hierarchical quality model that links internal design properties to external quality attributes. Stamelos *et al.* [22] reports from the use of the tool Tau Logiscope [28], which uses a similar strategy to produce combined measures meant as indicators of maintainability. The Maintainability Index [10] combines three (or four, in one version) traditional code measures into a polynomial to produce a single valued indicator of maintainability.

The weighted sum strategy is well known, and even used in every day situations. The technique belongs to the larger class of multi criteria decision aid (MCDA) techniques. Morisio *et al.* [29] have proposed the use of another MCDA technique, known as *Profile comparison*, in the context of software artifact evaluation. Profile vectors are constructed from threshold values for a set of structural measures. For example, if *Very High* values for measures m_1, m_2 and m_3 are judged to start at 20, 30 and 100, respectively, the profile vector is:

```
Very High =[m1>=20, m2>=30, m3>=100]
```

The performance vector, i.e., the actual measures for a software artifact is iteratively compared to each profile vector, testing whether a "sufficient" majority supports the classification, and classification is not "strongly" opposed by a minority. For example, the performance vector

```
ClassA =[m1=22, m2=20, m3=150]
```

is classified as Very High using the simple rule that the majority of the measures should support the classification. Weights can be assigned to reflect relative importance between the measures, and specific veto-rules can be specified. The use of this technique is illustrated in Section 4.3.

With *multivariate regression analysis,* historical data can be used to construct models that predict, e.g., error-prone classes or classes that will be difficult to maintain. A common strategy is to first use Principal Component Analysis (PCA) and univariate regression to identify candidate measures to be included in the model. Employing various variable selection heuristics, a multivariate prediction model is built for predicting the quality attribute of interest. The technique is described and used in [30].

Visualization. Kiviat charts are frequently used to support combinations that aim at comparing systems or comparing against threshold values. Drake used the shape of Kiviat charts to identify the "Albatross syndrome", which was a recurring pattern of undesirable values [14]. With simple goals, such as "Check that all aggregated values are below a threshold" or "Does Product A have consistent lower scores than Product B" this technique can be effective. *Chernoff faces* is an alternative technique that can be used for visualizing multi-dimensional data: Each dimension is represented by a facial feature, in order to take advantage of the capability of the human brain to recognize human faces.

If it is possible to collect historical data that we consider valid measures of the maintainability of the system, the regression-based methods are likely to produce the most trustworthy results. This is the strategy of most of the studies in the quality model survey by Briand&Wüst [4]. Since these models usually operate on the class level, combined measures must still be aggregated according to some of the techniques discussed in Section 3.3 to produce a system level measure. However, as already pointed out, historical data may not be available if the goal is to assess a system for aspects of maintainability while the system is still under development. Techniques that include elements of judgment must be used in these situations.

3.3 Aggregation

Summary statistics are simple and standard techniques to describe a larger data set using one or a few numbers, see for example [3, 15, 21, 22]. However, there are many choices to be made when calculating the summary statistics, as discussed below.

Sum values vs. central tendency. In the study by Sharble and Cohen [21], the sum of the measure values was used as a main aggregation method to compare the maintainability of two systems developed using two alternative design methods. This approach may be inappropriate. The relationship between the structural measures and maintainability may be nonlinear, but using the sum assumes a linear relationship. Furthermore, by using the sum, the measures are confounded with size, because larger systems will have higher measure values simply due to size. Obviously, size (e.g. the number of classes) is not unimportant, and can be a candidate as a separate measure, c.f., [6]. We thus believe that measures of central tendency (i.e., the mean and median) are more appropriate aggregation operators than *sum,* at least in the context of maintainability assessments.

Mean values vs. median values. Mean value tends to be the most frequently used measure of central tendency in the surveyed studies. In some cases, the median value would have been a preferred choice: Distributions of structural measures tend to be skewed to the left; hence the median is typically lower than the mean. When complementing the analysis with a specific analysis of the rightmost part of the distribution (high values and outliers) very high values will not be accounted for twice if the median is used instead of the mean. However, mean value remains the preferred choice when aggregation into one single number is necessary, because the important information resident in very high measures is hidden by median values.

Dispersion and distribution analysis. With increasing variance of complexity measures, a greater part of the classes have higher or lower complexity. Using the same reasoning as above, the penalty of analyzing a very complex class may more than outweigh the gain of analyzing the very simple class. Measures of dispersion are therefore important to consider. Low variance indicates a balanced design, with functionality and complexity distributed along a broad set of classes. One option is to calculate the variance or standard deviation of each measure. However, more information is retained from the original data set by creating frequency tables: A set of intervals are defined and the number of classes within each interval is counted. In the surveyed studies, this is the predominant method for analyzing the nature of the distributions, see e.g. [3, 15].

Outlier analysis. Outliers in measure values can be identified by using scatter plots, or with statistical methods. They may contain important information about the nature of design. There may be good reasons for a few classes in a system to have very high measures for individual structural attributes. For example, the use of some widely accepted design patterns can result in high measures of attributes, methods, or coupling. To be able to conclude whether the existence of an outlier can be defended, one may resort to the costly procedure of manual code inspection. Classes that are outliers with respect to several independent measures can more immediately be assumed to be an undesirable aspect of system design, even without manual inspection. Principal component analysis, discussed in Section 3.1, can be helpful in identifying the dimensions that should be included in such analysis. An example of detection of two-dimensional outliers using scatter plots is provided in Fig. 2.

Visualization: *Histograms* are frequently used for illustrating tabulated frequency of values of structural measures. *Box plots* provide a more compact technique to visually compare dispersions of systems. An example of the use of box plots is provided in Fig. 1.

In summary, using the sum or the mean values of structural measures at the class level provide very approximate measures of the overall design of a system. Unless linear relationships exist between the measures and the external quality attributes of interest, the sum or mean values may even be misleading. The median combined with measures of the variance and outliers might thus be a better choice in many situations. By using frequency analysis, more information from the original dataset is retained, and it is possible to take different kinds of non-linear relationships into account. However, retaining more information in the aggregation step will increase the complexity of the interpretation, discussed in the next section.

3.4 Interpretation

Interpretation is the assignment of a meaning to the measurement values with respect to the quality attribute of interest. Interpretation can occur as a final step after the combination and aggregation of measurement values, in which case the aim is to answers the questions related to some quality attribute. It can also occur at the class level, for example if the profile comparison technique discussed in Section 3.2 is employed. The relationships between the internal measures and the external quality attributes can only be established to a certain extent. The tolerated level of uncertainty is dependent on the intended use of the measures. For example, the uncertainty should be low if the goal is to test some contractually specified requirement to maintainability, hence assessment strategies that include elements of judgment may not be appropriate in this situation. However, if the goal is to support a development team in making reengineering decisions, judgment based strategies may provide considerable value.

Relative interpretation is the most basic principle for establishing relationships between internal and external characteristics of a software artifact. By assuming, say, that lower values are more desirable than high values with respect to maintainability, it is possible to rank software artifacts regarding maintainability. The assumption of a purely increasing or decreasing function may not hold in all cases: A system with deep inheritance trees may be difficult to maintain, while a system with no use of inheritance may not exploit useful features of object-oriented languages. Also, with a purely relative interpretation, the magnitude of observed differences cannot be determined. Finally, if individual measures show inconsistent patterns for a given software artifact, it can be difficult to conclude.

With *thresholds values*, the range of possible measurement values is sub-divided into intervals that are given specific interpretations. For example, intervals in a frequency table can be assigned names such as Good, Acceptable, Suspicious and Unacceptable. This type of interpretation is used in tools, such as Tau Logiscope [28]. The overall assessment can pay specific attention to the relative and absolute number of Suspicious and Unacceptable classes. The main problem with the method is to decide on interval thresholds. A similar strategy can be part of the profile comparison technique, described in Section 3.2. Outlier detection can be considered a special case, in which attention to extreme values are paid. Some tools, such as Borland Together [23], support the detection of outliers by highlighting classes or packages that exceed a predefined or user configured threshold value.

If measures from earlier versions of the product are available, *trend analyses* can provide useful insights. A system can be expected to be more resilient to change if measure values are stable between releases.

If *prediction models* based on historical data are built, the maintainability can be more precisely quantified. For example, based on historical data it may be predicted that the probability of a fault in a class doubles, if a measure of complexity increases by 50 %. Attempts have been made, most notably with the Maintainability Index [10], to create a model that is more generally applicable than local prediction models. It is difficult to argue in favor of the general validity of such a formula. However, adapted and used in local context, considerable value has been reported from using it [19, 31].

Visualization: Pie charts are frequently used to illustrate the relative number of classes receiving a specific classification when using threshold values. Line charts can be used to illustrate trends in measurement values. An example of the use of pie charts is provided in Fig. 3.

All studies in our survey use relative interpretation as an underlying principle, while a majority of the studies use threshold values as part of their interpretation [12, 14, 15, 18-20, 22]

3.5 Confidence Assessment

The discussion above shows that there are many uncertainties related to an assessment that is based on structural measures. This is not surprising, since the attempt is to draw conclusions on complex external quality attributes. General methods exist for assessing the confidence in methods or models that include sources of uncertainty.

The idea behind *triangulation* is that one can be more confident with a result if different methods lead to the same result. The options described in Table 1 can support the creation of alternative assessment strategies, the results of which can be cross examined to increase the confidence in the conclusions. With inconsistent results, it may not be possible to draw firm conclusions. In Section 4.2 and Section 4.3, an assessment is conducted with an aggregation-first and combination-first strategy, respectively.

Sensitivity analysis is a procedure to determine the sensitivity of the outcomes of a model to changes in its parameters. If a small change in a parameter results in relatively large changes in the outcomes, the outcomes are said to be sensitive to that parameter. The judgment based strategies that have been discussed in Section 3 can be regarded as models in where parameter settings are subject to uncertainty. For example, threshold values that are set by judgment during interpretation of measurement values can be varied within a range of reasonable values. If conclusions are insensitive to the threshold values used, more confidence can be put in the results. The number of alternative assessments will grow quickly when combinations of parameters with wide ranges of reasonable parameter values must be tested. However, this cost can be significantly reduced by automating the execution of the models.

The surveyed studies do not report the use of triangulation or sensitivity analysis. If model evaluation does not occur, it is difficult to put trust in the results. We provide examples of triangulation and sensitivity analysis in the next section.

4 Assessment of the DES Systems

The overall goal of the Database of Empirical Studies (DES) multi-case study was to investigate differences in development style of software providers, and their effects on software projects and products. In the study, we contracted four Norwegian software houses to independently construct a software system, based on the same requirement specification. Based on incoming proposals and company descriptions, we selected contractors that were likely to represent four dissimilar development cultures. Agreements and interaction between the client (us) and the contractors adhered to regular commercial and professional standards. The systems manage information about empirical studies conducted by our group, and emphasize is on storage and retrieval of such information. Each of the contractors spent between 431 and 943 man-hours on the project.

Our strategy for assessing and comparing the DES systems is based on the discussions in the previous section. The goal for the assessment is to rank the four systems with respect to future maintenance effort, and to explore the strategies described in Section 3. Since we do not yet possess rich empirical data from the maintenance phase, options involving regression analysis are not used; instead parts of the assessment are qualitative and judgment-based. We apply triangulation and simple sensitivity analysis as described in Section 3.5 to increase confidence in the results.

4.1 Selection of Measures

For tool support, we surveyed commercial tools, open source tools and tools from academia, and chose two tools that in sum covered a total of 71 measures. The tools selected were M-System from Fraunhofer IESE and JHawk from VirtualMachinery. This set of measures included most measures of size, complexity, coupling, cohesion and inheritance proposed in research literature. Due to differences in interpretation of measures, we chose to limit the number of different tools used, and ensured that related measures (i.e., measures that depend on common underlying information) were collected by the same tool.

Based on the discussions in Section 3.1 we investigated four alternative strategies for reducing the initial set of measures collected by the tools. An appropriate set of measures for our goal would be a minimal set that measures the dimensions of design that influence maintainability.

1. *Predefined set of measures.* The CK set is probably the most popular predefined set of measures. One problem with this set is that it includes only one measure for the concept of coupling, while it is known that fan-out (import) coupling has different effects than fan-in (export) coupling. Also, the LCOM measure has been shown to confound with size, and is not necessarily an appropriate measure of the concept of cohesion. The measures included in the CK set are shown in column "CK" in Table 2.
2. *Evidence-based.* We adjust the CK set of metrics to overcome the problems that were indicated above. We substitute the CBO coupling measures with separate measures for export coupling and import coupling (PIM, PIM_EC). LCOM is substituted by TCC, which is a normalized cohesion measure that has more discriminating power and is less influenced by size [32]. Also, we add the LOC measure as a straightforward measure of size, which is not included in the CK metrics. The selected measures with this strategy are shown in column "EV" in Table 2.
3. *Principal component analysis.* With the two above strategies it is uncertain whether the selected measures are orthogonal and have the discriminating power desired for the systems under study. We performed a principal component analysis to support the identification of such measures, and select the measure with highest loading for

each of the first eight principal components. We experienced that it was difficult to interpret some of the resulting principal components as distinct dimensions of design. Also, we found the analysis to be sensitive to the selection of input measures. The selected measures with this strategy are shown in column "PCA" in Table 2.

4. *Combination of the above*. In the last approach we fine-tune the selection from the CK and evidence-based strategy by making sure it does not contradict the PCA analysis. The measures TCC, DIT, NOC and WMC1 had high loadings on components that could be interpreted as "normalized cohesion", "inheritance height", "inheritance width" and "size and complexity", respectively. We therefore retain these as selected measures. For coupling measures we replace PIM and PIM_EC with OMMIC and OMMEC because the PCA indicated that the latter import/export coupling pair measures more distinct aspects of design. The LOC and WMC2 measures are removed, since they load moderately on the first principal components, already represented by the WMC1 measure. Instead, we choose to give double weight to the WMC1 measure in the following analysis. Since inheritance is not a widely used mechanism in the systems under study, we choose to halve the weight on each of the two inheritance measures. The selected measures, which constitute our final selection, are shown in column "Final" in Table 2.

As a result of this procedure, class level measures of WMC1, OMMIC, OMMEC, NOC, DIT and TCC were further analyzed[2].

Table 2. Analysis of DES systems: Selection of measures using four alternative strategies

Measure	Source	Short description	CK	EV	PCA	Final
loc	Trad.	Lines of code		X		
wmc1	[3]	Number of methods in class	X	X	X	X
wmc2	[3]	Cyclomatic complexity. Number of possible paths	X	X		
cbo	[3]	Coupling between objects	X			
ommic	[33]	Call to methods in unrelated class			X	X
ommec	[33]	Call from methods in unrelated class				X
ih_icp	[34]	Information-flow based coupling			X	
dac_	[35]	Data abstraction coupling			X	
pim	[36]	Polymorphically invoked methods		X		
pim_ec	[36]	Polymorphically invoked methods, export version		X		
ocaec	[33]	Class used as attribute type in other class			X	
noc	[3]	Number of children	X	X		X
nod	[37]	Number of descendants			X	
dit	[3]	Depth of inheritance tree	X	X		X
noa	[38]	Number of ancestors			X	
tcc	[32]	Tight class cohesion		X	X	X
lcom	[3]	Lack of cohesion	X			

4.2 Aggregation First Strategy

We here present the results of a quantitative and qualitative assessment, using an aggregation-first strategy. Summary statistics are provided in Table 3.

2 The raw measures and the PCA can be retrieved from http://www.simula.no/departments/engineering/projects/ooad/StudyData/StudyDataProfes2006

Table 3. Analysis of DES systems, named A, B, C and D: Summary statistics. For Mean and Standard deviation, values that deviate by more than 30% from Total values are in italics.

	Mean						Median					
	wmc1	om mic	om mic	dit	Noc	tcc	wmc1	om mic	om mec	dit	noc	Tcc
A	6.9	*7.7*	*7.7*	*0.46*	0.46	*0.26*	3.0	2	0	0	0	0.05
B	7.8	5.3	5.3	0.75	0.59	0.17	*6.0*	0	0	1	0	0
C	*11.4*	*8.6*	*8.6*	*0.0*	*0.0*	0.20	*8.0*	0.5	3	0	0	0.12
D	*4.9*	4.7	4.7	*0.83*	*0.76*	*0.11*	4.0	2	1	0	1	0.0
Tot	7.1	5.8	5.8	0.67	0.57	0.17	4.0	1.0	0.0	1.0	0.0	0
	Standard deviation						**Sum**					
	wmc1	om mic	om mic	dit	noc	Tcc	wmc1	om mic	om mec	dit	noc	Tcc
A	11.2	15.8	*20.6*	0.50	2.75	0.37	435	486	486	29	29	n.a.
B	10.3	11.8	15.6	0.81	2.37	0.31	1265	852	852	120	95	n.a.
C	*12.5*	*25.0*	*16.0*	0	0	0.23	273	206	206	0	0	n.a.
D	*4.5*	14.1	*10.1*	0.54	*3.81*	0.22	473	451	451	80	73	n.a.
Tot	9.6	14.4	15.6	0.69	2.83	0.30	2446	1995	1995	229	197	n.a.

Mean values: For mean values, the most distinct pattern can be observed for System C, which has relatively high values for size and complexity (WMC1) and coupling (OMMIC, OMMEC). Zero-value for the inheritance measures indicates that inheritance is not used in this system. Despite of a cohesion value (TCC) around average, this analysis is a first indication that the design of System C is non-optimal. System D has a low measure for WMC1 (considered desirable), but relatively high measures of inheritance, and low cohesion. System A has large coupling values (considered undesirable) and relatively low inheritance depth and high cohesion (considered desirable), while System B has no conspicuous mean values. This analysis indicates that System D will be the most maintainable system, while System C will be the least maintainable. It is difficult to rank System A and B, but since coupling measures are more than 30% larger than average for System A, we would rank B ahead of A.

Median values: We observe that due to the relatively large number of 0-values for all measures but WMC1, the median values become difficult to interpret. For WMC1, the pattern observed from the mean values recurs.

Standard deviation: System C has relatively large standard deviations for WMC1, OMMIC and OMMEC. System D has a small standard deviation for WMC1. This indicates that size and complexity is well distributed across the classes in System D, but not for classes in System C. System A has a rather large standard deviation for export coupling (OMMEC). There are no conspicuous values of standard deviation for System B. The suggested ranking from above is thus further supported from this analysis, however it is still difficult to distinguish between System A and System B.

Sum values: The sum values largely reflect the total size of the systems, measured in number of classes. The systems A, B, C and D contain 63, 162, 24 and 96 java classes, respectively. The low number of classes of System C introduces an uncertainty regarding the firm conclusion about this system from above. System B contains more than 2.5 times the classes than do System A. We interpret this as significant, given the close evaluation of these systems above. System B contains slightly more desirable code, but we rank it behind System A because 2.5 times the amount of classes must be comprehended and maintained.

Outliers: The box plots in Fig. 1 show that System D and System C contain extreme outliers for the OMMIC measure. The names of these classes, *StudyDAO* and *DB* respectively, indicate that the first uses the data access object pattern, while the

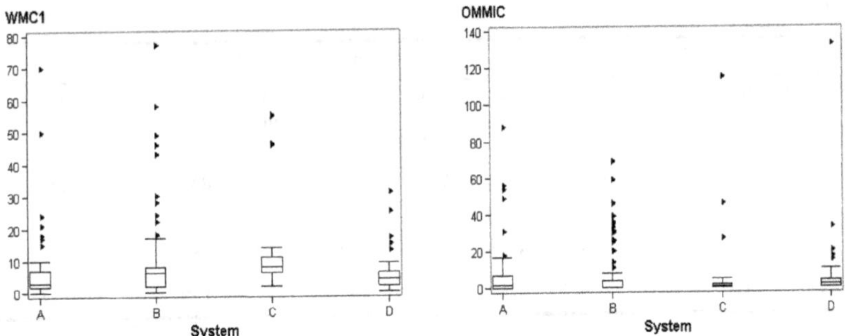

Fig. 1. Analysis of DES systems: Box plots for two structural measures

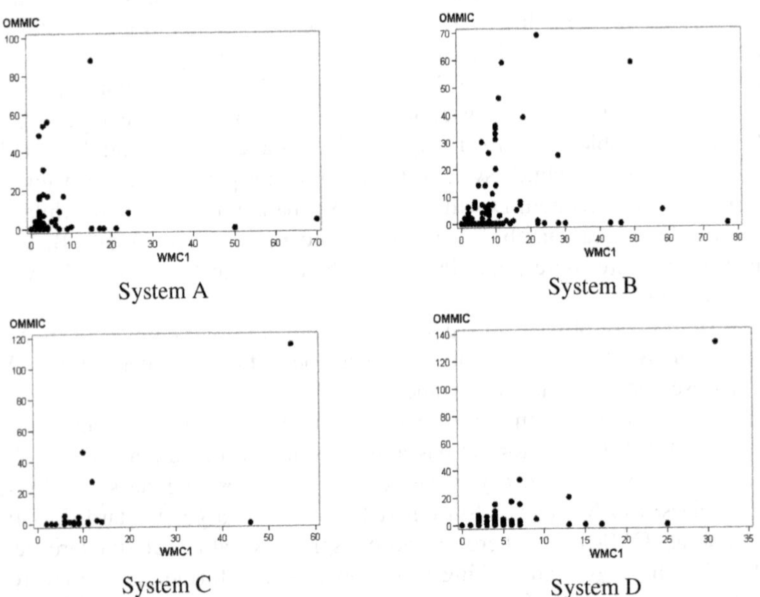

Fig. 2. Analysis of DES systems: Scatter plots of WMC1 vs. OMMIC

latter is likely to be a convenience based grouping of database access. System B contains one extreme outlier for the OMMEC measure, while System A contains one extreme outlier for the WMC1 measure. The name of these classes, *StudyForm* and *ObjectStatementImpl* respectively, indicates that these values are acceptable: A class handling a complex GUI may have many conditional paths, while a class supporting object persistence may be heavily used by other classes. Two-dimensional scatter plots, as shown in Fig. 2, show that System B, C and D contain one class that can be considered an outlier with respect to both size and complexity (WMC1) and import coupling (OMMIC). It counts to the advantage of System A that the system contains no such two-dimensional outliers.

4.3 Combination First Strategy

We conduct this analysis by combining measures at the class level, and then aggregating the combined values using a frequency table. Finally, the frequency table is interpreted by putting most weight on high measures.

Class-level combination: We use a simple version of the profile comparison method described in Section 3.2, and create four *profile vectors*, labeled Low, Average, High and Very High, see Table 4. The interval limits are calculated from the 0 to 50 percentile, 50 to 75 percentile, 75 to 95 percentile and above 95-percentile of the concatenation of all classes. We then construct the 345 performance vectors from the 345 classes in the systems.

Table 4. Analysis of DES systems: Profile vectors. Weight of measure in parentheses

	wmc1(2)	ommic(1)	ommec(1)	dit (0.5)	noc(0.5)	tcc (1)
Low	0-4	0	0	0-1	0	0.33+ or 0
Average	5-8	1-4	1-4	n.a.	n.a.	0.14-0.33
High	9-22	5-27	5-27	2	1-2	0.08-0.14
Very H.	>23	>28	>28	>3	>3	<0.13

The 345 performance vectors are compared against the profile vectors. The comparison criterion used is "The weighted sum of the criteria supporting the classification should be larger than the weighted sum opposing the classification".

To be able to interpret the results showed in Table 5, we assume that the classifications can be read as Good, Acceptable, Suspicious and Undesirable. 91.7% of the classes of System D are Good or Acceptable, while only 2% are Undesirable. For System C, one third of the classes are Suspicious or Undesirable. These observations support the conclusions for these systems from Section 4.2. System A and B fall between these extremes, with System A having slightly more desirable classifications than System B. The absolute numbers make the ranking clearer: 35 classes in System B are classified as Suspicious or Undesirable, while 10 classes in System A receive this classification. This analysis indicates that the ranking of the systems with respect to likely future maintenance effort is: D, A, B, C (least effort mentioned first).

Table 5. Analysis of DES systems: Categorization of combined class level measures

	System A	System B	System C	System D
Low	65.1% (41)	53.7% (87)	29.2% (7)	60.4% (58)
Acceptable	19.0% (12)	24.7% (40)	37.5% (9)	31.3% (30)
High	12.7% (8)	18.5% (30)	25.0% (6)	6.3% (6)
Very High	3.2% (2)	3.1% (5)	8.3% (2)	2.1% (2)

Sensitivity analysis: The classification procedure was automated using Microsoft Excel and a Visual Basic macro. We could therefore easily re-conduct the analysis to investigate the sensitivity for threshold values, weights and classification criteria. Classification was expected to be sensitive to these variations, but we obtained consistent results as far as ranking between the systems was concerned. The analysis was most sensitive to the weighing factors: With equal weight for all measures, it was difficult to differentiate between the systems A, B and D. However, we consider it fair to put less weight on the two inheritance measures, since inheritance is not a widely used mechanism in the systems under study.

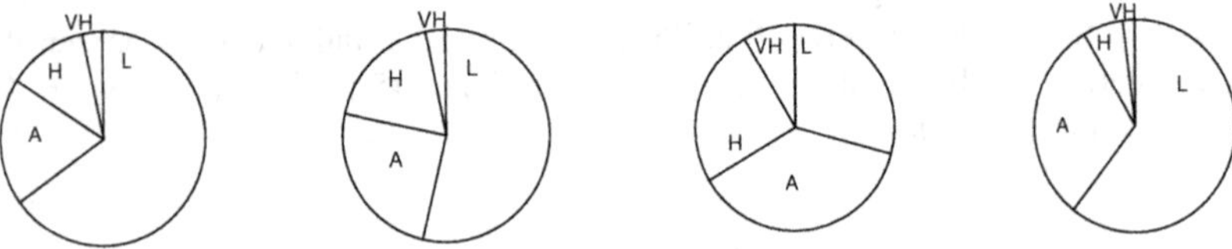

Fig. 3. Analysis of DES systems: Pie charts. Distributions of Low (L), Acceptable (A), High (H) and Very High (VH) classes, for system A, B, C and D respectively.

4.4 Summary of DES Analysis

Two parallel strategies were used for the DES analysis. The first strategy combined measures at the system level, while the second strategy created a derived measure at the class level. The latter strategy may be more intuitive for a developer who perceives the *class* as the main unit of analysis, change and testing during maintenance.

Systems C and D were consistently ranked lowest and highest, respectively. However, the significance of the small size of System C, measured in number of classes, leaves us with an uncertainty: It is quite possible that for some maintenance tasks, the effort involved in changing System C will not exceed that of the other systems. With the first strategy it was difficult to judge between System A and B, but we ended up with ranking A before B due to smaller overall size, and the absence of multi-dimensional outliers in System A. This ranking between System A and B was supported by the second strategy, which indicated a less desirable classification of classes in System B than in System A. The difference between the two systems was more evident when absolute number of classes was considered in place of relative number of classes.

The accuracy of the described predictions of maintainability will not become evident until empirical data is collected from the maintenance phase. However, we asked an experienced consultant, who had not been involved in neither the development projects nor the research, to assess the code with respect to maintainability using his own experience from maintaining object oriented code. The results were consistent regarding System C and D. The expert ranked A before B, largely because of the difference in size.

5 Conclusion and Further Work

We have investigated strategies for collecting structural measures at the class level to perform system level assessment of expected maintainability. A survey of reports from research and industry indicates that little emphasis is given on identifying the strategy that best fits specific measurement purposes. Although the specific purposes are special to every measurement initiative, this paper shows which decisions must be made while creating such a strategy, and suggests and discusses alternatives for each decision. The goal of the resulting strategy is to construct derived measures or views (through aggregation and combination) that can be interpreted so that specific questions can be answered with a certain level of confidence. In many cases and for many reasons, the historical data needed to create statistically based models are not available. Consequently, the interpretation of the derived measures needs to be partly based on judgments. This work promotes a systematic approach to the identification of alternative strategies for conducting system level assessment of maintainability. More empirical work is required to evaluate and improve the accuracy and precision of judgment-based strategies. A future scenario is to establish baselines of measurement values for specific software industry sectors, which could be used by software acquirers and providers as a basis for setting measurable goals on quality attributes that have previously been difficult to measure.

References

1. B. Boehm and H. In, "Identifying Quality-Requirement Conflicts," *IEEE Software*, vol. 13, pp. 25-35, 1996.
2. ISO/IEC, "Software engineering — Product quality — Part 1: Quality model," 2001.
3. S. R. Chidamber and C. F. Kemerer, "A Metrics Suite for Object Oriented Design," *IEEE Transactions on Software Engineering*, vol. 20, pp. 476-493, 1994.
4. L. Briand and J. Wuest, "Empirical Studies of Quality Models in Object-Oriented Systems," *Advances in Computers*, vol. 59, pp. 97-166, 2002.
5. V. R. Basili, G. Caldiera, and H. D. Rombach, "Goal Question Metrics Paradigm," *Encyclopedia of Software Engineering*, vol. 1, pp. 528-532, 1994.
6. J. Bansiya and C. G. Davis, "A Hierarchical Model for Object-Oriented Design Quality Assessment," *IEEE Transactions on Software Engineering*, vol. 28, pp. 4-17, 2002.
7. J. McCall, P. Richards, and G. Walters, "Factors in Software Quality," General Electric Command & Information Systems Technical Report 77CIS02 to Rome Air Development Center, Sunnyvale, CA 1977.
8. McCabe, "A complexity measure," *IEEE Transactions on Software Engineering*, vol. SE-2, pp. 308-320, 1976.

9. M. H. Halstead, "Elements of Software Science, Operating, and Programming Systems Series," vol. 7, 1977.
10. P. Oman and J. Hagemeister, "Construction and Testing of Polynomials Predicting Software Maintainability," *Journal of Systems and Software*, vol. 24, pp. 251-266, 1994.
11. D. Darcy and C. F. Kemerer, "OO Metrics in Practice," *IEEE Software*, vol. 22, pp. 17-19, 2005.
12. J. Barnard, "A new reusability metric for object-oriented software," *Software Quality Journal*, vol. 7, pp. 35-50, 1998.
13. L. Briand and J. Wüst, "Integrating scenario-based and measurement-based software product assessment," *Journal of Systems and Software*, vol. 59, pp. 3-22, 2001.
14. T. Drake, "Measuring Software Quality: A Case Study," *Computer*, vol. 29, pp. 78-87, 1996.
15. R. Ferenc, I. Siket, and T. Gyimothy, "Extracting Facts from Open Source Software," in *Proceedings of the 20th IEEE International Conference on Software Maintenance*: IEEE Computer Society, 2004.
16. R. Harrison, S. J. Counsell, and R. V. Nithi, "An Evaluation of the MOOD Set of Object-Oriented Software Metrics," *Software Engineering, IEEE Transactions on*, vol. 24, pp. 491-496, 1998.
17. R. Harrison, L. G. Smaraweera, M. R. Dobie, and P. H. Lewis, "Comparing programming paradigms: an evaluation of functional and object-oriented programs," *Software Engineering Journal*, vol. 11, pp. 247-254, 1996.
18. J. Mayrand and F. Coallier, "System Acquisition Based on Software Product Assessment," presented at 18th International Conference on Software Engineering, Berlin, 1996.
19. M. Saboe, "The Use of Software Quality Metrics in the Materiel Release Process — Experience Report," presented at Second Asia-Pacific Conference on Quality Software, Hong Kong, 2001.
20. M. Schroeder, "A Practical Guide to Object-Oriented Metrics," *IT Professional*, vol. 1, pp. 30-36, 1999.
21. R. C. Sharble and S. S. Cohen, "The Object-Oriented Brewery: A Comparison of Two Object-Oriented Development Methods," *SIGSOFT Software Engineering Notes*, vol. 18, pp. 60-73, 1993.
22. I. Stamelos, L. Angelis, A. Oikonomou, and G. L. Bleris, "Code quality analysis in open source software development," *Information Systems Journal*, vol. 12, pp. 43-60, 2002.
23. R. C. Gronback, "Software Remodeling: Improving Design and Implementation Quality," Borland 2003.
24. F. e. Abreu, "The MOOD Metrics Set," presented at ECOOP'95 Workshop Metrics, 1995.
25. T. Dybå, B. A. Kitchenham, and M. Jørgensen, "Evidence-based software engineering for practitioners," *IEEE Software*, vol. 22, pp. 58-65, 2005.
26. B. A. Kitchenham, T. Dybå, and M. Jørgensen, "Evidence-based Software Engineering," presented at Proceedings of the 26th International Conference on Software Engineering (ICSE), Edinburgh, Scotland, 2004.
27. I. T. Jolliffe, *Principal Component Analysis*, 2nd ed. New York: Springer-Verlag, 2002.
28. "Telelogic Tau Logiscope 6.1 Audit – Basic Concepts." Malmö, Sweden: Telelogic AB, 2004.
29. M. Morisio, I. Stamelos, and A. Tsoukias, "A New Method to Evaluate Software Artifacts Against Predefined Profiles," in *Proceedings of the 14th international conference on Software engineering and knowledge engineering*. Ischia, Italy: ACM Press, 2002.
30. L. Briand, C., J. Wüst, J. W. Daly, and D. V. Porter, "Exploring the Relationship between Design Measures and Software Quality in Object-Oriented Systems," *Journal of Systems and Software*, vol. 51, pp. 245-273, 2000.

31. K. D. Welker, P. W. Oman, and G. G. Atkinson, "Development and Application of an Automated Source Code Maintainability Index," *Journal of Software Maintenance: Research and Practice*, vol. 9, pp. 127-159, 1997.
32. J. Bieman, M. and B.-K. Kang, "Cohesion and Reuse in an Object-Oriented System," in *Proceedings of the 1995 Symposium on Software reusability*. Seattle, Washington, United States: ACM Press, 1995.
33. L. Briand, P. Devanbu, and W. Melo, "An Investigation into Coupling Measures for C++," in *Proceedings of the 19th international conference on Software engineering*. Boston, Massachusetts, United States: ACM Press, 1997.
34. Y. S. Lee, B. S. Liang, S. F. Wu, and F. J. Wang, "Measuring the Coupling and Cohesion of an Object-Oriented Program Based on Information Flow," presented at Conference on Software Quality, Maribor, Slovenia, 1995.
35. W. Li and S. Henry, "Object-Oriented Metrics that Predict Maintainability," *Journal of Systems and Software*, vol. 23, pp. 111-122, 1993.
36. L. C. Briand and J. Wüst, "The Impact of Design Properties on Development Cost in Object-Oriented Systems," presented at Software Metrics Symposium, London, UK, 2001.
37. A. Lake and C. Cook, "Use of Factor Analysis to Develop OOP Software Complexity Metrics," presented at 6th Annual Oregon Workshop on Software Metrics, Silver Falls, Oregon, 1994.
38. D. Tegarden, P., S. Sheetz, D., and D. Monarchi, E., "A software complexity model of object-oriented systems," *Decision Support Systems*, vol. 13, pp. 241-262, 1995.

Integrating Reuse Measurement Practices into the ERP Requirements Engineering Process

Maya Daneva

Department of Computer Science, University of Twente
P.O. Box 217, 7500 AE Enschede, The Netherlands
m.daneva@utwente.nl

Abstract. The management and deployment of reuse-driven and architecture-centric requirements engineering processes have become common in many organizations adopting Enterprise Resource Planning solutions. Yet, little is known about the variety of reusability aspects in ERP projects at the level of requirements. Neither, we know enough how exactly ERP adopters benefit from reuse as part of the requirements engineering process. This paper sheds some light into these questions and suggests a practical approach to applied ERP requirements reuse measurement by incorporating reuse metrics planning as part of the implementation of metrics on an ERP project. Relevant process integration challenges are resolved in the context of SAP R/3 implementation projects in which the author participated while being employed at the second largest telecommunication company in Canada.

1 Introduction

The business requirements for an Enterprise Resource Planning (ERP) solution in intra- or inter-organizational settings are the documents about the ERP adopter's organizational unit set-up, their business processes, data needs, and communication channels that are covered in the scope of the ERP implementation project. Requirements Engineering (RE) for ERP is the process concerned with all aspects of the reuse, the analysis, the adaptation, and the management of a large number of these descriptions. Its ultimate objective is to enhance the fit between the ERP adopting organization and its ERP system. The process begins ones a business case for the ERP implementation project is finalized and business drivers are identified and it continues throughout the entire implementation cycle in the form of tracking of the life history of any particular requirement and business issue. The better the resulting business requirements are conceptualized, the faster the progress in subsequent phases, because the necessary decisions concerning the future ERP solution have been made and agreed upon [4,5,24].

To streamline the RE process and to assure high quality results, the ERP vendors and their consulting partners have invented and marketed systematic requirements reuse approaches, infrastructures of processes, people and tools for ERP adopters to reuse, and, since 2000, industry-specific solution maps that are descriptions of the most important business processes within an industry sector, the technologies (ERP elements and add-ons), and services needed to support the processes. These can be

J. Münch and M. Vierimaa (Eds.): PROFES 2006, LNCS 4034, pp. 112 – 126, 2006.

seen as domain-specific frameworks [17] with three major features: an *architecture* defining the structure of integrated information systems within the business problem domain, a set of *business application components* engineered to fit the architecture, and a set of *tools* that assist the consultant in building component-based solutions using the domain knowledge within the architecture.

Nine years after the official launch of the first standardized ERP RE process by SAP, despite the increased attention to ERP requirements reuse, very few approaches have emerged to quantitatively measure the results from requirement reuse the customers have achieved [3]. As leading software metrics practitioners recognized earlier, we 'can not do effective reuse without proper measurement and planning' [19].

To obviate this issue, the present paper takes a measurement planning perspective [10]. We propose a practical solution that rests on a Goal-Question-Metrics-compliant process [1] of defining a requirements reuse measurement plan that links the reuse measurement needs to the ERP reuse goals and action items to be taken in the RE process. Our key objective is to provide a sound and consistent basis for incorporating reuse metrics planning as part of the implementation of metrics on an ERP project. We applied a case-study-driven research method [25] that was focused on the requirements reuse measurement activities in the context of implementing the SAP R/3 System, a leading product in the ERP software market [2,15,24]. However, our approach is generic enough and could easily be applied to any other ERP project implementation.

The layout of the paper is as follows: in the next section we motivate our approach. Section 3 is designed to answer some fundamental questions about the building blocks of our reuse measurement plan. Section 4 discusses how measurements are useful. Section 5 generalizes our experience. Section 6 concludes the paper.

2 Motivation

An ERP requirements reuse measurement process is a systematic method of (i) adopting or adapting standard reuse counting practices in ERP RE, (ii) measuring the ERP reuse goals, and (iii) indicating reuse levels targeted at the beginning and achieved at the end of each stage of the ERP implementation cycle. The main purpose of this process for ERP-adopters is to learn about their own business, technological and environment opportunities by learning how much reuse their ERP-supported business processes could practice. The motivation behind the integration of the reuse measurement process in the RE process is to achieve the following five goals:

- To enable the reuse process to be planned and reuse planning to be done as part of the RE process.
- To reduce the probability of errors and accidental omissions in the business process requirements.
- To spot requirements problems and conflict by identifying anomalous reuse measurements.
- To collect reuse data to serve as an input to an effort estimation model.

- To provide a foundation for (i) re-prioritizing the business requirements, (ii) communicating the value of ERP-reuse, (iii) increasing ERP users' understanding of the ERP functionality, and (iv) building and reinforcing partnerships,

3 The ERP Requirements Reuse Measurement Plan

Like any software development organization, an ERP adopter should document its requirements reuse measurement process in the form of a reuse measurement plan [6,10]. Its purpose is to establish a reuse measurement practice as part of a larger organizational process, namely, the ERP RE process. Moreover, it represents a communication vehicle to ensure that all the team members agree on the approach as well as serves as the on-going reference model to manage the implementation of reuse metrics. The plan defines the measurement process with exact information on stakeholders involved, measurement frequency, sources of metrics data, counting rules, metrics data interpretation rules, tools support, reports to be produces, and action items that can be taken based on the metrics data (Fig.1.).

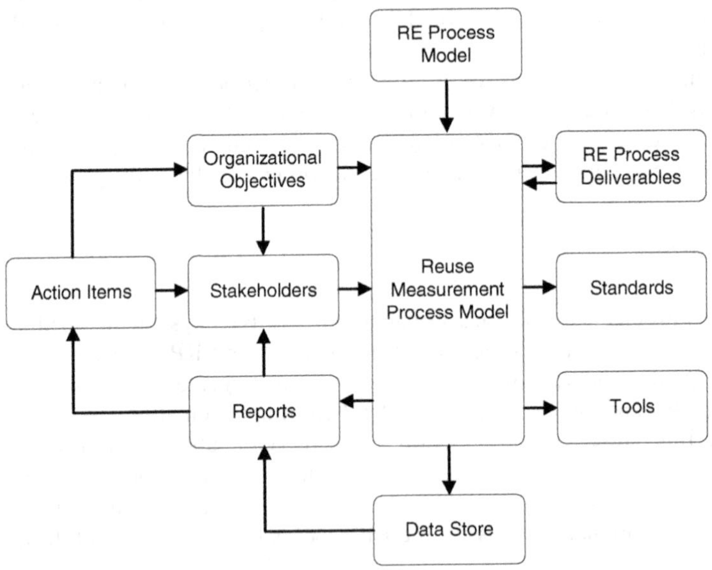

Fig. 1. The components of the SAP reuse plan

Stakeholders and their objectives define what is to be achieved by running a reuse measurement process. Next, as per the recommendations provided by software metrics researchers and practitioners [19,20], a model of the RE process is needed to capture the ERP reuse activities and to understand where measurements fit in. It should provide sufficient knowledge of (i) how to map reuse measures to RE activities, (ii) where and when in the RE process measurements could be taken, and (iii) how measurement activities could be integrated into the larger process. Given this context, a reuse measurement process model is required to specify what to count as requirements reuse, what units of measure to use, and how to count it. Furthermore, tools, data stores and standards for data collection, processing and packaging are to be selected to ensure the quality of the reuse metrics data. Finally, the plan concludes with strategies for using the reuse data. These are presented in terms of metrics data reports to be created and action items that can be formulated based on the reported data. The components of our ERP reuse measurement plan are discussed in detail in the next sections.

3.1 Understanding Stakeholders and Their Roles

Adequate and timely consultation of the ERP project stakeholders arties is a must to the planning of reuse metrics. It helped us (i) make sure that the definitions of our metrics are based on our SAP team members' goals, (ii) eliminate misunderstandings about how metrics data is expected to be used, and (iii) define relevant procedures for packaging, cataloguing, publishing and reporting reuse metrics data.

To identify the stakeholders, we applied the approach developed by Sharp et all in [23]. Based on early SAP project documentation, we developed stakeholder interaction diagrams that captured three important aspects of our team working environment: relationships between stakeholders, the relationships of each stakeholder to the system, and the priority to be given to each stakeholder's view. The organizational knowledge represented in the diagrams is needed to manage, interpret, balance and process stakeholders' input into the SAP requirements reuse measurement process. It was used to structure the SAP project team members in four groups: (i) *business decision makers*, who are corporate executives from the steering committee responsible for the optimization, standardization and harmonization of the business processes across multiple locations, and define the concept of ownership over the SAP R/3 system and are most interested in learning about the business benefits from SAP reuse, (ii) *business process owners*, who are department managers responsible for the project in specific business areas, and contribute the necessary line know-how, design new processes and procedures to be supported by the R/3 business application components and provide the project with the appropriate authority and resources, (iii) *technical decision makers*, who are SAP project managers responsible for planning, organizing, coordinating and controlling the implementation project, and (iv) *configurators*, who are both internal IT team members and external consultants involved in various work packages, e.g. process and data analysts, configuration specialists, ABAP programmers, system testers, documentation specialists. Each stakeholder had its own questions that should be answered by using the metrics data. Business decision makers wanted to know:

- What level of standardization could be achieved by reusing ERP software assets?
- What competitive advantages does the team get from ERP reuse?

- What are the implications of reusing ERP processes in a constantly changing business environment?
- How to align business processes across locations so that ERP reuse can yield significant cost reductions and enterprise-wide benefits?

Business process owners asked:

- How ERP reuse works with volatile process requirements?
- How much customization effort is required to implement minor/major changes in the business application components?
- What processes have the greatest potential for practicing reuse?
- What activities in our processes prevent us from reusing more?

Technical decision-makers needed to know:

- How much effort is required to produce the user and training documentation associated to the customized components?
- How much reuse the team did?

Configurators asked:

- Are there any rejected requirements that should be re-analyzed because of reuse concerns?
- What implementation alternative fits best?
- Which segments of the requirements are likely to cause difficulties later in the implementation process?

The questions relevant to each group have been documented and attached to the stakeholder interaction diagrams.

3.2 The RE Process in Point

The standard methodology for rapid R/3 implementation, called AcceleratedSAP (ASAP), provides a disciplined reuse-driven, architecture-centric process for coordination, controlling, configuring and managing changes of the R/3 business application components [2,15]. To investigate the ASAP RE process, we modelled it as a spiral (Fig. 2.). Its the radial arms represent the increasing collection of information by three types of activities: (i) *requirements elicitation* activities which deliver the foundation for the business blueprint and are concerned with finding, communication and validation of facts and rules about the business, (ii) *enterprise modelling* activities which are concerned with the business processes and data analysis and representation, and (iii) *requirements negotiation* activities which are concerned with the resolution of business process and data issues, the validation of process and data architectures and the prioritization of the requirements. The ASAP methodology suggests four iterations of the spiral. Level 0 iteration aims at developing a clear picture of the company's organizational structure based on the pre-defined organization units in the R/3 System. Next, the main objective of level 1 iteration is to define aims and scope for business process standardization based on the R/3 application components. Level 2 iteration aims at deriving company-specific business process architecture based on scenarios from the standard SAP process and data architecture components. Finally, level 3 iteration refers to the specification of data conversion, reporting and interfaces requirements. The major actors in these activities are business process owners who are actively supported by the SAP consultants and the internal SAP process and data architects. Next, the ASAP RE process is supported by the following tools: (i) the *ASAP Implementation Assistant* [15] which provides reusable questionnaires, project plans, cost estimates, blueprint presentations, blueprint templates, project reports and checklists, as well as manages the documentation base; (ii) the *SAP Business Engineer*, a platform including a wide range of business engineering tools fully integrated into the R/3 System [1]; (iii) *enterprise modelling tools* (ARIS-Toolset, LiveModel and Visio) which have rich model management capabilities and assist in analyzing, building and validating customer-specific process and data architectures based on the reusable reference process and data models.

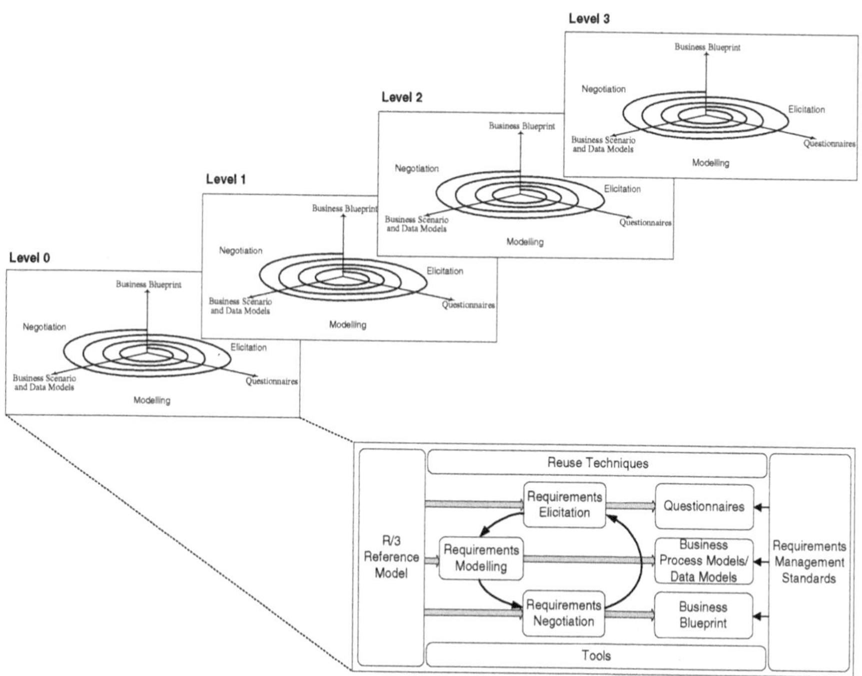

Fig. 2. The SAP requirements engineering process

The ASAP RE begins with reuse, ends with reuse and includes reuse in all the tasks in-between. It is based on proven reuse practices and techniques and it ensures that the requirements are correct, consistent, complete, realistic, well prioritized, verifiable, traceable and testable. This is achieved by using the R/3 Reference Model, a comprehensive architectural description of the R/3 System including four views: *business process* view, *function* view, *data* view and *organizational* view. Specifically, the R/3 Reference Process Models represent integrated and function-spanning collections of business processes that occur often in practice and can be handled to the greatest extend possible automatically if a corporation implements the complete R/3 System [15]. Instead of building an integrated information system from scratch, with the R/3 Reference Model we build a solution from reusable process and data architectures based on SAP's business experience collected on a large scale. Our analysis indicates that the R/3 Reference Model [2] supports the RE process in multiple ways: (i) in *requirements elicitation*, it provides a way for process owners and consultants to agree on what the SAP business application components are to do, (ii) in *requirements modelling*, it applies common requirements models [16] and serves two separate but related purposes: to quickly develop a requirement definition that shows to the business owners the process flow the solution is expected to support, and, then, to view it as a design specification document that restates the business specification in terms of R/3 transactions to be implemented, and (iii) in *requirements negotiation*, the R/3 Reference Model serves as a validation tool. It makes sure that the solution will meet the owners' needs, it is technically implementable and it is maintainable in future releases.

Reusing architectural components in the RE process is saving both time and money. As the business process requirement analysis is the most expensive consulting service in a business engineering exercise, the reuse of the R/3 Reference Model definitely provides the greatest savings.

3.3 Process Integration Model

This section presents how reuse measurement was integrated with the RE activities and where in the RE process reuse measurement data was taken (Fig. 3).

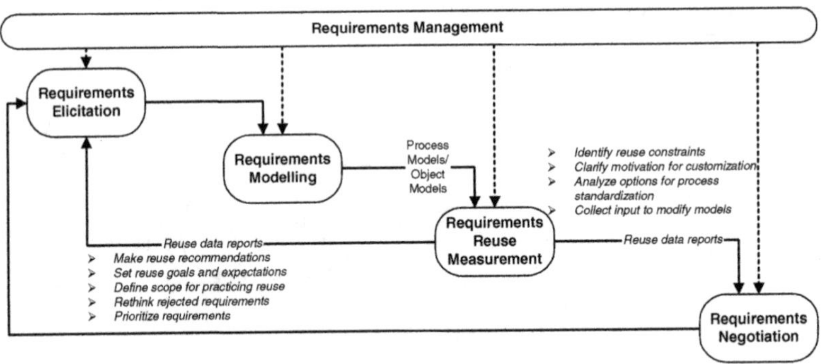

Fig. 3. Integration of requirements reuse measurement in RE

We adopted the following assumptions:

- reuse data are extracted by an SAP process analyst on the basis of two major RE deliverables: business scenario models and business object models [2];
- reuse metrics data analysis is based on quantitative indicators;
- reuse metrics data is used to support stakeholders' decision during the requirements negotiation and elicitation;
- reuse metrics data is reused at a later stage to support decision making in planning for future releases, upgrades and major enhancements.

We suggest reuse measurement be applied once the modelling activities of level 2 iteration are completed and the customer-specific process and data architectures are built (Fig.3). Given the reuse metrics data, the SAP process analyst may decide what negotiation / elicitation activities to take place next. The use of the metrics data is discussed in more detail in Section 4.

Our integration model implies that reuse measurement activities support the RE process in five areas: (i) definition of measurable reuse goals and expectations, (ii) quantitative analysis of process and data architecture reuse prior to solution design; (iii) assessment of the requirements specification, (iv) better understanding of the technical risks early in the ERP implementation cycle, (v) definition of the scope of ERP reuse and how it fits into the business environment.

3.4 The Measurement Process

As Pfleeger [14] recommends, we have to choose reuse metrics based on what is visible for the SAP project team in the requirements modelling process of level 2 iteration. Our approach uses the results of our previous research on the derivation of reuse indicators from SAP scenario process models and business object models [3]. It is based on the notion of "reuse percents" [20] and suggests a reuse indicator that includes reused requirements as a percentage of total requirements delivered [2]:

$$SAP\_Reuse = (RR / TR) * 100\%$$

where *RR* represents reused requirements, and *TR* represents total requirements delivered. In this paper, requirement borrowed from the R/3 Reference Model are classified as *reusable* if it does not require modification. If a borrowed requirement does require minor or major enhancement before use, we term it *'customized requirement'*.

To build well-defined and valid metrics [10], we selected a consistent and reliable means for structuring and collecting data to make up metrics. A standard functional size measurement methodology, namely Function Point Analysis (FPA) [11] was applied to size the total and the reused requirements in the project. It was chosen because of its appropriateness to the software artifact being measured [11,22] and its proven usage and applicability in software reuse studies [14,20]. However, we needed to adapt FPA the SAP requirements. This has been achieved in [3] by defining rules for mapping SAP business process models and data object models to the FPA counting components: we mapped SAP data entities to FPA data types, and SAP process components to FPA transaction types. As a result, the size of a scenario process model is assumed to be a function of the process components included in the model and the data objects defining the data that support the process. The step-by-step procedure for counting Function Points (FP) from scenario process models and business object models is described in [3] in terms of inputs, outputs and deliverables. Generally, it involves three stages: analysis of the process and data components, assignment of complexity values to the components and calculation of the final FP value.

Based on the analysis of the changes [15] that could be applied to the R/3 Reference Model throughout the reuse-based process modelling exercise, the measurement data collected throughout the FP sizing procedure [3], and the modes of component reuse investigated by Karllson [14], we have defined three levels of requirements reuse:

- *Level 3*: It refers to process and data components that were reused without any changes. This category of reuse would bring the greatest benefits to the SAP customer's organization. Scenarios with higher reuse rate at this level have greater potential of practicing reuse.
- *Level 2*: It refers to *minor enhancements* applied to reference processes and data components. A minor enhancement is defined as a change of certain parameter of a business process or a data component that does not result in a change of the process logic. This category of reuse refers to those processes and data components of the R/3 Reference Model that logically match the business requirements but their parameters need to be changed at code level to achieve their business purpose. Level 2 reuse is as desirable as level 3 reuse.
- *Level 1*: It refers to *major enhancements* applied to reference processes and data components. A major enhancement is any considerable modification in the definition of a process or a data component that affects the process logic from business user's point of view. This category of reuse refers to those processes and data components that do not match the business requirements and require changes at conceptual level, as well as at design and code level to achieve their business purpose. Level 1 reuse is at least desirable.

In these definitions, the term *process (component)* refers to the functional units of any SAP scenario process models and the term *data component* means a data entity, a relationship or an attribute from the data model describing the SAP business data requirements. Furthermore, we introduce a level of new requirements, *No_Reuse,* to acknowledge the fact that reuse is not practiced at all. It refers to newly introduced processes and data components. This does not mean a reuse category; it just helps us to partition the overall requirements and to get understanding of how much requirements are not covered by the standard scenario processes and business objects.

Given our definition of what to count as reuse and how to count it, we have derived three reuse indicators [3]:

$$\text{Level}_i\ \text{SAP\_Reuse} = (\ RR_i / TR\ )*100\%$$

where $i = \{1, 2, 3\}$, RR_i represents reused requirements at Level_i, and TR represents total requirements delivered. The indicator

$$\text{No\_Reuse} = (\ NR / TR\ )*100\%\ ,$$

where NR represents the new requirements, and TR has the above meaning, reports the percentage of requirements that can not be met by the R/3 application package unless some customer-specific extensions are not developed. Currently, case studies are being carried out to validate empirically our counting model and its application procedure. This exercise is being done on the basis of Jacqet's framework [13] for investigating measure validation issues and is carried out with the collaborators from Concordia University, Canada. It is part of a research project on building size and cost estimation models for inter-company ERP systems [5].

3.5 Assembling a Toolset for Data Collection

To assure the quality of the reuse data, we found that at least three tools were needed: (i) a form for recording all the counting details; (ii) a reuse metrics database, and (iii) a process knowledge repository. We extended the FP counting form suggested in [8] by including information needed for calculating the reuse indicators. Based on our FP counting model [3], we devised a counting form usage procedure that indicates at exactly what point each piece of data should be collected. information has been stored and processed in Excel spreadsheet software. Summarized and detailed reports have been extracted from Excel tables. For example, Table 2 reports on size numbers for six SAP business scenarios and Table 3 presents the summarized results from measuring reuse. Since reuse metrics provided knowledge about the business processes, reports on metrics data were treated as part of the SAP process documentation. can be We stored, packaged, catalogued and published reuse data by using a corporate intranet repository as well as standard process modelling tools and the ASAP Implementation Assistant. In this way, data was made available for review and analysis to all interested parties. Users of SAP documentation could easily navigate from scenario models to functional size and reuse metrics data.

Table 2. Functional size measurements in FP for six SAP scenarios

Business Scenarios	*Level*$_3$ *FP*	*Level*$_2$ *FP*	*Level*$_1$ *FP*	*New FP*
Recruiting	170	87	88	92
Business Trip Processing	120	41	20	25
Payroll Processing	236	26	16	32
Benefit Administration	195	87	102	91
Employee Relocation	165	21	10	16
Employee Numbers Processing	22	8	0	38

Table 3. Reuse levels for six SAP scenarios

Business Scenarios	*Level*$_3$ *Reuse*	*Level*$_2$ *Reuse*	*Level*$_1$ *Reuse*	*No Reuse*
Recruiting	39%	20%	20%	21%
Business Trip Processing	58%	20%	10%	12%
Payroll Processing	76%	8.5%	5%	10.5%
Benefit Administration	41%	18%	22%	20%
Employee Relocation	78%	10%	5%	7%
Employee Numbers Processing	32%	12%	0%	56%

3.6 How to Link Reuse Data to Action Items

Measurements are considered useful if they help stakeholders (i) understand what is happening during the ERP RE process, and (ii) control what is happening on the ERP project [10]. Typically, two types of reuse profiles could be derived from a requirements reuse measurement table (Table 3): *scenario-specific* profiles which present the levels of reuse pertinent to a given scenario, and *level-specific* profiles which show how the requirements are reused at a specific level within a project. Business decision-makers can use both types of profiles in at least three ways: (i) multiple reuse profiles of two or more different ERP products (SAP, Oracle, PeopleSoft) can be compared to determine which package best serves the needs of the company and offers the greatest opportunity for reuse; (ii) multiple reuse profiles of different releases (SAP R/3 4.0B, 4.5, 4.6) of one ERP package could be compared to determine which release brings biggest benefits to the company; (iii) multiple reuse profiles of a single ERP package (e.g. SAP R/3) can build an assessment of the overall level of standardization of the ERP solution in the organization. Reuse profiles of a single ERP package (e.g. SAP R/3) can be used by technical decision-makers to plan and control the reuse levels in the later phases of the ASAP implementation process. Business process owners and configurators can track requirements reuse levels over time to control the changes in overall reuse during the iterations of the RE process.

Furthermore, the specific use of each profile was systematically documented by using a Reuse Data Usage Table. We built it to characterize four aspects of a reuse profile: who needs to read the profile data, what the profile can help us understand, what the profile can help us control and what action items are likely to be taken based on the reuse profile. Tables 4 and Table 5 report on the current usage of the scenario-specific and level-specific profiles, respectively. (BDM, PO, TDM and C stand for business decision-makers, process owners, technical decision-makers and configurators, respectively.)

Table 4. Reuse data usage table for scenario-specific profiles

Usage	BDM	PO	TDM	C	Action items
Understand the customization risk for upgrade projects.	x	x	x	x	1. Assess the difficulty in the migration of processes with low reuse rates. 2. Reengineer the business requirements. 3. Budget and plan resources for extra gap analysis for the processes with low reuse rates.
Understand how much reuse the team did.		x	x	x	1. Set reuse expectations for later stages. 2. Define scope for practicing reuse. 3. Make process reuse recommendations.
Understand reuse constraints / Assess the level of standardization.	x	x		x	1. Elaborate alternative process flows to eliminate the need for customization. 2. Re-assess reuse levels. 3. Compare processes to select the best alternative.

Table 5. Reuse data usage table for level-specific profiles

Usage	BDM	PO	TDM	C	Action items
Define focus for negotiation meetings.		x		x	1. Review scenarios on a function-by-function basis to justify why customization is necessary. 2. Structure requirements in three categories: must-to-have, nice-to-have and possible-but-could-be-eliminated.
Select an implementation strategy.	x	x	x		1. Consider a step-by-step approach to a sequenced implementation, if Level 1 reuse dominates. 2. Consider a big-bang approach, if Level 3 reuse dominates.

4 Discussion on the Reuse Data Usage

Table 2 and 3 show example scenarios referring to the SAP Human Resource Management component. The *Level $_1$ Reuse* and *No_Reuse* ratings of the *Recruiting,* and *Benefits Administration* processes as well as the *No_Reuse* rating of the *Employee Number Processing* scenario are relatively high due to significant customization and numerous external interfaces required by the process owner. Next, the scenarios of *Payroll Processing* and *Employee Relocation* are the ones, which practice most *Level 3* reuse.

The scenario-specific data usage table suggests what benefits the reuse measurements bring to those stakeholders who are responsible for planning for reuse and assigning target reuse levels to each scenario to be achieved throughout the R/3 implementation project. Some examples of how these profiles were helpful include the following:

- The data was used in level 3 requirements elicitation to understand what prevented some teams from reusing more. In the *Recruiting* and *Employee Number Processing* scenarios, the low level of reuse was due to three reasons: (i) the standard R/3 functionality did not offer enough support to the business practices specific to a non-unionized mobile telecommunication services operator, (ii) many external interfaces to legacy systems had to be built, and (iii) hiring processes have not been standardized across locations in three Canadian provinces. We attempted to achieve requirements reuse trough re-engineering [12] of the major legacy systems.
- The data were useful in planning for both new implementations and upgrades. In the first case, unforeseen process modeling risks appeared for processes with high *Level $_1$ Reuse* or *No_Reuse* rates. They were likely to need additional resources (e.g. business process owners, internal training specialists, and documentation analysts) to get documented. In case of upgrades, reuse profiles helped the team assess the degree of difficulty involved in the migration to the new release. For example, Table 2 suggests that the process of *Employee Number Processing* needs to be migrated with extra caution.

Next, the level-specific usage table was important to requirements negotiation activities. Two illustrative examples of our experiences refer to the activities of (i) requirements prioritization and (ii) selection of an implementation strategy:

- The reuse data were used to decide what to focus the negotiation efforts on. As the process owners got a better understanding of the SAP reuse, and recognized customization options as one of the riskiest matters, they become more conscious to the avoidance of unnecessary adaptation and were willing to re-prioretize the requirements.
- The level-specific profiles helped both business and technical decision-makers determine what SAP implementation strategy fitted best with the organizational objectives. If *Level 1* reuse dominates and much customization efforts are anticipated, the team is likely to adopt a step-by-step approach to a sequenced implementation of the SAP components. If *Level 3* reuse rates are the highest ones, the customization risks are reduced and a big-bang approach to implementing multiple components seems to be reasonable.

5 Evaluating Experiences

SAP requirements sizing and reuse counting has been practiced in 13 SAP projects [4]. Each project was broken down in subprojects based on the number of SAP components to be implemented. For example, if a project implemented three components, it was broken done in three subprojects. The total number of all subprojects was 65. These varied in size and included new implementations, upgrades, and consolidations of system instances due to organizations' mergers and acquisitions. While applying the process, we collected and documented some facts and observations about the context of reuse measurement. Thus, we obtained a set of experience packages that suggested explanations of how and why the measurement process worked as part of the RE cycle [7]. We used these facts and observations to evaluate how the measurement process worked. Each package includes characteristics of the project context, a logical conclusion about specific aspects of the measurement process, and a set of facts and observations that support this conclusion. The conclusions represent either lessons learnt that tell us what and how worked in the process or critical success factors that suggest why it worked.

A summary of our lessons learnt is given in Table 6. It lists observations about what worked and how, and the number of subproject in which the observations occurred.

Table 6. Lessons learnt

Lessons learnt	Number of observations
Requirements reuse measurement helps understand in both qualitative and quantitative terms the role of the pre-defined process models in ERP RE.	60
The measurement process must be focused on defining action items based on the reuse data metrics, not on collecting and reporting data.	65
The process leads to consistent traceability information being maintained for all the business processes.	56
It increases the probability of finding poorly prioritized requirements.	48
Reuse data is a central record of all the process specific reuse information.	65
Reuse data helps to focus the validation process.	59
Reuse measurement should not be practiced as a short-term process that would be dropped at the end of the SAP implementation cycle.	53

Moreover, we identified 10 critical success factors:

- Apply a stakeholder identification method to the SAP project organization. This made sure that all important stakeholders have been captured, and yet that irrelevant actors have not been included.
- Use the ERP vendor's standard processes, deliverables, and tools. This significantly shortened the time needed to model the RE process and to spot where in this process measurements could be taken, analyzed, and used.
- Adopt (if possible) or adapt a standard methodology for sizing the business requirements. FPA proved its usefulness and applicability in ERP RE.
- Integrate the reuse measurement process incrementally. Pilot it by applying it to the business scenarios pertinent to a selected ERP component.
- Consider the metrics data reports as a supplement to the business blueprint. The business process owners should review reuse data as the other RE deliverables.

- Take extra efforts to experiment with the reuse measurement process and to collect and document the series of action items the team members suggest based on the metrics data.
- Understand the role of the reusable components and the reuse techniques in the ERP RE process.
- Maintain a limited number of requirements reuse measurement process documents: it is sufficient to start with a reuse measurement plan, a FP form and a customizable report template for presenting the results.
- Think out a strategy of how to maximize the benefits of the business engineering tools the team uses in the course of the ERP implementation. These can be of great support to the measurement process.
- Use the data for planning action items.

6 Conclusions

ERP requirements size and reuse measurement starts receiving the attention it deserves as a contributing factor in the success of ERP RE. This paper addresses both planning and technical aspects of making reuse indicators work in ERP project settings. We blended stakeholder interaction analysis with a process integration model to ensure the visibility of both reuse measurement and RE activities. This resulted in a practical requirements reuse measurement plan that one can apply incrementally to selected portion of the business requirements as well as to the entire project. The plan documents the components of a consistent measurement process: relevant stakeholders, a RE process model, a process integration model, counting rules, tools and reuse data usage tables. The process is reasonably simple so that RE teams can concentrate on their requirements elicitation and negotiation activities while functional size and reuse counting and data report generation playing a supporting role. Experiences of practicing the reuse measurement process have been packaged in 13 projects to derive lesson learnt and critical success factors for an on-going ERP reuse measurement initiative. We found that reuse requirements measurements were particularly valuable for highlighting anomalous customization requirements that may be unnecessary. ERP scenarios were then analyzed, then, in more detail.

We consider the work reported in this article as only the beginning of an ongoing effort to develop better requirements reuse measurement practices. In our future efforts, we plan to focus on answering the following research questions: How ERP requirements reuse relates to project cost? Does the claim that reuse decreases efforts [18,20,21,] remain valid in ERP settings? Which level of reuse dominates in each of the three project types, new implementation, upgrades, and instance consolidation? How to apply real options thinking [8] to ERP reuse as part of the RE process? What represents a good model for estimating the costs of keeping requirements reusable and estimating the future options [9] that this investment offers?

References

1. Basili, V.R., Caldiera, G. Rombach, H.D. The Goal Question Metric Approach, Encyclopedia of Software Engineering. Wiley (1994)
2. Curran, T., A. Ladd, SAP R/3 Business Blueprint, Understanding Enterprise Supply Chain Management, 2nd. Edition, Prentice Hall, Upper Saddle River, NJ (1999)

3. Daneva M.: Mesuring Reuse of SAP Requirements: a Model-based Approach, Proc. Of 5th Symposium on Software Reuse, ACM Press, New York (1999)
4. Daneva, M., ERP Requirements Engineering Practice: Lessons Learnt, IEEE Software, (2004) 21:26-33
5. Daneva, M., Wieringa, R.J., A Conceptual Framework for Research in Cross-organizational ERP Cost Estimation. Workshop on Requirements Engineering and Project Management in Software Projects (PROMan), in conjunction with the 13th IEEE Requirements Engineering Conference (RE'05), Paris (2005)
6. Desharnais, J.-M., A. Abran, How to Successfully Implement a Measurement Program: From Theory to Practice. In: Müllerburg, M., Abran A. (eds.): Metrics in Software Evolution, R. Oldenbourg Verlag, Oldenburg (1995), 11-38.
7. ESPRIT Project PROFES, URL: http://www.ele.vtt.fi/profes.
8. Erdogmus, H., A Real Options Perspective of Software Reuse, International Workshop on Reuse Economics "Redirecting Reuse Economics" Tuesday, April 16, 2002, Austin, Texas, USA
9. Favaro, J.M., K. R. Favaro, P.F. Favaro: Value Based Software Reuse Investment. Ann. Software Eng. 5: 5-52 (1998)
10. Fenton, N., Pfleeger, S.L.: Software Metrics: Rigorous and Practical Approach, PWS Publishing, Boston Massachusetts (1997)
11. Garmus D., D. Herron, Function Point Analysis: Measurement Practices for Successful Software Projects, Addison-Wesley (2001)
12. Guo J., Software Reuse through Re-engineering the Legacy Systems, Information and Software Technology, 45(9), pp. 597-609 (2003)
13. Jacquet, J.-P., Abran, A.: Metrics Validation Proposals: a Structured Analysis. In: Dumke, R., Abran, A. (eds.): Software Measurement, Gabler, Wiesbaden (1999), 43-60.
14. Karlsson, E.-A. (ed.): Software Reuse, John Wiley & Sons, Chichester (1998)
15. Keller, G., Teufel, T.: SAP R/3 Process Oriented Implementation, Addison-Wesley Longman, Harlow (1998)
16. Laguna, M.A., O. López, Y. Crespo, Reuse, Standardization, and Transformation of Requirements, Proc. of 8th Int. Conference on Software Reuse, LNCS, Springer, Berlin (2004)
17. McClure, C.: Reuse Engineering: Adding Reuse to the Software Development Process, Prentice-Hall, Upper Saddle River, NJ (1997)
18. Mili, H., Mili, A.: Reuse-Based Software Engineering, John Wiley & Sons, NY (2002).
19. Pfleeger, S.L.: Measuring Reuse: a Cautionary Tale, IEEE Software, June (1997)
20. Poulin, J. Measuring Software Reuse: Principles, Practices, and Economic Models, Addison-Wesley, Reading, MA (1997)
21. Rine D. C., N. Nada, An Empirical Study of a Software Reuse Reference Model, Information and Software Technology, 42(1), pp 47-65 (2000)
22. Robinson, S., J. Robinson, Mastering the Requirements Process, Addison-Wesley, Readings, MA (1999)
23. Sharp, H., A. Finkelstein, G. Galal, Shakeholder Identification in the Requirements Engineering Process, Proceeding of the 1st Intl. Workshop on RE Processes/ 10th Intl Conf. on DEXA, 1-3 Sept., 1999, Florence, Italy.
24. Welti, N., Sussessful R/3 Implementation, Practical Management of ERP Projects, Addison-Wesley, Harlow, England (1999).
25. Yin, R. K. *Case Study Research, Design and Methods,* 3rd ed. Newbury Park, Sage Publications, 2002.

Process Definition and Project Tracking in Model Driven Engineering

Ivan Porres[1] and María C. Valiente[2]

[1] Department of Computer Science, Åbo Akademi University
Lemminkäisenkatu 14, FIN-20520 Turku, Finland
ivan.porres@abo.fi
[2] Department of Computer Science, Carlos III University of Madrid,
Avda. Universidad 30, 28911 Leganés (Madrid), Spain
mcvalien@inf.uc3m.es

Abstract. This paper presents a software process definition language that is targeted towards the development of software and systems using Model Driven Engineering methods. The dynamics of a process model are based on Petri Nets. This allows us to use a process definition model to plan and track the execution of actual projects. This new language can be integrated with existing approaches for software process modeling such as Software Process Engineering Metamodel.

1 Introduction

Model Driven Engineering (MDE) is a software and system construction approach based on high-level abstract modeling. All the relevant information in a project is stored in models based on well-defined languages and development is then carried out as a sequence of model transformations. The MDE term was first proposed by Kent in [8] but it is derived from the OMG's Model Driven Architecture (MDA) initiative [13].

MDE is the result of recent developments on computer languages, awareness of the need of software and system development methodologies and the constant need to tackle larger and more complex system development projects. The two key elements in MDE are modeling languages and modeling tools to create and transform models. A modeling language is defined using standardized metamodeling languages such as MOF [11] or the UML 2.0 Infrastructure [16].

Automated model transformation is sometimes seen as the next silver bullet in software and system engineering. However, we consider that this is not the main advantage of MDE, since any non trivial development process will contain many development steps that cannot be automated. As a consequence, any MDE development step involves model transformations, but these transformations should be often performed by a skilled designer and not by a CASE tool.

On the other hand, we consider that the fact that we represent in MDE our software and system artifacts as models and that these models are based on a common metamodeling languages brings us many advantages to system development that have not been fully exploited. A uniform metamodeling approach enables us to build tools to manage complex relationships between the artifacts that form a complex project such as refinement [1] or retrenchment [2].

J. Münch and M. Vierimaa (Eds.): PROFES 2006, LNCS 4034, pp. 127 – 141, 2006.

In this paper, we study how recent advances in the area of software modeling languages and model transformations can be used in the context of software process modeling.

Different process modeling techniques have been used during decades. Software process modeling studies how to capture and describe a software process. A software process model is often a simplified representation of an actual process. However, this is one of its main advantages: a software process model should be easy to understand and follow by all the developers involved in a given project.

Approaches already exist to process definition that are integrated with modeling languages such as *Software Process Engineering Metamodel* (SPEM) [15] or the Rational Unified Process (RUP) [9]. However, these approaches do not address the definition of actual project tasks or development steps and tracking or execution of a project based on a process. This is a consequence of the fact that SPEM and RUP are generic process definition approaches that can be used in any development approach.

In this article, we propose a simple process definition modeling language that combines concepts from process definition languages such as SPEM with concepts from Model Driven Engineering such as model mappings and transformations. We define the execution semantics of the process models in terms of Petri nets. The result is a language that can be used to define a model-based development process in detail and, thanks to its behavioral semantics, to track the execution of projects based on a process.

We should note that our proposal is not a replacement to existing process definition approaches such as SPEM but a complement to them. Our approach focuses on the definition of process steps, but ignores other important aspects such as resource and role definitions since we consider that they are well supported in existing approaches such as SPEM.

We proceed as follows: In Section 2 we review the main concepts of Model Driven Engineering and how can be applied to software process modeling. We describe our new language for process modeling in Section 3 and we describe its dynamics in Section 4 using a practical example. Finally, we conclude in Section 5 with some final remarks and related work.

2 Definition of Software Development Processes in MDE

The execution of any complex software development process will include many different development steps that will produce internal and deliverable artifacts. A software development process contains the definition of each one of these steps and artifacts. Many organizations with complex projects have realized the need of better techniques and tools to support the management of software development process [4] and continue to demand more progress in the development process with acceptable results.

In short, software development process produces one tangible "thing" that is the software system. If we study the characteristics of software process to produce the "thing", we can conclude that there is a close relationship between software development process and business process. A software development process may be considered, and therefore managed as a business process. Like in business processes [21], in the software process there are cases (i.e., projects) that involve a process (i.e., software process that defines the life cycle of a project), conditions, tasks, work items, activities and resources that perform specific tasks in the process.

The development process used in a project should be well-defined and documented so it can be understood by all developers and its application can be monitored and evaluated. Software development processes can be described using natural language, but also modeling languages that are specific to the task such as the SPEM. Since models are supposed to raise the abstraction level of information processing, bring it near it to human understanding, and be less ambiguous than natural language [3], we prefer the last approach to describe a software development process. Furthermore, the development of a model of the software process facilitates reuse of the process by instantiation and execution of the model into multiple projects. Then, we consider that a modeling language for defining development processes should meet the following requirements [21]:

1. The structure of the software development process should be clearly documented. This makes the process recognizable to the user and reduces the chances of errors occurring both during the software development process definition and during the execution of a specific project (i.e., the instantiation and tracking of a process definition instance).
2. There should be an integrated approach, which also encompasses non-computerized tasks.
3. *A process definition model* must be set up so that the structure of the software development process can be modified easily. This enables organizations to respond flexibly to their changing environment and to restructure their software development processes accordingly.
4. It is important that the execution of the software development process can be tracked properly so that any problems can be discovered at an early stage. Interventions should also be straightforward and possible at the moment when something goes wrong. To this end, the execution of the software process should be easy to measure, and it should be possible to refine that execution.
5. The allocation of work to resources is a point of particular interest. Good workload management is crucial to achieving effective and efficient software development process.

However, we consider that SPEM does not address two important aspects: the definition of the actual development steps and the tracking or execution of a project based on a process defined using SPEM. However, if we consider a software development process as another business process, it is very important to separate process definition and process execution [21]. Therefore, we consider that in a software development process we always need to consider two aspects: *process definition model* that deals with the definition management of the software development process, and *project execution model* that deals with actual software development process definition instance, i.e. actual projects.

One of the reasons why SPEM cannot be used to define the execution of a project is that is a generic process engineering language that can be used to model any kind of process. This flexibility implies that a SPEM model cannot be specific on the exact nature of the artifacts and steps in a process. Therefore it cannot provide guidelines on the execution and tracking of a project.

These limitations can be lifted if we use SPEM to define a MDE process. In this case, most of the artifacts in a project will be models and the development steps model mappings. As a consequence, a step can be defined precisely as a mapping between a number of input models and a number of output models. All the input models should satisfy a given precondition and the output models a given post condition. A model mapping can be implemented using an executable transformation. However, many steps cannot be automated.

The OMG modeling standards already provide most of the technologies necessary to define a process as described above. The Meta Object Facility (MOF) and the UML Infrastructure are metamodeling languages that can be used to define other modeling languages, including the UML 2.0 or Domain Specific Languages (DSL) [22]. As such, we will distinguish between two kinds of artifacts: model artifacts that are based on a modeling language defined using MOF or the UML 2.0 Infrastructure, and uninterpreted artifacts that are defined using natural language or programming languages. Since we can consider, for instance, a Java program as a Java model, the uninterpreted artifacts can be considered as another kind of model as well. The Object Constraint Language (OCL) is another OMG standard that provides a language to define constraints over a model. OCL can be used to define the precondition or postcondition of a step. Finally, the OMG QVT [12] provides a language to define model mappings and executable model transformations.

The last element necessary to complete the specification of a process is a mechanism to combine and sequence the development steps as a business process. Again, we consider the solution is to reuse an existing OMG standard. The latest revision of UML 2.0 [17] offers a variety of notations modeling behavior, including workflow and business processes. Specially, the UML 2.0 Activity diagrams have been completely redefined and they are intended to be adopted as a standard for business process modeling.

UML 2.0 Activity diagrams may be applied to describe both computational processes and organizational modeling for business process engineering and workflow. Activity diagrams can show an entire business process from beginning to end. It can show a business process at any level, from a very high view down to one showing each individual task [20]. Besides, UML 2.0 Activity diagrams are redesigned to use a Petri net semantics instead of state machine semantics. The use of Petri nets as a formal concept has a number of mayor advantages since it enables the precise definition of behavioral models avoiding ambiguities, uncertainties, and contradictions. Besides, the formalism can be used to make strong statements about the properties of the process being modeled [21].

Based on this discussion, we consider that a software process engineering approach such as SPEM should be extended to embrace the main concepts of Model Driven Engineering. The result is an approach to software process definition that allows the precise definition of development steps using modeling languages to define artifacts, model mappings to define steps and activity models to define complex activities as a composition of simple steps.

3 Model-Based Software Development Process Definition and Execution

In this section we present a new approach to software process modeling that serves as a complement to SPEM. The proposed diagram considers MDA approach, UML 2.0 Activity Model, SPEM metamodel, and Petri nets semantics.

Like a business process (workflow), this diagram can be defined as the flow of information and control in a definition and execution of software development process. Therefore, the *process definition model* should depict the three *Rs* [20]: *Roles* (i.e., the resources who participate in the software development process), *Responsibilities* (i.e., the individual tasks that each resource is responsible for) and *Routes* (i.e., the control flow that connects the tasks together, and therefore defines the path that an individual task will take through the software development process).

On the other hand, since it is much easier to work with software development processes if there is an agreement on the things the process needs information about, a glossary with the definitions is very useful. Different interpretations could have a significant impact on the scope of some processes. Thus, a vocabulary or glossary should be always included in the *process definition model.*

A specification of software development process (i.e., life cycle process) definition in our diagram consists of the next model elements: *Work definitions* (*Activity*, *Step*, *Initial step* and *Final step*), *Models*, *Ancillary nodes* (*Comment*, *Constraint* and *Link*), *Resources*, and *Edges* (*Flow*).

An *Activity* is a work definition that represents a composite task, i.e., the specification of parameterized behavior consisting of other work definitions, models, ancillary nodes, resources and directed edges. An activity is identified by a *Name* and is performed by a *Resource*.

A *Resource* is the actor which is responsible of the performance of a task. This does not always mean to say that the resource necessarily carries out the task independently, but that it is responsible for it. We have considered two types of resources: *Role* when the task is performed by human beings and *Transformation tool* when the task consists in model transformation that is performed by a specific tool. A different notation is used for each resource. Figure 1 depicts these two notations.

Fig. 1. Human role (*left*) and transformation tool (*right*)

An activity has alternative *Parameter sets* and may have associated a *Precondition* and a *Postcondition.*

A *Parameter set* is a model element that provides alternative sets of input data (parameters in the left box in the parameter set) and output data (parameters in the right box in the parameter set) that a task may use. A parameter set acts as a complete set of inputs and outputs to a task, exclusive of other parameter sets on the task. When one set parameter or another has a complete set of input parameters, the task may begin.

A *Precondition* in a task is a constraint that must be satisfied when the execution of the task is started. A *Postcondition* in a task is the constraint that must be satisfied when the execution is complete.

An activity can be represented with two different notations: a) shorthand notation (*hierarchical structure*), or b) expanded notation. Figure 2 depicts these two notations.

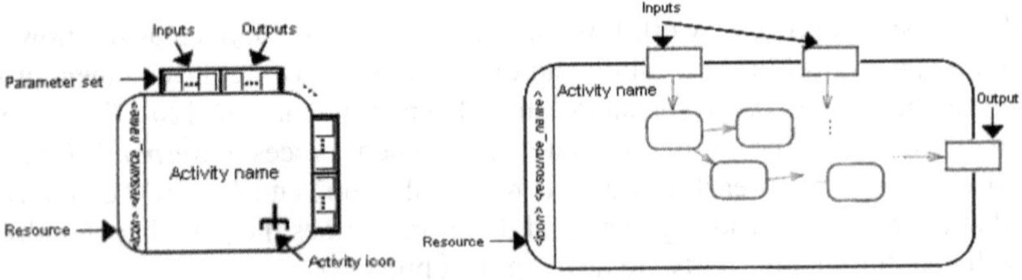

Fig. 2. Shorthand (*left*) and expanded (*right*) notation of an Activity

Since *Stakeholders* are the people who have a vested interest in the success of the project, or are involved in the implementation of the project, or even with the power to abolish the project, a list with the stakeholders is very useful. Stakeholders are associated with the full life cycle process. Therefore, an activity classified as a *Lifecycle* will keep this list.

Deliverable and *Milestone* are other key elements in a software development project. A *Deliverable* is a tangible event output from a task or a project (e.g., logical model, project agreement, database design or application). A *Milestone* is a tangible event used to measure the status of the project (i.e., markers during the execution of a project that shows the movement of a project in the right direction). Then, in this respect, we classify an activity as a *Phase* to indicate the grouping of tasks that lead to a *major project deliverable* or *milestone*. The output(s) of the *Parameter set(s)* in a *Phase* represent the corresponding deliverable(s) or milestone(s).

Figure 3 depicts the different specializations of an activity.

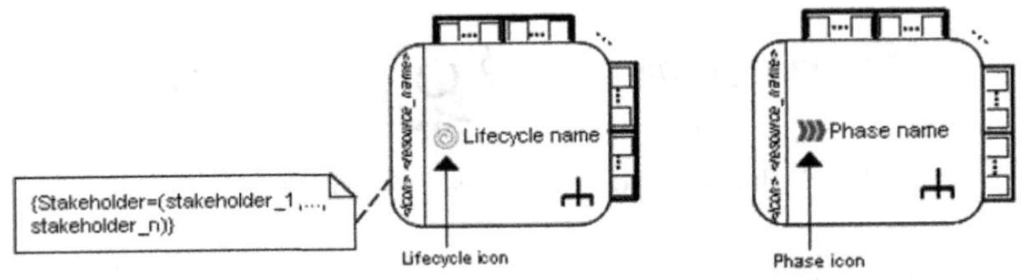

Fig. 3. Activity classified as a Lifecycle (*left*) or as a Phase (*right*)

A *Step* is a work definition that represents a single task to be performed by a resource. This is the fundamental unit of executable functionality. The execution of a step represents some transformation of processing in the modeled life cycle. A step is identified by a *Name* and is performed by a *Resource*, but in this case the resource is optional (if the resource is not indicated, it is assumed that the responsible of the step is the same responsible of the activity which the step is part of). Like an activity, a step has alternative *Parameter sets* and may have associated a *Precondition* and a *Postcondition*. The Figure 4 depicts this model element.

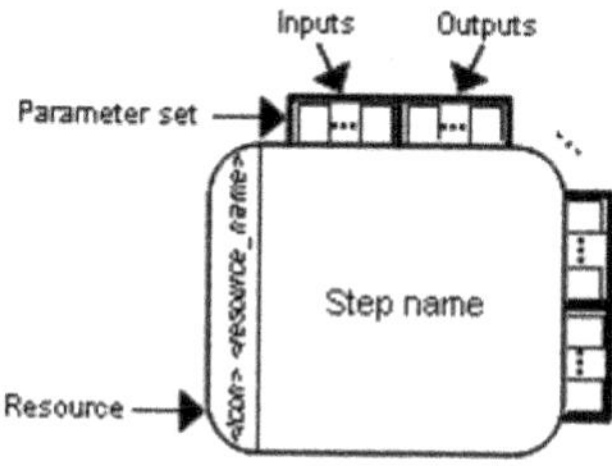

Fig. 4. Single step

Initial step and *Final step* are work definitions that represent *control* atomic tasks with specific functionality. An initial step provides the data that starts the life cycle. However, a final step stops all flows in the life cycle. This is the end of the life cycle. A life cycle may have more than one initial step and final step. Figure 5 depicts these two model elements.

Fig. 5. Initial step (*left*) and Final step (*right*)

A *Model* represents any artifact in a life cycle. We consider two types of models: *MOF-compliant* models and *Uninterpreted* models. The main difference between these two kinds of models is that we can easily define constrains over models based on MOF languages. These constraints are used as a model invariant, that tell us when a model is valid, but also as preconditions for an activity/step, so it is possible to know when an activity/step is enabled and can be carried out. We represent a model in a process definition diagram simply as a rectangle. The actual contents of the models are represented using the particular notation of the modeling languages used to create that model, and the type of model is indicated by a specific icon. Figure 6 depicts the notation for this model element.

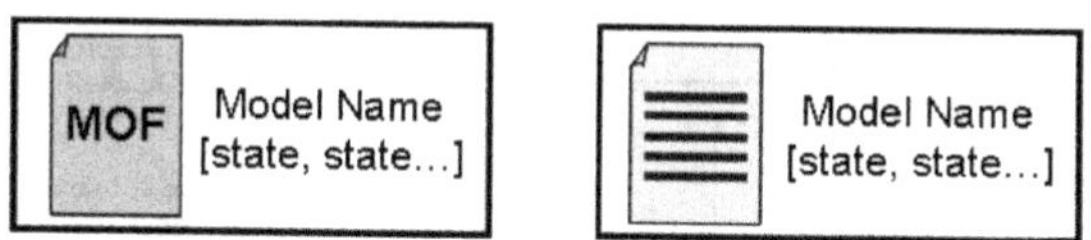

Fig. 6. MOF-compliant model (*left*) and Uninterpreted model (*right*)

A *Flow* is a directed edge that connects a *Work definition* with a *Model* or a *Model* with a *Work definition*. A flow may have associated the literal *{stream}* that indicates that there is a collection of models passing along the edge. More than one *Model* representation with the same name is not permitted, but in order to avoid complex and unreadable diagrams (e.g., crossing edges), the directed edge can be located inside the input and/or output parameters in a *Parameter set* next to the identification of the *Model* (without the rectangle). Figure 7 depicts this model element.

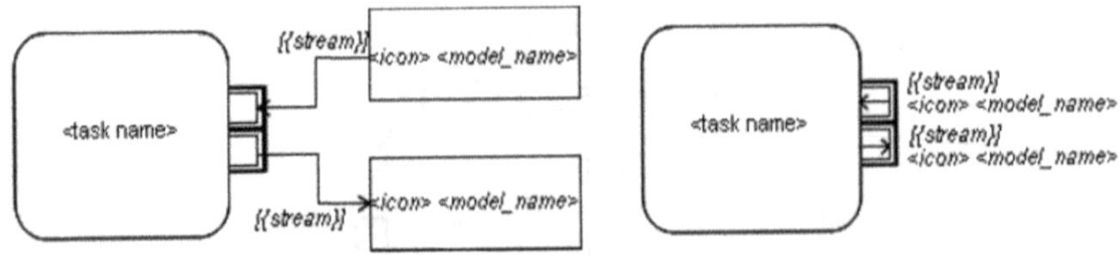

Fig. 7. Normal Flow notation (*left*) and the equivalent shorthand Flow notation (*right*)

Figure 8 illustrates an example of the notation. The diagram shows an overview of the Implementation phase in a specific software development process. Then, the activity *Implementation* classified as a *Phase* is performed by a *Hardware Designer* and is composed of two alternative parameter sets: (inputs*: {stream} Stream diagram*; outputs: *Detail Domain Model*), (inputs: *Defect list*; outputs: *Detailed Domain Model*); and three steps: *Model transformation* and *Generate code* performed by specific transformation tools, and *Defect removal* performed by *Hardware Designer.*

The *Model transformation* step takes as input a stream of MOF *Stream Diagram* and generates as a result a MOF *Detail Domain Model.*

The *Generate code* step takes as input a MOF *Detail Domain Model* and generates as a result a stream of uninterpreted *Code*.

The *Defect Removal* step takes as input an uninterpreted *Defect List* and generates as a result a MOF *Detail Domain Model* without defects.

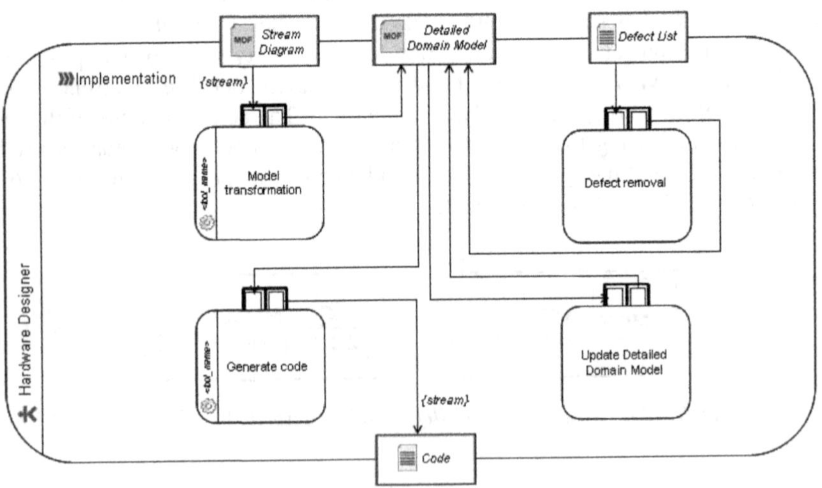

Fig. 8. An example of a diagram for process definition model

Finally, *Comment*, *Constraint* and *Link* are the ancillary nodes in our notation. A *Comment* is the textual annotation that provides additional information to the developer and can be attached to a set of model elements. A *Constraint* is the semantic condition of a model element that is expressed in natural language, formal notation, or in OCL. A *Link* indicates where the diagram continues by a numeric identification. It does not affect the underlying model. It is used for clarity. Figure 9 depicts this set of ancillary nodes.

Fig. 9. Ancillary nodes: Comment, Constraint and Link, respectively

Metamodel

Based on the above diagram, we propose the model illustrated in Figure 10 as our metamodel for software development process definition and execution models. *Process definition models* are the templates in which the *project execution models* are based on.

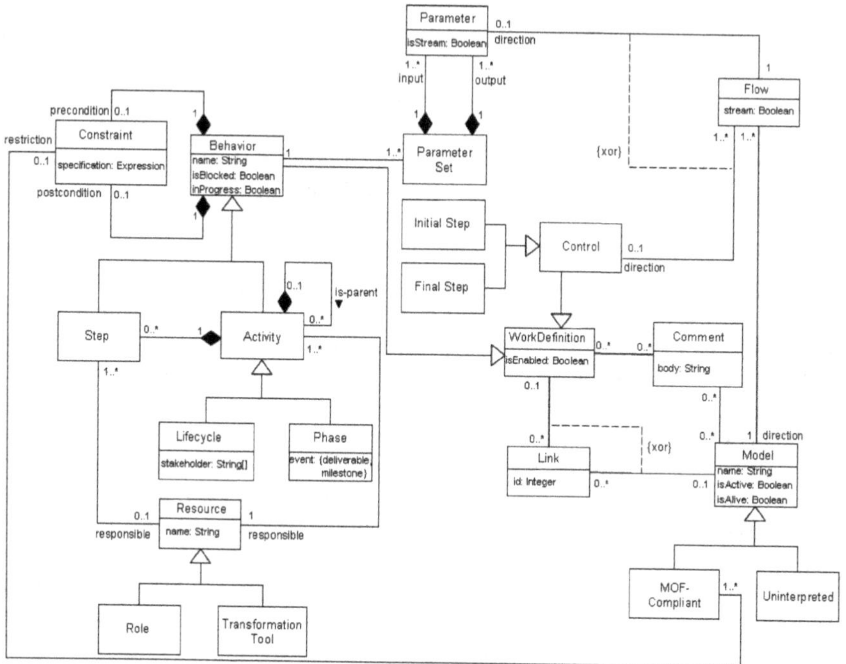

Fig. 10. UML class diagram representing the metamodel of the diagram for software development process definition and execution

The metamodel is at a higher level of abstraction than the models, and depicts the concepts considered in these models and the relationships between these concepts. *Process definition models* and *project execution models* will be instances of the concepts included in the metamodel. Therefore, these models have to conform to this metamodel in order to be valid.

Since information is provided by separate parts of the metamodel, it contributes to a clear separation of the different diagram concerns explained in the previous section. This separation of concerns makes modularity and reusability much easier.

Furthermore, the metamodel provides a repository of software development process definition and execution models. The repository stores agreed-on concepts and rules of the metamodel, so that users of the repository use common terminology for key terms in software development process definition and execution. The repository prevents model misinterpretation due to sketchy understanding of the true meaning and use of these models. Therefore, specific tools based on this metamodel could use the repository to specify and manipulate the *process definition models* and *execute* them into *project execution models*. By the automated creation of a *project execution model* based on a selected *process definition model*, and the use of the repository, tools can carry out project tracking.

4 Project Tracking

A *project execution model* is a model based on a *process definition model* template that represents the performance of a project. For a specific project, a *project execution model* provides a complete overview of the tasks that have to be performed, the responsible resources of the performance of each task, and the artifacts generated (in this case, models). Furthermore, when executing a *project execution model*, developers can keep track of what is the current state of the project, what has been done and what it is left.

Due to a recognized executable nature of *Petri nets* and their well-defined semantics allowing formal analysis, we define the execution semantics of the process models by establishing a mapping from our language to Petri nets. This behavioral semantics let us track the execution of projects based on a process. Petri nets are a formal approach based upon an established formalism for the modeling and analysis of processes. Petri nets have a strong mathematical basis and there are many analytical techniques and tools available for them. The use of Petri nets as a formal concept has a number of mayor advantages since it enables the precise definition of behavioral models avoiding ambiguities, uncertainties, and contradictions. Besides, the formalism can be used to make strong statements about the properties of the process being modeled [21].

A Petri net is a directed bipartite graph with two node types called *places* and *transitions* [6]. Places and transitions in a Petri net can be linked by means of a directed edge which is called *Arc*. Each arc connects a place with a transition or a transition with a place, but never two nodes of the same kind.

Places represent a control state or another condition in a Petri net. Places may contain zero or more *tokens*, and the number of tokens may change during the execution of the Petri net. The *state* of a Petri net is indicated by the distribution of tokens amongst its places.

Transitions are the active components in a Petri net. By firing a transition, the process being modeled shifts from one state to another. Therefore, a transition often represents an event, an operation or some kind of transformation. Transitions have *input places* and *output places*. An input place of a transition is any directed arc from a place to the transition. An output place of a transition is any directed arc from the transition to a place. A transition may only fire if it is *enabled*. A transition in a Petri net is said to be enabled (i.e., ready to fire) iff each input place of the transition contains at least one token. The firing of a transition will remove tokens from the input places, and will add completely new tokens to the output places.

Using Hierarchical Petri nets we can construct large models by combining a number of small Petri nets into a larger net (i.e., in a hierarchical Petri net, elements of the Petri nets contain Petri nets).

In our context, mapping the concepts of a specification of software development process onto Petri nets, transitions are described by *Work definitions* (*Activity*, *Step*, *Initial step* and *Final step*). *Activities* and *Steps* may have associated a *Precondition* and a *Postcondition*. *Activity* would be part of the hierarchical extension of a classic Petri net where compositionality, hierarchical structure is provided. *Control steps* (*Initial step* and *Final step*) are special tasks with specific functionality. The *Initial step* starts the *net* (i.e., the project) and the *Final step* removes all tokens in the net. The *Final step* represents the exit of the net (i.e., the firing of a *Final step* completes the project).

Models in our diagram represent variables that are used in a Petri net. When a *Model* has been initialized (i.e., the *Model* has a valid value), then the *Model* is considered *alive*. This property let developers know what *Models* have been already generated during the execution of the project.

Flows connect a *Work definition* with a *Model* or a *Model* with a *Work definition*. The firing of a *Work definition* will change the state to *active* of each model connected to an output parameter in the involved *Parameter set*. This operation is equivalent to add tokens to the output places of the transition. In short, each active *Model* indicates that there is a token in the corresponding place.

Only input parameters connected to active *Models* are considered valid inputs to the *Activity/Step*. Then, an *Activity/Step* is only *enabled* once there is an active *Model* connected at each input in an alternative *Parameter set* and the preconditions have been met. Therefore, active *Models* in a diagram determine the routing of a project (i.e., the tasks that may be performed and in which order).

In order to represent the above states in *project execution models*, we use several icons that are summarized in Table 1.

Table 1. Icons representing states in a Work definition and in a Model

Work definition		
Notation	**State**	**Description**
	Enabled	A member of the team project could select the task
	Not enabled	Selection is forbidden (i.e., invalid routing)
Model		
Notation	**State**	**Description**
	Active	The *Model* represents a valid input for an *Activity/Step*
	Alive	The *Model* has been initialized with a valid value

4.1 Example

We will use as a running example the definition of a development process for mobile phones peripherals called MICAS [10]. MICAS is a model-based development process based on a domain-specific modeling language. Many of the development steps are assisted by automatic model transformations. The complete definition of MICAS is out of the scope of this article.

Figure 11 exemplifies a *project execution model* with the MICAS case study. The diagram illustrates the model elements that are part of the MICAS life cycle and conforms to the metamodel described in the previous section.

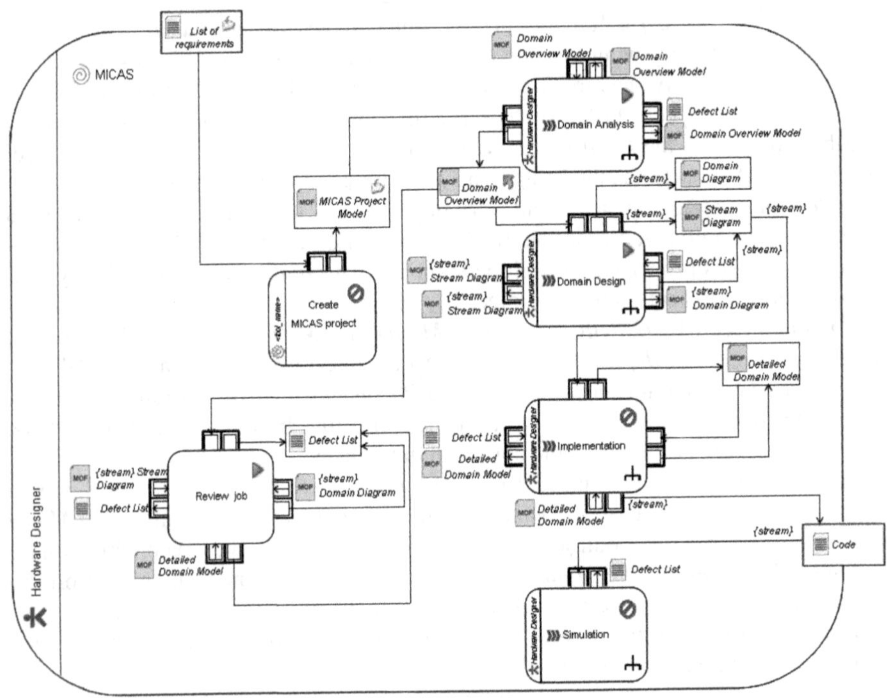

Fig. 11. Example of project tracking

The *project execution model* provides a well understanding of the applied process. The diagram provides an overview of the tasks that have to be performed, the responsible resources of the performance of each task, and the models that are part of the project. Besides, the diagram shows the current state of the project, what tasks have been done and what tasks are left. The *MICAS Project Model* was created and the *Domain Analysis Phase* has started.

The diagram shows that since the *Domain Overview Model* is active, the activities *Domain Analysis* and *Domain Design* (both classified as a *Phase*) and the step *Review job* are enabled. This model completes a set of inputs in one of their alternative *Parameter sets* and, in this case, there is not a precondition to meet. The developer could select either of them to continue with the project. If the user selects an activity, then the corresponding expanded diagram of the activity will be displayed until the user select a specific step to perform.

Since the rest of the work definitions do not have enough active models to begin, the selection is not permitted. Finally, models *List of requirements* and *MICAS Project Model* indicate that they are not active, but they are alive (i.e., they were initialized with a valid value).

5 Conclusions and Related Work

Software process modeling facilitates reuse of the process by instantiation and execution of the model into multiple projects. In this paper, we have proposed a software development process definition approach for Model Driven Engineering projects that improves the software process. Process models can be instantiated into specific projects. Our approach can be seen as a complement or extension to SPEM, but it can also be used independently.

The benefits of our approach are twofold: first we can introduce more detail in the software development process definition, allowing software development process precise and understandable with least effort. Also, a process model provides a complete overview of the tasks that have to be performed during a project, the responsible resources of the performance of each task, and the models generated. Furthermore, when executing a diagram, developers can keep track of what is the current state of the project, what has been done and what it is left.

Due to the executable nature of *Petri nets* and their well-defined semantics allowing formal analysis, we use Petri net as a foundation to provide project tracking features. The use of Petri nets as a formal concept has a number of mayor advantages since it enables the precise definition of behavioral models avoiding ambiguities, uncertainties, and contradictions. Besides, the formalism can be used to make strong statements about the properties of the process being modeled. We plan to extend our approach in this direction in the future and to build the corresponding tool that supports the proposed language.

UML 2.0 is a large modeling language that contains different mechanisms to organize and structure large projects. Some of the elements present in UML could be used to create process definition and model management diagrams as proposed in this article.

However, we consider that it is not a good idea to use UML 2.0, or any other existing language, for model management. Model management artifacts should be independent of the modeling language and be based on metamodeling approaches such as MOF and the UML infrastructure.

Data Flow Diagrams (DFDs) can identify, classify, and refine the data flows involved in a software process. However, DFDs only provide the functional view of the process (i.e., they describe only what is being done and what data is flowing). The diagrams do not describe the routing of a project neither the responsible resources of the performance of the process tasks.

Approaches already exist to process definitions that are integrated with modeling languages such as SPEM. SPEM is a known OMG's initiative that already supports the definition of the software development process specifically including those processes that involve the use of UML.

However, SPEM does not consider the execution of a project using a process definition described with SPEM. It neither tackles the definition of an actual task nor the actual tracking of a project that is what tasks should be performed at a given moment, what tasks have been done and what tasks are left.

Another modeling approach, *Statemate* by I-Logix, Inc. [5] seems to be a good alternative as representation formalism for software processes [7]. This system supports a unique methodology which was originally developed to aid in the design of real-time reactive systems (e.g., avionics software).

This system uses three types of diagrams to represent the specification of a process definition. Activity charts detail the functional viewpoint of a process. The first type, activity charts are basically DFDs with the addition of control activities and flows of information used for control purposes. The second type, statecharts provide the behavioral viewpoint (i.e., when and how). Statecharts extend conventional state-transition diagrams to deal with hierarchy, concurrency and communication. The third type, module charts provide the structural description of the models (i.e., they describe who performs tasks and where they are performed). Comparing to our proposed diagram, we offer a complete overview of the three diagrams (except timing issues) in a single diagram providing the useful information that developers need in order to understand the software development process. Besides, Statemate diagrams do not provide guidance in executing the process based upon its definition.

The *Programming Process Architecture* [19] is a related approach intended to define a homogeneous software development process across IBM's products. However, product development is not MDE-based and the architecture is not devised to contain specific tools or methodologies.

Finally, *Protégé* [18] is a tool that allows for the creation and manipulation of ontologies. Protegé uses a metamodel that can be used to model software processes involved in the creation of software products. However, the metamodel does not deal with hierarchy and for complex process definitions we could obtain unreadable diagrams. Furthermore, this metamodel does not provide project tracking.

Acknowledgments

The authors would like to thank Ian Oliver at Nokia Research Center, Helsinki for the enlighten discussions about the topics presented in this paper.

References

1. Ralph Back and Joakim von Wright, Refinement Calculus: A Systematic Introduction, Springer-Verlag, 1998.
2. Richard Banach and Mike Poppleton, Retrenchment, In Proceedings of Formal Methods, volume 1709 of LNCS, Springer,-Verlag 1999.
3. Gonzalo Genova, Maria C. Valiente, Jaime Nubiola. A Semiotic Approach to UML Models. In Proceedings of the 1st International Workshop on Philosophical Foundations of Information Systems Engineering (PHISE'05). June 13, 2005. Porto, Portugal. Esperanza Marcos, Roel Wieringa (eds.), 547-557.

4. Watts S. Humphrey. Managing the Software Process. Addison Wesley, 1989.
5. I-Logix Statemate. http://www.ilogix.com/
6. Kurt Jensen. Coloured Petri Nets. Basic Concepts, Analysis Methods and Practical Use. Volume 1. Second Edition. Springer-Verlag, 1996.
7. Marc I. Kellner, Gregory A. Hansen. Software Process Modeling. Software Engineering Institute, Carnegie Mellon University. Technical report, available at http://www.sei.cmu.edu/publications/documents/88.reports/88.tr.009.html, 1988.
8. Stuart Kent. Model Driven Engineering. In Proceedings of International Formal Methods 2002, volume 2335 of LNCS. Springer-Verlag, 2002.
9. Philippe Kruchten. Rational Unified Process. Addison-Wesley, 1998.
10. Johan Lilius, Tomas Lillqvist, Torbjörn Lundkvist, Ian Oliver, Ivan Porres, Kim Sandström, Glenn Sveholm, Asim P. Zaka. The MICAS Tool. In Proceedings of the NWUML'2005: The 3rd Nordic Workshop on UML and Software Modeling, pp. 180-192. Tampere, Finland, August, 2005.
11. OMG. Meta Object Facility (MOF) 2.0 Core Specification, version 2.0. Document ptc/04-10-15, available at http://www.omg.org/, October, 2004.
12. OMG. Meta Object Facility (MOF) 2.0 Query/View/Transformation Specification. Document ptc/05-11-1, available at http://www.omg.org/, November, 2005.
13. OMG. Model Driven Architecture. Document ormsc/2001-07-01, available at http://www.omg.org/, July, 2001.
14. OMG. Model Driven Architecture, MDA Guide, version 1.0.1. Document omg/2003-06-01, available at http://www.omg.org/, June, 2003.
15. OMG. Software Process Engineering Metamodel (SPEM) Specification, version 1.1. Document formal/05-01-06, available at http://www.omg.org/, January, 2005.
16. OMG. UML 2.0 Infrastructure Specification. Document ptc/04-10-14, available at http://www.omg.org/, November, 2004.
17. OMG. UML 2.0 Superstructure Specification. Document ptc/04-10-02, available at http://www.omg.org/, October, 2004.
18. Protégé. http://www.ics.uci.edu/~jgeorgas/ics225/index.htm
19. R. A. Radice, et al. A programming process architecture. IBM Systems Journal, v. 24, n. 2, pp. 79-90, 1985.
20. Alec Sharp, Patrick McDermott. Workflow Modeling. Tools for Process Improvement and Application Development. Artech House, 2001.
21. Wil van der Aalst, Kees van Hee. Workflow Management. Models, Methods, and Systems. The MIT Press, 2002.
22. Ariel van Deursen, Paul Klint, Joost Visser. Domain Specific Languages: An Annotated Bibliography. ACM SIGPLAN Notice, v. 35, n. 6, pp. 26-36. June 2000.

Difficulties in Establishing a Defect Management Process: A Case Study

Marko Jäntti, Tanja Toroi, and Anne Eerola

University of Kuopio, Department of Computer Science,
PL 1627, 70211 Kuopio, Finland
mjantti@cs.uku.fi

Abstract. A well-organized defect management process is one of the success factors for implementing software projects in time and in budget. The defect management process includes defect prevention, defect discovery and resolution, defect causal analysis, and the process improvement. However, establishing an organization-wide defect management process is a complicated task. The main research question in this paper is what kind of difficulties organizations have regarding the defect management process. Our findings show that problems are related to defect resolution reports, limited project resources for fixing defects, and challenges in creating a test environment. Results are based on our observations from four case organizations. The main contribution of this study is to help organizations to identify and avoid typical problems with defect management.

1 Introduction

Establishing a defect management process is an attractive way to improve the software quality. Early detection of defects provides cost and time savings for software projects because developers need to produce less new product versions and bug fixes. Moreover, reduced number of defects in applications increases the level of customer satisfaction, and reliable software is easy to sell to new customers.

Several studies have explored defect management activities. For example, different types of defect management models have been described by the Software Engineering Institute (SEI) [1], [2], IBM [3], the IT Infrastructure Library [4], and the Quality Assurance Institute (QAI) [4]. According to the QAI, the defect management process consists of six elements: defect prevention, deliverable baselining, defect discovery, defect resolution, process improvement, and management reporting. The Defect Prevention Model of IBM [3] is focused solely on defect prevention techniques, for example, Defect Causal Analysis method. The causal analysis is used to identify the root cause of the defect [5].

Additionally, there are a number of recent studies that have presented different defect classification schemes [6],[5]. Too detailed reporting and complex classification schemes might increase defect processing costs remarkably [7]. Defect management activities are also supported by various quality standards. CMM at Level 5 considers defect management as a key process area with the following

J. Münch and M. Vierimaa (Eds.): PROFES 2006, LNCS 4034, pp. 142–150, 2006.

goals: defect prevention activities are planned, common causes of defects are sought and identified, and common causes of defects are prioritized and systematically eliminated [8].

Currently, many organizations are adopting the Problem Management model described by the IT Infrastructure Library (ITIL) because ITIL has become a de facto standard for IT service management [4]. However, the ITIL model does not define how to perform testing and defect management activities as a part of IT service management. In fact, it seems to be that there is a need for both a problem management model used by the service support staff and a defect management model used by the application developers and testers. This might cause a communication gap if both counterparts use different data repositories for problems and defects.

However, few studies have examined the problems that organizations have with defect management. This study continues the work reported in our previous study [9], where we identified the advantages and problems of using an UML-based test model for creating test cases based on UML diagrams [10].

In this paper the research question is, what kind of problems do organizations have regarding defect management? First, we explore four case organizations' goals for defect management and defect management processes. After that, we will investigate what are their problem areas in defect management. Most of the previous research of defect management has focused solely on software companies, although customers are active participants in the defect management process. In our study we are going to examine defect management problems also from the IT customers' viewpoint.

As main findings we will show that instead of tool-related difficulties major problem areas in defect management are, for example, dealing with defect resolution reports, creating a test environment and a lack of commonly agreed defect management methods.

The rest of the paper is organized as follows. In Section 2 we describe the research methods of this study. In Section 3 findings of the case study are presented. Section 4 is the analysis of findings. The discussion and the conclusions are given in Section 5.

2 Research Methods

This case study is a part of the work of the research project SOSE (Service Oriented Software Engineering) at the University of Kuopio, Finland. SOSE is funded by the National Technology Agency TEKES, the European Regional Development Fund (ERDF), and four partner companies. The study was carried out partly with the research project PlugIT (2001-2004), which focused on research into application integration methods in the healthcare domain.

The main research purpose of this study was to explore the problems that organizations have in defect management. A case study method was used because it is well suited for the study of information systems in organizations. Yin [11] defines a case study as "an empirical inquiry that investigates a contemporary phenomenon within its real-life context, especially when the boundaries between phenomenon and context are not clearly evident". Both IT customers and software companies were selected for this study because our objective was to compare the difficulties in defect management between these two groups.

2.1 Data Collection Methods

Case A is a large IT service company with over 15 000 employees. It supplies information systems to various industries, such as banking and insurance, energy, telecom and media, and healthcare. The data collection methods in this case included personal interviews with a product manager and a customer support manager.

Case B is a project-oriented software company. Its core business is focused on implementing solutions for mobile communication: for example, solutions that enable operators to charge for GSM calls. The company employs 53 people. Their strategic partner is one of the leading GSM operators in Finland. The data collection methods included an interview with an IT manager.

Case C is an energy company group consisting of 1) the parent company, which is responsible for the network business and group administration; 2) a company specializing in selling electricity; and 3) the district heating company. They have 430 employees. The data collection methods included personal interviews with an IS manager and a risk manager.

Case D is an IS department of a hospital offering specialized services, including specialized nursing services, to the healthcare district. It is also a teaching hospital with medical, nursing science and healthcare students. The data collection methods included interviews with a system tester and a system designer. The interviews with the tester were conducted in the course of the UML-based testing experiment in the PlugIT project [9]. The purpose of the experiment was to explore how UML-based testing [12] helps in finding defects in a healthcare application.

Interviews were performed by the first author and were based on the questionnaire that was based on the research framework developed by the Quality Assurance Institute [13] containing the following questions:

1. Do you have a software quality program, a formal software development lifecycle model, a defect classification method or definition of defects?
2. What kind of defect information is collected?
3. Who collects defect data?
4. What are the sources of defect data?

2.2 Data Analysis Methods

A cross-case analysis technique [14] was used in this study to analyze data from interviews and to compare cases. In the data analysis, we tabulated the data on cases into four categories: existing defect management methods, type of defect information, defect data sources, units responsible for collecting defect data. Then we compared the results, looking for similarities and differences in defect management processes and problems. Finally, we analyzed how organizations could improve their defect management processes based on the results of this study.

3 Empirical Findings

This section presents our empirical findings from four cases. In this study, we explored the organizations' goals in defect management, their defect management processes, and problems related to the activities in defect management.

3.1 Defect Management Processes

Table 1 shows our findings regarding the four cases' defect management processes. Notes: N = no, Y = yes, - = missing data and P = partially.

Table 1. Defect Management processes in four case organizations

Question	A	B	C	D
The case organization has				
Software Quality Program	P	N	N	N
Formal software development lifecycle	Y	Y	N	N
Company-wide method of gathering defect information	Y	Y	Y	P
Method of classifying defects/problems	Y	Y	Y	Y
Definitions of defects and failures	Y	N	Y	Y
The case organization collects information on				
Development/Production failures	Y	Y	Y	Y
Development phase where a defect originated	Y	Y	-	Y
Activity which originated the defect/problem	N	Y	Y	-
Type of the defect/problem	Y	Y	Y	Y
Cause of the defect/problem	Y	N	Y	Y
Time to resolve the defect /problem	Y	Y	Y	N
Defect/problem resolution costs	N	N	Y	N
Sources of defect data are				
Change Request Form	Y	N	Y	Y
Problem Reports	Y	N	Y	Y
Reviews	Y	Y	Y	Y
Inspection measurements	Y	Y	Y	N
Operations/production reports	N	Y	Y	N
Change Management function	Y	Y	N	-
Defect data is collected by				
HelpDesk	Y	N	Y	N
Quality Assurance	Y	Y	Y	-
Project teams	Y	Y	Y	Y

Our case organization's goals in defect management were to 1) improve customer satisfaction and decrease costs, 2) to increase software quality, 3) to ensure that customers will get services with as few failures as possible, and 4) to ensure that purchased software works correctly in the system environment.

3.2 Problems Regarding the Defect Management Process

Personal interviews with the case organizations identified following problem areas, bottlenecks and challenges in defect management processes:

1. Defining good metrics for IT service problem management and Service Level Management is a challenge.
2. Creating a large amount of test data for testing is difficult.
3. Load testing and performance testing tools cannot test the whole system.
4. Informing customers of new defects is a challenge because not all customers use the function that containing the defects.
5. Limited resources for fixing defects.
6. Establishing a defect management framework takes a lot of time.
7. Teams use different methods: the challenge is how to combine methods.
8. IT companies often consider the bugs found by the customer as typical properties of the application.
9. IT companies do not send defect resolution reports to customers.
10. Establishing a test environment is always a challenge.
11. Some software vendors do not provide defect reporting services to customers.
12. No training in using a new defect management tool for reporting defects.
13. Negative attitudes towards defect reporting tools: long report forms.
14. Software vendors deliver applications containing many bugs that should have been found by the developer-side testing.

4 Analysis

4.1 The Analysis of Defect Management Processes

As expected, both customers reported that they do not have software quality programs or a formal software development lifecycle model. Case A stated that some units in their organization have quality programs. All cases had a company wide method for gathering defect data. Case D's answer was partially yes because they used defect reporting services provided by software vendors. They told that for some vendors defects must be reported by phone or by email.

All cases had a method for classifying defects. Case C also used a domain-specific problem classification (low voltage, medium voltage, high voltage faults). Similarly, all cases collected information on development / production failures and the type of defect. Surprisingly, only one of the cases systematically collected information on problem resolution costs, and even this was not related to software problems but to energy faults. Regarding the sources of defect data, on the basis of the interviews it seems that all the cases had used some informal reviews, and three cases had used inspections. Three cases mentioned problem reports. Defect data were collected by project teams in all cases. Cases A and C had a help desk function that was responsible for collecting incidents. Case D emphasized the importance of testers in collecting defects. Testers test each product version, and if the purchased product contains severe defects it will not be installed into the operation environment.

In the course of this study an interesting observation was made that Case A and Case D actually use the same defect reporting tool, but in different roles (A as an IT service provider and D as an IT customer). According to Case A, the advantages of the tool were an affordable price, a direct web interface for the customer, and good customization possibilities. The system designer of

Case D reported that the defect reporting tool is easy to use, and wished that other vendors offered similar tools. Another interesting finding was that while the customers reported that they use defect reporting tools provided by software vendors, the software company B used defect reporting tools provided by their customers.

4.2 The Analysis of the Identified Problems

Regarding the identified problem areas and challenges in defect management, probably the most interesting challenge was reported by an IT service provider that was looking for good metrics for IT service problem management and service level management because they were changing old processes to the processes that are compliant with the IT Service Management standard (ITIL). This was an interesting issue because when the company has a leading position in providing IT services in Scandinavia it can require that their partners and subcontractors must also use ITIL-based processes including problem management.

Most of the problems identified in our interviews were not surprising. Two case organizations stated clearly that it is difficult and expensive to create a test environment matching to the real production environment. A big problem is, for example, creating large amounts of suitable test data for testing. It is more expensive and difficult to create 100 Gb test data than only 1 Mb. Secondly, load testing and performance testing tools are often able to test only a part of the system. One of the software companies also stated that IT customers could use the review or inspection methods for the system specification phase in order to point out the issues that are unclear or that include problems. That would probably increase the customer's degree of involvement in project issues. One of the companies told that they have not had any problems with defect management tools but the major problem is that their project teams use different methods in managing defects.

Customers reported as a big problem that IT companies consider the bugs found by the customer often as typical properties of the application. "It is not a bug" has often been a statement from Help Desks of IT providers. An interesting question is why software companies do not admit that their application might have problems and state that problems will be carefully examined and possible improvements are implemented in the next product release. They also stated that IT providers should inform how the defects, reported by a customer, were handled or fixed. Often, customers do not understand defect resolution reports that they have received. Lack of resolution reports does not motivate customers to send problem reports to the IT provider in further projects.

One of our cases considered as a major problem that all the software vendors do not provide defect reporting systems to customers. In one case, a software vendor had offered a tool for reporting defects but a customer did not use the tool because they had not received any training. Additionally, IT companies reported some other problems, such as high prices of test tools. Especially, load testing is expensive with a large number of virtual users. Limited project resources also affect the use of dynamic and static techniques.

4.3 Lessons Learned

Based on our case study results, we emphasize that organizations should pay more attention to the following issues in performing defect management activities:

- The defect management process must be an organization-wide process, although Ahonen et al. have argued that it is practically impossible to ensure that all teams use good practices [15]. Henninger [16] has proposed that organizations should build an organizational repository of experiences. Learning from defects is a very good example of experience-based learning. There has to be clear rules and guides that define who are responsible for recording defect data, how to change a status of the defect, or how to classify a defect. Project teams should be motivated to share information on defects between different projects.
- The support staff of the IT organization must pay more attention to the service quality in the problem situation avoiding *this is not a bug* service. All problems reported by customers must first be recorded by the service desk that is usually capable to resolve most of the simple problems. Therefore, programmers will not be disturbed and they have more time to focus on serious problems.
- The defect/problem resolution reports, that an IT organization sends to customers, must be clear and consistent avoiding difficult IT terms.
- The organization's management has to allocate sufficient resources to defect management and testing teams, and motivate them to use diverse methods for preventing and finding defects, for example, UML-based testing [17], software inspections [18], and defect causal analysis [19]. In the long run, the defect management must be more proactive than reactive. Focusing on preventing defects and problems before they occur is more useful than correcting a large number of repetitive errors.
- Customers and end users must be trained to use automated defect reporting tools, FAQ sites and known error databases, if available. These tools will remarkably decrease the amount of work spent on processing defects.
- The defect management model must have clear connections to the neighbor processes such as service desk, change management, testing, and application development. Most of the current models (e.g. IBM, QAI) have ignored this issue. The major drawback of the ITIL problem management model is a poorly documented testing process. One possible method to test the connections between processes is to review the defect life cycle with ten sample defects and identify how they were processed in different units of the organization.
- Suitable metrics should be produced for both the defect management (e.g. defect removal efficiency, mean time to failure) [13] and monitoring service levels (e.g. a number of breached service level agreements, the resolution time for a problem) [20].

5 Discussion and Conclusions

This study aimed to explore problems regarding defect management. Our findings show that different stakeholders have different problems. A large part of the identified problems were not surprising. A lot of traditional problems were revealed in interviews. IT customers have problems getting defect resolution reports from IT companies, or interpreting them. They dislike being told by IT companies that the bugs they find are typical features of the application. Moreover, the software they purchase contains defects that should have been found by IT companies' testers.

IT companies' problems are related to decisions about whether to send defect resolution reports and bug fixes to customers or not. One major problem is the fact that project teams do not have commonly agreed methods of defect management. The developer side often has limited resources to fix defects. Creating a test environment seems to be a common problem for both IT customers and IT companies. Contrary to expectations, problems related to the usability of defect reporting tools were relatively unimportant to the participants in this study. Similarly, static methods for finding defects were used more often than expected. The IT service provider reported a new interesting challenge: how to create suitable metrics for IT service problem management and Service Level Management. This requires further investigation.

As with all case studies, there are threats to the validity of this study. First, construct validity is problematic in case study research. Data for the case study should be collected from several sources. We tried to avoid problems with construct validity by using multiple sources of evidence, such as conducting personal interviews with at leasttwo persons per case organization. One potential weakness is the fact that most of the interviewees in our study were managers. In order to get a richer view of the problems in defect management, we need to interview more ordinary programmers and testers. Second, there is the threat to external validity, i.e. to the generalizability of the results. The results of this study might not be generalizable to other organizations, since there were only four cases in this study, and all the cases were in different industries.

The main contribution of this study lies in helping IT companies and IT customers to identify and avoid typical problems in defect management. Future studies should explore more deeply the problems organizations face with regard to defect resolution reports. In future studies we intend to improve our research framework by exploring how our current defect management model and the problem management framework of the IT Infrastructure Library can be combined, and how service level agreements can be utilized in defect management.

References

1. Florac, W.: Software quality measurement a framework for counting problems and defects. Technical Report CMU/SEI-92-TR-22 (1992)
2. Hirmanpour, I., Schofield, J.: Defect management through the personal software process. Crosstalk, The Journal of Defense Software Engineering (2003)

3. Mays, R.G., Jones, C.L., Holloway, G.J., Studinski, D.P.: Experiences with defect prevention. IBM Syst. J. **29**(1) (1990) 4–32
4. Office of Government Commerce: ITIL Service Support. The Stationary Office, UK (2002)
5. Leszak, M., Perry, D.E., Stoll, D.: A case study in root cause defect analysis. In: ICSE '00: Proceedings of the 22nd international conference on Software engineering, New York, NY, USA, ACM Press (2000) 428–437
6. El-Emam, K., Wieczorek, I.: The repeatability of code defect classifications. Technical Report. International Software Engineering Research Network, ISERN-98-09. (1998)
7. Humphrey, W.S.: A personal commitment to software quality. In: ESEC. (1995) 5–7
8. Jalote, P.: CMM in Practise, Processes for Executing Software Projects at Infosys. Addison-Wesley (2000)
9. Jäntti, M., Toroi, T.: Uml-based testing: A case study. In: Proceedings of NWUML'2004. 2nd Nordic Workshop on the Unified Modeling Language, Turku: Turku Centre for Computer Science (2004) 33–44
10. Kruchten, P.: The Rational Unified Process: An Introduction. Addison-Wesley (2001)
11. Yin, R.: Case Study Research : Design and Methods. Beverly Hills, CA: Sage Publishing (1994)
12. Binder, R.: Testing Object-Oriented Systems: Models, Patterns, and Tools. Addison-Wesley (2000)
13. Quality Assurance Institute: A software defect management process. Research Report number 8 (1995)
14. Eisenhardt, K.: Building theories from case study research. Academy of Management Review **14** (1989) 532–550
15. Ahonen, J.J., Junttila, T., Sakkinen, M.: Impacts of the organizational model on testing: Three industrial cases. Empirical Softw. Engg. **9**(4) (2004) 275–296
16. Henninger, S.: Using software process to support learning software organizations. In: 1st International Workshop on Learning Software Organizations, Kaiserlautern (1999)
17. Hartmann, J., Imoberdorf, C., Meisinger, M.: Uml-based integration testing. In: ISSTA '00: Proceedings of the 2000 ACM SIGSOFT international symposium on Software testing and analysis, New York, NY, USA, ACM Press (2000) 60–70
18. Gilb, T., Graham, D.: Software Inspection. Addison-Wesley (1993)
19. Card, D.N.: Learning from our mistakes with defect causal analysis. IEEE Software **15**(1) (1998) 56–63
20. Office of Government Commerce: ITIL Service Delivery. The Stationary Office, UK (2002)

A Case Study on the Success of Introducing General Non-construction Activities for Project Management and Planning Improvement

Topi Haapio[1] and Jarmo J. Ahonen[2]

[1] TietoEnator Telecom & Media
P.O. Box 1779, FI-70601 Kuopio, Finland
topi.haapio@tietoenator.com
[2] Department of Computer Science
University of Kuopio
P.O. Box 1627, FI-70211 Kuopio, Finland
jarmo.ahonen@uku.fi

Abstract. The creation of a proper work breakdown structure (WBS) is essential in performing successful project effort estimation and project management. The use of WBS is required on the level 1 of CMMI. There is, however, no standard WBS available. In this paper, the results of a pilot project in which new activities were introduced into the TietoEnator's WBS are reported. The activities were non-construction activities which are necessary but not directly related to the actual software construction. The study shows that the success of the introduction of such activities very much depends on the naming of the activities and how they are introduced to the employees. Additionally, it turned out that the pre-thought set of non-construction activities included activities that should not have been in the set at all as individual activities.

1 Introduction

Since the beginning of software projects and their effort estimations, work has been broken down into smaller entities, i.e. project activities and phases to manage and estimate work easier. The work breakdown structure (WBS), a particular defined tree-structure the project work is broken into [1], was applied even in the early effort estimation models, e.g. the Wolverton Model [2] and COCOMO [3]. WBS is also required by the currently employed capability maturity models, e.g. the staged presentation of CMMI [4] requires WBS on its lowest maturity level 1. However, no standardized way of creating the WBS exists, thus the applied activity sets in software projects are either very general or project-specific. To benefit effort management in the project, the activities should be broken down into suitable granularity level, which in turn leads to activity sets that differ from each other from project to project.

This paper examines the adoption of general project activities to increase the reliability of registered effort and uniformity of the work breakdown structure. In the case study presented in this paper, a two-phased questionnaire survey was conducted to explore the adoption of a new set of project activities, namely the non-construction

J. Münch and M. Vierimaa (Eds.): PROFES 2006, LNCS 4034, pp. 151–165, 2006.

activities [5], i.e. the activities which are not directly related to software construction or project management. These activities include various management and support activities such as orientation, planning activities, quality assurance, configuration management, customer support, and documentation, each carried out by several members of the project. Neglecting the non-construction activities in project planning and effort estimation may result in significant effort proportion deviation between projects. Furthermore, regardless of the effort estimation method employed, even the best estimate cannot be accurate if the method neglects or undervalues the non-construction activities that are involved in the project. Effort estimation research has focused on software construction because the majority of the total effort is software construction effort [6], and because the customers are willing to pay for the construction work. However, the rest of the project effort is just as important when a higher estimation accuracy is pursued, and — in large projects — that effort can represent a significant amount of money. Considering the non-construction activities is useful also while comparing the efficiency of different projects.

This study is a part of a larger project aiming to improve effort estimation and effort management by focusing on activities other than the actual software construction or project management, and making the effort distribution proportions more stabile, thus more predictable and controllable, from project to project [5]. The larger project is a part of a company-wide CMMI effort at TietoEnator.

This paper is structured as follows. Section 2 describes the research methodology and the theoretical background, Sect. 3 outlines the effort management process with the adoption of new project activities. The case study is presented in Sect. 4. The analysis of the study is presented in Sect. 5, followed with a discussion in Sect. 6. Section 7 gives a brief conclusion and suggestions for future research.

2 Theoretical Background and Research Methodology

In many cases, the activities and lifecycle phases of software projects have served as the basis for the different factors used for effort-counting. However, no standardized way to divide different project lifecycle activities has been established: different effort estimation methods emphasize different activities and factors in their effort-counting by identifying and using the most important ones. For instance, the COCOMO models use activity breakdown. In the original COCOMO model, the activities were divided into eight major categories, namely requirement analysis, product design, programming, test planning, verification and validation, project office functions, configuration management and quality assurance, and manuals, each having specific activities in the four project lifecycle phases [3].

COCOMO was enhanced to COCOMO II in the mid-1990s in order to develop the model to address the new needs of evolving software engineering such as distributed software and component techniques. COCOMO II categorization is not, however, suitable for all project situations, and should be adjusted via context and judgment to fit individual projects [7]. In COCOMO II, software activity work was divided into five major categories: management, system engineering, programming, test and evaluation, and data [7]. This breakdown was adapted from COCOMO's eight categories, which were partly reorganized and renamed. The factors, used in COCOMO counting, comprise activities that correspond with the non-construction activities presented in this paper. These activities comprise project office functions, configuration management and quality assurance, and manuals. However, important factors such as the amount of documentation, management quality, and personnel continuity were excluded from COCOMO [3][8].

Although effort can be distributed in a project between project activities or project phases in many different ways, effort distribution is a less-investigated effort estimation area. Indeed, it has been disputed whether it is useful to distribute effort in the first place [6][9]. However, rightly modeled effort distribution could be used for effort estimation: for example, for predicting the effort needed for the latter phases using the effort information of the previous phases. Moreover, effort distribution can be used to compare different projects with each other.

The project activities, their estimated and realized effort and the success of the breakdown are analyzed in an effort analysis. Effort analyses are usually conducted as a part of project's post-mortem review, which is customary — or should be — in the software industry. The method used for post-project analysis is normally company proprietary [10]. A post-project analysis, also called the project closure or the post-mortem analysis [10][11][12] is a process of considering the project carefully in detail after the project has been completed in order to understand and explain it to learn from the experience, and improve the process based on learning.

Gathering data on project's actual effort and progress and comparing these with the estimates is essential for several reasons. As the effort estimating inputs and techniques are imperfect, the completed project data are needed to improve them. Moreover, not every project fits into the estimating model. Furthermore, as software engineering is constantly evolving and all estimating techniques are calibrated on previous projects, it is important to identify the differences due to the trends and incorporate them into improved effort estimates and techniques [3]. Besides the effort estimation methods, these differences may also affect estimation and software engineering processes, and vice versa. An evolved software engineering process may affect the effort estimation method, as in the case where the original COCOMO model was developed into the COCOMO II model.

The effort estimation models employed by companies normally require a follow-up system. This system both supports effective project management and benefits the long-range effort estimation capabilities. The data collected via control activities over several projects can be analyzed to determine how the realized effort distribution differs from the estimates. The differences are fed back to calibrate the model, e.g. the COCOMO models. For a new project, data collection should be considered at project start, at the end of major proper phases, and at the end of the development, as Boehm et al. [7] point out for the COCOMO II model. Projects can use the data to benchmark their progress, develop business cases and calibrate their estimating models [7]. A post-project effort analysis provides effort calibration information as a result to populate the effort repository from which the effort estimation method's factor weights can be derived.

Effort management can also be the focus of the software process improvement activity. The activity initiative can arise from employing a capability maturity model. The maturity models are used to improve the related processes. Software process improvement (SPI) means understanding the existing processes and improving them to achieve improved product quality and to reduce costs and development time, and it is usually an activity that is specific to an organization [13]. SPI has its origins in the Total Quality Management (TQM). The principles of statistical quality control in product quality management from the 1930's were further developed in the 1980's with a premise that real process improvement must follow a sequence of steps, i.e. make the process concrete, repeatable and measurable. The premise for improvement is that it is managed which in turn require that it is measurable [14].

SPI and the capability maturity model employment are under enormous interest of research. A number of studies have been conducted applying above mentioned models in software industry (e.g. [15][16][17][18][19]). However, studies describing improvement activity in software project effort management context, and adopting new project activities in particular, are not very common or their results applicable in the case analyzed in this paper. It is also argued that maturity models provide a good basis for SPI, but also an excessive overhead if deployed in full, and on the other hand, do not take enough in consideration that different businesses and situations require different processes [17]. Furthermore, it is argued that maturity models may not be the best models to measure maturity in management processes such as project management effort management included, as opposed to the technical processes of developing the software, since models have an underlying process model that view software development activities in an industrial production-like fashion, focusing attention on the flow of work from one process to another [18].

CMMI requires elements of the effort management. Mostly, the effort management relates to the project management process area in CMMI. Like CMM, CMMI requires an organization's measurement repository, which is used to collect and make available measurement data on processes, e.g. effort and cost estimates, and the realized actual effort and costs, to analyze the measurement data [20]. Moreover, the staged presentation requires work to be arranged as work elements and their relationship to each other and to the end product, i.e. into a work breakdown structure to estimate the scope of the project (at maturity level 1), and to plan the project resources and to manage configurations (at level 2) [4].

The primary research methodology for this paper is case study. Moreover, the research includes characteristics of action research: collaboration, implication and situation between the research and the project under examination. The research was carried out as a part of organization's SPI activity. Action research can be considered as a part of constructive research where both building and evaluating subprocesses closely belong to the same process [21]. Constructive research [21][22], also referred to as design science [23][24], consists of two basic activities: building products (constructs, models, methods, and instantiations) and evaluating them. The evaluation of the built product is based on user value or utility, i.e. feasibility is demonstrated when the created artifact serves human purposes [21][23]. Case studies can be used for evaluation [25][26]. Furthermore, as the research interest lies in the comprehension of the meaning of action, case studies can be used to interpret it [21]. This research employed structured questionnaires as the data gathering technique.

3 New Activities Adoption in Effort Management Process

The total project lifecycle can be divided into three main phases: pre-project, project, and post-project (Fig. 1) in which effort is first estimated, then collected, monitored and re-estimated, and finally analyzed. Besides several effort related activities and subactivities, these three phases also include phases related to project activities, and different information flows between them.

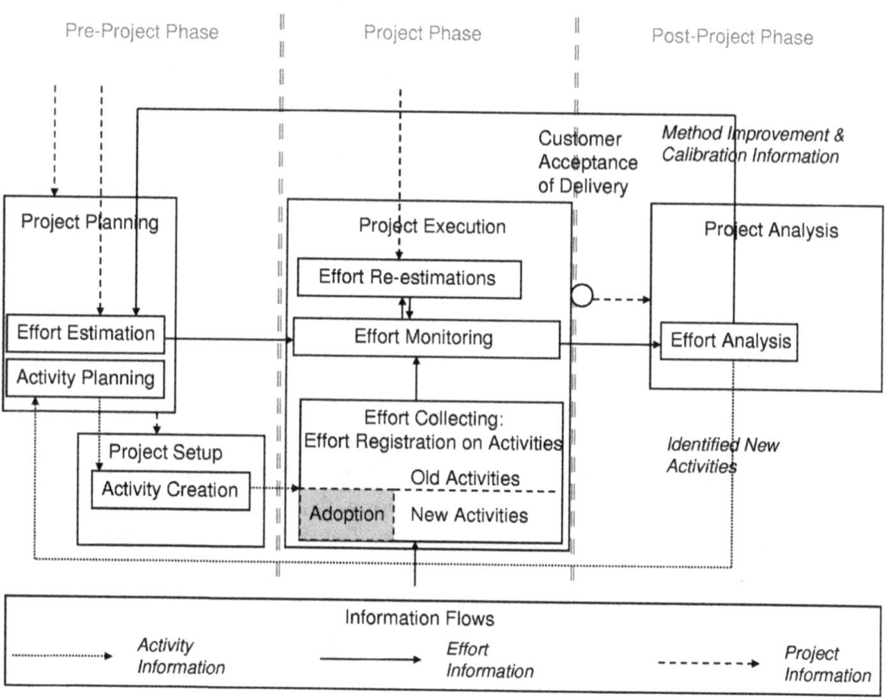

Fig. 1. The adoption of new project activities in the effort management process

During the pre-project phase, the project is planned and setup. Project planning includes project activity planning and effort estimation subactivities. Effort is initially estimated with the method in use with project information supplied by the customer, for example. At this point, the different activities concerning the projects are also planned. These activities include the activities related to actual software construction, the ones related to project management, and other activities. The planned activities are created, usually by the project manager, during the project setup into the work time registry system as registration entities for effort registrations during the project execution.

The adoption of new project activities steps in during effort collecting in project execution, the actual project phase. During project execution the project group registers effort on the activity entities that were created for the project in the work time registry system. The effort registration on old, familiar activity entities begins immediately, and effort is usually registered on the correct activity entity. The new project activities and new sets of activities, however, require an adoption period before effort can be registered on the new entities. At worst this period can last whole project execution which results in skewed effort data as effort is registered on wrong activities or is not registered at all. The correct registration of effort is essential for effort monitoring and effort re-estimations, since from this point on the project's own registered effort is the primary data for re-estimations.

During project closure, the post-project phase, the delivered project is analyzed, and a project final report is drawn. The delivery usually requires an acceptance from the customer after which the project is considered as executed. As a subactivity, effort analysis is conducted to produce input for a thorough, usually qualitative, project post-mortem analysis. In effort analysis the realized effort of specific project activities are compared with the estimated, and the reasons for accuracy or inaccuracy are analyzed and explained. Effort analysis can produce effort information for improving and calibrating the estimation method, thus improving the software engineering process. Moreover, if new significant project activities are identified, they are recorded for activity planning of future projects. The adoption of a particular new project activity set (the gray box in Fig. 1), namely non-construction activities, is analyzed in the reported case study (Sect. 4).

4 The Study

The study investigated the adoption of a set of project activities, namely the non-construction activities, within a project group at TietoEnator Telecom & Media, the largest business area within TietoEnator Corporation. TietoEnator Corporation is the largest IT services company in the Nordic countries with activity in more than 20 countries worldwide, and close to 15 000 employees. TietoEnator is building a common business system with reference models EFQM (ISO 9000:2000) and CMMI. Earlier, due to company diversity and acquisitions, TietoEnator applied both CMM and SPICE (ISO/IEC 15504). There are several internal research development projects on-going as a part of software process improvement including studies to improve effort management in the software engineering process.

The case study is on one enhancement project of custom client/server software system supplied by TietoEnator. The system's client/server technology is based on transaction management, and involves several programs with Windows GUIs and relational databases. The project, which took place in the beginning of 2005, was delivered to a Nordic customer operating in the telecommunication business domain. The duration of the project was six months. The project, which was carried out by one department, required 19 man-months of effort and consisted of five subprojects and an administrative umbrella project. The size of the total project group was 33 persons, all of which had experience of previous projects of similar kind. Since two of the subprojects were maintenance projects with separate effort accounting, they were excluded from the research. The umbrella project included activities concerning the whole project, e.g. management. The subprojects included software construction, subproject management and other activities related to the particular subproject.

The project constituted of 625 entries on 114 registration entities, i.e. project activities, in the work time registry system (Table 1). The registration entities and their corresponding titles were created in the work time registry system based on the identification of different project's activities during the pre-project planning. The registration entity titles (having a form of "AB_CDE_EFGH") consisted of eleven alfa digits which composed three parts. The work time registry system, however, would have allowed using maximum eighteen digits. The two first digits described the subproject in which the activity belonged (the umbrella project or one of the three subprojects). The three middle digits described the activity group the activity belonged to. For example, these activity group codes started with letter N (Non-Construction Activities), and, in the case of review activity the two latter letters were QA (for Quality Assurance activity group). This code was primarily for the project manager to sort the activities for reporting. The four last digits described the activity. The idea was to use as self-explanatory abbreviation as possible.

Table 1. The number of created registration entities

Activity set	Umbrella project	Subproject A	Subproject B	Subproject C	Total
Software Construction	4	13	24	16	57
Project Management	2	1	1	1	5
Non-Construction Activities	13	13	13	13	52
Total	19	27	38	30	114

In this study, the registration entities in focus are the non-construction activities (NCA), i.e. the activities which are not directly related to software construction or project management [5]. Software construction involves the effort needed for the actual software construction in the project's lifecycle frame, such as analysis, design, implementation, and testing. Without this effort, the software cannot be constructed. Project management involves activities that are conducted solely by the project group's project manager, such as project planning and monitoring, administrative tasks, and steering group meetings. All the activities in the project's lifecycle frame that do not belong to the other two main categories are non-construction activities. These activities include various management and support activities such as orientation, planning activities, quality assurance, configuration management, customer support, and documentation, which are carried out by several members of the project. Hypothetically, these activities can be eliminated from a software project and the software can still be constructed. In practice, however, a project would be more or less uncontrolled and unsupported without the non-construction activities. This increases both the software construction effort and project management effort needed to get the project accomplished.

The particular project was chosen for this study since the project organization, the concept of non-construction activities, and the activities were new to the project group and had not yet been established although the project is one in a continuing series of software enhancement projects. Neither were the project activities (registration entities) established for the project group because project managers emphasized and emphasize particular activities.

In project start-up, the first phase (initiation), the new project activities were introduced and the adoption process begun. The organization lacks a formal procedure to introduce the project activities to the project group. Hence, the prevailing introduction strategy depends on the project manager. In this case, the project manager send an initiative e-mail regarding the project activities to the prevailing project group. In the e-mail, both unfamiliar and familiar activities were listed, i.e. titles, work time registry system titles (codes), and a one-sentence description and example of the activity. The three-phased course of events for the project and the research is described in Table 2. The questionnaires were sent to whole project group totaling 33 persons. The response ratios for questionnaires 1 and 2 were 36.4% and 39.4%, respectively.

Table 2. The course of events

	Project	Study
Phase I — Initiation	– A set of project activities (non-construction activities) planned and created in the work time registry system – New project activities introduced and adopted	– The research strategy and procedure planned – Open-ended questionnaire 1 initially planned
Phase II — Active	– Effort registration on project activities into the work time registry system	– The adoption of the activities observed – The open-ended questionnaire 1 modified
Phase III — Closure	– Project post-mortem analysis including effort analysis and research survey	– The open-ended questionnaire 1 finalized – Questionnaire 1 survey carried out – The results of survey 1 analyzed for questionnaire 2 input – The closed-ended questionnaire 2 planned – Questionnaire 2 survey carried out – Quantitative data of effort registrations collected – Analysis – Reporting

The first section and its two first open-ended questions in the first questionnaire (QA1) solve whether the project group had comprehended the new activity set (what activities are grouped to a set: QA1.1: "By which common name would you call the following activities?") and its purpose (why this set and these activities were included as effort registration entities for the project: QA1.2: "Assess why these registration entities were included for the project."). From responses, only one was absolutely correct (activities that are not directly related into software construction or project management, i.e. non-construction activities). On the other hand, only one third of answers were completely wrong. Nine different reasons came up for why this set and these activities were included for the project, and only one respondent could not find any explanation. The most common reason was presumed to be a more detailed breakdown of hours these activities consumed (33.3% of given answers). The answers related to the actual reason (to find out how much these activities consume effort in a project) represented a clear majority (71.4%). Likewise, a great majority interpreted the digit codes in the beginning, in the middle, and in the end of the registration entity title correctly, which was explored in three open-ended questions in QA1 (Table 3).

Table 3. The comprehension of the registry entity compound

	Correct	Misunderstood	Do not know
QA1.3 (the first two digits)	66.7 %	8.3 %	25.0 %
QA1.4 (the three middle digits)	75.0 %	8.3 %	16.7 %
QA1.5 (the last four digits)	75.0 %	25.0 %	0.0 %

Two first questions in the latter questionnaire (QB1) sought answers for the relation of effort registrations in the project and the perceptions of and the attitudes to the new project activities (non-construction activities). In this paper we concentrate on the success of the adoption of the general non-constructive activities, which are intended to form a part of the general WBS for future projects. The results of the close-ended questions QB1.1: "Which of the following activities existed in the project?" and QB1.2: "Are the following activities useful or useless as individual activities?" are shown in Table 4.

Table 4. Perceptions on the non-constructive activities

Activity	QB1.1	QB1.2		
		Useful	Useless	Cannot answer
Configuration and Version Management	15.4 %	46.2 %	30.8 %	23.1 %
Customer Queries	53.8 %	23.1 %	23.1 %	53.8 %
Customer Support	0.0 %	69.2 %	23.1 %	23.1 %
Customer Training	0.0 %	46.2 %	38.5 %	15.4 %
Documentation	53.8 %	92.3 %	0.0 %	7.7 %
Orientation	38.5 %	92.3 %	15.4 %	0.0 %
Project Events	84.6 %	61.5 %	15.4 %	23.1 %
Project Group Working	61.5 %	46.2 %	23.1 %	23.1 %
Project Start-Up	15.4 %	30.8 %	30.8 %	30.8 %
Quality Assurance	23.1 %	76.9 %	7.7 %	15.4 %
Reviews	61.5 %	84.6 %	15.4 %	0.0 %
Technical Environment Maintenance	0.0 %	61.5 %	30.8 %	7.7 %
Technical Environment Setup	0.0 %	53.8 %	38.5 %	7.7 %

The three answers ("useful", "useless", "cannot answer") can be divided into three categories of expressed attitude: a positive ("useful"), a negative ("useless") or a puzzled ("cannot answer") attitude. The means to promote activity towards positivism are motivation (if negative attitude), and argumentation and motivation (if puzzled attitude). By argumentation we mean that the reasons for including new activities are shared with whole project group.

The amount of activities still unfamiliar at the end of the project was, however, of concern. The most confusing activities were Customer Queries and Project Start-Up, 53.8% and 30.8%, respectively. Also four other activities, namely Configuration and Version Management, Customer Support, Project Events, and Project Group Working remained unfamiliar (23.1%). These figures can, however, be partially explained. Customer Queries and Customer Support were probably confused with each other. The Project Start-Up, for one, concerned only some members of the project group. The most surprising results were the unfamiliarity of the activities related to project work: Project Events and Project Group Working. These activities were common in the project, i.e. the respondents attended on those activities. It is likely that by replying "Cannot Answer" the respondents replied that they cannot determine whether the activity is useful or not.

Table 5. Wherefrom the information on new activities was received

Activity	QB2.1 (%)	QB2.2 (%)		
		Good	Poor	Neither
Information by an e-mail:				
Initiative information e-mail on project activities	84.6	92.3	0.0	7.7
Another e-mail send by the Project Manager	30.8	69.2	0.0	23.1
E-mail send by a Subproject Manager	46.2	76.9	0.0	15.4
E-mail send by a project group member	15.4	23.1	23.1	38.5
Case-specific, along with the prescription of work task	30.8	84.6	0.0	15.4
Information in the project's internal kick-off event:				
Told by the Project Manager	61.5	84.6	0.0	7.7
By asking from the Project Manager	30.8	46.2	7.7	23.1
Information in the project's info meeting:				
Told by the Project Manager	61.5	84.6	0.0	7.7
By asking from the Project Manager	30.8	46.2	0.0	30.8
Information in a subproject's meeting:				
Told by a Subproject Manager	46.2	76.9	0.0	15.4
By asking from the Subproject Manager	30.8	46.2	0.0	30.8
Information in the project manager's meeting:				
Told by the Project Manager	15.4	53.8	0.0	23.1
By asking from the Project Manager	15.4	30.8	0.0	38.5
Personally:				
Told by the Project Manager	23.1	84.6	0.0	7.7
By asking from the Project Manager	46.2	61.5	0.0	23.1
Told by a Subproject Manager	38.5	76.9	0.0	15.4
By asking from the Subproject Manager	38.5	61.5	0.0	23.1
Told by a project group member	23.1	46.2	15.4	23.1
By asking from a project group member	30.8	53.8	7.7	30.8
Documented guide:				
A documented guide located in the network project folder	23.1	69.2	7.7	15.4
A shared project folder on project group member's work stations	—	7.7	—	—

The second section in the two questionnaires (QA2 and QB2) studied the exchange of information, i.e. how the project group was informed on new project activities. In general, in the open-ended questionnaire (QA2.1 and QA2.2) eight means of successful information exchange in this project were found against five different elements that failed. Information given by e-mail was mentioned as one of the successful elements in more than one response whereas other successful and failed elements all represented single opinions.

The detailed query on the different information sources in close-ended questionnaire (QB2.1) revealed that every respondent had gotten a project activity information e-mail at some stage of the project in some form or another. Other information sources were project's internal kick-off event (69.2%), project's info meetings (69.2%), subproject's meetings (53.8%), project manager's meetings (23.1%), and personal encounters (69.2%). A more detailed list of sources from the responses to the given alternatives in close-ended questionnaire (QB2.1) is presented in Table 5.

In conclusion, from the various ways to inform project group on project activities (QB2.2) e-mails seem to be the best (Table 5). The different ways to inform by e-mail collected a high respond for being a good method whereas an email send by a project group member was regarded as negative. However, in general, there were no absolute misjudgements in the ways of informing the personnel. Instead, the different information alternatives received good ratings, the attitude being either positive ("Good") or neutral ("Neither good or poor"). The most negative ratings came either from being forced to ask from the project manager (initiator is the member and not the manager of the project) or from the source from a lower organizational level (the information source is a project group member). Hence, the results indicate that the higher in the organization the information comes, the better.

5 Analysis

This research provided valuable lessons for TietoEnator regarding WBS. Furthermore, we believe that the results are extendable to software industry in general. The main findings concerning the recommendations for efficient new project activity adoptions include: versatile and frequent information on activities, both new and old, and by several sources, emphasized in the beginning of the project. Recommended sources of information include written guidelines sent by e-mails and verbal information given by management. It is notable that only five out of twenty choices for information sources were considered somewhat "poor", and these opinions were given by single respondents. Peer information, or self-initiated questions were considered as "poor" sources.

Emphasis on the consideration of an optimal number of activities for a project is beneficial. This consideration involves the funneling of effort on correct activity, since leaving project activities out increases the probability of misregistration. i.e. effort is registered on a wrong registration entity or left unregistered, which skews the effort data. From a project group member's view, the project should contain as a small number of different project activities (registration entities) as possible. Moreover, project activity (registration entities) views should preferably be customized by the project group member, i.e. only those entry alternatives are shown in the work time registry system's user interface that are necessary for a particular person. The registration entities (activities) should be titled clearly and consistently between projects. Therefore, the use of mandatory and optional project activity set templates is advantageous.

The main findings concerning the WBS and the non-construction activities in particular include: every project should contain a set of mandatory non-construction activities as registration entities for effort monitoring, post-mortem analyzing, and estimation purposes. The non-construction activities considered useful by the majority of the project group to be used as individual registration entities include customer support (69.2%), documentation (92.3%), orientation (92.3%), project events (61.5%), reviews (84.6%), quality assurance (76.9%), technical environment maintenance (61.5%), and technical environment setup (53.8%). Although none of the non-construction activities included for this project was considered useless by the majority of the project group, or more useless than useful, the following non-construction activities received rather high proportions for being useless as individual activities: configuration and version management (30.8%), customer queries (23.1%), customer training (38.5%), project group working (23.1%), and project start-up (30.8%). It seems that a suitable set of non-constructive activities would be: customer support (including customer support, queries, and training), documentation (non-related to software construction, e.g. user guides), orientation, project group working (including project start-up, events and project-related tasks), quality assurance, reviews, and configuration management (including setup and maintenance of technical environment, configuration and version management).

From the project aspect, the greatest difficulties were caused by naming the project activities as the registration entities in the work time registration system in project start-up. To benefit effort monitoring and analysis, the entities were named with somewhat cryptic coded titles instead of using longer and clear titles, which would have ensured better adoption and understanding. From the information point of view, the new project activities were introduced with an initiative e-mail from the project manager regarding the project activities and with an internal project kick-off event where these activities were also explained. Although these informative actions were appropriate and can be recommended, a more detailed prescription and examples of the activities and the registration of effort on them would have been necessary. Moreover, a documented guideline (e.g. the content of the e-mail) should be included in the project network folder in the future projects.

Getting the project group on auto-pilot with new project activities is a challenge. Although the information sources promoting self-steering were favored (e.g. a documented guide located in the network project folder and the initiative information e-mail on project activities (69.2% and 92.3% of "Good" ratings, respectively), the high ratios in active information both as favored information sources and the motivating and assisting factors give a clear statement. Furthermore, the project case study results revealed that without a strong commitment on promoting the adoption leaves the project group puzzled about the activities and registrations.

6 Discussion

This study complements the existing research on software process improvement and capability maturity models in particular by focusing on a special case of software project effort management improvement, especially the adoption of new project activities. Although there has been a vast interest in the concepts of software process improvement and effort in software projects within both information system and software engineering, researchers have, by and large, overlooked a total framework of effort management, as well as ignored the adoption mechanisms of new project activities. While the analysis of adopting new project activities presented in this paper is grounded to the particular case and project at TietoEnator Telecom & Media, we believe that the basic elements of our analysis can be generalized to other cases of adopting new project activities within the software industry. The responses are obviously case specific, but the tendencies for factors that promote or discourage the adoption are clear, although they lack statistical significance. Also, the framework of effort management is independent from the organization and is relatively general and likely applicable to similar situations, i.e. in software development. The practitioners, most likely the project or quality managers, can apply the results of this research to derive an organizational adoption plan to adopt project activities, in which we believe this study gives a good input. Also, a more complete view on the software project effort in the form of effort management framework combines the traditionally separate elements of managing the project effort to a single entity where every element influences the other.

From the research point of view, the survey suffered from both low sample and low response ratio. In software companies, these studies take time from actual business, which in many cases may reduce the willingness to respond to the surveys. In the future, the corporate management should motivate the project personnel, and the questionnaires should be more compact. As surveys like this are conducted among project groups and these groups are seldom large enough the results may not be statistically significant. On the other hand, expanding the study to larger population to satisfy statistical requirements would mean expanding the study from a project group to a larger unit of organization, e.g. a department or division, and this would extort the research results as analyzed cases are organization specific, i.e. a case study limits itself to one project.

7 Conclusion and Future Work

This paper explored the adoption of new project activities and proposed several factors that both motivate and assists a more efficient adoption of the activities, and factors that discourage the adoption. In addition to exploring the adoption mechanism, this research supplements also into the research of effort distribution by introducing a coherent set of project activities, namely non-construction activities, which is frequently ignored both in research and the effort management in software industry.

The reported study revealed that three issues should be avoided when building the general WBS: work assignments should not span over several projects or activities; the number of activities in WBS should be fairly limited and easy to understand; and the names of the activities should be self-evident.

Further, a replicated follow-up study on a project taking the measures to promote the adoption is recommended. Also, a higher response ratio might give statistically significant results. However, we believe that our findings can in fact be applied elsewhere in the software. Furthermore, research on non-construction activities effort is needed.

A deeper investigation into non-construction activities and their optimal effort proportions is currently being carried out. Moreover, research is needed to show how the project activities divided into the three categories proposed in this study bring stability into effort proportions and thus better predictability to effort estimation.

References

1. Wilson, D.N., Sifer, M.J.: Structured planning—project views. Software Engineering Journal **3** (1988) 134–140
2. Wolverton, R.W.: The cost of developing large-scale software. IEEE Transactions on Computers **23** (1974) 615–636
3. Boehm, B.: Software Engineering Economics. Prentice Hall (1981)
4. SEI: Capability maturity model integration (CMMI), version 1.1, staged representation. Technical Report CMU/SEI-2002-TE-029, ESC-TR-2002-029, CMU/SEI (2002)
5. Haapio, T.: The effects of non-construction activities on effort estimation. In: Proceedings of the 27th Information Systems Research in Scandinavia (IRIS'27). (2004) Available at http://w3.msi.vxu.se/users/per/IRIS27/iris27-1021.pdf.
6. MacDonell, S.G., Shepperd, M.J.: Using Prior-Phase Effort Records for Re-estimation During Software Projects, In: Proceedings of the Ninth International Software Metrics Symposium (METRICS'03), IEEE Computer Society (2003) 1–13
7. Boehm, B., Horowitz, E., Madachy, R., Reifer, D., Clark, B., Steece, B., Brown, A., Chulani, S., Abts, C.: Software Cost Estimation with COCOMO II. Prentice Hall (2000)
8. Hale, J., Parrish, A., Dixon, B., Smith, R.K.: Enhancing the cocomo estimation models. IEEE Software **17** (2000) 45–49
9. Blackburn, J.D., Scudder, G.D., Van Wassenhove, L.N.: Improving speed and productivity of software development: A global survey of software developers. IEEE Transactions on Software Engineering **22** (1996) 875–885
10. Collier, B., DeMarco, T., Fearey, P.A.: Defined process for project post-mortem review. IEEE Software **13** (1996) 65–72
11. Brady, S., DeMarco, T.: Management-aided software engineering. IEEE Software **11** (1994) 25–32
12. Jalote, P.: CMM In Practice: Processes for Executing Software Projects at Infosys. Addison-Wesley, Reading, MA (2000)
13. Sommerville, I.: Software Engineering. 6th edn. Pearson Education, Harlow, UK (2001)
14. Zahran, S.: Software Process Improvement. Addison-Wesley, London (1998)
15. Lee, H.Y., Jung, H.W., Chung, C.S., Lee, J., Lee, K., Jeong, H.: Analysis of interrater agreement in iso/iec 15504-based software process assessment. In: APAQS '01: Proceedings of the Second Asia-Pacific Conference on Quality Software, Washington, DC, USA, IEEE Computer Society (2001) 341
16. Damian, D., Zowghi, D., Vaidyanathasamy, L., Pal, Y.: An industrial experience in process improvement: An early assessment at the australian center for unisys software. In: Proceedings of the 2002 International Symposium on Empirical Software Engineering, ISESE'02, Washington, DC, USA, IEEE Computer Society (2002) 111–126
17. Rautianen, K., Lassenius, C., Vähäniitty, J., Pyhäjärvi, M., Vanhanen, J.: A tentative framework for managing software product development in small companies. In: HICSS '02: Proceedings of the 35th Annual Hawaii International Conference on System Sciences (HICSS'02)-Volume 8, Washington, DC, USA, IEEE Computer Society (2002) 251
18. McBride, T., Henderson-Sellers, B., Zowghi, D.: Project management capability levels: An empirical study. In: APSEC '04: Proceedings of the 11th Asia-Pacific Software Engineering Conference (APSEC'04), Washington, DC, USA, IEEE Computer Society (2004) 56–63

19. Yoo, C., Yoon, J., Lee, B., Lee, C., Lee, J., Hyun, S., Wu, C.: An integrated model of ISO 9001: 2000 and CMMI for ISO registered organizations. In: APSEC '04: Proceedings of the 11th Asia-Pacific Software Engineering Conference (APSEC'04), Washington, DC, USA, IEEE Computer Society (2004) 150–157
20. SEI: Capability maturity model integration (CMMI), version 1.1, continuous representation. Technical Report CMU/SEI-2002-TR-028, ESC-TR-2002-028, CMU/SEI (2002)
21. Järvinen, P.: On Research Methods. Opinpajan Kirja, Tampere, Finland (2001)
22. Iivari, J.: A paradigmatic analysis of contemporary schools of is development. European Journal of Information Systems **1** (1991) 249–272
23. March, S.T., Smith, G.F.: Design and natural science research on information technology. Decision Support Systems **15** (1995) 251–266
24. Hevner, A.R., March, S.T., Park, J., Ram, S.: Design science in information systems research. MIS Quarterly **28** (2004) 75–105
25. Kitchenham, B., Pickard, L., Pfleeger, S.L.: Case studies for method and tool evaluation. IEEE Software **12** (1995) 52–62
26. Fenton, N.E., Pfleeger, S.L.: Software Metrics: A Rigorous and Practical Approach. 2nd edn. PWS Publishing Company, Boston (1997)

The Concerns of Prototypers and Their Mitigating Practices: An Industrial Case-Study

Steve Counsell[1], Keith Phalp[2], Emilia Mendes[3], and Stella Geddes[4]

[1] School of Computing, Information Systems and Mathematics,
Brunel University, Uxbridge, Middlesex, UK
steve.counsell@brunel.ac.uk

[2] School of Computing and Engineering, Bournemouth University, UK
kphalp@bournemouth.ac.uk

[3] Department of Computer Science, University of Auckland., NZ
emilia@cs.auckland.ac.nz

[4] School of Crystallography, Birkbeck, University of London, UK
s.geddes@mail.cryst.bbk.ac.uk

Abstract. The use of formal models such as Role Activity Diagrams (RADs) for analysing a process often hide what really happens during that process. In this paper, we build on previous research on informal aspects of the prototyping process and look at the key concerns that prototypers had during the prototyping process. We contrasted those concerns with an analysis of whether documented practice during prototyping was likely to exacerbate or lessen those concerns. The basis of our analysis was a set of interviews with prototypers all of whom were part of a team actively producing evolvable prototypes in an industrial setting. Grounded Theory was used to extract the relevant data (concerns and mitigating practice) from the interview text. Interestingly, only a small number of the concerns of prototypers seemed to be supported by any supportive action, suggesting that there are factors that contribute to project success or failure beyond the control of the prototyping team. However, time and cost pressure seemed to figure largest in our analysis of prototyper concerns. The research highlights the problems that prototypers face and the benefits that an informal analysis can have on our understanding of the process. It also complements our understanding of the formal analysis of process using techniques such as RADs and the human factors therein.

1 Introduction

A commonly cited reason for systems being delivered late and over budget is inadequate requirements elicitation due to poor communication between developers and users. Prototyping, as an information systems discipline, provides an opportunity for free and unhindered interaction between developers and users in an attempt to overcome this problem [1, 2, 3, 5, 7, 20]. In theory, prototyping also offers the potential for requirements to be elicited more clearly through constant interaction with, and feedback from, the user. The prototyping process itself can be modelled formally using a technique such as Role Activity Diagrams (RADs) [13, 17] where actions and interactions between the different prototyping staff in the form of roles can be illustrated by lines joining, and internal to, the set of roles. What techniques such as RADs

J. Münch and M. Vierimaa (Eds.): PROFES 2006, LNCS 4034, pp. 166–176, 2006.

cannot show however, are the different concerns encountered during the process by the prototypers themselves and the supportive action that is taken to alleviate those concerns. Some of these concerns may be beyond the influence of the prototyper and hence detract severely from the effectiveness of that process.

In this paper, we focus on those concerns experienced by prototypers in the processes of five organisations, all of which used prototyping as part of their IS development strategy. Interview text with twenty different members (in ten interviews) of the prototyping team across the five organisations was analysed using principles of grounded theory [10] and their key concerns extracted. A number of centrally recurring concerns emerged from our analysis, in particular those related to restrictions of time and cost, the importance of experience and the effect of an overly bureaucratic environment in which protototpying took place.

We then carried out a further analysis to determine what actions perceived by the prototyper could *lessen* the threat that these factors posed in the prototyping process. Our analysis thus provides an insight into the tangible reasons why prototyping may not deliver the benefits it promises. It may also inform the manner in which future prototyping projects can be viewed and finally, highlights the importance of carrying out qualitative analysis as well as quantitative analysis of textual documents using theoretical techniques such as grounded theory.

The paper is arranged as follows. In Section 2, we describe the motivation for the research and related work. In Section 3 we describe the format of the interview text, the organisations studied and the grounded theory approach adopted for text analysis. In Section 4 we look at the extracted information and comment on the themes (i.e., concerns of the prototypers) and in Section 5 explore mitigating actions that prototypers perceived supported their practice. We then discuss some of the issues that arise as a result of our analysis (Section 6) and finally draw some conclusions and point to future work (Section 7).

2 Motivation and Related Work

The motivation for the work described in this study stems from a number of sources. Firstly, the prototyping process is widely promoted for the benefits it may provide; capturing user requirements accurately and pro-actively involving the user is bound to provide advantages, in theory at least. Yet very little literature has been published on some of the key human issues (i.e., qualitative issues) that may arise during this process [4]. Such issues could have a profound effect on how prototyping is perceived and carried out. In particular, our analysis highlights the dangers associated with any development, and in particular through that of the prototyping process.

Secondly, it is our belief that the majority of problems in the IS world stem from the *process* of IS development (we view the end product as only a function of that process). Getting the process right must be a priority for development staff, as well as addressing those problems related to the subtle influences during development. We also believe that whatever the type of information system, whether web-based or more traditional in nature, problems of an informal nature will always occur and therefore need to be documented.

A third motivation arises from a previous study using the same data [9]. A personality test carried out on prototyping development staff (including some of the staff used herein) concluded that prototypers tended to be extrovert in nature, while project managers tended to be less extrovert. Analysis of some of the problems during the prototyping process may give us further insight into the personalities, how they cope with the different pressures during development and what they do to alleviate those pressures.

The work in this paper extends a previous analysis [10] where the informal aspects of RADs were analysed. The study herein explores the chief concerns that prototyping staff have during the prototyping process and factors which potentially lessen those concerns. The work thus builds on the informal analysis in [10] by focusing specifically on the prime concerns that protoypers have. While our research does not specifically allude to the modelling of the prototyping process using RADs, the initial purpose of the research was to formally model the prototyping process using RAD notation. It is from that information about RADs however, that the research herein is founded.

In terms of related work, research by [19] used a RAD coupling metric based on interaction and role behaviour to establish traits in prototyping roles. It was found that the level of coupling in a RAD was highly correlated to the size of the prototyping team and the number of participants. In [17], metrics were applied to the same set of roles used for the analysis herein. Results showed that the project manager tended to exert control over the prototyper far more in large organisations than in small organisations. On the other hand, in small organisations, the project manager tended to interact with the end-user far more frequently, perhaps reflecting the lack of formality found in small organisations.

3 Grounded Theory

Grounded theory (GT) [11] was used as the mechanism for analyzing the interview text because it offers a means by which a corpus of data (including interview data) could be analysed in a rigorous way and the inter-relationships in that data uncovered mechanistically. According to [11], theories are developed through observation; scrutiny of text as we have done falls squarely into this category. The idea behind GT is to read and re-read text in order to reveal inter-relationships and categories. The motivation for analyzing the prototyping interview text in this case was to extract issues that prototyping staff identified as concerns during the prototyping experiences and to use that analysis as a basis for exploring what practice by prototypers addressed those concerns.

GT itself has been used in a number of situations to analyze qualitative interview text. It has also been applied to the analysis of organizational behaviour [16] as well as the use of ICASE tools in organizations [14]. Analysis of the interview text in the case of our research followed a series of four steps in accordance with GT principles. These were as follows:

1. Coding: each sentence in the interview text was examined. The questions: 'What is going on here?' and 'What is the situation?' were repeatedly asked. For the purposes of the analysis herein, each sentence in the ten interviews would be either identification of a 'concern' or 'mitigating action' and allocated

to the relevant category. We are not interested in any other information in the interview text. Coding is thus a process of filtering the text for the appropriate themes.

2. Memoing: A memo is a note to oneself about an issue or concern that you are interested in as part of the analysis. In other words, any point made by one of the interviewees which fell into the category of 'prototyping concern' could be used to pursue the analysis. This step should be completed in parallel with the coding stage. The memoing stage thus allows a certain amount of reflection and interpretation of the interview text as it is being read.
3. Sorting: a certain amount of analysis and arrangement of the collected data is then necessary.
4. Writing-up: the results of the analysis are written-up in a coherent way and conclusions drawn.

The process of categorizing the interview text according to the above principles took approximately one person week in total. In the next section, we describe the results of our analysis of the interview text, pointing to specific recurring issues and areas of concern.

4 Prototyping Concerns

Using GT, we categorized any such expression of concern by a member found in the interview text. We could thus cast our GT investigation in the form of the following two questions posed to the prototyper:

What most concerns (i.e., worries) you when you are carrying out prototyping?

and,

What is a key impediment to the success of the prototyping process?

Twenty-five different occurrences of a concern were extracted as a result of our GT analysis. Table 1 shows the three most common themes running through that text in ascending order of their 'occurrence'. We remark that these three themes repeatedly occurred across all the interview texts analyzed. We attach a 'Ranking' to each concern for brevity of explanation.

Table 1. The three most common concerns of the prototypers

Ranking	Concern
1.1	Time and Cost Constraints
1.2	Lack of Experience (in prototyping) and Lack of Business Knowledge
1.3	A Bureaucratic Infrastructure

The most common concern amongst prototyping staff was that of the time and cost imposition. Clearly, with the prototyping process, time and costs are, by definition, a constraint on the process. Moreover, prototyping theory would dictate that time should purposely be restricted to prevent 'over-prototyping', i.e., spending too long developing a prototype with consequent diminishing returns on time. There will always be cost pressures, but perhaps for prototyping (which some organizations would consider more of a luxury than a potentially cost-effective practice) the pressure is that much greater. In previous work [18], it was suggested that in relatively large organizations, pressure for project success falls much more heavily on the prototyping process simply because it occurs early in the development lifecycle and the consequences of getting a 'large' project wrong at the start are serious.

Clearly, it would seem that far from helping the prototyping process, the time and cost constraints play a large part in the concerns of the prototyper during the prototyping process, irrespective of organisation size. In particular, the need to prioritise activities and not waste the time of either customer or prototyper, came across strongly through analysis of the interview text.

The second major concern of the prototypers interviewed was the lack of experience of prototyping by certain prototypers together with a general lack of business knowledge of the prototypers. This feature suggests that there are a set of experience skills which any developer has to acquire to be effective during the prototyping process. Included in those skills is an awareness of business knowledge to inform the prototyping process. Evidence from the interview texts and given in Table 1 thus points to the need for experienced and well-rounded developers to do the prototyping as of paramount importance. The choice of the right people for the task in hand with the required skills thus emerged as a crucial aspect of prototyping, supported throughout the interview text.

The third major concern relates to the bureaucratic infrastructure of the prototyping process. This is an interesting concern since it supports our belief that rigid control structures can impair the effectiveness of the prototyping process; a laissez-faire approach is favoured by prototypers. It also supports our other strong belief that personality of the prototyper is an important factor in how the process should work. In previous work by three of the same authors [8], prototypers were found to be largely extrovert in nature; we believe that imposing a rigid control structure does not fit well with this personality profile. This result also helps to understand why in previous tables, there is opposition to formal standards and formal change request procedures.

As well as the key recurring themes in the interview text, there were a number of other concerns worth stating. Table 2 shows, in no particular order, these remaining concerns on the part of prototypers which seem to contradict the whole ethos of prototyping and in certain cases conflict with that ethos.

Table 2. Other concerns of prototyping staff

Ranking	Concern
2.1	The company is getting too big
2.2	Requirements overkill (customers getting angry)
2.3	The quick and dirty approach causes problems later on
2.4	Conventional development standards are an imposition
2.5	The existing life cycle is inappropriate for RAD
2.6	Getting it right for the user/user satisfaction
2.7	The ripple effect of changes
2.8	Time prioritization

The first contradiction relates to the fact that there is the inevitable desire by the user to have changes made to prototypes (as a key part of prototyping). However, the associated concern by prototypers of the 'ripple effect' that this causes at later stages of the prototyping process seems to be a warning against making changes of certain types (2.7); this contradiction is further compounded by the evidence from the interview text that customers do not seem to like overbearing requirements gathering (they 'get angry' if too many questions are being asked by the prototyper).

Secondly, there is the conflict between autonomy of the prototyping process and the need to meet organizational standards (2.4). Thirdly, there is the conflict between the need for prioritizing functionality/features of the prototype under time and cost pressures and user satisfaction (2.6). Keeping the user happy is a common theme that comes across in the interview text analyzed, but this is obviously not an easily achieved goal in the time available (time prioritization (2.8) seems to be one possible solution to this problem).

Finally, there is the 'quick and dirty' concern (2.3) which would seem to conflict with both standards adherence and user satisfaction. Since the prototype is evolutionary, then this approach may not yield the benefits later on. Perhaps this explains why there is a need for prioritization of time (2.8) to extract the best use of the resources available in the limited time available.

It is interesting that 'the company is getting too big' was stated as a concern (2.1). This suggests that perhaps, in keeping with results in [17], that prototyping works best in small companies (where there is relatively low bureaucracy). It is also interesting to note that in one case it was felt that the 'existing lifecycle was inappropriate for RAD'. This could suggest that the prototyping phase is not an isolated, independent activity, but like any stage of development, feeds into, and is dependent on, the larger development process. For that to happen, there have to be appropriate interfacing structures in place. More evidence would be needed before any concrete conclusions could be drawn, however, for each of these two points.

Overall, the data analysed as part of these concerns highlight two key principles of prototyping. Firstly, it is a far more complex process than it at first seems which influences, and is influenced by, a relatively few key factors. The strengths of prototyping are often the very *cause* of concern by prototypers (time and cost constraints). Secondly, that extremely skilled IS staff are needed in the prototyping process to manage and cope with the inherent complexity. Prototyping brings with it many risks, both from a cost and time perspective and not least of these risks is the potential for alienating the user. It is also interesting that of the concerns listed in Tables 1 and 2, there are various factors outside the immediate control of the prototyping team and are far more organization-centered. In particular, concerns 1.3, 2.1, 2.4 and 2.5.

5 Evidence of Mitigating Action

As well as extraction of data relating to the concerns of the prototyping team, we also collected evidence from the same interview scripts concerning supportive action that the prototypers believed important for mitigating their concerns during the prototyping process (and noted in the previous section). From a grounded theory perspective, the question which drove this analysis was:

"*What practices (whether formal or informal) are necessary during that process for end-prototype success*".

This is a very different question to that asked in the previous section. Here, we are analysing the *positive* actions suggested by prototypers during the course of the process, rather than the problems and concerns they perceive existing during the same process. The first theme of the previous section addresses the issue of what the prototyper sees as a problem during the prototyping process. The question now being posed is:

"*What do you do to address and mitigate that concern?*"

From our GT analysis, the answer to this question emerged on thirty-five occasions. Table 3 shows the top three responses; 'effective use of time' is the most frequent mitigating action that prototypers expressed as important to address during prototyping. It is also interesting that this result is in keeping with the most frequent 'concern' expressed by the same prototypers from Table 1.

Table 3. Actions deemed necessary for prototyping effectiveness

Ranking	Mitigating action	Occurrences
3.1	Effective use of time	6
3.2	Effective use of appropriate experience	5
3.3	Standards adherence	4
3.4	Estimation	3

Clearly, effective use of time is both a concern of the prototyping team and uppermost in the minds of the prototyping team during the process. A sample of the detailed responses within this category was:

- It is important to do just "enough" work during the process to show what the system is capable of.
- Time-boxing: "…..first choose a relatively arbitrary time and then build whatever you can build in during that period".
- Keeping the time with the user short (and the task small and manageable).
- Deliver "something" on time.
- The importance of placing time limits.

The second most frequent mitigating action during our analysis of the prototyping process and again, in keeping with the data in Table 1 – is that of making effective use of the experience of staff available. A sample of the responses in this category was:

- Application of appropriate mix of skills to the tasks. This response suggests that for any one project there are a variety of different skills needed (both personal and technical).
- Selection of more experienced prototypers for the more important projects. This would seem to make both practical ad economic sense.

- Movement of staff around the different projects should be done in order that they obtain the required experience *and* the project has the right staff.

The third most frequent mitigating action found was adherence to standards. This is interesting, since it suggests that while standards according to traditional development are an 'imposition' (see concern 2.4), it is widely recognized that standards related specifically to the prototyping process are of value. The fourth most frequent response related to the importance of estimation. This was also interesting, since it highlights one of the skills that is difficult to acquire without experience (itself a concern during the prototyping process). A sample of the responses in this category was:

- Estimation (time/cost) is done just after initial requirement gathering.
- Requests for cost estimation of projects from the customer to the prototyper.
- Requirements should be gathered in order to make an estimate of how important the work is.

Table 4 shows the next most frequent actions extracted using our analysis and the two occurrences of each action found. The importance of educating the customer (in terms of what prototyping can do for them) was one mitigating action that emerged from our analysis (4.1). Awareness of technology change was another important facet of the prototyping process according to the prototypers (4.2). Surprisingly, talking to users seemed to fare very badly on the list of mitigating actions that the prototyper seems to believe important (4.3). One possible explanation for this may be that in terms of prototyping effectiveness, talking too much to the users may be detrimental. To support this view, there is evidence in the interview text and described in [10], where the prototyper has deliberately hidden information from the user and a general feeling that users expect too much from the prototyping process – they are thus best kept away from the decision-making process.

Table 4. Other mitigating actions found

Ranking	Mitigating action	Occurrences
4.1	Educating the customer	2
4.2	Awareness of technology change	2
4.3	Talking to users	2
4.4	Review	2
4.5	Development of improvement plan	2

Finally, the instigation of a plan for improving the process of development featured in two responses (4.5). The overall impression amongst those interviewed was that planning was a good idea and permitted some level of control into the process without being too over-bearing. Table 5 shows the remaining responses, each of which occurred just once. The most remarkable feature from this table is the relatively low importance attached to *core* prototyping activities.

Table 5. Isolated mitigating actions

Ranking	Mitigating action
5.1	Trust between prototyper and customer
5.2	Informal discussion with users
5.3	Clarify requirements
5.4	Explore Feasibility
5.5	Proper Library management
5.6	Develop mock-ups
5.7	Controls

For example, we would expect informal discussion (5.2), clarification of requirements (5.3), exploration of feasibility (5.4) and develop mock-ups (5.6) to have figured more prominently in our analysis. This result highlights the point that the most obvious features of the prototyping process are not necessarily those that concern the prototyper unduly. Controls were also suggested as a useful mechanism during prototyping (5.7), but only in a limited sense. Most prototypers expressed dislike for excessive controls being imposed.

To conclude, it is clear that prototypers engage in various actions to mitigate the concerns they have during the prototyping process. However, it is worrying that the user seems to play very little part in any of those actions and that only indirectly is the purpose of prototyping served. In the next section, we discuss some of the issues arising from our analysis.

6 Discussion

A number of issues are raised by the analysis. Firstly, the over-riding emphasis and focus on cost and time as factors in the prototyping process was surprising. While we would have expected time to be an important consideration, it also seemed to permeate many of the other concerns. Furthermore, there is evidence that the same factors influenced the way that prototypers worked and ultimately how they viewed the user/customer. On some occasions, this had a negative effect on the way that prototypers treated and perceived the user.

A further issue to emerge from the analysis was the many conflicts that the prototyping process seems to engender. There is the need to satisfy the user, while at the same time avoiding requirements overkill. There is the need for prototyping to fit in with the overall system development approach of the organisation without too many standards or controls. Finally, the balancing act required to ensure that time pressures do not compromise the whole point of prototyping – the clear elicitation of requirements. The actions which we imagined would support this activity most, seem to have been given a low priority.

Interestingly, the use of software tools does not figure prominently in the interview text which we have studied (in common with the study in [10]). Only on two occasions was the significance of development tools mentioned. A recent survey of tools used for web development showed relatively simple tools such as Visio and Dreamweaver to be the most commonly used tools [12] by developers.

Finally, we have to consider a number of threats to the validity of the study described. Firstly, the interview text has been assumed to reflect accurately the prototyping as it existed in each organisation. We have to accept that the interviewees may have lied and/or withheld information about the true situation in the organisation. In defence of this threat, the investigator did return to clarify points with interviewees which they had not been clear about and certain cross-checking would have been inevitable (especially with multiple interviews in the same organisation). Secondly, we have not yet any indication of what factors truly reflect good practice during prototyping. Many of the factors we have suggested as highly important to the process may in due course turn out to be as unimportant as the prototypers would have use believe. This investigation is the subject of future work. Finally, we believe the interview questions gave the prototyper *carte blanche* to say what they wanted, both good and bad about the prototyping process. We also believe the questions allowed as much freedom expression of with respect to what actions they thought mitigated the problems they stated. Often, as would be expected, a prototyper would state a concern and in the same response suggest action that they took to mitigate that concern. In the next section, we draw some conclusions from the research and point to future work.

7 Conclusions and Future Work

In this paper, we have described an analysis of the concerns that prototypers have during the prototyping process. Interestingly, time and cost pressures seemed to figure prominently in both the concerns of the prototypers and in the actions they took to mitigate the pressures that these two factors induced. A number of factors were found to be outside the control of the prototyper, for example, the standards imposed by a traditional systems development. This seemed to be a cause of annoyance and worry by the prototyper. It also implies that the prototyping process is not an isolated activity that can be achieved unilaterally.

The chief conclusion we draw from our analysis is that investigation of the human factors in the development of systems can tell us as much about development as a formal model such as that embodied by Role Activity Diagrams (RADs). As such, the informal analysis complements the RAD as a tool for exploring software development issues. It is clear that any process involving IS staff is likely to be exceptionally complex. In terms of future work, we intend to investigate how the corresponding RADs could be modified in some way to accommodate the features we have uncovered herein. We also intend assessing the impact of making such changes, from a performance point of view, using appropriate metrics.

The research suggests that in an ideal prototyping environment, there is no limit on time or cost, every prototyper has a wide range of skills and experience and that standards and controls are limited, with no outside influence or interference. Obviously in any organization, sadly, this scenario is unlikely.

Acknowledgements

We gratefully acknowledge the help given by Liguang Chen of the University of Bournemouth for access to the interview script material [6].

References

1. Baskerville, R., and Pries-Heje, J. Short cycle time systems development, Information Systems Journal (14:3), July 2004, pp. 237-264.
2. Baskerville, R., and Stage, J., Controlling Prototype Development through risk analysis, MIS Quarterly, December 1996.
3. Beynon-Davies, P, Mackay, H. and Tudhope, D. It's lots of bits of paper and ticks and post-it notes and things ...: a case study of a rapid application development project, Information Systems Journal (10), 2000, pp. 195-216.
4. J. Brooks, People are our most important product, In E. Gibbs and R. Fairley, ed., Software Engineering Education. Springer-Verlag, 1987.
5. D. Card, The RAD fad: is timing really everything? IEEE Software, pp. 19-22, Jan. 1995.
6. L. Chen, An Empirical Investigation into Management and Control of Software Prototyping, PhD. dissertation, Department of Computing, University of Bournemouth, 1997.
7. G. Coleman and R. Verbruggen. A quality software process for rapid application development, Software Quality Journal, 7(2):107-122, 1998.
8. S. Counsell, K. Phalp and E. Mendes. The 'P' in Prototyping is for Personality. Proceedings of International Conference on Software Systems Engineering and its Applications, Paris, France, December 2004.
9. S. Counsell, K. Phalp and E. Mendes. The vagaries of the prototyping process: an empirical study of the industrial prototyping process, Proceedings of The International Conference on Software Systems Eng. and its Applications, Paris, France, December 2005.
10. S. Counsell, K. Phalp, Mendes, E. and Geddes, S. (2005). What formal models cannot show us: people issues during the prototyping process, Proceedings of 6th International Conference on Product Focused Software Process Improvement (PROFES 2005), Oulu, Finland, June. Pages 3-15 (Springer Lecture Notes in Computer Science Series Volume 3547, Ed. Frank Bomarius, Seija Komi-Sirvio).
11. B. Glaser and A. Strauss. The Discovery of Grounded Theory. Strategies for Qualitative Research. Aldine Publishers, 1967.
12. GUUUI survey. Results from a survey of web prototyping tools usage. The Interaction Designer's Coffee Break. Issue 3, July 2002. available from: `www.guuui.com/issues01_03_02`.
13. C. Handy, On roles and Interactions. Understanding Organisations, Penguin.
14. C. Knapp. An investigation into the organisational and technological factors that contribute to the successful implementation of CASE technology. Doctoral Dissertation, City University, New York, 1995.
15. H. Lichter, M. Schneider-Hufschmidt and H Zullighoven. Prototyping in industrial software projects: Bridging the gap between theory and practice. IEEE Transactions on Software Engineering, 20(11):825-832, 1994.
16. P. Martin and B. Turner. Grounded Theory and Organisational Research. Journal of applied Behavioural Science. 22(2), pages 141-157.
17. M. Ould. Business Processes: Modelling and Analysis for Re-engineering and Improvement, Wiley, 1995.
18. K. Phalp and S. Counsell, Coupling Trends in Industrial Prototyping Roles: an Empirical Investigation, The Software Quality Journal, Vol. 9, Issue 4, pages 223-240, 2002.
19. K. Phalp and M. Shepperd, Quantitative analysis of static models of processes, Journal of Systems and Software, 52 (2000), pages 105-112.
20. J. Reilly. Does RAD live up to the hype? IEEE Software, pages 24-26, Jan. 1995.

An Industrial Case Study on the Choice Between Language Customization Mechanisms

Miroslaw Staron[1,2] and Claes Wohlin[1]

[1] Department of Systems and Software Engineering
School of Engineering
Blekinge Institute of Technology
{miroslaw.staron, claes.wohlin}@bth.se
[2] Department of Applied IT
IT University in Gothenburg
miroslaw.staron@ituniv.se

Abstract. Effective usage of a general purpose modeling language in software engineering poses a need for language *customization* – adaptation of the language for a specific purpose. In the context of the Unified Modeling Language (UML) the customization could be done using two mechanisms: developing profiles and extending the metamodel of UML. This paper presents an industrial case study on the choice between metamodel extensions and profiles as well as the influence of the choice on the quality of products based on the extensions. The results consist of a set of nine prioritized industrial criteria which complement six theoretical criteria previously identified in the literature. The theoretical criteria are focused on the differences between the extension mechanisms of UML while the industrial criteria are focused on development of products based on these extensions. The case study reveals that there are considerable differences in effort required to develop comparable products using each mechanism and that the quality (measured as correctness of a product) is different for these comparable products by an order of magnitude.

1 Introduction

Effective usage of a general-purpose modeling language (like the Unified Modeling Language – UML, [1]) in the course of software development strives for a customization of the language – i.e. its fine-tuning and adaptation for a specific purpose. For example in the context of code generation, customizing the language could be done by defining additional modeling constructs that would enable generating a complete source code. The customized languages can be primary assets of MDA (Model Driven Architecture [2]) frameworks for automating software construction through model transformations – for example as presented in our previous case study [3]. UML has two extension mechanisms which can be used for its customization – profiles and metamodel extensions [4]. The option of creating a metamodel extension (as opposed to creating profiles) was usually not supported in UML modeling tools and thus not considered so far in the enterprises customizing UML. The situation, however, changes as modern modeling tools expose mechanisms for extending the metamodel of UML. Examples of this kind of tools are Telelogic

J. Münch and M. Vierimaa (Eds.): PROFES 2006, LNCS 4034, pp. 177–191, 2006.

Tau G2 and Coral Modeling Framework [5]. These tools are modeling tools with metamodeling capabilities – i.e. tools primarily dedicated for creating UML models with possibility of altering the metamodel of UML. It should be noted that these tools are dedicated for the modeling of software and not for the development of modeling tools – which makes them representative for modeling tools used in software development companies. As the new customization possibilities emerge in modeling tools, companies willing to use the modeling language more effectively consider customizing the language and hence need to choose the appropriate extension mechanism.

The case study presented in this paper is performed at a UML modeling tool vendor which regularly develops language extensions, with significant experience in this area – Telelogic AB in Malmö, Sweden (referred to as Telelogic hereafter). The extensions are the basis for some of the products developed by the company. Examples of these products are domain specific modeling tool extensions for modeling real-time software, full source code generation for embedded systems or architecture frameworks. The products are based on the extensions of the modeling language but they also require supporting software components to provide additional functionality defined by the extension. These products are dedicated mostly for companies developing software for the domains of real-time and embedded software. The domains pose strict requirements, e.g. that the products should allow for early verification based on models – thus the models created with Telelogic's modeling tool – Tau G2 – can be executable which in turn leads to strict requirements on the quality of the customizations of the tool. The language customization endeavors at Telelogic are conducted within a UML modeling tool which is a similar situation to companies customizing the modeling language while not being tool vendors themselves. The large number of developed extensions by Telelogic provided us with a unique opportunity of studying products which are based on each of the extension mechanisms thus allowing comparison of products which are very similar yet based on different extension mechanisms. This unique opportunity provides an evidence of influences of choosing the mechanisms in industrial context.

As a starting point in designing our case study we used the theoretical differences between the extension mechanisms identified previously in the literature [4]. The initial set of criteria based on these differences does not contain considerations on the implications on the products based on the customized notation, for example in terms of the quality. The products based on the customized language are adaptations of tools used in software development as presented in Section 3. In addition to identifying the industrial criteria focused on developing complete products based on the extensions, studying comparable metamodel extensions and profiles provided us with differences in quality (measured as correctness) of the products. In addition to the quality we also studied effort required to develop the language extensions in order to investigate whether there are differences between profiles and metamodel extensions in this aspect. We discuss the relevance of the results of this case study in the context of the results of our previous industrial case study at an enterprise working with customizing UML in order to enable automating part of their software development process [3].

The paper starts with the presentation of the related work in the field in Section 2. The two compared techniques and the differences between them are presented in Section 3 followed by the description of the design of the case study performed and its operation in Section 4. The results of the study and their analysis are presented in Section 5 with the evaluation of the validity of the study in Section 6. The conclusions of the paper are presented in Section 7.

2 Related Work

Language customization is one of the core elements of MDA. The MDA related literature often discusses the use of both profiles and metamodels for language customization (for example [6, 7]), but does neither give guidelines when to use one over the other nor criteria for choosing between the extension mechanisms. The discussions presented in these papers are taken into account while considering the differences between metamodels and profiles in Section 3. The authors of [8] in the context of MDA conclude that profiles should always be used over metamodels due to their simplicity. The suggestion, however, is based on an analytical evaluation of the expressiveness of profiles and metamodel extensions without considering industrial applications of profiles or products based on the customizations.

The issues of creating custom modeling notations are similar to problems studied while creating Domain Specific Modeling Languages (DSLs). In particular, while considering such initiatives as software factories or generative programming [9]. As opposed to that work this paper considers creating DSLs based on a general-purpose language, not creating DSLs from scratch.

In this paper we discuss the issues of choosing between metamodel extensions and profiles in the context of language customization. The issues related to extending metamodels, however, are a part of a bigger aspect – language engineering. Details on language engineering – in particular creating a language from scratch – can be found in [10]. Furthermore, it is not always the case that metamodels and profiles can both be used for the same purpose. Considerations on this matter are discussed in [11]. The authors classify metamodel extensions in a similar way as in [12] and draw conclusions in the context of domain modeling and code generation. Despite the similarity of the purpose of that study to ours, the context (specific domain of extensions) does not allow drawing conclusions from the study in [11] in other cases than code generation or domain modeling.

3 Language Customization

Usually using an off-the-shelf modeling language like UML is dictated by the tool support and the knowledge base. Benefits from using a general-purpose language can be increased if a company is willing to *customize* it for the specific needs. This means that the language is adapted for a specific purpose and a tool that takes advantage of the customization is created. In the context of code generation, customizing the language could be done by defining dedicated constructs that would provide (along with customizing the code generators) means for generating a complete source code for the developed system.

Advanced industrial usage of UML (as studied at Volvo IT [3] and ABB Robotics in Sweden) showed that creating the language customization can (and should) be handled by modelers within the enterprise since they possess the necessary domain knowledge. The motivation behind the research presented in this paper is that practitioners improving the practice of modeling in their enterprises need support in choosing between costly (but powerful) metamodel extensions and cheaper (but limited) profiles since these practitioners are usually not language engineers. They also need to be able to assess potential consequences of their decision in terms of quality of the customization and the effort required to develop them. The scenario in which a language is customized in a company using a modeling tool with metamodeling capabilities for the development of models is presented in Figure 1.

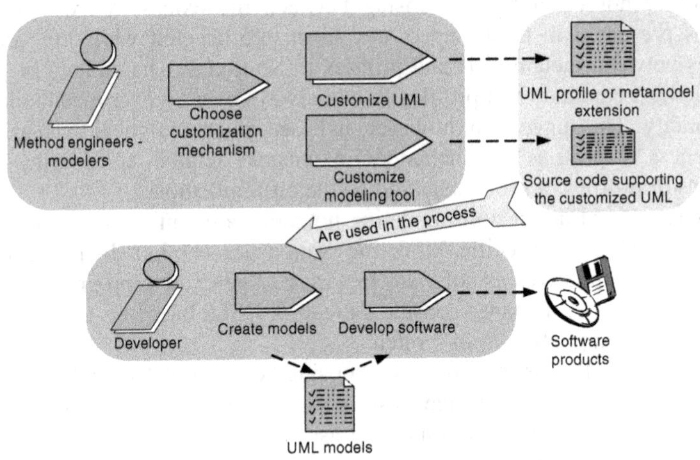

Fig. 1. Language customization in companies – an abstract view

Method engineers (who are also modelers) are specialists possessing the necessary skills to develop language extensions and to customize the appropriate tools. They customize the modeling language by creating language extensions and they customize the tools by developing add-ins extending the functionality of the tools. The add-ins are required so that the developers (at the bottom of Figure 1) can use the extensions in an effective way. In their work the method engineers need to choose the appropriate customization mechanism for a particular task. It was found in this study and it was observed in the study presented in [3] that there are usually a handful of people (a dedicated small team with a designated architect) in a company who can play this role. The results of the work of the method engineers are the customized modeling language and the customized tool which is used by developers in the company to create models.

In the case of Telelogic the products based on the customized language are add-ins for the tool, which provide such functionality as, for example code generation for C++, architecture modeling with DoDAF (US Department of Defense Architecture Framework) or providing new diagrams for the tool. In the case of other companies, the products are additional components which can take advantage of the extensions to the base language. For example in the case of a company developing an MDA framework, the product was a framework for model driven software development, including add-ins for software development and project management. This company also regarded extensions of UML to be of primary importance in this kind of products.

3.1 Theoretical Differences Between Profiles and Metamodel Extensions

As a starting point for elaborating criteria in our case study we adopted theoretical differences based on the analysis of criteria for choosing techniques for building language families [4]. The differences are numbered T1 – T6 (where the letter *T* indicates that they arise from theoretical analysis). The differences are applicable to the issue of language customization and as such are evaluated in this study.

T1: **Profiles are easier to construct.** Not as much knowledge is required to develop a profile as to develop a metamodel extension.

T2: **Profiles promote reusability.** Profiles might be applied (thus reused) to different metamodels provided the extended elements (and the mechanisms of profiles) are presented in both metamodels.

T3: **Profiles are better supported in tools.** Metamodeling tools are not yet common on the market (with the exception of [10]), which is quite the opposite to UML modeling tools. Defining profiles is specified in the UML specification and thus is supported in the growing number of UML tools, not requiring special tools.

T4: **Profiles are better for smaller solutions.** For a small language customization (i.e. when the customization requires only making a single certain language construct more precise in a given context), the profiles are possibly better since they provide means of refining single existing constructs.

T5: **Metamodels are more expressive.** Profiles are a restricted way of metamodeling, and as such are less expressive than metamodels. The mentioned lack of ability of defining new associations between extended model elements is only one of the restrictions of profiles, which makes them suitable only for some of the purposes for which metamodels can be used.

T6: **Metamodels are harder to integrate.** Due to the strict metamodeling principle [13] each element in the model can be an instance of only one element in the language definition. While this limits the integration possibilities of metamodels, it does not affect profiles since several stereotypes can be applied to the same element in the model.

Evaluation of whether these differences are used in the choice between the two language customization mechanisms is one of the goals of our case study.

4 Case Study Design

Telelogic is a vendor of multiple software development tools, among others a modeling tool for UML – Tau G2. The tool is constructed in such a way that it supports the mechanisms of profiles in the way defined in the UML 2.0 specification and allows extending the metamodel in the tool. Creators of language extensions at Telelogic often (several times per release, which is usually every other month) need to make the decisions of which is the preferred extension mechanism in a certain situation. The modelers perceive UML as a framework for language definition. Such a perception is similar to the vision of UML as a family of languages as presented in [4] and it is also known as the language product line, since the main – core – language elements are reused by all languages. The existence of the common core allows using both profiles and metamodels for language extension.

Three employees were interviewed in the case study: (i) chief architect of the tool responsible for the decision process; (ii) two modelers responsible for development of profiles and metamodel extensions. The chief architect and the two modelers are actually the whole population of people involved in choosing between profiles and metamodel extensions hence no sampling was conducted. The chief architect is the person who makes the major decisions whether a given product is to be based on a metamodel extension or a profile. His experience in the field of UML and tool development allows us to regard his opinion as the expert.

We facilitated data source triangulation [14] to cross-validate the data from different sources, which were:

- Comparable profiles and metamodel extensions – profiles for interaction overview diagrams, component diagrams, and deployment diagrams; metamodel extensions for activity diagrams and Java add-in. They were used to obtain data on their size and to verify whether the products can be directly compared.
- The specification of requirements and the high level designs of the products which (i) provided the necessary information to characterize the products, (ii) ensure compatibility in the scope, purpose and size, and (iii) were used to explore purposes of customizing UML at Telelogic.
- Fault database – to investigate the quality of the products. The faults were obtained by querying the database. The data available in the fault database consists of the faults found in the software, their severity and history of their fixes.
- Decision process – obtained during the interviews – was used to elaborate industrial criteria considered while choosing between profiles and metamodel extensions.

It should be noted that diagrams are treated uniformly with other modeling elements in Tau G2, which allowed us to use the diagrams as objects of the study without any threat to generality. In this study we studied metamodels and profiles which were close to each other as they were: (i) developed by the same modelers in the same tool; (ii) found to provide similar functionality; (iii) were of similar complexity. Due to the above we were able to compare the quality of the different products in spite of the fact that they are not created to provide identical functionality. With this respect we see these products as *sister projects* [15] typical for the studied company and representative for other companies.

In our study we pose the following research questions:

RQ_1: *What are the criteria used in choosing between profiles and metamodel extensions in order to customize a modeling language in industry and how important is each criterion?*

RQ_2: *Is there a difference in the quality of products based on profiles and metamodel extensions?*

We pose the first research question – RQ_1 – in order to get insight into the decision process from the software engineering perspective. The differences between metamodel extensions and profiles in the expressive power and the degree to which they affect the other elements of the language – i.e. how deeply they alter the base language (which is important for metamodel extensions) – can have implications on the quality of the products based on these extensions. Therefore, the second question – RQ_2 – is posed. The quality was measured as the number of reported faults (along with severity) in the behavior of the product as observed during the testing phase and by users of the tool.

We used several methods for collecting the data, thus facilitating method triangulation [14]. The methods are: (i) interviews with chief architect and modelers, (ii) investigations of documents and fault database, and (iii) a prioritization technique – one hundred dollar test [16]. The interviews were in the form of a structured questionnaire (to verify the criteria) with additional open questions (to complement the criteria). In particular the questions to the chief architect were about: the process of choosing between profiles and metamodel extensions, resources required and available for development of the extensions, and differences between processes of developing profiles and metamodel extensions. The questions for the modelers contain aspects related to products development: the purposes of customization of UML at the company, the process of developing profiles and metamodel extensions, quality assurance of the developed products, and development effort required to develop profiles and metamodel extensions.

Data was collected sequentially during the case study during three months. The interviews with the chief architect and one modeler as well as the fault database investigation were conducted during a one day visit to the company headquarters. The prioritization of the industrial criteria was done by the chief architect a week later via e-mail. The interview with the second modeler was performed after one and a half months (due to summer holidays). During the interviews, documentation of the requirements for extensions and specification of the metamodel and profiles to be developed were provided by the interviewees. The fault database was studied during the first visit and it was later checked (during the last visit) that there were no additional faults reported. After the study, the results were discussed during a half-day workshop in order to verify whether the conclusions drawn and the obtained data were valid. During that workshop we performed a simple experiment to check whether the views on language customization are consistent among all subjects. The results were positive – the subjects had uniform views.

5 Results

The results of the study are presented according to the research questions posed in the case study. The results are analyzed in a qualitative way.

5.1 Criteria and Prioritization

In the course of the interviews and the subsequent data analysis it appeared that there are two levels at which the criteria are considered: high level (business level) and low level (technical level). The two levels of criteria introduced in the interview are equally important while choosing between the two ways of customizing the language.

The business value, i.e. market related elements, are considered at the business level. They relate to the following question – "Which way of customizing the language would be more profitable?" The technical criteria are considered at the lower level and they relate to the following question – "Can we do it in a certain way?"

The criteria presented in this section are numbered I1 to I9 (the letter *I* indicates that they were identified in the course of the industrial case study). The process of making the decision consists of two phases – first, the business level criteria are considered and then the technical level criteria are considered.

I1: **User expectations.** The expectations can explicitly state that one of the mechanisms should be used or implicitly require that a specific one should be used. The expectations might be altered if other criteria point to the alternative extension mechanism.

I2: **Cost** is virtually the most important from the perspective of profits that the company provisions from the customization. The cost is measured in person-hours. The considered aspect of cost is how much the development of the product would cost if it was to be included in the next release.

I3: **UML compliance** is considered since it affects the level of compatibility with the UML 2.0 language and other tools that implement it. The level of compatibility with the UML standard is taken into considerations by customers of Telelogic[1].

The set of technical criteria consists of criteria I4 – I9.

I4: **Limitations of Tau** are considered, although the company is itself the manufacturer of Tau, since there is a constant non-functional requirement – the tool's extendable architecture. The decision taken should aim at increasing extensibility of the architecture.

I5: **Expression power of the approach (includes the limitations of the approaches).** This criterion corresponds to difference T5 which states that metamodels are more expressive than profiles.

I6: **Possibility of integration of a profile/metamodel with other profiles/metamodels.** This criterion corresponds directly to the difference T6.

I7: **Versioning of the product to be developed** – is considered since according to the company's configuration management practices metamodels' versions need to be controlled while the profiles required less strict control over versions.

I8: **Effort required so that the product can be included in the next release** – is considered on this level although it is not strictly a technical criterion. Nevertheless, since each product influences the components of the tool to a different extent, the effort required to include the product (including the effort of integration into the architecture) is considered. The question that is asked based on this criterion is how much effort the product would require if it was to be included in the next release and whether such resources are available. This criterion is derived from difference T1 which states that profiles are easier to construct, but it complements it with a software engineering perspective – the effort required to include the product in the next release. It also relates to the difference in reusability T2 as profiles reuse more than metamodels.

---

[1] The metamodel of UML used in the tool differs at some places from the standard UML metamodel which might be an effect of choosing different extension mechanisms in particular situations.

I9: Knowledge known by the persons who potentially can make the work. The availability of staff that can actually develop each extension determines whether it is feasible to include the product in the desired release (c.f. section 5.3).

As it can be observed in the criteria, they are focused on the complete product based on the language customizations. The aspects of development effort, knowledge required to develop the products, versioning and the business criteria have not been identified previously in the literature.

Although it seems that T3 is similar to I4, there are differences between them. While T3 relates to the way in which the metamodels are defined (and the lack of support for it) I4 (limitations of Tau) relates to the fact that the architecture should be extendable. The theoretical difference is very strict – either there is a support for metamodel extensions or not. The criterion I4 is a "relaxed" version of criterion T3. For companies adopting effective usage of models, however, it is a significant criterion since one of the factors determining the success of the introduction of customized way of modeling is the evolution in company's way of working (c.f. [3, Factors 13-14]) which can be seen as a limitation on the introduction of the extension (or on the architecture of enterprise tools).

Criterion I7 is a new one and relates to configuration management, which is part of software engineering, but it is not a theoretical difference between profiles and metamodels. The last new criterion is the knowledge of the employees who potentially can do the work (I9). Once again this criterion is important for software development companies which usually do not possess extensive expertise in language engineering. This criterion seems to be related to the overall quality of the products developed based on the language extensions.

It should also be noted that the interviewee regarded some of the theoretical criteria as not important. In particular the interviewee has not considered size of the customization as one of the criteria in making the choice although it was identified in literature (c.f. difference T4). The prioritizations at both levels (Table 1) were done with the same technique. The prioritization was conducted by the chief architect as he is the person making choices between metamodel extensions and profiles in most cases. Modelers were consulted after the study whether the percentages reflect their opinions.

Table 1. Prioritization results

Level	Importance [%]	Criterion
Business	40	I1: User expectations
	40	I2: Cost
	20	I3: UML compliance
Technical	25	I5: Expression power of the approach
	25	I9: Knowledge known by the persons who potentially can perform the work
	20	I4: Limitations of Tau
	20	I8: Effort required so that the product can be included in the next release
	5	I6: Possibility of integration
	5	I7: Versioning of the product to be developed

The low importance of the UML compliance indicates that in industry the UML compliance is not as important as the business value. The low importance of the criterion shows that it does not have a decisive influence on the decision although it is considered due to the market-driven nature of software development at Telelogic. The equal importance of user expectations and cost indicate a constant trade-off between the expectations of the product and the cost that is required to implement it in the next release. High expectations can be reconsidered if the cost of their fulfillment is significant.

The technical criteria prioritization reflects the importance of technology related issues. There is no single decisive factor whether to choose profiles or metamodels but the most important criteria are the expressiveness of the approaches and the knowledge required for development. These criteria are related to both the difference between products and the software engineering perspective on the difference – knowledge required to develop them. The issues of knowledge required to customize the language are related to several factors determining successful adoption of customized modeling language [3].

Slightly lower importance (20%) characterizes the limitations of Tau (I4) and the effort required for development and integration of the product into the next release (I8). The extensible architecture requirement limits to some extent the possibilities of extending the metamodel. An equally important aspect is the effort required to develop the product in a given time – since no delays are allowed. Any potential delays of product development are compensated in decreasing the size of the product – i.e. if there is not enough time, the time is not extended, but functionality is being restricted or if it is not possible, the integration is postponed until a later release. Issues related to the delivery of the product were also observed in the previous study – in the course of the studied industrial MDA realization there was an internal deadline: the profiles were to be finished before developing transformations.

The low priority of the criterion related to integration issues (I6, 5%) is in contradiction to the theoretical analysis, in which the integration issues were indicated as one of the main drawbacks of using different metamodels in the course of model driven software development. From the practical perspective in the company the integration issue is not as important as there is always only one metamodel used at a time in the tool. So the only integration issue is how the new elements are incorporated in the existing metamodel and what the effects of this activity are, which are reflected in criteria I4 and I5 (together 45%).

The names of these industrial criteria seem to be specific for the studied company, but they represent issues that are not specific for Telelogic. Three of the criteria need generalization as presented in Table 2.

Table 2. Generalization of the names of the criteria

Criterion	Telelogic specific name	General name
I1	User expectations	Requirements for customization
I4	Limitations of Tau	Limitations of the tool to support each mechanism
I8	Effort required so that the product is included in the next release	Effort required so that the customization is finished before it is needed

Criterion I1 can be renamed as the requirements for the customization are essentially the user expectations for the extension. Criterion I4 is renamed since it is important to keep in mind that the customization is done in the context of modeling tools (not metamodeling) and these – even though they can be metamodel driven – have some limitations (c.f. [17]). Thus we advocate for making the criterion closer to the original understanding stemming from theoretical difference T3. Criterion I8 can be renamed as the given deadline for the customization of the language in a company is defined by the time in which the customization is to be used in the course of software development (c.f. [18]).

5.2 Quality

The quality of the products is measured as the number of faults reported in the fault database, as presented in Table 3.

Table 3. Normalized number and severities of faults and sizes of the extensions

Severity	**Metamodels**		**Profiles**		
	Activity	Java	Deployment	Interaction overview	Component
1	1	3	1	0	0
2	12	10	0	1	1
3	58	7	2	4	0
4	6	2	1	0	0
5	9	4	0	4	2
6	2	2	0	0	0
Non-classified	3	1	1	2	0
Total number of faults	91	29	5	11	3
Avg. Severity	3.2	3	2.8	3.8	4
Size	21	37	11	7	13

The faults correspond to incompliance with user requirements and erroneous behavior of the products based on the extensions which can be regarded as the measure of quality as defined in [19]. The extensions included which are analyzed in this section are comparable in terms of the implemented functionality (c.f. section 4.2) and therefore analyzed in this paper. The normalized number of faults for the studied extensions are presented in Table 3, grouped according to their severity (1 – catastrophic, 2 – critical, 3 – non-critical, 4 – minor, 5 – suggestion, 6 – question).

In total it seems that the products based on profiles are of better quality (less faults reported in the fault database). We found (and it was confirmed by the interviewees) that the elements potentially contributing to the differences are: (i) high level of reusability that is facilitated by profiles; (ii) technical differences in introducing profiles and changes in the metamodel in the tool. The technical differences in the way the extensions are introduce stem from the fact that when developing a profile certain support is already provided (e.g. adding graphical icons to stereotypes). In the case of metamodel extensions, these mechanisms are not present and therefore, similar functionality (e.g. representing a model element on a diagram) needs to be implemented in the final product. One of the main technical differences

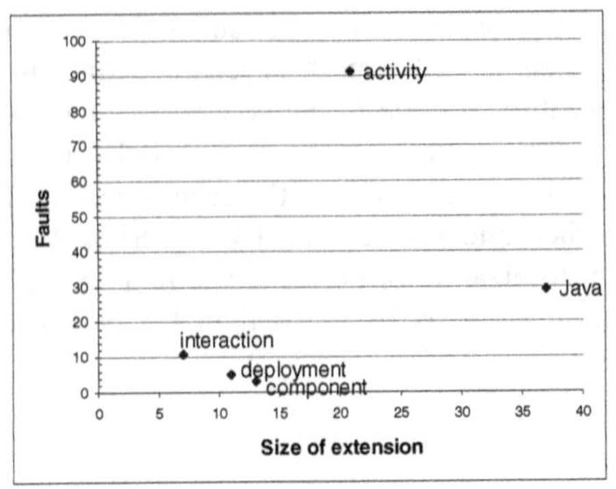

Fig. 2. Scatter plot of size and number of faults

seems to be the way in which the extensions are integrated into the tool. In the interview with the modelers on the process of developing profiles and metamodels it appeared that there are minor differences which do not have an influence on the quality directly. It is the fundamental integration issues that potentially affect the quality. However, the fault data in the fault database does not allow distinguishing whether the fault is caused by the implementation (integration) or by an extension to the metamodel itself (i.e. a modeling error). Although it might be initially perceived as a confounding factor in our study it is not since the additional implementation is expected to be present while customizing a language (as it was the case of Volvo IT [3]). The source code often supports the extensions.

The scatter graph for size and number of faults is shown in Figure 2. It seems that the faults are not related to size (wide spread of the points), for example the largest product – the Java add-in contains fewer faults than the smaller activity diagrams. This in turn indicates that the quality of the product is not dependent on the size of the extension measured as the number of elements in it. This might explain why the size is not considered during the decision process.

Another important aspect in the analysis is the relationship between the size and the average severity, which is shown in Figure 3. The small number of data points (only five products) does not allow calculating the correlations coefficients. Although it would be possible to include several more profiles or metamodel extensions, it was our intention to include only the products which are directly comparable. Furthermore, the lack of visible relationship between the size of the extension and the quality of the products could be caused by: (i) measures of size which are not done with stereotype and metamodel specific metrics (these are part of our current work); (ii) implementation of an additional functionality specific for the product – e.g. support for graphical representation of new model elements in case of metamodel extensions. In order to minimize the threat of drawing conclusions based on descriptive statistics while evaluating a very small set of profiles and metamodel

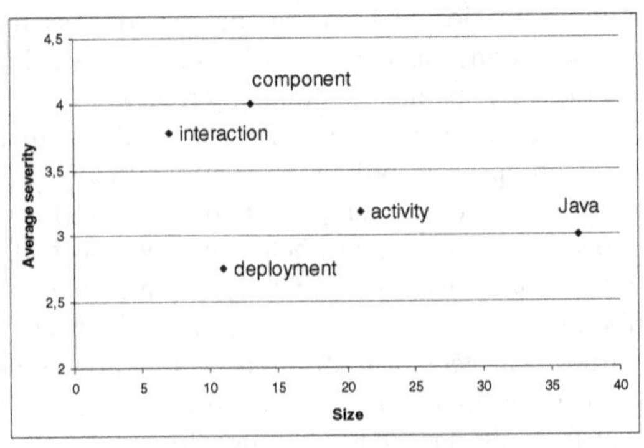

Fig. 3. Scatter plot of size and average severities

extensions our respondents were consulted after the study. Our interpretation of the results is consistent with their expert opinion.

5.3 Effort and Resources

The development effort for creating profiles and metamodel extensions determines the cost of the product and has a potential influence on quality. In the course of the interviews it was found that developing an extension to the metamodel takes approximately three to four weeks depending on the size of the extension and usually involves several engineers (one modeler creating the metamodel extension and several developers integrating the extension with affected components of the tool). The development of a profile takes approximately one week and usually is done by a single modeler. According to the chief architect's experience extending the metamodel requires ten times more effort than developing a profile. This impacts the development effort. In the project (or release) planning phase, the potential influences of the metamodel extension on other components need to be considered.

Table 4. Development time and resources available for developing profiles and metamodel extensions

	Metamodel extension	**Profile**
Development time (calendar time)	3-4 weeks	1 week
Resources available – who can potentially do the work	2 modelers	5 modelers

There is a difference between the metamodels and profiles in terms of resources available for their development. There are five modelers who have the knowledge and expertise to develop profiles although only two of them have enough expertise to fully develop metamodel extensions. The two modelers who develop both profiles and metamodels were interviewed. The remaining three modelers develop very small profiles on irregular basis and thus were not included in the study.

6 Validity Evaluation

In evaluating the validity of the presented study we follow the schema presented in [20], describing four kinds of validity threats to empirical studies.

The main threat to the *external validity* is related to the fact that the company might not be representative for the population of companies in which decisions on the choice between profiles and metamodels are taken. The results can be transferred to other companies customizing their modeling language (e.g. Volvo IT, ABB Robotics); particularly as the case study was performed based on the needs identified in these enterprises. The sizes of products studied in this paper were similar to the sizes of products used in the previous case study (c.f. [3]) which indicates that the objects of this case study are representative not only for Telelogic.

The main *internal validity* threat to the study is there is a risk that while measuring the quality of products the metamodel and the profiles under study were specific and the result is only due to chance factors. To minimize this threat, the most representative sister profiles and metamodel extensions were chosen. All interviewees provided the same estimations of differences in development effort between profiles and metamodel extensions. This similarity increases the validity of their claims.

We have identified a *construct validity* threat. Measuring of the quality can be confounded by the lack of distinction whether the problems reported arise from the modeling issues or the code that accompanies the extensions. Nevertheless, we have found that the accompanying code is often required to introduce changes into the metamodel so the influence of the code on quality is expected to be similar for other metamodel extensions and profiles (even in other companies).

As a *conclusion validity* threat we see the lack of inferential statistics used in the analysis of results caused by a small number of data points even though we have interviewed the whole population of modelers at Telelogic who develop profiles and metamodels in their daily work. The conclusions are similar to observations in our previous case study [3] which increases their validity. The small number of persons involved in the decision process is a representative situation, which was also observed in our previous case study.

7 Conclusions

In the case study presented in the paper we investigated a company with extensive expertise on language customization. The case study was stimulated by the need identified in our previous case studies on issues related to industrial adoption of model-driven software development [3] in which the language customization is a prerequisite for automation of software development. The customizations are the basis for the development of products, which usually are customized modeling tools. In choosing the appropriate mechanism, the criteria should consider the whole products and not only the differences between the mechanisms, which was the case so far. In this case study the identified set of nine criteria for choosing between these mechanisms complement an existing set of theoretically elaborated criteria existing in literature. The criteria allow making the decision in considering two different levels – business and technical. Three industrial criteria at the business level relate to the issues of profitability of using the language customization mechanism (which is crucial in industrial software development). The remaining industrial criteria at the technical level allow assessing whether the chosen extension is technically sound, feasible, and can be the basis of a product.

In addition to identifying the criteria, in the case study the quality of a set of sister products was investigated. The results show that the products based on metamodel extensions usually have more faults and they require up to ten times more effort to develop than profiles. Together with the criteria the quality investigations provide a basis for taking informed decisions on the way in which the modeling practices in enterprises can be improved based on language customization.

During the study we have also observed that the quality of profiles depends on the quality of the base metamodel. If the metamodel is well-suited for the customization at hand, then the profiles are easier to construct. This observation has not been described in the paper, and its further investigation will be done in our upcoming research.

Acknowledgments

We would like to thank Telelogic AB, Sweden for letting us perform the study. We would like to thank Dr. Ludwik Kuzniarz for his valuable comments on the paper.

References

1. Object Management Group: Unified Modeling Language Specification: Infrastructure version 2.0, Object Management Group (2003).
2. Miller, J., Mukerji, J.: MDA Guide, Object Management Group (2003).
3. Staron, M., Kuzniarz, L., Wallin, L.: A Case Study on Industrial MDA Realization - Determinants of Effectiveness, Nordic Journal of Computing **11** (2004) 254-278.
4. Evans, A., Maskeri, G., Sammut, P., Willians, J.S.: Building Families of Languages for Model-Driven System Dev, Workshop in Sw. Model Eng., San Francisco, CA (2003).
5. Centre for Reliable Software Technology: Coral Modeling Framework, CREST (2004).
6. Kleppe, A.G., Warmer, J.B., Bast, W.: MDA explained: the model driven architecture: practice and promise, Addison-Wesley, Boston (2003).
7. Mellor, S.J.: Make models be assets, Communications of the ACM **45** (2002) 76-78.
8. De Miguel, M., Jourdan, J., Salicki, S.: Practical Experiences in the Application of MDA. In: Stevens, P., Whittle, J., Booch, G. (eds.): The 6th Int. Conf. on UML, Vol. 2460, Springer-Verlag (2002) 128-139.
9. Greenfield, J., Short, K.: Software factories: assembling applications with patterns, models, frameworks, and tools, Wiley, Indianapolis, IN, USA (2004).
10. Clark, T., Evans, A., Sammut, P., Willans, J.: Applied Metamodeling - A Foundation for Language Driven Development, Xactium (2004).
11. Schleicher, A., Westfechtel, B.: Beyond stereotyping: metamodeling approaches for the UML. Hawaii Int. Conf. on System Sc., IEEE Comp. Soc, Maui, HI, USA (2001) 10-17.
12. Berner, S., Glinz, M., Joos, S.: A classification of stereotypes for object-oriented modeling languages, 2nd Int. Conf. on UML, Fort Collins, CO, USA (1999) 249-264.
13. Atkinson, C., Kühne, T.: Profiles in a strict metamodeling framework, Science of Comp. Programming **44** (2002) 5-22.
14. Martella, R.C., Nelson, R., Marchand-Martella, N.E.: Research methods: learning to become a critical research consumer, Allyn & Bacon, Boston (1999).
15. Fenton, N.E., Pfleeger, S.L.: Software metrics: a rigorous and practical approach, International Thomson Computer Press, London (1996).
16. Leffingwell, D., Widrig, D.: Managing software requirements: a unified approach, Addison-Wesley, Reading, MA (2000).
17. Alanen, M., Porres, I.: The Coral Modeling Framework, In: Koskimies, K., Kuzniarz, L., Lilius, J., Porres, I. (eds.): 2nd Nordic Workshop on UML, Turku (2004) 93-98.
18. Staron, M., Kuzniarz, L., Wallin, L.: Factors Determining Effective Realization of MDA in Industry, In: Koskimies, K., Kuzniarz , L., Lilius, J., Porres, I. (eds.): 2nd Nordic Workshop on UML, Turku, Finland (2004) 79-91.
19. IEEE: Standard glossary of sw. eng. terminology, Std 610.12-1990, New York (1990) 84.
20. Wohlin, C., Runeson, P., Höst, M., Ohlsson, M.C., Regnell, B., Wesslèn, A.: Experimentation in Sw. Eng.: An Introduction, Kluwer, Boston MA (2000).

Preliminary Results from a Survey of Multimedia Development Practices in Australia

Anne Hannington and Karl Reed

Department of Computer Science and Computer Engineering
La Trobe University, Victoria 3086, Australia
a.hannington@latrobe.edu.au, kreed@cs.latrobe.edu.au

Abstract. In this paper we present our preliminary findings from a survey conducted during 2005 of Australian Multimedia Application Developers. Our objective was to understand what development processes and techniques are used and how these relate to practices cited in the literature. We were also interested in what impact the presence of multimedia content has on the process, as well as the differing skill sets it requires in relation to "traditional" software development. In our findings we report on the process models used and the process tasks most often performed, as a first step to determining what is considered best practice in the industry. We found that developers appear to have a much keener sense of their processes than previous studies have suggested.

1 Introduction

The Australian Multimedia Industry is a major developer of "software-like" products, ranging from multimedia CDs and DVDs, to online applications. A fundamental characteristic that differentiates product creation from conventional software development is the inclusion of various combinations of visual media and audio, often providing an interactive experience for users. While these may include significant amounts of "traditional" software the presence of media content requires additional tasks and differing skills to those in conventional software development [1, 2]. To gather information on multimedia development a survey of industrial multimedia practice was undertaken. Our objective was to gain an understanding of the current state of practice and its relationship to multimedia and "traditional" software development practices cited in the literature.

Earlier surveys into multimedia application development have described the approach to design, and as a result the development processes undertaken, as inconsistent [3]. They have also commented on the apparent use of design techniques based in software development being used to capture multimedia design, particularly by those who are crossing over into the industry from "non-multimedia" software development [4]. Further, they show that techniques from film and video production, such as the use of storyboards, scripts and mock-ups are also being used, even when these too can be ineffective in capturing critical aspects, such as interaction [4].

These observations have been attributed to factors such as the diversity of developer backgrounds, the newness of the discipline, and the limited industrial

J. Münch and M. Vierimaa (Eds.): PROFES 2006, LNCS 4034, pp. 192–207, 2006.

take-up of specifically designed techniques from academia [3, 4]. However, the impact of these factors on actual development processes and outcomes has yet to be established.

The survey questionnaire was targeted at tying together the factors impacting multimedia processes, to allow us to establish which parameters influenced developers' decisions to follow certain processes, employ particular techniques, and use particular tools. By doing this we hope to identify "best practice", and guide our research in the direction of industry needs. Due to space limitations, we focus here on respondents' profiles, team skills, process models/methods and process tasks.

The following section describes our survey method and the profile of our resulting sample. In Section 3 we discuss the preliminary results of our data analysis, in Section 4 we discuss implications for our work on a multimedia process framework, and in Section 5 we discuss our findings and areas for further work.

2 Survey Instrument and Method

Based on our review of previous studies and processes described in the literature [5-7], we constructed a list of survey goals and questions. We applied a GQM [8] style approach to assess the fitness of our questions to the realisation of our goals. Once we had mapped questions to goals, we assessed a question's capability of providing us with the data we required by looking at the statements we wished to make using the data collected, i.e. technique *x* is being used to model *y*. The resulting survey instrument was organised into the following sections: Company Profile, Team Profile, Development Process, Treatment of Content, Design Techniques, Authoring Tools, and Project Management. The pilot survey had a further section that asked for feedback on the survey instrument, to try and identify likely problems before the survey was distributed to a larger sample.

To facilitate responses and assist in keeping consistent terminology amongst respondents, closed questions were used where possible. However, where applicable the opportunity to give an alternate response by use of an "other" option was also provided. In addition, open-ended questions were used to help elicit reasons for particular responses.

2.1 Pilot Survey

During 2004 we conducted a pilot study to assess the suitability of our survey instrument. The study involved three companies obtained using convenience sampling [9]. To determine the applicability of our response options and terminology each company represented one of our target domains: educational systems, business communication systems, and games.

2.2 Survey Sample

Prospective participants for the survey were initially selected from company listings publicly available via the VicIT Web Directory [10], and the Australian Interactive Media Industry Association (AIMIA) member listing [11].

The VicIT directory is a self-serve web site established by Multimedia Victoria, a government body responsible for the maintenance and expansion of the information and communications technology industry in Victoria [12].

AIMIA is a national industry body that represents the Interactive Media and Digital Content sectors in Australia. It is focused on the commercial development of its members, and the industry as a whole, through the provision of a wide range of services and events [13].

To determine the target population for the survey, suitable inclusion and exclusion criteria were established, as not all companies listed in these directories were involved in the development of multimedia applications. A detailed discussion is beyond the scope of this paper. Companies identified to be developing multimedia applications based on the information they provided were included, as were companies/individuals where it was unclear, to avoid biasing the sample.

Due to the well-known difficulty of obtaining appropriate response rates (to be discussed in section 3) the survey was sent to all members of the target population. The main reason for this was while the AIMIA sample was derived from a membership listing where membership is renewed annually, the VicIT sample was derived from a database that has been in operation since 2001. It was therefore not known how many of the businesses listed had up-to-date profiles or were still in operation.

Four other individuals (two from the same team) working in the eLearning sector were included, and two others requested the survey after seeing the publicity on the AIMIA web site.

2.3 Survey Distribution

Table 1 shows details of the distribution of the survey to the two sample groups. In an effort to improve the response rate an advance notice was sent via email.

Members of the VicIT sample were sent the survey in both an electronic format (by email) and a paper-copy by regular mail. Members of the AIMIA sample were sent the survey by email only. This was done as there was concern about people's preferred method of response.

Of the actual surveys sent 37 were returned "unknown at this address" from the VicIT mail-out, and a number of the emailed surveys "bounced". Further to this, responses were also received indicating when the company was no longer in business, did not develop multimedia, or was no longer developing multimedia. Some people advised they were too busy to complete the survey; others simply declined participation.

Three reminders notices were sent, the first to all those who had not yet responded, the next two to those who had indicated a willingness to respond.

Table 1. Target sample

	Sample Group	
	AIMIA	vicIT
Original target sample size	223	430
Badly formed or no email address	2	4
Number of advance notices sent	221	426
Number of advance notices undeliverable	8	80
Declined participation from advance notice	0	4
Actual surveys sent	213	342

3 Results and Analysis

We received responses from 40 companies. Of these, 5 have been excluded from this discussion as they either did not fit the multimedia application developer profile, or did not provide enough information. The remaining 35 companies have their main operations based in 4 states: Queensland (5.7%), New South Wales (22.9%), Tasmania (2.9%) and Victoria (65.7%). One company's main operations are split between New South Wales and Victoria. 94.3% of these companies are 100% Australian owned, while one is 50% Australian owned, and the other had no Australian ownership.

Our low response rate is consistent with the experiences of others [4, 14], however our number of respondents compares favourably to those used in other studies of the multimedia industry [1, 3, 4, 15, 16]. In addition, the experience base of the respondents is also encouraging with 90.6% of companies ($n = 32$) more than 5 years old.

3.1 Respondents' Development Profile

To obtain a picture of the impact application domain has on processes and techniques used by developers, we asked respondents to indicate the percentage of their total production in each domain. Five broad domains were given, the first four adapted from [17]: Multimedia Business Systems, Multimedia Education Systems, Multimedia Entertainment Systems, Multimedia Communication Systems and Multimedia Application Development Tools. While Multimedia Application Development Tools are not strictly multimedia development, we were interested in whether there were any tool developers in the sample. The option of specifying additional categories through the use of *other* was also provided. Within the first four domains sub-domains were listed. These are shown in Table 2.

The majority of respondents were involved to varying degrees in developing applications within the Multimedia Business Systems or Multimedia Education Systems categories, with Multimedia Communication Systems also well represented. No respondents were primarily games producers. Given the detailed response received from the games company included in our pilot this was unfortunate. Only three companies were not involved solely in multimedia development.

Within the multimedia business domain those who used the *other* option cited non-specific "applications" and "websites". One respondent specified "ecommerce" web sites with marketing/advertising - a hybrid of options offered.

Multimedia education developers reported producing custom packages for specific sections of the market, "interactive learning objects", "mobile learning", and "online learning" (which may be used for distance learning). In addition, utilities such as "document database repositories" and "learning management systems" were also developed. "New media art" was specified in *other* for Multimedia Communication Systems, as was "instant messaging", "broadcast television", "public websites", "facilitating/managing weblogs", and "e-Newsletters and e-Calenders".

Other areas included "interactive documentaries", "knowledge management systems", and "corporate" and "community" web sites.

Multimedia application development tools being produced included: "professional development tools for accessibility and usability", and tools to assist web site development, content management, and authoring of online learning.

Table 2. Percentage of respondents' development within each domain/sub domain, $n = 35$

Application Development Domain			Percentage Level of Production in each Domain					
			0.5 - 20%		21 - 40%	41 - 60%	61 - 80%	81 - 100%
			0.5 - 10%	11 - 20%				
Multimedia Business Systems (MBS)	Sub-domain	Electronic Commerce	25.7%	2.9%	0.0%	0.0%	0.0%	2.9%
		Online Shopping	20.0%	5.7%	0.0%	2.9%	0.0%	0.0%
		Marketing/Advertising	5.7%	8.6%	8.6%	5.7%	5.7%	2.9%
		Intranet	17.1%	5.7%	0.0%	0.0%	0.0%	0.0%
		MBS Other	2.9%	0.0%	5.7%	0.0%	0.0%	0.0%
Multimedia Education Systems (MEduS)	Sub-domain	Corporate Training	8.6%	8.6%	0.0%	5.7%	5.7%	0.0%
		Automated Assessment	14.3%	0.0%	0.0%	0.0%	0.0%	0.0%
		Distance Learning	11.4%	0.0%	0.0%	0.0%	0.0%	0.0%
		Instruction Manuals	8.6%	0.0%	0.0%	0.0%	0.0%	0.0%
		Simulation Systems	8.6%	0.0%	2.9%	0.0%	0.0%	0.0%
		Training Manuals	11.4%	2.9%	2.9%	0.0%	0.0%	0.0%
		General Education Packages	14.3%	5.7%	2.9%	0.0%	2.9%	5.7%
		MEduS Other	2.9%	5.7%	5.7%	0.0%	2.9%	5.7%
Multimedia Entertainment Systems MEntS)	Sub-domain	Infotainment	0.0%	5.7%	2.9%	0.0%	2.9%	0.0%
		Games	8.6%	5.7%	0.0%	0.0%	0.0%	0.0%
		MEntS Other	0.0%	0.0%	0.0%	0.0%	0.0%	0.0%
Multimedia Communication Systems (MCS)	Sub-domain	Chat Systems	8.6%	0.0%	0.0%	0.0%	0.0%	0.0%
		Bulletin Boards	17.1%	0.0%	0.0%	0.0%	0.0%	0.0%
		Presentations	14.3%	2.9%	0.0%	0.0%	0.0%	0.0%
		Teleservices	0.0%	0.0%	0.0%	0.0%	0.0%	0.0%
		Videoconferencing	2.9%	0.0%	0.0%	0.0%	2.9%	0.0%
		MCS Other	5.7%	2.9%	0.0%	0.0%	2.9%	2.9%
Multimedia Application Development Tools			2.9%	2.9%	0.0%	0.0%	0.0%	5.7%
Other			0.0%	0.0%	2.9%	5.7%	0.0%	2.9%

Few developers specialised in one domain. This is not surprising as the domains are not mutually exclusive, especially with regard to Communication Systems, where applications such as Chat Systems and Bulletin Boards may also feature in education applications. Another reason may be the need to meet changing markets.

Mediums and Platforms. Most companies used more than one delivery medium for application distribution. The most common was the Internet (80.0% of companies), followed by CD ROM (68.6%). Companies also used multiple delivery platforms, the most common being the PC (97.1% of companies) and Macintosh (60.0%). Interestingly 22.9% of companies were building applications for hand-held devices.

For 68.6% of respondents, the development and delivery platforms were the same. However, the use of Macintoshes in development (due to their graphics capability) with final applications running on or accessed by PCs was also reported.

Project Output. Table 3 shows the number of projects that were completed by companies from 2002 – 2004 (n = 30, as two companies did not answer this question, one responded for only one year of business, and the other two had not been in business for the full three years and so were omitted to allow any trends to be observed). This historical data indicates a consistent growth in the volume of company output over the 3 years, as shown by decreases in the *Less than 5* category coupled with compensating increases across the remaining categories.

Table 3. Number of projects completed by companies 2002 - 2004, n = 30

	Year		
No. of projects	2004	2003	2002
Less than 5	26.7%	33.3%	43.3%
6 – 10	26.7%	30.0%	20.0%
11 – 15	13.3%	10.0%	13.3%
16 – 20	6.7%	6.7%	3.3%
21 – 25	6.7%	3.3%	3.3%
More than 25	20.0%	16.7%	16.7%

86.7% of companies reported 90% or more of their projects were adopted in 2004, with 90% reporting in the same year that less than 10% were cancelled before completion (note that we neglected to include a 0% option). This paints the picture of a very successful sample. As one respondent put it, "I don't build shelf-ware". However, given our small sample size we can not determine whether this is an industry-wide characteristic. Companies may have been reluctant to report their failures, as respondents who indicated projects had been cancelled were usually part of a larger company where projects were initiated internally.

3.2 Team Profile

All respondents reported average team sizes of ten or less members, with 68.6% having five or less. This is consistent with the findings of Britton [15].

Skills and Roles. We asked respondents about the skill background of their team members, the roles they filled and the roles filled by temporary staff. To determine the skill background we provided a list of skills, each skill with its own code, and asked respondents to indicate which skills each member of their team possessed. The number of skills of each staff member varied in the range of 1 – 20, with a median of 1. Smaller project teams required members to utilise more of their skills. Some respondents included temporary staff in describing the skills of their development team while others did not. For a company to include the skills of a temporary staff member in their response to this question we reasoned that this could be a skill they require in most of their projects, and so hire someone to fill, though it may not always be the same person. Therefore in our preliminary analysis we included these cases when we looked at the number of companies who had at least one person with a particular skill. This is shown in Figure 1.

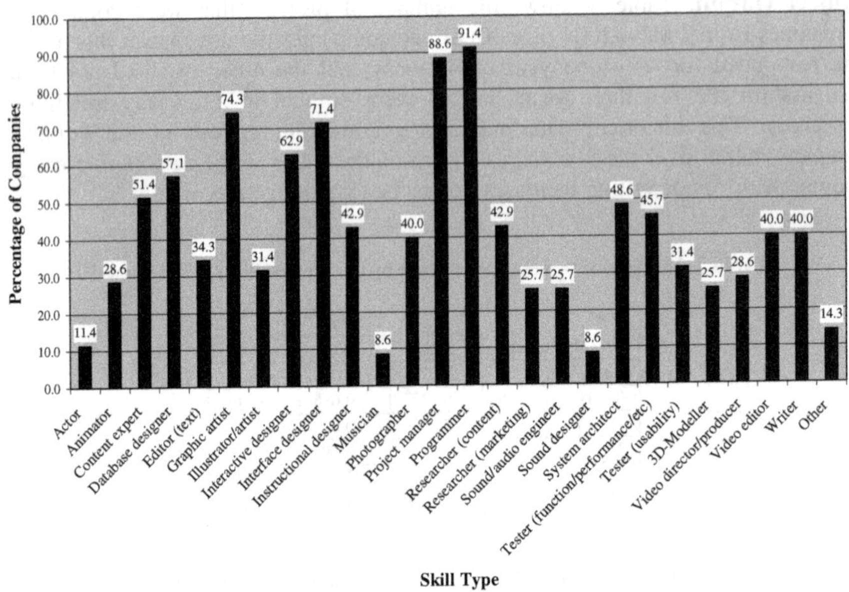

Fig. 1. Percentage of companies employing at least one person with a particular skill, $n = 35$

As can be seen from Figure 1 the five most common skills are those of programmer, project manager, graphic artist, interface designer and interactive designer. This ranking mapped to those skills considered by respondents as essential to multimedia development teams with 68.6% of respondents considering programming skills essential followed by project management and graphic artist (62.9%), interface design (51.4%) and interactive design (37.1%). This shows an increase in recognition of interface and interactive design skills when compared to [15]. Instructional design was also listed by 37.1% reflecting the slightly higher portion of respondents specialising in educational titles. Team skill composition may of course vary depending on the requirements of each project. Further analysis will look at the matching of skills to roles and vice-versa.

Temporary staff mainly filled the roles of Content Expert (25.7% of companies), Usability Tester (25.7%), Actor (22.9%), Photographer (22.9%), Sound/Audio Engineer (22.9%) and Functional and Performance Tester (22.9%). The bringing in of testers from outside aligns with good practice recognised in "traditional" software development [7]. Content experts may be expected to change from project to project as the content changes. Actors, Photographers and Sound/Audio Engineers could also be expected to be used on an as-needed basis, especially within this sample as audio and video were reportedly less used (see section 3.3).

3.3 Development Process

Respondents were given a list of process models/methods and asked to select those that best described their organization's development approach on a typical project.

Table 4 shows the percentage of respondents using the models listed either alone or in combination. There were 33 (94.3%) valid responses to this question and two invalid. One (2.9%) of these was not familiar with the concepts presented. This is to be expected given the differing backgrounds of multimedia developers. However, this outcome indicates a reasonable level of familiarity with these concepts. By way of contrast a survey of "traditional" software developers [18] found 9.5% were not familiar with the concept of software development methodologies. Our higher perceived familiarity may, however, have been achieved by the provision of a list of options.

Most companies include some kind of prototyping in their development process, with many classifying their process as in-house proprietary. This is consistent with the findings of Barry and Lang [4]. As commented by one respondent there is substantial crossover in this area. While nearly 50% of respondents used only one model, the other 50% used from 2 (12.1%) to 7 (6.1%). Combinations for two models included: prototyping and iterative, iterative and component-based, and prototyping and in-house. The first is fairly intuitive as prototyping by its nature may lead to iterative development. The combination of prototyping and in-house gives some insight into the nature of the proprietary method. Table 5 shows all the combinations cited.

The reports of combinations involving some form of Waterfall model and Agile process appear contradictory, particularly with regard to the difference in the level of documentation they prescribe. The pairing is less surprising from the view that Royce's original model included both prototyping and iteration [19]. However, as this is not the common interpretation it could be due to the users' associating it with a clear delineation of phases, and therefore using it to assist project management [4]. Another view is that the responses may not all be for a typical project but instead represent the range of processes used for different kinds of projects.

Amongst single method/model users (n = 16) an In-house Proprietary method was most common (37.5%) followed by Prototyping (25.0%), Iterative (12.5%), Other (12.5%), Agile – Feature Driven Development (6.25%) and Component Based

Table 4. Process models/methods used in multimedia development, n = 33

Process Model/Method	Percentage of affirmative responses
Prototyping Model	45.5%
Iterative Model	39.4%
In-house Proprietary	39.4%
Component Based Model	27.3%
Concurrent Development Model	18.2%
Incremental Model	15.2%
Waterfall Model	12.1%
Agile Process (other than XP)	12.1%
Waterfall Model (with prototyping)	9.1%
Other	9.1%
RAD Model	6.1%
Unified Process Model	3.0%
Extreme Programming (XP)	3.0%
Spiral Model	0.0%

(6.25%). Examination of the tasks performed by those using an in-house method (n = 6) shows that on most or all of their projects 83% build a structural prototype and 67% create a prototype to achieve an early visualisation. Whether these prototypes are just throwaway (as may be expected in the case of the early visualisation) or evolve into the final system is unclear.

One respondent commented that the client's processes are often adopted. Another noted that due to projects mainly being simple Internet sites extensive project management was not required. Overall 93.9% of respondents tailored the method(s)/model(s) used to meet individual project needs, however only 53.1% of these stated that they kept a record of their tailored process.

Table 5. Process model/method combinations reported where two or more used, n = 17

Company	Waterfall	Waterfall (with prototyping)	Prototyping	Incremental	Iterative	RAD	Unufued Process Model	Componet Based	Concurrent	Extreme Programming (XP)	Agile Process (other than XP)	In-house Proprietary	Other
c1			■									■	
c2			■		■								
c3		■			■						■		■
c4	■	■	■		■		■				■		
c5			■		■								
c6				■					■			■	
c7	■	■	■		■				■				
c8	■			■				■	■				
c9	■			■	■								
c10			■		■	■							
c11			■					■				■	
c12			■		■			■	■	■	■	■	
c13				■				■				■	
c14			■	■	■	■		■	■			■	
c15			■		■			■					
c16					■			■					
c17			■					■	■			■	

Process Tasks. Responses were sought on actual tasks performed to provide more detail on processes used and inform our work on a multimedia process framework. In addition, developers' varying backgrounds may have meant they were not familiar with the software engineering process models listed, so this provided a way of still capturing process information. The list of tasks was derived from the multimedia and software development literature [5-7]. We asked respondents to indicate whether they performed these tasks in the development of every, most, half, few, or none of their projects. The tasks were assigned to the following phases of development adapted from [6]:

1. *Concept and Planning* – determines the feasibility of the project, outlining required product functionality and development resources
2. *Design and Prototype* – outlines the structural, behavioural and media design
3. *Production* – results in the production of all required media and their integration
4. *Application Testing* – tests the application works correctly
5. *Distribution* – sees the product delivered to the client or end-users
6. *Maintenance* – deals with correcting post-delivery errors, and assessing/ maintaining the product's performance/viability to provide feedback to new versions until the product is retired

Table 6 shows the tasks performed by 75% or more companies, in order of ranking, on at least half of their projects. As a comparison the far right column shows the percentage of companies who perform these tasks on every project.

Tasks related to scoping a project ranked highest as a group. This may be because these tasks are common across all projects regardless of domain or process model used, as establishing a project's purpose and delivery mechanisms are inherent in assessing its feasibility. It may also be due to the high task granularity with which the "Approach Exploration" activity was represented. The top two tasks performed on half or more of projects, *Determine software (functional) requirements* (97% of companies) and *Function Testing* (94%) compare to tasks considered good practice in Software Engineering. Interestingly, 86% created a requirement specification document and 80% had the client sign off on this document. User interface screens were also used to "sign-off" requirements. Over 90% of respondents reported that determining content and structuring content were tasks performed on half or more of their projects.

Graphics production appears highest of all media production, as, aside from text, this is the most common media used by our sample. All companies that responded to this question (n = 31) use text in their applications to varying degrees. 93.5% of companies used graphics, with 41.9% using graphics in 21 – 30% of their applications. 83.9% of companies had animation in applications they produced, with 45.2% of companies using it in 6 – 10% of their products. Audio and video were included in applications developed by 74.2% and 77.4% of respondents respectively; however the majority used these media in less than 10% of their total production. While in a creative sense the choice of media used is based on its ability to convey or support the idea presented, distribution medium also plays a large part. Reasons cited for the limited use of video related to bandwidth - as noted earlier the majority of distribution was online. Audio was mainly used by those developing musical instrument instruction, or eLearning with full voice-over for the text.

We asked respondents if there were any tasks that they considered important to development, yet rarely undertook and the reasons for this. Responses included: application testing, due to limited resources; documentation and evaluation of the project, due to being too busy seeking or undertaking the next project; archiving for reuse; and prototyping, due to lack of time and budget. While the responses indicate prototyping is incorporated into most development processes, knowledge of the extent of its use and nature would be valuable. Fully rendering graphics etc. for an early visualisation, for example, would be a waste of resources if the client changed their mind. This will be further investigated when we incorporate our findings on the use of design techniques (in this instance wire-frames).

Table 6. Tasks performed on half or more projects by at least 75% of companies, $n = 35$. Also shown is the percentage of companies that perform these tasks on all projects.

Task	Phase	Percentage of companies performing task on half or more projects	Percentage of companies performing task on all projects
Determine software (functional) requirements	Concept and Planning	97	77
Function testing	Application Testing	94	66
Establish the project's intended audience	Concept and Planning	94	80
Determine delivery platform	Concept and Planning	94	77
Determine content	Concept and Planning	94	69
Function testing (Design and Prototype)	Design and Prototype	94	66
Establish the project's purpose in terms of its resulting benefits	Concept and Planning	91	71
Establish the project's themes and major points	Concept and Planning	91	71
Determine delivery medium	Concept and Planning	91	83
Determine level of interactivity	Concept and Planning	91	60
Structure content	Design and Prototype	91	60
Interface/Screen design	Design and Prototype	91	74
Determine hardware requirements	Concept and Planning	89	54
Determine content source	Concept and Planning	89	63
Interactivity design	Design and Prototype	89	63
Navigation design	Design and Prototype	89	69
Test the delivery medium	Design and Prototype	89	71
Determine development platform	Concept and Planning	86	66
Determine non-functional system requirements (security, accuracy, speed, reliability…)	Concept and Planning	86	51
Create proposal	Concept and Planning	86	54
Create requirement specification	Concept and Planning	86	43
Establish legal (content ownership) issues	Concept and Planning	83	57
Have client sign-off on proposal/requirement specification	Concept and Planning	83	60
Maintenance	Maintenance	83	29
Usability testing (interface and navigation)	Application Testing	80	57
Content testing	Application Testing	80	43
Graphics design	Design and Prototype	80	51
Establish content (asset) naming conventions	Design and Prototype	80	51
Have client sign-off on design document	Design and Prototype	80	51
Final Sign-off	Distribution	80	66
Support	Maintenance	80	40
Establish naming conventions (Production)	Production	80	51
Graphics production	Production	80	60
Performance testing	Application Testing	77	40
Create an early visualisation (prototype)	Concept and Planning	77	31
Integrate working content with structural design	Design and Prototype	77	46
Evaluate design with respect to objectives	Design and Prototype	77	51
Archive budget and planning information	Distribution	77	63

The necessity and yet difficulty of establishing a project's purpose and benefits was noted by one respondent, as clients are at times unable or unwilling to justify a business case. In one case it was reported that the graphic design was signed-off as the design document. While the respondent noted it would be useful on occasion to write-up the design rationale, they find that the client "rarely, if ever, reads the documentation – particularly documentation that could be described as "optional"".

Respondents were also asked if they performed any tasks in phases other than in those specified. Understandably, a few cited testing as occurring throughout development rather than in a dedicated phase. One respondent reported a process similar to that described in [20] for computer assisted learning, where their instructional designers get the project first, specify the structure, content frame and assessment strategies, then further refine with graphic designers and programmers.

Comparing the highly ranked tasks performed in all domains combined to those for business and education showed little deviation from Table 6. Notable additions for education included content archiving and text production, while the only addition for business was the archiving of formal documents (requirements, design, test, code etc).

When asked what percentage of total development time was usually spent within each development phase the most common responses were: 11 – 20% of their time on *Concept and Planning* (55.9% of companies, n = 34); 11 – 20% on *Design and Prototype* (38.2%); 41 – 50% on *Production* (32.4%); 6 – 10% on *Application Testing* (52.9%); 1 – 5% on *Distribution* (47.1%); and 1 – 5% on *Maintenance* (44.1%). It is not surprising that most time is spent in production given the fuzzy distinction between it and design due to the role content plays in the need for an early visualisation.

Impact of Content on the Development Process. As the presence of content makes it important to provide the client with an example of the "look and feel" of the application, especially when the client is new, we asked what was the earliest phase in which media design would begin. 40.6% (n = 32) indicated media design could start in the *Concept and Planning* phase, illustrating the overlap of tasks between the phases, while 34.4% indicated it might not start until the *Design and Prototype* phase. One respondent stated that while the media design didn't begin until *Design and Prototype* the design concepts were still referred to in *Concept and Planning* as outlines or abstracts. Another stated that during planning they would draft ideas and sketches, and depending on the bid, prototype a sample. Other respondents stated a particular milestone as the trigger for media design such as: a complete specification that allows the basic site structure to be implemented; approval of the interface design concepts; and the provision of the basic content (instructional and information architecture and basic flowcharts).

The majority of respondents indicated *Design and Prototype* as the earliest phase in which media production would begin (41.9%, n = 31), with *Production* (25.8%) and *Concept and Planning* (9.7%). Other responses included: "once everything (content particularly) has been locked down", "early in the project to give authors visual feedback on ideas developed, [to] better evaluate the methods", "after interface design concepts have been approved", and "after programming". The need to prototype before production to get clients "excited" about what can be done for them, as well as to assess technical risks (e.g. 3D animations running on minimum spec PCs) was reported. The comment was also made that while "routine media production will occur as required", "look and feel (i.e. interface design) will be the first step in the production phase, as all the rest must follow style and colour guides".

4 Implications for a Multimedia Process Framework

Considering the majority of projects were delivered via the internet, we compared multimedia specific tasks in Table 6 to those defined in the Web OPEN framework [21], an extension of the OPEN framework [22].

Table 7. Compatibility of multimedia specific tasks identified as common practice in our respondent sample with Web OPEN tasks

Multimedia Tasks from Survey	Web OPEN Task/ [Fitness (0-3)]	Comments
Determine Content	- [0]	Requirements level. Web OPEN's *Create Content (on website)* appears more design/production oriented.
Determine Level of Interactivity	- [0]	-
Create an early visualisation (prototype)	Build White Site [2]	Our task focus is more visual than structural, and may also be used in offline projects.
Structure Content	Create Content (on website) [2]	-
Interface/Screen Design	Design User Interface (OPEN Task) [3]	While not multimedia specific, this task is extremely important to multimedia development.
Interactivity Design	- [0]	-
Navigation Design	Create Navigation Map for Website[3]	While not multimedia specific, this task is extremely important to multimedia development.
Integrate working content with structural design	Prototype the Human Interface / Build White Site [2.5]	"Working" content refers to content that may not yet be complete and is being used to assist in a structural prototype
Graphics Design	Create Content (on website) [1]	The Web OPEN task is seemingly not granular enough to capture the design of specific media.
Graphic Production	As above	As above for "production"

Based on our findings in Table 7, we suggest that a framework to support multimedia development (online and offline) should also include the tasks: *Determine Content*, *Determine Level of Interactivity*, *Interactivity Design*, *Graphic Design* and *Graphic Production*. Individual design and production tasks should also exist for media other than graphics, in order to provide an appropriate level of detail for management of the differing technical considerations and resources.

The important Web OPEN task *Integrate Content with User Interface* [21] was split between *Integrate Using Programming Language* and *Integrate Using Authoring Package* in our study, hence these tasks did not appear in Table 6. Future work will ascertain which tasks can and are being performed at the expense of one another and explore common task combinations.

5 Conclusion

This paper presents the preliminary analysis of the profile, skill and process data collected on multimedia development practices in Australia. While the response was small and therefore cannot be considered representative of a national industry, the results do provide useful insights into the nature of current practices. As noted earlier, small responses seem to be common in such studies [1, 3, 4, 15, 16].

Our responses suggest an industry were development occurs predominantly by teams of less than 10 members, with relatively high success rates in terms of product adoption compared to those traditionally cited for conventional software development [23]. While, due to our response size, we cannot confidently generalise these findings to the industry as a whole, our finding relating to team size is in line with the findings in the AIMIA Survey relating to the number of staff employed by companies [24]. The high success rate reported by respondents may be due to them belonging to a more successful cohort within the sample, and hence being more willing to respond. However, there are suggestions that even within conventional software development success rates may be better than is widely acknowledged [23].

A significant factor in terms of project success may be the relatively small size of multimedia projects. These averaged about 560 person hours (about 0.3 person years), with projects in the range 100 to 500 person hours predominating ($n = 27$).

With regard to the development process our analysis shows use of a variety of models that are predominantly iterative and incremental in nature. Prototyping (both of structure and visuals) plays a major role, as would be considered inherent in the visual and interactive nature of the work.

The differing skills and tasks required for multimedia development compared to conventional software development were recognised, and the implications for a multimedia process framework introduced. Further investigation of the relationship between skills, roles and specialisation will be particularly interesting, since the specialist tasks from outside the "software" development domain require what might be called "artistic" skills and illustrate the need to further explore the impact of creative processes. These considerations will provide a basis for our future work on design and project management techniques, and tools used, to determine how these influence process. Coupled with the impact of multimedia domain this should identify common development practices and lead to a tailorable multimedia process model.

Acknowledgements

The authors would like to thank AIMIA for endorsing the survey and kindly promoting it in their newsletter and on their website. We would also like to thank Neela Khan from the Faculty of Life and Social Sciences, Swinburne University, for her assistance, and the reviewers for their comments. Most importantly, many thanks go to all those who gave of their time to respond to the survey.

References

1. MacDonell, S.G., Fletcher, T., and Wong, B.L.W.: Industry Practices in Project Management for Multimedia Information Systems. In: International Journal of Software Engineering and Knowledge Engineering, Vol. 9(6). World Scientific Publishing Company (1999) 801-815
2. Hannington, A. and Reed, K.: Towards a Taxonomy for Guiding Multimedia Application Development. In: Ninth Asia-Pacific Software Engineering Conference. IEEE (2002) 97-106
3. Augusteyn, D., Gunn, K., and Leung, Y.K.: Formalised Approaches for Multimedia Design - Are they being used by Australian Designers? In: 3rd Asia Pacific Computer Human Interaction. IEEE (1998) 279-284
4. Barry, C. and Lang, M.: A Survey of Multimedia and Web Development Techniques and Methodology Usage. In: IEEE Multimedia, Vol. 8(2). IEEE (2001) 52-60
5. England, E. and Finney, A.: Managing Multimedia - Project Management for Web and Convergent Media, Book 1 - People and Processes. Addison-Wesley, London (2002)
6. Multimedia Demystified: A Guide to the World of Multimedia from Apple Computer, Inc., Apple-new media series. Random House, New York (1994)
7. Pfleeger, S.L.: Software Engineering: Theory and Practice. Prentice-Hall, Inc., NJ (2001)
8. Basili, V.R. and Weiss, D.M.: A Methodology for Collecting Valid Software Engineering Data. In: IEEE Transactions on Software Engineering, Vol. 10(6). IEEE (1984) 728-738
9. Fink, A.: How to Sample in Surveys. 2nd ed, The Survey Kit, Vol. 7. Sage Publications, Inc. (2003)
10. Multimedia Victoria: Find - IT Companies. Accessed January 2005 from www.vicit.com.au
11. AIMIA: AIMIA - Member Listing. Accessed January 2005 from www.aimia.com.au
12. Multimedia Victoria: About Multimedia Victoria. Accessed 3 March 2005 from www.mmv.vic.gov.au
13. AIMIA: AIMIA - About Us. Accessed 28 September 2005 from www.aimia.com.au
14. Ng, S.P., et al.: A Preliminary Survey on Software Testing Practices in Australia. In: Australian Software Engineering Conference 2004. IEEE (2004) 116-127
15. Britton, C., et al.: A survey of current practice in the development of multimedia systems. In: Information and Software Technology, Vol. 39. Elsevier (1997) 695-705
16. Bailey, B.P., Konstan, J.A., and Carlis, J.V.: DEMAIS: Designing Multimedia Applications with Interactive Storyboards. In: Multimedia Modeling 2001. ACM (2001) 241-250
17. Gonzalez, R.: Disciplining Multimedia. In: IEEE Multimedia, Vol. 7(3). (2000) 72-78
18. Verner, J.M. and Cerpa, N.: Australian Software Development: What Software Project Management Practices Lead to Success? In: Australian Software Engineering Conference 2005. IEEE (2005) 70-77
19. Royce, W.W.: Managing the Development of Large Software Systems. In: IEEE WESCON. IEEE (1970) 1-9
20. Kopka, C. and Wellen, U.: Role-based Views to Approach Suitable Software Process Models for the Development of Multimedia Systems. In: IEEE Fourth International Symposium on Multimedia Software Engineering. IEEE (2002) 140-147
21. Haire, B., Henderson-Sellers, B., and Lowe, D.: Supporting Web Development in the OPEN Process: Additional Tasks. In: Proceedings of the 25th Annual International Computer Software and Applications Conference. IEEE (2001) 383-389

22. Firesmith, D.G. and Henderson-Sellers, B.: The OPEN Process Framework - An Introduction. Addison-Wesley (2002)
23. 23. Glass, R.L.: IT Failure Rates - 70% or 10-15%. In: IEEE Software, Vol. 22(3). IEEE (2005) 112, 110-111
24. 24. AIMIA: AIMIA Digital Content Industry Survey. Accessed 23 February 2006 from www.aimia.com.au/dcis

An ISO 9001:2000 Certificate and Quality Awards from Outside – What's Inside? – A Case Study

Darja Šmite[1] and Nils Brede Moe[2]

[1] Riga Information Technology Institute
Darja.Smite@riti.lv
[2] SINTEF ICT
Nils.B.Moe@sintef.no

Abstract. In order to survive in a strong competition software houses need to design high-quality software. To achieve this some companies try to certify their software development processes in accordance with well-known industrial standards. Through a case study we investigated what characterizes the use of a quality system among developers and project managers in a large software company that has successfully achieved an ISO 9001:2000 certification. We found that certification not always indicates that the company successfully uses the practices in accordance with quality standards. This caused serious problems, such as projects that follow outdated practices, project managers faking quality documentation before audits, resources wasted by producing documents no one needs, problems created for new employees since they cannot find descriptions of the processes people are working in accordance with, and an expensive system no one uses.

1 Introduction

Along with global market expansion, competition among software development organizations has been growing. Reduction of costs has for a long time been the leading driver when selecting a subcontractor or outsourcing provider (subcontracting parts or whole software development), but lately productivity and quality indicators have become essential when choosing suppliers [9, 18]. Implementing a quality system based on the ISO model [5] or a maturity model, is nowadays one of the most common approaches in achieving the above mentioned objectives.

Quality certificates are meant to give buyers of goods and services an impression of the quality of the suppliers. Therefore many companies are eager to obtain a quality certificate because of market pressure. In Europe, the ISO 9001 set of quality standards are widely used standards for quality management in software development, and the Capability Maturity Model® Integration (CMMI) [17] is one of the common standards in the USA.

Getting the certificate often means that a minimum set of procedures and quality handbooks are developed in the company without a quality system really being implemented or quality awareness being created among the employees. In such cases, the possession of certificates does not guarantee the quality of the software production process or a reasonable price performance ratio for the products delivered to the client [21].

J. Münch and M. Vierimaa (Eds.): PROFES 2006, LNCS 4034, pp. 208 – 221, 2006.

Moreover, even when a company maintains a quality system that meets the ISO 9001:2000 standards, the quality of the final product cannot be guaranteed. Worse still, adhering to strict software quality standards can, in some circumstances, be counterproductive[21].

1.1 ISO Quality Management Systems

The intention of an ISO 9001:2000 quality management system (QMS) is to provide "an orderly and systematic way of providing quality services to the customers"[7]. The key advantages provided by an ISO Quality Management system are: "improve your product and service quality; give your customers confidence that their needs will be met; standardize your business by giving it a consistent approach to its operations; improve work processes, efficiencies, morale and reduce waste" [5].

For useful implementation of the Quality Management systems they are often introduced on the companies' intranet, containing detailed descriptions of the companies software life cycle processes, also known as an Electronic Process Guide (EPG) [3, 11, 16]. Such process guides usually include activities (how things are done), artifacts (descriptions of products created or modified by an activity), agents (description of entities that can perform activities, roles (roles and agents involved in performing the activities) and resources (tools and techniques used to support or automate the performance of an activity) [6].

However, the potential of QMS/EPG's can only be realized when key capabilities are not only adopted, but also infused across the organization. There is also a growing body of studies focusing on the determinants of technology acceptance and utilization (e.g. [1, 3, 22]).

1.2 Research Question

The motivation for the work described in this paper is to understand how a quality system is used in a company that successfully has achieved an ISO 9001:2000 certification and several quality distinctions. The core research question has been:

What characterizes the use of a quality system among developers and project managers in a large software company that has successfully achieved an ISO 9001:2000 certification?

1.3 Related Research

Since software organizations have been pressured or required to conform to certain standards, many researchers have been focusing on software process improvement (SPI) and quality system implementation investigation and discussion (such as [4, 8, 13, 14, 20]). However, according to Emam and Madhavji [4] most of the empirical case studies tend to show only success stories, as organizations that have not shown process improvement or have even regressed over time is reluctant to publicize their results.

In this paper we present a case study that investigates a quality certified and awarded company that still faces problems with employee involvement and commitment to quality. By investigating the level of usage of a quality tool, we look into the environmental and cultural aspects.

The rest of the paper is organized as follows: the next section describes the case company where we investigate our research question as well as the case study design. Section 3 describes the findings that emerged from the case study, followed by a discussion in section 4. Finally, we conclude and state further work in section 5.

2 Method

This study is a single-case study [23] using semi-structured interviews with employees as the data source. The data was analyzed according to principles in grounded theory as described by Strauss and Corbin [19]. Grounded theory is a research method that seeks to develop theory that is grounded by data that has been systematically gathered and analyzed. It is a form of field-study that systematically applies procedural steps to develop an exploration about a particular phenomenon.

In grounded theory, data collection, analysis, and eventually theory stand in close relationship to one another. A researcher does not begin a project with a preconceived theory in mind (unless his or her purpose is to elaborate and extend an existing theory). Rather, the researcher begins with an area of study and allows the theory to emerge from the data. Constant comparison is the heart of the process. In this study the interviews were compared to other interviews. From comparing the interviews a theory quickly emerged, and when it began to emerge, the data was compared with the existing theory. A theory derived from data is more likely to resemble the "reality" than a theory that is derived by putting together a series of concepts based on experience or solely through speculation (how one expects things to work). Grounded theories, because they are drawn from data, are likely to offer insight, enhance understanding, and provide a meaningful guide to action. Although grounding concepts by data is the main feature of this method, creativity of researchers when explaining the data, is also an essential ingredient. How we used this method is described in detail in Sections 2.3 and 2.4.

2.1 Case Overview - LatSoftware

The context for this research is the Latvian software development company LatSoftware (the company name is changed due to confidentiality). The company was established in the late 80s and was reshaped several times. It has been orientated towards the international market, focusing on providing software development outsourcing services for the public sector, telecommunications, insurance and banking, as well as tourism and logistics. LatSoftware has successfully accomplished more than 200 projects both in Latvia, Western Europe and Scandinavia. At the present time the company has 345 employees, 260 of them have a software engineering background and are directly involved in software development.

While LatSoftware extended its operation in global markets, quality certification has been given a high priority. Therefore a quality management system (QMS) has been developed and the company was certified in the late 90s according to ISO 9000:1994 and 3 years later according to ISO 9001:2000 standards in both cases using the TickIT scheme. In addition, LatSoftware received several national quality awards at the turn of the century.

The following section will provide more detail about the quality management system and its implementation in LatSoftware.

2.2 LatSoftware's Quality Management System

2.2.1 Development

The introduction of the quality management system (QMS) was motivated by the owners desire to sell the company. Therefore, an implementation of a QMS to achieve a future certification in compliance with internationally recognized standards was given a high priority since 1994. At this time the company already employed about 300 employees. According to the Quality Director - who is responsible for the QMS, only 1/3 of the employees supported the decision of implementing a QMS. Nevertheless, the owners provided significant resources for implementing a QMS by establishing a quality department.

The quality department was responsible for educating themselves in the ISO 9001:2000 practices, and collecting current LatSoftware best practices by means of interviews with key specialists. The process descriptions, procedures and guidelines were then developed over a short period of time, in accordance with the ISO standards and real work practices.

The QMS consists of a wide variety of quality documents including a Quality handbook, Software development lifecycle process descriptions and procedures, Methodological guidelines, Templates and forms, Job instructions, Administrative reports and audit summaries for limited access.

Today the quality system consists of more than 500 documents and around 100 process descriptions.

2.2.2 Implementing

The Quality Management System was introduced to the employees during seminars and training. The system's use was mandatory for all projects; however the Quality Director reported that "many managers actually ignored it".

Currently the quality management department employs 3 specialists who maintain the quality system, perform internal audits and provide consulting on quality issues for the company employees. Large projects also have their own quality managers who are responsible for product and process quality.

In the beginning the company used a Windows directory-based quality document storage called the "ISO Directory", but during the last three years a web-based tool "Skapis" (Latvian for Shelf), which is a MS Share Point based tool, has been implemented. It structures the content of the QMS, provides searching opportunities and access control. At the present time the tool is not being developed further due to a possible transition to a different technological platform within the company.

The projects are being audited externally twice a year. In addition internal audits are being conducted to check the consistency of project practices with the quality system.

2.2.3 Promoting Quality Issues

LatSoftware quality department has developed various activities to promote quality issues among the employees, which include newsletters, annual conferences called Quality Days, and quality seminars for new employees. Nevertheless, there has been a slowdown in these activities since none of them were organized during the last two years.

In 2004 LatSoftware organized a Project Managers Symposium with social events afterwards. The aim of the Symposium was to share quality management practices. The results of the seminar were quite shocking – it showed a low level of knowledge transfer within the company; e.g. there were two project managers who developed and implemented traceability tools in parallel. This indicated an area of concern within LatSoftware considering project managers' poor awareness of existing practices, which precludes the accumulation and reuse of organizational knowledge assets. Although the seminar was seen as a good start of a good tradition, it has not been repeated so far.

2.3 Data Sources

We gathered data through semi-structured interviews, using the following questions as a starting point:

- What do you see as the main purpose of the quality system?
- What tasks do you use the quality system to help you with?
- Do you find „Skapis" as a good tool for quality management?
- Do you like using tools like the quality system?
- Have you used tools like the quality system previously?
- Who do you think benefits most from using the quality system?
- Do you think there are disadvantages with the quality system?
- What do you think should be improved about the quality system?
- How would you assess your use of „Skapis" considering the following content (Never used; Used once; Used occasionally; Regularly used in most activities/ projects; Regularly used in all activities/ projects):
  - Quality handbook;
  - Software Life Cycle Procedures;
  - Administrative procedures;
  - Methodological guidelines;
  - Templates and forms?

LatSoftware is divided into 6 Business Units (BU). We interviewed 9 persons – five project managers and four developers to cover various kinds of roles within LatSoftware (see Table 1). Although we only interviewed 9 Developers and Projects Managers from 5 out of 6 BUs, we believe the interviewees reflect the major practices within LatSoftware. All the interviewees had 2-5 years working experience in LatSoftware. The representatives were involved in various roles, such as Systems Analyst / Developer; Project Manager / Project Quality Manager.

In addition, we have conducted interviews with all three employees from the Quality Department (QD) using the same questions, and several interviews with the Quality Director. These interviews provided insight in the QMS maintaining body and implementation history.

Table 1. Interviewed Employees

Roles	*BU1*	*BU3*	*BU4*	*BU5*	*BU6*	*QD*	*Number of interviewees*	*Total number of employees*
Project Managers		2	2		1		5	28
Developers	1		1	1	1		4	205
Quality Specialists						3	3	3
						Total:	12	260

2.4 Data Analysis

The answers from the interviews were written down, translated into English, and then imported into a tool for analysis of qualitative data, Nvivo1. In the data analysis we first used open coding followed by axial coding, and then selective coding [19]. During open coding we read all interviews and coded interesting expressions of opinions in the text by assigning the expression to a category with similar expressions. Open coding is the analytic process through which concepts are identified and their properties and dimensions are discovered in data. Events, happenings, objects and actions/interactions that were found to be conceptually similar in nature or related in meaning, were grouped under more abstract concepts termed "categories". A category represents a phenomenon, that is, a problem, an issue, or an event that is defined as being significant to the respondents. The product of labeling and categorizing are the basic building blocks in grounded theory construction.

An example of open coding are the expressions “there’s too many documents” and “there’s too much of everything, and it’s hard to orient oneself,” that was coded into “too big”.

After the open coding, where we created concepts and categories, we created connections between categories and their sub-categories. The coded pieces of text from the open coding were again categorized with other expressions, e.g. of disadvantages of the QMS, such as “too detailed”, “too big” and “hard to find documents and templates”. This is referred to as axial coding.

Finally, we tagged all interviews with information (attributes in Nvivo) about use level, and interviewees’ roles. During the selective coding, where we integrated and refined the theory, the matrices generated by NVivo were very important analytical tools.

3 Results

We generated reports for 5 main groups of axial codes to get the results. These are described next:

[1] Nvivo is a tool for analyzing qualitative data available from QSR International, www.qsrinternational.com.

- Purpose of the Quality Management System;
- Use level of Skapis;
- What is used in Skapis?
- When is Skapis used?
- Why is Skapis not used?

We use quotes from the interviews in the following presentation of the results.

3.1 Purpose of the Quality Management System

When we asked about the purpose of the QMS we counted 18 different purposes in total (table 2). The persons from the Quality department reported 10 difference purposes reported by the persons from the Quality department. They specially mentioned marketing, process performance, satisfied customers and getting the certificate. One from the Quality Department said "... at the very beginning someone had the opinion that we need the certificate for any price, even by telling lies to the auditors ... although it didn't happen".

The project managers also reported 10 purposes, and the most frequently reported purposes were: improve product quality, guarantee for the customer, guarantee for a minimal performance and satisfied customers. One said "Well, QMS implementation costs, but it is more expensive to work without a quality system. It brings us even more satisfied customers, more new customers".

Table 2. Purpose reported by 4 developers, 5 project managers and 3 quality specialists

Purpose	Developer	QA department	Project manager	Total all
Improve product quality	1	0	3	4
Satisfied customers	0	2	2	4
Process performance	1	2	0	3
Marketing	1	2	0	3
Flag waiving	1	1	1	3
Improve the process quality	1	1	1	3
Getting the certificate	1	2	0	3
Guarantee for the customer	0	1	2	3
Support work	0	1	1	2
Improve quality of products and doc	1	0	1	2
Less to think about	0	0	2	2
Successful projects	1	0	0	1
Order manufacturing	0	1	0	1
Long term operation	1	0	0	1
Things are done similar	0	0	1	1
Approve that there is a QA system	0	1	0	1
Guarantee for a least performance	0	0	1	1
Do things correct	1	0	0	1
Sum	**10**	**14**	**15**	

The developers also reported 10 different purposes. They were focused on process, project and product quality. One reported that "The quality system's main purpose is to provide successful projects… "

It seems that the project managers and those from the Quality Department were more focused on issues related to the market, customers and the certificate. The developers saw the main purpose as improving their daily work.

3.2 Use Level of Skapis

While investigating the use level of Skapis, the storage of the QMS's content, persons from the quality department were not asked about that, since they are not involved in software development projects and are not using the QMS in the projects. Among the nine developers and project managers, only one of the project managers claimed she used Skapis on a regularly basis. The rest claimed they did not use it at all. Three of the project mangers and two of the developers said they did not know about Skapis. One project manager said "An electronic one? I have never heard about that before. So, I might say that I don't use it". Another project manager said "Unfortunately, I am hearing about it for the first time today".

When we asked about what they used instead when they needed information about quality issues and software lifecycle processes, they all said they had local copies on their computer. These local copies consisted either of documentation from earlier projects, or templates and checklists from earlier versions of the quality system. One developer said "We reuse testing documentation from the previous projects".

Even though the use level of Skapis was very low, it was clear that the developers and project managers used older parts of the Quality Management System.

3.3 What Is Used in Skapis?

Since almost no one seemed to use the system we were surprised that they still used parts of the QMS content. Everyone used a local copy of their own quality documentation, and in most cases this was inspired by earlier projects or older version of the quality system. The local copies included templates, forms and checklists. One said "Our project has its own processes. We made our own process descriptions. … In the previous projects I have used checklists, examples for process descriptions".

3.4 When Is Skapis Used?

Since the use level was so low, we received answers about the usage of the content of the QMS. Three project managers and one developer said they accessed it only to get ready for the audits. One project manger said "It disturbs me, when the audits come, because I have to make all the documents. Otherwise, to tell the truth, I don't use it". One developer said "Write something, so that I can show it to the auditor – that's what our project manager says, when he needs test plans and test cases".

3.5 Why Is Skapis Not Used?

There were two main reasons for the system not being used. The main issue was the system itself (Table 3), because it was seen as cumbersome to use and did not support work. The other issues were related to organizational problems (Table 4).

3.5.1 Tool and Content Related Issues

When the interviewed persons were asked about the problems with the tool or the content of the QMS, they all listed similar problems. The persons form the Quality department and the project mangers came up with most of the issues. This was probably because they knew the tool and/or the content better. The most frequent problems reported were:

- Too big;
- Too detailed;
- Hard to understand documents and templates;
- Does not make work easier;
- Hard to find documents and templates;
- Not tailored to small projects;
- Not reflecting real work practice.

One from the Quality department said "... there are too many documents in it, too much of everything. Therefore it's hard to orient oneself, for an ordinary worker". A project manager said "There are a lot of details. For big projects, it would be OK, but for small ones nobody will read such a mountain of paper", and another manager said "Our quality system doesn't correspond to the company's current organizational structure". Also a developer stated "Software Life Cycle Procedures, I have used once; they are too far from project reality".

Table 3. Tool and content related issues reported by 4 developers, 5 project managers and 3 quality specialists

Tool and content related issues	Developer	QA department	Project manager	Total all
Too big	1	3	3	7
Too detailed	0	2	1	3
Hard to understand documents and templates	0	1	2	3
Does not make work easier	0	1	2	3
Hard to find documents and templates	1	0	2	3
Not reflecting real work practice	2	0	0	2
Not tailored to small projects	0	0	2	2
Search not working	0	2	0	2
Not user friendly	0	1	1	2
Not integrated with other tools	0	2	0	2
Does not coorespod to org structure	0	2	0	2
Do not improve the tool any more	0	2	0	2
No knowledge base	0	0	2	2
System not efficient	0	1	0	1
Updates are not spread	0	0	1	1
Not flexible	0	1	0	1
Hard to get an overview	0	1	0	1
Sum	**4**	**19**	**18**	

3.5.2 Organizational Issues

The interviewed persons also mentioned several problems within the organization that could explain why the tool was not used. The most frequently reported issues were:

- Lack of training;
- Top management not involved;
- No motivation in the company;
- Low employee involvement;
- The quality system is only for the management.

One of the developers said “People have to be shown what is good, where are the benefits. To give a try to work with it”, and one from the Quality department said “There should be a common understanding why the system is necessary; every manager should clarify that. It won’t work if the (company) president will say we need that. It needs a culture”.

Table 4. Organizational issues reported by 4 developers, 5 project managers and 3 quality specialists

Organizational issues	Developer	QA department	Project manager	Total all
Lack of training	2	1	2	5
Top management not involved	1	2	0	3
No motivation in the company	1	0	1	2
Low employee involvement	2	0	0	2
The quality system is only for the management	0	1	0	1
Quality manager’s attitude	1	0	0	1
No culture for using	0	1	0	1
LCP internalized	0	0	1	1
Lack of quality in small projects	0	0	1	1
Don’t see the benefit from the QMS	0	0	1	1
Sum	**7**	**5**	**6**	

4 Discussion

We have examined the use of a tool called Skapis through qualitative interviews. Skapis was created to support the Quality Management System in LatSoftware, a large software company in Latvia.

The results show that almost no one used the tool. We found however that the Quality Management System, or parts of an earlier version, was used to some degree.

We also discovered that although the company was successfully certified, the employees both lacked awareness about the tool and did not use the content of the QMS when developing software. For most developers and project mangers, using the QMS meant producing project documentation before audits.

4.1 Effect of Failure

We found several effects of the problem with the Quality Management System not really implemented in this company:

- Everyone developed their own best practices and used own local copies from earlier projects or former Quality Management System. No one knows how the local copies corresponded with the QMS.

- Employees did not see the benefits of following the QMS. They lacked understanding of what and why they should follow.
- The majority of the projects produced documentation for auditing purpose only. Faking the documentation retrospective, resulted in a lot of non-productive work and particular dissatisfaction by employees.
- The Quality Management System did not correspond to real work practices. New employees did not get support from the Skapis system when they joined the company, because it was not possible to use the system to find out how project work should be really done.
- Process improvement was very difficult since there was no any common process to improve. Improving or changing a process within the QMS would not make much sense since such processes were not followed.
- Since the use level of the tool was so low, the SW implementation of Skapis and the effort used to develop the QMS has been a waste of money (except for auditing purpose).

4.2 Reason of Failure

In our work we found the following reasons for why this certified company with several national awards for quality management has problems with employees not using or following the Quality Management System.

- Pitterman [13] warns that without high levels of senior management commitment to a quality system, most quality improvement efforts are doomed to fail. In LatSoftware there was a **low top management involvement** in motivating the employees to work in accordance with the QMS practices. The motivation of the QMS implementation was getting a certificate, and since the employees did not see the benefits with the QMS, they had a strong resistance against it from the very beginning.
- **Lack of employee involvement** in the early stages when implementing the QMS caused low motivation to use the system. In [10] and [12] we found that involvement resulted in a high usage levels of such systems in small and medium sized companies. We assume that involvement also is important for large companies like LatSoftware.
- The potential users of Skapis have not been **trained** in using it. Such training is presumably important for making the users understand the system and its benefits.
- Despite the huge amount of effort expended by the quality department, the system was disregarded, because **it was too big, too heavy and didn't reflect real work practices**. Besides, Skapis as **the quality system tool didn't support the work** of software developers and project managers. Those few persons who actually used the tool reported that it contained faulty functionality and had poor usability. We cannot expect infusion of a system that is not perceived as useful or easy to use in daily practice, as well as consistent with the existing values, past experiences, and needs of the software developers. Employees tend to ignore any activities if the perceived desirable benefits do not outweigh the perceived undesirable effects. Rogers [15] and Dybå [3]) found that perceived usefulness is a fundamental driver of both usage and use intentions and thus the prospects for successfully infusing such systems will be severely undermined if they are not regarded as useful by the developers.

4.3 Limitations

The first limitation of this study is the number of interviewees. We interviewed only nine software developers and project managers because of limited resources. We interviewed the whole Quality Department, and the findings these confirmed the results we got from the developers and project leaders. We also presented the results to the Quality Director and he confirmed the results that we found. Since we didn't record the interviews, we sent the interviews back to the interviewees to make sure we didn't miss anything.

Secondly, we expected that the role of the interviewed person would affect the reported use level of the tool. Skapis is seen as a project manager's support tool (it is also mandatory for them to use). The tendency is the same for the developers and the project managers.

5 Conclusion and Further Work

In this study we conclude that even though a company might be certified in accordance with e.g ISO standards; it doesn't prove successful implementation and usage of the company's quality system. You really need to look inside a company to find out what is happening.

Investigation on the usage of the Quality Management System and Skapis, the tool for storing the system's content, confirmed our anticipation about the problems faced by the company. We discovered that although quality management was set as a mandatory activity for all projects within the company, most of the users were not aware about the tool that supports quality documentation; they accessed only parts of an older version of the Quality Management System and quality documentation from their previous projects. This caused serious problems for the company, such as projects that followed outdated practices, project managers faking quality documentation before audits, wasted resources producing documents no one needed, problems created for new employees since they couldn't find descriptions of the processes people are working in accordance with, and an expensive system no one used.

The Quality Director really appreciated the outcome of the study although he was disappointed and surprised by some of the results. Most of all he was concerned about the fact that there are employees who fake documentation before audits.

The company needs to exert a lot of effort in order to solve these problems. The first step should focus on developing a culture and environment that would lead to convincing the company's employees to focus on software process improvement, and demonstrate upper management commitment to quality. We recommend involving the users when the quality system is being improved by establishing a joint responsibility between the Quality Department and the project teams for maintaining the quality system. Involvement can be achieved by using the process workshop approach [2]. A set of workshops with project managers and developers could fill the gap between the existing Quality Management System and the common work practices. This should also be accompanied by regular employee seminars and training on quality issues, to minimize the lack of awareness within the company. We also recommend improving the Skapis user interface, as well as the usability and accessibility of the content and a possibility to share feedback by the users.

Although the given recommendations might refer to well-known knowledge areas as senior management commitment [13], attitudes and motivation [20], resistance to change [8], etc., the results from this case study can be seen as a useful checklist of which pitfalls to avoid when implementing a quality system in your organization.

Because of the results, the Quality Director will plan further improvements in this area. He plans to include the same set of questions used in this study, in the company's annual anonymous employee survey in order to observe this situation in the long term. We are planning to continue studying the Quality Management System usage in LatSoftware over time, including additional data sources for further evaluation such as annual survey results, tool usage logs, quantitative surveys and inspection of project documents.

Acknowledgement

We appreciate valuable discussions with the Quality Director, and research input received from the Quality Department personnel, developers and project managers from the studied company. We would also like to thank Tore Dybå, Torgeir Dingsøyr, Karlis Rumpe and Fergal McCaffery for helpful comments.

This research was partly supported by the Research Council of Norway under Grant 156701/220, European Social Fund and the Latvian Council of Science project Nr. 02.2002 “Latvian Informatics Production Unit Support Program in the Area of Engineering, Computer Networks and Signal Processing”.

References

1. Davis, F. D., "Perceived Usefulness, Perceived Ease of Use, and User Acceptance of Information Technology," Mis Quarterly, vol. 13, (1989) 319-340
2. Dingsøyr, T. and Moe, N. B., "The Process Workshop - A Tool to Define Electronic Process Guides in Small Companies," presented at Proceedings of the Australian Software Engineering Conference (ASWEC), Melbourne, Australia, (2004) 350 - 357
3. Dybå, T., Moe, N. B., and Mikkelsen, E. M., "An Empirical Investigation on Factors Affecting Software Developer Acceptance and Utilization of Electronic Process Guides," presented at Proceedings of the International Software Metrics Symposium (METRICS), Chicago, Illinois, USA, (2004) 220-231
4. ElEmam, K. and Madhavji, N. H., "Does organizational maturity improve quality?," IEEE Software, vol. 13, (1996) 109-110
5. ISO, "ISO 9001:2000 Quality management systems -- Requirements," 2000.
6. Kellner, M. I., Becker-Kornstaedt, U., Riddle, W. E., Tomal, J., and M, V., "Process Guides: Effective Guidance for Process Participants," presented at Proceedings of the Fifth International Conference on the Software Process: Computer Supported Organizational Work, Lisle, Illinois, USA, (1998) 11-25
7. Mariun, N., "Assuring Quality in Engineering Education via Implementation of ISO 9000," Department of Electrical and Electronic Engineering, Faculty of Engineering, University Putra Malaysia, Publications by Simply Quality 2005.
8. Markus, M. L., "Power, Politics, and Mis Implementation," Communications of the ACM, vol. 26, (1983) 430-444

9. McCaffery, F., Šmite, D., Wilkie, F. G., and McFall, D., "How European Software Industries Can Prepare For Growth Within The Global Marketplace - Northern Irish Strategies," presented at Industry Proceedings of the European Software Process Improvement Conference (EuroSPI 2005), Budapest, Hungary, (2005) 3.23-3.32.
10. Moe, N. B. and Dingsøyr, T., "The Impact of Process Workshop Involvement on the Use of an Electronic Process Guide: A Case Study," presented at EuroMicro, Porto, Portugal, (2005) IEEE: 188-195
11. Moe, N. B., Dingsøyr, T., Dybå, T., and Johansen, T., "Process Guides as Software Process Improvement in a Small Company," presented at Proceedings of the European Software Process Improvement Conference (EuroSPI), Nürnberg, Germany, (2002) 177-188
12. Moe, N. B. and Dybå, T., "The Adoption of an Electronic Process Guide in a Company with Voluntary Use," presented at Proceedings of the European Software Process Improvement Conference (EuroSPI), Trondheim, Norway, (2004) 114-125
13. Pitterman, B., "Telcordia technologies: The journey to high maturity," IEEE Software, vol. 17, (2000) 89-96
14. Pyzdek, T., "To Improve Your Process - Keep It Simple," IEEE Software, vol. 9, (1992) 112-113
15. Rogers, E. M., Diffusion of Innovations, vol. Fourth Edition. New York: The Free Press, 2003.
16. Scott, L., Carvalho, L., Jeffery, R., D'Ambra, J., and Becker-Kornstaedt, U., "Understanding the use of an electronic process guide," Information and Software Technology, vol. 44, (2002) 601-616
17. SEI, "Capability Maturity Model ® Integration (CMMISM), Version 1.1," 2002.
18. Smite, D., "A Case Study: Coordination Practices in Global Software Development," presented at Proceedings of the 6th International Conference on Product Focused Software Process Improvement (PROFES 2005), Oulu, Finland, (2005) Springer-Verlag: 234-244
19. Strauss, A. and Corbin, J., Basics of Qualitative Research: Techniques and Procedures for Developing Grounded Theory. Thousand Oaks, CA: Sage Publications, 1998.
20. Thomas, S. A., Hurley, S. F., and Barnes, D. J., "Looking for the human factors in software quality management," presented at International Conference on Software Engineering: Education and Practice (SE:EP '96), Dunedin, New Zealand, (1996) 474-480
21. van der Pijl, G. J., Swinkels, G. J. P., and Verrijdt, J. G., "ISO 9000 versus CMM: Standardization and certification of IS development," Information & Management, vol. 32, (1997) 267-274
22. Venkatesh, V. and Davis, F. D., "A theoretical extension of the Technology Acceptance Model: Four longitudinal field studies," Management Science, vol. 46, (2000) 186-204
23. Yin, R. K., Case Study Research: design and methods, vol. vol. 5, 2 ed. Newbury Park, CA: Sage Publications, 1994.

Implementing Software Process Improvement Initiatives: An Empirical Study

Mahmood Niazi[1], David Wilson[2], and Didar Zowghi[2]

[1] School of Computing and Mathematics, Keele University, ST5 5BG, UK
mkniazi@cs.keele.ac.uk

[2] Faculty of Information Technology, University of Technology Sydney, NSW 2007, Australia
{davidw, didar}@it.uts.edu.au

Abstract. In this paper we present findings from our empirical study of software process improvement (SPI) implementation. We aim to provide SPI practitioners with insight into designing appropriate SPI implementation initiatives in order to achieve better results. Thirty-four interviews were conducted with Australian practitioners. Three SPI implementation issues were investigated: reasons for embarking on SPI initiatives, SPI benefits to the management, and factors that play a positive role in SPI implementation.

We have found that most common reasons for embarking on SPI initiatives are to: improve the quality of software developed, reduce software development cost, and increase productivity. Our results show that 71% of the practitioners said that SPI initiatives provided clear benefits to the management. We have also found that most frequently cited SPI implementation factors are: SPI awareness, defined SPI implementation methodology, experienced staff, staff time and resources, senior management commitment and training.

Our aim of conducting this study is to provide a SPI implementation framework for the design of effective SPI implementation initiatives.

1 Introduction

Information Technology failure has been a common topic in the literature over the last 25 or more years with the annual CHAOS Report [1] perhaps being the most cited regular report. These failures are often seen as being due to issues of software quality, which has accordingly received much attention in both academia and industry. Software quality problems are widely acknowledged to affect the development cost and time [1; 2]. A recent study, conducted by a group of Fellows of the Royal Academy of Engineering and British Computer Society, shows that despite spending 22.6 billions pounds on IT projects in UK during 2003/2004, significant numbers of projects still fail to deliver key benefits on time and to target cost and specification [3]. In addition to such disappointing performance, some software projects result in operational failure (e.g. Airbus A320 [4], the London Ambulance Service [5], and the explosion of the Ariane 5 [6]) or even the demise of organisations (e.g. Greyhound's TRIPS System [7], FoxMeyer's ERP project [8], Oxford Health's 'computer glitch' [9] and One.Tel billing system [10]).

J. Münch and M. Vierimaa (Eds.): PROFES 2006, LNCS 4034, pp. 222–233, 2006.

There have been increasing calls for the software industry to find solutions to software quality problems [11]. Software developing organizations are realizing that one of their fundamental challenges is to effectively manage the software development process [12; 13]. In order to address the effective management of software process different methods have been developed, of which Software Process Improvement (SPI) is the one mostly used.

Different advances have been made in the development of SPI standards and models, e.g. CMM, CMMI, and ISO's SPICE. Despite the significant development of standards and models for SPI, the failure rate for SPI programmes is high. The recent report from the Software Engineering Institute puts the rate of failure at around 70% [14]. This may be due to the fact that not enough attention has been paid to SPI implementation issues.

In this paper we present empirical findings of a study into SPI implementation that points to the issues that have to be addressed when developing SPI implementation initiatives. Our study uses data from interviews of 34 Australian practitioners in 29 Australian companies. The objective of this paper is to provide insight to SPI practitioners into designing appropriate SPI implementation initiatives in order to achieve better results. Our overall aim of this study is to develop a SPI implementation framework in order to guide practitioners in designing effective SPI implementation strategies.

There are four research questions that have motivated our work:

RQ1. Why different companies embark on SPI initiatives?
RQ2. Have SPI initiatives provided clear and expected benefits to the management?
RQ3. What factors, as identified by mature companies, have a positive impact on SPI implementation?
RQ4. What factors, as identified by immature companies, have a positive impact on SPI implementation?

This paper is organised as follows. Section 2 describes the background. Section 3 describes the research design. In Section 4 findings are presented and analysed. Discussion is provided in Section 5. Section 6 provides the conclusion.

2 Background

McDermid and Bennet [15] have argued that the human factors in SPI have been largely ignored and this has damaged the effectiveness of SPI implementation programmes. Hall and Wilson [16; 17] have also suggested that the experiences, opinions and perceptions of software practitioners impact indirectly on the quality of software produced. This also implies that such attributes influence how software practitioners behave towards SPI implementation approaches. It is, therefore, very important to identify the views and perceptions of different practitioners about factors that play a positive role in the implementation of SPI initiative. These views, experiences and perceptions collectively may provide practitioners with sufficient knowledge about the nature of issues that play a positive role in the implementation of SPI programmes in order to assist them in effectively planning SPI implementation strategies.

Since the introduction of Capability Maturity Model, a number of related studies have been conducted to identify SPI factors [18-22]. Following is a summary of some of the well known studies.

- A survey of 138 individuals in 56 software organizations [18] identified the factors necessary for implementing a successful SPI programme. The authors have identified a number of factors associated with successful SPI programmes. In this study factors associated with unsuccessful SPI programmes are also identified [18].
- A review of 56 software organizations that have either implemented an ISO 9000 quality system or that have conducted a CMM-based process improvement initiative, determined ten factors that affect organizational change in SPI [19].
- El Emam et al. [20] have investigated some of the important success factors and barriers for SPI. This study is a follow-up study to [18]. They have used data from 14 companies involved in the SPICE trials in order to identify which of the factors are most strongly related to the success of SPI efforts and which factors have no impact.
- A questionnaire survey of 85 UK companies [21] identified the key success factors that can impact SPI implementation. The results show that the four factors that practitioners considered had a major impact on successfully implementing SPI. These factors are: reviews, standards and procedures, training and mentoring and experienced staff. The authors have also identified four further factors (internal leadership, inspections, executive support and internal process ownership) that more mature companies considered had a major impact on successfully implementing SPI.

Many of the studies mentioned above have adopted the questionnaire survey method for the identification of factors. A disadvantage of the questionnaire survey method is that respondents are provided with a list of possible factors and asked to select from that list. This tends to pre-empt the factors investigated and to limit them to those reported in existing studies - respondents only focus on the factors provided in the list. In order to provide more confidence in the study it is important that practitioners' experiences and perceptions should be explored independently and without any suggestion from the researcher. So this motivated us to use interviews for data collection in this study.

The work reported in some of the other studies is based on single case study. This type of work has been assessed for being company-specific and therefore potentially unrepresentative [23]. In our study, we not only conducted 34 interviews, but data was collected as an impartial third party.

3 Study Design

In order to address research questions, we collected and analysed empirical data using a combination of qualitative and quantitative methods. Qualitative and quantitative methods are complementary [24]. Qualitative data can be converted through coding to become frequency data, and hence quantitative [25; 26]. Seaman [26] adds that although this process of coding transforms qualitative data into quantitative data, it does not affect its subjectivity or objectivity. Bryman [27] noted that reverse can also occur. One of the examples in which quantitative research can facilitate qualitative research is by the selection of case studies for further research.

This overview of methods indicates that empirical methods help researchers move towards well-founded decisions [28]. In line with recommendations, this research uses a combination of qualitative and quantitative methods for data collection and analysis.

3.1 Sample Profile

From November 2002 to August 2003 we visited 29 software companies and conducted 34 interviews. The sample profile is shown in Appendix A. All of the 29 companies responded to a request for participants which was posted via the email. The target population in this research was those software-producing companies that have initiated SPI programmes. Although we do not claim this is a statistically representative sample, appendix A does show that companies in the study range from a very small software house to very large multinational companies and cover a wide range of application areas. It is further important to acknowledge that the data was collected from companies who were tackling real issues on a daily basis; therefore we have high confidence in the accuracy and validity of data [29].

It is important to acknowledge that the practitioners sampled within companies are representative of practitioners in organisations as a whole. A truly representative sample is impossible to attain and the researcher should try to remove as much of the sample bias as possible [30]. The sample of practitioners researched includes developers, business analysts, methodology analyst, technical directors, project managers and senior management.

3.2 Data Collection Method

Interviews were conducted with three groups of practitioners: developers, project managers and senior managers. Questioning was both open and close-ended with frequent probing to elaborate and clarify meaning. The negotiated interview duration was half an hour, however, the researcher and interviewee would determine the pace of the interview. Before the interview the researcher arranged the time and place with which the interviewees were comfortable. Most of the interviews took place in the interviewee's offices.

3.3 Data Analysis Method

This research seeks to identify perceptions and experiences of practitioners about SPI implementation. In order to identify common themes for the implementation of SPI programmes, the following process has been adapted in this research [25; 29]:

- Identifying themes for SPI implementation from transcripts: All the interview transcripts were read to identify the major themes for SPI implementation. These themes were noted down and compared to the notes made during the interviews in order to reassure that the transcripts being analysed are indeed a true reflection of the discussion in the interviews. These two process steps also verify that the transcription process has not changed the original data generated in the interviews.

- Generate categories: All the interview transcripts were read again to generate categories for responses. Different themes were grouped together under different categories. For example, budget, funds etc were grouped together under critical success factor (CSF) category "resources". Each category represents a CSF for the implementation of SPI programme.

In order to reduce researcher's bias we conducted inter-rater reliability in this process. Three interview recordings were selected at random and a colleague, who was not familiar with the issues being discussed, was asked to identify CSFs that appeared in the interviews. The results were compared with our previous results and no disagreements were found.

4 Findings

In this section we discuss the results relating to RQ1 to RQ5.

4.1 Reasons for Embarking on an SPI Initiative

In order to answer RQ1, Table 1 shows a list of reasons for embarking on SPI initiatives. The percentage shows the proportion of practitioners that cited a particular reason.

It shows that most of the practitioners want to improve the quality of software. Nearly half of the practitioners embark on SPI initiative to reduce the development cost and to increase productivity. It shows that practitioners are interested to reduce time-to-market and to shorten software development cycle times. Table 1 also shows that few companies introduced SPI initiatives because of marketing purpose.

Table 1. Embarking reasons

Reasons for embarking on SPI initiatives	**Occurrence in interviews n=34**	
	Freq	%
To improve the quality of the software developed	26	77
To reduce software development cost	17	50
To increase productivity	16	47
To reduce time-to-market	12	35
To shorten software development cycle times	9	27
To improve management visibility	8	24
For public relations/ marketing purposes	6	18
To automate the production of relevant development documentation	4	12
To meet vendor/supplier qualification	3	9
To make procedures and processes optimal	3	9
CEO directive	2	6
Industry requirements	2	6
To bring discipline to the company	2	6
Desire to change	1	3
To reduce maintenance	1	3
To reduce risks	1	3

4.2 Clear and Expected Benefits of an SPI Initiative

Table 2 shows that 71% of the practitioners say that SPI initiatives provided clear and expected benefits to the management. Only 6% of the practitioners say SPI initiatives did not provide any benefits to the management. Our results are in line with other studies that showed that the effort put into SPI can assist in producing high quality software, reducing cost and time, and increasing productivity [12; 13; 31-33].

Table 2. Expected SPI benefits

Clear and expected benefits to the management	**Occurrence in interviews n=34**	
	Freq	%
Yes	24	71
No	2	6
Do not know	8	23
Total	34	100

4.3 Mature Versus Immature Companies

We partitioned the 29 companies according to their appraisal status. Each company was either formally appraised, informally appraised (self rated) or no appraisal. In this research, the companies that have been assessed (formally or informally) to be in CMM level-2 or above are considered mature companies. Similarly, the companies with ISO 9001 certification are also considered to be mature companies. We have collapsed a sample of companies with CMM level-2 and above with a sample of companies with ISO 9001 certification.

The companies that did not achieve CMM level-2 or ISO 9001 certification are considered to be immature companies. Similarly, the companies that are using some internal methodologies for software development but they did not provide any appraisal information are considered to be immature companies.

In order to answer RQ3, Table 3 shows the list of critical success factors (CSFs) cited in the empirical study. The most frequently cited factor by mature companies is training and mentoring, i.e. 79%. This suggests that in practitioners' opinion training can play a vital role in the implementation of SPI programs. Other frequently cited factors by mature companies are senior management commitment (71%) and SPI awareness (64%). It shows that practitioners of mature companies consider management commitment and awareness of the benefits of SPI programs imperative for the successful implementation of SPI initiatives. The results also show that defined SPI implementation methodology, experience staff and staff time and resources are also important factors.

In order to answer RQ4, Table 3 shows the list of CSFs cited in the empirical study. Table 3 shows that the most frequently cited factor by immature companies is senior management commitment, 65%. The factor training and mentoring is cited by 60% of practitioners. The results show that most of the practitioners of immature companies consider SPI awareness and resources critical for the implementation of SPI. The results also suggest that practitioners want their involvement in SPI initiatives. They also want experience staff and an SPI implementation methodology. The practitioners of immature companies also require facilitation during SPI implementation process.

Table 3. Mature and immature companies

Success Factors	**Mature companies (n=14)**		**Immature companies (n=20)**	
	Freq	%	Freq	%
Company culture	2	14	0	0
Creating process action teams/external agents	1	7	1	5
Customer satisfaction	1	7	1	5
Defined SPI implementation methodology	6	43	6	30
Encouraging communication and collaboration	4	29	1	5
Experienced staff	6	43	7	35
Facilitation	2	14	7	35
Formal documentation	1	7	2	10
Formalised relationship between development team	0	0	1	5
Higher staff moral	1	7	0	0
Logical sequence/order of SPI implementation	1	7	1	5
Managing the SPI project	2	14	3	15
Measurement	2	14	0	0
Quality assurance	2	14	3	15
Reviews	1	7	2	10
Senior management commitment	10	71	13	65
SPI Awareness	9	64	11	55
Staff involvement	3	21	8	40
Staff time and resources	5	36	11	55
Tailoring improvement initiatives	2	14	0	0
Training and mentoring	11	79	12	60
Tools/packages	0	0	2	10

5 Discussion

Table 4 shows that SPI approach is strongly established in many companies. Only a 6% of companies say SPI is less than one year old and 56% say it has been in operation for more than five years. These results show that companies have been using SPI approach over a relatively long period of time. Despite this, less companies in this study report high software process maturity (i.e. 14 out of 29). Companies in our sample seem to be accelerating SPI as slow as has been reported in SEI [34]:

- Maturity level 1 to 2 is 22 months
- Maturity level 2 to 3 is 19 months
- Maturity level 3 to 4 is 25 months
- Maturity level 4 to 5 is 13 months

Our results suggest that the most frequently cited reasons for embarking on SPI initiatives are to: improve quality of product, reduce cost, increase productivity and reduce time-to-market.

Our results also suggest that the most frequently cited factors by mature and immature companies are: training, senior management commitment and SPI awareness. However, comparison of the CSFs in the two data sets provides evidence that there are more similarities than differences between the findings of two sets (as shown in Table 3).

CSFs represent few key areas where management should focus their attention in order to successfully achieve the desire results [35]. In order to decide criticality of a factor, we have used the following criteria:

- If a factor is cited by the respondents in the interviews with a frequency percentage of >=30%) then we treat that factor as a critical factor in this empirical study

A similar approach has been used by other researchers [21]. However, instead of having 50% limit in this criteria, which is the more common approach, we have reduced this limit to 30%. This is because we wanted to have a sufficient number of implementation factors and with a 50% limit the identified implementation factors were not sufficient for the required research project. Our ultimate aim was to utilize these common factors in the development of the SPI implementation framework [36; 37].

Using this criterion, six factors from mature companies have been identified that are generally considered critical for successfully implementing SPI. These factors are: training and mentoring, higher management support, SPI awareness, defined SPI implementation methodology, experienced staff and staff time and resources.

Using this criterion, eight factors from immature companies have been identified. These factors are: higher management support, training and mentoring, SPI awareness, staff time and resources, staff involvement, experienced staff, facilitation and defined SPI implementation methodology.

Table 4. SPI life

How long has your process improvement programme been in operation?	**Occurrence in interviews n=34**	
	Freq	%
Less than 1 year	2	6
1 - 2 years	6	18
3 - 5 years	7	20
More than 5 years	19	56
Total	34	100.0

Six factors are common between two data sets. The results suggest that companies should focus on these common CSFs in order to successfully implement SPI programs because we have more confidence that a factor does indeed have an impact on SPI implementation if it is critical in both data sets.

6 Conclusion

We report on findings from our recent empirical study of SPI implementation with thirty-four Australian practitioners. We aim to provide SPI practitioners with some insight into designing appropriate SPI implementation initiatives in order to achieve better results. Our ultimate aim of conducting this empirical study is to develop a SPI

Table 5. Summary of results

Research Question	Answer
RQ1. Why different companies embark on SPI initiatives?	Our results suggest that the most frequently cited reasons for embarking on SPI initiatives are to: • improve quality of product • reduce cost • increase productivity • reduce time-to-market
RQ2. Have SPI initiatives provided clear and expected benefits to the management?	Our results show that 71% of the practitioners say that SPI initiatives provided clear and expected benefits to the management. Only 6% of the practitioners say SPI initiatives did not provide any benefits to the management
RQ3. What factors, as identified by mature companies, have a positive impact on implementing SPI?	Factors are: • Training and mentoring • Senior management commitment • SPI Awareness • Defined SPI implementation methodology • Experienced staff • Staff time and resources
RQ4. What factors, as identified by immature companies, have a positive impact on implementing SPI?	Factors are: • Senior management commitment • Training and mentoring • SPI Awareness • Staff time and resources • Staff involvement • Experienced staff • Facilitation • Defined SPI implementation methodology

implementation framework in order to assist practitioners in the design of effective SPI implementation strategies. We analysed the experiences, opinions and views of practitioners in order to identify issues that have some impact on the implementation of a SPI programs. We identified the important reasons for embarking on SPI initiatives. We also identified factors that are critical for successful implementation of SPI efforts. Our results provide advice to SPI practitioners on what needs to be addressed when developing SPI implementation initiatives. We have summarised our results in Table 5.

Our findings generally indicate that SPI is progressing in the Australian software industry. It shows that more than half of the companies said that SPI has been in operation for more than five years. However, companies in our sample are not maturing at a reasonable speed. Overall, mature and immature companies showed a good understanding of factors that can play a positive role in the implementation of SPI initiatives. There are more similarities than differences in CSFs identified by two types of companies. It shows that these companies are aware of what is imperative for successful implementation of SPI initiatives.

References

1 Standish-Group: Chaos - the state of the software industry. (2003).
2 Standish-Group: Chaos - the state of the software industry. Standish group international technical report, 1-11. (1995).
3 The-Royal-Academy-of-Engineering: The Challenges of Complex IT Projects, The report of a working group from The Royal Academy of Engineering and The British Computer Society. ISBN 1-903496-15-2 (2004).
4 Randell, B.: Airbus A320, The Risks Digest: Forum on Risks to the Public in Computers and Related Systems 8 (57). (1989)
5 Finkelstein, A.: Report of the Inquiry Into The London Ambulance Service. International Workshop on Software Specification and Design Case Study Electronic: http://www.cs.ucl.ac.uk/staff/A.Finkelstein/las/lascase0.9.pdf: Site visited 4-3-2003, 1993. (1993)
6 Lions, J. L.: http://www.ima.umn.edu/~arnold/disasters/ariane5rep.html, Site visited 4-3-2003. (1997).
7 Tomsho, R.: Real Dog: How Greyhound Lines Re-Engineered Itself Right Into A Deep Hole, Wall Street Journal 20 (October). (1994) A1-A6.
8 Scott, J., E: The FoxMeyer Drugs' Bankruptcy: Was it a Failure of ERP? In Proc. of the Association for Information Systems 5th Americas Conference on IS, Milwaukee, WI, August. (1999) 223-225.
9 Khasru, B., Z: Former Oxford Health Directors Settle Lawsuit, Fairfield County Business Journal, Stamford. (2nd July). (2001) 5.
10 Paul, B.: On for young and old as James and Kerry began to fret. The Sydney Morning Herald. http://www.smh.com.au/articles/2002/03/20/Pbonetel.htm: Site visited 12-9-2003 (2002).
11 Crosby, P.: *Philip Crosby's reflections on quality*. McGraw-Hill.(1996).
12 Pitterman, B.: Telcordia Technologies: The journey to high maturity, IEEE Software (July/August). (2000) 89-96.
13 Yamamura, G.: Software process satisfied employees, IEEE Software (September/October). (1999) 83-85.
14 SEI: Process maturity profile of the software community. Software Engineering Institute, Carnegie Mellon University, (2002).
15 McDermid, J. and Bennet, K.: Software Engineering research: A critical appraisal, IEE Proceedings on software engineering 146 (4). (1999) 179-186.

16 Hall, T. and Wilson, D.: Views of software quality: a field report, IEEE Proceedings on Software Engineering 144 (2). (1997)
17 Hall, T. and Wilson, D.: Perceptions of software quality: a pilot study, Software quality journal (7). (1998) 67-75.
18 Goldenson, D. R. and Herbsleb, J. D.: After the appraisal: A systematic survey of Process Improvement, Its benefits, And Factors That Influence Success. SEI, CMU/SEI-95-TR-009 (1995).
19 Stelzer, D. and Werner, M.: Success factors of organizational change in software process improvement, Software process improvement and practice 4 (4). (1999)
20 El-Emam, K., Fusaro, P. and Smith, B.: Success factors and barriers for software process improvement. Better software practice for business benefit: Principles and experience, IEEE Computer Society (1999)
21 Rainer, A. and Hall, T.: Key success factors for implementing software process improvement: a maturity-based analysis, Journal of Systems & Software (62). (2002) 71-84.
22 Rainer, A. and Hall, T.: A quantitative and qualitative analysis of factors affecting software processes, Journal of Systems & Software, Accepted awaiting publication (2002)
23 Herbsleb, J. D. and Goldenson, D. R.: A systematic survey of CMM experience and results. 18th international conference on software engineering (ICSE-18). Germany (1996) 323-330.
24 Walker, R., Briand, L., Noktin, D., Seaman, C. and Tichy, W.: Panel: Empirical validation - what, why, when, and how. Proceedings of the 25th International Conference on Software Engineering (ICSE '03). (2003)
25 Burnard, P.: A method of analysing interview transcripts in qualitative research, Nurse education today (11). (1991) 461-466.
26 Seaman, C.: Qualitative methods in empirical studies of software engineering, IEEE Transactions on Software Engineering 25 (4). (1999) 557-572.
27 Bryman, A.: *Quantity and quality in social research.* London, Routledge.(1996).
28 Perry, D., Porter, A. and Votta, L.: Empirical studies of software engineering: a roadmap. Proceedings of the Twenty-second Conference on Software Engineering. Ireland (2000) 347-355.
29 Baddoo, N. and Hall, T.: Motivators of software process improvement: An analysis of practitioner's views, Journal of Systems and Software (62). (2002) 85-96.
30 Coolican, H.: *Research Methods and Statistics in Psychology.* Hodder and Stoughton, London.(1999).
31 Butler, K.: The economics benefits of software process improvement, CrossTalk (July). (1995) 14-17.
32 Ashrafi, N.: The impact of software process improvement on quality: in theory and practice, Information & Management 40 (7). (2003) 677-690.
33 Jiang, J., Klein, G., Hwang, H.-G., Huang, J. and Hung, S.-y.: An exploration of the relationship between software development process maturity and project performance, Information & Management (41). (2004) 279-288.
34 SEI: Process Maturity Profile. Software Engineering Institute Carnegie Mellon University, (2004).
35 Rockart, J. F.: Chief executives define their own data needs, Harvard Business Review (2). (1979) 81-93.
36 Niazi, M., Wilson, D. and Zowghi, D.: A Framework for Assisting the Design of Effective Software Process Improvement Implementation Strategies, Journal of Systems and Software Vol 78 (2). (2005) 204-222.
37 Niazi, M., Wilson, D. and Zowghi, D.: A Maturity Model for the Implementation of Software Process Improvement: An empirical study, Journal of Systems and Software 74 (2). (2005) 155-172.

Appendix A. Participant Company Information

Company	Scope	Age (yrs)	Size	Software size	SPI in operation (yrs)
1	Australian	3	38	14	< 1
2	Multi-national	21-50	>2000	DK	> 5
3	Multi-national	>50	>2000	101-500	> 5
4	Multi-national	11-20	>2000	501-2000	1-2
5	Australian	6-10	<10	<10	> 5
6	Australian	21-50	11-100	30	3-5
7	Multi-national	21-50	>2000	DK	> 5
8	Multi-national	>50	501-2000	26-100	> 5
9	Multi-national	>50	>2000	>2000	>5
10	Australian	>50	101-500	11-25	3-5
11	Multi-national	>50	>2000	>2000	3-5
12	Australian	<5	<10	<10	1-2
13	Multi-national	>50	>2000	DK	>5
14	Multi-national	11-20	>2000	>2000	3-5
15	Australian	21-50	>2000	101-500	1-2
16	Multi-national	21-50	>2000	>2000	>5
17	Multi-national	11-20	>2000	11-25	>5
18	Multi-national	>50	>2000	101-500	>5
19	Australian	11-20	11-100	11-25	1-2
20	Australian	21-50	>2000	DK	>5
21	Multi-national	<5	11-100	11-25	1-2
22	Australian	11-20	11-100	11-25	3-5
23	Multi-national	6-10	101-500	26-100	3-5
24	Australian	<5	<10	<10	3-5
25	Australian	6-10	>2000	101-500	>5
26	Australian	6-10	11-100	26-100	>5
27	Australian	>50	101-500	<10	1-2
28	Multi-national	>50	>2000	11-25	>5
29	Multi-national	>50	>2000	501-2000	>5

Using Linear Regression Models to Analyse the Effect of Software Process Improvement

Joost Schalken[1], Sjaak Brinkkemper[2], and Hans van Vliet[1]

[1] Vrije Universiteit, Amsterdam, Department of Computer Science
{jjp.schalken, jc.van.vliet}@few.vu.nl
[2] Utrecht University, Institute of Information and Computing Sciences
s.brinkkemper@cs.uu.nl

Abstract. In this paper we publish the results of a thorough empirical evaluation of a CMM-based software process improvement program that took place at the IT department of a large Dutch financial institution. Data of 410 projects collected over a period of four years are analysed and a productivity improvement of about 20% is found. In addition to these results we explain how the use of linear regression models and hierarchical linear models greatly enhances the sensitivity of analysis of empirical data on software improvement programs.

1 Introduction

To improve the management and work processes in software development, the software process improvement field has proposed improvement models (such as the Capability Maturity Model [1], ISO-SPICE [2], and the Capability Maturity Model Integrated [3]) that are based on best practices and guidelines for software developing organisations. As each of these models focuses on a wide range of interacting practices, the benefits of an improvement model are not always intuitive. Therefore empirical data about the benefits of SPI is needed.

There is a lack of empirical studies on the effects of SPI in industry. Even for the most widely used improvement model, the Capability Maturity Model [1], little empirical data is available. In a recent meta analysis on the effects of the CMM, Galin and Avrahami [4] were only able to identify three studies that give details on productivity gains when an organisation progresses to CMM level 2 and only twelve studies that provide details on productivity gains when an organisation progresses to CMM level 3.

In this study we investigate the success of a software process improvement program at a large, Dutch financial institution. In this program the Capability Maturity Model has been used as the reference model for software process improvement and the Dynamic Systems Development Method (DSDM) [5] as the new project management methodology. We analysed the productivity of 410 projects during a period of four years and found a productivity increase of 20%.

If is often claimed that extensive measurement programs are ineffective in an immature organisation. We however believe that in immature organisations the

J. Münch and M. Vierimaa (Eds.): PROFES 2006, LNCS 4034, pp. 234–248, 2006.

effects of SPI are invisible because the data is too noisy to be analysed with simple statistical techniques. In this paper we explain how regression models [6] and hierarchical linear models [7] help interpreting the productivity data. Regression models offer an improved sensitivity to changes in productivity and hierarchical linear models allow researchers to study SPI programs that take place in heterogeneous organisations. *Heterogeneous organisations* consist of departments that use different technologies and work on different products.

Using these statistical techniques results in an explained variance of over 60% for our data, as opposed to a mere 2% when a straight-forward productivity index is used.

This paper provides an answer to the following two questions:

1. What is the impact of a project's CMM level on its productivity?
2. To what extent do the outcomes of a CMM study depend on the choice of proper statistical techniques?

2 Related Work

Related work for this study consists of two bodies of literature: studies of the empirical results of software process improvement and literature of statistical techniques used in empirical software engineering.

In [8, 9, 10, 11] studies of software process improvement are described. The studies report the (solely positive) changes in productivity of software developing organisations, expressed in ratios of lines of code delivered per unit of effort (usually man months).

In their paper *"Do SQA Programs Work"* [4] Galin and Avrahami provide an overview of the above mentioned case studies and others that contain empirical evidence on the effects of software process improvement. They identified 22 studies relating to the effects of Capability Maturity Model based software process improvement. Of these 22 studies, only 19 contained sufficiently detailed quantitative data to allow a meta analysis of the SPI effects. The meta analysis examines the effects of CMM on error density, productivity, rework schedule time, conformance to schedule and the effectiveness of error detection.

The authors were able to locate three studies that examine the change in productivity when a software development organisation increases its maturity from CMM level 1 to CMM level 2 and ten studies that examine the change in productivity when an organisation increases its maturity from CMM level 2 to CMM level 3. On average an organisation increases its productivity by 42.3% when it matures to CMM level 2. And an organisation that increases its maturity to CMM level 3 improves its productivity by an additional 44.4%.

Related work on the analysis of productivity data is hard to find in software process improvement papers, however research in cost-estimation provides instructions on how to apply regression models to relate effort to size [12, chap. 5] [13, chap. 12] and therefore how to analyse productivity. Unfortunately the statistical techniques used for cost-estimation models are not used to elucidate changes in productivity caused by software process improvement. Related work on hierarchical linear models applied to software process improvement has not been found[1].

A subset of the data that we examined in this study, has also been analysed using different statistical techniques in [14], where a method is demonstrated to validate size measurements made by the organisation and time series are used to analyse the changes of productivity over time (irrespective of CMM level).

3 Research Methodology

3.1 Research Design

To answer our research questions, we use the experimental design of a cohort study [15, p. 126]. We collected data on 410 software development projects and compared the productivity of projects that were executed in an CMM level 2 or 3 environment with projects that were executed in an environment that did not already fulfil the CMM requirements. For this comparison we used three different statistical techniques.

The cohort study design has some weaknesses that create threats to the validity of the study, of which the maturation effect poses the biggest threat. Changes in the organisation occur over time that are unrelated to CMM, but that do have an effect on the productivity of the projects (c.f. [16]). We found similar results in the different organisational departments that implemented SPI at different moments in time, which improves our confidence in the results.

3.2 Research Context

This study has been performed within an internal Information Technology department of a large financial institution. In this department over 1500 people were employed during the course of study. The organisation primarily builds and maintains large, custom-built, mainframe transaction processing systems, most of which are built in COBOL and TELON (an application-generator for COBOL). Besides these mainframe systems, a large variety of other systems are implemented, constructed and maintained by the organisation. These systems are implemented in a large variety of different programming languages (such as Java and COOL:Gen), run under various operating systems (such as Microsoft Windows and UNIX) and are distributed over different platforms (batch, block-based, GUI-based and browser-based).

The organisation has undertaken a major software process improvement program (SPI) to improve the internal IT processes and cooperation with the business in the period of 1999 until 2004. The SPI program included the introduction

[1] We did not find any relevant results in ACM's Portal, Springer-Verlag's SpringerLink, Elsevier's ScienceDirect or in IEEE Computer Society's Digital Library that contained both a relevant statistical term ("hierarchical linear model", "multi-level linear model", "mixed-effects model", "random-effects model", "random-coefficient regression model", or "covariance components model") and a relevant application domain term ("spi", "cmm", or "software process improvement").

of a software metrics program, the introduction of the Dynamic Systems Development Method (DSDM) [5] as the iterative development and project management method, the introduction of a tailor-made quality system consisting of two levels that comply with the requirements of CMM [1] level 2 and 3 respectively, and a culture change program to support the above mentioned changes.

To successfully implement the changes required for the software process improvement, a program with a dedicated senior vice-president was initiated. Through the SPI program the individual departments of the line organisation received assistance and coaching by dedicated internal and external consultants; IT staff received the required training and certification in CMM, DSDM and company-specific procedures; and improvement goals were set to maintain the commitment of upper management.

In the process the organisation designed an on-line knowledge base containing reference information about the DSDM method and the supporting management and quality processes, templates for documentation and review check-lists and background information about development tools. The on-line knowledge base was a replacement of an existing on-line knowledge base, that was based on the prior (linear) development method.

3.3 Data Collection

To perform the evaluation of the software process improvement program, two sources of data were used: the project database and a log of the assessment results. The project database contains generic information on all projects executed in the organisation and the assessment log contains information on which domains have been assessed and what the outcomes of the CMM assessment were. From the database, data about 410 closed projects has been extracted.

From the project database the size in function points, the effort, the end date and the department in which the project was executed has been extracted for each project. To obtain the maturity of the organisation in which the project has been executed, the end date of a project was compared with the assessment date of its domain. If the project has been executed before the assessment, the project has been considered to have been executed in an organisation with CMM maturity level 1. The decision rule to determine the maturity of the department in which the project has been executed leads to a conservative estimate of the effects of SPI.

Please note that before we analysed the data, we have multiplied the effort data with a random constant ($0.75 < \alpha < 1.5$) for the sake of confidentiality of the actual productivity figures. This linear scaling of the data does not in any way affect the improvement ratios that are provided in this paper.

3.4 Analysis Methods

We examined three distinct ways of comparing the productivity of an organisation before and after a software process improvement program. The methods of comparing productivity increase in sophistication and complexity.

Classical Approach. In most studies, productivity is defined as size divided by effort. Conte, Dunsmore and Shen [12, chap. 5] define productivity as *"the number of lines of source code produced per programmer-month (person-month) of effort"*. This leads to the following formula to estimate the productivity of an organisation (1):

$$\hat{L} = \frac{1}{n}\sum_{i=1}^{n} l_i = \frac{1}{n}\sum_{i=1}^{n}\frac{s_i}{e_i} \quad \text{where} \quad \begin{array}{ll} \hat{L} & \text{is estimated organisational productivity,} \\ l_i & \text{is productivity of project } i\text{, and} \\ s_i & \text{is size of the software } i\text{, and} \\ e_i & \text{is effort of project } i\text{, and} \\ n & \text{is the number of projects executed} \\ & \text{in the organisation} \end{array} \tag{1}$$

Size measurements of a project can also be expressed in function points [17] or other size metrics and effort can also be expressed in other measures without loss of generality. Although function points have certain desirable properties, such as technological independence [18], Galin and Avrahami [4] observe that "most of the reporting organisations applied the classic lines of code (LOC) measure for productivity". In our study a productivity index consisting of function points (S_{fp}) per hour of effort of IT personnel (E_{hr}) is used. The effort of IT personnel includes not only programmer effort, but also the effort of requirements engineers, technical designers, architects and project management.

Productivity indices (L) can be used to determine whether the productivity has changed. To estimate the productivity index ($\hat{L}$) of an organisation the productivity indices of projects carried out in that organisation are averaged (1). To determine the effect of software process improvement, the productivity index of the organisation before the software process improvement initiative ($L^{\neg spi}$) is compared with that of the organisation after the software process improvement initiative (L^{spi}). A t-test [19] can be used to test whether the productivity of the organisation has changed significantly (2):

$$\begin{array}{l} \mathrm{H}_0 : L^{\neg spi} = L^{spi} \\ \mathrm{H}_1 : L^{\neg spi} \neq L^{spi} \end{array} \tag{2}$$

Cost-Model Comparison Approach. In studies of productivity, changes in productivity are often measured in lines of code per man month [4] or in another ratio of size divided by effort. We believe however that better comparisons of productivity changes can be made based on the same data.

Instead of describing the productivity with a single productivity index L, the productivity also can be described by a regression equation that models effort as a function of size. The parameters of the regression model $\beta_{1\ldots n}$ now function as a measure for productivity. The simplest regression model is a linear regression model (3):

$$e_{hr_i} = \beta_0 + \beta_1 \cdot s_{fp_i} + r_i \quad \text{where} \quad \begin{array}{ll} e_{hr_i} & \text{is effort of a project in hours,} \\ s_{fp_i} & \text{is size of effort in function points, and} \\ r_i & \text{is unexplained, residual variance} \\ & (R \sim N(0, \sigma^2)) \end{array} \tag{3}$$

In order to build a valid regression model, the relation must satisfy the assumptions of linear regression: (a) linearity of the relation, (b) independence of residuals, (c) residuals have constant variance and (d) residuals follow the normal distribution [6].

Unfortunately, in most organisations productivity data does not satisfy the assumptions of linear regression. In most organisations larger projects are less predictable and more prone to overrun their budget and schedules. This is an indication that the residuals (difference between observations and the regression model) are related to the size of a project, which is a violation of assumption (c) and can lead to invalid conclusions.

If the relation between effort and size violates one of the assumptions of the linear regression model, it is possible to scale the dependent (E_{hr}) and or independent (S_{fp}) variables before they are used in the regression equation. Although in principle every transformation is allowed, involution, extraction of roots and taking a logarithm are often used transformations. Based on diagnostic information, one can choose an appropriate transformation. This leads to the more general regression model (4):

$$e_{hr}{}'_i = \beta_0 + \beta_1 \cdot s_{fp}{}'_i + r_i \qquad \text{where} \quad \begin{array}{ll} e_{hr}{}'_i & \text{is scaled effort of a project in hours,} \\ s_{fp}{}'_i & \text{is scaled size of effort in function points,} \\ r_i & \text{is unexplained, residual variance} \\ & (R \sim N(0, \sigma^2)) \end{array} \tag{4}$$

Regression equations that model effort as a function of size are usually employed to build cost prediction models (such as COCOMO-II [20]). Their use however is not limited to cost estimation, as regression models are also useful to compare the productivity of organisations or to determine the productivity effects of a software process improvement initiative. Productivity of organisations can then be compared by comparing the parameters $\beta_{1 \ldots n}$ of the regression models.

To determine the effects of software process improvement, the process maturity (C) of the organisation can be factored into the equation (5) to determine the influence of software process improvement. If software process improvement has no effect, the regression parameters β_2 and β_3 should be equal to zero (6), which can be tested with ANOVA [19]. By examining the parameters β_2 and β_3 we obtain an estimate of the effect of software process improvement.

$$\begin{array}{rl} e_{hr}{}'_i = & \beta_0 + \beta_1 \cdot s_{fp}{}'_i + \\ & \beta_2 \cdot c_i + \\ & \beta_3 \cdot s_{fp}{}'_i \cdot c_i + r_i \end{array} \qquad \text{where} \quad \begin{array}{ll} e_{hr}{}'_i & \text{is scaled effort of a project in hours,} \\ s_{fp}{}'_i & \text{is scaled size of effort in function points,} \\ c_i & \text{is the maturity level of the organisation} \\ & \text{in which the project is executed,} \\ r_i & \text{is unexplained, residual variance} \\ & (R \sim N(0, \sigma^2)) \end{array} \tag{5}$$

$$\begin{array}{l} \mathrm{H}_0 : \beta_2 = 0 \quad \text{and} \quad \beta_3 = 0 \\ \\ \mathrm{H}_1 : \beta_2 \neq 0 \quad \text{or} \quad \beta_3 \neq 0 \end{array} \tag{6}$$

The advantage of the regression model approach is that regression models take the effect of project size on the productivity of a project into account. After all, projects can have startup costs and projects can experience (dis-)economy of scale. Ignoring the effect of project size on project productivity increases the residual, unexplained variability in the data. This increased residual variance means that larger sample sizes are needed to obtain significant results. In certain situations it is even possible that, by ignoring the effect of size on productivity, invalid conclusions are drawn (e.g. if the size of projects before and after the software process improvement changes significantly).

Hierarchical Model Approach. Large organisations structure their work according to the principle of division of labour. These large organisations consist of different departments that perform different projects. These departments either specialise on the group of products they work on or specialise on the technology or skills that the department uses. We call these organisations with specialised departments heterogeneous organisations. In this section we explain why data from heterogeneous organisations cannot be adequately analysed using classical linear regression models and how hierarchical models [21, 7] can be used to analyse this data.

Linear regression models are based on the assumption that residuals in a model are independent, and therefore the observations need to be drawn from a single homogeneous pool of subjects. The characteristics of such a homogeneous pool from which the observations are drawn should have the same statistical distribution. Because the characteristics of departments in a heterogeneous organisation differ, the assumption of independent residuals does not hold.

We illustrate the problems sketched above with a hypothetical example. If we want to understand the effects of a type of fertiliser on the growth-rate of fruit, an experiment could be set up with eight plots of apples and eight plots of pears, four plots of bananas and two plots of pineapples. Half the plots are assigned with the new fertiliser (the treatment group) and half the plots are assigned with no fertiliser (the control group). At the moment the plants bear fruit, the yield of each of the plots is weighed. To determine the effect of the fertiliser (a) the yields of all plots with fertiliser could be compared with the yields of all plots without the fertiliser or (b) for each type of fruit the average yields of plots with fertiliser could be compared with the plots grown without fertiliser. In the first approach, we literally compare apples with pears, which severely increases error variance and therefore reduces the chance we detect the effect of the fertiliser. If we on the other hand take the second approach to gauge the effect of the fertiliser, we have to make four comparisons, which increases the chance of making an error by fourfold.

When determining the effect of software process improvement on productivity, the productivity of projects that took place before and after the software process improvement initiative are compared. Unfortunately the number of projects that take place within a single department of a company is usually too small to find significant results of software process improvement. If the productivity of projects that took place in different departments is compared, effectively 'apples' are compared with 'pears'. Hierarchical linear models can be used to make a single comparison of the overall effects of changes in software process (or fertiliser) and at the same time take into account that we are comparing 'apples' with 'pears'. Multi-level linear models, mixed-effects models, random-effects models, random-coefficient regression modes, and covariance components models are other names for hierarchical level models. To measure the overall effects of software process improvement, hierarchical linear models should be used to take the differences of the departments into account.

Hierarchical linear models are an extension of ordinary linear regression models. In a hierarchical linear model, the regression model is split up in two components: a level 1 model and a level 2 model. Hierarchical linear models extend linear regression models by fitting a new set of regression parameters for each group of data, the department in which the project took place. For each group a different set of regression parameters $\beta_{0\,j} \ldots \beta_{n\,j}$ is found. The level 2 model brings structure in the regression parameters; an overall $\gamma_{n\,0}$ value for a group of parameters $\beta_{n\,j}$ is determined, from which each group j is allowed to deviate by $u_{n\,j}$.

The level 1 model (7) for effort looks similar to the regression model from the previous section. Note however that the observations i are grouped according to the department j in which they were made. Also note that the parameters in the level 1 regression model also have a subscript for their group j.

$$
\begin{aligned}
e_{hr}{}'_{i\,j} = \beta_{0\,j} + \beta_{1\,j} \cdot s_{fp}{}'_{i\,j} + \\
\beta_{2\,j} \cdot c_{i\,j} + \\
\beta_{3\,j} \cdot s_{fp}{}'_{i\,j} \cdot c_{i\,j} + \\
r_{i\,j}
\end{aligned}
\quad \text{where} \quad
\begin{array}{ll}
e_{hr}{}'_{i\,j} & \text{is scaled effort of a project in hours,} \\
s_{fp}{}'_{i\,j} & \text{is scaled size of effort in function points,} \\
c_{i\,j} & \text{is the maturity level of the organisation} \\
 & \text{in which the project is executed,} \\
r_{i\,j} & \text{is unexplained, residual variance} \\
 & (R \sim N(0, \sigma^2))
\end{array}
\tag{7}
$$

We also have a level 2 model (8) for productivity, which breaks up each $\beta_{n\,j}$ in the level 1 model into an organisation wide parameter $\gamma_{n\,j}$ and a deviation $u_{n\,j}$ from that organisation average for each department j.

$$
\begin{array}{ll}
\beta_{0\,j} = \gamma_{0\,0} + u_{0\,j} & u_{0\,j} \sim N(0, \tau_{0\,0}) \\
\beta_{1\,j} = \gamma_{1\,0} + u_{1\,j} & u_{1\,j} \sim N(0, \tau_{1\,1}) \\
\beta_{2\,j} = \gamma_{2\,0} + u_{2\,j} & u_{2\,j} \sim N(0, \tau_{2\,2}) \\
\beta_{3\,j} = \gamma_{3\,0} + u_{3\,j} & u_{3\,j} \sim N(0, \tau_{3\,3})
\end{array}
\tag{8}
$$

Bryk and Raudenbush [7, chap. 3] provide a conceptual explanation of how these models can be fitted and a more thorough mathematical description of how values for these parameters can be found is provided by Pinheiro and Bates [22, chap. 2].

To determine whether software process improvement has an effect, the parameters $\gamma_{2\,0}$ and $\gamma_{3\,0}$ should be tested for equality with zero (9). The parameters $\gamma_{2\,0}$ and $\gamma_{3\,0}$ are related with the maturity of the organisation (c_i) and if the parameters are equal to zero that would indicate that SPI has no effect.

$$
\begin{array}{llll}
\mathrm{H}_0 : \gamma_{2\,0} = 0 & \text{and} & \gamma_{3\,0} = 0 \\
\mathrm{H}_1 : \gamma_{2\,0} \neq 0 & \text{or} & \gamma_{3\,0} \neq 0
\end{array}
\tag{9}
$$

The advantage of using hierarchical linear models in determining the effects of SPI in heterogeneous organisation is that by taking the department into account, the residual variance of the data is reduced, which reduces the amount of data required to make an analysis. Furthermore the usage of hierarchical linear models can guard against making erroneous conclusions. Such erroneous conclusions could be made if workload of departments that perform easy assignments increases at the expense of the workload of departments that perform difficult assignments. In such cases the productivity of the organisation would seem to have increased, whereas in reality the work has changed and no real performance increase has occurred.

4 Results

4.1 Classical Approach

In this section we use the classical approach to determine the effects of software process improvement. Table 1 shows the average productivity of projects that are executed in a CMM Level 1, 2 and 3 organisation.

Table 1. Productivity Indices per Maturity Level

Maturity	*CMM Level*	Productivity $L_{hr/fp}$
low	1	14.46
medium	2	12.08
	3	8.50
	2 & 3	11.54

From Table 1 we can conclude that projects executed in a CMM level 2 or level 3 organisation are on average 20.19% more productive than projects that are executed in a CMM level 1 organisation. When we use a t-test to test hypothesis (2), which states that $L^{spi}_{hr/fp} \neq L^{\neg spi}_{hr/fp}$, we find that have to reject H_0 with $p = 0.002$ ($t = 3.13, df = 267$). We can therefore conclude that there is a significant productivity increase after the implementation of SPI.

Although we do find statistically significant results with the classical approach, the results are not satisfactory if we look at the amount of explained variance. When we fit productivity as a function of process maturity (level 1 vs. level 2 and 3), we obtain $R^2 = 0.02$. This means that only 2% of the differences in productivity can be explained by process maturity.

4.2 Cost-Model Comparison Approach

We use linear regression models to determine the effect of software process improvement on productivity. As explained in Sect. 3.4, we first need to find a suitable linear regression model between effort and size.

In Table 2 we tabulated diagnostic information on six different combinations of transformations on both the dependent (effort) and the independent variable (size). The Shapiro-Wilk test [23] is used to test for normality and the Breusch-Pagan test [6, p. 115] is to test the constance of variance of the residuals. The residuals of the linear model and the log-transformed model ($log(E) = \beta_0 + \beta_1 log(S) + R$) are shown in Fig. 1. From Fig. 1 we can see that the residuals from the linear model are correlated with the fitted values (show heteroscedascity) and that the residuals from the logistic model are uncorrelated with the fitted values (homoscedastic). Homoscedasticity, or constance of variance, is assumed in linear regression models and therefore the logistic model is superior to the simple linear model. For goodness of fit we used the unadjusted multiple coefficient of determination R^2, which tells us how much of the variation in effort can be explained by size.

Table 2. Diagnostic Information on Effort Regression Models

		Residuals			
	Goodness of fit	*Constance of Variance*		*Normality*	
Formula	R^2	X^2_{bp} [a]	p	W^b	p
$E = \beta_0 + \beta_1 S + R$	0.493	86.07	¡ 0.001	0.798	¡ 0.001
$E = \beta_0 + \beta_1 S^2 + R$	0.315	87.29	¡ 0.001	0.748	¡ 0.001
$E = \beta_0 + \beta_1 log(S) + R$	0.407	33.14	¡ 0.001	0.830	¡ 0.001
$log(E) = \beta_0 + \beta_1 S + R$	0.436	27.26	¡ 0.001	0.981	¡ 0.001
$log(E) = \beta_0 + \beta_1 S^2 + R$	0.202	54.24	¡ 0.001	0.988	0.002
$log(E) = \beta_0 + \beta_1 log(S) + R$	0.576	4.43	0.035	0.995	0.283

[a] Breusch-Pagan X^2 to test for dependence between predictors and residuals.
[b] Shapiro-Wilk W to test deviation of residuals from the normal distribution.

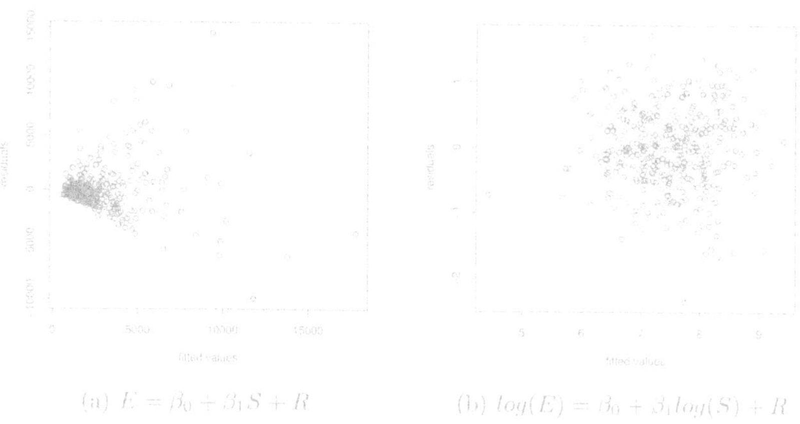

(a) $E = \beta_0 + \beta_1 S + R$ (b) $log(E) = \beta_0 + \beta_1 log(S) + R$

Fig. 1. Residuals of Linear Models plotted against the Fitted Values

If we examine the diagnostic information in Table 2, we see that the log-transformed model ($log(E) = \beta_0 + \beta_1 log(S) + R$) has the best characteristics; 58% of the variance is explained and its residuals are normally distributed and the variance of the residuals only has negligible relation with size.

We can transform the model for log-transformed effort to a model for effort by raising both sides of the equation to the power e, which leads to equation (10). It turns out that we effectively arrive at an exponential effort estimation model [12, p. 281] of the form $effort_i = \beta_0 * size_i^{\beta_1} * e^{\epsilon_i}$. To determine if the maturity of an organisation has an effect on the productivity, we effectively are comparing cost-estimation models.

$$e_{hri} = exp(\beta_0) \cdot s_{fp_i}{}^{\beta_1} \cdot exp(r_i) \quad \text{where} \quad \begin{array}{ll} e_{hri} & \text{is effort of a project in hours,} \\ s_{fp_i} & \text{is size of effort in function points} \\ r_i & \text{is unexplained, residual variance} \\ & (R \sim N(0, \sigma^2)) \end{array} \tag{10}$$

Having selected an appropriate regression model, we continue by testing the hypothesis (6) that process maturity influences on productivity with ANOVA, the results of which can be seen in Table 3.

Table 3. ANOVA on Linear Regression Model ($log(E_{hr}) = \beta_0 + \beta_1\ log(S_{fp}) + \beta_2\ C + \beta_3\ log(S_{fp})\ C + R$)

	df	*SSE*	*MSE*	*F*	*p*
$log(S_{fp})$	1	199.725	199.725	580.082	¡ 0.001
C	2	6.937	3.469	10.075	¡ 0.001
$log(S_{fp})$:C	2	0.966	0.483	1.403	0.2471
residuals	404	139.099	0.344		

From the ANOVA we can see that both size ($log(S_{fp})$) and process maturity (C) have a significant effect on the effort ($log(E_{hr})$. Furthermore we can observe that there is no interaction between size and process maturity, which means that software process improvement has a similar (positive) effect on both large and small projects. If we examine the regression coefficients, we arrive at the following relations between effort and size, which overall is a 20.86% improvement of productivity for CMM level 2 & 3 projects over CMM level 1 projects.

$$\begin{aligned} \text{CMM level 1: } E_{hr} &= 31.68 \cdot S_{fp}{}^{0.80} \\ \text{CMM level 2: } E_{hr} &= 26.35 \cdot S_{fp}{}^{0.80} \\ \text{CMM level 3: } E_{hr} &= 18.93 \cdot S_{fp}{}^{0.80} \end{aligned} \tag{11}$$

If we look at the explained variance, we see an $R^2 = 0.60$. This means that 60% of the variation in effort can be explained by process maturity and size. This leave less chance that the results can be explained in an alternative way.

4.3 Hierarchical Model Approach

In this section we examine the effects of software process improvement with hierarchical linear models. In the previous section we established that that the log-scaled model best fits the data ($log(E) = \beta_0 + \beta_1 log(S) + \beta_2 C + R$). In a similar manner we examine the influence of domain on the regression coefficients ($\beta_{1...3}$) in Table 4. This table contains the Akaike Information Criterion (AIC) and the Bayesian Information Criterion (BIC) [22] and the log-likelihood of each model.

From Table 4 we see that model $log(E) = \beta_{0\,j} + \beta_1 log(S) + \beta_2 C + R$ has the lowest AIC and therefore is the best balance between goodness-of-fit and number of parameters. If we compare the likelihoods with the optimal regression model from the previous section, we obtain that the hierarchical linear model is significantly better (log-likelihood ratio=22.27645, $p < .0001$). Although some other hierarchical linear models have an even lower log-likelihood, this difference is not significant.

Table 4. Diagnostic Information on Hierarchical Linear Models

Formula	AIC	BIC	*Log-likelihood*
$log(E) = \beta_0 + \beta_1 log(S) + \beta_2 C + R$	733.17	753.25	-361.58
$log(E) = \beta_{0\,j} + \beta_1 log(S) + \beta_2 C + R$	712.89	736.90	-350.45
$log(E) = \beta_{0\,j} + \beta_{1\,j} log(S) + \beta_2 C + R$	715.94	748.07	-349.97
$log(E) = \beta_{0\,j} + \beta_1 log(S) + \beta_{2\,j} C + R$	718.60	762.77	-348.30
$log(E) = \beta_{0\,j} + \beta_{1\,j} log(S) + \beta_{2\,j} C + R$	725.92	786.16	-347.96

When we obtain an ANOVA on model $log(E) = \beta_{0\,j} + \beta_1 log(S) + \beta_2 C + R$ to test whether process maturity has an influence on productivity, hypothesis (9), we obtain the results as shown in Table 5:

Table 5. ANOVA on Hierarchical Linear Model ($log(E) = \beta_{0\,j} + \beta_1\, log(S) + \beta_2\, C + R$)

	num df	*den df*	*F*	*p*
$log(S_{fp})$	1	369	630.06	¡ 0.001
C	2	369	8.06	¡ 0.001

So, significant effects of process maturity on productivity are not only found if we analyse the data with linear regression models, but also if we analyse the data using hierarchical linear models. As hierarchical linear models take the impact of both size and organisation into account, we rejected that these obvious alternative explanations explain the change in productivity instead of software process improvement. Taking organisation into account when analysing the data increases the explained variance from 60% to 67% ($R^2 = 0.67$). This increases the confidence in our results.

If we examine the regression coefficients, we obtain an 23.42% overall productivity increase for CMM level 2 & 3 organisation when compared with a CMM level 1 organisation. Examining the regression coefficients leads to the following, organisation-wide models for productivity:

$$\begin{aligned} \text{CMM level 1: } E_{hr} &= 33.09 \cdot {S_{fp}}^{0.82} \\ \text{CMM level 2: } E_{hr} &= 26.68 \cdot {S_{fp}}^{0.82} \\ \text{CMM level 3: } E_{hr} &= 20.40 \cdot {S_{fp}}^{0.82} \end{aligned} \tag{12}$$

5 Conclusions

From the study we have found clear evidence that CMM does increase the productivity of an organisation. We found a productivity increase of 20%. More planning and more attention to management and work processes do seem to have a positive effect on the productivity of the organisation. The improvements made in this study are smaller than found in certain similar studies, but we believe that this can might be explained because in some studies small convenience samples are analysed instead of the productivity data on all projects in that organisation.

In addition we found that the classical method of comparing productivity indices has a lot of disadvantages, as only a tiny part of the variance can be explained by the maturity level. By using more sophisticated statistical techniques, linear regression models and hierarchical linear models, we gain confidence in the results of the analysis as the underlying assumptions of the analytical techniques are met and the influence of alternative explanations for the change in productivity are excluded. Linear regression models allow us to exclude the impact of project size on changing productivity and hierarchical linear models allow us to exclude the impact of the department or organisational unit in which the project takes place. It gives confidence in the results that the increases found in productivity using both statistical methods are approximately equal.

Acknowledgements

We would like to than Jean Kleijnen, Marcel Uleman, Ton Groen for their insights into the SPI program and their help in obtaining the required data. Frank Harmsen's guidance and supervision at the beginning of the project is greatly appreciated, as is Geurt Jongbloed's helpful statistical advice.

References

1. Paulk, M.C., Curtis, B., Chrissis, M.B., Weber, C.V.: Capability maturity model for software, version 1.1. Technical Report CMU/SEI-93-TR-24, DTIC ADA263403, Software Engineering Institute, Carnegie Mellon University, Pittsburgh, PA, USA (1993) Available from: http://www.sei.cmu.edu/.
2. ISO/IEC: Information technology - software process assessment. Technical Report ISO/IEC TR 15504:1998, International Organization for Standardization/ International Electrotechnical Commission (1998)

3. CMMI Product Development Team: CMMI for systems engineering/software engineering/integrated product and process development/supplier sourcing, version 1.1 continuous representation. Technical Report CMU/SEI-2002-TR-011, ESC-TR-2002-011, Software Engineering Institute, Carnegie Mellon University, Pittsburgh, PA, USA (2000) Available from: http://www.sei.cmu.edu/.
4. Galin, D., Avrahami, M.: Do SQA programs work – CMM works. A meta analysis. In Amir Tomer, R., Schach, S.R., eds.: Proceedings of the International Conference on Software - Science, Technology & Engineering (SwSTE'05), Washington, DC, USA, IEEE Computer Society Press (2005) 95–100
5. Stapleton, J.: Framework for Business Centred Development: DSDM Manual version 4.1. DSDM Consortium, Ltd., Kent, United Kingdom. (2002)
6. Peter, J., Kutner, M.H., Nachtsheim, C.J., Wasserman, W.: Applied Linear Statistical Models. 4 edn. WCB/McGraw-Hill, Boston, MA, USA (1996)
7. Bryk, A.S., Raudenbush, S.W.: Hierarchical Linear Models: Applications and Data Analysis methods. 1st edn. Volume 1 of Advanced Quantitative Techniques in the Social Sciences. Sage Publications, Newbury Park, CA, USA (1992)
8. Diaz, M., King, J.: How CMM impacts quality, productivity, rework, and the bottom line. CrossTalk: The Journal of Defense Software Engineering **15**(3) (2002) 9–14
9. Diaz, M., Sligo, J.: How software process improvement helped Motorola. IEEE Software **14**(5) (1997) 75–81
10. Wohlwend, H., Rosenbaum, S.: Software improvements in an international company. In: Proceedings of the 15th International Conference on Software Engineering (ICSE-93), Washington, DC, USA, IEEE Computer Society Press (1993) 212–220
11. Oldham, L.G., Putman, D.B., Peterson, M., Rudd, B., Tjoland, K.: Benefits realized from climbing the CMM ladder. CrossTalk: The Journal of Defense Software Engineering **12**(9) (1999) 7–10
12. Conte, S.D., Dunsmore, H.E., Shen, V.Y.: Software Engineering Metrics and Models. Benjamin/Cummings Publishing, Menlo Park, CA, USA (1986)
13. Fenton, N.E., Pfleeger, S.L.: Software Metrics: A Rigorous and Practical Approach. 2nd edn. International Thomson Computer Press, London, UK (1998)
14. Verhoef, C.: Quantifying software process improvement. Technical report, Vrije Universiteit Amsterdam, Amsterdam, NL (2005) Available from: http://www.cs.vu.nl/~x [Accessed: 05/12/2005].
15. Cook, T.D., Campbell, D.T.: Quasi-Experimentation: Design & Analysis Issues for Field Settings. Rand McNally College Publishing Company, Chicago, IL, USA (1979)
16. McGarry, F., Decker, B.: Attaining level 5 in cmm process maturity. IEEE Software **22**(6) (2002) 87–96
17. Albrecht, A.J.: Measuring application development productivity. In: Proceedings of the Joint SHARE/GUIDE/IBM Applications Development Symposium. (1979) 83–92
18. Furey, S.: Point: Why we should use function points. IEEE Software **14**(2) (1997) 28–30
19. Bhattacharyya, G.K., Johnson, R.A.: Statistical Concepts and Methods. Wiley Series in Probability and Statistics. Wiley-Interscience, New York, NY, USA (1977)
20. Boehm, B.W., Abts, C., Brown, A.W., Chulani, S., Clark, B.K., Horowitz, E., Madachy, R., Reifer, D.J., Steec, B.: Software Cost Estimation with Cocomo II. Prentice-Hall PTR, Upper Daddle River, NJ, USA (2000)

21. Lindley, D.V., Smith, A.F.M.: Bayes estimates for the linear model. Journal of the Royal Statistical Society **34**(1) (1972) 1–41
22. Pinheiro, J.C., Bates, D.M.: Mixed Effects Models in S and S-Plus. 1st edn. Statistics and Computing. Springer-Verlag, Berlin, D (2000)
23. Shapiro, S.S., Wilk, M.B.: An analysis of variance test for normality (complete samples). Biometrika **52**(3 & 4) (1965) 591–611

Taba Workstation: Supporting Software Process Deployment Based on CMMI and MR-MPS.BR

Mariano Montoni, Gleison Santos, Ana Regina Rocha, Sávio Figueiredo, Reinaldo Cabral, Rafael Barcellos, Ahilton Barreto, Andréa Soares, Cristina Cerdeiral, and Peter Lupo

COPPE/UFRJ - Federal University of Rio de Janeiro
POBOX 68511 – ZIP 21945-970 – Rio de Janeiro, Brazil
{mmontoni, gleison, darocha}@cos.ufrj.br

Abstract. Deployment of software processes based on reference models is a knowledge-intensive task, i.e., a great amount of technical knowledge must be applied in order to guarantee conformance and adherence of processes deployed to the reference models adopted. Moreover, software process deployers have to deal with organizational and individual cultural problems on a regular basis, for instance, resistances to organizational changes. Therefore, the success of software process deployment within an organization or organizational unit depends on both technical and social aspects of the software process deployment strategy definition and execution. This paper presents the Taba Workstation, an enterprise-oriented Process-centered Software Engineering Environment (PSEE) constituted of an integrated set of tools to support software process deployment based on the Capability Maturity Model Integration (CMMI) and the Reference Model for Brazilian Software Process Improvement (MR-MPS.BR). Software process appraisals demonstrated that the Taba Workstation constitutes one of the most important organizational assets to facilitate the success of software process deployment initiatives and to overcome the inherent difficulties.

1 Introduction

Deployment of software processes based on reference models is a knowledge-intensive task, i.e., a great amount of technical knowledge must be applied in order to guarantee conformance and adherence of processes deployed to the reference models adopted. Moreover, software process deployers have to deal with organizational and individual cultural problems on a regular basis, for instance, resistances to organizational changes [1, 2]. Therefore, the success of software process deployment within an organization or organizational unit depends on both technical and social aspects of the software process deployment strategy definition and execution.

One important characteristic of a software process deployment initiative is the selection of an appropriate reference model to base the definition of the software processes and evaluation of the organization. International standards like ISO 12207 [3] and ISO 15504 [4] and software process quality models like CMMI (Capability Maturity Model Integration) [5] were developed aiming to define the requirements of an ideal organization, i.e., a reference model to be used in order to assess the maturity of

J. Münch and M. Vierimaa (Eds.): PROFES 2006, LNCS 4034, pp. 249 – 262, 2006.

the organization and their capability to develop software. Based on these standards and models, Brazilian industry and research institutions have worked together during the last two years aiming to define the Reference Model for Brazilian Software Process Improvement (MR-MPS.BR) [6, 8, 9]. This model has been deployed in many companies in Brazil and official appraisals were already conducted.

This paper presents the Taba Workstation, an enterprise-oriented Process-centered Software Engineering Environment (PSEE) constituted of an integrated set of tools to support software process deployment based on the Capability Maturity Model Integration (CMMI) and the Reference Model for Brazilian Software Process Improvement (MR-MPS.BR).

Section 2 presents the Reference Model for Brazilian Software Process Improvement and the appraisal method developed. Section 3 presents the main characteristics of PSEE approaches to support software process definition, deployment and enactment. Section 4 describes the main objectives of the Taba Workstation, and how it supports software process deployers during the deployment of processes according to reference models. Section 5 presents the conclusions and points out future directions for the presented work.

2 The Reference Model for Brazilian Software Process Improvement

The Reference Model for Brazilian Software Process Improvement (MR-MPS.BR) was created with the objective to provide an adequate model to Brazilian public and private organizations with different characteristics and sizes based on the most important reference models for software process definition and improvement (ISO/IEC 12207 [19], ISO/IEC 15504 [20], and CMMI [21]).

The reference standard for the software processes of MR-MPS.BR is the ISO/IEC 12207, i.e., this standard is the framework for the definition of the processes that constitute the MR-MPS.BR. Similarly to the ISO/IEC 12207 standard, the MR-MPS.BR defines fundamental processes, supporting processes and an adaptation process. Each company interested in deploying the MR-MPS.BR should select the pertinent processes from that set according to the adaptation process. The expected results for the deployment of the MR-MPS.BR processes are an adaptation of the expected results of the ISO/IEC 12207 processes and activities.

Seven maturity levels were established in the MR-MPS.BR: Level A (Optimization), Level B (Quantitatively Managed), Level C (Defined), Level D (Largely Defined), Level E (Partially Defined), Level F (Managed), and Level G (Partially Managed). For each of these maturity levels, processes were assigned based on the ISO/IEC 12207 standard and on the process areas of levels 2, 3, 4 and 5 of CMMI staged representation. This division has a different graduation of the CMMI staged representation aiming to enable a more gradual and adequate deployment in small and medium size Brazilian companies. The possibility of rating companies maturity considering more levels, not only diminishes the cost and effort of achieving a certain maturity level, but also allows the visibility of the results of the software process improvement within the company and across the country in a shorter time when compared to other models, such as CMMI. The criteria used to divide the processes across the maturity levels G-C were the importance of the process to the company, the facility to implement it and the dependency of the process to the others.

The MR-MPS.BR Appraisal Method for Process Improvement was defined based on the ISO/IEC 15504 standard. The level of deployment of the expected results related to a specific process is evaluated based on indicators that evidence such deployment. These indicators are defined for each company, related to the expected results of a process, and can be one of the following types: (i) Direct, (ii) Indirect, or (iii) Affirmations. Direct indicators are intermediate work products that result from an activity. Indirect indicators are generally documents that indicate that an activity was executed. Affirmations are results of interviews with the project teams of the evaluated projects. The implementation of an expected result is evaluated according to four levels: (i) TI – Totally Implemented; (ii) LI – Largely Implemented; (iii) PI – Partially Implemented, and (iv) NI – Not Implemented. The appraisal method adheres completely the ISO/IEC 15504 standard appraisal method defined to the staged representation.

A company is considered MR-MPS.BR level A, B, C, D, E, F or G if and only if all of its units, divisions or sectors had been rated as such level. Since one or more appraisals can be executed in a company, it is possible that parts of a company are rated with different levels. No matter the appraisal context, the evidential document of the appraisal must explicitly state the objective of the appraisal (appraisal scope), and the maturity level ratings.

3 PSEE Approaches to Support Software Process Definition, Deployment and Enactment

A great variety of PSEE approaches have been defined, designed and implemented over the past years. Many of these approaches have been developed to cope with the software engineering dynamic environments, such as software process evolution, decentralization of software process modeling and enactment, and support of cooperative activities. In the following, some of the most significant approaches to process model definition, deployment and enactment will be discussed.

EPOS (Expert System for Program and ("og") System Development) is a SEE (Software Engineering Environment) with emphasis on Process Modeling, Software Configuration Management and support to cooperative work [13]. EPOS supports a reflexive, object-oriented software process modeling language called SPELL. EPOS facilitates basic mechanisms for incremental (re)planning and enactment of the process models by process tools like Planner and Process Engine. An evolution of EPOS is EPOSDB built to store versioned software products, as well as their related process models. EPOS also supports cooperative transactions. EPOS is constituted of a meta-process for managing model evolution, and mechanisms for managing process evolution: retrieval of project experience, recording of project experience and manipulation of task-network layout. Although EPOS efficiently supports process modeling, evolution and enactment, there are not knowledge management mechanisms to provide knowledge to process executants during process enactment. Moreover, EPOS provides a meta-model only to software process domain. The connection between this domain and other areas of Software Engineering is not allowed.

Oz is a Process-centered Software Engineering Environment (PSEE) that implements the requirements for a decentralized PSEE based on a design for decentralization of process modeling and enactment [14]. The Oz environment supports process modeling using two popular families of Process Modeling Languages (PMLs), rules and Petri-Nets. Although the Oz environment implements a decentralized Process Centered Environment architecture, there is no integration of the process models to other software engineering tools. Moreover, the formalisms for process modeling sometimes become a burden for process modeler due to lack of intuition. This creates significant barriers to entry and, consequently, limits the possibility for the PMLs to be adopted in practice [2].

SPADE is a research project with the goal of developing an environment for Software Process Analysis, Design and Enactment [15]. SPADE is centered on a process modeling language called SLANG, an extension of a high-level Petri nets. SPADE-1 evolved to support cooperation in software development. Although SPADE-1 has demonstrated to be efficient to deal with synchronous and asynchronous activities among distributed, there is no evidence of applicability of such approach in the industry in large scale.

MILOS (Minimally Invasive Long Term Organizational Support) aims at offering support for agile processes by providing collaboration and coordination technology for distributed software development [16]. It also supports project planning and knowledge management. MILOS is constituted of the following components: a workflow engine, an experience base, and a resource pool. MILOS also supports agile software development with the use of some Extreme Programming (XP) practices. The MILOS PSEE does not provide support to important knowledge management tasks, such as consultation of organizational members' skills and knowledge that fulfill projects specific needs. Moreover, the MILOS PSEE does not model a comprehensive set of the Software Engineering Domain. Therefore, efficient integration of MILOS tools to other tools that support different areas of Software Engineering is not to be guaranteed.

Artemis 7 is a Web-based software developed to support business processes and roles associated, and to enable deployment of multiple solutions on a common platform [17]. Artemis 7 allows configurable access levels based on role and rights granted that allow users to access the various modules and features of the solution based on their individual needs. This approach ensures that each user need only see the functionality and information necessary to perform their responsibilities, thereby making the application easier to use for all stakeholders. Since Artemis 7 were developed to be used in general domains, the definition, design, implementation and integration of tools to support specific needs in the Software Engineering area are not feasible.

4 The Taba Workstation

The Taba Workstation is an enterprise-oriented Process-centered Software Engineering Environment (PSEE) that supports individual and group activities, project management activities, enhancement of software products quality, and increase of the productivity, providing the means for the software engineers to control the project and measure the activities evolution based on information gathered across the development. It also integrates knowledge management activities within software processes aiming to preserve organizational knowledge, and to foster the institutionalization of a learning software organization. The workstation also provides the infrastructure to the development and integration of tools to support the execution of software processes. Moreover, this infrastructure maintains a useful repository containing software project information gathered across its life cycle [7, 10, 11, 12].

In order to support the definition, deployment, and improvement of software processes, the Taba Workstation supports the definition of organizational standard processes and tailoring of these processes to specific projects aiming to increase the control and improve the quality of software products. Therefore, the Taba Workstation not only supports software engineers in the execution of software development processes activities, but also provides the means to execute these processes according to organizational software development processes.

During the last years, the Taba Workstation evolved to comply with the different levels of capability maturity models of software organizations. Therefore, the main objectives of Taba Workstation are:

- to support the configuration of process-centered software engineering environments for different organizations (Configured PSEE);
- to support the automatic generation (i.e., instantiation) of software engineering environments for specific projects (Enterprise-Oriented PSEE);
- to support software development using the instantiated environment; and
- to support the management of organizational knowledge related to software processes.

The Taba Workstation has been used by the Brazilian software industry since 2003. The Taba Workstation was identified during three official SCAMPI appraisals for CMMI Level 2 as one of the greatest organizational strengths to facilitate the success of software process deployment initiatives and to overcome the inherent difficulties. Moreover, the Taba Workstation was also identified as an important organizational asset to guarantee the quality of software process and product quality in other three official MR-MPS.BR appraisals.

The Taba Workstation is constituted of integrated tools to support software processes definition, deployment and enactment. These tools are adherent to the practices of the CMMI levels 2 and 3 process areas. The functionalities of other tools to support Knowledge Management activities are integrated into the environment to facilitate the preservation of organizational knowledge and support activities execution.

The next section presents the software process definition approach adopted in the Taba Workstation. The functionalities of specific tools to support software process deployment and enactment are presented in section 4.2. Section 4.3 presents the main characteristics of the Taba Workstation that helps organizations to obtain success in their software process deployment initiatives based on CMMI and MR-MPS.BR.

4.1 Software Process Definition Approach

The Software Processes definition approach adopted in the Taba Workstation establishes phases and intermediary products using the ISO/IEC 12207 [3] as a basis for defining standard software processes from the Taba Workstation. Figure 1 depicts the presented approach.

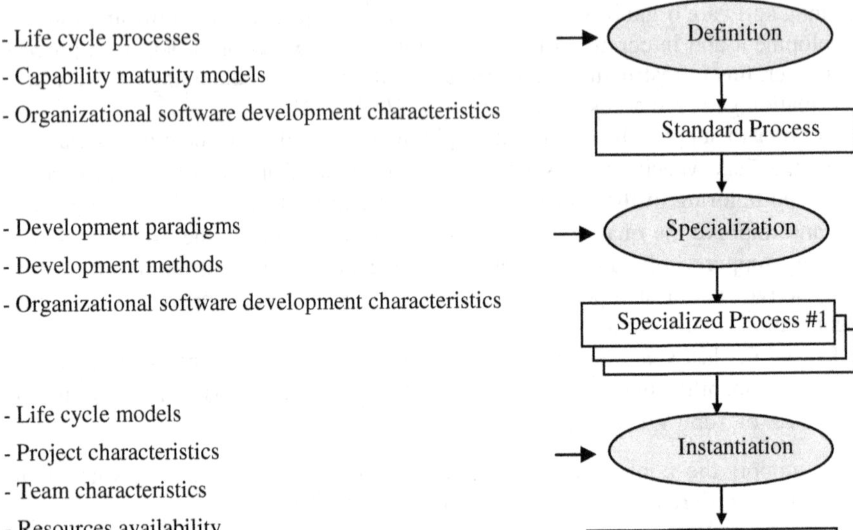

Fig. 1. Software processes definition approach

The standard processes and the specialized processes are considered to be organizational level processes. The instantiated processes are project level processes. This approach guarantees some practices of CMMI level 3 process areas, for instance, the establishment of defined processes for each process area.

4.1.1 Defining Organizational Software Process

During the Standard Process definition phase we not only consider the ISO/IEC 12207, but organizational software development characteristics related to the work environment, knowledge and experiences of the teams involved and the organizational software development experience and culture are also considered.

From the Standard Process, different software processes can be specialized according to different software types produced by the organization, (for instance, specialists systems and information systems) and to development paradigms adopted (for instance, object oriented or structured). During this phase, new activities can be defined and inserted into the specialized processes and the activities execution description can be adapted. Nevertheless, all the basic elements defined in the Standard Process must always be presented in the specialized processes.

The definition of organizational standard process for a specific organization is done during the configuration of a specific environment for the organization. The tool responsible for supporting this configuration is named Config. This tool supports the following activities:

- Configuration contextualization;
- Definition of environment configuration proposal;
- Definition of standard process;
- Definition of specialized processes;
- Definition of domain theory and tasks descriptions;
- Generation of configured environment

The configured environment for the organization contains not only the standard process and the specialized processes, but also specific knowledge related to software development and maintenance. By using this environment, the software engineers are enabled to generate instantiated environments to each of the projects to be developed.

4.1.2 Instantiating Software Process to Specific Project

In order to be used in a specific project, the most adequate specialized process to a specific project must be instantiated to satisfy the characteristics of the project (for instance, size and complexity of the product and relevant quality characteristics), development team characteristics, etc. In this phase, the life cycle model, methods and tools are selected.

The figure 2 presents a screenshot of a tool named AdaptPro that supports the institutionalization of the organizational processes since it facilitates the adoption of these processes in all the projects of the organization. By using the AdaptPro tool, the

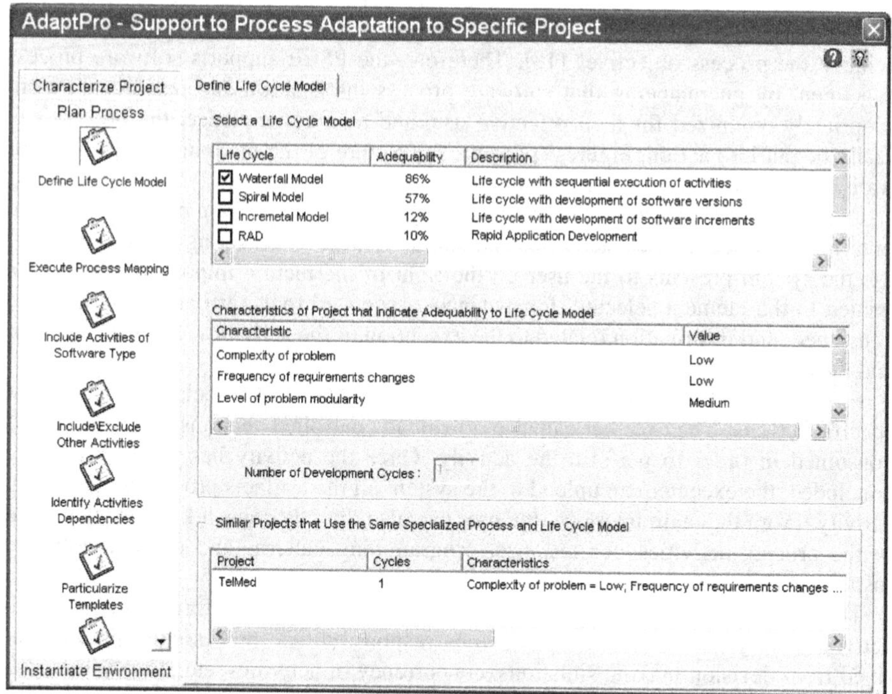

Fig. 2. AdaptPro tool to support instantiation of software process to specific project

software engineer can execute the following activities: (i) characterize the project; (ii) plan the process that will guide the project through the adaptation of the organizational standard process considering the project characteristics; and (iii) instantiate a PSEE to support the execution of the planned process.

On the left side of figure 2, the system presents the activities that guide the execution of the tool. On the right side of the figure, the system presents another screen to support the execution of the selected activity; in this case, it is presented the screen that supports the definition of a life cycle model to a specific project as part of the process planning activity. A list of life cycle models and the respective level of adequability to the project considering its characteristics are presented on the right side of the screen. Besides that, the user can consult the justification of the automatic identification of the adequability level and can consult the software processes defined for similar projects that used the same specialized process and life cycle model facilitating the selection of an adequate project life cycle model by the user.

The next sections present specific Taba Workstation tools to support software process deployment and enactment.

4.2 Supporting Software Process Deployment and Enactment

Once the software process for a specific project has been defined and a Software Engineering Environment has been instantiated, the basic means for software process deployment and enactment are established. Software process enactment involves coordination of relevant team members to enact various tasks, i.e., the enactment of a software process is the procedure of enacting various partially-ordered tasks to achieve the process objectives [18]. Therefore, the PSEE supports software process enactment by guaranteeing that software process information and resources are appropriately organized for their effective use, and as a consequence, the process can easily be put into action. Figure 3 presents the picture of the main interface of a Software Engineering Environment instantiated to a specific project.

On the left of the picture, it is presented the instantiated software process organized in terms of project phases, activities and sub-activities. By selecting a phase or activity, the system presents to the user on the right of the picture important information related to the element selected, for instance, associated tools, artifacts produced and consumed, and information related to the execution of the activities (for instance, time and effort estimates).

From the PSEE, the process's executers can execute tools associated to perform a specific activity. The executer can also download controlled versions of artifacts to be consumed in order to perform the activity. Once the activity has been initiated or concluded, the executer can upload to the system all the artifacts produced during that activity. From the main interface, the user can also directly consult knowledge related to the process activities, for instance, programming patterns and detailed software inspection procedures and techniques.

The process enactment is supported through the control of information related to activities entry and exit criteria, activities responsibilities, processes sequences derived from decision making situations, concurrency of activities, etc. The system also provides the means to identify process critical paths in order to support the monitoring and controlling of processes execution.

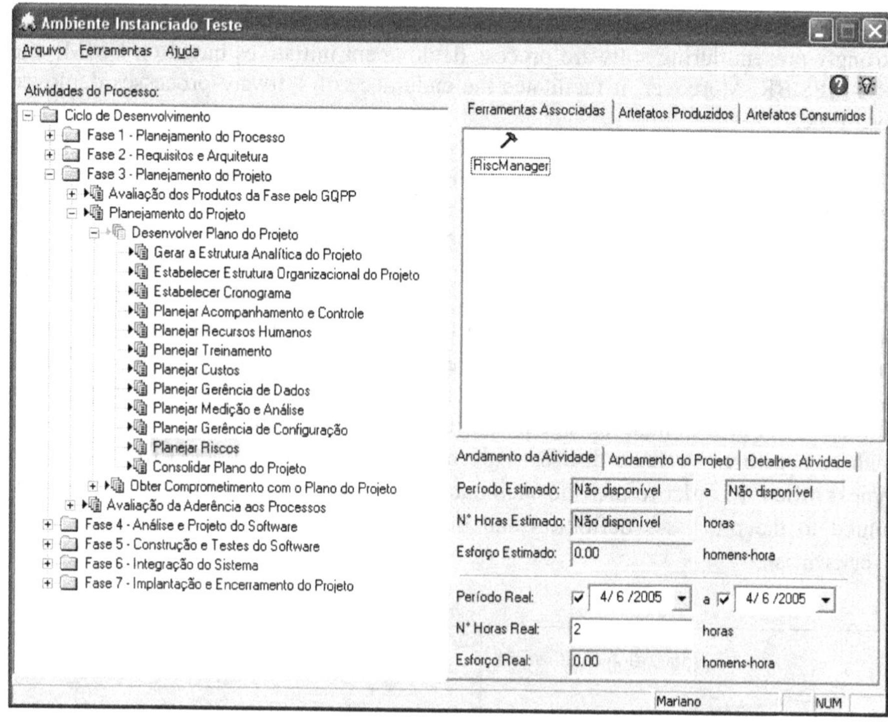

Fig. 3. Software Engineering Environment to support specific project software process deployment and enactment

4.3 Using the *Taba Workstation* to Guarantee the Success of Software Process Deployment Based on CMMI and MR-MPS.BR

In the context of software process deployment, we executed a survey with the objective to identify success factors and difficulties related to software process deployment experiences. The participants of the survey were members of COPPE/UFRJ, an institution of the Federal University of Rio de Janeiro with vast experience in software process research and deployment [7, 8, 10, 11, 12]. The success factors and difficulties identified through this survey were grouped according to the category of the findings. 12 categories were identified related to success factors and 16 categories related to difficulties in software process deployment experiences based on CMMI and MR-MPS.BR. From a comparative analysis of these findings, we identified important factors that contribute significantly to the success of software process improvement programs in small, medium and large organizations.

The consideration of such factors during software deployment initiatives can significantly increase the success of software process improvement programs, because they can help organizations to tailor their process deployment strategies considering particularities of the software development organizations and available resources. Figure 4 depicts the distribution of those factors according to categories of the findings.

The Taba Workstation provides the means to assure that most of those factors are strongly present during software process deployment initiatives based on CMMI and MR-MPS.BR. Moreover, it facilitates the endurance of software processes deployed over time.

The most relevant success factor in software process deployment is related to the commitment obtained from organization members and high management. Our experience demonstrated that the results are often satisfactory when the organization members are committed with the deployment process and the high management continuously supports the execution of the activities. The lack of commitment of the high management with the deployment process, and the lack of involvement of the organization members were also considered to be great difficulties in deploying software processes. Since, the Taba Workstation efficiently supports the enactment of software process and provides accurate project status reports to high level managers, the probability of lack of high management commitment is significantly reduced, because high management strategic decisions are based on the data extracted from the Taba Workstation. In order to provide such data, the organization members must be committed to the processes definition and the procedures deployed through the Taba Workstation.

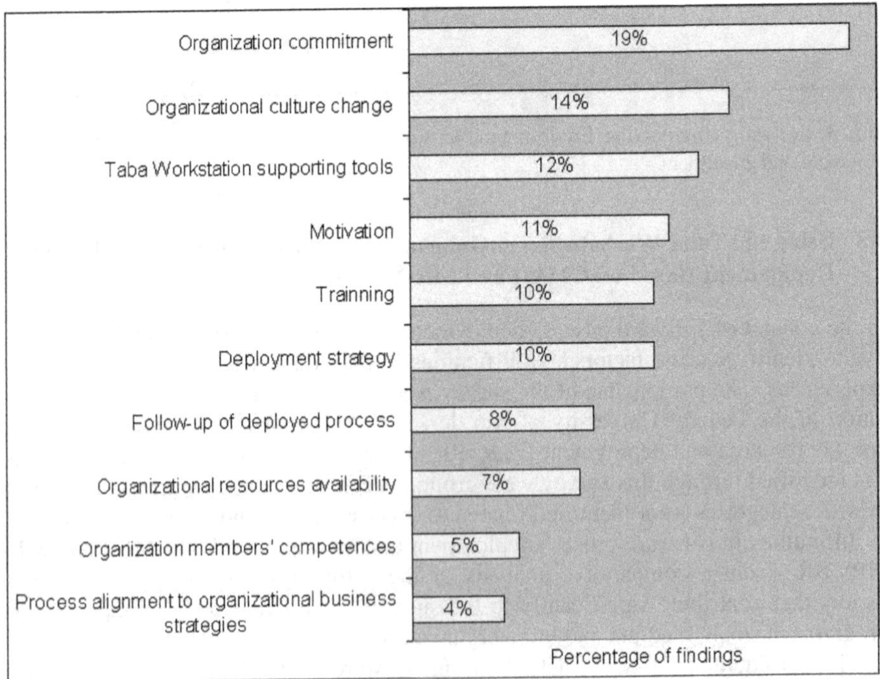

Fig. 4. Important factors that contribute significantly to the success of software process deployment based on the CMMI and the MR-MPS.BR

Another difficulty found in software process deployment is related to organizational culture change. In our deployment experiences, we found great difficulty in customizing the standards process according to organizational needs when a not completely correct culture about Software Engineering procedures (system analysis, testing, documentation, etc) were already disseminated within the organization. Moreover, we noticed great resistance from software project developers during the deployment of process activities that were traditionally executed *ad hoc*.

One of the main characteristics of the Taba Workstation is to guarantee the institutionalization of the organization processes through automated support of important software engineering tasks, such as project process definition, and collection of project measures. Therefore, most of the culture change impact can be minimized by reducing the effort of software process activities deployed. Moreover, since all Taba Workstation tools are process driven and integrated to a knowledge base, most of the difficulties of executing a new process demonstrated to be easily overcome by providing important knowledge related to the current process activity in the exact moment that the executer needs it, such as organizational directives and lessons learned from past project experiences.

The organization members' motivation was also a very important factor in software process deployment. This motivation occurred in various levels. The high management was motivated to deploy software process, because their main objective was to successfully achieve an official certification/appraisal of the software process reference models due to clients' pressure and market competitive needs. The motivation of other organization members was related to the need to learn and improve the execution of their activities. The Taba Workstation could satisfy both needs, because the institutionalization of the PSEE speeded the execution of the processes deployment and enactment, and provided the means for deployment of new and competitive technologies, i.e., organizational competitive advantages and members satisfaction increased due to the fact that organizational members were able to not only learn about new technologies, but also to apply them in real projects in a reduced time.

Since the delivery of software engineering trainings was considered essential to deal with the lack of organization members deficiencies in software engineering and to guarantee and adequate execution of the software process, the Taba Workstation tools integrated to knowledge management applications were also identify as an important factor, because it helped to diminish the training effort necessary to execute the process.

Many difficulties were related to the deployment strategy adopted by the software process deployment team. For instance, deployment strategies that required approval of many organization members in order to deploy a specific practice usually took a great amount of time since many conflicting needs had to be dealt with. In order to deal with this difficulty, our software process deployment strategy supported by the Taba Workstation defines that, no matter the level of the capability of the organization, all processes of the projects will have to be based on an organizational standard process defined by our consultants and a specific organization process group.

That aspect of our strategy requires less time to define organization processes, and speeds the institutionalization of organizational processes. Adjustments of these processes are executed on-the-fly and new processes definitions are derived through the

Taba Workstation Software Process Modeling tool. This characteristic of our deployment strategy also contributes to another important aspect: alignment of software process with the organization business strategies to obtain software processes that satisfy organizational development characteristics. This characteristic also helps to diminish the impact of organizational culture changes.

The greatest difficulty found in our software process deployment experience is related to deficiency of organization members' competences. The most relevant deficiency was the little knowledge in Software Engineering. Once this difficulty was found in an organization, most of the procedures, methods and techniques used to support software development had to be taught, for instance, how to describe a use case, classes' diagrams and requirements specifications, etc. This difficulty is related to the lack of organization members' computer science background knowledge.

In order to overcome that difficulty, before deploying the software processes in the organization, we fill the Taba Workstation Knowledge Base with important theoretical knowledge related to software engineering area and systems analysis methodologies. During the follow-up of the projects, our consultants are instructed to access the knowledge stored in that base and to discuss it with the organization members. This practice allows the organization members to learn about Software Engineering during the execution of their daily activities.

Another important consideration to be stated is that the amount of time dedicated to support software process deployment in the organization especially during pilot projects, and the dedication of the deployment team in the organization are key factors to guarantee the success of the deployment. Technology and knowledge transference demands a lot of involvement of the people related to the deployment process.

The results of the software process improvement program are not satisfactory when the cost of deployment restricts the amount of time dedicated to support software process deployment. This factor is directly related to the availability of financial resources to spend on software process deployment activities. During these activities, the organization must be able to provide sufficient financial resources in order to cope with dynamic deployment necessities.

5 Conclusions

This work presented the Taba Workstation, an enterprise-oriented PSEE developed to support software process deployment based on the CMMI and the MR-MPS.BR. Characteristics of Taba Workstation that increases the efficiency and efficacy of software process deployment initiatives and reduces the inherent difficulties were also presented by comparing these characteristics to important factors that contribute significantly to the success of software process deployment based on the CMMI and the MR-MPS.BR.

Since the Taba Workstation is based on a Software Engineering Ontology, the integration of Taba Workstation tools to other tools that support different areas of Software Engineering is facilitated. Moreover, the Taba Workstation software process definition approach demonstrated to support process modeling and evolution in an efficient and efficacy way. One of the mayor contributions of the Taba Workstation is that its architecture and software development supporting tools were modified over the past years to become more adequate to the necessities of software organizations executing real projects in dynamic and evolving environments. Another important aspect of Taba Workstation in this evolution is that it supports important knowledge management tasks, such as consultation of organizational members' skills and knowledge that fulfill projects specific needs. These characteristics facilitate preservation of organizational memory.

The Taba Workstation is continually evolving. The next steps is to evaluate the adequacy of the tools that support CMMI Level 3 process areas, and to define and integrate other tools to support CMMI Level 4 and 5 process areas and to facilitate the elevation of organization software development maturity to higher levels.

References

1. Arent, J. and Norbjerg, J.: Software process improvement as organizational knowledge creation: a multiple case analysis. In: Proceedings of the 33rd Annual Hawaii International Conference on System Sciences, pp 1-11, Jan 4-7 (2000)
2. Fuggetta, A.: Software Process: A Roadmap. In: The Future of Software Engineering, Ed. Anthony Finkelstein, 22nd Int. Conference on Software Engineering, pp. 27-34 (2000)
3. ISO/IEC 12207:2000 - Information technology – software process life cycle (2000)
4. ISO/IEC 15504 –1 Information Technology – Process Assessment, - Part 1: Concepts and Vocabulary (2003)
5. Chrissis, M. B., Konrad, M, Shrum, S.: CMMI: Guidelines for Process Integration and Product Improvement. Addison-Wesley (2003)
6. MPS.BR – Melhoria de Processo do Software Brasileiro, Guia Geral (v. 1.0) (2005)
7. Santos G., Montoni M., Rocha A. R., Figueiredo S., Mafra S., Albuquerque A., Paret B. D., Amaral M.: Using a Software Development Environment with Knowledge Management to Support Deploying Software Processes in Small and Medium Size Companies. In.: Lecture Notes in Artificial Intelligence, ISBN 3-00-016020-5, pp 72-76, presented at the 3rd Conference Professional Knowledge Management Experiences and Visions, Kaiserslautern, Germany, April 10-13 (2005)
8. Rocha, A. R., Montoni, M., Santos, S., Mafra, S., Figueiredo, S., Albuquerque, A., Mian, P.: Reference Model for Software Process Improvement: A Brazilian Experience. In.: Lecture Notes of Computer Science (LNCS), ISBN 3-540-30286-7, pp. 130-141, presented at the European Software Process Improvement and Innovation Conference (EuroSPI 2005), Budapest, Hungary (2005)
9. Weber, K.C., Araujo, E.R., Rocha, A.R., Machado, C., Scalet, D., Salviano, C.: Brazilian Software Process Reference Model and Assessment Method. In.: Computer and Information Sciences – ISCIS 2005, LNCS 3733, pp 403-411 (2005)
10. Montoni M., Santos G., Villela K., Rocha A. R., Travassos G. H., Figueiredo S., Mafra S., Albuquerque A., Mian P.: Enterprise-Oriented Software Development Environments to Support Software Products and Process Quality Improvement. In.: Lecture Notes of Computer Science (LNCS), ISBN 3-540-26200-8, pp. 370-384, presented at the 6th Int. Conference on Product Focused Software Process Improvement, Oulu, Finland, June (2005)
11. Montoni, M., Santos, G., Villela, K., Miranda, R., Rocha, A.R., Travassos, G.H., Figueiredo, S., Mafra, S.: Knowledge Management in an Enterprise-Oriented Software Development Environment. In.: Lecture Notes of Computer Science (LNCS), ISBN 3-540-24088-8, pp. 117–128, presented at the 5th Int. Conf of Practical Aspects of Knowledge Management, Vienna, Austria, (2004)

12. Montoni, M., Miranda, R., Rocha, A. R., Travassos, G. H.: Knowledge Acquisition and Communities of Practice: an Approach to Convert Individual Knowledge into Multi-Organizational Knowledge, In.: Lecture Notes in Computer Science (LNCS), ISBN 3-540-22192-1, pp. 110-121, presented at the 6th International Workshop on Learning Software Organizations (LSO'2004), Banff, Canada, June (2004)
13. Minh, N. N., Wang, A.I., Conradi, R.: Total Software Process Model Evolution in EPOS Experience Report. In: Proc. of the 19th Int. Conf. on Software Engineering, pp: 390–399, May 17-23 (1997)
14. Ben-Shaul, I.Z., Skopp, P.D., Heineman, G.T., Tong, A.Z., Popovich, S.S., Valetto, G.: Integrating groupware and process technologies in the Oz environment. In: Proc. of the 9th Int. Software Process Workshop, pp.: 114–116, 5-7 Oct. (1994)
15. S. Bandinelli, Di Nitto, E., Fuggetta, A.: Supporting Cooperation in the SPADE-1 Environment. IEEE Trans. on Software Engineering, Vol. 22, No. 12, pp. 841-865 (1996)
16. Bowen, S., Maurer, F.: Process support and knowledge management for virtual teams doing agile software development. In.: Proc. of the 26th Annual Int. Computer Software and Applications Conference (COMPSAC) pp:1118–1120, 26-29 Aug. (2002)
17. Artemis 7, http://www.aisc.com/Product/1 (2006)
18. Yan, J., Yang, Y., R., G. K.: Decentralized Coordination for Software Process Enactment, F. Oquendo (Ed.): EWSPT 2003, LNCS 2786, pp. 164–172 (2003)
19. ISO/IEC 12207:2000 - Information technology –software process life cycle, (2000)
20. ISO/IEC 15504 –1 Information Technology – Process Assessment, - Part 1: Concepts and Vocabulary, (2003)
21. Chrissis, M. B., Konrad, M, Shrum, S.: CMMI: Guidelines for Process Integration and Product Improvement, Addison-Wesley, (2003)

Analysis of an Artifact Oriented Test Process Model and of Testing Aspects of CMMI*

Paulo M.S. Bueno[1,**], Adalberto N. Crespo[1], and Mario Jino[2]

[1] Divisão de Melhoria de Processo de Software - CenPRA
Rodovia Dom Pedro I, km 143,6 - Campinas - São Paulo CEP 13069-901
[2] Faculdade de Engenharia Elétrica e de Computação - Unicamp
{paulo.bueno, adalberto.crespo}@cenpra.gov.br,
jino@dca.fee.unicamp.br

Abstract. The CMMI model for Software Engineering provides guidance for improving an organization's processes and the ability to develop software systems. The CenPRA test process is a generic software testing model defined by selecting software testing "best practices"; it evolved over the last years and has been published in specific forums. The CenPRA test process, which defines a set of partially ordered activities and test artifacts, has been validated and improved based on the experience of its application at software development companies in Brazil. In this work we carried out an evaluation of the CenPRA test process under the perspective of CMMI. We evaluated essentially which aspects of CMMI are taken into account by the CenPRA test process. We also evaluate how the CenPRA model can be used to supplement software testing related aspects of CMMI. Our results pointed to improvements in the CenPRA test process, and also identify testing tasks and artifacts not considered by CMMI, which can significantly improve an organization testing practices.

1 Introduction

Software testing is the process of executing a program in a controlled way aiming to check if the program behaves as defined in its specification. It is an essential activity to achieve a good quality level in software products. A testing process defines a set of partially ordered activities, methods and practices used for testing software, as well as the artifacts used and produced in these activities. Taking into account the fact that the quality of the test process is directly related to the final quality of the developed product, improving the test process is crucial for the success of software development organizations. Improving testing practices may lead to a testing process which is more efficient (within budget and schedule) and more effective (fewer bugs deployed to users).

Software process assessment and improvement models define a set of best practices, methods for the assessment of processes capabilities, and provide a rational guide for the process improvement. These models have been recognized as an effective way for the controlled and stepwise improvement of the practices used for software development [9, 10].

* Work partially supported by CNPq and HP-Brazil.
** Teacher at Faculdade Comunitária de Campinas (FAC), Anhanguera Educacional.

J. Münch and M. Vierimaa (Eds.): PROFES 2006, LNCS 4034, pp. 263 – 277, 2006.

This paper reports results of the analysis of a test process model under the perspective of a process improvement model and the opposite, that is, the analysis of a process improvement model under the perspective of a test process model. More specifically, we evaluate the generic test process model defined at CenPRA (Centro de Pesquisas Renato Archer) [3] using as a reference the process improvement model CMMI [11]; conversely, we use the test process model defined at CenPRA as a basis for supplementing testing aspects of CMMI.

The evaluation reveals strong aspects in the CenPRA process and confirms our experience that development organizations can achieve significant improvements in their testing practices by using the CenPRA testing process as a basis for the definition of the organization's testing processes. Aspects in CMMI which are not considered in the CenPRA test process model point to improvements in this model. On the other hand, important testing aspects not detailed in CMMI were identified and used for the definition of a set of Supplementation Notes for the standard. In a previous work we performed a similar analysis using the ISO/IEC 15504 model [1].

Section 2 of the paper presents concepts of software testing and of software process improvement models; Section 3 describes succinctly the CMMI model; Section 4 presents the CenPRA testing methodology; Section 5 describes the assessment of the CenPRA Test Process Model under the perspective of CMMI and discuss the analysis results; Section 6 presents the analysis and supplementation of CMMI software testing practices; Section 7 discuss briefly the results of our analysis and summarizes the conclusions of this work.

2 Software Testing and Software Process Improvement Models

Testing is a fundamental activity for ensuring that the software meets the user requirements, it is the final evaluation of the quality of the developed product. [7]. A test process is a set of partially ordered steps composed of activities, methods and practices used for testing a software product. Testing is usually performed through levels which correspond to the different development phases and is based on techniques that define how the test cases are selected and evaluated [3].

Process improvement is an approach for furthering an organization's objectives by improving the capability of the organization's most important processes. The capability of a process in an organization is the extent to which the process is executed, explicitly managed, defined, measured, controlled, effective and continually improved. Process improvement models have shown in practice to be a viable, effective and efficient approach for the improvement of software development organizations [10].

Process improvement approaches use as reference a process model that systematizes and represents the best practices, defines a metric for the evaluation of processes capabilities, and provides a rational roadmap for process improvement. Examples of models are: the SW-CMM [8], the ISO/IEC 12207 standard, the ISO/IEC 15504 model [12] and the CMMI model [11]. In this paper we use the CMMI model as a reference for the analysis.

3 The CMMI Model

The CMMI model provides guidance for improving an organization's processes reflecting different bodies of knowledge or "disciplines" (e.g., systems engineering, and software engineering). It can be used for setting process improvement objectives and priorities and for improving the processes towards stable and capable processes.

Table 1. Verification process area - specific goals and practices related to software testing

Specific Practices (Capability Level)	Description
Specific Goal VRSG 1 Prepare for Verification	
VRSP 1.1-1 Select Products for Verification (1)	Work products are selected based on the contribution to meeting objectives and requirements. Verification methods mentioned: path coverage testing, load, stress and performance testing, decision-table-based-testing, functional-decomposition-based-testing, test-case reuse and acceptance tests. Work products: list of products for verification and verification methods. **Subpractices:** Identify work products; Identify requirements; Identify methods; Define methods; Integrate with project plan.
VRSP 1.2-2 Establish the Verific. Environment (2)	The environment is established based on the selected work products and methods. It may require: simulators, scenario generators, data tools, environmental controls and interfaces. **Subpractices:** Identify environment requirements; Identify verification resources for reuse; Identify verification equipment and tools; Acquire verification equipment and tools.
VRSP 1.3-3 Establish Verification Procedures and Criteria (3)	Verification criteria are defined. Examples of sources for verification criteria: product requirements; standards; organization policies, test parameters, parameters for the tradeoff between quality and cost of testing, type of work products. **Subpractices:** Generate the set of verification procedures; Develop verification criteria, Identify expected results; Identify environmental components.
Specific Goal VRSG 3 Verify Selected Work Products	
VRSP 3.1-1 Perform Verification (1)	Verify work products incrementally. **Subpractices:** Perform verification of selected work products against specification; Record the results; Identify actions resulting from verification; Document verification method and deviations from the method.
VRSP 3.2-2 Analyze Verification Results Identify corrective action (1)	Compare actual results to established verification criteria. Work Products: analysis reports, problem reports; change request for verification methods; corrective actions to verification methods. **Subpractices:** Compare actual results with expected results; Identify products that have not met requirements and problems with methods, procedures, and criteria; Analyze defects; Record all results; Use results to compare measurements to performance parameters; Provide information on how defects may be resolved.

Table 2. Validation process area - specific goals and practices

Specific Practices (Capability Level)	Description
Specific Goal VLSG 1 Prepare for Validation	
VLSP 1.1-1 Select Products for Validation (1)	Product and components of products are selected for validation based on their relationships and the user needs. Scope of validation should be determined; validation methods should be selected early in the project. Work products: Lists of products; validation methods; requirements and constraints for validation. **Subpractices:** Identify key principles, features and phases for product validation through the life of project; Determine categories of user needs to be validated; Select the products; Select methods; Review selection constraints and methods with stakeholders.
VLSP 1.2-2 Establish the Validation Environment (2)	Requirements for the environment are driven by the product selected and by method of validation. Elements in the environment include: test tools; recording tools; simulated components; interface systems (real and simulated); network. **Subpractices:** Identify environment requirements; Identify customer-supplied products; Identify reuse items; Identify test tools; Identify resources for reuse; Plan availability for resources
VLSP 1.3-3 Establish Validation Procedures and Criteria (3)	Validation procedures and criteria are defined. Examples of sources for verification criteria: product requirements; standards; customer acceptance criteria; environmental performance; and thresholds of performance deviations. **Subpractices:** Review product requirements to ensure the identification of issues affecting validation; Document the environment, scenario, procedures, inputs, outputs and criteria for validation; Assess the design to identify validation issues.
Specific Goal VLSG 2 Validate Product or Product Components	
VLSP 2.1-1 Perform Validation (1)	Perform validation activities and collect the resulting data according to the established methods, procedures and criteria. The procedure should be documented and deviations noted. Work products: validation reports; results; cross-reference matrix; procedure log, operation demonstrations.
VLSP 2.2-1 Analyze Validation Results (1)	Test data resulting from validation tests are analyzed against the defined criteria. **Subpractices:** Compare actual results to expected results; Identify products that do not perform suitably in their intended operating environments, problems with methods, criteria or environment; analyze data for defects; record results of the analysis and identify issues; compare actual measurements and performance to intended use.

As we aim to assess specific aspects in the software development related to software testing, we selected the CMMI continuous representation of Software Engineering Discipline. We analyzed the CMMI Process Areas that can more directly influence software testing practices as a reference for assessing the software testing practices and artifacts of the CenPRA testing process model. We also make the opposite analysis, that is, we use the CenPRA testing process model for identifying software testing aspects not mentioned anywhere in the CMMI model

The CMMI model components are: process areas, specific goals, specific practices, typical work products, subpractices, notes, discipline amplifications, generic goals, generic practice elaborations and references.

Table 3. Capability levels, generic goals and practices

Capability level 0: Incomplete process – not performed or partially performed **Generic Goals:** – **Generic practices:** –
Capability level 1: Performed – process satisfies all specific goals of the process area **Generic Goals:** GG1 Achieve Specific Goals **Generic practices** GP1.1 Perform Base Practices
Capability level 2: Managed – process is performed, planned and executed according to a police, employ skilled people with adequate resources to produce controlled outputs. Is monitored, controlled, reviewed, and is evaluated for adherence to process description. **Generic Goals:** GG 2 Institutionalize a Managed Process **Generic practices:** GP 2.1 Establish an Organizational Policy; GP 2.2 Plan the Process; GP 2.3 Provide Resources; GP 2.4 Assign Responsibility; GP 2.5 Train People; GP 2.6 Manage Configurations; GP 2.7 Identify and Involve Relevant Stakeholders; GP 2.8 Monitor and Control the Process; GP 2.9 Objectively Evaluate Adherence; GP 2.10 Review Status with Higher Level Management.
Capability level 3: Defined – a managed process tailored from organization's standards according to tailoring guidelines. Contribute with process-improvement information. **Generic Goals:** GG3 Institutionalize a Defined Process. **Generic practices:** GP 3.1 Establish a Defined Process; GP 3.2 Collect Improvement Information.
Capability level 4: Quantitatively Managed – a defined process that is controlled using statistical and other quantitative techniques. Quantitative objectives for quality and performance are established and used in managing the process. **Generic Goals:** GG4 Institutionalize a Quantitatively Managed Process. **Generic practices:** GP 4.1 Establish Quantitative Objectives for the Process; GP 4.2 Stabilize Sub process Performance.
Capability level 5: Optimizing – process continually improve performance through both incremental and innovative technological improvements. **Generic Goals:** GG5 Institutionalize an Optimizing Process. **Generic practices:** GP 5.1 Ensure Continuous Process Improvement; GP 5.2 Correct Root Causes of Problems.

In the CMMI structure each process area is assigned to a set of specific goals and a set of generic goals. Specific goals organize specific practices, which apply to an individual process area. The generic goals organize generic practices that apply to multiple process areas. The generic goals and generic practices define a sequence of capability levels representing improvements in the effectiveness of the processes. Therefore a capability level associates specific and generic practices which, when performed, achieve a set of goals that lead to improved process performance.

This structure allows to focus on the best practices the organization can use to improve processes in the process areas it has chosen to address. It builds an organization's ability to pursue process improvements and to evaluate the progress on target process area.

In the analysis presented in the next sections we focused on the specific goals and practices related to software testing activities. Therefore the scope of our analysis consists of the Verification and Validation Process Areas for identifying software testing aspects, and the Project Management Process Area for identifying planning issues that can be applied to planning software testing. The Product Integration Process Area is also related to the integration testing activity, but for space reasons we did not include this Process Area in our analysis.

Table 1 and Table 2 describe specific goals and practices of the, respectively, Verification and Validation Process Areas[1]. Table 3 describes capability levels and their generic goals and practices.

4 The CenPRA Testing Methodology

A testing methodology is a set of steps and tasks used to implement or improve a software testing process of a software development organization or company that produces software. A testing methodology supports the selection of techniques and the choice of tools. The methodology enables the organizations to develop testing activities which result in good quality products. The CenPRA testing methodology encompasses: i) a generic testing process; ii) a process for instantiation of the test process; and, iii) training courses in testing.

The CenPRA methodology has been used for improving the testing process in software development companies of the State of São Paulo, Brazil. These experiences have contributed to the evaluation and continual improvement of the methodology.

4.1 The CenPRA Generic Testing Process

To characterize a testing process it is necessary to specify: the testing levels corresponding to the development phases; the types of testing; the testing techniques and criteria; and to detail the activities: test planning, design, execution and recording of testing.

The CenPRA testing process is based on testing artifacts defined by the standard IEEE Std 829-1998 [4] and its activities are defined and ordered aiming at an effec-

[1] Note that Verification Process Area includes also SG2: Perform Peer Reviews, SG not described in Table 2. The Project Management and Monitoring PAs are not described here to save space, please refer to [11].

tive and efficient testing process. The CenPRA testing process is composed of testing sub processes and associated artifacts. Figure 1 shows the testing activities and artifacts in CenPRA testing process. The sub processes Planning, Design, Execution and Recording are described next.

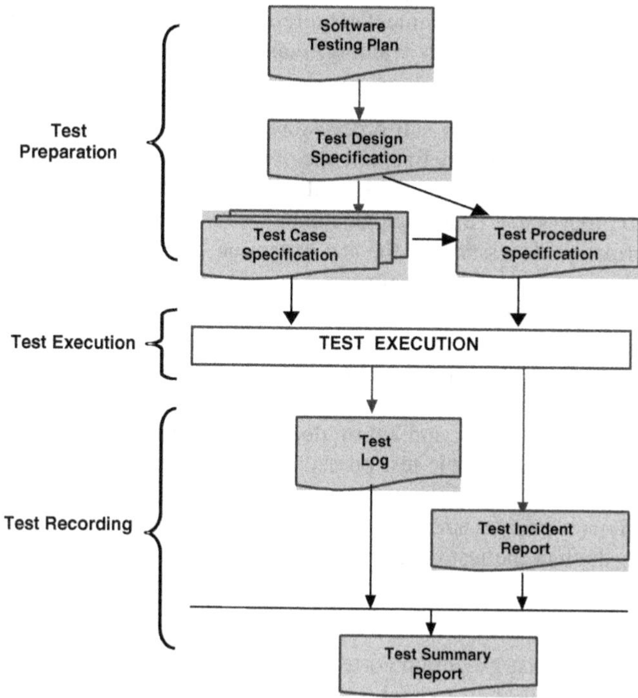

Fig. 1. Testing Activities and Artifacts – adapted from [4]

Planning Sub Process: The product of this sub process is the document Software Testing Plan, which describes the planning of all activities involved in testing a software product. In addition to the activities the testing plan must contain the testing scope, the approach used in testing, the needed resources, the schedule and the definition of the operational environment for test execution.

The testing plan identifies the software items to be tested and contains references to the test items documentation and software project documentation (project plan, policies, standards, item's requirements, design, user guide, etc.), features to be tested and features not to be tested, the level at which the items have to be tested, the overall approach to be used for testing each item (for the identification of major tasks, estimation of necessary time, and definition of minimum degree of comprehensiveness desired – such as level of code coverage), the tasks involved in each testing activity, the deliverables documents (test design specification, test case specification, etc), responsibilities for managing, designing, preparing, executing, checking and resolving the testing, staffing and training needs, testing schedule and risks an contingencies. The Software Testing Plan can be a document for all testing activities of a given product – a complete software testing project, or can be a document related to one of the testing levels, such as: Unit Testing Plan, Integration Testing Plan and System Testing Plan.

The activities of this sub process are: define the testing context; characterize the testing items; identify features; establish approaches and criteria; define deliverables; define testing activities; establish environment requirements; establish responsibilities; establish the team and the necessary training; construct the schedule; identify risks and establish contingencies.

Design Sub Process: The goals of this sub process are: refine the software testing approach defined in the planning step; define and specify the test cases; establish the requirements of the testing environment; define and specify the testing procedures. The product of this sub process can be a single document – Test Design Specification containing all the information necessary for the test execution. Alternatively, this sub process can generate three documents: a document – Test Design Specification, containing basically the details about the testing approach and an initial description of test cases and the associated testing procedures; a second document – Test Case Specification, containing the specification of the test cases listed in the Test Design Specification, the testing environment requirements, the requirements of special procedures, and the dependencies among test cases; and a third document – Test Procedure Specification, containing the description of the test procedures steps listed in the Test Design Specification.

The activities of this sub process are: refine the testing approaches and criteria; specify the test cases; establish the test environment requirements; elaborate the purpose of the testing procedures and identify the special requirements of the testing procedures.

Execution Sub Process: The test execution corresponds to the execution of the steps in a Testing Procedure. The activities are: set up (actions to prepare for execution of the procedure); start of the test procedure; proceed (actions necessary during the execution of the procedure); measure; shut down (suspend testing because of unscheduled events); resuming testing; stopping testing (orderly halt); wrap up (restore the environment) and contingency actions (deal with anomalous events).

Recording Sub Process: The goals of this sub process are: record chronologically in a document named Test Log the relevant details related to the execution of tests defined in a set of Test Procedures; record in a document named Test Incident Report any event that occurs during the test execution and that requires analysis (software failure or any anomaly in the environment - referred as Test Incidents); describe summarily in a document named Test Summary Report the results of the testing activities associated to the Test Project, as well as the evaluations based on these results.

The activities for the Test Log generation are: describe the test (items being tested, attributes of the environment, hardware and software descriptions); describe the execution (identifier of the procedure being executed, personal present and their functions); record procedure execution (test executions and visually observable results, successful execution or fail); record environment information; record anomalous events (what happened before and after unexpected events); record identifiers of each test incident report generated.

The activities for the Test Incident Report generation are: incident description (inputs, expected results, actual results, anomalies, date and time, procedure step, environment, attempts to repeat, testers and observers) and test incident impact determination (impact on the test plan, test design, test procedure and test plan specifications). The activities for the Test Summary Report generation are: summary description of the test items (with references to related test documents); report variances of the test items from their specifications and variances from the test plan, test designs and test procedures; evaluate comprehensiveness of the testing process against the planed comprehensiveness; summarize the results of testing (resolved incidents with their resolutions, and unresolved incidents); provide a overall evaluation of each test item, including its limitations and estimates of failure risk; summarize data about testing activities and about resource consumption.

4.2 Development Phases and Testing Phases

The CenPRA methodology proposes using the V model [7], one of the most usually adopted for software testing. This model considers the main phases of software process and assigns each phase to the corresponding software testing level.

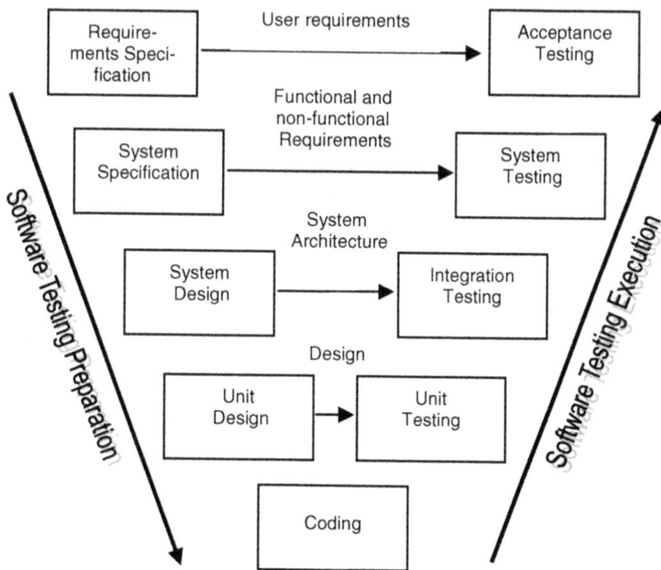

Fig. 2. The V model

Figure 2 shows the V Model. The left branch in the model corresponds to the software testing preparation, using as a reference the phases of software process. The right branch in the model corresponds to testing execution and recording, using as reference the software testing levels.

With this model the test planning starts with the User Requirements analysis and proceeds being detailed along the software project and implementation phases. The

Test Design comprises detailing the testing approach previously defined in the Testing Plan. The details include the testing levels that will be performed; in this way, for each testing level a corresponding Testing Project is elaborated.

On the right side of the V model we have the test execution at the several levels defined in the Testing Plan (Unit, Integration, System and Acceptance). In the execution of each testing level the corresponding Testing Designs are used to direct the testing activity; in these activities the Test Cases and Test Procedures specifications are used. Each testing level can be iterated in cycles of: fault detection, debugging and fault correction, and re-application of test cases. The progress of the test execution activities is recorded in detail in the Test Log. The events that deserve special attention are recorded in the Test Incident Report and a summary of the testing process is saved in the Test Summary Report.

5 Assessing the CenPRA Testing Process Under the Perspective of CMMI

The analysis consists in the evaluation of whether specific and generic goals and practices in the CMMI model are taken into account by the Subprocesses and artifacts in the CenPRA generic testing process. The goals are: i) evaluate the potential capability of testing activities reached by organizations adopting the generic testing process; and ii) identify the aspects in the CenPRA process that can be improved.

Note that different customizations of the CenPRA generic testing process, for different organizations, may present variations that depend on the organization's goals and necessities. Therefore the evaluation shows the potential capacity of customized processes. The capacity of an organization process naturally depends on decisions made in the customization of the generic testing process.

Due to space reasons we restrict our analysis to Generic Goals 1 to 3. We performed the analysis through the following procedures.

Procedure 1: Evaluating essential test aspects of the CenPRA testing model
Considering the Verification and Validation Process Areas:
For each CMMI Specific Goal, Specific Practice, Subpractices, Work Products **and**
For each CMMI Generic Goal, Generic Practice, Subpractices and Elaborations:

- Examine each testing Sub Process and the corresponding Artifacts in the CenPRA testing process.
- Classify the Goal, Practice or Subpractice concerning the *adherence* of the CenPRA testing Subprocesses-Artifacts to them:
  i) It is unequivocally present: *adherence* = "Total".
  ii) It is present but not completely satisfied: *adherence* = "Partial".
  iii) It is not present: *adherence* = "Null" (see explanation below).

Procedure 2: Evaluating marginal test aspects of the CenPRA testing model
Considering the Process Areas: Project Planning and Project Monitoring and Control.
For each CMMI Specific Goal:

- Evaluate if it is applicable to software testing activity
- If it is applicable, examine the CenPRA testing Subprocesses-Artifacts and Classify the Goal, Practice or Subpractice *adherence* as in Procedure 1.

To classify the "adherence levels" of Goals and Practices we evaluate if the information in the CenPRA testing Subprocesses-Artifacts satisfy the Goals, Practices, Subpractices and Elaborations described in the CMMI model. If the CenPRA testing Subprocesses-Artifacts clearly and unequivocally satisfy CMMI requirements we set adherence = "total". If some aspects of CMMI requirements are not addressed in the CenPRA testing Subprocesses-Artifacts we set adherence = "partial". If CenPRA testing Subprocesses-Artifacts do not address CMMI requirements we set adherence = "Null".

Table 4 summarizes the results from the application of Procedures 1 and 2. For each CMMI Process Area it shows how each Subprocess in the CenPRA model deals with CMMI Practices and Goals. Practices and goals are marked T, P or N indicating, respectively, a practice or goal with Total, Partial or Null adherence. Table line "Generic Results" shows Generic Practices and Generic Goals adherence with respect to all Process Areas and Practice or Goals with adherence = "Null".

Table 4. Adherence to CMMI practices and goals of the CenPRA testing model

Subprocess of CenPRA process	**CMMI Process Area**		
	Verification and Validation	**Project Planning**	**Project Monitoring and Control**
Planning	VRSP1.1-1(T), VRSP1.2-2(T), VRSP1.3-3(T), VLSP1.1-1(T), VLSP1.2-2(T), VLSP1.3-3(T).	SG1(T), SG2(P), SG3(N).	SG1(N), SG2(N).
Design	VRSP1.1-1(T), VRSP1.2-2(T), VRSP1.3-3(T).		
Execution	VRSP 3.1-1(T), VLSP2.1-1(T).		
Recording	VRSP3.2-2(T), VLSP2.2-1(T).		
Generic Results	VRSG1(T), VRSG2(N), VRSG3(T), VLSG1(T), VLSG2(T), VRSP2.1-1(N), VRSP2.2-1(N), VRSP2.3-2(N), GG1(T), GG2(P), GP2.1 up to GP2.5(T), GP2.6(P), GP2.7(T), GP2.8(P), GP2.9(N), 2.10(N), GP3.1(P), GP3.2(N), GG3(P).		

The main remarks on the analysis are:

- The Verification and Validation Specific Goals and Practices are satisfied by CenPRA testing subprocesses. The exceptions are the Verification Specific Goal and Practices related to Peer Review activity (VRSG2, VRSP2.1-1, VRSP2.2-1, VRSP2.3-2). Peer review activities are not part of the CenPRA testing model.
- Project Planning SG1 (Establish Estimates) is totally satisfied: testing scope, work products, task, testing life cycle and effort are estimated in the testing planning. For SG2 (Develop a Project Plan) 5 out of 7 Specific Practices are satisfied: plan for test data management and for stakeholder involvement are not part of CenPRA planning subprocess. SG3 (Obtain Commitment to the Plan) is not addressed: Testing Plan must be approved and signed by the designated persons; however, specific activities for review and reconcile the plan are not defined.

- Project Monitor and Control SG1 (Monitor Project Against Plan) and SG2 (Manage Corrective Actions) are not addressed. There is no mention in the Test Procedure Specification, Incident Report and Summary Report of information or activities about monitoring testing and taking corrective actions. Summary reports elaboration includes the activity "report variances from the plan" but does not explicitly include testing monitoring.
- Generic practices not addressed or partially addressed are: Manage Configuration (GP2.6); Monitor and control process (GP2.8); Evaluate Adherence (GP2.9); Review Status (GP2.10); Establish a defined process (GP3.1); and Collect improvement information (GP3.2).

6 Assessing and Supplementing CMMI Software Testing Practices

The analysis performed consists in evaluating the software testing practices and information embodied in the CMMI Specific Goals, Specific Practices, related Subpractices and Typical Work Products; as well as in the Generic Goals, Generic Practices and their Elaborations. We use as a reference a model specific for software testing – the CenPRA generic testing process model, which defines outstanding practices and is based on the IEEE Std. 829 testing documentation standard [4]. The goal is to identify testing aspects missing in CMMI model or aspects that require further descriptions to be applicable.

Note that, as a specific testing model, it is expected the CenPRA testing process to provide more complete and detailed information related to software testing than CMMI (a generic model) does. The idea is therefore, to take advantage of these different perspectives (specific and generic) to supplement the testing aspects of CMMI. As a result we provide additional guidelines for organizations that adopt CMMI and intend to pay special attention to improving their testing practices. We performed this analysis through the following procedure.

Procedure 3: Evaluating the test aspects of CMMI
For each testing Sub Process and the corresponding Artifacts in the CenPRA testing process we examined:

- The practices (or activities) defined for the CenPRA sub process (we call these "CenPRA-practices");
- The testing information used or produced in the practices (we call these "CenPRA-information");
- If the CenPRA-practices and CenPRA-information are present in the:
  a) Verification Process Area.
  b) Validation Process Area.
  c) Project Management Process Area.
  d) Product Integration Process Area.

  Note: in all Process Areas above we examined: Specific Goal, Specific Practices, Subpractices, Work Products, Generic Goals, Generic Practices, Subpractices and Elaborations.

If the CenPRA-practices or CenPRA-information are <u>not</u> found in any process area **or** If the CenPRA-practices or CenPRA-information are present in a Process Area, but requires additional explanations to be applied, we create a "Supplementation Note".

Results from application of Procedure 3 are presented in Table 5, which shows Supplementation Notes related to each Subprocess in the CenPRA testing process model.

Table 5. Testing Supplementation notes for CMMI

Planning Subprocess – Artifact: Testing Plan
When specifying test items mention versions and the testing level, supply references for items documentation. Items that will not be tested should be identified
When defining features or methods, identify the Test Design that details this information (different items may be tested with different methods).
Define features not to be tested and present reasons.
At this level define the technique to be used (Functional testing, structural testing, etc.) for testing features or group of features. Specify the major activities and tolls to be used. Consider the testing level (unit, integration, etc.) and the quality requirements for the item.
Specify criteria to suspend the planned testing activity and actions that must be repeated when testing is resumed.
Specify the minimum degree of comprehensiveness desired and how to measure it (e.g., test all features or only main features, all program statements executed once).
Identify pass-fail criteria for test items (e.g., "low severity problems allowed," or "no failures accepted"). Note that test items and features can be prioritized for the definition of adequate completion and pass-fail criteria.
When defining test environment care should be taken to specify all facilities, including hardware, tools (testing evaluation, simulation, capture and playback, test data generators, test data management and tracking), communication and system software, and aspects of security
When identifying responsibilities include developers, testers, operations staff, users, technical support and quality support. Identify the roles for: managing, designing, preparing, executing and checking tests.
Design Subprocess – Artifacts: Test Design Specification, Test Case Specification, Test Procedure Specification
Test design can provide more detailed information on the testing approach and about features to be tested. Several design specifications may be created for different test items or for different features to be tested in a given test item.
For each test design describe the test items (components, aggregates of components, or the entire system), features to be tested under the test design (e.g., functions, performance) and provide references to the items specifications.
Refine the testing approach defined in the testing plan: detail techniques to be used, methods for analyzing results and the error tolerance (how to distinguish valid from invalid inputs). Testing criteria (such as equivalence partitioning, boundary values, branch testing, condition testing, essential paths testing, data flow testing) can be determined. Specific testing literature should be used for criteria definition.
Summarize common aspects for all test cases in the design specification (e.g., constraints for all test inputs or shared environmental needs).

Table 5. (*contitnued*)

Test cases can be assigned to a test design specification and to a test procedure specification. Test cases can be reused for different test items and be related to different design specifications. Information on test cases must be useful for their reuse.
For each test case assign an identifier and specify: inputs (specific values, tables and file names, system parameters, database states) and outputs (values or features – e.g., response time); specify environmental needs (hardware and system software to execute the test case); special procedure requirements (set up, output checking); inter-case dependencies.
Test procedure specifications can be used to describe the purpose, special requirements, and procedure steps. Information include: methods for logging results; set up actions (prepare for execution); starting actions; measures to be made; actions for stopping and resuming testing and to restore the environment; contingency actions.
Execution Subprocess
Identify the testing procedure specification associated to the test items and execute it.
Recording Subprocess – Artifacts: Test Log, Test Incident Report, Test Summary Report
Record in a testing log information about: test items; test environment; responsible for test execution; testing results and testing incidents.'
Record in a test incident report each incident description and analysis of the impact in the testing plan.
A test summary report present results of the testing activities and provide evaluations. It can include: a summary evaluation of test items; variances of the test items from their specifications; variances from the test plan, design, or procedures and correspondent reasons; comprehensiveness assessment, summary of incidents and solutions.
Process Model
Testing activities should start early in software life cycle. Each step in the software development can provide information (development artifacts) to be used in testing planning and design.

7 Conclusions

In this work we evaluate the CenPRA testing process under the perspective of the process improvement model CMMI and, conversely, evaluate the testing practices of CMMI using as a reference the CenPRA testing process.

Due to the fact that the Testing Process highlights the technical aspects of the testing activity and the CMMI is a generic model for software process assessment and improvement, we found complementary natures in the addressed aspects. This allowed the identification of aspects of the testing process that can be improved by taking into account the Generic Goals and Generic Practices of CMMI. Analogously, the CenPRA testing process can be the basis for improving the testing technical aspects in organizations that adopt the CMMI model and that wish to improve the testing process.

The analysis in Section 5 clearly points to possible improvements in the CenPRA testing process model: consider including specific practices of Peer Review; improve the test planning activities using hints from CMMI Project Planning Process Area; include Practices for project monitoring and control and for manage corrective actions.

We propose a set of "Supplementation Notes" which reflects important testing aspects not treated by CMMI and aspects of this model that can be refined under a software testing perspective.

The main contributions of this work are:

- The application of a generic process improvement model for evaluating the capability of a testing process model;
- The identification of potential improvements to the CenPRA testing process;
- The proposition of a supplementary software testing content to be used in addition to CMMI for improving software testing processes.

Future work can explore standards specific to software testing, such as SW-TMM [2] and the TPI [6].

References

1. Bueno, P.M.S., Crespo, A., Jino, M., (2006), "Analysis of an artifact oriented test process model and of testing aspects of ISO/IEC 15504", Technical Report, CenPRA, 2006.
2. Burnstein, I. Suwanassart, T., Carlson, R., (1996), "Developing a Testing Maturity Model for Software Test Process Evaluation and Improvement". Proc. of Int. Test Conference.
3. Crespo, Adalberto .N., Jino, Mario, (2005), "Processo de Teste de Software", Technical Report CenPRA, (in Portuguese).
4. IEEE Std 829 (1998), "IEEE Standard for Software Test Documentation", IEEE, New York.
5. ISO/IEC 15504 (2004), "The International Organization for Standardization and the International Electrotechnical Commission", ISO/IEC 15504.
6. Koomen, T. and Pol M., (1999), "Test Process Improvement: A practical step-by step guide to structured testing". ACM Press, London, England.
7. Myers, G.J., (1979), "The Art of Software Testing", Addison-Wesley, New York.
8. M. C. Paulk, Charles V. Weber, B. Curtis and M. Chrissis, (1994), "The Capability Maturity Model - Guidelines for Improving the Software Process", CMU-SEI, Addison-Wesley.
9. Ana R. C. Rocha, José C. Maldonado e Kival C. Weber (Editores), (2001), "Qualidade de Software: Teoria e Prática", Prentice Hall, (in Portuguese).
10. Salviano, Clênio F., (2004), "Introdução à melhoria de processo de software com ISO/IEC 15504 e CMMI", Technical Report CenPRA - TRT1351, (in Portuguese).
11. SEI (2005), Web Site of the Software Engineering Institute – SEI, (CMMI documentation), http://www.sei.cmu.edu/cmmi/.
12. SPICE (2005), Web Site of the SPICE project, http://www.sqi.gu.edu.au/spice/.

The Impact of Pair Programming and Test-Driven Development on Package Dependencies in Object-Oriented Design — An Experiment

Lech Madeyski

Institute of Applied Informatics, Wroclaw University of Technology,
Wyb.Wyspianskiego 27, 50370 Wroclaw, Poland
Lech.Madeyski@pwr.wroc.pl
http://madeyski.e-informatyka.pl/

Abstract. Background: Test-driven development (TDD) and pair programming are software development practices popularized by eXtreme Programming methodology. The aim of the practices is to improve software quality.

Objective: Provide an empirical evidence of the impact of both practices on package dependencies playing a role of package level design quality indicators.

Method: An experiment with a hundred and eighty eight MSc students from Wroclaw University of Technology, who developed finance-accounting system in different ways (CS — classic solo, TS — TDD solo, CP — classic pairs, TP — TDD pairs).

Results: It appeared that package level design quality indicators (namely package dependencies in an object-oriented design) were not significantly affected by development method.

Limitations: Generalization of the results is limited due to the fact that MSc students participated in the study.

Conclusions: Previous research revealed that using test-driven development instead of classic (test-last) testing approach had statistically significant positive impact on some class level software quality indicators (namely CBO and RFC metrics) in case of solo programmers as well as pairs. Combined results suggest that the positive impact of test-driven development on software quality may be limited to class level.

1 Introduction

Test-driven development (TDD) [1] and pair programming (PP) [2] have recently gained a lot of attention as the key software development practices of eXtreme Programming (XP) methodology [3]. The main idea of test-driven development is that programmers write tests before production code. Pair programming is software development practice where two programmers work together, collaborating on the same development tasks. The basic aim of both practices, described

J. Münch and M. Vierimaa (Eds.): PROFES 2006, LNCS 4034, pp. 278–289, 2006.

in section 3.5, is to improve software quality. The question is whether both practices (used separately or together) really improve software quality.

Researchers and practitioners have reported numerous, often anecdotal and favourable studies of XP practices and methodology. Empirical studies on pair programming often concern productivity [4, 5, 6, 7, 8]. A few studies have focused on pair programming or test-driven development as practices to remove defects [5, 6, 9, 10], influence external code quality (measured by the number of functional, blackbox test cases passed) [11, 12, 13] or reliability of programs (a fraction of the number of passed tests divided by the number of all tests) [14, 15, 16]. Janzen [17] has pointed out that there was no research on the broader efficacy of test-driven development, nor on its effects on internal design quality outside a small pilot study [18]. Recently, Madeyski [19] pointed out that using test-driven development instead of classic (test-last) development had significant positive impact on two Chidamber and Kemerer (CK) [20] class level software quality indicators — Response For a Class (RFC) and Coupling Between Object classes (CBO). Obtained results did not support similar, positive impact of pair programming practice [19]. Hulkko and Abrahamsson [21] also suggested that pair programming might not necessarily provide as extensive quality benefits as suggested in literature. The key findings from empirical studies concerning software quality are summarized below in table 1.

Table 1. Pair programming and test-driven development literature review

Study	Environment	Subjects	Key findings
PP studies:			
[5, 6]	Academic	41(14P/13S)	P had 15% less code defects than S
[15, 16]	Academic	37(10P/17S)	P did not produce more reliable code
[21]	Acad./Ind.	4x(4–6)	P did not provide extensive quality benefits
TDD studies:			
[14]	Academic	19(9CS/10TS)	T did not produce more reliable code
[11, 12]	Industrial	24(6CP/6TP)	TP products passed 18% more tests than CP
[9, 10]	Industrial	13(5CS/9TS)	Minimal/no difference in *LOC* per person-month T reduced defect rate by 40–50%
[18]	Academic	8(1Cx4/1Tx4)	No meaningful differences in package dependencies between T and C project
Combined study:			
[13, 19]	Academic	188 (28CS/28TS/ 31CP/35TP)	TS passed significantly less acc. tests than CS TP passed significantly less acc. tests than CP No difference between CS and CP as well as TS and TP in *NATP* (Number of Acc.Tests Passed) T had significant positive impact on *RFC* and *CBO* CK metrics in case of S and P

Abbreviations: S(Solo programmers), P(Pairs), x4(groups of four), T(TDD), C(Classic)

In spite of a wide range of empirical studies there is still limited evidence concerning the impact of pair programming and test-driven development on quality of an object-oriented design in terms of dependencies between packages (collections of related classes), which in turn may have impact on external qualities e.g. fault-proneness or maintainability. The aim of this paper is to fill in this gap.

An experiment, performed in 2004 at Wroclaw University of Technology, was aiming to investigate the impact of test-driven development and pair programming practices on different aspects of software development. One of the interesting results of the experiment is that using test-driven development instead of classic testing approach has statistically significant positive impact on class level software quality indicators (RFC and CBO) in case of solo as well as pair programming [19]. The interesting research question, investigated in this paper, is whether the positive impact of test-driven development on software quality is limited to the class level. It is important question because test-driven development practice (also known by names such as, test-first design and test driven design) is considered not only one of the core programming practices of XP but also one that we use instead of writing detailed design specifications [22]. Practitioners emphasize that test-driven development is primarily a method of designing software, not just a method of testing [23] and that pair programming tend to come up with higher quality designs [24].

The quality of an object-oriented design is strongly influenced by a system's package relationships. Loosely coupled and highly cohesive packages are qualities of good design. Therefore to investigate the impact of test-driven development and pair programming on object-oriented design we used Martin's package level dependency metrics [25, 26] that can be used to measure the quality of an object-oriented design in terms of the interdependences between the packages of that design. Designs which are highly interdependent tend to be rigid, unreusable and hard to maintain [25].

Martin's metrics, investigated in this study and measured by our tool [27], are defined as follows [25]:

- Ca (Afferent Couplings) — The number of classes outside the package that depend upon classes within the package.
- Ce (Efferent Couplings) — The number of classes inside the package that depend upon classes outside the package.
- I (Instability) — The ratio ($Ce/(Ca+Ce)$) of efferent coupling (Ce) to total coupling ($Ce+Ca$). This metric is an indicator of the package's resilience to change and has the range $[0, 1]$. $I = 0$ indicates a maximally stable package. $I = 1$ indicates a maximally instable package.
- A (Abstractness) — The ratio of the number of abstract classes to the total number of classes in package. This metric range is $[0, 1]$. 0 means concrete package and 1 means completely abstract package.
- Dn (Normalized Distance from Main Sequence) — This is the normalized perpendicular distance of the package from the idealized line $A + I = 1$. This metric is an indicator of the package's balance between abstractness and stability. Dn metric's results are within a range of $[0, 1]$. A value of zero indicates perfect package design.

Underlying theory about a relationship between the object-oriented metrics and fault-proneness as well as maintainability due to the effect on cognitive complexity has been provided in [28] and [29].

2 Problem Statement

The following definition determines a foundation for the experiment [30]:

Object of study. The objects of study are software development products — developed code.
Purpose. The purpose is to evaluate the impact of test-driven development and pair programming practices on software development products.
Quality focus. The quality focus is the object-oriented design quality in terms of the interdependences between packages of that design.
Perspective. The perspective is from the researcher's point of view.
Context. The experiment is run using MSc students as subjects involved in finance-accounting system development.

Summary: The analysis of *the developed code* for the purpose of *evaluation of the test-driven development and pair programming practices impact on the developed code* with respect to *interdependences between packages* from the point of view of *the researcher* in the context of *finance-accounting system development performed by MSc students.*

3 Experiment Planning

The planning phase of the experiment can be divided into seven steps [30]: context selection, hypotheses formulation, variables selection, selection of subjects, experiment design, instrumentation and validity evaluation.

3.1 Context Selection

The context of the experiment was the Programming in Java (PIJ) course, and hence the experiment was run off-line [30]. Java was the programming language, Eclipse 3.0 was the IDE (Integrated Development Environment). All subjects had prior experience at least in C and C++ programming (using object-oriented approach). The PIJ course consisted of seven lectures (90 minutes per each) and fifteen laboratory sessions (also 90 minutes per each). The course introduced Java programming language using test-driven development and pair programming as the key XP practices. The subjects' practical skills in programming in Java using pair programming and test-driven development were evaluated during the first seven laboratory sessions. The experiment took place during the last eight laboratory sessions. The problem (development of the finance-accounting system) was close to the real one (not toy-size). The requirements specification consisted of 27 user stories. The subjects participating in the study were mainly second and third-year (and few fourth and fifth-year) computer science MSc students of Wroclaw University of Technology. In total 188 students were involved in the experiment, see table 2. A few people were involved in the experiment planning, operation and analysis.

3.2 Quantifiable Hypotheses Formulation

The crucial aspect of the experiment is to know and formally state what we intend to evaluate in the experiment. This leads us to the formulation of the following quantifiable hypotheses to be tested:

- $H_{0\ X,\ CS/TS/CP/TP}$ — There is no difference in the mean value of X metric (where X is Ca, Ce, I, A or Dn) between the software development projects using any combination of classic (test-last) / TDD (test-first) testing approach and solo / pair programming development method (CS, TS, CP and TP are used to denote development methods).
- $H_{A\ X,\ CS/TS/CP/TP}$ — There is a difference in the mean value of X metric between the software development projects using any combination of classic (test-last) / TDD (test-first) testing approach and solo / pair programming development method.

If we reject null hypotheses $H_{0\ X,\ CS/TS/CP/TP}$ (where X is Ca, Ce, I, A or Dn) we can try to investigate more specific hypotheses concerning differences between development methods (CS vs. TS, CP vs. TP, CS vs. CP, and TS vs. TP).

3.3 Variables Selection

The independent variable is the software development method used (CS, TS, CP or TP). The dependent (response) variables are mean values of Ca, Ce, I, A and Dn (denoted as M_X where X is Ca, Ce, I, A or Dn).

Table 2. The context of the experiment

Context factor	ALL	CS	TS	CP	TP
Number of MSc students:	188	28	28	62	70
– on the 2nd year	108	13	16	40	39
– on the 3rd year	68	12	11	18	27
– on the 4th year	10	3	0	3	4
– on the 5th year	2	0	1	1	0
– with industry experience	33	4	6	8	15
Mean value of:					
– Programming experience in years	3.8	4.1	3.7	3.6	3.9
– Java experience in months	3.9	7.1	2.8	3.4	3.5
– Another OO language experience in months	20.5	21.8	20.9	19.2	21.1

3.4 Selection of Subjects

The subjects are chosen based on convenience — the subjects are students taking the PIJ course. Prior to the experiment, the students filled in a pre-test questionnaire. The aim of the questionnaire was to get a description of the students' background, see table 2 for sample results. The ability to generalize from this context is further elaborated when discussing threats to the experiment.

3.5 Design of the Experiment

The design is one factor (the software development method) with four treatments (alternatives):

- Solo programming using classic testing approach — tests after implementation (CS).
- Solo programming using test-driven development (TS).
- Pair programming using classic testing approach — tests after implementation (CP).
- Pair programming using test-driven development (TP).

Pair programming is a practice in which two programmers (called the driver and navigator) work together at one computer, collaborating on the same development tasks (e.g. design, test, code). The driver, is typing at the computer or writing down a design. The navigator observes the work of the driver, reviews the code, proposes test cases and considers the implementations strategic implications [5, 31]. In case of solo programming all activities are performed by one programmer.

Test-driven development is a practice based on specifying piece of functionality as a low level test before writing production code, implementing the functionality so that the test passes, refactoring (e.g. removing duplication) and iterating the process. Tests are run frequently, while writing production code. In case of classic (test-last) development tests are specified after writing production code and less frequently [32].

The assignment of subjects to groups was performed first by stratifying the subjects with respect to their skill level, measured by graders, and then assigning them randomly to test-driven development or classic testing approach treatment groups. However the assignment to solo or pair programming teams took into account the people preferences (as it seemed to be more natural and close to agile software development practice).

Students who did not complete the experiment were removed from the analysis. Sixteen teams dropped out, did not check in the final version of their program or did not fill in questionnaires. Therefore, we retained data from 122 teams. The design resulted in an unbalanced design, with 28 solo programmers and 31 pairs using classic testing approach, 28 solo programmers and 35 pairs using test-driven development practice.

3.6 Instrumentation

The instrumentation of the experiment consisted of requirements specification (user stories), pre-test and post-test questionnaires, Eclipse project framework, detailed description of software development methods (CS, TS, CP, TP) and duties of subjects, instructions how to use the experiment infrastructure (e.g. CVS Version Management System) and examples (e.g. sample source code of applications developed using TDD approach and JUnit tests). Martin's metrics were collected using aopmetrics tool [27] developed and supported by members of e-Informatyka development team at Wroclaw University of Technology.

3.7 Validity Evaluation

The fundamental question concerning results of each experiment is how valid the results are. When conducting the experiment, there is always a set of threats to the validity of the results. Shadish, Cook and Campbell [33] defined four types of threats: *statistical conclusion*, *internal*, *construct* and *external validity.*

Threats to the *statistical conclusion* validity are concerned with issues that affect the ability to draw the correct conclusion about relations between the treatment and the outcome of the experiment. Threats to the *statistical conclusion* validity are considered to be under control. Robust statistical techniques, tools (e.g. Statistica) and large sample sizes to increase statistical power are used. Measures and treatment implementation are considered reliable. However, the risk in the treatment implementation is that the experiment was spread across laboratory sessions. To avoid the risk, access to the CVS repository was restricted to the specific laboratory sessions (access hours and IP addresses). Validity of the experiment is highly dependent on the reliability of the measures. The basic principle is that when you measure a phenomenon twice, the outcome should be the same. The measures used in the experiment are considered reliable because they can be repeated with the same outcomes.

Threats to the *internal* validity are influences that can affect the independent variable with respect to causality, without the researcher's knowledge. Concerning the *internal* validity, the risk of rivalry between groups must be considered. The group using the traditional method may do their very best to show that the old method is competitive. On the other hand, subjects receiving less desirable treatments may not perform as well as they generally do. However, the subjects were informed that the goal of the experiment was to measure different development methods not the subjects' skills. Possible diffusion or imitation of treatments were under control of the graders.

Construct validity concerns generalizing the results of the experiment to the concepts behind the experiment. Threats to the *construct* validity are not considered very harmful. Inadequate explication of constructs does not seem to be the threat as the constructs were defined, before they were translated into measures or treatments. The mono-operation bias is a threat as the experiment was conducted on a single software development project; however, the size of the project was not a toy-size. Using a single type of measure would be a mono-method bias threat; however, different measures were used in the experiment.

Threats to *external* validity are conditions that limit our ability to generalize the results of our experiment to industrial practice. The largest threat is that students (who had short experience in pair programming and test-driven development) were used as subjects. However, Kitchenham et al. [34] state that students are the next generation of software professionals, so, are relatively close to the population of interest. In summary, the threats are not regarded as being critical.

4 Experiment Operation

The experiment was run at Wroclaw University of Technology in 2004 during eight laboratory sessions. The data was primarily collected by automated experiment infrastructure. Additionally, the subjects filled in pre-test and post-test questionnaires, primarily to evaluate their experience. The package for the experiment was prepared in advance and is described in section 3.6.

5 Analysis of the Experiment

The experiment data are analysed with descriptive analysis and statistical tests.

5.1 Descriptive Statistics

Descriptive statistics of gathered Martin's metrics are summarized in table 3. Columns "Mean", "StdDev", "Max", "Median" and "Min" state for each metric and development method ("DevMeth") the mean value, standard deviation, maximum, median, minimum, respectively.

The first impression is that development methods performed similarly. Results shown in table 3 also indicate imperfect package design (e.g. values of normalized distance from main sequence are close to 1), no matter which development method was used.

Table 3. Descriptive statistics of Martin's metrics

Metric	DevMeth	Mean	StdDev	Max	Median	Min
Ca	CS	.46	1.12	4.50	0	0
	TS	.20	.72	2.75	0	0
	CP	.31	.98	3.60	0	0
	TP	.11	.50	2.80	0	0
Ce	CS	.24	.53	1.67	0	0
	TS	.17	.53	2.25	0	0
	CP	.15	.49	2.00	0	0
	TP	.07	.31	1.60	0	0
I	CS	.08	.17	.54	0	0
	TS	.07	.22	1.00	0	0
	CP	.03	.10	.34	0	0
	TP	.03	.12	.50	0	0
A	CS	.00	.02	.08	0	0
	TS	.01	.02	.08	0	0
	CP	.01	.03	.17	0	0
	TP	.00	.02	.09	0	0
Dn	CS	.92	.18	1.00	1.00	.42
	TS	.92	.22	1.00	1.00	0
	CP	.96	.10	1.00	1.00	.66
	TP	.97	.12	1.00	1.00	.50

5.2 Hypotheses Testing

Experimental data are analysed using models that relate the dependent variable to the factor under consideration. The use of these models involves making assumptions concerning the data that need to be validated. Therefore we run some exploratory analysis on the collected data to check whether they follow the assumptions of the parametric tests:

- Normal distribution — the collected data come from a population that has a normal distribution.
- Interval or ratio scale — the collected data must be measured at an interval or ratio level (since parametric tests work on the arithmetic mean).
- Homogeneity of variance — roughly the same variances between groups or treatments (as we use different subjects).

We find that — according to the Kolmogorov-Smirnov and Shaprio-Wilk statistic (see table 4) — the data are not normally distributed. This finding alerts us to the fact that a nonparametric test should be used.

Hypotheses $H_{0\ X,\ CS/TS/CP/TP}$ (where X is Ca, Ce, I, A or Dn) are evaluated using the Kruskal-Wallis one way analysis of variance by ranks. The

Table 4. Tests of Normality

Metric	DevMeth	Kolmogorov-Smirnov[1]			Shapiro-Wilk		
		Statistic	df[2]	Significance	Statistic	df[2]	Significance
M_{Ca}	CS	.480	28	.000	.481	28	.000
	TS	.536	28	.000	.287	28	.000
	CP	.529	31	.000	.350	31	.000
	TP	.529	35	.000	.232	35	.000
M_{Ce}	CS	.494	28	.000	.495	28	.000
	TS	.519	28	.000	.370	28	.000
	CP	.527	31	.000	.353	31	.000
	TP	.536	35	.000	.254	35	.000
M_I	CS	.496	28	.000	.494	28	.000
	TS	.517	28	.000	.366	28	.000
	CP	.529	31	.000	.348	31	.000
	TP	.539	35	.000	.251	35	.000
M_A	CS	.509	28	.000	.342	28	.000
	TS	.535	28	.000	.295	28	.000
	CP	.539	31	.000	.176	31	.000
	TP	.539	35	.000	.161	35	.000
M_{Dn}	CS	.466	28	.000	.521	28	.000
	TS	.455	28	.000	.400	28	.000
	CP	.514	31	.000	.409	31	.000
	TP	.518	35	.000	.284	35	.000

[1] Lilliefors Significance Correction.

[2] Degrees of freedom.

Kruskal-Wallis test is used for testing differences between the four experimental groups (CS, TS, CP, TP) when different subjects are used in each group. Table 5 shows test statistics and significances.

Table 5. Kruskal-Wallis Test Statistics — grouping variable: DevMeth

	M_{Ca}	M_{Ce}	M_I	M_A	M_{Dn}
Chi-Square	2.917	2.323	2.402	2.039	2.420
Asymp. Significance	.405	.508	.493	.564	.490

We can conclude that the software development method used by the subjects do not significantly affected interdependencies between the packages.

6 Summary and Conclusions

It appeared that package level design quality indicators (namely package dependencies in an object-oriented design) were not significantly affected by development method. Using test-driven development instead of classic (test-last) testing approach as well as pair programming instead of solo programming had not significant impact on package dependencies. Previous research revealed that using test-driven development instead of classic testing approach had statistically significant positive impact on some class level software quality indicators (namely CBO and RFC) in case of solo as well as pair programming [19]. Combined results suggest that the positive impact of test-driven development on software quality may be limited to class level. Therefore software engineers and academics may benefit from using test-driven development but they should take care of package level design issues. Further research is needed to replicate the study, to evaluate the impact in other contexts (e.g. in industry) as well as on other package level software quality indicators and to establish evidence.

Acknowledgments

The author would like to thank the students for participating in the investigation, the graders and the members of the e-Informatyka team (Michał Stochmiałek, Wojciech Gdela, Tomasz Poradowski, Jacek Owocki, Grzegorz Makosa, Mariusz Sadal) for their help during development of the measurement infrastructure (e.g. aopmetrics tool [27]). This work has been financially supported by the Ministry of Education and Science as a research grant 3 T11C 061 30 (years 2006-2007).

References

1. Beck, K.: Test Driven Development: By Example. Addison-Wesley (2002)
2. Williams, L., Kessler, R.: Pair Programming Illuminated. Addison-Wesley (2002)

3. Beck, K.: Extreme Programming Explained: Embrace Change. 2nd edn. Addison-Wesley (2004)
4. Nosek, J.T.: The case for collaborative programming. Communications of the ACM **41**(3) (1998) 105–108
5. Williams, L., Kessler, R.R., Cunningham, W., Jeffries, R.: Strengthening the case for pair programming. IEEE Software **17**(4) (2000) 19–25
6. Williams, L.: The Collaborative Software Process. PhD thesis, University of Utah (2000)
7. Nawrocki, J.R., Wojciechowski, A.: Experimental evaluation of pair programming. In: ESCOM '01: European Software Control and Metrics. (2001) 269–276
8. Nawrocki, J.R., Jasiński, M., Olek, L., Lange, B.: Pair Programming vs. Side-by-Side Programming. In Richardson, I., Abrahamsson, P., Messnarz, R., eds.: EuroSPI. Volume 3792 of Lecture Notes in Computer Science., Springer (2005) 28–38
9. Williams, L., Maximilien, E.M., Vouk, M.: Test-Driven Development as a Defect-Reduction Practice. In: ISSRE '03: Proceedings of the 14th International Symposium on Software Reliability Engineering, Washington, DC, USA, IEEE Computer Society (2003) 34–48
10. Maximilien, E.M., Williams, L.A.: Assessing Test-Driven Development at IBM. In: ICSE '03: Proceedings of the 25th International Conference on Software Engineering, IEEE Computer Society (2003) 564–569
11. George, B., Williams, L.A.: An Initial Investigation of Test Driven Development in Industry. In: SAC '03: Proceedings of the 2003 ACM Symposium on Applied Computing, ACM (2003) 1135–1139
12. George, B., Williams, L.A.: A structured experiment of test-driven development. Information and Software Technology **46**(5) (2004) 337–342
13. Madeyski, L.: Preliminary Analysis of the Effects of Pair Programming and Test-Driven Development on the External Code Quality. In Zieliński, K., Szmuc, T., eds.: Software Engineering: Evolution and Emerging Technologies. Volume 130 of Frontiers in Artificial Intelligence and Applications. IOS Press (2005) 113–123
14. Müller, M.M., Hagner, O.: Experiment about test-first programming. IEE Proceedings - Software **149**(5) (2002) 131–136
15. Müller, M.M.: Are Reviews an Alternative to Pair Programming? In: EASE '03: Conference on Empirical Assessment In Software Engineering. (2003)
16. Müller, M.M.: Are Reviews an Alternative to Pair Programming? Empirical Software Engineering **9**(4) (2004) 335–351
17. Janzen, D.S.: Software Architecture Improvement through Test-Driven Development. In: OOPSLA '05: Companion to the 20th annual ACM SIGPLAN conference on Object-oriented programming, systems, languages, and applications, New York, NY, USA, ACM Press (2005) 222–223
18. Kaufmann, R., Janzen, D.: Implications of Test-Driven Development: A Pilot Study. In: OOPSLA '03: Companion of the 18th annual ACM SIGPLAN conference on Object-oriented programming, systems, languages, and applications, New York, NY, USA, ACM Press (2003) 298–299
19. Madeyski, L.: An empirical analysis of the impact of pair programming and test-driven development on CK design complexity metrics. Technical Report PRE I31/05/P-004, Institute of Applied Informatics, Wroclaw University of Technology (2005)
20. Chidamber, S.R., Kemerer, C.F.: A Metrics Suite for Object Oriented Design. IEEE Transactions on Software Engineering **20**(6) (1994) 476–493

21. Hulkko, H., Abrahamsson, P.: A Multiple Case Study on the Impact of Pair Programming on Product Quality. In: ICSE '05: Proceedings of the 27th International Conference on Software Engineering, New York, NY, USA, ACM Press (2005) 495–504
22. Object Mentor, Inc.: Test Driven Development (2005) http://www.objectmentor.com/writeUps/TestDrivenDevelopment.
23. Wikipedia, the free encyclopedia: Test-driven development (2005) http://en.wikipedia.org/wiki/Test_driven_development.
24. Wikipedia, the free encyclopedia: Pair programming (2005) http://en.wikipedia.org/wiki/Pair_programming.
25. Martin, R.C.: OO Design Quality Metrics, An Analysis of Dependencies (1994)
26. Martin, R.C.: Agile Software Development, Principles, Patterns, and Practices. Prentice Hall (2004)
27. Wroclaw University of Technology, e-Informatyka and Tigris developers: aopmetrics project (2005) http://aopmetrics.tigris.org/.
28. Briand, L.C., Wüst, J., Ikonomovski, S.V., Lounis, H.: Investigating quality factors in object-oriented designs: an industrial case study. In: ICSE '99: Proceedings of the 21st International Conference on Software Engineering, Los Alamitos, CA, USA, IEEE Computer Society Press (1999) 345–354
29. Emam, K.E., Melo, W.L., Machado, J.C.: The Prediction of Faulty Classes Using Object-Oriented Design Metrics. Journal of Systems and Software **56**(1) (2001) 63–75
30. Wohlin, C., Runeson, P., Höst, M., Ohlsson, M.C., Regnell, B., Wesslén, A.: Experimentation in Software Engineering: An Introduction. Kluwer Academic Publishers, Norwell, MA, USA (2000)
31. Williams, L.A., Kessler, R.R.: All I really need to know about pair programming I learned in kindergarten. Commun. ACM **43**(5) (2000) 108–114
32. Erdogmus, H., Morisio, M., Torchiano, M.: On the Effectiveness of the Test-First Approach to Programming. IEEE Transactions on Software Engineering **31**(3) (2005) 226–237
33. Shadish, W.R., Cook, T.D., Campbell, D.T.: Experimental and Quasi-Experimental Designs for Generalized Causal Inference. Houghton Mifflin (2002)
34. Kitchenham, B., Pfleeger, S.L., Pickard, L., Jones, P., Hoaglin, D.C., Emam, K.E., Rosenberg, J.: Preliminary Guidelines for Empirical Research in Software Engineering. IEEE Transactions on Software Engineering **28**(8) (2002) 721–734

Applying an Agility/Discipline Assessment for a Small Software Organisation

Philip S. Taylor[1], Des Greer[1], Paul Sage[1], Gerry Coleman[2], Kevin McDaid[2], Ian Lawthers[2], and Ronan Corr[3]

[1] Queen's University Belfast, School of Computer Science, Belfast BT7 1NN, Northern Ireland, UK
{p.taylor, des.greer, p.sage}@qub.ac.uk
[2] Dundalk Institute of Technology, Department of Computing and Maths, Dublin Road, Dundalk, Co. Louth, Ireland
{gerry.coleman, kevin.mcdaid, ian.lawthers)@dkit.ie
[3] Servasport, 102 Lisburn Road, Belfast BT9 6AG, Northern Ireland, UK
ronan.corr@servasport.com

Abstract. The adoption of agile software development methodologies may appear to be a rather straightforward process yielding instantly improved software in less time and increasingly satisfied customers. This paper will show that such a notion is a misunderstanding and can be harmful to small software development organisations. A more reasonable approach involves a careful risk assessment and framework for introducing agile practices to address specific risks. A case study with a small software development organisation is provided to show the assessment in practice and the resulting risk mitigation strategies for process improvement.

1 Introduction

Readers of software process research papers and books may find it difficult to believe that there are software development organisations with no discernable process to help guide development. The authors of this paper have spent over six months observing development meetings and interviewing software engineers and managers from a range of companies varying in size and product domain. Some of the large organisations, particularly in the telecoms domain, have been using specific established processes for years. Some of the smaller organisations have developed their own process and are very successful.

However, there is also a set of smaller organisations, typically with fewer than ten employees, that are not using any defined process. This paper is concerned with such organisations. They can still develop successful products and provide excellent support for their customers but they are at great risk from issues such as an increasing number of new contracts, employee turnover, misunderstood requirements and so forth. Such organisations, to be successful, often work at an unsustainable pace. This situation is obviously detrimental for a small business and something which an agile approach attempts to address. It is in such organisations that an agile approach to development is often seen to be the quick and easy solution for preparing the business to grow by building better products and satisfying more customers. A cursory glance at

J. Münch and M. Vierimaa (Eds.): PROFES 2006, LNCS 4034, pp. 290–304, 2006.

some of the agile literature or hearing a short talk on the topic can give the mistaken belief that an agile development approach will be straightforward to adopt and result in instant success.

A better approach for adopting agile methods is to take the time to assess what an organisation's risks are and what it does to manage these risks. This understanding can then be used to inform process improvement.

This paper aims to show how the authors adapted the assessment developed by Boehm and Turner [1], [2], [3], [4] to help a small software development organisation take a reasoned step towards process improvement and an Agile approach to satisfying their customers.

The paper is organised as follows. The second section provides a short historical context for agile methods by discussing their evolution. The third section will discuss approaches to adopting agile methods and the fourth section will introduce Boehm and Turner's Agility/Discipline assessment. Section five presents the case study with the company Servasport and how the authors utilised Boehm and Turner's Agility/Discipline assessment. Section six generalizes the risk mitigation process for introducing agile methods. The seventh section concludes this paper, summarising the key findings.

2 Agile Methods in Context

This section will briefly present a historical evolution of agile methods and thereby counter some of the misunderstandings that software organisations may have regarding their validity. For overviews of individual agile methods the reader can consult Abrahamsson et al [5] and Highsmith [6].

Larman and Basili [7], [8] have carefully provided the context for current agile methods. They argue convincingly that many of the practices which appear to be novel in agile methods, most notably incremental and iterative development (IID), have actually been practiced since software began to be developed in the 1950's.

Figure 1 shows the context of agile methods. When software began to be developed there were two approaches, IID and ad hoc. The waterfall process [9] was developed to improve those ad hoc development efforts and not necessarily to replace IID. At some point the waterfall process became the dominant approach, possibly due to its conceptual simplicity, and was used on many projects which would have been better suited to IID. This issue began to be addressed in the early to mid 1990's resulting in what would later be known as Agile Methods.

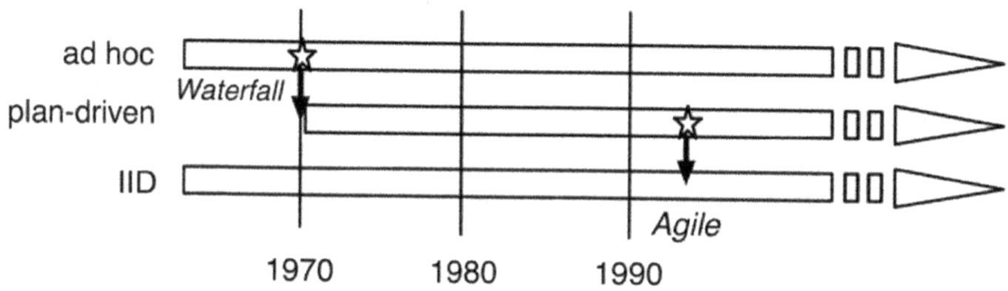

Fig. 1. The historical context for agile methods

Agile methods have been derived from the failure of the plan-driven waterfall processes to be successful with all varieties of software product and team and are now in the IID family. Agile methods are not ad hoc and their empirical nature requires discipline on the part of the team using them. All three streams of software development are likely to continue into the future.

3 Adopting Agile Methods

This research has arisen from the Software Process Agility for Competitive Edge (SPACE) project [10]. This project has the primary aim of promoting the merits of agile methods for smaller software development organisations and to enable the adoption of these methods to increase efficiency and competitiveness.

As stated previously, adopting an agile development approach is not a simple solution to an organisation's problems and may, in fact, lead to further problems. Turk et al [11], [12] have discussed some of the problems they perceive with agile methods. Their work is based primarily on examining the underlying assumptions of agile methods and determining for which development scenarios the assumptions do not hold. They arrive at two groups of limitations:

Personnel limitations

Limited support for distributed development environments
Limited support for subcontracting
Limited support for large teams

Product limitations

Limited support for building reusable artifacts
Limited support for developing safety-critical software
Limited support for developing large, complex software

There is a certain amount of truth in each of these perceived limitations and, obviously, if a development scenario involved any of the above situations then a careful risk analysis would have to be completed. Agile method proponents are quick to state that much work has yet to be done in each of these areas. Other studies by Keefer [13] and McBreen [14] focus specifically on perceived weaknesses with Extreme Programming (XP) [15]. They also note similar limitations to Turk et al [11], [12].

Given such perceived limitations it is clear that small software organisations require a straightforward guide to adopting, or rejecting, an agile approach to development.

4 Boehm and Turner's Agility/Discipline Assessment

As early as 2002 Boehm [1] had already produced an approach to assessing an organisation's suitability for agile methods. Boehm and Turner [4] present the sets of conditions under which agile and plan-driven methods are most likely to succeed:

Application characteristics – primary project goals, project size, and application environment.

Management characteristics – customer relations, planning and control, and project communications.

Technical characteristics – approaches to requirements definition, development, and test.
Personnel characteristics – customer characteristics, developer characteristics, and organisational culture.

For example, agile methods work best when the application environment has a high amount of change and plan-driven methods are better suited to stable environments with low change. Five critical factors, as shown in Figure 2 and described in Table 1, are summarised from Boehm and Turner's [4] analysis of the strengths of agile and plan-driven methods.

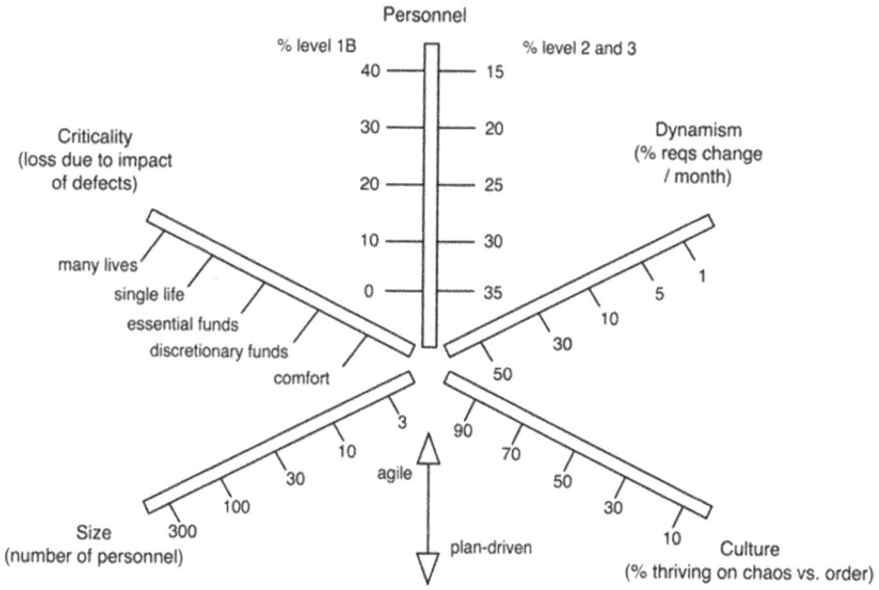

Fig. 2. Five critical factors affecting method selection [4, p. 56]

Building upon the five critical factors Boehm and Turner [4] describe a five-step, risk-based method. The risks are categorised as follows:

Environmental – risks resulting from the project's general environment. An example is technology uncertainties in the particular project domain.
Agile – risks specific to the use of agile methods. For example, agile methods rely on tacit knowledge as the small number of team members communicate on a daily basis, but if there is personnel turnover the tacit knowledge also leaves.
Plan-driven – risks specific to the use of plan-driven methods. For example, emerging requirements will cause strain for a plan-driven method as it is structured for up-front requirements elicitation.

Table 1. Five critical factors described [4, p. 55]

Factor	Agility Discriminators	Plan-Driven Discriminators
Size	Suited to small products and teams. Not very scalable.	Methods suited to large products and teams. Difficult to scale down.
Criticality	Little testing on safety-critical products. Informal documentation and simple design may be potentially difficult.	Methods suited to highly critical products. Overkill for low-criticality products.
Dynamism	Simple design and continuous refactoring good for dynamic environments. Can be a source of expensive rework in stable environments.	Detailed plans and Big Design Up Front excellent for highly stable environments. Can be a source of expensive rework in dynamic environments.
Personnel	Requires highly skilled software engineering experts. Risky to use inexperienced people.	Requires highly skilled software engineering experts during project definition. Later in project can work with fewer experts and more inexperienced people.
Culture	Thrives on chaos.	Thrives on order.

The assessment is based on a five step process:

Step 1. Rate the project's environmental, agile, and plan-driven risks. If uncertain about the ratings use prototyping, data collection, and analysis.
Step 2a. If agility risks dominate, use a risk-based plan-driven approach.
Step 2b. If plan-driven risks dominate, use a risk-based agile approach.
Step 3. If the risks are a mixture of 2a and 2b then architect to encapsulate the agile parts. Use risk-based agile approach on the agile parts and risk-based plan-driven elsewhere.
Step 4. Establish an overall project strategy by integrating individual risk mitigation plans.
Step 5. Monitor project progress and risk/opportunities; readjust balance and process as appropriate.

A further explanation of factors and how the authors adapted the Agility/Discipline assessment as a tool to aid software process improvement in small organisations will be given in Section Five.

5 Servasport Case Study

The SPACE project organises regular industrial events to discuss and inform regarding agile methods. At these events, overviews of various agile methods are presented and industrial speakers who are using agile methods describe their experiences. Through such events the SPACE team promotes the Agility/Discipline assessment primarily to small software development organisations.

Servasport is a specialist sports management company providing a range of internet-based software solutions to meet the information management, administration, communication, marketing and revenue generation needs of sports organisations and their associated clubs. They have four software developers and a graphic designer and are relatively successful in their product domain. On average a project will generally take between ten and twelve weeks from initial requirements to customer handover. The contract model used requires them to agree a price and time-scale before commencing the development work. If the deadline is missed further work must be completed within the original budget. Servasport had previously been operating without much specific process guidance. Such an approach worked well but their reputation in the product domain continues to increase and hence they are getting further projects, leading them to explore the benefits of agile methods.

This scenario is common and Servasport are not alone in wanting to be prepared for increased project activity and the vital revenue it generates. They have sought guidance on how to improve the management of parallel projects, prioritise changing and emergent requirements, retain fast development cycles and so forth.

Given the nature of Servasport and the products they produce, it would seem inevitable that an agile approach to development would be particularly beneficial. However, small software organisations such as Servasport cannot risk losing contracts and revenue due to the adoption of a new process that does not suit the team, product domain, or customer relationship.

5.1 Adapting the Assessment

Boehm and Turner's intention is "to offer a way to plan your program and incorporate both agility and discipline in proportion to your project's needs." [4, p. 99]. Although this aim suggests that a software team leader or manager should be knowledgeable and confident enough to make process improvements the Agility/Discipline assessment can also prove useful for those small software organisations.

Boehm and Turner do not explicitly split their Agility/Discipline assessment into stages but for the purposes of engaging software organisations with straightforward process improvement strategies we have established two explicit stages.

The first stage was to use the five critical factors graph to reassure Servasport that they are suited to an agile development approach. Before introducing Servasport to the five factors, they were asked to describe their most crucial problems. Customer related issues were deemed most important and entailed most risk. As product providers many small software organisations can be made to feel privileged that they are getting the contract and revenue and the customer will give them initial requirements and remain practically uninvolved until the handover deadline. This scenario was also noticeable in some large software development organisations. As a result, we added a sixth factor, *Client Involvement*, to the graph as shown in Figure 3.

The sixth factor, *Client Involvement*, has the following categories:

> *On AB* – Client is on-site and an agile believer. This is the ideal when a client is fully persuaded of the agile approach and makes themselves available on-site to work with the team.
>
> *Off AB* – Client is off-site but an agile believer. Although off-site, the client fully understands the nature of agile development and is open to frequent communication.

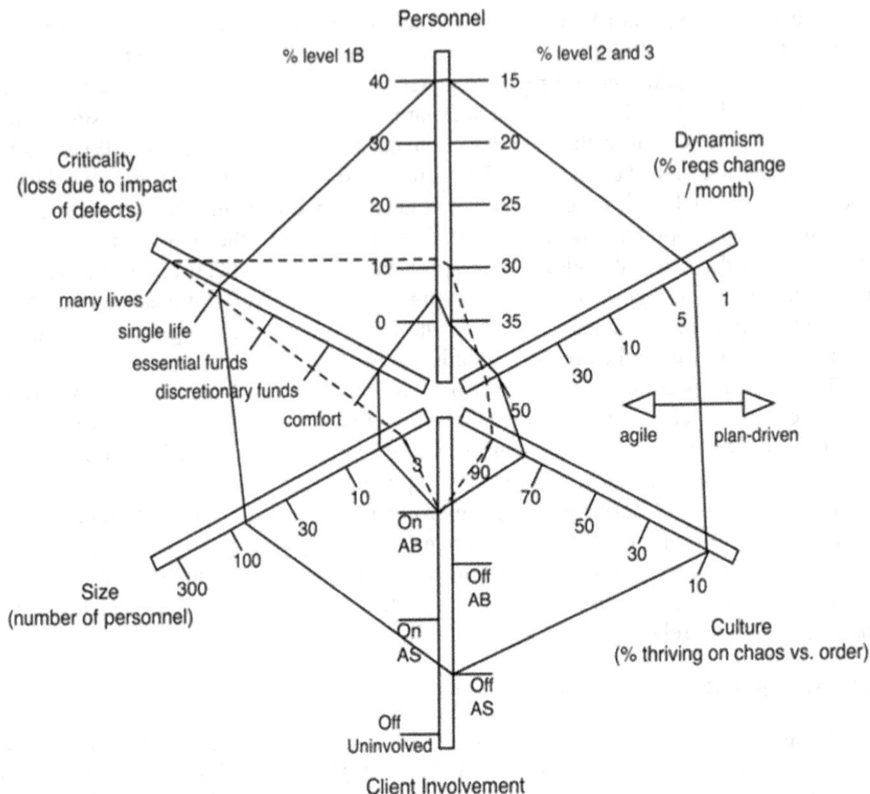

Fig. 3. Six critical factors affecting method selection. This is an update of Figure 2 after surveying industrial risks.

On AS – Client is on-site but is an agile skeptic. They may be on-site but they are not convinced about the agile development approach.
Off AS – Same as On AS except the problem is compounded by the client being off-site.
Off Uninvolved – Not only is the client off-site but they want no involvement between providing the initial requirements and getting the right product delivered.

Servasport then performed a self assessment, using the six critical factors graph and accompanying instructions. The aim was to get the developers discussing process improvement and forming opinions about how their process should be improved.

Plotting the data on the graph is simple. If the project *criticality* is 'comfort' and the team *size* is 3, draw a line from one to the other. The other factors require more explanation. *Personnel* is an important part of the self assessment. Each team member is required to give an accurate assessment of themselves and each other. The categories are described in Table 2.

Table 2. Personnel characteristics

Level	Characteristics
3	Able to revise a method (break its rules) to fit an unprecedented situation.
2	Able to tailor a method to fit a precedented new situation. Can manage a small, precedented agile or plan-driven project but would need level 3 guidance on complex, unprecedented projects.
1A	With training, able to perform discretionary method steps (e.g. sizing tasks for project timescales, composing patterns, architecture re-engineering). With experience, can become level 2. 1A's perform well in all teams with guidance from level 2 people.
1B	With training, able to perform procedural method steps (e.g. coding a class method, using a CM tool, performing a build/installation/test, writing a test document). With experience, can master some level 1A skills. May slow down an agile team but will perform well in a plan-driven team.
-1	May have technical skills, but unable or unwilling to collaborate or follow shared methods. Not good on an agile or plan-driven team.

The *Personnel* axis requires more explanation. The outer solid line shows that approximately 15% of staff are level 2 or 3, approximately 40% are level 1B and the remaining at level 1A. An agile approach will be better supported if there is a higher percentage of level 2 or 3 staff as shown by the inner solid line and dashed line. The agile related *Personnel* risk with the outer solid line is that most of the level 2 or 3 staff will be expending much time training and overseeing level 1B staff and therefore contributing less directly to the product. As a team gains more practical knowledge with an agile development approach the *Personnel* percentages should move towards the centre indicating more level 1B staff becoming level 1A.

Dynamism can be an exact figure if metrics are kept or a notional estimate if metrics do not exist. Requirements changes include all functional and non-functional requirements. *Culture* is a notional estimate of how much your team or organisation likes to work on the edge of chaos or with more planning and defined procedures.

The self assessment then outlines how a graph, such as that in Figure 3, can be interpreted. The outermost solid line suggests a project that is suited to a plan-driven approach and the innermost solid line indicates a project to be suited to an agile approach. The dashed line suggests that the project would be suited to an agile approach but has a significant risk on the *Criticality* axis. When such a risk is encountered more planning is required than an agile approach typically recommends.

The second stage of the self assessment involved using Boehm and Turner's Agility/Discipline risk ratings. Each team member was asked to provide a rating for each risk item. Once each team member had completed the self assessment we collated the results and discussed with Servasport the issues arising from the exercise.

5.2 Primary Risks

As Figure 4 shows, the biggest risk from stage one of the assessment is the situation where there are off-site uninvolved customers who have the potential to break the agile development approach. The aim was to find a way to bring this risk down to the dashed section of the line in Figure 4 resulting in customers who were off-site agile believers (Off AB clients). Such customers work well with internet-based product development due to the relatively straightforward nature of accessing working versions of the product. Before reaching the Off AB category for *Client Involvement* the risk needs to be more specifically defined and a workable plan implemented.

Servasport have experienced a customer who desired new functionality at the product handover stage. In this circumstance, the contract arrangement meant that Servasport did not obtain full payment until the customer was satisfied which lead to further development having to be completed within the budget of the original timescale. For a small software team providing competitively priced work based on the originally approved project such a scenario can leave them in a vulnerable position in the working relationship. The subsequent work to satisfy the customer can lead to unplanned and badly paced software development. There is also the danger that the customer perceives an inability to meet their desires first time. Figure 4 also shows that 25% of the staff are at level 2 and the rest are level 1A.

Table 3 presents the risk ratings for Servasport from the second stage of the assessment. Looking at the total risk ratings clearly shows that the company are relatively unaffected by environmental risks. The technology they use, whilst changing regularly, is not uncertain. Their systems are not overly complex and there are few stakeholders. Using a plan-driven approach has greater risk when compared to using an agile approach resulting in the decision to work towards adopting an agile approach.

The primary risk with using the agile approach is personnel turnover. Many small software organisations can lose employees to bigger organisations offering a more stable future and better benefits packages. It is crucial for them to manage this risk as best they can.

5.3 Risk Mitigation as a Framework for Adopting Agile Methods

Having used the adapted two stage Agility/Discipline assessment with the company the following risks require careful management if using an agile development approach:

Risk 1. Off-site uninvolved customers.
Risk 2. Personnel turnover.

The authors believe that highlighting the risks of a software organisation focuses the need for process improvement and effectively acts as a framework for the introduction of agile methods. Such an approach enables the organisation to see that the new agile method is actually helping to mitigate real risk and hence reduces resistance to the changes required. The risk mitigation strategies developed for the company are described in the following paragraphs. These strategies introduced certain agile practices to Servasport and are a first step towards process improvement. Introducing the agile practices in small stages enables the staff to feel confident using them and provides space to tailor them to the company's specific context.

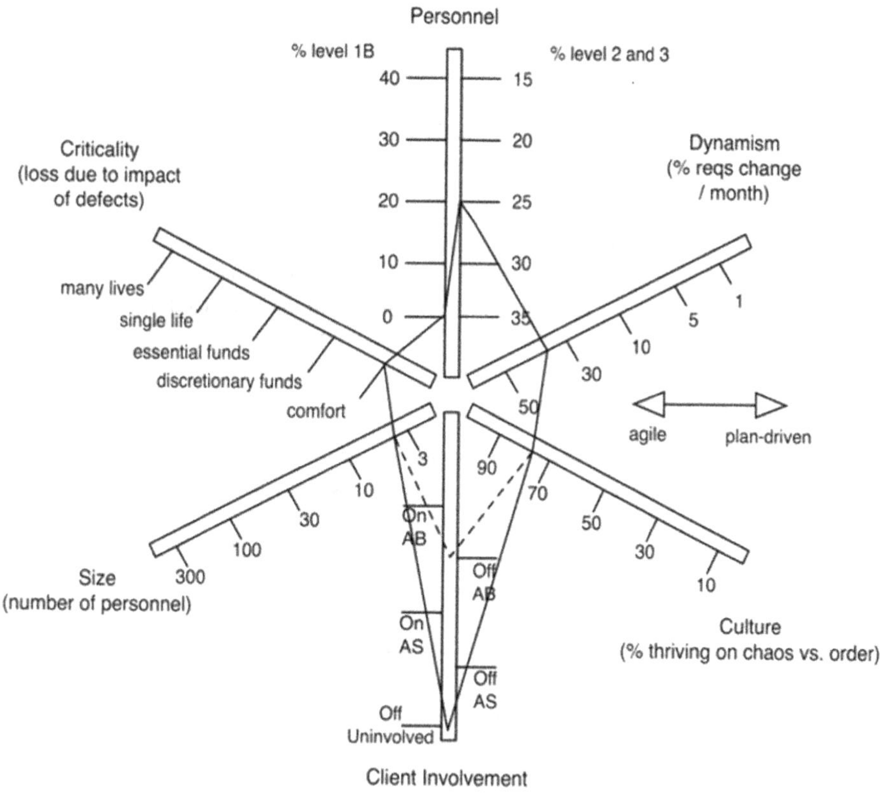

Fig. 4. Six critical factors affecting method selection for Servasport

5.3.1 Off-Site Uninvolved Customer Risk

Given an average development cycle of between ten and twelve weeks a risk mitigation strategy making use of incremental delivery was agreed.

- The company should have a weekly incremental delivery for at least the last three weeks of any project. The rationale for this decision is to begin moving an Off-Site Uninvolved customer to an Off AB (see Figure 4).
- The final increment shall typically result in the handover release.

This new approach should be made visible to the customer with the following requirements:

- The customer should understand that involvement in the incremental releases is contractually required. Contractual conditions with small software organisations usually favour the customer. This type of clause ensures active participation by the customer.
- User acceptance testing will be part of the incremental approach. User acceptance testing is the means by which customers can verify their requirements. The tests should be developed with input from the company and the customer. They should be written in the language of the customer, for example:

Test 1
"The user must be able to click the bike icon and receive new content."

Test 1.1
"Receiving this new content must be in the following manner – a bulleted list shown on the left side of the news window."

The objective is not to have the product totally finished before the incremental delivery phase begins. Rather, the company will have planned the work needs to completed in each increment. The first attempt at this was based on previous experience with the time to complete certain types of requirement. The accuracy of planning the amount of work for the increments will increase with each product.

Table 3. Risk ratings for Servasport

Risk Items	**Risk Rating**
Environmental risks	
Technology uncertainties	1
Many stakeholders	1
Complex system of systems	1
	total = 3
Risk of using agile methods	
Scalability and criticality	1
Use of simple design	1
Personnel turnover	4
Not enough poeple skilled in agile methods	2
	total = 8
Risk of using plan-driven methods	
Rapid change	4
Short development cycles	4
Emergent requirements	4
Not enough people skilled in plan-driven methods	3
	total = 15
1 – minimal risk, 2 – moderate risk, 3 – serious but manageable risk, 4 – very serious but manageable risk, 5 – showstopper risk	

The company are aware that each incremental delivery will result in issues arising from failed user acceptance tests or unspecified new requirements. In relation to this, Servasport must discern between a user acceptance test failing because the customer has implicitly changed their requirement or because the specified requirement has not been implemented correctly. Unspecified new requirements must be prioritised with previously specified requirements. In some instances the new requirement will replace a specified requirement and in other instances the new requirement will be previously unspecified. In either scenario the company must work with the customer to determine what can realistically be done in the next increment.

If new requirements arise at the last increment during final user acceptance tests then the customer must provide reasons why they were not originally specified or discovered in a previous increment. At this point it will be necessary to negotiate further increments if the customer must have the new requirements. If all the user acceptance tests pass at the final planned increment then discuss and agree a new costing for any subsequent increments.

The above strategy has helped to mitigate the risk from off-site uninvolved customers by bringing them closer to being off-site agile believers. It also makes the balance of power fairer in the working relationship as Servasport are seen to be driving certain aspects of the product development. The customer was also given the opportunity to be more involved in product development resulting in greater commitment to the product. As the company prepares for larger projects running in parallel the careful use and planning of increments will become essential if they are to continue to be successful in satisfying their customers. When such development situations arise further agile practices will be investigated for suitability.

5.3.2 Personnel Turnover Risk

The mitigation strategy for this risk has yet to be refined with Servasport but the following paragraphs outline the basic practices. The advantage of a small development team often relates to the natural occurrence of face to face communication. It is generally accepted that small teams benefit from the ability to communicate frequently about each other's development problems and successes. However, the disadvantages are that if a team member becomes ill or leaves for another employer the other team members find it difficult to orient themselves with often undocumented work practices and development. This scenario is common for many small software development organisations working at or near to their limits.

Contrary to the popular misunderstanding agile methods do use documentation but the emphasis is on working software. Documentation may not be comprehensive but it will relate to the essential aspects of a project. Ruping [16] suggests that agile documentation should be governed by the following principles:

- Project documentation should be lightweight and only include what is necessary.
- Necessary documents can only prove useful if they are high-quality.
- Tools and techniques for documentation are only useful if they aid the production of high-quality documents and make their organisation and maintenance easier.
- The documentation process must adapt to each specific project.

Regarding tools, Servasport use standard word processing software for the production of formal documents for customers such as contractual agreements and user manuals. They use the open source SugarCRM [17] tool as a version control system for documents. SugarCRM can also be used to manage tasks but it is not possible to produce burn-down statistics hence limiting its applicability to other agile practices. It is recommended that Servasport use a standard spreadsheet to track all tasks and manage it with their chosen version control system.

Servasport follow a standard set of coding guidelines and code comment standard. However, more important than this type of documentation is that related to the product architecture. One of the developers is primarily responsible for deciding the shape of the architecture and the tools used to implement it. It should be evident to all members how to update such tools and integrate other tools within the architecture. In order to keep such documentation lightweight and current it is advised that a wiki [18] system be used which is accessible and editable by all team members. The wiki system used in conjunction with periodic mentored role changing will help reduce the risk accompanying personnel turnover. For example, the developer responsible for architecture changes should change roles temporarily with the developer responsible for interface design. This will at least highlight where the wiki documentation is incorrect or unclear and at most lead to more than one developer who can adequately maintain or change the architecture and interface.

The documentation could be more rigorous but, given the nature of Servasport and the product domain, what has been described above is adequate to begin mitigating the risk of personnel turnover and contribute to process improvement.

6 A Risk Based Process for Adopting Agile Methods

Figure 5 summarises the risk based process for adopting agile methods in small software development organisations. Given that many such organisations work near or at their limits, the process for adopting agile methods has to be minimally intrusive yet effective enough to actually begin mitigating risks. The process begins with the two stage self assessment. The results are collated by those skilled in agile methods and process improvement and the risk strategies are developed in conjunction with the software development organisation. Only at this point are agile practices introduced which relate directly to the risks resulting in the overall risk mitigation framework. Feedback and refinement is essential for continual process improvement and changing product domains. This risk based process will also help to reduce the limitations mentioned in Section 3.

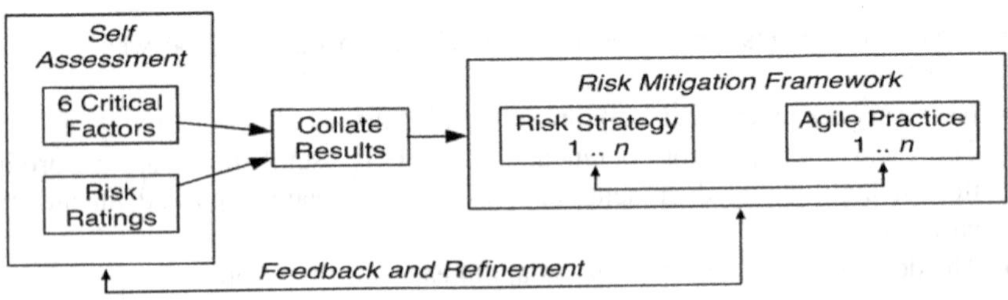

Fig. 5. Minimally intrusive risk assessment process for introducing agile methods

7 Conclusions

Many small software development organisations, seeking to improve the efficiency and effectiveness of their development processes, are being drawn by the hype surrounding agile methods.

The aim of this paper has been to present a method, with an accompanying case study, to assess the risks that a small software organisation has and to introduce agile practices to help mitigate these risks. Based on observation and numerous discussions with small software development organisations the approach presented, derived from Boehm and Turner's Agility/Discipline assessment, is a more reasonable attempt to introduce agile methods. The self assessment presented in Section 5.1 highlights the primary risks which then function as a framework for the new agile practices. The framework approach has the advantages of focusing the efforts of those responsible for process improvement and of reducing resistance to the required changes.

The case study has helped to show how the self assessment can be used. It has been effective at highlighting the risks and providing the framework for process improvement with agile practices. For organisations like Servasport it is more likely that such small improvements will need to be made and refined as the business grows rather than a complete change to agile methods in one step. The potential for failure is simply too great to risk complete process change in one step.

Acknowledgements

The work described in this paper arises from the SPACE project, supported by the EU Programme for Peace & Reconciliation, administered by Co-operation Ireland.

References

1. Boehm, B.: Get Ready for Agile Methods, with Care. IEEE Computer, Vol. 35(1), IEEE Computer Society (2002) 64 – 69
2. Boehm, B., Turner, R.: Rebalancing Your Organization's Discipline and Agility. In: Maurer, F., Wells, D (eds.): XP/Agile Universe 2003. Springer-Verlag, Berlin Heidelberg (2003) 1 – 8
3. Boehm, B., Turner, R.: Using Risk to Balance Agile and Plan-Driven Methods. IEEE Computer, Vol. 36(6), IEEE Computer Society (2003) 57 – 66
4. Boehm, B., Turner, R.: Balancing Agility and Discipline – A Guide for the Perplexed. Addison-Wesley (2004)
5. Abrahamsson, P., Warsta, J., Siponen, M. T., Ronkainen, J.: New Directions On Agile Methods: A Comparative Analysis. Proc. 25th Int. Conf. Software Engineering. IEEE Computer Society (2003) 244 – 254
6. Highsmith, J.: Agile Software Development Ecosystems. Addison-Wesley (2002)
7. Larman, C., Basili, V. R.: Iterative and Incremental Development: A Brief History. IEEE Computer, Vol. 36(6), IEEE Computer Society (2003) 47 – 56
8. Larman, C.: Agile & Iterative Development – A Manager's Guide. Addison-Wesley (2004)
9. Royce, W. W.: Managing the Development of Large Software Systems. Proc. WESCON. IEEE Computer Society (1970) 1 – 9. Available for download at http://www.cs.umd.edu/class/spring2003/cmsc838p/Process/waterfall.pdf (last visited January 2006)
10. www.agileireland.com

11. Turk, D., France, R., Rumpe, B.: Limitations of Agile Software Processes. In: Wells, D., Williams, L. A. (eds): XP/Agile Universe 2002. Springer-Verlag, Berlin Heidelberg (2002) 43 – 46
12. Turk, D., France, R., Rumpe, B.: Assumptions Underlying Agile Software Development Processes. Journal of Database Management, Vol. 16(4), Idea Group Inc (2005) 62 – 87
13. Keefer, G.: Extreme Programming Considered Harmful for Reliable Software Development 2.0. Available at http://www.avoca-vsm.com/Dateien-Download/ExtremeProgramming.pdf (last visited January 2006). AVOCA GmbH 2003
14. McBreen, P.: Questioning Extreme Programming. Addison-Wesley (2003)
15. Kent, B., Andres, C.: Extreme Programming Explained: Embrace Change. 2nd Ed. Addison-Wesley (2005)
16. Ruping, A.: Agile Documentation – A Pattern Guide to Producing Lightweight Documentation for Software Projects. John Wiley & Sons (2003)
17. http://www.sugarcrm.com (last visited January 2006)
18. http://en.wikipedia.org/wiki/Wiki (last visited January 2006)

Lessons Learned from an XP Experiment with Students: Test-First Needs More Teachings

Thomas Flohr[1] and Thorsten Schneider[2]

[1] Software Engineering Group, University of Hannover, Welfengarten 1, 30167 Hannover, Germany
Thomas.Flohr@Inf.Uni-Hannover.de
[2] S²e (Secure Software Engineering), Lange Strasse 33, 32051 Herford, Germany
Schneider@secure-software-engineering.com
http://www.secure-software-engineering.com

Abstract. For most XP techniques only a few experimental results on their effects are available. In October 2004 we started a medium-term experiment to investigate the impact of test-first compared to a classical-testing approach. We carefully designed a controlled experiment and conducted it with 18 graduated students randomly assigned to 9 pairs. Hypotheses dealt with development speed, number of test-cases and the test-coverage when applying the testing approaches. Results show differences however not significant ones. This paper also addresses other observations we made during the experimental run. Two major problems strongly affect the results of the experiment: the low number of data points and the non-trivial question, whether students really applied test-first all the time. Although we cannot provide any new results on testing to the research community, this paper contains valuable information about further experimental studies on this topic.

1 Introduction

The test-first approach is an XP technique [1] answering the question, when test-cases should be written. When applying the test-first approach one normally traverses a cycle similar to:

1. Write one single test-case.
2. Run this test-case. If it fails continue with step 3. If the test-case succeeds, continue with step 1.
3. Implement the minimal code to run the test-case successfully.
4. Run the test-case again. If it fails again, continue with step 3. If the test-case succeeds, continue with step 5.
5. Refactor the implementation to achieve the simplest design possible.
6. Run the test-case again, to verify that the refactored implementation still succeeds the test-case. If it fails, continue with step 5. If the test-case succeeds, continue with step 1, if there are still requirements left in the specification.

One claimed advantage of test-first is that one never writes more code than absolutely necessary. It is also said, that test-first leads to greater confidence in code correctness and when performing refactorings, etc.

J. Münch and M. Vierimaa (Eds.): PROFES 2006, LNCS 4034, pp. 305 – 318, 2006.

Of course these are hypotheses, which must be proven through experimental runs and depends on how good developers follow the process of test-first.

But what about the normal approach of testing? We called this approach classical-testing. It can be defined by the following process:

1. Read the specification.
2. Design the program
3. Write a few lines of code, some method(s), class(es), package(s) or the whole application.
4. Write some (new) or no test-suites, tests-sets, tests or test-cases gained from the specification.
5. Run the tests. If they succeed, continue with step 1, 2, 3 or 4. If the tests fail, continue with step 6. If there are no more further requirements and the code has been tested enough (perspective of the developer), exit the classical-testing cycle.
6. Remove the errors in the implementation and continue with step 5.

The classical-testing approach is less specified and does not give a good answer when to write a test-case. Our main research question concentrated on several aspects:

1. The difference between both testing approaches regarding the amount of time needed to complete the same number of story-cards (development speed).
2. The difference between both testing approaches regarding the test-coverage.
3. The difference between both testing approaches regarding the number of test-cases.

To verify (or falsify) our hypotheses, we conducted an experiment with students in October 2004. We opted for a medium-term experiment of several weeks (altogether 40 hours) because short-term studies observing development processes are limited to use small and artificial tasks. We had two groups: one applied test-first and the other one was our control group applying the classical-testing approach. Each group contained several pairs, so in fact the pairs were our subjects. The design of the experiment is outlined in section 3 and a much more detailed description can be found in [2].

Overall, this paper is structured as follows: section 2 contains the hypotheses we had using parts of the GQM approach as proposed by Basili [3, 4]. Section 4 contains the threats to validity. Section 5 deals with the execution of the experiment. In section 6 we give an overview of the results we received from the experimental run. Section 7 contains the discussion of the observations we made and how we judge their significance. A final conclusion follows in chapter 8.

1.1 Related Work

There is only small number of publications dealing with the observation of test-first in controlled experiments. Most empirical studies about XP techniques report on pair programming [5], XP or agile methods in general [6, 7].

Müller and Hagner observed 19 graduate students with some experience in XP [8]. In their experiment test-first was compared to traditional development separately. The students were divided in two groups to apply one of the approaches each. Each group had to implement the main class of a graph library which only contains declarations of methods. The experiment included unit and acceptance tests. Objects of investigation were programming speed, reliability of the final code and program understanding (reuse of code). The authors conclude that test-first for a traditional developer is not faster than traditional development.

Hulkko and Abrahamsson [9] report on the impact of pair programming in four software projects. There is no clear answer, whether pair programming or solo programming results in better product quality. Nevertheless, they give an answer in which project phases or activities the application of pair programming is useful based on their empirical findings.

2 Our Hypotheses

We apply the versatile GQM goal template [4] to express the purpose of our study (the keywords of the GQM goal template are bold):

> **Conduct a study with the purpose** to **evaluate the object of study** test-first **with a focus on** (1) development speed, (2) test-coverage, (3) number of test-cases and (4) attitude **from the point of view of the** researchers **in the context of** a university computer laboratory and a simulated XP environment with Master's students as subjects.

Basically, we compared the results gained from the test-first approach with the data gained from the control group, who applied the classical-testing approach. Our alternative hypotheses and corresponding null hypotheses were:

Test-coverage (tc)

$\mathbf{H_{a\_tc}}$: $\mu_{tf} \neq \mu_{ct}$
The test-coverage when applying test-first (tf) and classical-testing (ct) is significantly different.
$\mathbf{H_{0\_tc}}$: $\mu_{tf} = \mu_{ct}$
There is no difference in the test-coverage between the two testing approaches.

Number of test-cases (nt)

$\mathbf{H_{a\_nt}}$: $\mu_{tf} \neq \mu_{ct}$
The number of test-cases when applying test-first and classical-testing is significantly different.
$\mathbf{H_{0\_nt}}$: $\mu_{tf} = \mu_{ct}$
There is no difference in the number of test-cases between the two testing approaches.

Development speed (ds)

$\mathbf{H_{a\_ds}}$: $\mu_{tf} \neq \mu_{ct}$
The development speed when applying test-first and classical-testing is significantly different.
$\mathbf{H_{0\_ds}}$: $\mu_{tf} = \mu_{ct}$
There is no difference in the development time between the two testing approaches.

3 Design of Experiment

We had a one factor (testing approach) with two treatments (test-first and classical-testing) scenario and we opted for a completely randomized design [10]. Our independent variable was the testing approach. The dependent variables were: the development time for a fixed number of story-cards, the test-coverage and the number of tests.

Chronologically, the experiment was limited to the length of the winter semester. We had a total of 13 weeks and in each week the experiment session lasted 4 consecutive hours. The experiment took place in our computer lab. Some sessions were dropped because of Christmas and New Year. Each student could get 6 credit points (ECTS) for participation.

The experiment itself was divided into 3 phases: a training phase, a development phase and an analysis phase. Table 1 shows the schedule of the experiment.

Table 1. Phases of Experiment and Schedule

20.10.2004	27.10.2004	27.10.2004	27.10.2004	3.11.2004	26.1.2005	2.2.2005
Introduction Eclipse (all students) Testing with JUnit (all students)	Introduction Test-First (10 students) Classical-Testing (8 students)	Introduction Flow (all students)	Introduction Practical trail (all students)	10 weeks of development 4 hours per week = 40 hours total	Release of final version	Announcement of empirical data
General Trail	Special Trail	Prog. Task Trail	Practical Trail			
Training Phase				Development Phase		Analysis Phase

The main part of the experiment was the development phase of 10 weeks. In this time the students should implement a library for our research project FLOW [11]. FLOW is concentrating on the graphical description of communication flows in software processes, so these flows can be analyzed systematically. Each pair started to develop their library from scratch by using the Eclipse tool platform and Java as development language. The subjects should exactly follow the detailed steps of their testing approach being explained in the introduction. Each group only received an introduction to the testing approach they applied later in the experiment, to minimize the impact the other approach could have on the group. Test-cases were written with the help of the JUnit framework [12]. In the training phase students also got an introduction to Eclipse and testing with the JUnit framework.

Instead of observing the two testing approaches in an isolated way, we integrated three other XP techniques to simplify measurement, gain more data points and to better control the experiment: (1) Pair Programming, (2) On-site Customer and (3) User Stories. Both testing approaches were combined with these three techniques, but the testing approaches were the only object of investigations. The story-cards (user stories) were the project's milestones and with each story-card at least one feature was added to the library. Additionally, the milestones were our points of measurement. At each milestone we checked in the project's state together with its current set of test-cases in our CVS system, so we could extract any project's state for later evaluation. A story-card was considered completed when all customer tests run successfully. The story-cards were given in a fixed order, so there was no XP planning game included in the experiment. The on-site customer was always available to answer question regarding the library's requirements and to hand out new story-cards. The students worked in pairs at one single workstation all the time.

4 Threats to Validity

In experimental designs there are four validity key terms which always must be considered [10]: conclusion, internal, construct, and external validity. Conclusion validity concerns with the relationship between the treatment and the outcome. Threats to internal validity concern issues that may indicate a causal relationship, although there is none. Construct validity refers to the extent to which the experiment setting actually reflects the construct under study. Finally, external validity addresses the question how good the observed and analyzed results can be generalized beyond the experimental setting.

4.1 Conclusion Validity

Many experiments in software engineering suffer from very poor conclusion validity, because of a lack of enough data points. Especially medium- and long-term studies with a complex design are affected, because their replication is complex and only a few subjects want to attend an experiment for a very long time. Our computer lab could only support 10 subjects at one time. Because of this low capacity and lack of enough staff to handle a second session per week, our experiment had low conclusion validity. In fact only 19 students (9 real pairs/subjects) attended our experiment. With an alpha of 0.05 and an effect size of 0.8 the power of a two-sided t-test is only 0.18, which is a very poor power. We used a two-sided Wilcoxon rank sum test for two samples so we have approximately 95% of the power of the t-test: 0.17. This means that we only have a probability of 0.17 to show a difference between the testing approaches, if there is any. Normally, only experiments with a power of at least 0.8 are approved to show real effects. Other threats to conclusion validity are considered to be low.

4.2 Internal Validity

We applied several methods to ensure the internal validity:

- Every team could only program in the four hours of every session. Homework was not possible; otherwise diligent students will start to develop the program, while others may not. Therefore we also forbid to transfer any of the source code to another computer outside the laboratory environment.
- During the sessions every team had access to the same electronically library of documents. Access to the Internet was disabled. Anyone had the same body of knowledge.
- We asked the students not to talk about anything regarding the experiment to other participants of the experiment (except the team mate), because discussion about the experiment could influence the results. Overall, the imitation of other treatments is hard to control in a multi-session design. We only appealed to student's honour to avoid this problem.

– Each group only got an introduction to the testing approach they also would use later in the experiment. This minimized the danger to use the wrong testing approach.

A problem we could not handle is boredom in experiments lasting a longer time. We tried to hand out an interesting programming task (with each story-card there was a new challenge) to prevent this, but there was no guarantee. Boredom endangers the process conformance i.e. bored subjects will not follow a detailed process very consequently.

4.3 Construct Validity

Threats to construct validity must be considered, because the results can be influenced by the other XP techniques we included in the design. Maybe pair programming, story-cards or the on-site customer favoured one of the approaches. Other threats to construct validity are considered to be low, especially social threats. We avoided mentioning any results we observed in the experiment, because it could influence the students. None of the participants knew any of our hypotheses. To avoid evaluation apprehension students were not graded for their results, otherwise it is likely that students will try to cheat in some way e.g. will ask for help. In fact the participants could receive a fix amount of credit points as a reward regardless of their project's code quality.

4.4 External Validity

Ensure external validity in experiments conducted with students as subject is always a problem. Researchers often seek for results, which are also valid in an industrial environment. Students and university are always different from the development in reality which is driven by money- and time-pressure. We tried to establish an environment as real as possible. We decided for a medium-term study and a not too abstract programming task (a toy problem), because industrial projects are seldom short and very abstract.

5 Experimental Run

In October 2004 we started to conduct the experiment with a total number of 19 students. The students were randomly paired resulting in 9 pairs and a one person team. Since the observed results of the one person team can not be compared to the pairs, we will neglect any results regarding this one student for the rest of this paper. Five pairs applied the test-first approach and the other 4 pairs adopted the classical-testing approach.

All students had attended a software engineering course and 12 of them had prior knowledge of test-first. 16 students had knowledge of JUnit and understood how to use it. One student even used it in a professional way.

14 students had average (average = conducted a medium-size Java project before) or above average knowledge in Java, the remaining 5 students had at least some basic knowledge in Java. Only 3 students never used Eclipse. 7 participants only had experiences with software projects in university, 7 had an industrial project before (6 months maximum) and 5 designed software in a professional way in the industry for many years. 12 students attended at least one meeting with a real customer before.

There were no major differences between the design and execution, so the experiment was run according to schedule. Some minor problems are mentioned in [2], including for example the exact location of the TFT screen, when pair programming is applied.

6 Results and Analysis

This section presents an overview of the results we got. We also will give an analysis of these results and information about how we gathered data. Since we have a measure point after the completion of each story-card, we draw a curve of the development over time for some of the focuses. All teams completed at least 10 story-cards, so we will especially observe the project's state immediately after the completion of the 10th story-card. Some teams completed more than 10 story-cards, but this section lays only one time attention on the state of the projects at story-card 11 or later. For statistical evaluation we used a two-sided Wilcoxon rank sum test for two samples (equivalent to the Mann-Whitney test) requiring no assumptions on a given distribution. We chose $\alpha = 0.05$ as significance level for the following statistical tests. The last part of this section deals with other observations of the experimental run being not included in any of the hypotheses.

We start with an observation of the development speed showing the most intriguing result.

6.1 Development Speed

To obtain the development speed, we calculated the time needed to complete each story-card. The time was measured from the time, when the customer handed out the story-card to the pair until the time the customer's acceptance tests run successfully.

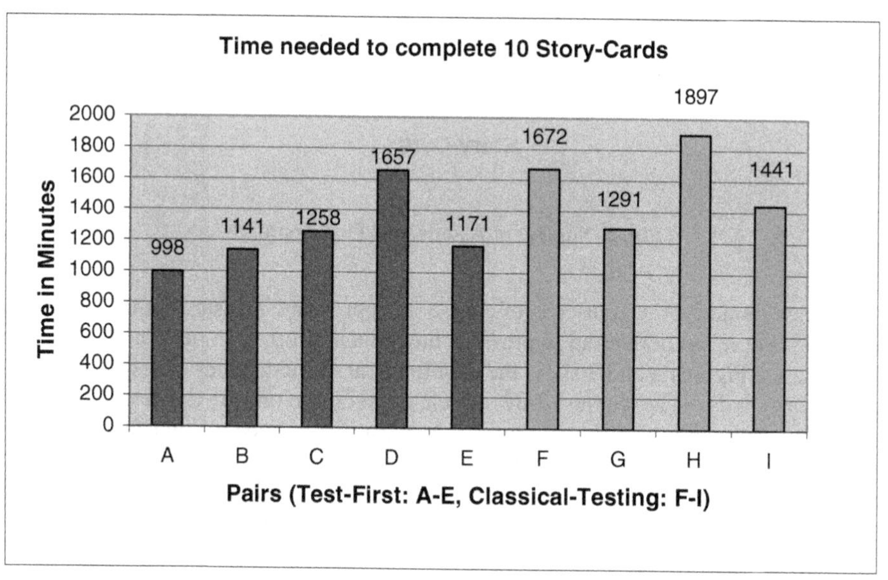

Fig. 1. Development Time

Figure 1 shows the total time needed to complete the first ten story-cards. Our results show, that the test-first pairs needed less time than the classical-testing pairs to complete the same amount of ten story-cards. The median time off all pairs is 1291 minutes and all classical-testing pairs needed more (or at least the same) time than the median time. The Wilcoxon rank sum test delivers a p-value of 0.063, which exceeds our chosen significance level. Therefore the null hypothesis H_{0_ds} can not be rejected.

6.2 Number of Test-Cases

After the test-cases had been checked in, we calculated the current number of test-cases. In our scenario a test-case is a synonym for an assert-statement of the JUnit framework.

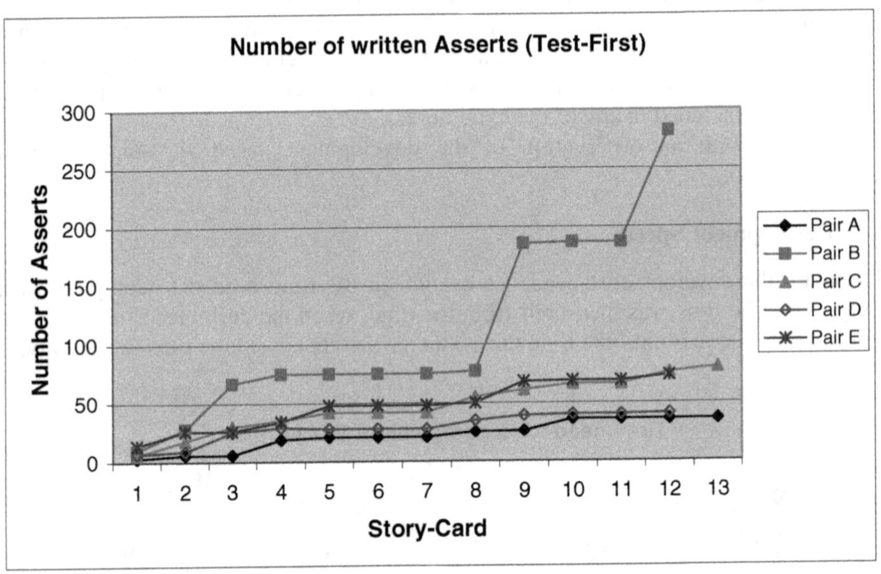

Fig. 2. Number of Asserts Test-First Approach

The raw number of test-cases is of course no appropriate measure for the quality of test-cases, but it can deliver an impression how much effort was spent on the creation of test-cases. Figures 2 and 3 show the development of the number of tests-cases over time (story-cards). The curves show no clear favor for one of the test-approaches (with the exception of outliers of pair B). At most, we can see a slight favor for test-first in the means measured after the check in of story-card 10: 79.6 (test-first) and 61.5 (classical-testing). The reason for this favor is the very high number of asserts of pair B. A hypotheses test showed no difference between the two approaches ($p = 1$). Therefore we can not reject the null hypothesis $H_{0\ nt}$.

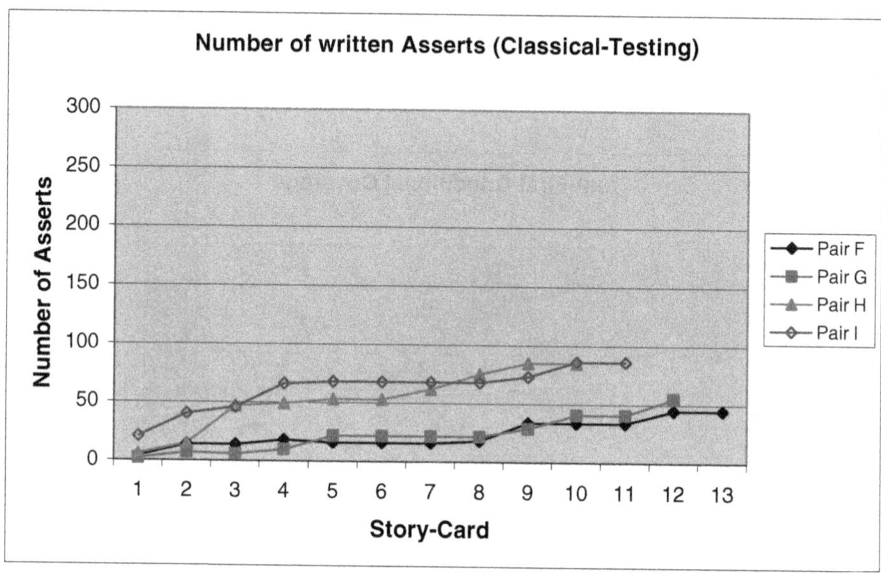

Fig. 3. Number of Asserts Classical-Testing Approach

6.3 Test-Coverage

We determined different types of coverage with the code coverage tool Clover [13], which can compute three different types: Method Coverage, Statement Coverage and Conditional Coverage. Our special attention lied on the percentage of conditional coverage, because method and statement coverage can easily produce very extreme values depending on which conditional expressions or methods are evaluated and which are not evaluated. When applying test-first, we could hypothesize that we should get a conditional coverage very close to 100%, but our observations show that the mean conditional coverage of 36.1% is far below this (story-card 10). Classical-testing even provides a slightly better mean conditional coverage of 39.9%. Figures 4 and 5 give an overview of the development of the conditional coverage. With story-card 11 we had a new design decision:

To run the customer's acceptance tests the pairs were asked to provide a simple command line based UI to use the library from beginning (story-card 1), but with each story-card the UI became larger (even larger than the library code) and very hard to test. Therefore, students did not write any test-cases to test the UI, but the UI was part of the same project and measurements regarding the code coverage also included the UI. Finally, it resulted in a quite low conditional coverage until we decided to exclude the UI from any further measurement with story-card 11. After this conditional coverage increases dramatically for nearly all pairs, but the effect was much stronger for the test-first pairs.

We could not get a significant difference between the two approaches in the percentage of conditional coverage after the check in of story-card 10 ($p = 0.904$, library and UI were measured). Even at story-card 11 (after excluding the UI from measurements) we could not get a significant difference ($p = 0.786$).

Some pairs improved their conditional coverage over time (mainly at project's early phases). So we can assume there was some learning effect. It is hard to discover any major differences over time between both approaches.

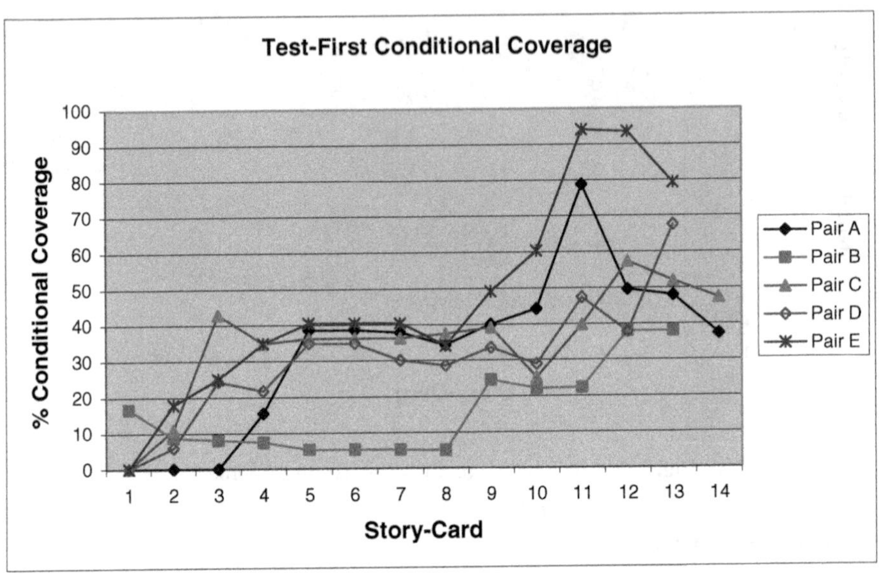

Fig. 4. Conditional Coverage Test-First Pairs

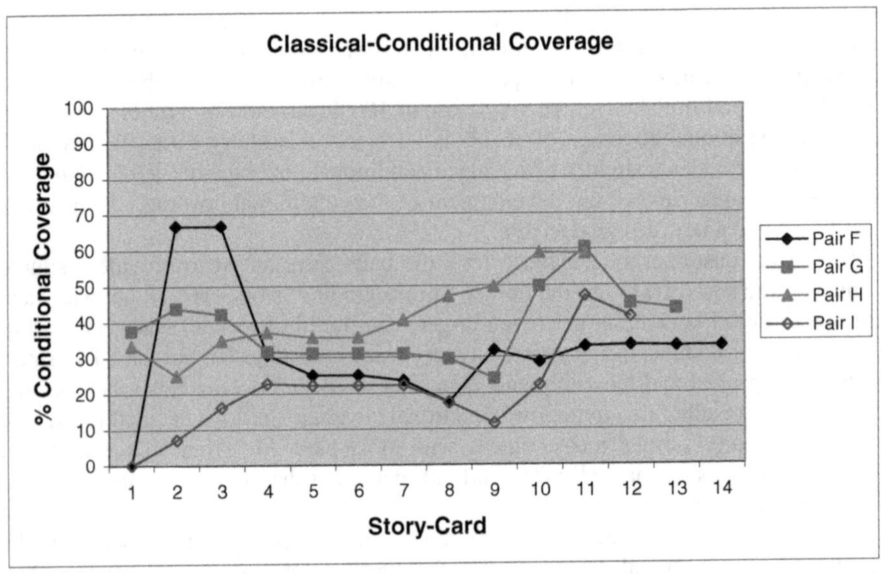

Fig. 5. Conditional Coverage Classical-Testing Pairs

We also analyzed the data from the two other coverages (story-card 10), but can not get any significant difference. Table 2 summarizes the p-values we calculated for each of the coverages. So in fact there is no statistical significant difference between the testing approaches regarding the coverages.

Table 2. P-Values of Coverages

type of coverage	**p-value**
method coverage	0,286
statement coverage	0,73
conditional coverage	0.904

6.4 Other Observations

We assumed that students' acceptance for test-first can be mapped to the curve shown in Figure 6 (black line). After a test-first training students have a slight rejection towards test-first, because they suppose that it will slow down the development process. Shortly after, they change their opinion, because they realize that test-first can guide through the development process. Afterwards the acceptance steadily increases until the hot spot (final hours of development) is reached. After the hot spot the acceptance decreases rapidly, because time is short and will not be "wasted" for testing.

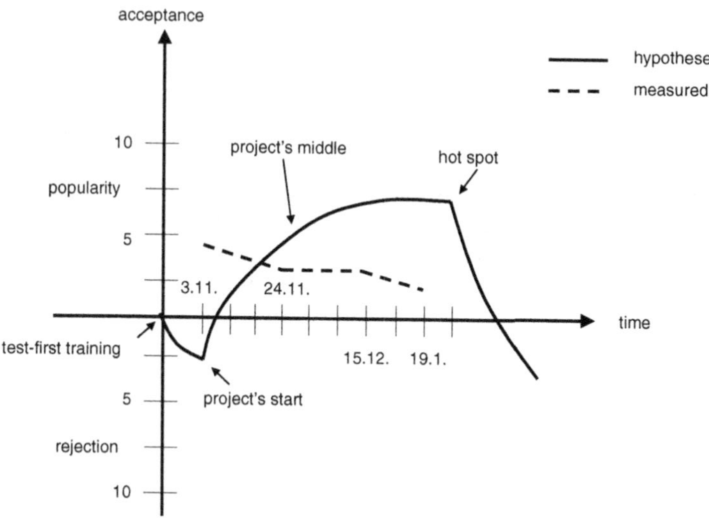

Fig. 6. Attitude of Students over Time

From questionnaires we obtained the students' attitude towards test-first (dashed line). We only asked the pairs following the test-first approach to fill out the questionnaires. The questionnaires were handed out four times during the run of the experiment. We had not enough data point to draw a complete line over the duration of the experiment. But it is obvious, that the real attitude differs from our assumed curve. The measured curve showed a clear trend: the attitude decreased over time. Nevertheless, students never rejected test-first. Negative attitude could be a result of boredom, which finally could results in low process conformance. A positive attitude indicates that the students were not bored.

The questionnaires included questions regarding the attitude towards test-first. With each questionnaire we also asked if the students support several statements about test-first. Table 3 gives an overview of these statements and how many people (measured in %) supported the statement.

Table 3. Supported Statements

statement: Test-first helps…	mean percentage
not to write more code than necessary.	73%
to write code with less flaws.	63%
to understand the customer's requirements better.	38%
to write more structured code.	28%
To design the application.	18%

85% of the test-first subjects said, that test-first is not better or worse than the programming style they used before. 70% were the opinion, that development with test-first is not faster or slower than their preferred way of programming. 20% even said test-first slows down their development.

Another interesting observation is that pair programming provoked the subjects to program more concentrated and to follow their testing approach more consequently. We assume this is because of one team member always had an eye on the other team member, so no one could disregard the testing approach.

7 Discussion

Designing perfect software engineering experiments is a difficult task, because skilled developers are needed and there is always a human factor that is hard to control. There are also a large number of context variables an experiment's designer has to pay attention to. Therefore, there is always a tension between environments with controlled variables (good internal validity) and environments, which should be real (good external validity). We tried to fulfill both aspects, which is very hard. On the one hand, we opted for a medium-term experiment with a programming task, which is not too abstract. On the other hand, we had to include rules in our experiment, to establish basic internal validity. Additionally, we suffered from a very low number of data points resulting in a low statistical power. Another problem could be the influence of further XP techniques included in the experiment on the dependent variables.

Despite we provided a good setup, which addressed a lot of problems, we faced two major problems:

Our experiment strongly suffered from a small amount of data points resulting in a poor experiment's power. Even if there are differences between the test approaches, it is very unlikely, that our experiment was able to show them. So it was very likely that none of the null hypotheses could be rejected.

The other major problem was the process conformance: It is very hard to control, whether subjects follow a technique or not. From figure 4 we can conclude, that test-first was not applied consequently and a large portion of code was left untested. We suppose that students applied a testing-approach being neither test-first nor classical-testing., but rather a combination of both approaches. This is rather likely for test-first and testing novices.

Students might not have followed the process in our experiment:

- Because of the UI large parts of the code could not be tested very easily.
- The introduction to test-first and testing was not deep enough, so students were not able to test the complex data structures needed for an appropriate implementation of the FLOW library.
- The experiment was not taken seriously enough.

Nevertheless we think that pair programming helped to ensure a minimal process conformance in our experimental setup, because students had one eye on each other.

8 Conclusion

Our experiment strongly suffered from a lack of data points resulting in a very low power of 0.17, but with our limited resources there was no way to obtain a higher power. The second major problem concerns process conformance.

In any case a further replication of our controlled experiment (strict replication [4]) is necessary to increase the conclusion validity. So the next logical step will be a creation of an experimental package for strict replications or maybe variations of the experiment.

From the small number of data points we could draw the following conclusions:

- There is no evidence that there is a significant difference in the development speed, number of test-cases and code coverage.
- Conditional coverage became better over time, because of better understandings towards testing.
- Students do not reject test-first after an introduction to test-first.
- Pair programming is a good way to ensure a minimal process conformance.
- Students consider test-first development neither faster (better) nor slower (worse) than the programming style the used before.

We strongly suggest anyone wanting to replicate our experiment or at least conducting an experiment dealing somehow with test-first and testing:

- Students need more lecture hours in testing and test-first. Two hours are not enough, even if students had some experience with testing before. We suggest at least a special testing course of one semester combined with practical sessions. The experiment could be last one of the practical sessions, so everyone should have enough prior knowledge and practical experience.
- Enough subjects are necessary to gain statistical power, whereas pair programming reduces the number of subjects, but increasing process conformance. Without pairs our experiment would have the double number of subjects resulting in a power of 0.354. This is of course not good enough, but much better. Maybe it would be better to conduct a short-time experiment combined with pair programming and a much greater number of subjects.

References

[1] Beck, K.: *Extreme Programming Explained*. 2000: Addison-Wesley

[2] Flohr, T., Schneider, T.: *An XP Experiment with Students - Setup and Problems*. in *Profes 2005*. 2005. Oulu, Finland: Springer-Verlag

[3] Basili, V., Caldiera, G., Rombach, H.: *Goal question metric paradigm*, in *Encyclopedia of Software Engineering*, J.J. Marciniak, Editor. 1994, John Wiley & Sons: New York. p. 528-532

[4] Basili, V.R., Shull, F., Lanubile, F.: *Building Knowledge through Families of Experiments*. IEEE Transactions on Software Engineering, 1999. **Vol. 25**

[5] Müller, M.M., Tichy, W.F.: *Case Study: Extreme Programming in a University Environment*. in *International Conference on Software Engineering*. 2001. Toronto, Ontario, Canada: IEEE Computer Society

[6] Noll, J., Atkinson, D.C.: *Comparing Extreme Programming to Traditional Development for Student Projects: A Case Study*. in *XP 2003*. 2003. Genova, Italy

[7] Lindvall, M., et al.: *Empirical Findings in Agile Methods*. in *Extreme Programming and Agile Methods - XP/Agile Universe 2002*. 2002: Springer-Verlag

[8] Müller, M.M., Hagner, O.: *Experiment about Test-first programming*. IEEE Proceedings Software, 2002. **149**(5)

[9] Hulkko, H., Abrahamsson:, P.: *A multiple case study on the impact of pair programming on product quality*. in *ICSE*. 2005. St. Louis, Missouri, USA

[10] Wohlin, C., et al.: *Experimentation In Software Engineering: An Introduction*. Kluwer Academic Publishers. 2000, USA

[11] Schneider, K., Lübke, D.: *Systematic Tailoring of Quality Techniques*. in *3rd World Congress for Software Quality*. 2005. Munich, Germany

[12] Gamma, E., Beck, K.: JUnit framework, http://www.junit.org/index.htm

[13] Clover Code Coverage for Java, http://www.cenqua.com/clover/

An Empirical Study on Design Quality Improvement from Best-Practice Inspection and Pair Programming

Dietmar Winkler and Stefan Biffl

Vienna University of Technology, Institute of Software Technology
Karlsplatz 13, A-1040 Vienna, Austria
{Dietmar.Winkler, Stefan.Biffl}@qse.ifs.tuwien.ac.at

Abstract. The quality of the software design often has a major impact on the quality of the final product and the effort for development and evolution. A number of quality assurance (QA) approaches for inspection of early-life-cycle documents have been empirically evaluated. An implicit assumption of these studies was: an investment into early defect detection and removal saves higher rework cost. The concept of pair programming combines software construction with implicit QA in the development team. For planning QA activities, an important research question is how effective inspectors can be expected to be at detecting defects in software (design and code) documents compared to programmers who find defects as by-product of their usual construction activities.

In this paper we present an initial empirical study that compares the defect detection effectiveness of a best-practice inspection technique with defect detection as by-product of constructive software evolution tasks during pair programming. Surprisingly, in the study context pair programmers were more effective to find defects in design documents than inspectors. However, when building a larger team for defect detection, a mix of inspection and pair programming can be expected to work better than any single technique.

Keywords: Verification & Validation, Inspection, Pair-Programming, Nominal Teams, Empirical Software Engineering.

1 Introduction

Traditional software development life cycle processes typically consist of five steps: requirements definition, system design, implementation, integration, and operation. Quality assurance (QA) activities embedded within the software development process are a key to achieve a higher level of software quality. In industrial practice a low number of defects in a software product are a measure for product quality. Product improvement also leads to a reduction of repair effort due to defects in artifacts, e.g., specification documents, requirements definitions, or code. Rework effort for defect repair can increase rapidly the later a defect is detected and removed [18]. Thus, early removal of defects in design documents and the requirements specification is expected to lead to better-quality products and to improve project performance, i.e., result in overall lower effort and cost.

J. Münch and M. Vierimaa (Eds.): PROFES 2006, LNCS 4034, pp. 319–333, 2006.

Inspection and testing are common analytical methods for software product improvement along the life cycle to minimize the number of remaining defects. Obviously, both techniques can require considerable effort in the face of scarce resources in a project. To reduce this effort, an option is to strengthen constructive QA approaches in order to detect and remove defects shortly after they occur. Pair Programming (PP) aims at supporting the construction of higher-quality software products using a small-team approach that is expected to reduce rework effort.

An important parameter for planning QA activities is how effective a best-practice analytical QA approach (inspection) is compared to just using a constructive approach with implicit QA, such as PP. In this paper we report on an initial empirical study in an academic environment [6] that compares the performance of a best-practice constructive approach (PP) and a best-practice QA technique. We applied usage-based reading (UBR), a well-investigated reading technique for software inspection, as representative approach for best-practice defect detection. Further, we investigate the impact of team size and team composition involving PP teams and UBR individuals for improving software product quality, i.e., detecting defects. The comparison of the effort of the different methods is more difficult because of the different emphasis, proceedings, and outcomes of the two approaches. However, even the comparison of quality measures provides an interesting initial baseline and deeper understanding of the defect reduction characteristics of the investigated approaches.

The reminder of this paper is structured as follows. Section 2 describes related work on pair programming, software inspection, and team composition. Section 3 summarizes the research hypotheses; Section 4 outlines the experiment setting. Section 5 presents the results of the empirical study and Section 6 discusses these results. Finally, Section 7 concludes and sketches directions for further research.

2 QA Aspects of Usage-Based Inspection and Pair Programming

Software processes structure development to systematically achieve higher-quality software products. In this context we define software quality based on the number of (important) defects in a software product. In most software processes reviews (or inspections) are performed at milestones to check artifacts for quality compliance and correctness. An important goal is to reduce the number of defects effectively.

Recently, agile programming practices have been introduced that foster rapid QA feedback during software construction activities. A particularly promising approach is pair programming, where two persons jointly conduct construction tasks; one team member implicitly supports QA by questioning unclear work results of the other partner and by pointing out defect candidates as they occur. However, there are very few studies on the QA effect of PP in direct comparison to software inspections. In this initial study we pay special attention to the benefits of usage-based inspection and constructive software development approaches, as proposed in [6].

2.1 Defect Reduction with Usage-Based Reading During Design Inspection

Software inspection is a well-known, team-oriented, and empirically evaluated static verification and validation approach for the improvement of software artifacts [15][23]. The nature of inspection makes the method applicable to all types of software documents, i.e., design documents and source code documents [9][10], because inspection does not require executable code.

In industrial practice, inspection processes consist of four major steps: inspection planning, defect detection, defect collection, and defect repair [23]. The inspection process includes a defect detection task, where individual inspectors (within an inspection team) traverse the document under inspection following a reading technique for guidance. A reading technique is a structured process for defect detection that uses predefined roles, scenarios, checklists, etc. Inspectors follow a set of guidelines and/or checklists defined by the reading technique. Several reading technique approaches have been discussed and investigated experimentally [1][3][15][17].

Requirements and use cases are the units of interest for usage-based reading (UBR) [15][16]. Use cases describe business cases on a defined level of detail to achieve full coverage of requirements in design specification and source code.

In this paper we use UBR as baseline for an active approach for defect detection [22] in design and code documents. UBR is a best-practice approach that focuses on scenarios and a pre-defined order of use cases (ranked according to their business value contribution) [2], which are understandable for customers and developers as well, using graphical representation and additional textual information for scenario and business case description. Experienced domain experts prioritize the use cases according to their business importance. UBR inspectors apply prioritized uses cases sequentially to the inspection artifacts starting with the most important use case and report candidate defects. Candidate defects are subjectively raised issues, recognized by the inspectors during the individual reading process. Note that inspectors do not fix defects during defect detection. Defect candidates are labeled as real defects or false positives after individual inspection by a group of experts in the project context. Use case prioritization is part of the preliminary inspection preparation phase and not in the scope of this paper. In the empirical study environment UBR inspectors perform the following sequence of steps [23]:

1. Choose the use case with the highest priority.
2. Apply use case to the documents under inspection and record candidate defects.
3. Continue with the next use case until time is up or all use cases are covered.

The third step of the traditional software inspection process is defect collection. Because of the team-oriented approach of inspection, a set of individual defect detection lists exist after individual inspection. Team meetings are one option for defect detection list aggregation. An alternative is a nominal team, i.e., a non-communicating team for defect collection after independent individual inspection [4][5]. The application of nominal teams ignores the impact of real team meetings and real interaction between team members [3]. Some studies [4][5] doubt the net benefit of team meetings. Nominal teams can be built from a permutation of the available individual inspectors.

2.2 Defect Reduction with Pair Programming in Design Artifacts

Pair programming (PP) is a constructive development technique that includes QA tasks for agile software development. Agile software processes [8] use smaller and more frequent iterations for better cooperation between customers and developers and to foster communication in the software engineering team. These smaller steps support the project team in constructing software products that better meet the needs of the customers, partly due to smaller entities for QA [8].

A PP team consists of two persons, sharing one keyboard and one monitor. While the first person implements tasks according to pre-defined use cases and scenarios, the other person looks over her shoulder to raise issues in the new work results or defect candidates in the specification and code documents. The roles of team members can change frequently. Due to the involvement of "two brains" [19][20], the team can achieve a twofold benefit: (a) higher-quality development of the software product because of the effective involvement of two persons who work together, and (b) improvement of software quality within all parts of the project during software construction. The latter benefit is also a twofold one: (a) increasing quality because of a lower number of defects in the new software code due to continuous reviews [7] and (b) increasing quality of existing software artifacts; thus defect reduction is a by-product of PP. The key question of this paper focuses on the comparability of defect detection capabilities of traditional inspection approaches and constructive approaches, where defect detection is considered as a by-product.

In this paper we use a PP variant, proposed in [6], to accelerate agile processes by adding QA tasks as part of the constructive phase. The pair programmers follow the prioritized list of expert-ranked use cases and perform their construction tasks. In these tasks, they have to use existing material (requirements specification, existing code fragments, etc) to understand their working environment and also check the plausibility and consistency (analytical tasks); then they evolve the existing source code following the predefined order of use cases (constructive tasks).

While one part of the pair implements and completes open programming tasks, defined within the work package, the other person looks over her shoulder to check the code for correctness. In more detail, this process consists of four steps:

1. Select the use case with the highest priority.
2. Compare requirements and use cases to the design specification and already implemented code fragments. Report candidate defects in case of deviations.
3. Work on requirements (including previous check for correctness).
4. Continue with the next use case until all use cases are covered or time is up.

To our knowledge, there is an increasing number of empirical studies on PP [12][13][14][21], however, very few investigate the quality improvement effect on existing software products [11]. Müller et al. [11] propose additional review and testing phases after PP tasks to achieve internal validity in an experiment environment. In the empirical study reported in this paper, we did not perform additional QA tasks, but asked pair programmers to note defect candidates as by-product of construction. PP's primary task is the implementation of new software code fragments and defect detection as a by-product with focus on software code (using the usual development environment, i.e., computer, compiler, and tool support).

3 Research Issues

The main focus of this paper is the comparison of the defect reduction effect as by-product of a constructive software development to a focused defect detection technique. To achieve comparability of defect detection rates, we focus on finding defects in input documents to inspection and evolution, i.e., design and code.

3.1 Variable Definition

We define dependent and independent variables. The independent variable is the technique applied: PP (with 2-person teams) and UBR (with individual inspectors). We controlled the influence of participant capability by randomly assigning them to techniques (PP and UBR) and PP teams.

Dependent variables capture the performance of the individual techniques applied in the experiment. We focus on defect detection effectiveness, i.e., the share of defects found in relation to all defects seeded, as performance measure to investigate the influence of each approach on defect detection capability of existing software artifacts. In addition to the overall number of defects we also apply defect severity classes: critical defects (class A), major defects (class B), and minor defects (class C). For evaluation purposes we focus on important defects, i.e., the summary of critical and major defects (class A+B).

Furthermore we provide data on the effort of technique application for background information. Because of a different focus of the individual approaches, a comparison of effort would not seem useful. Note that we cover experiment participation duration, not the duration of experiment setup and artifact preparation.

In addition to measuring the effectiveness of PP teams and individual inspectors we measure the performance of teams with the parameters team size and team composition (the techniques participants in a team used) to investigate the impact of nominal teams on defect reduction.

3.2 Hypotheses

In the experiment we first observed effectiveness of techniques according to important defects (classes A+B) for PP teams and UBR individuals. In a second round we build nominal teams [4] from the performance of average experiment participants to investigate the effectiveness contributions of the two techniques.

In this paper we investigate hypotheses: on the effectiveness of work units (H1); on the effectiveness of 2 persons in a nominal UBR team or a PP team (H2); and on the effectiveness of technique variations in nominal teams of different sizes (H3).

- *H1.1: Effectiveness (PP) > Effectiveness (UBR) for source code documents.* To analyze the benefits of "natural work units" we compare PP teams with one UBR inspector. Note that PP involves higher effort and more persons, but also has a focus that is different from finding defects. PP focuses primary on implementation including defect detection as a by-product. Therefore, we expect a higher effectiveness of PP teams for source code documents.
- *H1.2: Effectiveness (PP) < Effectiveness (UBR) for natural-language text documents.* In contrast, the main scope of UBR inspectors is defect detection with

focus on written text documents, e.g., design documents (DD). Therefore, we expect a higher effectiveness of UBR regarding written text documents.

To improve comparability among the techniques according to team size, we build nominal 2-person UBR teams (so-called minimal teams, MT) randomly (complete permutation). The hypotheses are similar to H1.

- *H2.1: Effectiveness (PP) > Effectiveness (UBR-MT) for source code documents and minimal teams.* The argument is similar to H1.1 because of the different main focus of both approaches. Because of an additional UBR inspector we expect a somewhat higher effectiveness.
- *H2.2: Effectiveness (PP) < Effectiveness (UBR-MT) for natural-language text documents and minimal teams.* Because of an additional UBR inspector we expect strengthened results similar to H1.2 with higher deviation of design document effectiveness.

Because both approaches focus on different issues, we assume a team consisting of members from both techniques to combine their benefits.

- *H3.1: Effectiveness (PP+) > Effectiveness (UBR+) for source code documents and nominal teams.* We expect a higher effectiveness in a team from adding a PP team (PP+) rather than compared to adding a similar number of UBR inspectors (UBR+).
- *H3.2: Effectiveness (PP+) < Effectiveness (UBR+) for design documents and nominal teams.* Additionally we expect a higher defect detection rate for written text documents from additional UBR individuals (UBR+) in a team.

3.3 Experiment Description

The study material is based on a taxi management system, provided by Thelin et al. [15][16], who investigated different reading technique approaches. We proposed an empirical investigation of analytical QA activities (best-practice inspection) with constructive approaches (PP) in [6]. First empirical results were published in [23].

The main task of UBR inspectors was defect detection in software documents. PP teams used similar artifacts including a constructive task, i.e., extending the source code according to prioritized use cases. The main purpose of this paper is the investigation of the performance of defect detection, i.e., the number of found defects in relation to the total number of seeded defects (effectiveness) for important defects and depending on defect locations in documents (source code documents and written text documents). All participants applied a pre-defined set of prioritized use cases, a business case description, a requirements document, a design specification, and a set of guidelines for method application. The design specification and the source code documents contained seeded defects.

The experiment was conducted in three steps: (a) experiment preparation, (b) experiment execution, and (c) data evaluation.

During *experiment preparation* experts prepared the software artifacts, i.e., the requirements definition including use cases description and prioritization according to business process importance. Selected parts of the software code were provided by the experiment preparation team. The design document and source code documents were seeded with a pre-defined set of defects. The other documents were improved in extensive review cycles until they were found to be correct.

The *execution phase* consisted of 3 steps: (a) tutorials where participants got an overview on the software system and the application domain (45 min) as well as training on the application of their technique (45 min), (b) the individual application of the technique (up to 300 min for inspection and up to 600 min for PP individuals), and (c) data submission to a database. The participants were supported by experiment supervisors, to clarify upcoming questions and to check the produced products for accuracy and usability. Concerning team evaluation, we counted multiple matched defects (within a team) only once. During individual application, the inspectors/pair programmers found candidate defects in the software artifacts and submitted them to the defect database.

Data evaluation: Members of the experiment team mapped defect candidates to seeded defects ("real defects"). Candidate defects that matched to seeded defects were classified as matched defects. Note that multiple candidate defects, which matched to one specific seeded defect, were counted only once, i.e., at the first time of detection and reporting. We built nominal teams from UBR individuals and PP teams by applying full permutation of all available data for the desired team size. For UBR-MT, the team size was 2 UBR persons. For statistical testing we applied the Mann-Whitney test at alpha level 0.05.

3.4 Software Artifacts

The system describes a taxi management system, presented by Thelin et al. [17]. We extended the experiment package to UML notation and included additional constructive approaches, i.e., PP [6]. First empirical results on the replication part (without constructive approaches) were published in [23].

The taxi management system consists of 2 parts, a central and a taxi. In our evaluation context we investigated defect detection capability in both parts (view on systems level).

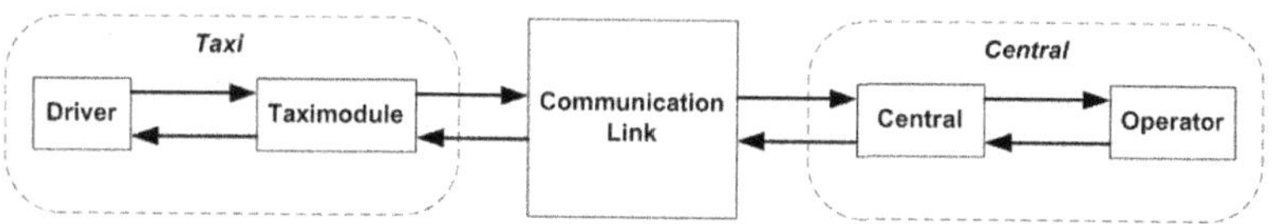

Fig. 1. Taxi management system – overview according to [17]

The experiment setup consists of (a) a textual description of the requirements and the use cases in users view, (b) the design document as well as the source code containing seeded defects and (c) the guidelines for the techniques applied as well as questionnaires for determining inspector capability and feedback.

- The textual requirements document consists of 8 pages including 2 UML2 component diagrams. The textual requirements document describes the basic functionality of the system in a user-friendly way.

- The design document spans 8 pages (including about 2,400 words, 2 component diagrams and 2 UML diagrams). We describe an overview of the software modules as well as their context including internal (relationships between two or more modules) and an external representation (relationships between the user and the system). Furthermore, we provide prioritized use case descriptions containing 24 use cases from user point of view and an overall number of 23 sequence diagrams. This artifact describes the technical dimension of the taxi management system.
- We provide source code fragments (some 1,500 lines of code) written in Java2, seeded with defined defects, and a method description of about 9 pages. These source code fragments were used in a twofold way: (a) to investigate the inspection effectiveness for source code, and (b) to investigate the QA effectiveness of PP and when extending the existing modules.
- The participants use guidelines for application of the assigned technique. Furthermore we provide questionnaires to measure inspector/programmer experience, capability indicators, and feedback on the individual techniques.

The design specification and the source code documents were seeded with a pre-defined number of defects by highly experienced experts.

Table 1. Distribution of Seeded Defects

Defect class	Design	Source	*Sum*
A (critical)	10 (17%)	19 (32%)	*29 (49%)*
B (major)	12 (20%)	12 (20%)	*24 (40%)*
C (minor)	5 (8%)	2 (3%)	*7 (11%)*
Sum	*27 (45%)*	*33 (55%)*	*60 (100%)*

Critical defects (class A) would have a severe and frequent impact on important functionality. Class B (major) defects are rarely occurring important defects or less important frequent defects (medium risk). Minor defects appear seldom and have little influence on functionality and quality. The document package (design specification and source code documents) contains overall 60 seeded defects according in three defect severity classes and two defect locations. Table 1 presents the nominal numbers of seeded defects according to defect severity classes and document types. In this paper we focus on important, i.e., critical and major (classes A and B), defects.

3.5 Subjects

The subjects in this initial study were 41 graduate software engineering students. We used a PP qualification test for candidate participants to ensure sufficient implementation skills. All participants were assigned randomly to the techniques, PP and UBR, to control the influence of inspector capability and to achieve better external validity. The experiment was integrated in a practical part of a software engineering and quality assurance workshop. We assigned 15 inspectors (54%) to UBR and 26 persons (46%) to 13 PP teams.

3.6 Threats to Validity

We controlled the external validity by randomly assigning participants to UBR and PP. Additionally, all candidates had to pass a PP qualification test to ensure their sufficient programming skills. 41 subjects (of about 60 candidates) passed this test. This qualification test was used to enable comparability to an industrial setting and to minimize the influence of variance of inspector capability. We did not perform a qualification test for inspectors; however, all participants had had classes on the skills needed for inspection in their regular curriculum.

We seeded representative defects in the design specification and source code documents according to different types of defects and defect locations. The seeded defects were representative of defects found during the development of the documents under study. For achieving higher external validity with defects in specific industry setting, replicated studies would be appropriate that consider the typical range of defects in the target context.

The correctness of the requirements document was achieved with extensive review cycles. To achieve better internal validity the experiment preparation team set up the experiment package under guidance of experienced researchers including several reviews. To achieve comparability to previous studies [15][16], we used approved material modified to fit the experiment context.

Note different focus of inspection and PP. Inspection focuses on defect detection as primary task. PP focuses on the construction of software code and defect detection as a by-product.

4 Experiment Results

In this section we present results of the initial empirical study concerning effectiveness of work units, minimal teams, and some preliminary results of nominal team composition to investigate the influence of mixtures of both approaches.

4.1 Effort

We report effort to illustrate the background of the study. In the study context, we define effort as the overall session duration, including individual preparation (reading the documents and getting familiar with the technique applied) and technique application time. We do not consider experiment preparation time which was done by experts as preliminary work packages before the experiment started.

PP teams needed 1,030 min (about 17 person-hours (ph)) on average and a standard deviation of 120min (2ph). Inspectors required 273 min (about 4.5 ph) with a standard deviation of 38 min (0.6 ph). Note that PP involves 2 persons and took much longer than UBR because of the main focus on the implementation of additional software code. Defect detection is considered as by-product of PP in this study.

4.2 Effectiveness of Work Units

Effectiveness is the number of defects found in relation to the number of seeded defects according to defect class and defect location in a document (design document and source code documents). The evaluation covers important defects (class A+B), which should be supported by prioritized use cases.

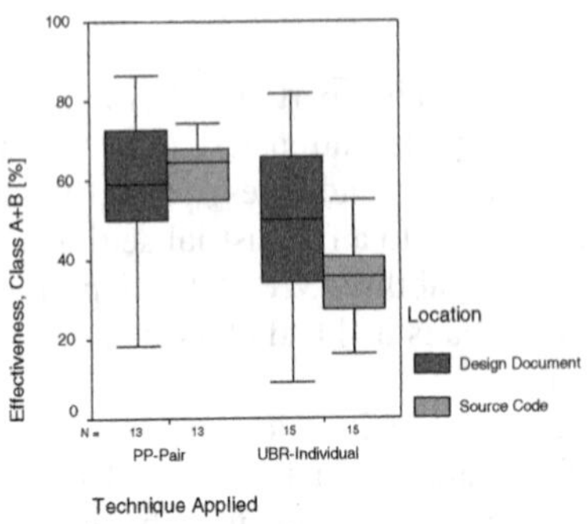

Fig. 2. Effectiveness of important defects acc. to defect location

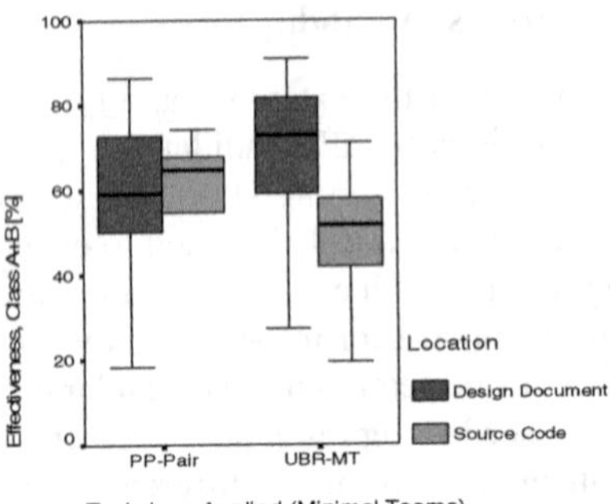

Fig. 3. Effectiveness of important defects from minimal teams

Effectiveness of Work Units. We concern "work units" as the original configuration of participants applying each technique: PP team and UBR inspector. The results presented in Figure 2 show best effectiveness for important defects according to all defect locations for PP teams. We observe a smaller difference (9 defects on average) for design document effectiveness, but a higher difference (21 defects on average) for source code effectiveness.

Table 2. Effectiveness, important defects

	Location	PP-Pair	UBR-Individuals	P-value
Mean	DD+SC	56.3	40.3	0.013 (S)
	DD	56.3	47.3	0.212 (-)
	SC	56.3	35.3	0.004 (S)
Std.Dev	DD+SC	20.6	13.6	-
	DD	26.7	20.6	-
	SC	17.9	11.4	-

Nevertheless, PP outperforms UBR for all defect severity classes. Note also a higher standard deviation for design defects found by UBR inspectors. Table 2 presents an overview of effectiveness according to technique applied and defect location. Applying the Mann-Whitney-Test to investigate significant differences, we observe significant differences for all documents (DD+SC) and source code (SC), but no significant difference with respect to design documents (DD). Obviously, the investigated implementation approach (PP) outperforms the individual inspection approach (UBR) for SC documents.

A more detailed investigation of this defect type shows the benefits of the PP approach more clearly. A subset of the seeded source code defects (4 defects) focus on logic, dataflow, and visibility defects, e.g., private and public statements, which may be found more easily applying an implementation approach rather than a paper-based inspection approach. Additionally, PP uses a computer and a compiler to find defects, which supports defect detection in source code documents. The results show an effectiveness of about 79% according to these defect types for PP and 23% for UBR a significant difference.

4.3 Effectiveness of Minimal Teams (MT)

To achieve comparability of team size, we compare the original work unit of PP teams to a nominal team of 2 UBR inspectors. Figure 3 displays the results of minimal team effectiveness for important defects according to defect locations. Table 3 depicts mean value and standard deviation of effectiveness according to important defects (class A+B) with respect to minimal teams, i.e., PP team and randomly assigned 2 person UBR nominal teams (UBR-MT).

Table 3. Effectiveness of Minimal Teams (MT)

	Defect	PP-Pair	UBR-MT	p-value
Mean	DD+SC	56.3	57.8	0.292 (-)
	DD	56.3	68.6	0.680 (-)
	SC	56.3	50.1	0.014 (S)
Std.Dev	DD+SC	20.6	10.5	-
	DD	26.7	15.8	-
	SC	17.9	9.9	-

The UBR-MT approach achieves a notably, but not significantly, higher average effectiveness with respect to the all documents and design documents, but there is a difference for PP teams. Concerning defect detection regarding source code defects, PP teams outperform UBR-MT significantly.

4.4 Effectiveness of Nominal Teams

Because the two techniques focus on different aspects of a software document, we expect a higher defect detection effectiveness of teams, consisting of participants of UBR and PP. Team composition can achieve a twofold benefit: (a) more efficient handling of source code documents with tool support (naturally available for PP) and (b) higher defect detection rate in written text documents due to the application of reading techniques (in our study: UBR). Table 4 depicts the team composition regarding PP-teams and UBR individuals to a team size up to 5 team members. Note that PP teams consist of 2 persons and the table shows individual persons (we did not split PP teams). The "team size" describes the overall number of participants (persons) within a nominal team. The participants were assigned to a nominal team randomly, performing full permutation. Regarding team notation, *P* defines the integration of a number of PP-teams in the team, while *R* indicates the number of UBR individuals included.

Figure 4 displays the mean of effectiveness according to the nominal teams with respect to important defects (class A+B). Note that the figure includes also the overall effectiveness according to all matched defects as control value for nominal team evaluation. The analysis shows an increasing effectiveness, regarding defect detection rates for design documents, independent of the technique applied. A closer view shows somewhat smaller gain including another PP-Pair within the nominal team. Concerning source code location, we observe an increasing effectiveness for PP-teams and a constant value (team size 4) and decreasing value (team size 5) when including UBR individuals.

Table 4. Nominal team composition (individuals)

	Team-Members	PP Ind.	UBR Ind.	Team Size (number of individuals per team)
Teams	PR	2	1	3
	PP	4	0	4
	PRR	2	2	4
	PPR	4	1	5
	PRRR	2	3	5

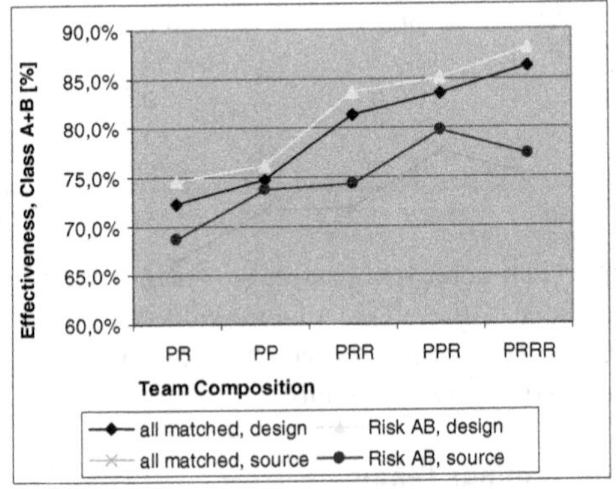

Fig. 4. Effectiveness of nominal teams

Table 5. Team effectiveness, class A+B

	A+B	PR	PP	PRR	PPR	PRRR
	Team Size	3	4	4	5	5
Mean	DD+SC	71.2	74.8	78.1	**82.0**	81.8
	DD	74.6	76.2	83.6	85.1	**88.2**
	SC	68.7	73.7	74.2	**79.7**	77.4
Std.Dev	DD+SC	12.6	13.3	9.1	8.6	7.2
	DD	16.4	17.2	11.3	10.9	8.1
	SC	11.8	11.6	9.6	8.5	8.5

We observe a similar trend for all matched defects and for important defects (class A+B). Table 5 displays mean value and standard deviation for effectiveness of important defects according to defect location.

5 Discussion

In Section 3.2 we presented hypotheses on the expected effectiveness of individuals, real teams, and nominal teams regarding the defects in different documents. This section discusses the hypotheses with the experiment results.

Effectiveness of Work Units (H1). Concerning the effectiveness of work units (PP team and UBR individuals) according to defect location and important (classes A+B) defects, we expected a higher effectiveness of PP for source code documents and a higher effectiveness of UBR for text documents. The results show a higher effectiveness of a PP team for both aspects. PP significantly outperforms UBR concerning defect in the whole experiment package (DD+SC). We did not recognize a significant difference for design documents. The results support hypothesis (H1.1), that effectiveness of PP outperforms UBR according to source code documents. Hypothesis (1.2) that UBR performs better than PP for design documents could not be supported in the study context. We assume two possible reasons for this effect: (a) PP requires additional effort for implementation and defect detection (therefore more defects were found), and (b) implementation tasks support defect detection in design specifications because of immediate observation of the corresponding impact of defects. While implementing, defects in the design specifications might be detected easier than during reading a document.

Effectiveness of Minimal Teams (H2). Because PP involves 2 persons and UBR is a single person defect detection approach, we set up minimal nominal UBR teams to compare effectiveness according to team size, defect location, and defect severity. Again, we assume a better performance of PP for source code defects and a better performance of UBR for defects in the design document.

Hypothesis (H2.1), PP outperforms UBR-MT for source code defects, was confirmed. We observe a significant difference for SC defects. Again we assumed that UBR-MTs perform better (H2.2) than PP teams for design documents. UBR-MTs find more defects than PP. The Mann-Whitney test does not flag significant differences. Therefore the results did not agree to our assumptions.

Effectiveness Team Composition (H3). The combination of PP and UBR approaches promises to deliver better results, summarizing the benefits of PP for the detection of source code defect and UBR for defect detection in written design documents. We investigate teams up to a size of 5 persons, regarding PP and UBR. The results describe an increasing effectiveness concerning an increasing team size. We also record, that additional PP participants improve defect detection in source code documents and additional participants of UBR inspectors support defect detection in design documents. Therefore, both assumptions agree to the results.

Our expectations, that additional PP teams improve defect detection in source code (H3.1) were confirmed by the observed results. Additionally, the expectations, that additional UBR inspectors improve defect detection capability regarding design specifications (H3.2), were also confirmed by the observed results. These observations might be used in decision support processes for combining analytical and constructive QA approaches in a given project context to achieve a certain level of product quality, e.g., building a QA team to find 70% of important defects.

6 Conclusion and Further Work

Software product improvement is an important issue in software development. Defect prevention, defect detection, and defect removal should be established as early as possible during development. Software inspection is a defect detection approach applicable to written text documents early in the development process. The main task of inspection is defect detection, in best practice applying reading techniques, e.g., UBR based on expert-prioritized use cases. As inspections do not require executable code, they may be performed in early software development phases.

Pair programming (PP) is a method, applicable to agile software processes and focuses on implementation of code fragments, involving two persons. While one person implements the software code, the other performs continuous reviews of code documents and specification documents. Therefore, PP performs defect detection as a by-product of software implementation, also rather early in low-level development. Note that code implementation is still the main focus of PP.

The results of our initial empirical study showed that PP is a promising method for both implementation and defect detection regarding the seeded defects in our study context. However, PP requires higher effort because of the involvement of two persons and the focus on software construction. Nevertheless, PP performed better than best-practice inspection concerning defect detection in code documents, which may partly be attributed to tool support for some defect detection tasks. UBR as a paper-based defect detection approach performed better for design documents. Regarding design documents, we do not recognize any significant difference between PP and UBR. Combinations of both approaches lead to overall best results.

Further work is necessary to validate the results of this study, including more participants to achieve a higher level of external validity. The replication and extension of the initial study enabled a closer look on agile software development methods, like pair programming, including quality assurance approaches. Further work is necessary to investigate the impact of inspector capability on defect detection effectiveness and on defect profiles for typical target contexts in practice.

References

[1] Basili V., Caldiera G., Lanubile F., Shull F.: "Studies on Reading Techniques", 21st Annual Software Engineering Workshop, NASA/Goddard Software Engineering Laboratory Series, SEL-96-002, pp 59-65, College Park, Maryland, 1997.

[2] Biffl S., Aurum A., Boehm B.: "Value-Based Software Engineering", Springer, 2005.

[3] Biffl S.: "Software Inspection Techniques to support Project and Quality Management", Shaker Verlag, 2001.

[4] Biffl S., Halling M.: "Investigating the Defect Detection Effectiveness and Cost Benefit of Nominal Inspection Teams", IEEE Transactions on Software Engineering 29 (5), pp.385-397, 2003.

[5] Biffl S., Gutjahr W.: "Influence of Team Size and Defect Detection Methods on Inspection Effectiveness", Proc. of IEEE Int. Software Metrics Symposium, London, 2001.

[6] Biffl S., Winkler D., Thelin T., Höst M., Russo B., Succi G., “Investigating the Effect of V&V and Modern Construction Techniques on Improving Software Quality”, Poster presented at ISERN 2004, Los Angeles.

[7] Cockburn A., Williams L.: "The Costs and Benefits of Pair Programming in Extreme Programming Examined", Addison Wesley, 2001.
[8] Cockburn A.: "Agile Software Development", Addison Wesley, 2002.
[9] Fagan M.: "Design and Code Inspections To Reduce Errors In Program Development", IBM Systems J., vol. 15, no. 3, pp. 182-211, 1976.
[10] Gilb T., Graham D.: "Software Inspection", Addison-Wesley, 1993.
[11] Müller M.: "Are Reviews an Alternative to Pair Programming?", Conference on Empirical Assessment In Software Engineering (EASE), pages 3- 12, UK, 2003.
[12] Nawrocki J., Wojciechowski A.: "Experimental Evaluation of Pair Programming", Proceedings of the 12th European Software Control and Metrics Conference, pages 269-276, April 2001.
[13] Padberg F., Müller M.: "Analyzing the Cost and Benefit of Pair Programming", International Symposium on Software Metrics METRICS 9, 2003.
[14] Parrish A., Smith R., Hale D., Hale J.: "A field study of developer pairs: Productivity impacts and implications", IEEE Software, 21(2), Pages 76-79, 2004.
[15] Thelin T, Andersson C., Runeson P., Dzamashvili-Fogelström N.: „A Replicated Experiment of Usage-Based and Checklist-Based Reading", 10th IEEE International Symposium on Software Metrics, pp. 246-256, 2004.
[16] Thelin T., Runeson, P., Regnell B.: "Usage-Based Reading - An Experiment to Guide Reviewers with Use Cases," Information and Software Technology, vol. 43, no. 15, pp. 925-938, 2001.
[17] Thelin T., Runeson, P., Wohlin, C.: "An Experimental Comparison of Usage-Based and Checklist-Based Reading, IEEE Trans on Software Engineering, 29(8), pp. 687-704, 2003.
[18] Westland J. C.: "The cost of errors in software development: evidence from industry", Journal of Systems and Software 62, 1-9., 2002.
[19] Williams L., Kessler R., Cunningham W., Jeffies R.: "Strengthening the Case for Pair Programming", IEEE Software 17(4):19-25, 2000.
[20] Williams L. Kessler, R.: "All I really need to know about pair programming I learned in Kindergarten", Communication of the ACM, Volume 43, Issue 5 (May 2000), ACM Press, New York, pp. 108-114, 1999.
[21] Williams L., McDowell C., Nagappan N., Fernald J., Werner L.: "Building Pair Programming Knowledge through a Family of Experiments", IEEE, Proceeding of the 2003 International Symposium on Empirical Software Engineering, ISESE, 2003.
[22] Winkler D., Biffl S., Thurnher B.: "Investigating the Impact of Active Guidance on Design Inspection", Proc. of Profes 05, 2005.
[23] Winkler D., Biffl S., Riedl B.: „Improvement of Design Specifications with Inspection and Testing", Proc. Of Euromicro 05, 2005.

A Variability-Centric Approach to Instantiating Core Assets in Product Line Engineering*

Soo Ho Chang, Soo Dong Kim, and Sung Yul Rhew

Department of Computer Science
Soongsil University, Seoul, Korea
shchang@otlab.ssu.ac.kr,
{sdkim, syrhew}@comp.ssu.ac.kr

Abstract. As a key activity in product line engineering (PLE), instantiation is a task to generate target applications by resolving variability embedded in core assets. However, instantiation is often conducted in manual and ad-hoc fashion, largely replying on domain knowledge and experience. Hence, it can easily lead to technical problems in precisely specifying decision model consisting of product-specific variation points and variants, and in handling inter-variant conflicts/dependency. To overcome this difficulty, it is desirable to develop a systematic process which includes a set of systematic activities, detailed instructions, and concrete specification of artifacts. In this paper, we first propose a meta-model of a core asset to specify its key elements. Then, we represent a comprehensive process that defines key instantiation activities, representations of artifacts, and work instructions. With the proposed process, one can instantiate core assets more effectively and systematically.

1 Introduction

Product line engineering (PLE) is one of the recent and effective reuse approaches, and it consists of two processes; *domain engineering* and *application engineering*. Domain engineering is to develop a core asset which captures common functionality and quality attributes among family members in the domain. Application engineering is to generate target applications by instantiating the core asset with a product-specific decision resolution model (DRM)[1].

In PLE, modeling the variability among applications is a key activity because it allows a number of potential applications to reuse the same core asset [2]. A harder part of modeling variability is to identify the conflicts and dependencies among variation points and variants. Once the variability model is constructed, it is further refined and designed into a decision model (DM) which specifies concrete variation points and their relevant variants.

Once a core asset with a DM is constructed as either a model or an implementation, it is instantiated for each application. A key step of instantiation is to define a DRM which specifies application-specific variants for the variation points, and to bind the variants to relevant variation points of the core asset. However, this instantiation is

* This work was supported by grant No. (R01-2005-000-11215-0) from the Basic Research Program of the Korea Science & Engineering Foundation.

J. Münch and M. Vierimaa (Eds.): PROFES 2006, LNCS 4034, pp. 334 – 347, 2006.

carried out largely in manual and ad-hoc fashion, replying on domain knowledge and experience. Moreover, current research works on core asset instantiation have not yet identified the comprehensive instantiation process and detailed instructions.

In this paper, we define a process to instantiate core assets to application specific assets. The process consists of activities which have detailed steps and instructions and produces an instantiated core asset as the final deliverable. We first define a meta-model of core assets, i.e. the key elements and their representation of core assets in section 3. Then, we present an instantiation process and instructions in section 4. Then, we assess our proposed framework with process evaluation criteria in section 5.

2 Related Works

PuLSE (Product Line Software Engineering) is a process for developing product line developed by fraunhofer institute for experimental software engineering (IESE) [3]. It consists of three sub-elements; *Deployment Phases*, *Technical Components*, and *Support Components*. *Deployment phases* is to produce reusable assets and products using related technical components of *PuLSE–BC*, *PuLSE-Eco*, *PuLSE-CDA*, *PuLSE-DSSA*, *PuLSE-I*, and *PuLSE-EM*.

PuLSE-I is used to develop applications and it includes an activity of instantiating product line model and reference architecture [4]. The product line model which is essentially an object model and storyboards representing a core asset is hierarchically resolved with a decision model and application specific characteristics. The reference architecture is refined into an intermediate architecture which embeds an architectural variability and it defines an architectural resolution decision. This identifies activities for instantiating, however, step-wise and detailed instructions are not given. Moreover, elements of each artifact are not defined.

KobrA is a component-based product line engineering method based on UML. It consists of *Framework Engineering* and Application *Engineering*[1]. Framework engineering defines a framework which is a set of reusable assets among family members and Application engineering is to produce applications by instantiating the framework with a decision model. During Instantiation activity, a generic *Komponent* is translated into a specific Komponent by using DM. DM is tailored to a DRM for a specific application. A process to instantiate core assets is also represented by analyzing the overlap between a framework and application requirements and tailoring a Komponent framework. This work defines a process of instantiation at macro level. The instructions given here need to be further refined in order to automate the instructions.

Deelstra's work starts with motivation that deriving products from shared software assets is a time-consuming and expensive activity contrary to the popular belief [5]. This work presents a product derivation framework which defines a number of terminologies, product family classifications according to two dimensions of scope, and generic software derivation process. It also presents a set of identified problems and issues associated with product derivation based on a case study at two large industrial organizations. Case studies conducted in this work show well application of their proposed framework with appearance of well known company, explicit number of components, variation points, LOC, etc.

3 Meta Models of Core Assets

There are several kinds of abstraction levels for artifacts (e.g. requirement, analysis, design, implementation, etc) in developing application. In accordance with the level, several kinds of binding time (e.g. design, compile, and install time, etc) can be applied. In this paper, we focus on the design level core assets in which level variability is resolved because we assume that MDA approach is used to implement development automation.

Most of definitions given in PLE research works specify that a core asset consists of product line (PL) architecture, components and their interfaces, and a decision model defining variability realization[1][6][7][8]. We now summarize and refine sub-elements of each key element based on the works as in shown Figure 1.

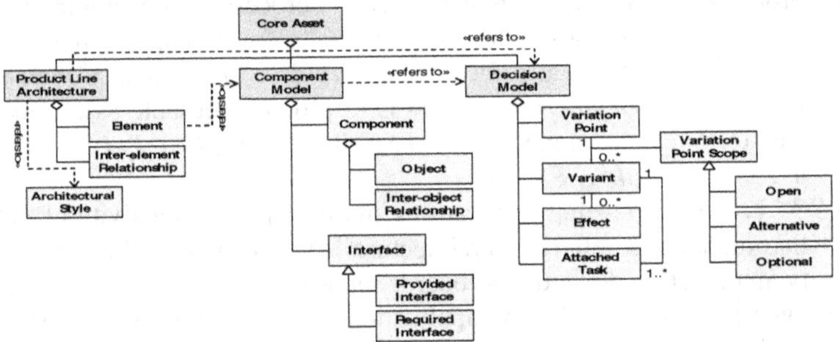

Fig. 1. Meta-model of Core Assets

Product Line Architecture (PLA): Software architecture realizes both functional and non-functional requirements. Architecture design begins with choosing most appropriate architectural styles which can realize the both types of requirements. *Element* and *inter-element relationships* in PLA are derived from the requirements and especially inter-element relationships are guided by styles. Hence, the style is not a constituent of product line architecture, but an abstract element to which architecture conforms.

PLA may be represented by a class diagram, package diagram, or others in UML[9], and architectural variability may be represented in the model by defined expressions such as stereo types in UML [10].

Component Model: The component model represents a design of component internal which is represented with structural and behavioral model of objects, inter-object relationships, and interfaces. Generally component-base development (CBD) is based on object-oriented development (OOD) and in this section we assume that functionality of core asset is realized by components in CBD. And the component model is linked to elements in PLA.

Object-oriented model is generally represented by use case models, static models, and dynamic models. Therefore, component models can be represented by use case diagrams, class diagrams, and sequence diagrams in UML. Expression of variability on the models has generally been proposed by using stereo types [1].

Decision Model (DM): Decision Model is a specification of variations in core assets and includes *variation points, variants, effects,* and *attached task* [1]. We believe that it is essential to precisely define the representations and semantics of the variation.

- *A variation point* is a place where slight differences among member may occur. Depending on elements of core asset, variations can be distinguished such as architecture and component internal as shown in Figure 2

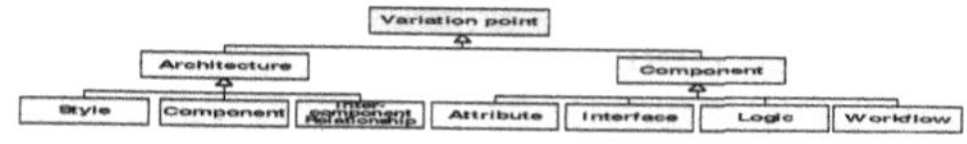

Fig. 2. Specialization of Variation Point

In architecture design, some architectural styles may be not selected depending on non-functional requirements of target application. Variable components and their relationships may be optionally used in some applications or alternatively used in some applications. Therefore component variability on DM may be divided into alternative and optional. In components, several types of variation points may be appeared as referred in [11].

- *Variants* are valid values which can appropriately fill in a variation point. As the types of variation points and variability types such as optional and alternative, the variants may be designed into various formats.
- *Effect* means a range of relationships among variations points and it is represented with dependencies or conflicts among variability. That is, a variant for a variation point should be selected with other variants for other variation points, but some variants should not. The relationships are an essential problem which should be specified and resolved in product line engineering [12].
- *Attached Task* is a set of activities to resolve a variation point for one selected variant, that is, to instantiate. Through the attached tasks, post-conditions of an instantiated variation point should satisfy specified effects for a variation point. The tasks typically utilize to customization mechanisms. Since a variation point is realized as one of different types [11], each type of variation points may require different customization mechanisms.

We now refine DM[1] and variability range table in [13] into 3 types of decision models to represent variations for each element of core assets. Table 1 shows a possible specification of the variability, a *Decision Model.*

Table 1. Decision Model for Style Variability

Variation Point	Scope	Variant	Effect	Attached Task
VP_i	*Alternative* | *Optional* | *Open*	$Variant_i$	· Some $variant_a$ *can not be selected.* · Some $variant_b$ *should be selected.* · …	· *Remove* some $variant_b$. · *Add* variant. · *Replace* a variant which will be defined. · …
…	…	…	…	…

The VPs is specialized to style, components, inter-component relationships, or elements in a component. Scope means the relationship between a variation point and its relevant variants and is classified with *Alternative*, *Optional*, and *Open*. To describe dependency, we use two cases; *can not be selected* and *should be selected.* Moreover, depending on the two cases, attached task can be classified into *remove*, *add*, and *modify*.

4 Process and Instruction

Based on the meta-models and representations of core assets, we now present a process and work instructions for instantiating core assets. It is assumed that a core asset for a product line is available, so that the process takes a core asset as the input.

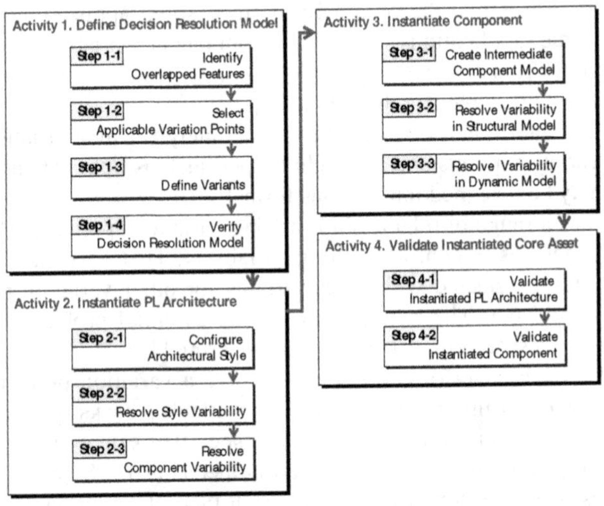

Fig. 3. Process to Instantiate Core Assets

The process consists of 4 activities where each activity has steps with input/output artifacts and instructions and it produces an instantiated core asset as the final deliverable.

4.1 Activity 1. Define Decision Resolution Model (DRM)

This activity is to define a DRM which refers to application requirement and indicates variants for relevant variation points. Hence, DRM specifies applicable variation points and their variants of a target application, and it is used for resolving variability during activities 2 and 3. This activity has four steps as shown in Figure 4.

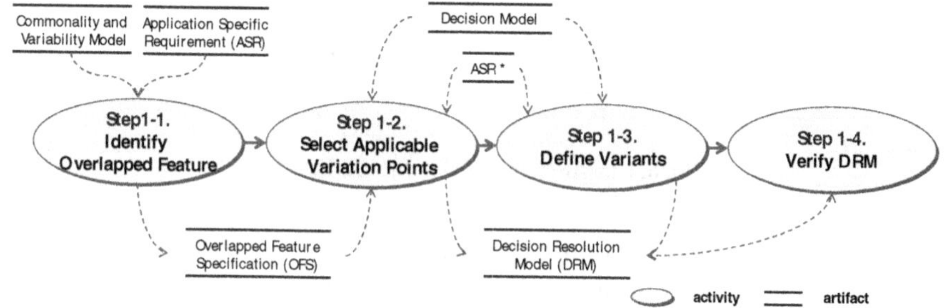

Fig. 4. Steps for Activity 1

Step 1-1. Identify Overlapped Features

In PLE, a feature is a basic unit for designating common functional or non-functional characteristics among applications. However, some applications may not need to use all of the features in a core asset. This situation is shown as '*Features Not Used by Application*' in Figure 5. In contrast, a core asset may not provide all the features required by an application. This situation is shown as '*Features Not Covered by Core Asset*' in the figure. These kinds of mismatches especially arise when a new application is added to the product line after a core asset has been developed.

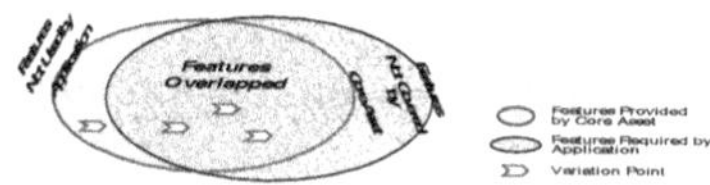

Fig. 5. Mismatch between Core Asset and Application Requirement

Step 1-1 is to identify the features that are overlapped between a core asset and a target application. Only the overlapped features need to be instantiated onto the target application. The input is both commonality and variability(C&V) model of a product line and an application specific requirement specification (ARS). C&V model describes common and variable features where features in the model can be classified to functional and non-functional features. This step produces a list of overlapped features (LOF).

Instruction: This step is divided into two sub-steps. The first sub-step is to extract non-functional overlapped features. The non-features can be represented into quality attributes such as performance or security and each quality attribute may be specified into detailed requirements. From the detailed requirements, we identify architecture-relevant non-functional requirements as well as other non-functional requirements related to fine-grained functionality.

The second sub-step is to identify functionally overlapped features. The functionality may be generally itemized as subsystem units and use case units. Figure 6 shows a classification of the overlapped features which are identified in this step.

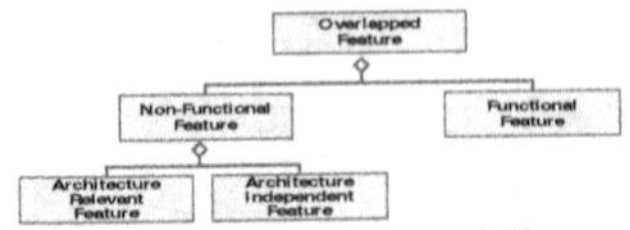

Fig. 6. Classification of Overlapped Features

Step 1-2. Select Applicable Variation Points

This step is to identify the features which have variation point from the overlapped features. Note that, since there are features which are not used by application as shown in the Figure 6, not all variation points specified in a decision model are applicable to each application. That is, an application may typically take a subset of those variation points.

Input and Output: The inputs are LOF, DM, and ARS which specifies application specific functionality in detail. Especially the representation of DM in the section 3 is referred in this step. The output is an initial DRM which includes a *list of variation points* but the VP is not filled yet.

Instruction: As inferred in section 3, variability can be appeared in architecture and component internals. We first identify variation points on architecture and initialize an architectural decision resolution model. The architectural variation points are classified into those of styles and components. Style variability can be derived from non-functional and architecture-relevant features, that is, style variability of DM. In styles, some components may be discarded or replaced other component, that is, component variability of DM.

Once architectural variation points are identified, variation points in components should be selected. Since variability in components is relatively fine-grained, specific requirements of ARS may be referred to find variation points.

Step 1-3: Define Variants

This step is to define appropriate variants for associated to variation points identified in step1-2. The scope of variability can be either *closed* or *open*[13]. The scope of closed variability is determined by a set of known valid values for a variation point, where the scope of open variability includes currently unknown future variants. Therefore the variants may be selected a decision model or defined as new variants fitted into variation points, as shown in Figure 7.

Input and Output: The inputs in this step are the initial DRM from stpep1-2 and ARS. Through this step, we output a DRM.

Instruction: this step is divided into sub-steps for closed variability and open variability. First, in the closed case, we choose an appropriate variant for identified variation points in DRM. And then associated effects and attached task can easily be taken from the DM.

Next sub-step is to resolve open variability. In this step, a variant is newly defined for an application by exploring application specific requirement. In this case, effects and attached task should also be newly defined. That is possible because core assets have already had an extension point in which the new variants can be plugged due to an open scope expectation.

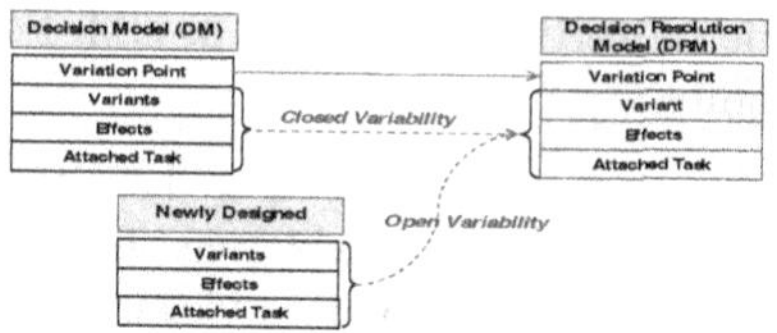

Fig. 7. Defining Variants

As inferred section 3, the variation points may be classified to architectural styles, components, component internals. To choose appropriate variants of style variability, quality attributes are referred.

Step 1-4. Verify Decision Resolution Model
This step is to verify DRM by reviewing application requirement specification. Followings are check list for verifying DRM

- Check whether the decision resolution specification includes all the necessary variation points.
- Check the validity of variants for each variation point.
- For open variability, verify that the supplied variant satisfies the specification of valid variants in DM.

4.2 Activity 2. Instantiate PL Architecture

This activity is to resolve architectural variability, including 3 steps as in Figure 8.

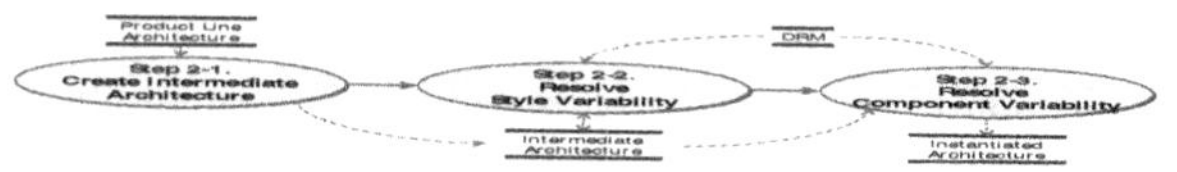

Fig. 8. Steps for Activity 2

Step 2-1. Create Intermediate architecture
To instantiate PL architecture, we first create an intermediate architecture which has the same set of elements in PL architecture. Subsequent steps 2-2 and 2-3 modify this intermediate architecture through resolving architectural variability.

Step 2-2. Resolve Style Variability
PLA consists of a set of architectural styles which include commonality and variability. In this step, we realize a valid configuration of applicable styles by referring DRM. Therefore this step requires DRM and outputs a refined intermediate architecture in which style variability is resolved.

Instruction: This step should be guided by effects and attached tasks of style variability of DM. We first trace the attached tasks. The tasks generally show which elements should be removed and which should be not removed depending on selection of a style. In the selected case, attached tasks of DM may be not proposed because intermediate architecture already contains the selected style. After tracing, the post condition should be verified for effects of DM. Followings are observations of resolving style variability.

- Extent of overlapped area between styles may be different. While one style may be extent over architecture, other style may occupy limited portion of the architecture. Therefore effect on removing styles may have different propagations.
- Since a style is realized by components and inter-component relationship, removing style may be confused by removing components and their relationships. However, some component may be removed, but some components may be just changed their relationships in architecture since a style describes components' configuration.

Step 2-2. Resolve Component Variability
Component variability may be occurred in both common and variable styles. In this step, we resolve component variability by removing not selected variants. The input is intermediate architecture from step 2-2 and the output is instantiated architecture.

Instruction: This step is also guided by effects and attached tasks in DM like style variability in step 2-2. However, component are linked to other components, tasks are slightly different from style variability in that the tasks should cover dependency between variable components and linked components. Followings are observations of resolving component variability.

- Variable components have links in PLA. Once an optional component is removed, the relationships to other components should be traced and removed.
- When one of alternatives in component variability is selected, compatibility with other components should be verified.

Figure 9 shows an example of instantiated PLA in a rental domain which include tow members; *book rental system* and *car rental system*. Instantiation in this example is for the book rental system. PLA has variability on four components; *LggingMgr, WebUI, AuthenticationMgr, and OnlinePaymentMgr*. And the LogingMgr is selected as only variant.

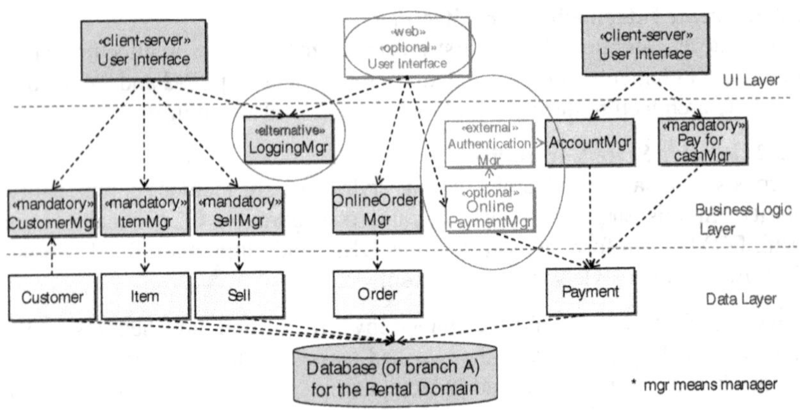

Fig. 9. An Example of Instantiated PLA of the Rental Domain

4.3 Activity 3. Instantiate Components

This activity is to resolve component variability designed in structural and dynamic models.

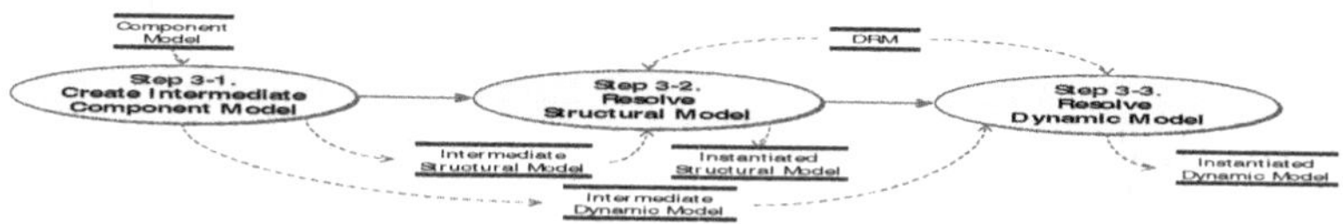

Fig. 10. Steps for Activity 3

Step 3-1. Create Intermediate Component Model
In this step, we first create an intermediate component model like the intermediate architecture. Contrary to the intermediate architecture, intermediate component model is divided into structural model and dynamic model which will be used in step 3-2 and 3-3. The input is component models the output is intermediate structural and dynamic component model.

Step 3-2. Resolve Structural Model
Structural models of a component are generally represented by class diagrams. In the models, variability of component internal such as attributes, logic, and interface may be designed. In this step, the variability is resolved and structural models for a target application are established. The detailed steps to resolving structural model are similar to step 2-2. However observations of resolving variability of component internal structural model are as followings.

- Attributes variability may largely affect signature of many operations or interfaces which use the variable attributes.
- In case of open variability, attributes, operations, and even objects may be newly designed in the structural model.
- Logic variability is represented in specification of structural model rather than the structural diagram since it needs detailed description.

Step 3-3. Resolve Dynamic Model
Dynamic models of a component are generally represented by collaboration diagrams. In the models, workflow variability of component can be designed. In this step, the variability is resolved, and then dynamic models for a target application are established. The detailed steps to resolving structural model are same to step 2-2. However, observations of resolving variability of component internal dynamic model are different as followings.

- Some workflow variability may be limited to component internal, i.e. micro workflow, whereas other workflow variability may affect component outside, i.e. macro workflow.
- The macro workflow variability may affect architecture configuration since they modify inter component relationship as inter-component dependency.

4.4 Activity 4. Validate Instantiated Core Asset

Activity 4 is to validate instantiated core assets against application specific requirement. The task of validating instantiated core assets is a lot more complicated than validating assets for a single system. Hence, the steps and detailed instructions for this activity are out of the paper scope. Instead, we give a few check items as examples:

- All and only the variation points specified in DRM should have been resolved in an instantiated core asset.
- All the variation points specified in the DRM must be resolved with the specified variants.
- Pre-condition and inter-variation point relationships specified in the *effect* should have been preserved in an instantiated core asset.
- Variants unselected by the DRM must have not presented in an instantiated core asset.

5 Assessment

5.1 Evaluation Criteria

To assess the proposed process, we first define evaluation criteria. These criteria are derived from the commonly referred process evaluation works found in systems and software engineering area [14][15].

Criterion #1. Process Architecture: This criterion is to evaluate the overall organization of processes. A process should have a hierarchical representation for various granularities of work units [16]. For example, larger-grained work as phases, medium-sized work as activities and small-grained work as steps. A logical numbering system is desirable in practical processes and methodologies.

Criterion #2. Coverage of Key Activities: This criterion is to evaluate how comprehensively a process provides the required key activities for the development paradigm. In the case of PLE, they should include instantiation activities such as selecting and setting variants, and handling inter-variability dependency with different core asset elements. To apply this criterion, a set of key and common instantiation activities must be identified from a survey of PLE methodologies. With the identified activities, a generic set of instantiation activities can be defined as a consequence. These generic instantiation activities are then compared to the proposed process under evaluation.

Criterion #3. Comprehensiveness and Precision of Work Instructions: This criterion is to evaluate how *comprehensively* and *precisely* the instructions are provided. Activities specified in a process typically carry some degree of instructions on how to carry out the activities. For the comprehensiveness, we evaluate the coverage of process for its instructions. A process lacking instructions will be difficulty to apply in practice. For the precision, we evaluate the level of details and effectiveness for the given instructions. Some instructions can be stated at abstract and vague level, while others can be quite specific and easy to follow in practice.

Criterion #4. Specification of Key Artifacts: This criterion is to evaluate how well the key artifacts are defined in terms of key elements, template, example and related artifacts/activities. A process with well-defined artifacts will provide a clear goal and vision on what should be delivered.

Criterion #5. Seamlessness of Process: This criterion is to evaluate the how cohesively activities and artifacts of a process are related and organized. In a process, activities and artifacts should be seamlessly related to yield a high degree of traceability among them. That is, one should be able to produce an artifact of an activity using one or more preceding artifacts without putting excessive amount of new information, creativity and effort.

5.2 Discussion

We now discuss how our proposed process framework satisfies the evaluation criteria.

Satisfying Criterion #1. Process Architecture: While current works on instantiation methods and process only define coarse-grained units of work, we organize the process with four activities where each activity includes several steps as shown in Figure 3. That is, our process specifies all the fine-grained units of instantiation work. We incorporated a numbering system to distinguish activities and steps, and to arrange the tasks in order. A process with fine-grained work units tends to yield a more systematic and effective application of the process.

Satisfying Criterion #2. Coverage of Key Activities: The key activities of core asset instantiation are found in representative PLE works in [1][17]. They include comparing core asset scope with the application scope to find the overlapped scope, defining product-specific variants, binding variants to variation points, especially resolving architectural variability, instantiating components required in the core asset, and validating instantiated core assets. All of these key activities are found in the *12 steps* of our process.

Satisfying Criterion #3. Comprehensiveness and Precision of Work Instructions: The specification of the process in section 4 is structured with an overview, detailed instructions, and artifacts. That is, some instructions are described with more detailed sub-task such as the steps in activity 1, while others are listed for observations or check-list such as steps in activity 3 and 4. Since these instructions are focused on a step which is already in fine-grained and detailed level, the instructions are regard to be comprehensively defined. And the process gives some examples so that it can be followed in practice easier.

Satisfying Criterion #4. Specification of Key Artifacts: In PLE, the variability model including DM is a key artifact, in that, it largely affects the reusability of core assets and the efficiency of reusing them. And, in AE process, resolving the variability is another key activity. The proposed process handles the variability around all activities by utilizing DRM. There is its concrete template in section 3 and lots of steps show the instructions managing the elements of DRM represented in the template.

Satisfying Criterion #5. Seamlessness of Process: We defined the process with a great focus on traceability among tasks and artifacts. Hence, we are able to show a traceability map in Figure 11. This map focus on traceability of variability between C&V model, application specific requirement, and a core asset, and instantiated model including architecture, static, and dynamic model. The traceability shown in the map implies that the process can be more consistently and correctly applied in practice.

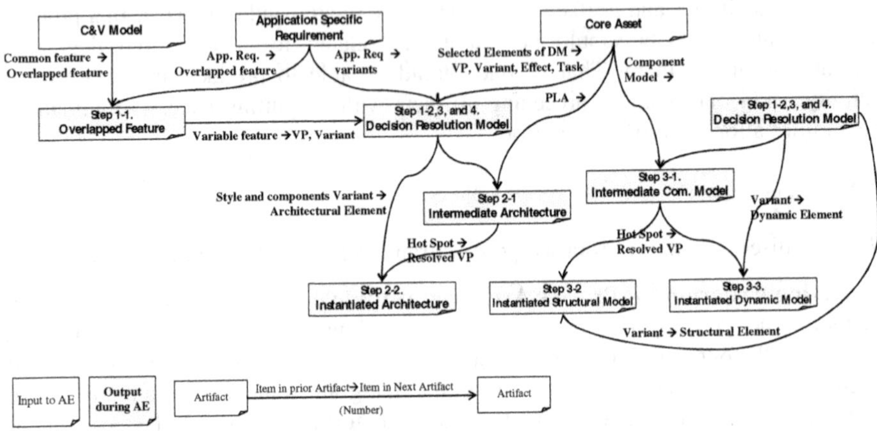

Fig. 11. Traceability Map

6 Concluding Remarks

As an effective reuse approach, PLE consists of two processes; core asset engineering and application engineering. Though instantiation is a key activity of application engineering, there is still a room for defining practical instantiation methods and artifact representations that can be applied in commercial projects and tool implementations. Moreover, it has not been clearly identified yet how to instantiate variable features of core assets such as architectural variability, required components, and component internals. Also, it should be dealt in a process to resolve inter-variation point dependencies during instantiation.

In this paper, we first defined a meta-model to specify the key elements of core assets and representation templates. And, we proposed a process containing instructions of instantiating core assets. We also proposed mechanisms for a tool implementation which support proposed process. Using the proposed process and a tool utilizing proposed mechanisms, one can efficiently generate high-quality artifacts for instantiation and the large portion of instantiation process can be automated.

References

[1] Atkinson, C., et al., *Component-based Product Line Engineering with UML*, Addison Wesley, 2001.

[2] Geyer, L., Becker, M., "On the Influence of Variabilities on the Application-Engineering Process of a Product Family," *Proceedings of SPLC2 2002, LNCS 2379*, Springer, pp. 1-14, 2002.

[3] Bayer, J., Flege, O., Knauber, P., Laqua, R., Muthig, D., Schmid, K., Widen, T., and DeBaud, J., "PuLSE: A Methodology to Develop Software Product Lines," *Proceeding of symposium for Software Reusability '99*, ACM, 1999.

[4] Bayer, J., Gacek, C., Muthig, D., and Widen, T., "PuLSE-I: Deriving Instances from a Product Line Infrastructure," *Proceedings of 7th International Conference and Workshop on the Engineering of Computer Based Systems*, IEEE, 2000.

[5] Deelstra, S., Sinnema, M., and Bosch, J., "Product derivation in software product families: a case study", *The Journal of Systems and Software*, Vol.74, No.2, p.174-194, Jan. 2005.

[6] Clements, P. and Northrop, L., *Software Product Lines: Practices and Patterns*, Addison Wesley, 2001.

[7] Bayer, J., Flege, O., Knauber, P., Laqua, R., Muthig, D., Schmid, K., Widen, T., and DeBaud, J., "PuLSE: A Methodology to Develop Software Product Lines," *Proceeding of symposium for Software Reusability '99*, ACM, 1999.

[8] Kyo C. Kang et. al., "FORM: A Feature-Oriented Reuse Method with Domain-Specific Reference Architectures," *Annals of Software Engineering*, 5, 1998, pp. 143-168.

[9] Clements, P., et al., *Documenting Software Architectures Views and Beyond*, Addison-Wesley, 2003.

[10] Gomma, H., *Designing Software Product Lines with UML from Use Cass to Pattern-Based Software Architectures*, Addsion-Wesley, 2004.

[11] Kim S., Her, J., and Chang, S. , "A Theoretical Foundation of Variability in Component-Based Development ," *Information and Software Technology(IST),* Vol. 47, p.663-673, 2005.

[12] Sinnema, M., Deelstra, S., Nijhuis, J., and Bosch, J., "COVAMOF: A Framework for Modeling Variability in Software Product Families," *Proceedings of the Third Software Product Line Conference (SPLC 2004), Springer Verlag Lecture Notes on Computer Science Vol. 3154 (LNCS 3154)*, August 2004.

[13] Choi, S., et al., "A Systematic Methodology for Developing Component Frameworks," *Lecture Notes in Computer Science 2984, Proceedings of the 7th Fundamental Approaches to Software Engineering Conference*, 2004.

[14] IEEE, *Guide to the Software Engineering Body of Knowledge*, 2004.

[15] Pressman, R, *Software Engineering: A Practitioner's Approach 6th edition*, McGraw-Hill, 2005.

[16] ISO/IEC 12207 Standard for Information Technology-Software life cycle processes, 1995.

[17] Pohl, K, Bockel., G., and Linden, F., Software Product Line Engineering, Springer, 2005.

Improving the Development of e-Business Systems by Introducing Process-Based Software Product Lines*

Joachim Bayer, Mathias Kose**, and Alexis Ocampo

Fraunhofer Institute for Experimental Software Engineering (IESE)
Fraunhofer-Platz 1, D- 67663 Kaiserslautern, Germany
{joachim.bayer, alexis.ocampo}@iese.fraunhofer.de
**ehotel AG
Greifswalder Strasse 207, D-10405 Berlin, Germany
mkose@ehotel.de

Abstract. In the e-Business domain, workflows are central artifacts that are used to specify application systems. To realize reuse at a large scale for e-Business application systems, therefore, workflows need to be reused systematically. To this end workflows must be classified, documented, and stored in a way that enables their identification, evaluation, and adaptation in order to integrate them in an application. Software product line engineering is an established and approved software engineering approach that addresses these issues by handling a number of similar software systems together, enabling large scale reuse during the development and maintenance of the different systems covered by the product line.

In this paper, we transfer the concepts of software product line engineering to the domain of e-Business systems by applying the product line techniques to workflows and present initial validation results.

1 Introduction

Survival in today's highly dynamic business environments requires that organizations continuously adapt their business processes. Success and growth rather than mere survival require that this adaptation be rapid enough to realize the competitive advantage offered by new business opportunities. The conduction of business in the internet (e-business) including buying and selling but also services and collaboration can be seen as one of these new important business opportunities. Mechanisms for rapid description, implementation, and deployment of such business processes become important. Currently, business processes are often represented by business process models. Business processes models are partially implemented through workflows [9] and deployed and executed in workflow environments, which show graphically the different steps of a business process (i.e., the business logic). According to [16],

* This work has been partially funded by the PESOA project (Process Family Engineering in Service-Oriented Applications) funded by the German federal ministry of education and research (BMBF) (Förderkennzeichen: 01 ISC 34E).

J. Münch and M. Vierimaa (Eds.): PROFES 2006, LNCS 4034, pp. 348 – 361, 2006.

business processes connect a set of business functions, where the connections are controlled by business rules. Those business rules are specific for an enterprise and specific at a certain point in time. However, changes in business rules and objectives are an everyday issue that demands capabilities to be able to react and adapt to such changes. Therefore, new rules and objectives can inevitably result in a large number of processes that vary in relatively minor ways. One way to control this proliferation and its attendant risks is to analyze commonalities and differences between the different process models in order to identify process variants and justifications for them [13], and to systematically integrate them in a software product line [6].

The following sections describe briefly the basic concepts of product line engineering and the mapping that we have done to process-based product lines, describe the details of the approach we have developed, and provide a preliminary validation (in terms of an example of its use).

2 Conceptual Foundation

2.1 Product Line Engineering Concepts

The underlying idea of product line engineering is to reuse common parts of related software systems. To this end, varying aspects of software systems, that is, differences among them are explicitly documented. Product line engineering distinguishes two development phases – domain and application engineering – as presented in Figure 1. The initial activity, scoping, defines which systems are members of a product line and which systems are outside the product line. Scoping is done by investigating a set of concrete products, be it already existing, planned, or envisioned products. The result of scoping is a set of products that make up the product line along with the features of the different product line members.

Based on a scope definition, domain engineering identifies the common features (commonalities) and the variable features (variabilities) of the identified products. Commonalities define the skeleton of the systems in the product line; variabilities bound the space of required and anticipated variations of the products in the product line. Each artifact produced during domain engineering contains the commonalities

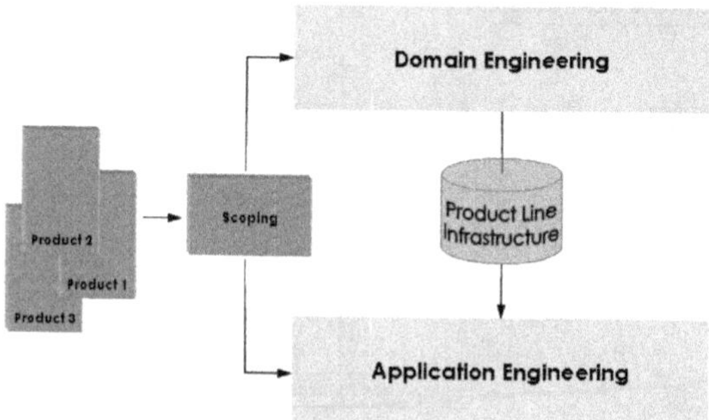

Fig. 1. Product Line Engineering

and specially labeled variabilities. These so-called variant-rich artifacts are stored in the product line infrastructure.

During application engineering, the product line infrastructure is instantiated to create a concrete product; the commonalities are reused and the variabilities are resolved for the specific product.

2.2 Process Based-Oriented Product Lines

A number of approaches for software product line engineering have been proposed [4],[7],[12]. Application domains that use processes, such as workflow or technical processes, as driving software development artifacts are, however, neglected to a large extent by product line research. The main problem in applying product line engineering techniques in such domains is that processes describe flows of activities and, consequently, variability covers different flows. The techniques traditionally proposed in product line engineering, however, provide means for the modeling of static diagrams rather than for dynamic ones. For example, the modeling of variability that results in different sub-processes that are exchanged for different products is not well supported. Another issue is that software generation traditionally also focuses on static models.

In this section, we present our approach for process-based product line engineering. The approach is based on PuLSE™ [2] (PuLSE™ is a registered trademark of Fraunhofer IESE) that is an approach for product line engineering that is developed and used in technology transfer projects since 1997. To adapt PuLSE™ for process-based product line engineering, we combined it with variability mechanisms [14] and software generation [8].

The core concepts of our approach to process-based product line engineering are variant-rich workflows or processes, which are workflows or processes that contain variabilities. To augment workflows used to model e-Business systems with the possibility to model variability in an explicit way, we use the approach proposed in [11]. This approach forms the basis for variability and decision modeling in PuLSE ™ and provides a systematic way to extend any given software engineering artifact to be generic, that is, to enable the explicit modeling of variability in that artifact.

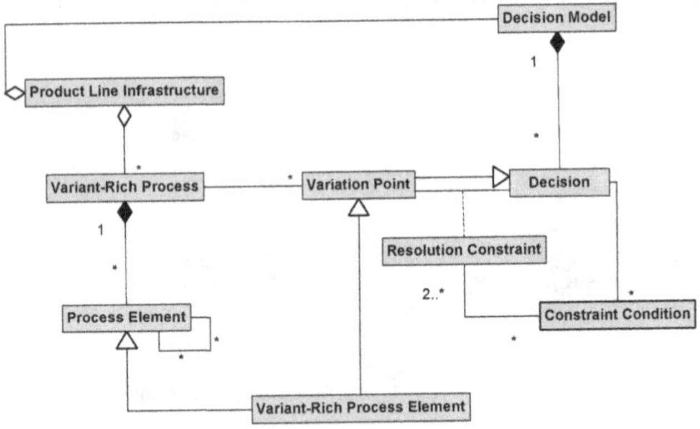

Fig. 2. Process-based Product Line Concepts

As presented in Figure 2, a product line infrastructure contains variant-rich processes and decision models. A variant-rich process contains variation points that represent its variability. A decision model contains the relationships among the variations of a product line infrastructure. Such decision models contain decisions, which are variation points that constrain the resolution of other variation points. A variant-rich process contains process elements, for instance activities, inputs, outputs, or roles. Those process elements that contain variation points are called variant-rich process elements.

Figure 3 provides an example that illustrates these concepts. It shows the flow between the "Create Order", "Pay Order", and "Send Invoice" process elements of an online shop. The "Pay Order" process element contains three alternatives (telephone, credit card, and bank transfer). The process element has one interface that interacts with the "Create Order" process element. At this point three alternatives split, and one of them must be chosen in order to resolve this variation. The resolution of the variation determines the path taken by the flow. The three alternatives converge in another interface that joins them. This interface is used to communicate the output of the "Pay Order" process element. The same can be observed in the case of the "Invoice" process element, an output that contains two alternatives (America or Europe), and two interfaces. This means that depending on the continent of destination, the invoice to be sent to the customer will have different fields of information (e.g., currency, address). One optional variation point can be assigned to the "Email" output process element. "Email" has only two alternatives i.e., yes or no. Therefore, once the variation points are resolved, the client has the possibility of receiving the invoice both as printed document or email.

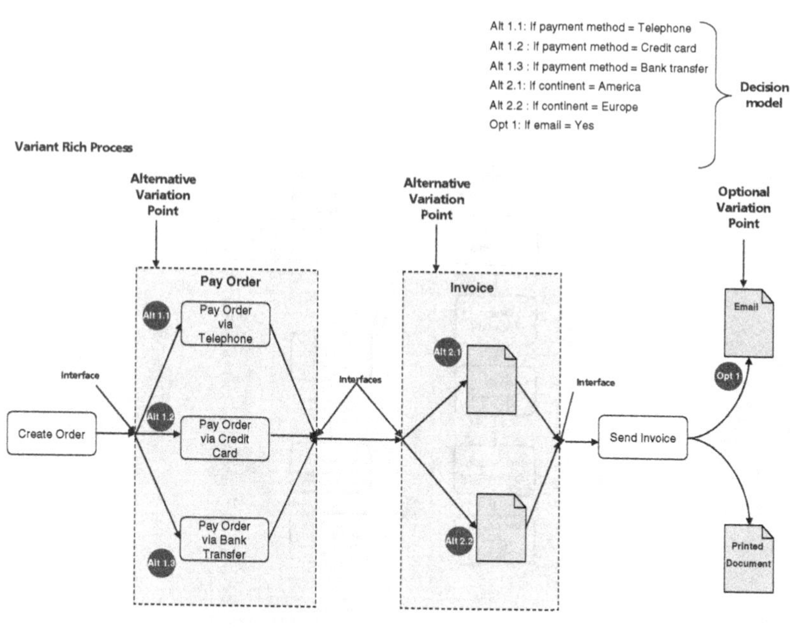

Fig. 3. Variant-rich Process Example

2.3 The Systematic Approach for Developing Process-Based Product Lines

Figure 4 shows our systematic approach for developing a process-based product line.

As mentioned above, the initial activity in product line engineering is *scoping*. The underlying idea of *scoping* is on the premise that one shall obtain as much return on investment as possible from the effort of establishing a process-based product line infrastructure. Using as input an existing or a planned set of process-based products a subset of such products is selected. Afterwards, the selected products are related to the features that they should offer. This information is recorded in a *domain scope definition*.

The *domain analysis* begins by using the defined domain scope as input for identifying relationships among features (e.g., consists-of, requires). Afterwards, in the activity *model features*, such relationships are captured in a hierarchical structure [10] or a tabular representation.

The resulting feature model can be used as basis for *identifying* and documenting the requirements for those processes that will be part of the process-based product line infrastructure. Such processes shall be conceived as building blocks that can be reused.

The domain design begins with the *design processes* activity. Here, using as input the list of identified processes, a commonality analysis among processes is performed in order to identify variant-rich process elements. At the moment there are not many techniques or approaches on how to perform such a comparison. One idea can be taken from [12], where a systematic comparison of a set of software process models is illustrated. The commonalities and variabilities detected among variant-rich process elements are then integrated into their respective variant-rich process.

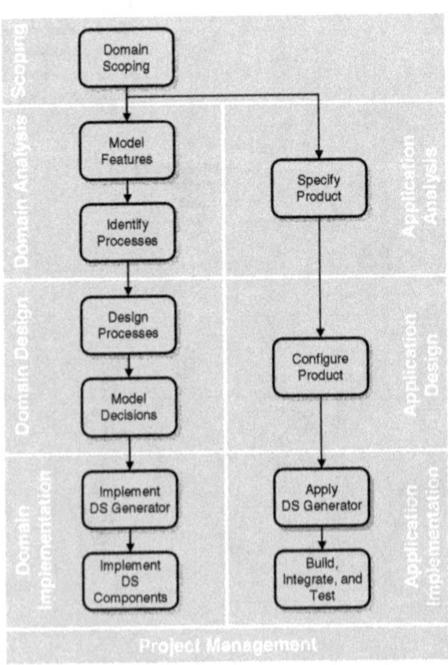

Fig. 4. Process-based Product Line Engineering

Relationships among variation points are identified and documented in the *decision model.*

This way, a process-based product line infrastructure that contains variant-rich processes elements, process elements, and a decision model has been produced.

The next step is *domain implementation.* It starts with the activity *implement domain-specific generator* that consists of identifying the domain-specific functionalities to be covered by a generator based on the commonalities and variabilities contained in the process-based product line. Code fragments implementing these functionalities are defined. They are connected to the process' variabilities, that is, each variation point is annotated by one or more code fragments.

Once the domain-specific functionalities have been identified, *DS components are implemented* as follows: First, functionalities that are to be implemented by generic components are identified based on the commonalities present in the process-based product line. Such components are referred to as *runtime components.* Then, components that are needed to process the generator's output are identified. They are referred to as *infrastructure components.* Once the DS components are implemented, a process-based product line infrastructure can be used for automatically generating new products according to new requirements.

The first step to derive a concrete product from the product line infrastructure is *application analysis.* It starts by *specifying the new product* based on the scope definition of the existing process-based product line infrastructure, and the feature model. Those features that are estimated to be realizable are mapped to the actual products from the process-based product line infrastructure. Such mapping must be documented in a *product feature model.* Those features that are not yet planned in the process-based product line shall be documented in a list of not covered features, which will be later integrated in the scope of the process-based product line.

The next step is to *configure the product,* in which the decision model is used for resolving the variation points based on the new product features. The resolution of the variation points and their relationships are documented in the *resolution model.*

Finally, the *appliance of the domain-specific generator* starts with importing data from a resolution model, followed by triggering the generation of *target code.* If there are additional variabilities that are not part of the process-based product line, for example technical ones specific for the target platform, they can be configured and resolved before triggering the code generation.

The generated target code is subject to further processing by the use of infrastructure components, including the domain-specific ones. The resulting executables have to be *built and integrated* with the needed runtime components. Together they form the product that might be *tested* in order to complete the implementation.

More details on the approach can be found in [3].

3 Validation

ehotel AG is a technology organization that specializes on developing software suitable for processing hotel reservations. It distinguishes because of its software development experience and know-how in the traveling business but especially in the hotel industry. ehotel AG develops and operates a software platform that supports hotel booking operations. The platform can be accessed through a browser interface or through a XML-/Web service interface. The XML-/Web service interface allows the integration of the platform in external IT-Systems. The rationale behind having such an interface was to integrate ehotel's solution with as many different systems as possible such as traveling systems of large corporate groups, traveling services offered by other web-Sites, or travel companies' internal applications. It was found that those systems supported a common hotel booking process. However, due to the different needs and scenarios of such systems, different types of requirements applied for functions such as search, select, reserve, or cancel. Each system type, therefore, needed a customized version of ehotel's product.

This is a classical situation where the product line approach can be used for better reusability of software products. ehotel has followed this approach systematically in the context of the PESOA project. The PESOA project's main goal is the design and prototype implementation of a platform for process family engineering and their application in the e-business and automotive areas. This goal is addressed by enhancing the approved technologies from the area of domain engineering, product line engineering, and software generation with new methods from the area of workflow management.

The following sections present example of artifacts produced when process-based product line engineering was applied at ehotel in the context of the PESOA project. We focus in the case study on analysis and design, and thus leave out implementation. More details on the case study can be found in [14].

3.1 Domain Scope Definition

The selection of a subset of e-hotel's process-based software was driven by the customer's point of view. Use cases helped to sketch this point of view and to identify the following set of sub-processes: "informing", "booking", "canceling", and "charging". Figure 5 shows the respective use case diagram for the "informing" sub-process that identifies the different ways ehotel customers can retrieve information.

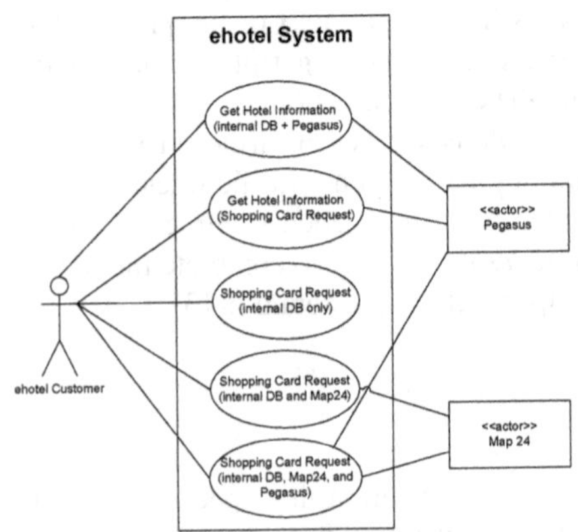

Fig. 5. Informing Use Case Diagram

3.2 Feature Model

A feature model captures and relates the characteristics of the different product line members. Common and varying characteristics are distinguished in feature models.

Figure 6 shows an excerpt of the feature model for ehotel's booking engine. The features for the "informing" and the "booking" sub-processes are modeled in detail. For the booking engine, there are common characteristics (denoted by full circles), like hotel details expressing that every booking system provides the possibility to acquire information on hotels. There are also optional characteristics (denoted by hollow circles). For example, pictures, description, and map in the hotel details express that these are the different possibilities for hotel details that are provided by the different booking systems. The third type of characteristics shown in the figure is alternative. Alternatives denote different ways to realize characteristics from which one is chosen for a specific booking system. In the example, an alternative feature is the map that can be realized either as static map or as dynamic map. The figure shows that for the varying characteristics all possible values are captured.

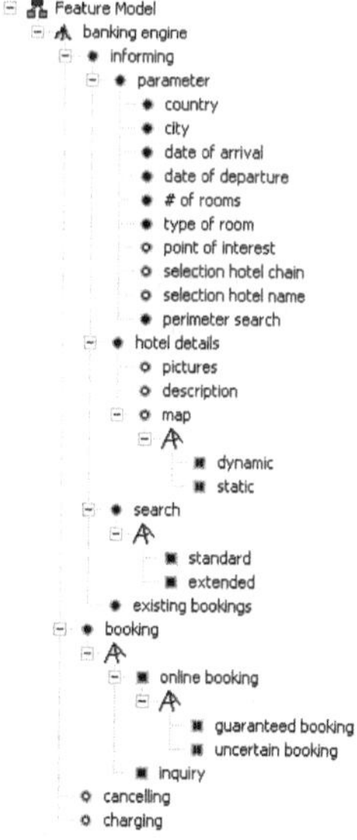

Fig. 6. Feature Model (modeled with fmp [1])

3.3 List of Processes

The next step in process-based product line engineering is the elicitation of processes that are needed to provide the features collected in the previous step. The list of processes mostly reflects the hierarchical organization of the feature model. The list of processes that was elicited based on the feature model in Figure 6 is:

- Informing
    - Search
        - Standard
        - Extended
    - Parameter
        - get countries
        - get cities
        - get Points-of-Interest (POIs)
        - get hotel chain
    - Hotel details
        - get Pictures
        - get Description
        - get Map
        - existing bookings
            - get All Bookings
            - get booking details
- Booking
    - online booking
        - guaranteed booking
        - uncertain booking
    - inquiry
- Canceling
- Charging

These are the (sub-) processes that have been identified for the ehotel booking engine and that will be modeled as variant-rich processes in the next step.

3.4 Variant-Rich Processes

Variant-rich processes are the core artifact in a process-based product line. They describe the behavior of the different product line members and thus determine the process-based product line. Variant-rich processes contain variation points to determine process elements that vary between different product line members. We use the variability mechanisms described in [14] for modeling variation points. These variability mechanisms enable the expression of different types of variation using stereotypes and other notation-specific modeling mechanisms.

Figure 7 shows the booking engine top-level process using the BPMN notation [4]. The top-level process contains "informing", "booking", "canceling", and "charging" as sub-processes. The process contains three types of variation points. The "charging" and the "cancellation" sub-processes are optional, denoted by the Null stereotype that expresses that the respective sub-processes are either present or not in a specific booking engine. "Booking" has an abstract stereotype; this means that there are different realizations possible for this sub-process.

The variable stereotype for the "informing" sub-process expresses that there are variabilities within the sub-process. This is shown in Figure 8 that depicts the "informing" sub-process. Figure 9 refines the "search" sub-process and shows for the abstract activity perform search two possible realizations, a standard and an extended search.

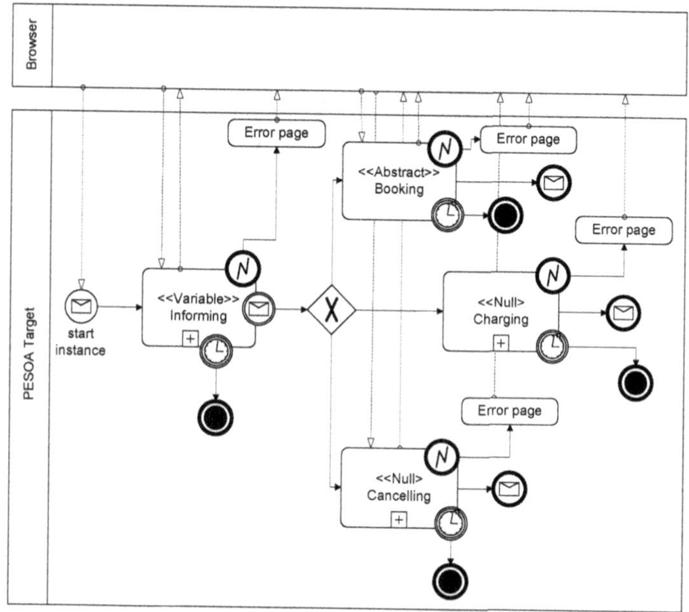

Fig. 7. Variant-rich Booking Engine Process

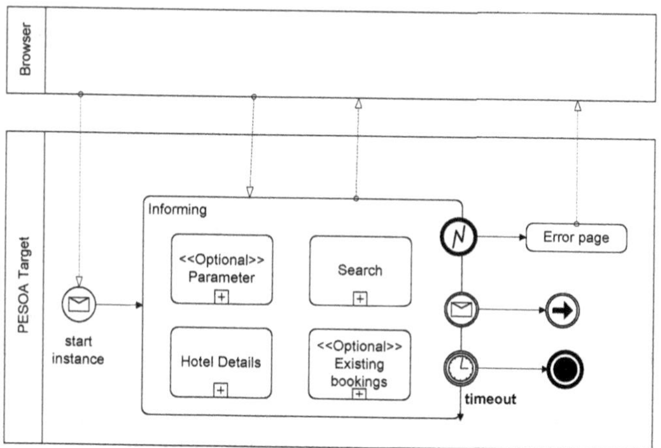

Fig. 8. Variant-rich Informing Process

3.5 Decision Model

The variation points in the variant-rich processes must be resolved in order to derive specific processes that describe concrete booking engines. This resolution is supported by decision models that relate features to variation points and document how a

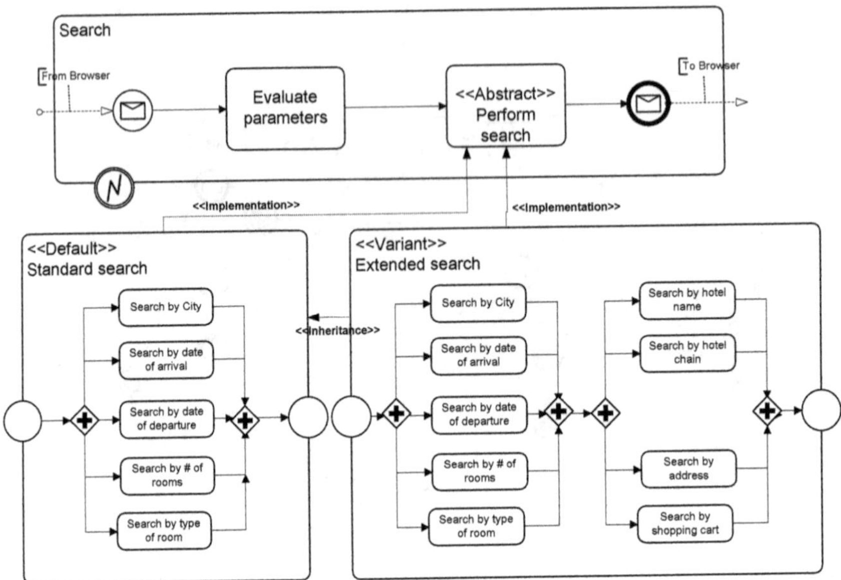

Fig. 9. Variant-rich Searching Process

Table 1. Decision Model Excerpt

ID	Process	Question	process element	Resolution	Effect
Searching.1	searching	Is extended search required?	Perform search	yes	Perform search = extended search
				no	Perform search = standard search

variation point must be resolved if a booking engine provides a given feature. Table 1 shows the decision model excerpt for the "searching" process shown in Figure 9.

The decision shown in Table 1 describes how the "searching" process is instantiated for the two possible cases, standard and extended search. When the effect is applied to the respective process, the abstract activity "perform search" in Figure 9 is replaced by either a sub-process realizing the standard or the extended search, respectively, depending on the decision taken.

The decision model is a collection of the decisions for all variation points in the different variant-rich processes.

3.6 Product Feature Model

In the following, we describe the instantiation of the variant-rich processes for a hypothetical ehotel customer that uses an instance of the ehotel booking engine derived from the process-based product line infrastructure.

As a first step, the required features from the feature model (compare Figure 6) are selected. The result is shown in Figure 10.

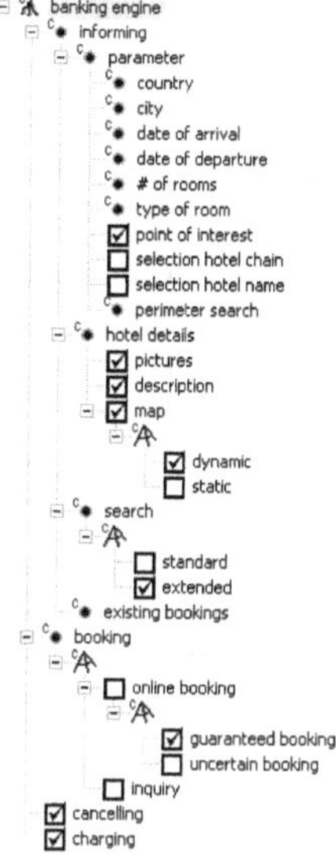

Fig. 10. Product Configuration (modeled with fmp [1])

3.7 Configured Product

Using the selected features, the decision model can be instantiated by answering the different questions. The application of the appropriate effects on the variant-rich processes resolves the processes leading to concrete processes for the product. In Figure 11, the variant-rich search process in Figure 9 is instantiated using the features selected in the product feature model in Figure 10. The result is a "search" process providing extended search features.

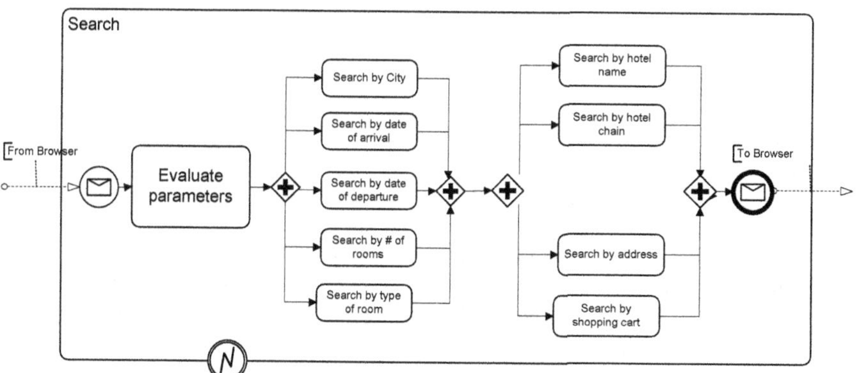

Fig. 11. Search Process Instance

4 Summary and Outlook

The booking engine plays a dominant role in the software system of the ehotel AG. A large variety of functionalities are implemented because of different requirements of individual users as well specific requirements of corporate customers. The result of the different market requirements is of high complexity for the ehotel-system. The process-based product line engineering shows a practical way to handle this complexity.

Based on existing specific business processes a generic, variant-rich process is derived. With feature diagrams and decision models this generic process can be configured. By using software generators customer specific software instances can be produced.

Process-based product line engineering forces a better structuring of the existing ehotel software system and future developments. After the setup of the process-based product line infrastructure, a faster and more reliable delivery of a customized version of the booking engine to new customer requirements is possible. The quality of the overall software system is improved and the time to market is reduced. This improved agility helps the ehotel AG on the customer side for example, to offer products to niche markets and has therefore a positive impact to the company. Overall the planning process of the development is improved; this results in higher delivery reliability. At the end ehotel achieves a higher customer satisfaction.

Acknowledgements

We want to thank our colleagues in the PESOA project that supported us in the development of the presented example, namely Paul Bouché (ehotel AG), Dennis Plötner (ehotel AG), Thomas Hering (University of Leipzig), and Andrej Werner (University of Leipzig). We especially want to thank Frank Puhlmann (Hasso-Plattner-Institut at the University of Potsdam) for supporting the example development and for reviewing an early version of the paper.

References

[1] M. Antkiewicz, K. Czarnecki.: FeaturePlugin: feature modeling plug-in for Eclipse, Proceedings of the 2004 OOPSLA workshop on eclipse technology eXchange, p.67-72, October 24-24, 2004.

[2] J. Bayer, O. Flege, P. Knauber, R. Laqua, D. Muthig, K. Schmid, T. Widen, and J. –M. DeBaud. PuLSE: A Methodology to Develop Software Product Lines. In Proceedings of the Fifth Symposium on Software Reusability (SSR'99), May 1999.

[3] J. Bayer, W. Buhl, C. Giese, T. Lehner, A. Ocampo, F. Puhlmann, E. Richter, A. Schnieders, J. Weiland, M. Weske. Process Family Engineering: Modeling variant-rich processes. PESOA-Report No. 18/2005, Juni 2005.

[4] G. J. Chastek (ed). Software Product Lines. Proceedings of the Second International Software Product Lines Conference (SPLC2), San Diego, California, USA, August 2002.

[5] Business Process Management Initiative (BPMI): Business Process Modeling Notation (BPMN), Version 1.0, www.bpmi.org, Mai 2004.

[6] P. Clements and L. Northrop. Software Product Lines. Practices and Patterns. Addison-Wesley, 2002.

[7] P. Donohoe (ed.) .Software Product Lines - Experience and Research Directions. Proceedings of the First International Software Product Lines Conference (SPLC1), Denver, Colorado, USA, August 2000.

[8] C. Giese, H. Overdick, W. Buhl. Realisierungsstrategien für Prozessfamilien: Werkzeuge für Modellierung und Generierung. PESOA-Report No. 15/2005, Process Family Engineering in Service-Oriented Applications, Juni 2005.

[9] D. Hollingsworth. The Workflow Reference Model. Technical report, Workflow Management Coalition, Hampshire, 1995.

[10] K. Kang, S. Cohen, J. A. Hess, W. E. Novak, A. S. Peterson; "Feature-Oriented Domain Analysis (FODA) Feasibility Study". Technical Report CMU/SEI-90-TR-21, 1990.

[11] D. Muthig: A Light-weight Approach Facilitating an Evolutionary Transition Towards Software Product Lines. Stuttgart: Fraunhofer IRB Verlag, 2002 (PhD Theses in Experimental Software Engineering Vol. 11). Kaiserslautern, Univ., Diss., 2002.

[12] R. Nord (ed.). Software Product Lines. Proceedings of the Third International Conference (SPLC 2004), Boston, MA, USA, August - September, 2004.

[13] A. Ocampo, F. Bella, J. Münch. Software process commonality analysis. Software Process: Improvement and Practice. Vol. 10(3), pp. 273-285, 2005.

[14] D. Plötner, M. Kose, T. Hering, A. Werner. Prozesse im E-Business am Beispiel ausgewählter Geschäftsprozesse des Partners ehotel AG. PESOA-Report No. 20/2005, Juni 2005.

[15] F. Puhlmann, A. Schnieders.: Process Family Engineering: Variability Mechanisms, Technical Report PESOA-Report No. TR 17/2005, Process Family Engineering in Service-Oriented Applications, Jun. 2005.

[16] G. van de Putte, T. Benedett, D. Gagic, P. Gersak, K. Krutzler, M. Perry. Intra-Enterprise Business Process Management. IBM Corporation. IBM International Technical Support Organization. IBM Reedbook. October 2001.

Assessing Requirements Compliance Scenarios in System Platform Subcontracting

Björn Regnell[1,3], Hans O. Olsson[1], and Staffan Mossberg[2]

[1] Sony Ericsson, Lund, Sweden
http://www.sonyericsson.com
[2] Ericsson, Lund, Sweden
http://www.ericsson.com
[3] Lund University, Sweden
bjorn.regnell@telecom.lth.se
http://serg.telecom.lth.se

Abstract. In the mobile industry, system platforms are offered to device developers to enable rapid product development while sharing expensive technology development investments. This paper presents a framework for assessment of requirements engineering collaboration related to statements-of-compliance negotiation in platform subcontracting. The framework includes a classification of platform compliance scenarios and results from analysis of interviews with engineers at two collaborating companies, a device vendor and a platform vendor. Case study findings particular to the compliance scenarios of the framework are provided. The purpose of the framework is to provide a basis for process improvement in collaborative requirements engineering.

1 Introduction

Collaborative systems engineering and multi-partner development impose special opportunities and challenges [6]. A strategic combination of a number of specialised organisations, each with their specific expertise, can hopefully provide cheaper and more advanced products. However, the collaborative mode adds extra complexity to the development and special measures needs to be taken to address barriers of communication [5]. This paper focuses on the assessment of a specific mode of collaboration: subcontracting of technical platforms in embedded systems development. Embedded systems are often based on a number of components such as real-time operating systems, special-purpose hardware, communication protocol software, and user interface software. These components are included in a system architecture that enable separate development of each component that communicate with other components through well-defined interfaces. Developments of specific components or architectural layers are often subcontracted, which impose the need for collaborative engineering between the integrator and the subcontractor [1].

The presented work is based on a case study in the domain of mobile devices. The mobile device industry is facing challenges of rapid technology development in combination with increasing market demands on expanding product portfolios targeting a wide scope of different capabilities and price ranges. Strategic alliances are formed among companies providing technology that can be reused among products to

J. Münch and M. Vierimaa (Eds.): PROFES 2006, LNCS 4034, pp. 362 – 376, 2006.

increase productivity. Collaborative product line engineering where platforms are developed by subcontractors impose special challenges to requirements engineering compared to in-house platform development. At each platform release a contractual scheme needs to be set up, which often is based on statements of compliance representing agreed intentions by the subcontractor to deliver specific requirements in specified releases. Further work on challenges in this context can be found in [10], [11], 12].

This paper focuses on the assessment of the requirements negotiation outcome in collaborative requirements engineering, and the results of the presented work is a framework to be used in systematic analysis of compliance scenarios in order to find improvements for the future advancements of a collaborative requirements engineering process.

The paper is structured as follows. Section 2 provides a description of the industrial case under study, including an overview of the artefacts that are transferred in the collaborative engineering process. Section 3 gives an account of the research methodology applied. Section 4 presents the main result packaged in a compliance scenario framework. Section 5 concludes the paper.

2 The Industrial Case

This section provides an overview of the industrial case of the presented work. The domain is mobile device development and the products include a range of features related to communication, business applications and entertainment. The technological content is complex and includes advanced system engineering areas such as radio technology, memory technology, software design, communication protocols, security, audio & video, digital rights management, gaming etc.

As the investment of keeping up with the fast technology development is high, there is a market for providing *mobile platforms* that can be used by mobile handset vendors as a basis for rapid device and application development. A mobile platform typically offers ready-to-use capabilities of radio network access, communication protocols, local connectivity, multimedia encoding and decoding, encryption and decryption, and much more. These capabilities are implemented as an open-ended system of both hardware and software and the mobile platform is delivered as a *reference package design* including application specific integrated circuit (ASIC) designs and application programming interfaces (API), as well as documentation and test procedures.

The presented research case study involves two collaborating companies: a mobile device product company and a mobile platform product company. The collaboration is strategic and involves requirements engineering of mobile devices and the technology needed for future products. The two companies offer their respective products at different positions in the mobile industry value chain and they have different competitors and customers. Fig. 1 shows a simplified[1] overview of the actors in the mobile device domain with focus on the collaboration between the device product company and the platform product company.

---

[1] Many other actors such as network system providers, 3rd party application providers, standardization bodies, legislation authorities, manufacturing subcontracting, are not shown.

The primary actors are the consumers that buy and use the mobile device. The key players are operators that offer network capacity through subscription to consumers as well as additional services. Often devices are subsidised by operators if the consumer signs a subscription for a certain period. Devices and subscriptions are sold by operators directly or by independent retailers. Many mobile device vendors are competing on the market, and many mobile platform companies are competing to offer technology to device vendors.

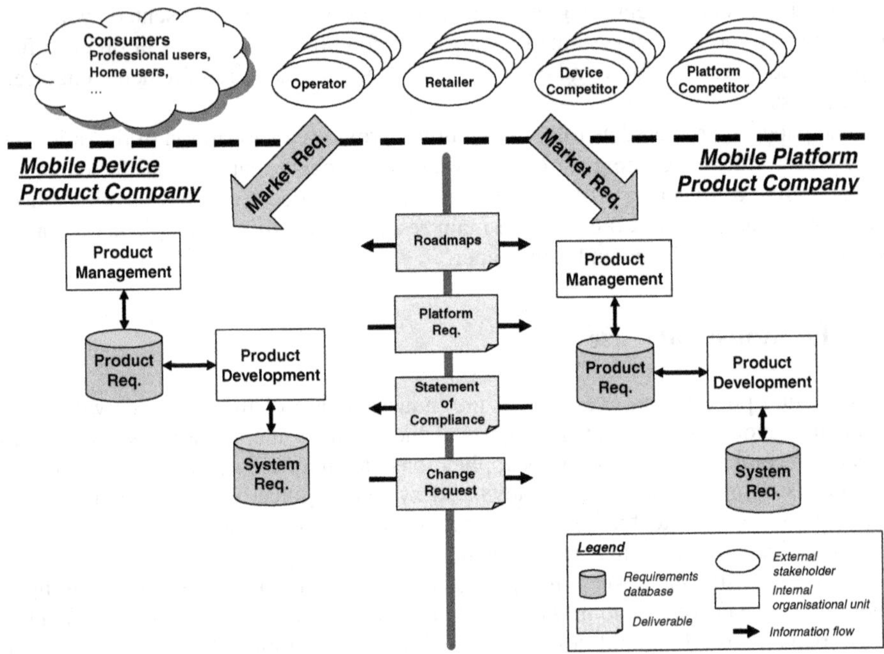

Fig. 1. An overview of the case study domain

The two companies in the case study have a tight collaboration on requirements engineering for mobile platforms. Both companies have very large requirements repositories at various abstraction levels [9]: roadmaps (~100), product level requirements (~1000) and system level requirements (~10 000). Roadmaps are strategic plans for specific high-level technology areas, product requirements are high-level product feature requirements from a market perspective, and system level requirements are detailed software and hardware requirements from a development perspective that are the basis for system design and testing. Requirements are continuously managed to repeatedly initiate development projects delivering new product versions to their respective markets at regular intervals (several times each year).

The alignment of the two companies' requirements repositories is not trivial as they are formulated for different types of products; the product level requirement on mobile devices is not the same as the product level requirement on mobile platforms, and similarly for system requirements. Furthermore, both companies have their own internal product family approach with reusable code bases and internal product platforms that are used to provide new versions of families of products [14]. Other platforms and third party products are also integrated into the products such as operating systems and communication protocol components, making it even more complex. The repeated task of release planning [3] is thus not trivial.

The collaboration process in fig. 2 is represented through an interface of exchanged deliverables: *roadmaps* are continuously shared to align strategies; *platform requirements* are periodically transferred from the device product company and *compliance statements* are transferred back from the platform product company answering which requirements that is the intention to be supported by the platform; down-stream requirements are handled as *change requests*.

3 Research Methodology

The presented work was conducted within an industrial case study on collaborative requirements engineering process improvement. The presented framework is a result of insights gained in retrospective analysis of previous projects and archival analysis of platform requirements from a series of releases in the case study. The methodology is thus qualitative, explorative and conducted in an action research mode where the researchers also are involved in the actual change of the object of study. The proposed framework is a result of an attempt to make a systematic classification of the particular phenomena that were encountered during the case study. The framework was not a part of the originally planned research products, but was developed when needed and found useful in assessing the process under study.

The research was conducted within these interrelated activities that were iterated during the work: (1) collection of entities and relationships in the case study domain; (2) interviews with selected roles across organisations; (3) analysis of interviews; (4) framework construction; (5) initial framework validation.

The collection of entities and relationships in the case study was based on initial problem formulations and process descriptions that preceded and constituted the case study as well as results from analysis of interviews. The entities and relationships were recorded as intermediate codes. Interviews were iterated with interview analysis and the interviews were either unstructured or semi-structured. The interview analysis was conducted based on interview notes and resulted in informal drawings and lists of interesting concepts. Interview analysis was input to subsequent interviews and the explorative information gathering was adapted to the findings as the understanding of the problem increased. More than 15 interviews have been conducted with the general aim of finding improvement opportunities and the interviews will continue as the action research progresses. Persons from both the device product company and the platform product company were interviewed. Interviewed roles include market researchers, usability engineers, product managers, project managers, requirements coordinators, researchers, developers, and supply chain managers.

Step 4 and 5 was not initially anticipated, but emerged as an opportunity for a systematic way of assessing the collaborative requirements engineering process. The focus on decisions originated from the results of the interview analysis, and the use of a decision tree as a basis for the proposed framework emerged when compliance decision types where analysed and structured.

The first author contributed with the construction of the framework based on interview analysis and the second and third authors contributed with the initial framework validation by bringing their experience as requirements coordinators at the device and platform companies respectively. The initial validation concentrated on determining for each compliance scenario if it was (a) principally possible and (b) if it has occurred at least once, (c) a subjective and relative assessment of its frequency (a detailed frequency assessment is not reported here for reasons of confidentiality), and (d) the potential reasons behind the scenario was analysed based on expert experience.

4 Requirements Compliance Scenario Framework

The framework resulting from interview analysis and structuring of decision alternatives in the platform subcontracting case study is depicted in fig. 2. For each new requirement a strategy is selected by the device product company to either implement the requirement in its own internally developed application platform, or to require an external platform solution by the subcontracted platform product company. In the latter case, the timing of the requirement determines what happens in the collaborative requirements engineering process enacted across organisational boundaries.

If the requirement is elicited before the requirements for the current release are put in baseline, the requirement is incorporated in upstream requirements engineering [7] where specification, prioritisation and compliance negotiation is invoked according to the process described in Section 2. This process results in a declaration of intention by the platform product company, called Statement of Compliance (SoC), resulting in either the intention to make the platform compliant to the requirement or not.

If the requirement is (1) elicited after the point in time when the requirements for the current release are put in baseline by the platform product company, and (2) the requirement is not compliant with the current release plans, and (3) the device product company finds that it is too late to wait until the upstream requirements engineering for the next release, then it is forwarded to the change management procedures in downstream requirements engineering [7] for the current release. The Change Control Board (CCB) is responsible for initiating and judging the analysis of the change request and arrives at a decision to accept or reject the change request.

The leaf nodes of the platform requirements in fig. 2 are generated when the decision alternatives for two releases are combined including both what is actually delivered in the current release and the SoC decision for the next release.

If the decision by the device product company is to develop a proprietary solution, the leaf node scenarios are generated depending on if flexibility still is needed in the platform in the form of an enabler or not. An enabler can e.g. be an API extension or an architectural change. The leaf level scenarios are generated depending on if the platform product company has a competing solution to offer to competitors or not.

Subsequently each leaf node scenario is explained and the case study findings are reported in terms of reasons behind the decision made that has been encountered in the industrial case under study. The scenarios are also assessed in terms of the benefit to each party in the collaborative requirements engineering process.

4.1 Upstream Compliance Scenarios

After the decision has been made that it is best to implement a certain requirement in the subcontracted technical platform, the requirement is included in the collaborative requirements engineering process between the device product organisation and the platform product organisation.

If the requirement is elicited (invented or discovered) *before* the platform system requirements are baselined, the normal statement-of-compliance negotiation process is invoked upstream [7]. Depending of the outcome of the negotiation and the outcome of the actual implementation, a number of scenarios may occur, as described subsequently.

Inclusion. This is the normal case for a requirement that has been stated compliant and delivered according to plan in the current release. The requirement is normally continued to be compliant also in the next release.

Case study findings: This is a very common scenario that occurs when the device developer and the platform subcontractor have similar objectives and strategies for a given requirement. It is also the likely result of development going as planned, with cost estimates for this requirement turning out as expected.

Assessment: This scenario is good for both the device developer and the platform subcontractor, given that the requirement inclusion is in line with a good trade-off between cost and value.

Transient inclusion. This is a special case where a requirement has been stated compliant, delivered according to plan in the current release, but then been excluded in the next release.

Case study findings: A typical reason behind *transient inclusion* is that a certain feature has been excluded based on technology development or market considerations, old technology may be replaced by new or a certain feature was never taken up by the market. Another reason may be that there have been backward traceability problems between architecture and requirements resulting in loss of legacy requirements in architectural evolution.

Assessment: Being responsive to technology and market changes is crucial. If the device and platform developers are aligned in the views on technology this scenario is good for both, and the sooner changes can be discovered the better. If the reason is traceability problems, it is not good for any of the parties: the device developer misses desired features and the platform developer loses goodwill.

De-scoped to next; De-scoped indefinite. These scenarios represent requirements that were stated compliant but then not delivered as promised in the current release. Some of them are delivered in the next release and some are delayed even further.

Case study findings: Several reasons were identified, including: (1) there may be problems with the interpretation of a requirement resulting in a misunderstanding of what was meant by the statement of compliance; (2) the customer has changed its assessment of the requirement's priority and ceased to require it due to e.g. market changes, and thus the platform development resources can be utilised more efficiently by concentrating on other things; (3) the cost estimates were unrealistic and the requirement was not possible to implement within the available resources.

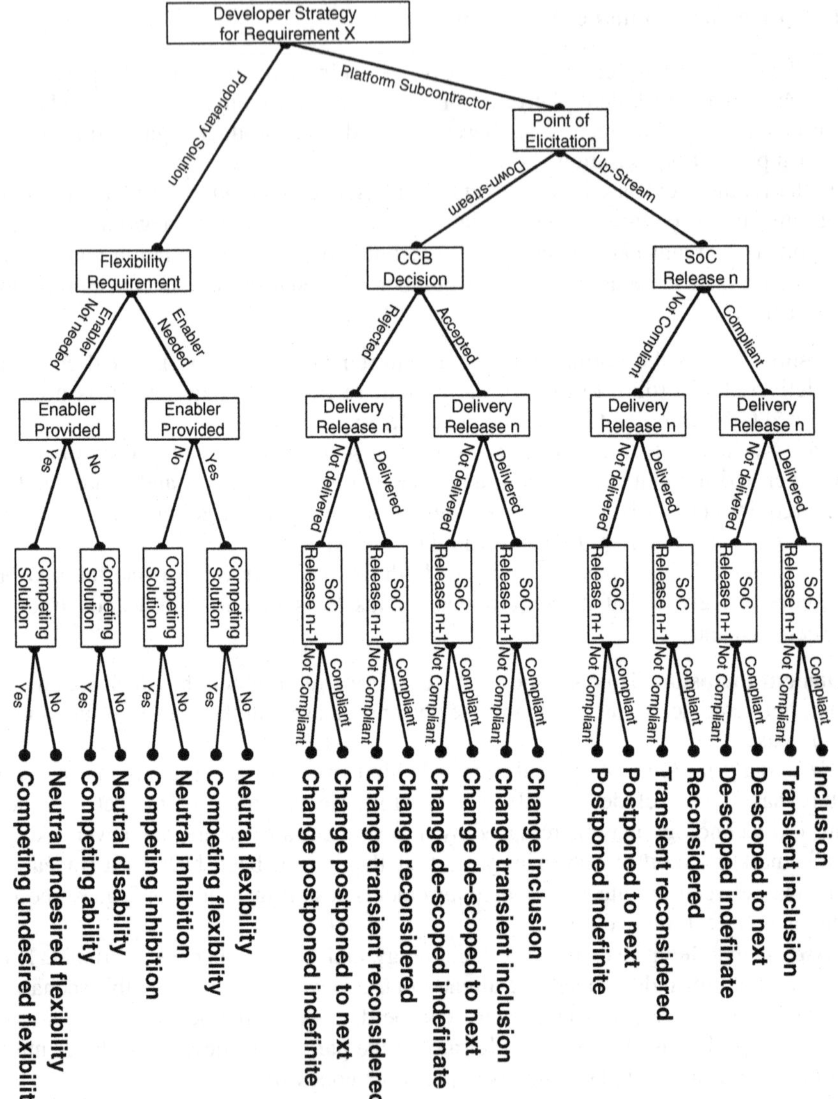

Fig. 2. Requirements Compliance Scenario Framework. (CCB = *Change Control Board*; SoC = *Statement of Compliance*).

Assessment: Reason (1) is bad for both parties and such instances should be minimised through improved requirements specification quality; (2) and (3) occur more frequently than desired due to the great uncertainties in market and cost estimation and are bad for both parties, and may be minimised through improvements in estimation techniques.

Reconsidered. This scenario represents the case where a requirement initially was stated not compliant, however delivered anyway in the current release.

Case study findings: One identified reason for this rather uncommon scenario is that several competing device developers also has declared firm interest in this requirement and the platform product company has upgraded accordingly the priority of the requirement based on platform market considerations.

Assessment: This scenario is generally beneficial to both parties, although less turbulence may have been created if the requirement was stated compliant earlier in the negotiation process.

Transient reconsidered. This is a special case of the previous scenario, where a reconsidered requirement is stated not compliant in the next release.

Case study findings: One identified reason for this rare scenario is that a requirement is only partly implemented using a temporary work-a-round that subsequently in the next release is excluded due to permanent architectural changes.

Assessment: If this scenario is a result of incomplete solutions and work-a-rounds it may be a pragmatic outcome based on resource constraints and therefore acceptable by both parties given the circumstances.

Postponed to next; Postponed indefinite. These scenarios represent the cases where the statement of compliance for the current release is negative and the requirement is accordingly not delivered. Some of the requirements are implemented in the next release and some are postponed even further.

Case study findings: These scenarios are rather common and are a natural result of the not surprising fact that the number of desired requirements is larger than what the available platform development resources can cope with. Postponed to next may also be a result of that the necessary technology is not part of the current release, but will be incorporated in the next release as the platform architecture evolves. Postponed indefinite may be a result of a strategic decision by the platform developer to not support a certain technology or set of features. Another common reason behind postponed requirements is that the market value does not justify the anticipated development costs. Or it may be unfeasible to reach a cost per device unit that is attractive to the targeted market segment.

Assessment: These scenarios are in general not desirable to the device developer, although it is of course necessary to prioritise among requirements that exceed available resources. It is crucial to the platform developer not to over-allocate development resources as there otherwise is a risk that pressure results in sub-optimal decisions and to late de-scoping, which generates further turbulence. There is a difficult trade-off involved in the decision of postponing, as it in effect may mean balancing decreased reliability versus lost market opportunities and disadvantageous competitor lead.

4.2 Downstream Compliance Scenarios

If the requirement is elicited (invented or discovered) *after* the platform system requirements are put in baseline, the change control process is invoked and the requirement may be incorporated in downstream requirements engineering as a change request [4, 13]. This means that a formal decision procedure needs to be followed involving the Change Control Board (CCB) which is set up by the platform company specially for the collaborative requirements engineering with this particular device product company. The CCB is responsible for balancing the benefits of the change with the effects of disturbing the ongoing development of the current platform release. Estimates regarding impact and cost are needed and available developer competence needs to be assessed. Depending on the outcome of the CCB decision a change request may be accepted or rejected, and depending on the actual implementation of the change request, a number of scenarios may occur, as described subsequently.

Change inclusion. This is a typical scenario for a change request. It is the result of a decision to accept a change request, and hence the requirement is allowed to change the plans of the on-going development. This scenario also imply that the development was successful, resulting in a satisfactory implementation of the requirement. Normally, a successful change is persistent in subsequent releases.

Case study findings: Change requests are an order of magnitude fewer than normal requirements (~100 rather than ~1000), as only a few change requests can be handled during on-going development. If too many change requests are accepted, the development is trashed by disruptive rework (cf. [8]). The reasons behind change requests (cf. [13]) that have been identified include: (1) late incoming requirements from operators or incomplete elicitation in general, (2) late discovery of platform performance problems, (3) spill-over of the most important *de-scoped* or *postponed* requirements (cf. Section 4.1), and (4) late discovery of requirements specification quality problems that has resulted in misaligned interpretation of what will be delivered. The decision to include a change may be paired with an agreement to separately pay for a customer specific project dedicated to this requirement in order to enable an increase in the available resources, e.g. through additional personnel from consultancy firms.

Assessment: This scenario is positive to the device product company as desired requests are fulfilled. It also gives the platform product company goodwill and if the estimates and assessments underpinning the decision to accept the change are sound and a budget for changes is planned in advance, it can be handled in an undisruptive manner that does not excessively impact on-going construction.

Change transient inclusion. This scenario represents the acceptance of a change request and the requirement is implemented and delivered in the ongoing release, but then the requirement is not compliant in the subsequent release and its implementation is for some reason excluded, as opposed to the normal case of persistent changes.

Case study findings: This scenario is rare but less rare than for normal requirements, as change request implementations more often are of a work-around nature to enable late inclusion in on-going development. If backward requirements traceability in architectural evolution is incomplete, change requests may accidentally be lost in later releases.

Assessment: This scenario may be reasonable to both parties, given that an agreement on superseding a work-around with another more general solution that better covers the needs is reached. Temporary changes lost in coming up-stream requirements engineering due to traceability problems is not beneficial to any party, in a similar way as *transient inclusion* in Section 4.1.

Change de-scoped to next release; Change de-scoped indefinite. These scenarios are resulting from decision changes during ongoing construction. First a change request is accepted and the implementation of the requirement is incorporated in the plans, but then for various reasons, the change is excluded from the scope of the current release. If this happens the change is normally included in the next release or it may also be indefinitely delayed.

Case study findings: These scenarios are relatively rare in comparison to de-scoping in up-stream requirements engineering, due to the fact that change requests are very carefully scrutinised as changes often have large impact and dedicated resources often need to be reallocated. If it happens it may be that the acceptance decision has come too late for it to be feasible to include in on-going construction or that an even more important change request has emerged. Another reason may be that unforeseen implementation problems need urgent re-allocation of resources resulting in de-scoping.

Assessment: These scenarios are not desirable to any party as much time already has been spent on change of plans and impact analysis. It may, however, be necessary given the circumstances and the best choice given the market situation or the actual outcome of construction efforts.

Change reconsidered; Change transient reconsidered. These scenarios result from rejected changes that are then reconsidered during on-going construction. Depending on if the implemented requirement is compliant or not in the next release, the reconsidered change may be persistent or transient.

Case study findings: These scenarios are very uncommon, especially change transient reconsidered. The reasons behind these scenarios resemble the reasons behind upstream reconsidered requirements (see Section 4.2), and are based on reconsidered estimations of e.g. the platform product market value. Incomplete or intermediate solutions may be superseded causing transient compliance.

Assessment: These scenarios are, as the previous *change de-scope* scenarios, symptoms of a changing environment and uncertain predictions of future market and outcome of implementation. When they occasionally occur, they are results of trying to adapt to facts of reality, and they often have the consequence that value of previous efforts are shredded and that rework is needed. The gains may include rectified competitive advantage.

Change postponed to next release; Change postponed indefinite. These scenarios are results of rejected change requests. This means that the current release is not compliant with the requirement in the change request. Either the change is included as a compliant requirement in the next release or it may be postponed even further.

Case study findings: These scenarios are common for change requests, especially *change postponed to next release*. The later in down-stream development that a change request comes, the more likely it is that it gets postponed as the impact and cost of rework is increased as construction proceeds. Only really important change requests are accepted. If the change is in line with the platform product company strategy it may be included in the next release in the upstream requirements engineering as a compliant requirement. If the strategic fit is not perfect or if the architecture is not ready for such features, it may be further delayed to an uncertain future. Sometimes changes are postponed due to lack of competent resources, and it may not even be possible to find resources through additional personnel from consultancy firms.

Assessment: These scenarios are in general not beneficial to the device product company. Change requests are most often made on really important requirements and if not included, the market value of the device may be substantially reduced. It is also crucial that the CCB decision comes as soon as possible in order to give time for potential development of proprietary solutions. This scenario may give serious bad-will for the platform product company with regard to this particular device customer, but it may very well be necessary given the global optimisation of resource utilisation as seen by the platform product company.

4.3 Proprietary Solution Chosen

If the strategy chosen for a given requirement by the device product company is to implement it in the device application platform that is developed internally by the device developer, the requirement is not forwarded to the platform subcontractor.

Case study findings: One reason behind the choice to make a proprietary solution is that this gives a competitive advantage in relation to other competing device vendors. Even if the platform company offers a standard solution to, e.g., a certain communication technology, it may not be as advanced, production economical, or high performing as the device company wants it, and thereby a proprietary solution is selected. Another reason may be that the device product company has the competence and the necessary resources to implement the requirement and finds that the platform product company's development resources and competences are better utilised on other requirements. Yet another reason may be that the requirement is application specific and is out of scope of the mobile platform, or the proprietary solution may be a spill-over as a result of a previous decision by the platform company not to comply with a certain requirement.

Often a requirement, although not to be implemented in the platform, needs an *enabler* in the platform in order to facilitate its implementation in the device application platform or in the product-specific part of the design. This often manifests itself in the need for opening up access to platform-internal entities through extensions to the application programming interface (API) of the platform. Subsequently, this is called a *flexibility requirement*.[2]

The flexibility requirement scenarios generated based on the proprietary solution branch of fig. 2 are described below, firstly the four scenarios that come from the need of an enabler, and secondly the four scenarios implied if no enabler is needed.

Neutral flexibility; Competing flexibility. These scenarios represent the case where an enabler in the platform is needed. Two cases exist: either the platform company offers only the enabler (through e.g. API extensions) or the platform company also offers a complete solution to all device developers using the platform. This complete solution is thus a competing alternative to the proprietary solution of the specific device product company.

Case study findings: The *neutral flexibility* case is the normal case and is rather common. The reason for providing neutral flexibility through enablers in the platform is to support device developers in application development, which is in line with the general goal of the platform company. Often the device company pays extra for the effort needed to provide enablers not planned as part of the standard platform

[2] There are other types of flexibility requirements not discussed here. For example, there may be requirements to exclude certain capabilities in order to have reduced processor load and thereby enable manufacturing of devices with cheaper hardware and thus lower cost per unit.

proposition. *Competing flexibility* is a special case, although not uncommon, and occurs when a platform solution is offered to those device product companies that do not want to, or would not be able to implement the application-level requirement themselves if the competing solution would not be present.

Assessment: The *neutral flexibility* scenario is in general beneficial to the device product company, although sometimes the result of an unfavourable non-compliance. It is often no problem to provide an enabler and the platform company increases the capabilities of the platform through the inclusion of an enabler. The competing flexibility scenario is in general a disadvantage to the device product company; whereas it is beneficial to the platform company as the platform market opportunities are enhanced.

Neutral inhibition; Competing inhibition. These scenarios are based on the case where the device product company needs an enabler but the platform product company does not offer one. This results in that the application implementation by the device developer is inhibited to various degrees. A special case is when a solution in the platform is offered that the device developer does not want to use and at the same time there is no needed enabler available to support proprietary solutions.

Case study findings: The decision by the platform product company not to provide an enabler may come from a choice that this is not in line with the architectural strategy. There may also be a shortage of resources internally or the right competence may not be available through additional personnel from consultancy firms, even if the device vendor is prepared to pay extra for the enabler. Every customer-specific addition to the platform adds extra complexity in configuration management as variants in the code base increases. We have not found examples of the competing inhibition scenario in our interviews, but it is in principle possible as a result of, e.g., resource constraints at the platform product company.

Assessment: Inhibition scenarios are not good for the device product company, as a competitive advantage is spoiled. The competing inhibition is worse than the neutral inhibition, if the device company is not satisfied with the standard platform solution offered and cannot make its own proprietary solutions due to a lacking enabler. The platform company may lose goodwill, but act according to a global assessment of the platform market taking all device vendor customers into account.

Neutral disability; Competing ability. These scenarios are resulting from an absence of support to proprietary solutions, although different to the inhibition scenarios in that the enabler is not needed. Thus, the platform support is not necessary for the particular device product company. A special case is when the absence of an enabler is paired with a competing solution in the platform to other device product companies that may not want or be able to implement the application without this support.

Case study findings: The neutral disability scenario occurs rather frequently as the internal application platform developed by the device company includes many features outside the scope of the platform. It can be seen as the result of a beneficial division of responsibilities between the device product company and the platform product company. The competing ability scenario is a natural result of the platform company striving to offer standard solutions for those device developers that refrain from implementing proprietary variants.

Assessment: The neutral disability scenario is generally beneficial to the device company, as competitors gain no advantage through the platform, while a proprietary solution is preferred and possible without an enabler in the platform. The competing ability is most often tolerable to the specific device company although from its point of view, the platform company resources could have been used better. For the platform company, however, this may be a good strategy in the competition with other platform product companies.

Neutral undesired flexibility; Competing undesired flexibility. These special case scenarios of undesired flexibility occur if the device product company does not need an enabler although provided by the platform company. This may occur e.g. if the proprietary solution is replacing a significant part of the subcontracted platform with internally developed application and platform technology. The platform company may in this case offer not only an enabler for proprietary technology add-on to the competing device companies, but also a competing solution supporting direct application realisation.

Case study findings: These scenarios seem to occur rarely as the special relationship between these particular companies ensures that the respective strategies are mostly aligned. However, the business model of the platform company is based on making propositions to competing device vendors, and undesired flexibility as seen from a specific vendor's viewpoint, having proprietary solutions to platform features, is happening at occasions.

Assessment: Neutral undesired flexibility is often acceptable to the device vendor, as the competition situation is not often significantly impacted by an enabler. In some cases competing undesired flexibility is also acceptable, as the device product company finds their own proprietary solution superior to what is available in the platform.

5 Conclusion

The presented results of the collaborative requirements engineering case study includes a framework for assessing compliance scenarios as outcomes of collaboration in platform subcontracting. The framework is based on decisions in upstream and downstream development as well as platform flexibility issues and the outcomes of the development of subsequent releases are taken into account. The main findings of the case study analysis is that the framework is useful as a basis of analysing compliance issues in system platform subcontracting and that the scenarios are relevant in the understanding of collaboration performance. Particular examples of compliance scenarios are discussed and a qualitative assessment is given for each scenario or scenario group.

The intention of the presented framework is to enable continuous assessment of an *ongoing* subcontracting relationship, to complement the existing support for *selecting* subcontractors such as MASS [1]. Process improvement based on prescriptive models such as e.g. CMMI [2] can be complemented with retrospective analysis of past projects and the presented framework can be used to find both positive and negative scenarios. By analysing the frequency of scenarios of the framework and focusing on the reasons behind collaboration outcomes for particular classes of requirements, the aim is to increase collaboration efficiency by focusing on improvements that yield maximal impact.

Future work includes further investigation of how the framework can be utilised in process improvement in subcontracting, through analysis of compliance scenario frequencies and impacts. Analysis of reasons behind change requests similar to [13] but specific for platform subcontracting, may complement this case study findings with more understanding of downstream requirements engineering issues. Non-functional requirements, especially performance and flexibility are of particular interest based on the findings of this case study, and further investigation on how these types of requirements are handled in the collaborative situation is interesting. It would also be interesting to compare the case study findings in the telecom domain with similar case studies in other domains where technology platforms for embedded systems are common, such as the automotive industry.

Acknowledgements. This work is supported by VINNOVA (Swedish Agency for Innovation Systems) within the ITEA project MERLIN. We would like to give special thanks to Lena Karlsson and Dr. Martin Höst for careful reviewing and valuable comments. Special thanks to Niklas Rystedt for valuable input on change requests.

References

1. Assmann, D.; Punter, T. (2004) "Towards partnership in software subcontracting", Journal of Computers in Industry, 54(2):137-150, Elsevier.
2. Chrissis M. B.; Konrad M.; Shrum S. (2003) CMMI: Guidelines for Process Integration and Product Improvement, Addison-Wessley ISBN: 0-321-15496-7.
3. Carlshamre P., Regnell B. (2000) "Requirements Lifecycle Management and Release Planning in Market-Driven Requirements Engineering Processes", Int. Workshop on the Requirements Engineering Process: Innovative Techniques, Models, and Tools to support the RE Process (REP'00), 11th IEEE Conference on Database and Expert Systems Applications (DEXA'00), September 6-8, Greenwich UK, pp. 961-965.
4. Damian, D., Chisan, J., Vaidyanathasamy, L., Pal, Y. (2005) "Requirements Engineering and Downstream Software Development: Findings from a Case Study", Empirical Software Engineering, 10(3): 255-283, Springer.
5. Damian, D. and Zowghi, D. (2003). Requirements Engineering challenges in multi-site software development organizations. Requirements Engineering Journal, 8(3):149-160, Springer.
6. Ebert, C. De Neve, P. (2001). "Surviving Global Software Development", IEEE Software March/April 2001. pp. 62-69.
7. Ebert, C. (2005) "Requirements BEFORE the Requirements: Understanding the Upstream Impact", Proc. 13th IEEE International Conference on Requirements Engineering, Paris, France, pp. 117-124.
8. Fairley, R.E.; Willshire, M.J. (2005) "Iterative Rework: The Good, the Bad, and the Ugly", IEEE Computer, 38(9):34-41.
9. Gorschek, T.; Wohlin, C. (2005) "Requirements Abstraction Model", Requirements Eng Journal, 11:79–101.
10. Hietala, J.; Kontio, J.; Jokinen, J.-P.; Pyysiainen, J. "Challenges of software product companies: results of a national survey in Finland", Proc. 10th International Symposium on Software Metrics, pp. 232-243.

11. Karlsson L., Dahlstedt Å. G., Natt och Dag J., Regnell B., Persson A., (2002) Challenges in Market-Driven Requirements Engineering - an Industrial Interview Study, 8th International Workshop on Requirements Engineering: Foundation for Software Quality (REFSQ'02), September 09-10th, Essen, Germany, pp. 37-49.
12. Lormans, M; van Dijk, H.; van Deursen, A.; Nöcker, E.; de Zeeuw, A. (2004) "Managing Evolving Requirements in an Outsourcing Context: An Industrial Experience Report", Proc. IEEE Int. Workshop on Principles of Software Evolution, Kyoto, Japan, pp. 149-158.
13. Nurmuliani, N.; Zowghi, D.; Powell, S. (2004) "Analysis of requirements volatility during software development life cycle" Proc. IEEE Australian Software Engineering Conference, pp 28-37.
14. Svahnberg, M.; Bosch, J. (1999) "Evolution in software product lines: two cases", Journal of Software Maintenance: Research and Practice, 11(6):391-422, Wiley.

Software Inspections in Practice: Six Case Studies

Sami Kollanus[1] and Jussi Koskinen[2]

Department of Computer Science and Information Systems
P.O. Box 35 (Agora), FI-40014 University of Jyväskylä, Finland
[1]sami.kollanus@jyu.fi, [2]koskinen@cs.jyu.fi

Abstract. Software inspections have been acknowledged as an important method in software engineering, but they are not well applied in practice. This paper discusses the current practices and the related problems based on six case studies in industrial settings. The analysis of inspection practices was organized according to ICMM, which is a model for systematically assessing and improving software inspection process maturity. The sample case organizations used inspections relatively regularly. The involved units are compared and the revealed practices, their characteristics, inspection problems and implications of the study discussed. The main problem areas were non-existent inspection training, limited formality of inspections and immaturity of inspection metrics.

1 Introduction

Since Michael Fagan published his original software inspection method [2] in 1976, inspections have been acknowledged as an important method in software development. Several researchers have reported great savings or improved effectiveness when using inspections [7]. Unfortunately, regardless of the fact, that inspection is known as a useful method within the software engineering research community, it is not widely applied in practice. There also is very little systematic research conducted, attempting to study the real state of the industrial practices. There are, however, some relevant experience reports. Johnson [3] refers in his paper to an informal survey, where 80% of the 90 respondents practiced inspections irregularly or not at all in their organizations. Ciolkowski *et al.* [1] conducted a survey, which aimed to study the practice of any kinds of software reviews. Based on 226 responses, they also concluded that reviews are irregularly used in software industry.

This paper reports six case studies, which were conducted in organizations producing commercial software. We will later sometimes refer to this set of studied units simply as *case units*. The focus of the paper is to identify strengths and weaknesses in inspection subpractices in the units by using *Inspection Capability Maturity Model* (ICMM) [5]. Since it was necessary to understand the whole organizational context of applying software inspections, data was gathered via interviews. There is an earlier study [6], which provided preliminary problem analysis based on data from two case studies. This paper extends that study by a larger set of involved organizations, by providing information regarding the state of the covered inspection processes, and by gathering discussion concerning the implications.

J. Münch and M. Vierimaa (Eds.): PROFES 2006, LNCS 4034, pp. 377 – 382, 2006.

2 Inspection Capability Maturity Model

This section briefly introduces Inspection Capability Maturity Model (ICMM) [5], which is used in this paper as a framework in analyzing existing inspection practices in the involved organizations. ICMM supports: 1) inspection process maturity assessment, and 2) inspection process improvements. It resembles the internationally well known and well established CMM [9] model, but focuses on the assessment of the maturity of inspection practices instead of the whole software development process. Only the ICMM-levels 2-3 were used in this study, because the upper levels were not currently relevant in the case units.

The second level is called 'Practicing level' in ICMM. It requires an organization to practice inspections regularly. It includes the following specific *process areas*:

P1. *Requirement Inspections.* Requirements have to be inspected in organization's every project. Inspections have to include preparation and reporting.
P2. *Design Inspections.* At least the system architecture description and some other central design documents should be inspected.
P3. *Training for Leaders.* Training should be provided at least for inspection leaders.

The third, 'Defined level' requires an organization to have a well defined inspection process and it has focus on inspection effectiveness. The required process areas are the following:

P4. *Test Case Inspections.* This process area requires inspection of test cases.
P5. *Code Inspections.* The most important parts of the code must be inspected in every project. In addition, project plan should define, which documents are required to be inspected within the project.
P6. *Defined Process.* Inspection process must be defined and documented.
P7. *Training for all.* This includes training for all relevant stakeholders.
P8. *Customized Material.* Inspection support materials must be created and customized for the organization. The material may include for example standards, rules, checklists and scenarios.
P9. *Data Collection and Use.* Inspection data should be collected and used to monitor, control and improve the inspection process.
P10. *Organizational Policy.* There must be clear organizational policy and management's commitment to the inspection practices.
P11. *Assigned Responsibilities.* This refers to the formal responsibilities which concern the inspections.
P12. *Allocated Resources.* This refers to the formal allocation of resources for the inspections.

3 Data Gathering

These case studies had two main goals related to the involved organizations: 1) to find out *how inspections* (or less formal reviews [8]) *are practiced*, and 2) to find out *what are the faced inspection related problems*. The case studies were conducted in six software supplier units within five Finnish companies. These companies produce and tailor software products for their customer organizations. The sample represented different kind of units. All invited units participated to the study. Interviews, see e.g. [4], were used as a means of data gathering in order to reveal the actual way of practicing inspections and the possibly related problems. We did have the following main assumptions: 1) there are some serious problems in the inspection processes, since regardless of their theoretical importance, they are evidently relatively rarely applied in software industry, 2) defects are caused by poor process maturity level in terms of ICMM, 3) problems may concentrate on some process areas which need to be identified within each case unit. The organizations were asked to find proper interviewees on different organizational levels. The case studies included three interviews in each involved unit. The total number of interviewees was 18. All interviewees were experts (*quality managers*, *project managers* and *software developers*) with average 11 years of SE-experience. In the beginning interviewees were asked to estimate in scale from 1 to 5 (5 is the best), the quality of the applied inspection practices. First main part of the interviews charted the currently applied inspection practices. This part was mainly based on ICMM. Another main part focused on the experienced inspection problems.

4 Results

This section presents the results. The six industrial units were compared based on ICMM. The presented observations, characterizations of the process areas, comparisons of the units, recommendations regarding SPI, and identification of the implications for research regarding inspections are the main results of this study. Results of the case unit comparisons are summarized in Table 1. It lists the required process areas from ICMM and evaluation results from each of the units (U1…U6). The process areas are evaluated as fully implemented (F), partially implemented (P) or not implemented (-). Additionally, there is an average subjective score (scale 1-5, where 5 is the best), which the interviewees gave to their current inspection practices.

The applied inspection practices and levels of satisfaction varied a lot in the case units. In the best case, based on the coverage of the process areas, inspections were well defined on general level and all documents were inspected in every project. However, as can be seen from Table 1 even in the best cases only about half of the listed requirements from ICMM levels 2 and 3 were fully satisfied. In two of the case organizations there is still some work to do to get inspections run regularly. This means that: 1) it appears to be relatively hard to fully achieve even the ICMM levels 2&3, and 2) there were real gaps in the maturity profile of the case units. Due to the problems in the inspection processes, the performed inspections probably were less effective than they should have been.

An interesting finding was that the subjective estimates about inspection performance do not correlate at all with the ICMM profiles. For example interviewees in units U1 and U2 gave the same average score, but they were opposites in the comparison, achieved based on ICMM. Another example is that units U4 and U5 had almost identical profiles, but interviewees in U4 were somewhat more satisfied to their inspections. There may be several reasons for the different scores. For example, some interviewees may have felt comfortable with the applied informal practices, which however do not satisfy ICMM requirements. Also general knowledge about inspections appeared to affect the scores. Higher knowledge usually caused more critical attitude. Regardless of the different subjective estimates, all the case units saw many improvement needs in their inspection practices.

Table 1. Level and comparison of the inspection process maturity as applied in the case units

Process areas \ Units	**U1**	**U2**	**U3**	**U4**	**U5**	**U6**
Level 2						
P1. Requirement inspections	P	F	F	F	F	P
P2. Design inspections	P	F	P	F	F	P
P3. Training for leaders	-	-	-	-	-	-
Level 3						
P4. Test case inspections	P	F	P	F	F	P
P5. Code inspections	-	P	-	P	P	-
P6. Defined process	-	F	F	F	P	F
P7. Training all	-	-	-	-	-	-
P8. Customized material	-	P	P	-	-	-
P9. Data collection and use	-	-	-	-	-	-
P10. Organizational policy	-	F	F	F	F	-
P11. Assigned responsibilities	P	P	P	P	P	P
P12. Allocated resources	-	P	-	-	-	-
Levels 2-3: Subjective process quality estimate (Avg., scale: 1-5)	2.8	2.8	3.3	3.0	2.7	2.0

Table legend: F means fully implemented and P partially implemented process area.

We also analyzed the qualitative data from the interviews to understand organizations and possible trends in their inspection practices. We regarded the following findings as the most interesting ones:

- All the case units review more or less formally and regularly requirements, but it is quite rare in the units to review any parts of code. This trend was not so clear in the survey by Ciolkowski *et al.* [1]. In their study 42% of the respondents reviewed requirements and 28% code regularly.
- Surprisingly, there was not any kind of training concerning inspections in the case organizations. In addition, motivating people to carefully read others' work products was one of the biggest challenges in all units regardless of their maturity levels. So, training with primary goals to motivate and increase general knowledge could be recommended for every case organization.
- Only one unit (U1) did not have any kind of process documentation about inspections. However, the interviewees in the other units knew quite little about their process. Many of them could only guess what the process definitions include. This was one of the findings, which emphasize the need for training.
- Inspection support material was one of the really weak process areas in the case organizations. Two units had some kind of checklists for inspections, but even they

did not apply those lists in practice and some interviewees did not know anything about the checklists.

- None of the case organizations collected inspection data systematically. Inspection report (in case that it was written) was a text document in all case units and it's information was not further gathered or used within the units. Moreover, no one appeared to be interested in that data.
- All case organizations have a quality manager or some similar kind of role, responsible of quality, but they did very little to monitor and control inspection practices. So, the control is left to the project managers. This often appeared to lead to the situation, where inspections are properly practised only when it is a customer requirement.
- Only one of the case organizations usually allocated distinct resources for inspections and it was done only roughly and only on project level. If resources are not allocated specifically for inspections, the employees may feel they have to do something "productive" instead of inspections.

5 Discussion and Conclusions

This paper reported current inspection practices in six case units in software industry. ICMM served as an organizing framework for systematically comparing the units and evaluating inspection processes and process areas. It fulfilled that task quite well and helped to identify the maturity levels and central problems of the inspection practices. However, it should be noted that ICMM is still under development. The inspection capability and focus of the analysis was on the 12 process areas of ICMM levels 2-3. Sample case units are only starting their systematic improvements of software inspections. Therefore the results should not be generalized beyond those levels. Nevertheless, the observations received are useful in characterizing the pitfalls of inspection process improvement on these levels in industrial settings.

The case organizations had weaknesses in their inspection practices, especially related to the ways in which inspections are performed, their focus areas, training related to inspections, and definition and gathering of proper metrics as a basis for systematic and continued software inspection process improvements. The study supported our main assumptions. Typical practical problems of applying inspections appeared to be serious. Therefore, the quality of inspection processes should be improved. However, especially the following problems make this harder. 1) The general knowledge about inspections, defined processes and related organizational policies was very low and there was no inspection training. 2) Formality of the applied inspections was limited. 3) Inspection data was not collected and therefore there were no control over inspections. All these findings suggest that the case units might not have fully understood the benefits which inspections probably would provide for their software development processes if they were organized effectively.

Lack of inspection training was the most common weakness in every case unit. General knowledge about inspections appeared to be quite limited. Almost all interviewees agreed on the need for more formal inspections. There are differences in the inspection focus areas, coverage, and their effectiveness within the organizations. One clear weakness was lack of metrics and process control. Metrics would at least give guidance for how to achieve quality [10]. Objective inspection effectiveness could not be formally studied because of that lack of proper metrics. In addition, inspections do not seem to be an intuitively pleasant part of software engineers' work. There also were some interesting similarities and differences between this study and the survey by Ciolkowski *et al.* [1]. The case organizations of our study appeared to review requirements and designs much more regularly. However, the respondents in that earlier survey reviewed code more regularly. Another identified issue was that customer interest on inspections correlates positively with the level of discipline of conducting inspection practices by the software supplier organization. Nevertheless, customers are rarely interested in very technical documentation.

The next SPI-step is to conduct inspections systematically and to improve the effectiveness of the current inspection practices. ICMM and similar models can support the SPI needed in these cases, but the identified problems need to be identified and resolved casewise. This study has its rightful place among the empirical case studies in this relatively scarcely studied area. Each conducted case study helps in its part to form the "bigger picture" of the industrial practices, characteristics of the needed processes, and problems of the software inspection area. Problems of inspection practices in different kinds of organizations could be studied further.

References

1. Ciolkowski, M., Laitenberger, O., Biffl, S.: Software Reviews, the State of the Practice. IEEE Software, Vol. **20**, 6 (2003) 46-51.
2. Fagan, M.E.,: Design and Code Inspection to Reduce Errors in Program Development, IBM Systems Journal, Vol. **15**, 3 (1976) 182-211.
3. Johnson, P.M.: Reengineering Inspection. Comm. of the ACM, Vol. **41**, 2 (1998) 49-52.
4. Kitchenham, B.A., Pfleeger, S.L., Pickard, L.M., Jones, P.W., Hoaglin, D.C., Emam, K.E., Rosenberg, J.: Preliminary Guidelines for Empirical Research in Software Engineering. IEEE Transactions on Software Engineering, Vol. **28**, 8 (2002) 721-734.
5. Kollanus, S.: ICMM – Inspection Capability Maturity Model. Proc. of the 2nd IASTED International Conference on Software Engineering (IASTED-SE'2005), ACTA Press, Innsbruck, Austria (2005) 372-377.
6. Kollanus, S.: A Problem Based Approach to Inspection Improvement? Proc. of the 6th Int. Conf. on Product Focused Software Process Improvement (PROFES'2005), Springer LNCS Vol. **3547**, Oulu, Finland, (2005), 429-442.
7. Laitenberger, O., DeBaud, J.-M.: An Encompassing Life-Cycle Centric Survey of Software Inspection. Journal of Systems and Software, Vol. **50**, 1 (2000) 5-31.
8. Sauer, C., Ross, J., Land, L., Yetton, P.: The Effectiveness of Software Development Technical Reviews: A Behaviorally Motivated Program of Research. IEEE Transactions on Software Engineering, Vol. **26**, 1 (2000) 1-14.
9. SEI: Capability Maturity Model Integration, version 1.1. Software Engineering Institute (2002) <URL: http://www.sei.cmu.edu/cmm/>
10. Voas, J.: Software Quality's Eight Greatest Myths. IEEE Software, Vol. **16**, 5 (1999) 118-120.

Productivity of Test Driven Development: A Controlled Experiment with Professionals

Gerardo Canfora[1], Aniello Cimitile[1], Felix Garcia[2], Mario Piattini[2], and Corrado Aaron Visaggio[1]

[1] RCOST- Research Centre on Software Technology
University of Sannio, Italy
{canfora, cimitile, visaggio}@unisannio.it

[2] ALARCOS Research Group- Information Systems and Technologies Department
UCLM-Soluziona Research and Development Institute
University of Castilla-La Manch Paseo de la Universidad, 4 – 13071 Ciudad Real, Spain
{Felix.Garcia, Mario.Piattini}@uclm.es

Abstract. With the growing interest for Extreme Programming, test driven development (TDD) has been increasingly investigated, and several experiments have been executed with the aim of understanding if and when it is preferable to the traditional practice of testing the code after having written it (named TAC in the paper). However, the research concerning TDD is at its beginning and the body of knowledge is largely immature. This paper discusses an experiment carried out within a Spanish software company with the aim of comparing productivity in TDD and TAC.

1 Introduction

Test driven development (TDD) belongs to the set of the extreme programming [1] practices, even if it might be adopted in any kind of software development process. According to TDD, unit testing results drive code development. As a first step, the developer defines the classes of the system in terms of public interfaces. Then, the test suite for each class is written: the suite must contain all the tests helpful for verifying that each method in the class exposes the correct behavior. Finally, the body of each method is completed throughout an iterative process, consisting of two activities: to execute the tests and, when some of them fail, to change the code in order to remove the bugs that potentially caused the failure. The process ends when all the tests succeed. TDD is widely considered a practice of code development rather than code testing, although the role of unit testing is relevant for defining the design strategy to adopt. TDD might be considered also an alternative to the traditional approach of testing the code after having written it, named 'test after coding' (TAC) in this paper. Recently some researchers investigated TDD: some experiments [2], [4], [7], and [9] produced evidence about the improvement of code quality achieved with TDD; however, some authors [2], and [6] did not find particular differences between TDD and TAC. There is not a wide consensus about the relationship between TDD and productivity, despite several studies obtained evidence that TDD is able to increase the productivity with respect to TAC [3], and [4]. Since both the practices involve

J. Münch and M. Vierimaa (Eds.): PROFES 2006, LNCS 4034, pp. 383 – 388, 2006.

coding and testing in a tightly interleaved process, we aim at understanding differences in the productivity in the two practices. We have carried out an experiment with the collaboration of professionals working in a Spanish Software Company, aiming at meeting the following research goal: **Analyse** *Test Driven Development and Test After Coding* **With the purpose of** *comparing them* **With respect to** *productivity* **From the point of view of** *the developers* **In the context of** *a group of professionals.* The work comprises two research questions:

R.1 *Is test driven development more productive than TAC from the viewpoint of testing?* In this case, productivity is intended as the time needed to write and execute assertions.

R.2 *How is the time employed in the two practices?* In order to have a deep insight of the two practices, we try to understand if the increasing of productivity means reducing the time for developing or for coding.

The paper proceeds as follows: section 2 describes the experimental design; data are analyzed in section 3; and, finally, section 4 draws the conclusions.

2 The Experiment Characterization

The experiment aimed at testing the following null hypotheses:

$\mathbf{H_{01}}$ **:** there is no difference in the productivity between test driven development and test after coding (helps to answer the research question R.1).

$\mathbf{H_{02}}$ **:** there is no correlation between productivity and the number of assertions in test driven development (helps to answer the research question R.2).

$\mathbf{H_{03}}$ **:** there is no correlation between the productivity and the number of assertions in test after coding (helps to answer the research question R.2).

The experiment was carried out in the facilities of the company Soluziona Software Factory located in Ciudad Real (Spain). The variables used in the data analysis are described in Table 1.

Table 1. Variables used in the experiment

Variable	Description
MeanTPA	*Mean Time per Assertion.* It is the time required to write and execute an assertion in the test suite. In both the practices the time for executing the assertion includes also the changing in the code, suggested by the failures of the test. It is assumed as an indicator of the *productivity.*
AssertTot	*Total Number of Assertions.* It is the total amount of assertions in the project. It is an indicator of the *quality of test* in the overall project. The greater is the number of assertions the greater is the number of aspects of the code which are tested.
MeanAPM	*Mean Assertion per Method.* It is the mean number of assertions written for a method. It is an indicator of the *accuracy of testing.* A high value of this metrics could indicate that all the methods of the classes received the same attention in the test.

28 employees of the company took part to the experiment: they have a BsC in Computer Science and a wide knowledge in software programming and modeling (UML, databases, etc.). The subjects were required to implement two assignments in two different runs, one assignment per run. The programming language was java, while ECLIPSE [10] and JUnit [11] were chosen as development environments. Subjects received a form for each run, which they had to fulfill with the information about the time and the assertions written for each assignment.

The experiment consisted of two runs; each run lasted five hours. Every subject implemented both the requirements and performed both the practices but in two different runs. The experimental design is illustrated in Table 2.

Table 2. The Experimental Design

	RUN I		RUN II	
Subjects	Treatment	Assignment	Treatment	Assignment
S_1	TDD	A1	TAC	A2
S_2	TAC	A1	TDD	A2
S_i	TDD	A2	TAC	A1
S_n	TAC	A2	TDD	A1

3 Data Analysis

Figure 1 compares the performances of the subjects when using the two practices, TAC and TDD.

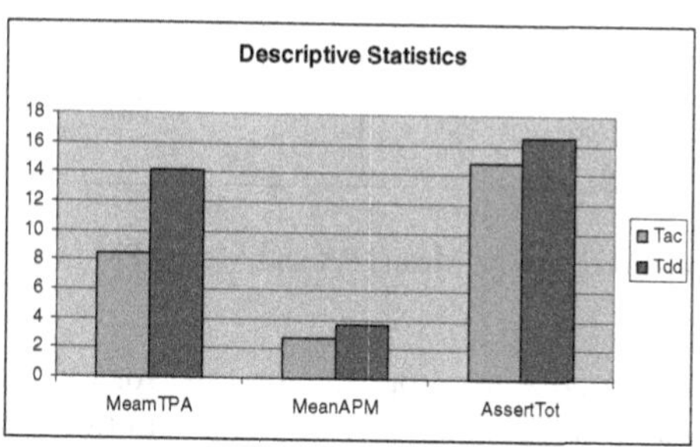

Fig. 1. Performances of the experimental samples

The data suggests that differences between the two practices exist. TAC reduces the mean time spent for each assertion (MeanTPA) , thus it is more productive than TDD; conversely, TDD increases the density of assertions per method (MeanAPM) and the total number of assertions (AssertTot); thus, TDD might determine more accuracy and quality in the testing than TAC. On one hand, the iterative approach of TDD requires more time than TAC in order to deliver a method. On the other hand, since the developer writes the tests before the code, greater attention is devoted to testing and, consequently, the developer increases the number of assertions. Table 3 shows that the difference in productivity is statistically significant; Mann-Whitney test was used and the p-level was fixed at 0.05. Analysis of correlation can help answer the research question R.2, and understand more precisely how the additional time in TDD is employed.

Table 3. Tests of Hypothesis H_{01}

Testing	Rank Sum (a)	Rank Sum (b)	p-level
MeanTPA (TDD)-MeanTPA (TAC)	846.0000	585.000	**0.0037374**

Fig.2 shows that in TDD the MeanAPM decreases when the MeanTPA increases; this might be due to the iterative process of TDD which forces the developer to modify recursively the code of a method until the correspondent tests do not succeed. The tests are defined before the code and the additional time is mainly used to improve the code rather than the tests.

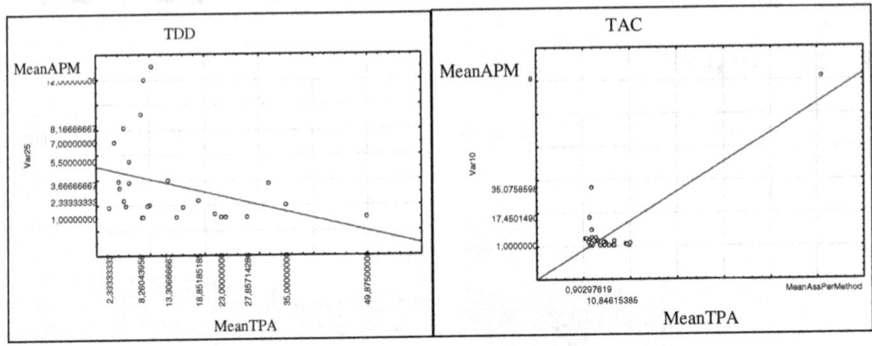

Fig. 2. Correlation between MeanTPA and MeanAPM in TDD and TAC

In TAC the opposite phenomenon appears: the time for writing assertions increases with the number of assertions. This indicates that the additional time is used mainly to improve the test cases for each method, by defining further assertions, rather than to modify the code: as a matter of fact the developer writes the tests only after having defined the code. Fig. 3 shows that in both the techniques the mean time for assertions determines a decrement in the total number of assertions. This is explainable by deriving the variables with respect to the MeanTPA variable.

If we consider that AssertTot= (number of Methods*MeanAPM), then:

d(AssertTot)/d(MeanTPA)=(MeanAPM)*d(number of Methods)/d(MeanTPA)
+ (number of Methods)*d(MeanAPM)/d(MeanTPA).

If d(AssertTot)/d(MeanTPA) < 0, then:

- in TAC d(MeanAPM)/d(MeanTPA) > 0, and consequently d(number of Methods)/d(MeanTPA) should be negative. This means that to increase the time spent for the assertions reduces the number of methods, which is an indicator of modularity: the additional time is not used to increase the number of methods in the code;
- in TDD d(MeanAPM)/d(MeanTPA) <0, thus it is not possible inferring the sign of d(number of Methods)/d(MeanTPA). It is possible to deduce only that if it is positive, it grows slower than the absolute value of d(MeanAPM)/d(MeanTPA). In TDD, if the additional time is dedicated to increase modularity (number of methods), this is smaller than the increasing of assertions density, anyway: TDD advantages the testing aspect.

Table 4 shows that there is statistical evidence for the correlation of all the discussed cases. Spearman's method was applied for testing hypotheses because the sample data set is not normally distributed and the p-level was fixed at 0.05.

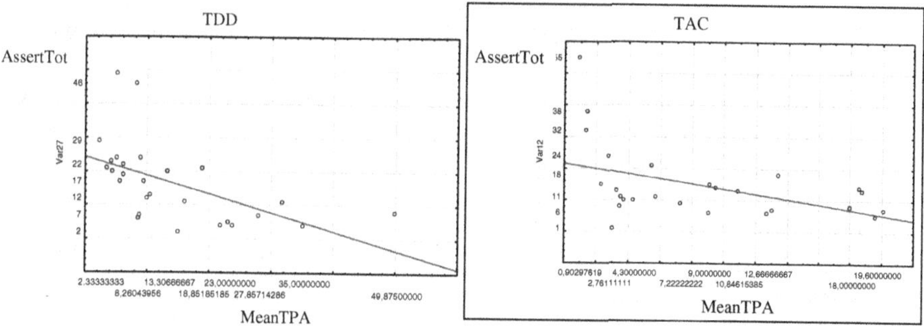

Fig. 3. Correlation between MeanTPA and AssertTot in TDD and TAC

Table 4. Statistical Tests of Hypotheses H_{02} and H_{03}

Correlation	Valid N	Spearman R	T(N-2)	p-level
MeanTPA-MeanAPM [TDD]	27	-0.442272	-2.46561	**0.0208**
MeanTPA-MeanAPM [TAC]	31	-0.387853	-2.26603	**0.003108**
MeanTPA-AssetTot [TDD]	27	0.549229	3.286153	**0.00300**
MeanTPA-AssetTot [TAC]	27	0.777829	6.188211	**0.00002**

4 Conclusions

This paper discusses the results of an experiment carried out in a Spanish Software Company. The research aimed at comparing productivity in test driven development and testing after coding. It emerged that: TAC reduces the time for writing assertions and modifying the code, according to the feedback of the tests; TDD increases the total number of assertions and the density of assertions per method, which could be indicators of unit testing quality and accuracy; and, finally, the additional time while testing is mainly exploited to improve code in TDD, whereas in TAC it is used to improve the testing strategy. In both the practices, the additional time is never used to increase the number of methods, which is indicator of modularity.

Acknowledgements

We would like to thank professionals of Soluziona Software Factory for their active participation and collaboration. This research has been partially funded by the projects: MAS (Dirección General de Investigación del Ministerio de Ciencia y Tecnología, TIC 2003-02737-C02-02), MECENAS (Junta de Comunidades de Castilla-La Mancha, Consejería de Educación y Ciencia, PAI06-0024-2494) and FAMOSO (Ministerio de Industria, Turismo y Comercio, FIT-340000-2005-161).

Bibliography

[1] Beck K. Extreme Programming explained: Embrace change. Addison-Wesley: Reading, Massachusetts, 1999.

[2] Edwards S. Using test-driven development in the classroom: Providing students with automatic, concrete feedback on performance. *Proc. of the Int'l Conference on Education and Information Systems: Technologies and Applications*, EISTA'03, Orlando, Florida, USA, 2003.

[3] Erdogmus, H. and Morisio, M. On the effectiveness of test-first approach to programming. *IEEE Transactions on Software Engineering*, 31(1), 2005, IEEE CS Press), pp. 1-12.

[4] George B. and Williams L. A structured experiment of test-driven development, *Information and Software Technology*, 46(5), 2004, Elsevier,pp.337–342.

[5] Geras A., Smith M. and Miller J. A Prototype Empirical Evaluation of Test Driven Development. *Proc. of the 10th Inter'l Symposium on Software Metrics (METRICS'04)*, Sidney, Australia, 2004, IEEE CS.

[6] Muller M. and Hagner O. Experiment about Test-first programming, *Proc. of Empirical Assessment in Software Engineering*, Keele, UK, 2002.

[7] Pankur M., Ciglaric M., Trampus M. and Vidmar T. Towards empirical evaluation of test-driven development in a university environment. Proc. of EUROCON 2003. Computer as a Tool. Ljublijana, Slovenia, 2003,IEEE CS Press.

[8] Sjoberg D., Anda B., Arisholm E., Dyba T., Jorgensen M., Karahasanovic A., Koren E. and Vokác M. Conducting Realistic Experiments in Software Engineering. *Proc. of the 2002 Int'l Symposium on Empirical Software Engineering (ISESE'02)*, Nara, Japan, 2002, IEEE CS Press.

[9] Williams L., Maximilien E., and Vouk M. Test-driven development as a defect-reduction practice. *Proc. of the 14th IEEE Int'l Symposium on Software Reliability Engineering*, Denver, Colorado, USA, 2003, IEEE CS Press.

[10] The ECLIPSE IDE. Available in http://www.eclipse.org/

[11] The JUnit Testing Framework. Available in http://www.junit.org

Results and Experiences from an Empirical Study of Fault Reports in Industrial Projects

Jon Arvid Børretzen and Reidar Conradi

Department of Computer and Information Science,
Norwegian University of Science and Technology (NTNU),
NO-7491 Trondheim, Norway
borretze@idi.ntnu.no, conradi@idi.ntnu.no

Abstract. Faults introduced into systems during development are costly to fix, and especially so for business-critical systems. These systems are developed using common development practices, but have high requirements for dependability. This paper reports on an ongoing investigation of fault reports from Norwegian IT companies, where the aim is to seek a better understanding on faults that have been found during development and how this may affect the quality of the system. Our objective in this paper is to investigate the fault profiles of four business-critical commercial projects to explore if there are differences in the way faults appear in different systems. We have conducted an empirical study by collecting fault reports from several industrial projects, comparing findings from projects where components and reuse have been core strategies with more traditional development projects. Findings show that some specific fault types are generally dominant across reports from all projects, and that some fault types are rated as more severe than others.

1 Introduction

Producing high quality software is an important goal for most software developers. The notion of software quality is not trivial, different stakeholders will have different views on what software quality is. In the Business-Critical Software (BUCS) project [1] we are seeking to develop a set of methods to improve support for analysis, development, operation, and maintenance of business-critical systems. These are systems that we expect and hope will run correctly because of the possibly severe effects of failure, even if the consequences are mainly of an economic nature. In these systems, software quality is important, and the main target for developers will be to make systems that operate correctly all the time [1]. One important issue in developing these kinds of systems is to remove any possible causes for failure, which may lead to wrong operation of the system.

The study presented here investigated fault reports from two software projects using components and reuse strategies, and two projects using a more traditional development process. It compares the fault profiles of the reuse-intensive projects with the other two, in several dimensions; Fault type, fault severity and location of fault.

J. Münch and M. Vierimaa (Eds.): PROFES 2006, LNCS 4034, pp. 389 – 394, 2006.

2 Previous Studies on Software Faults and Fault Implications

Software quality is a notion that encompasses a great number of attributes. When speaking about business-critical systems, the critical quality attribute is often experienced as the dependability of the system. According to Littlewood et al. [2], dependability is a software quality attribute that encompasses several other attributes, the most important are reliability, availability, safety and security.

Faults in the software lessen the software's quality, and by reducing the number of faults introduced during development you can improve the quality of software. *Faults* are potential flaws in a software system, that later may be activated to produce an error. An *error* is the execution of a fault, leading to a failure. A *failure* results in erroneous external behaviour, system state or data state. Remedies known for errors and failures are to limit the consequences of a failure, in order to resume service, but studies have shown that this kind of late protection is more expensive than removing the faults before they are introduced into the code [3]. Faults are also known as *defects* or *bugs*, and a more extensive concept is *anomalies*, which is used in the IEEE 1044 standard [4]. Orthogonal Defect Classification – ODC – is a way of studying defects in software systems [5, 6, 7, 8]. ODC is a scheme to capture the semantics of each software fault quickly.

It has been debated if faults can be tied to reliability in a cause-effect relationship. Some papers like [6, 8] indicate that this is valid, while others like [9] are more critical. Still, reducing the number of faults will make the system less prone to failure, so by removing faults without adding new ones, there is a good case for the system reliability increasing. This is called "reliability-growth models", and is discussed by Hamlet in [9]. Avizienis et al. states [10] that fault prevention aim to provide the ability to deliver a service that can be trusted. Hence, preventing faults and reducing their numbers and severity in a system, the quality of the system can be improved in the area of dependability.

3 Research Design

Research questions. Initially we want to find which types of faults that are most frequent, and if there are some parts of the systems that have more faults than others:

RQ1: *Which types of faults are most typical for the different software parts?*
When we know which types of faults dominate and where these faults appear in the systems, we can choose to concentrate on the most serious ones in order to identify the most important issues to target in improvement work:

RQ2: *Are certain types of faults considered to be more severe than others by the developers?*

Research method. This study is based on data mining, where the data consists of fault reports we have received from four commercial projects. The investigation has mostly been a bottom-up process, because of the initial uncertainty about the available data from potential participants. After establishing a dialogue with the projects, and acquiring the fault reports, our initial research questions and goals were altered accordingly.

The metrics used. The metrics have been chosen based on what we wanted to investigate and on what data turned out to be available from the projects participating in the study. The frequency number of *detected faults* is an indirect metric, attained by counting the number of faults of a type or for a system part etc. The metrics used directly from the data in the reports are type, severity and location of the fault.

3.1 Fault Categories

There are several taxonomies for fault types, two examples are the ones used in the IEEE 1044 standard [4] and in a variant of the Orthogonal Defect Classification (ODC) scheme [6]. The fault types used in *this study* is shown in Table 1. They have been derived by using the existing data material in the reports, combined with two taxonomies found in literature, IEEE 1044 and ODC.

Categorization of faults in this investigation has been performed partly by the projects themselves and completed by us as a part of this investigation, based on the fault reports' textual description and partial categorization. Also, grading the faults' consequences upon the system and system environment enables fault severities to be defined. All severity grading has been done by the fault reporters in the projects.

Table 1. Fault types used in this study

Fault types		
Assignment fault	Functional fault - logic	Missing data
Checking fault	Functional fault - state	Missing functionality
Data fault	GUI fault	Missing value
Documentation fault	I/O fault	Performance fault
Environment fault	Interface fault	Wrong functionality called
Functional fault - computation	Memory fault	Wrong value used

3.2 Data Collection

The data sample. We contacted over 40 different companies that we believed had relevant projects we could study. In the end four projects fit our criteria and were willing to proceed with the study. The reasons for the low participation rate among the contacted companies were most likely issues like skepticism towards releasing sensitive information, lack of organized effort in fault handling and lack of resources. Table 2 contains information about the participating projects.

Table 2. Information about the participating projects

Project	A	B	C	D
Project description	Financial system.	Real-time embedded system.	Public administration application.	Task management system.
Domain	Finance	Security	Publ. administration	Publ. administration
Platform	MVS, OS/2	VxWorks	J2EE, EJB	J2EE
# reports	52	360	1684	379
Dev. effort	~27400 hours	~ 32000 hours	~17600 hours	2165 hours

Note that projects C and D have been developed using modern practices, including component-based development, while projects A and B have been developed using more traditional development practices.

4 Research Results

RQ1 – Which types of faults are most typical?

To answer RQ1, we look at the distribution of the fault type categories for the projects, shown in Table 3. For projects C and D, we see that functional logic faults are dominant, with 49% and 58% of the faults for those projects. Functional logic faults are also a large part of the faults in projects A and B.

In the same manner, the distribution of faults with a severity rating of "high" is shown in Table 4. Functional logic faults are still dominant in projects C and D, with 45% and 69% of the faults, respectively. Project A is a special case here, as only one single fault was reported to be of high severity.

Table 3. Distribution of all faults in fault type categories

	Project			
Fault type	A	B	C	D
Assignment	7 %	4 %	1 %	1 %
Checking	4 %	3 %	2 %	1 %
Data	4 %	6 %	5 %	4 %
Documentation	0 %	1 %	6 %	3 %
Environment	0 %	2 %	1 %	0 %
Funct. comp.	13 %	1 %	1 %	0 %
Funct. logic	20 %	29 %	49 %	58 %
Funct. state	0 %	25 %	3 %	5 %
GUI	2 %	8 %	8 %	7 %
I/O	0 %	2 %	1 %	0 %
Interface	0 %	4 %	0 %	0 %
Memory	0 %	1 %	0 %	0 %
Missing data	2 %	0 %	1 %	2 %
Missing funct.	13 %	8 %	8 %	3 %
Missing value	4 %	1 %	1 %	1 %
Performance	0 %	1 %	3 %	1 %
Wrong funct.	0 %	1 %	2 %	1 %

Table 4. Distribution of high severity faults in fault type categories

	Project			
Fault type	A	B	C	D
Assignment	100 %	1 %	0 %	0 %
Data	0 %	6 %	15 %	4 %
Documentation	0 %	0 %	2 %	0 %
Environment	0 %	4 %	5 %	0 %
Funct. logic	0 %	19 %	45 %	69 %
Funct. state	0 %	36 %	8 %	9 %
GUI	0 %	10 %	2 %	0 %
I/O	0 %	1 %	5 %	0 %
Interface	0 %	3 %	0 %	0 %
Memory	0 %	3 %	0 %	2 %
Missing data	0 %	0 %	2 %	4 %
Missing funct.	0 %	7 %	2 %	4 %
Missing value	0 %	1 %	2 %	0 %
Performance	0 %	3 %	9 %	0 %
Wrong funct.	0 %	0 %	0 %	2 %
Wrong value	0 %	6 %	6 %	4 %

When looking at the distribution of faults, especially for the high severity faults, we see that two categories of dominate the picture, "Functional logic" and "Functional state". We also see that for all faults, "GUI" faults have a large share (around 8% for projects B, C, D) of the reports, while for the high severity faults the share of GUI faults are strongly reduced in projects C and D to 2% and 0% respectively.

RQ2 – Are certain types of faults considered to be more severe?

To answer RQ2, we need to look at the number of "high" severity rated faults for different fault categories. Figure 1 shows the percentage of high severity faults found in some fault categories for three of the projects. Project A is left out because of having only one high severity fault reported.

From Figure 1, we see that some fault types seem to be judged as more severe than others. In the projects that do report them, "Memory fault" stands out as a high severity type of fault. For Projects C and D, "GUI faults" are not judged to be very severe, while Project B rates them in line with other fault types. We also see that Project B has generally rated more of their faults as being highly severe than Projects C and D.

By comparing the two projects C and D, which had employed reuse strategies in development, with the other two projects, there is no evidence that development with reuse has had any significant effects on fault distribution or severity.

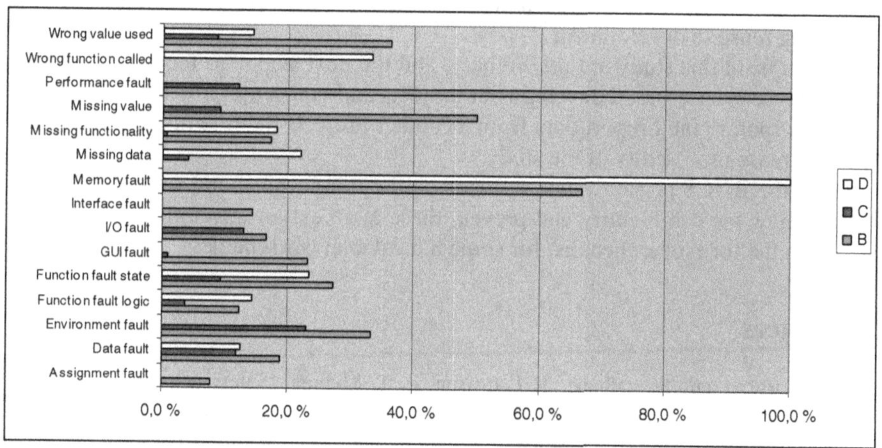

Fig. 1. Percentage of high severity faults in some fault categories

5 Discussion

A major issue when doing the analysis of the data collected was the heterogeneity of the data. These are four different companies where data collection has not been coordinated beforehand, and as each company used their own proprietary fault report system, no standards for reporting was followed. Another issue was cases of missing data in reports, e.g. missing information about fault location. Because the reports have been used for development rather than for research purposes, the developers have not always entered all data into the reports. A final issue was incompatibility between fault reports for one of the projects and other information concerning the project. No satisfactory link between the functional and structural modules was available in project D. This prevented us from separating the reused parts from the rest of the system, and hindered a valid study of comparing reused to non-reused system parts at this time.

Concerning validity, the most serious threats to **external validity** are the small number of projects under investigation and that the chosen projects may also not necessarily be the most typical. As for **conclusion validity,** one possible threat is low reliability of measures, because of some missing data or parts of the data.

6 Conclusion and Future Work

This paper has presented some preliminary results of an investigation on fault reports in industrial projects. The results answer our two questions:

RQ1: *Which types of faults are most typical for the different software parts?* - Looking at all faults in all projects, "functional logic" faults were the dominant fault type. For high severity faults, "functional logic" and "functional state" faults were dominant.

RQ2: *Are certain types of faults considered to be more severe than others?* -We have seen that some fault types are rated more severe than others, for instance "Memory fault", while the fault type "GUI fault" was rated as less severe for the two projects employing reuse in development.

Results from this study are preliminary, and the next step is to focus on the differences between reuse-based development projects and non-reuse projects. We will also try to incorporate fault report data from 2-3 other projects into the investigation in order to increase the validity of the study.

Later, the BUCS project wants to focus on the most typical and serious faults, and describe how we can identify and prevent these at an earlier development stage. This may be in the form of a checklist for some hazard analysis scheme.

References

1. J. A. Børretzen; T. Stålhane; T. Lauritsen; P. T. Myhrer, "Safety activities during early software project phases". *Proceedings, Norwegian Informatics Conference*, 2004
2. B. Littlewood; L. Strigini, "Software reliability and dependability: a roadmap", *Proceedings of the Conference on The Future of Software Engineering,* Limerick, Ireland, 2000, Pages: 175 - 188
3. N. Leveson, *Safeware: System safety and computers,* Addison-Wesley, Boston, 1995
4. IEEE Standard Classification for Software Anomalies, IEEE Std 1044-1993, December 2, 1993
5. K. Bassin; P. Santhanam, "Managing the maintenance of ported, outsourced, and legacy software via orthogonal defect classification", *Proceedings. IEEE International Conference on Software Maintenance, 2001*, 7-9 Nov. 2001
6. K. El Emam; I. Wieczorek, "The repeatability of code defect classifications", *Proceedings. The Ninth International Symposium on Software Reliability Engineering, 1998,* 4-7 Nov. 1998 Page(s):322 – 333
7. R. Chillarege; I.S. Bhandari; J.K. Chaar; M.J. Halliday; D.S. Moebus; B.K. Ray; M.-Y. Wong, "Orthogonal defect classification-a concept for in-process measurements", *IEEE Transactions on Software Engineering*, Volume 18, Issue 11, Nov. 1992 Page(s):943 - 956
8. R.R. Lutz; I.C. Mikulski, "Empirical analysis of safety-critical anomalies during operations", *IEEE Transactions on Software Engineering*, 30(3):172-180, March 2004
9. D. Hamlet, "What is software reliability?", *Proceedings of the Ninth Annual Conference on Computer Assurance, 1994.* COMPASS '94 'Safety, Reliability, Fault Tolerance, Concurrency and Real Time, Security', 27 June-1 July 1994 Page(s):169 - 170
10. A. Avizienis, J.-C. Laprie, B. Randell, and C. Landwehr; Basic Concepts and Taxonomy of Dependable and Secure Computing, IEEE Transactions on Dependable and Secure Computing, vol. 1, no. 1, January-March 2004

Software Process Improvement: A Road to Success

Mahmood Niazi

School of Computing and Mathematics, Keele University, ST5 5BG, UK
mkniazi@cs.keele.ac.uk

Abstract. Software process improvement (SPI) has received much attention in both academia and industry. SPI aims to improve the effectiveness of the software development process. Several different approaches have been developed for SPI, including the SEI's Capability Maturity Model (CMM), more recently the Capability Maturity Model Integration (CMMI) and ISO's SPICE. Research shows that the effort put into these approaches can assist in producing high quality software.

This paper has a two-fold objectives: first to review and summarise the empirical evidence thus far on the costs and benefits of SPI approaches; second to establish a relationship between different approaches to SPI and to seek and identify whether these approaches fulfil all the needs for an effective SPI initiative. The aim of this review is to analyse material about SPI approach and to set the scene for future research in the area of Software Process Improvement.

1 Introduction

Problems associated with software quality are widely acknowledged to affect the development cost and time [1]. The annual Standish Group report showed that on average the percentage of software projects completed on-time and on-budget was only 34% in 2003 [2]. A recent study, conducted by a group of Fellows of the Royal Academy of Engineering and British Computer Society, shows that despite spending 22.6 billions pounds on IT projects in UK during 2003/2004, significant numbers of projects still fail to deliver key benefits on time and to target cost and specification [3].

There have been increasing calls for the software industry to find solutions to software quality problems [4]. Software organizations are realizing that one of their fundamental problems is to have an effective software development process [5; 6]. In order to have an effective software development process different methods have been developed, of which Software Process Improvement (SPI) is the one mostly used.

The objective of this paper is to discuss and analyse different approaches to SPI in order to identify the issues that can undermine these approaches. The other objective is to analyse empirical evidence on the costs and benefits of SPI approaches. The overall aim is that SPI practitioners would utilise the results of this paper to support the business case for initiating SPI initiatives. To focus this study, I investigated the following research questions:

RQ1. Does SPI really impact on organizations' capabilities?
RQ2. What is missing in current SPI approaches?

J. Münch and M. Vierimaa (Eds.): PROFES 2006, LNCS 4034, pp. 395 – 401, 2006.

The main purpose of addressing these research questions is to provide software practitioners with some insight into initiating SPI programmes. To answer these research questions, a literature review technique was adopted. Furthermore, results of the previously conducted empirical study were also used to answer these two research questions [7]. This two step process has given confidence that the findings of this paper are indeed important to provide some insights into initiating SPI initiatives.

2 Research Methodology

The SPI literature consists of case studies, experience reports and high-level software process texts. Most of the studies describe real life experiences of SPI implementation and provide specific guidelines and recommendations for SPI implementation. I have analysed these published experience reports, case studies and articles in order to answer research questions described in Section 1.

There were 3 categories of papers. Firstly, papers in which the authors have summarised the impact of SPI initiative on quality factors (time, cost, productivity and customer satisfaction). Secondly, papers in which SPI implementation was discussed but authors did not provide any summary of SPI impact on the quality factors. In this case, I have had to read each paper carefully to identify the SPI impact on any quality factor. Thirdly, I have also analysed a few papers in which the results of empirical studies were described.

In order to reduce researcher's bias I have conducted inter-rater reliability test in this process. Three research papers were selected at random and a colleague, who was not familiar with the issues being discussed, was asked to identify SPI impact on quality factors. In the end results were compared with previous results.

In this paper a literature review technique was adopted in order to analyse SPI impact on cost, time, productivity and customer satisfaction. This means that a secondary source was used to analyse SPI impact of quality factors. The primary data used in the literature was not verified directly.

Because this study is limited to the software industry, the gathered data reflects the perceptions of those individuals employed in this industry, and generalizations to other industries should be undertaken with extreme caution.

3 Does SPI Really Impact on Organizations' Capabilities?

In the previously conducted empirical study with 34 Australian practitioners [8], I asked SPI practitioners "Have SPI initiatives provided clear and expected benefits to the management?" Results show that 71% of the practitioners say that SPI initiatives provided clear and expected benefits to the management. Only 6% of the practitioners say SPI initiatives did not provide any benefits to the management. Conducting previous research has convinced me that the SPI impact on organizations capabilities would be best viewed in terms of cost, time, productivity and customer satisfaction.

3.1 Impact on Cost

There are several accounts that describe the impact of an SPI initiative on project cost. A few of the key studies are described below:

- Prior to the CMM initiative at Raytheon in 1988 [9] the average rework costs was about 41% of project costs. After CMM initiative, these costs dropped to about 20%. Fixing source code problems dropped by 80% and cost of retesting dropped by 50%.
- The process improvement resulted Hughes annual savings about $2 million annually [10].
- Diaz and Sligo [11] have computed return on investment for Motorola's process improvement initiatives, which is $611,200 for an $90,180 investment (i.e. total return of 677%).

These results are very positive and show that efforts put into SPI can reduce overall development cost.

3.2 Impact on Time

Many studies have described SPI impact on time.

- Dion [12] described that before SPI initiative at Raytheon most projects were completed behind schedule and now most projects are finishing on schedule.
- Herbsleb *et al* [13] described the yearly reduction in time to market in the range of 15% to 23% (i.e. 19% Median).
- Herbsleb and Goldenson's [14] found a correlation between higher maturity and meeting schedules. For example, ability to meet schedule increased from 40% (companies in CMM Level 1) to 80% (companies in CMM Level 3).
- These results show that the SPI is an effective approach that can help organizations in reducing time to market.

3.3 Impact on Productivity

The following studies have highlighted SPI impact on productivity:

- Herbsleb and Goldenson's [14] results showed development productivity of companies has increased from 50% (companies in CMM Level 1) to 90% (companies in CMM Level 3).
- Herbsleb *et al* [13] described the yearly gain in productivity in the range of 6% to 67% (i.e. 35% Median).
- SPI initiative at Raytheon obtained an average productivity increase of about 130% from 1988 to 1992 [12].
- Butler [15] described a most recent development project 10 time more productive than the baseline project.

The results show that organizations productivity has been increased with the passage of time after adopting SPI initiatives.

3.4 Impact on Customer Satisfaction

There are several studies that describe SPI impact on customer satisfaction. A few of the key studies are described below:

- Yamamura [6] results showed a correlation of employee satisfaction to process maturity, e.g. the average satisfaction was increased from 57% (before process improvement activities) to 83% (after process improvement activities).
- Herbsleb and Goldensons [14] showed that customer satisfaction has increased from 80% (companies in CMM Level 1) to 100% (companies in CMM Level 3).
- Pitterman [5] reported an overall customer satisfaction increased at Telcordia Technologies from 60% in 1992 to above 95% in 2000.

The results show that increased organizations' process maturity has also increased customer satisfaction with the products.

3.5 Discussion

The analysis of the literature shows that large enterprises using processes based on SPI models and standards can produce higher quality software, reduce development cost and time, and increase development productivity. However, most research on the impact and benefits of SPI approach has focused on large organizations [11; 16]. There is a world-wide academic and industrial interest in similar research on Small and Medium-sized Enterprises (SMEs). Research shows that SPI models like CMMI is difficult to apply to (SMEs), due to distinguishing characteristics of SMEs [17]. Due to these distinguishing characteristics, it is important to analyse the impact of SPI approach on SMEs. This is because SMEs may need to know that SPI is proven before they may be drawn to complex issues of SPI which require lot of funds, expertise and management time.

4 What Is Missing in Current Approaches to SPI?

Different models and standards have been developed in order to improve software processes. The CMM is developed by software engineering institute (SEI) in order to improve organizations' software processes. The Capability Maturity Model Integration (CMMI) [18] is the latest SPI model from the SEI. SPICE is a set of international standards for software process assessment [19]. SPICE is intended to harmonize many different approaches to software process assessment and to provide an approach that encourages self-assessment. The ISO 9000 series of standards [20] were developed with the intent of creating a set of common standards for quality management and quality assurance.

4.1 Discussion

In order to address the effective management of software process different approaches have been developed, of which SPI is the one most often used. Research shows that the effort put into these model and standards can assist in producing high quality software [6; 21].

Despite these documented benefits, SPI initiatives exhibit low levels of adoption and limited success [22]. Deployment is often not only multi-project, but multi-site and multi-customer type and the whole SPI initiative typically requires a long-term approach. It takes significant time to fully implement an SPI initiative [23]. Such time frames mean that the SPI approach is often considered an expensive approach for many organizations [22] as they need to commit significant resources over an extensive period of time. Even organizations willing to commit the resources and time do not always achieve their desired results. The failure rate of SPI initiatives is very high, estimated as 70% [24; 25]. The significant investment and limited success are reasons for many organizations being reluctant to embark on a long path of systematic process improvement.

Despite the importance of SPI implementation process, little empirical research has been carried out on developing ways in which to effectively implement SPI programmes [16; 22]. Much attention has been paid to developing standards and models for SPI. This suggests that the current problems with SPI are not a lack of standards or models, but rather a lack of an effective strategy to successfully implement these standards or models. A thorough literature review [11; 14; 21; 26; 27] and previously conducted interviews with 34 Australian practitioners [7] revealed that in general no standard approach has been adopted by practitioners for the implementation of SPI initiatives. Organizations typically adopt ad hoc methods instead of standard, systematic and rigorous methods in order to implement SPI initiatives [28]. So far no approach has been identified that could assist specifically in the design of effective SPI implementation initiatives. There is a great need to develop some mechanism that could assist SPI practitioners in the design and implementation of effective SPI initiatives. This has the potential to reduce SPI implementation time, cost and failure risks.

In order to address some of the missing SPI issues a research project with SPI practitioners is being carried out [7]. The objective of this project is to develop SPI implementation framework to assist SPI practitioners in the design of effective SPI implementation initiatives. The results will be published as soon as the evaluation is completed.

5 Conclusion

This paper has examined the domain of SPI. I have set out to answer two research questions in this paper:

- RQ1. Does SPI really impact on organizations' capabilities?

SPI literature shows that the SPI approach can help organizations in reducing development cost and in improving time-to-market, productivity, and customer satisfaction. However, in order to support the business case for initiating SPI initiatives in SMEs, it is important to analyse the impact of SPI approach on SMEs.

- RQ2. What is missing in current SPI approaches?

Thorough literature review revealed one topic of SPI missing, i.e. many standards and models exist for SPI but little attention has been paid to their effective implementation. Literature also shows that in real life different organizations adopted chaotic methods instead of standard methods in order to implement SPI initiatives. So far no approach has been identified that could assist specifically in the design of effective SPI implementation initiatives. Therefore, further research is needed in the domain of SPI implementation in order to reduce SPI implementation time and cost, higher SPI implementation quality and higher SPI practitioners' satisfaction.

References

1. Sommerville, I.: *Software Engineering Fifth Edition.* Addison-Wesley.(1996).
2. Standish-Group: Chaos - the state of the software industry. (2003).
3. The-Royal-Academy-of-Engineering: The Challenges of Complex IT Projects, The report of a working group from The Royal Academy of Engineering and The British Computer Society. ISBN 1-903496-15-2 (2004).
4. Crosby, P.: *Philip Crosby's reflections on quality.* McGraw-Hill.(1996).
5. Pitterman, B.: Telcordia Technologies: The journey to high maturity, IEEE Software (July/August). (2000) 89-96.
6. Yamamura, G.: Software process satisfied employees, IEEE Software (September/October). (1999) 83-85.
7. Niazi, M., Wilson, D. and Zowghi, D.: A Framework for Assisting the Design of Effective Software Process Improvement Implementation Strategies, Journal of Systems and Software Vol 78 (2). (2005) 204-222.
8. Niazi, M., Wilson, D. and Zowghi, D.: A Maturity Model for the Implementation of Software Process Improvement: An empirical study, Journal of Systems and Software 74 (2). (2005) 155-172.
9. Hally, T.: Software process improvement at Raytheon, IEEE Software November (1996)
10. Humphrey, W. S., Synder, T. R. and Willis, R. R.: Software process improvement at Hughes Aircraft, IEEE Software 8 (4). (1991) 11-23.
11. Diaz, M. and Sligo, J.: How Software Process Improvement helped Motorola, IEEE software 14 (5). (1997) 75-81.
12. Dion, R.: Process improvement and the corporate balance sheet, IEEE Software 10 (4). (1993) 28-35.
13. Herbsleb, J., Caarleton, A., Rozum, J., Siegel, J. and Zubrow, D.: Benefits of CMM-based software process improvement: Initial results. Technical report, CMU/SEI-94-TR-013 (1994).
14. Herbsleb, J. D. and Goldenson, D. R.: A systematic survey of CMM experience and results. 18th international conference on software engineering (ICSE-18). Germany (1996) 323-330.
15. Butler, K.: The economics benefits of software process improvement, CrossTalk (July). (1995) 14-17.
16. Goldenson, D. R. and Herbsleb, J. D.: After the appraisal: A systematic survey of Process Improvement, Its benefits, And Factors That Influence Success. SEI, CMU/SEI-95-TR-009 (1995).
17. Cater-Steel, A.: Process Improvement in Four Small Software Companies. 13th Australian Software Engineering Conference (ASWEC'01). (2001)
18. SEI: Capability Maturity Model® Integration (CMMISM), Version 1.1. SEI, CMU/SEI-2002-TR-029 (2002).
19. ISO/IEC-15504: Information technology - Software process assessment. Technical report - Type 2 (1998).
20. ISO-9000: Internation Standard Organization, http://www.iso.ch/iso/en/iso9000-14000/iso9000/iso9000index.html, Site visited 23-02-2004. (2004).

21. Ashrafi, N.: The impact of software process improvement on quality: in theory and practice, Information & Management 40 (7). (2003) 677-690.
22. Leung, H.: Slow change of information system development practice, Software quality journal 8 (3). (1999) 197-210.
23. SEI: Process Maturity Profile. Software Engineering Institute Carnegie Mellon University, (2004).
24. SEI: Process maturity profile of the software community. Software Engineering Institute, (2002).
25. Ngwenyama, O. and Nielsen, P., A.: Competing values in software process improvement: An assumption analysis of CMM from an organizational culture perspective, IEEE Transactions on Software Engineering 50 (2003) 100-112.
26. Butler, K.: Process lessons learned while reaching Level 4, CrossTalk (May). (1997) 1-4.
27. Dyba, T.: Factors of software process improvement success in small and large organizations: an empirical study in the scandinavian context, ACM SIGSOFT Software Engineering Notes 28 (5). (2003) 148-157.
28. Zahran, S.: *Software process improvement - practical guidelines for business success.* Addison-Wesley.(1998).

Characterization of Runaway Software Projects Using Association Rule Mining

Sousuke Amasaki, Yasuhiro Hamano, Osamu Mizuno, and Tohru Kikuno

Graduate School of Information Science and Technology
Osaka University, 1-5 Yamadaoka, Suita, Osaka 565-0871, Japan
amasaki@computer.org,
{y-hamano, o-mizuno, kikuno}@ist.osaka-u.ac.jp

Abstract. In this paper, characteristics of a runaway project are revealed based on combinations of risk factors which appear in the project. Concretely, an association rule mining technique is applied with an actual questionnaire data to induce rules that associate combinations of risk factors with runaway status of software projects. Furthermore, the induced rules are integrated and reduced based on a certain rule obtained from experts' perception to simplify the representation of characteristics of a runaway project. Then, for confirming the effectiveness of this characterization, it is evaluated how many runaway projects in distinct data set were identified by the reduced rules. The result of the experiment suggested that the induced rules are effective to characterize runaway projects.

Keywords: association rule mining, risk factors, project characterization.

1 Introduction

Recently, software development projects have often been put in a very risky situation because of increasing demand for high quality, short period, and low cost. Thus, detecting signs of problems at an early stage of the software project is important. So, much research has been carried out on the detection of problem signs of a software development project [1, 2]. So far, we have proposed methods to predict runaway status of projects using responses of questionnaire [3, 4].

During past works, the following question is recognized: "How can the runaway-prone projects avoid the runaway status?" One answer to this question is a set of parameters in a logistic regression model. Although these parameters can indicate dominant risk factors,the number of parameters included in a model is restricted by the property of the regression analysis [5]. On the other hand, some risk factors are simultaneously found in the same runaway project frequently. As the result, we consider that there exist combinations of risk factors which significantly affect to the runaway status of projects.

In this paper, we propose an approach using a data-mining technique to induce combinations of risk factors related to runaway status of software projects significantly. The proposed approach consists of the following two phases:

Phase 1: To characterize runaway projects by combinations of risk factors, the association rule mining technique [6] was applied for response data of a questionnaire checking potential risks, collected in a certain company.

J. Münch and M. Vierimaa (Eds.): PROFES 2006, LNCS 4034, pp. 402–407, 2006.

Phase 2: To evaluate the effectiveness of the rules induced in **Phase 1**, the rules were applied to distinct response data collected in the same company.

From the result of experiment, we can conclude that the induced combinations of risk factors can characterize runaway projects.

2 Preliminaries

2.1 Definition of Runaway Projects

In the company cooperating with us, the Software Engineering Process Group (SEPG) has tried to analyze characteristics of runaway projects. In this paper, a definition established by the SEPG is used to judge a "runaway project". The definition is as follows: 1) Cost and duration is out of a certain range, and, 2) A project fell into an uncontrollable situation during development. The SEPG in the company judges whether these conditions are satisfied.

1. Requirements		Eval.
Q1.1	Ambiguous requirements.	
Q1.2	Insufficient explanation of the requirements.	
Q1.3	Misunderstanding of the requirements.	
Q1.4	Lack of commitment regarding requirements between the customer and the project members.	
Q1.5	Frequent requirements or specification changes.	
2. Estimations		**Eval.**
Q2.1	Insufficient awareness of the importance of estimation.	
Q2.2	Insufficient skills or knowledge of estimation methods.	
Q2.3	Insufficient estimation for the implicit requirements.	
Q2.4	Insufficient estimation for the technical issues.	
Q2.5	Lack of stakeholders commitment for estimation.	
3. Planning		**Eval.**
Q3.1	Lack of management review for the project plan.	
Q3.2	Lack of assignment of responsibility.	
Q3.3	Lack of breakdown of the work products.	
Q3.4	Unspecified project review milestones.	
Q3.5	Insufficient planning of project monitoring and controlling.	
Q3.6	Lack of project members' commitment for the project plan.	
4. Team Organization		**Eval.**
Q4.1	Lack of skills and experience.	
Q4.2	Insufficient allocation of the resources.	
Q4.3	Low morale.	
5. Project Management Activities		**Eval.**
Q5.1	Lack of resource management of project managers throughout a project.	
Q5.2	Inadequate project monitoring and controlling.	
Q5.3	Lack of data needed to keep track of a project objectively.	

For each item, please answer with one of "Strongly agree", "Agree", "Neither agree nor disagree", and "Disagree".

Fig. 1. Questionnaire for risk identification

2.2 Questionnaire to Identify Problems

For early identification of runaway status, a questionnaire was constructed that includes possible risk factors in the software development projects. The questionnaire is distributed to and filled out by a project manager. All questions in the questionnaire and applicable answer types are shown in Figure 1. The questionnaire consists of five viewpoints: requirements, estimations, planning capability, team organization, and project management activities. Each sub-item regarding risk factors in the questionnaire must be filled in according to the Likert scale.

2.3 Association Rule Mining

The association rule mining [6] is one of the data mining techniques. It finds interesting associations among the database according to given criteria. The notion of rule is explained as follows: Let the item set I be a set of n distinct items, and a set of transactions D, where each transaction T is a set of items such that $T \subseteq I$. When a rule exists between the subsets X and Y of item set I ($X \subseteq I, Y \subseteq I, X \cap Y = \phi$) in a database, the rule is expressed as $X \Rightarrow Y$ where X means antecedent and Y means consequent.

Confidence and support are two measures of rule interestingness. The confidence is a percentage of transactions in the given database containing X that also contain Y. The support is the percentage of transactions in the given database that contain both X and Y. Typically, rules are considered interesting if they satisfy both a user-specified minimum support and minimum confidence threshold.

3 Mining Rules (Phase 1)

3.1 Applied Data

In order to characterize runaway projects by using the association rule mining, responses of the questionnaire in Figure 1 of 40 projects was used. These projects was carried out from 1996 to 1998 in the company cooperating with us. Each case in the dataset is evaluated whether a project resulted in a runaway status or not by the SEPG according to the definition shown in subsection 2.1.

For further analysis, the responses are classified into two classes: For the responses with "Strongly agree" and "Agree", we classified them into "H", and for the responses "Disagree", "Neither agree nor disagree", and no response,we classified as "L".

3.2 Rule Mining Operation

The association rule mining is applied to 40 project data by using Weka [7]. Here, the minimum confidence and the minimum support are set to 0.6 and 0.25, respectively.

As a result, 107487 rules are obtained. Because the aim is to induce the rules that related conclusively whether a project becomes runaway status or not, we then selected only rules that antecedent includes high risk factors and consequent is runaway. Finally, we got the 11 rules shown in Table 1.

3.3 Rule Reduction

Actually, the preliminary investigations with a company providing the dataset concluded that plural risks often emerged simultaneously in a runaway project while a successful project often has only a single risk. Furthermore, it is observed from Table 1 that a longer antecedent in a rule tends to contain a shorter antecedent in the other rules. Thus, to simplify a rule application in practical use, the induced rules in Table 1 is reduced according to the following optimistic strategy:

1. From the induced rules, rules having the longest antecedent are extracted.
2. From remained induced rules, rules having antecedent which is contained in one of antecedents of the extracted induced rules are removed.
3. Repeat Step 1 and Step 2 while induced rules remain.

Table 2 shows the specific rule set obtained by using the optimistic strategy.

Table 1. Rules for characterizing runaway projects

Rule ID	Antecedent	Consequent	Confidence
R_1	$Q_{1.4} = H \wedge Q_{2.3} = H \wedge Q_{3.3} = H$	S=Runaway	0.91
R_2	$Q_{2.3} = H \wedge Q_{3.3} = H$	S=Runaway	0.91
R_3	$Q_{1.4} = H \wedge Q_{1.5} = H \wedge Q_{2.3} = H$	S=Runaway	0.77
R_4	$Q_{1.4} = H \wedge Q_{3.3} = H$	S=Runaway	0.77
R_5	$Q_{1.1} = H$	S=Runaway	0.71
R_6	$Q_{1.4} = H \wedge Q_{2.3} = H$	S=Runaway	0.69
R_7	$Q_{1.2} = H \wedge Q_{1.4} = H \wedge Q_{2.3} = H$	S=Runaway	0.67
R_8	$Q_{1.5} = H \wedge Q_{2.3} = H$	S=Runaway	0.67
R_9	$Q_{3.3} = H$	S=Runaway	0.65
R_{10}	$Q_{1.2} = H \wedge Q_{2.3} = H$	S=Runaway	0.63
R_{11}	$Q_{1.2} = H \wedge Q_{1.5} = H$	S=Runaway	0.63

Table 2. Rules obtained in Phase 1 for characterizing runaway projects

Rule ID	Antecedent	Consequent
R_1	$Q_{1.4} = H \wedge Q_{2.3} = H \wedge Q_{3.3} = H$	S=Runaway
R_3	$Q_{1.4} = H \wedge Q_{1.5} = H \wedge Q_{2.3} = H$	S=Runaway
R_5	$Q_{1.1} = H$	S=Runaway
R_7	$Q_{1.2} = H \wedge Q_{1.4} = H \wedge Q_{2.3} = H$	S=Runaway
R_{11}	$Q_{1.2} = H \wedge Q_{1.5} = H$	S=Runaway

4 Rule Evaluation (Phase 2)

4.1 Applied Data

In this section, the effectiveness of the specific rule set is confirmed by applying the specific rule set to distinct project data. In order to remove influences from difference in software development environments, the project data used for evaluation was collected in the same company.

The dataset is from 12 projects and these projects have been performed from 2003 to 2004. This dataset is distinct from the project data used for rule mining in two points: 1) all members in these projects must respond to the new questionnaire, and, 2) some of questions were integrated or modified according to experts' opinion. Note that we do not apply cross-validation methods in this research since we prepare distinct test data for evaluation.

Table 3 shows a part of the correspondence of questions between two questionnaires and the instructions of questions in the new questionnaire. Because of page limitation, only questions in antecedents of the rule set are shown in Table 3. By replacing questions in the rule set with those corresponded questions, we can produce new rule set for the dataset used in this section. Finally, the new 2 rules shown in Table 4 is obtained.

Table 3. Correspondence between new questionnaire and Fig. 1

Questions used in 12 projects	Instructions	Corresponded questions in Fig.1	Remark
q_1	Lack of clarity, sufficiency, or stability of requirements.	Q1.1, Q1.5, Q2.3	
q_4	Lack of commitment regarding requirements between the customer and the project members.	Q1.4	
q_{23}	Ambiguity of the organization of the project, the roles, and authorities of its members, etc.	Q3.3	Lack of work breakdown usually causes ambiguous organization and authorities.
q_{31}	Lack of communication with customers	Q1.2	

Table 4. Rules used for an evaluation in Phase 2

Rule ID	Antecedent	Consequent
r_1	$q_1 = H \wedge q_4 = H \wedge q_{23} = H$	S=Runaway
r_2	$q_1 = H \wedge q_4 = H \wedge q_{31} = H$	S=Runaway

4.2 Rule Application Procedure

Using the new rule set shown in Table 4, the effectiveness of the rule set induced in **Phase 1** is verified. Here, in contrast to optimistic strategy taken for rule reduction in subsection 3.3, pessimistic strategy is taken for dealing with responses of the questionnaire. Because members in a project have different roles, experience, and skill, and thus they are able to notice different risks which the other members couldn't notice.

By using Table 5, we show a pessimistic rule application procedure for responses of the questionnaire. In Table 5, we assume that three members A, B, and C responded the questionnaire with respect to an example project.

1. First, responses of all members in a project are evaluated with antecedents of rules r_1 and r_2. For instance, Table 5 showed that member B responded $q_1 = H$, $q_4 = H$, and $q_{31} = H$. Thus, antecedent of r_1, which is $q_1 = H \wedge q_4 = H \wedge q_{31} = H$, is obviously true. If antecedent of r_1 or r_2 is true, "T" is specified in r_1 or r_2 column in Table 5, respectively; otherwise "F" is specified.
2. Next, for each of antecedent columns r_1 and r_2, OR logic (pessimistic decision) is applied. If there is any "T" in r_1 column, then "OR logic result" takes "T". Similarly if there is any "T" in r_2 column, it takes "T".
3. Finally, predicted result is calculated by applying OR logic to the "OR logic result" row. That is, if there is any "T" in the row, then the project is predicted as a runaway project. Thus, a project in Table 5 is predicted as a runaway project.

Table 5. Explanation of risk evaluation an example project

Member	Answer to the questions	Evaluation of antecedent	
		r_1	r_2
A	$q_1 = H,\ q_4 = H,\ q_{23} = L,\ q_{31} = H$	F	T
B	$q_1 = H,\ q_4 = H,\ q_{23} = H,\ q_{31} = L$	T	F
C	$q_1 = H,\ q_4 = H,\ q_{23} = H,\ q_{31} = H$	T	T
	OR logic result	T	T
	Predicted result	Runaway	

4.3 Result of Evaluation

The result of rule application is shown in Table 6. Table 6 shows that the accuracy of prediction is relatively good (75%) and all projects predicted as "Runaway" are actually "Runaway". It seems that the first point means that the rules are effective for characterizing runaway projects with a certain generality and that the second point is a result of the optimistic strategy used for reducing rules.

Table 6. Result of experimental prediction

		Predicted result	
		Successful	Runaway
Actual status	Successful	5	0
	Runaway	3	4

Accuracy: 0.75

5 Conclusions

In this paper, we proposed an approach to characterize runaway software projects using the association rule mining technique. The result of experiment showed that the induced rules can characterize runaway status of projects successfully.

By the way, our use of rule mining was not sufficient since induced rules were obvious ones only. As a future work, evaluation with larger datasets to refine generality of rules is considered. Our next step is to find unexpected rules which cause serious situations in software development. To do so, reconstruction of questionnaire maybe needed.

References

1. Boehm, B.W.: Software risk management: Principles and practice. IEEE Software **8**(1) (1991) 32–41
2. Wohlin, C., Andrews, A.A.: Prioritizing and assessing software project success factors and project characteristics using subjective data. Empirical Software Engineering **8** (2003) 285–303
3. Takagi, Y., Mizuno, O., Kikuno, T.: An empirical approach to characterizing risky software projects based on logistic regression analysis. Empirical Software Engineering **10**(4) (2005) 495–515
4. Mizuno, O., Hamasaki, T., Takagi, Y., Kikuno, T.: An empirical evaluation of predicting runaway software projects using bayesian classification. In: Proc. of 5th International Conference on Product Focused Software Process Improvement (PROFES2004). (2004) 263–273
5. Kantardzic, M.: Data Mining: Concepts, Models, Methods, and Algorithms. IEEE Press (2003)
6. Han, J., Kamber, M.: Data Mining: Concepts and Techniques. Morgan Kaufmann Publishers (2001)
7. Weka Machine Learning Project: Weka 3: Data mining software in java. (http://www.cs.waikato.ac.nz/~ml/weka/)

A Framework for Selecting Change Strategies in IT Organizations

Jan Pries-Heje[1] and Otto Vinter[2]

[1] The IT University of Copenhagen, Denmark
jph@itu.dk
[2] DELTA IT Processes, Denmark
otv@delta.dk

Abstract. In this paper we describe a framework which combines several models for organizational change. The framework enables an organization to decide which strategies will be most successful when implementing a specific change in its particular setting. The conditions for change is assessed in relation to each of the strategies for organizational change and a list-of-fit is produced, which reveals the degree to which each of the strategies fits the specific setting. The framework was developed and evaluated within a field study involving four companies in the financial sector. The IT organizations in two of these collaborated with the researchers in providing promising evaluations of the framework.

1 Introduction

The Danish Talent@IT project [26] (www.talent-it.dk) studies parameters in organizations which promote or impede changes in organizations. This has led to a model of 20 parameters in 4 categories, the *ImprovAbility*™ model [20] (see Fig. 1). The *ImprovAbility*™ model and accompanying assessment method provides an organization with a view of their strengths and weaknesses on each of these parameters.

In addition, the project studies different change approaches [25] and their relevance for improving each of the parameters of the model. An *ImprovAbility*™ assessment therefore also produces recommendations for change approaches that can be used in the specific organizational setting to improve the success of its change efforts.

Our study of change approaches employed in practice by IT practitioners and their management lead us to distinguish three types: Means (methods, techniques, and tools), Approaches (principles, practices, or conducts), Strategies (overall rationale for how changes are perceived by the organization).

Means and Approaches belong to the operational level. The selection of a change strategy, however, belongs to the top level of the organization. It is heavily influenced by the vision or goals for the change as well as by issues in the organizational culture. These issues determine the conditions that make certain change strategies successful and others a failure. In this paper, we are concerned with the design and evaluation of a framework for change strategies and a tool, which enables organizations to select among those which will be most successful, and avoid those most probable to fail.

J. Münch and M. Vierimaa (Eds.): PROFES 2006, LNCS 4034, pp. 408–414, 2006.

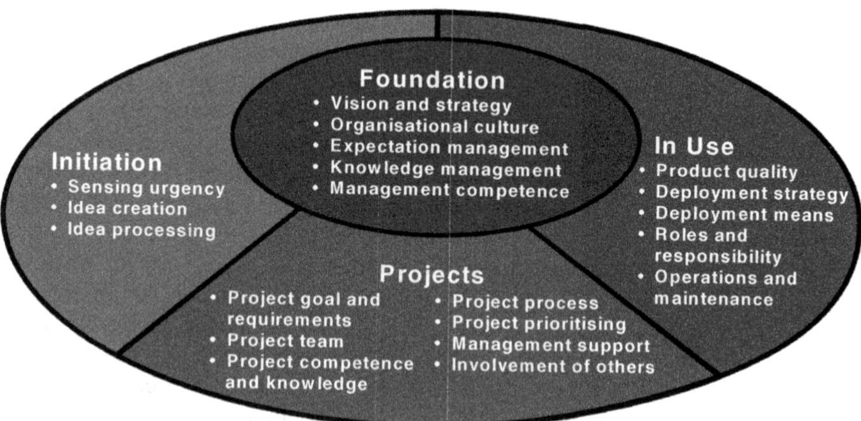

Fig. 1. The *ImprovAbility*™ model

2 Theories and Models for Organizational Change

Since management became a discipline, the study of change has been important. Authors have written about organizational change from different perspectives including psychology, sociology and business. Academic and practitioner contributions to organizational change have been built on empirical work in many organizations. Examples of this include descriptive accounts of change, normative models to guide change processes, theoretical models for understanding and analyzing change, typologies of approaches to organizational change, and empirical studies of success and failure.

In terms of the descriptive accounts of change, three different schools of organizational thinking have provided metaphors for organizations. The first school (and oldest) descends back to the end of the 19th century where Taylor, Fayol, and Weber were key figures. Taylor invented "Scientific Management" including the key belief that "it is possible and desirable to establish, through methodological study and the application of scientific principles, the one best way of carrying out any job." ([6], p. 28). The metaphor for this is an organization as a production system where it is possible to optimize its efficiency and effectiveness. Organizational change is about optimizing planning through observation, experimentation, calculation and analysis.

In the 1930s and 1940s the second school challenged the classical view of organizations to provide a new perspective. In relation to change this perspective is characterized by [6][4] the belief that organizations are co-operative, social systems rather than mechanical ones, where people seek to meet their emotional needs. So the metaphor for an organization is a (large) group of people with an organizational culture and visible communication and interaction processes between them.

The 3rd school of thought has been called the political-emergent perspective [6][4]. It is characterized by the belief that organizations and change are shaped by the interests and commitments of individuals. It is also characterized by the belief that decisions often arise from power-struggles between special-interest groups or coalitions. "Organizations are not machines, even though some of those running them would dearly like them to be so. They are communities of people, and therefore behave just like other communities. They compete amongst themselves for power and resources; there are differences of opinion and of values, conflicts of priorities and goals" [11].

An interesting approach to combining change strategies is found in Huy [12], who identifies four ideal types of interventions. He distinguishes between episodic and continuous change. Changing formal structures is an episodic change involving something tangible. Thus the ideal type of change will be "commanding". He suggests that every ideal type is relatively more effective than the other ideal types. For example, the "engineering" intervention is relatively best at changing work processes.

Organizational change management thought has now developed so many approaches to change that no one approach can claim that it is suitable for all organizational goals and settings. There is a need for analysis of available approaches in developing a particular organizational change strategy. However, few (if any) comprehensive analytical tools are available to support this analysis. The contingency approach exemplified by Huy [12] provides the right direction, but its two-by-two analytical structure is simplistic compared to the complexity of most practical settings.

3 A Framework for Selecting Organizational Change Strategies

How can an organization select the best change strategy from the abundance of different foundational theories for organizational change? Each theory has its advocates and adherents, and there is little comparative research to aid the selection. The theories are so varied that comparisons are usually drawn between only a few alternatives [24]. Our research focuses on this selection issue, the lack of formulated tools to help organizational change managers to select from these change theories. Our intention is to improve the ability for organizational change managers to rationally select the most appropriate change strategies.

In connection with our survey of the organizational change literature, we conducted a number of search conferences involving participants from the companies in the Talent@IT consortium in order to assemble a catalogue of change approaches, which have been used successfully in practice. From the search conferences we identified a number of high-level overall approaches. We analyzed them to determine their distinguishing characteristics and related them to theories in literature. We focused on the essential goals of each change strategy (the ends) and the essential processes (the means), and refined them into ten prominent change strategies (Table 1).

4 Development of a Change Strategy Selection Tool

Following this analysis, we set out to create a tool to guide change managers in evaluating and choosing which of the ten change strategies that would be most appropriate in an actual organizational setting. For each of the ten organizational change strategies in Table 1 we formulated a number of assertions that would reveal in a given organizational setting to which degree the conditions were present. E.g. for the change strategy called "Commanding," we formulated the following assertions:

- Right now we need change to happen fast
- It is primarily organizational structures that need to be changed
- In the past we have had successes in requiring or dictating change

Table 1. An overview of the ten organizational change strategies

Strategy	Definition	Conditions	Literature
Commanding	Change is driven and dictated by (top) management. Management takes on the roles as owner, sponsor and change agents.	*Where* formal structures needs change. *Where* change is needed fast	[12] the approach called Commanding
Employee driven	Change is driven from the bottom of the organizational hierarchy when needs for change arise among employees.	*Where* the need for change arises among the employees. *Where* the result is more important than the process; there is no need for a standardized approach. *Where* an open management style allows change to arise from the bottom.	[1] on a grassroots approach. [13], [14] on participatory design
Exploration	Change is driven by the need for flexibility, agility, or a need to explore new markets, technology or customer groups.	*Where* dynamic and complex surroundings make it important to explore opportunities.	[3], [17]
Learning driven	Change is driven by a focus on organizational learning, individual learning and what creates new attitudes and behavior.	*Where* employees learn from the experience of others. *Where* there is a need for change in attitudes and/or behavior. *Where* relationships between means and goals are unclear.	[12] the approach called Teaching
Metrics driven	Change is driven by metrics and measurements	*Where* there are relatively stable surroundings so measurements from the past can be used to decide the future. *Where* the result of change is measurable	Total Quality Management thinking [18]. Six Sigma thinking [19]
Optionality	Change is driven by the motivation and need of the individual or group. It is to a large degree optional whether the individual takes the innovation into use	*Where* target group is very diverse and has large individual or contextual differences. *Where* individuals that should (could) change are highly educated, very knowledgeable and self-aware.	[21] studies groups that took innovations into use voluntarily.
Production organized	Change is driven by the need for optimization and/or cost reduction	*Where* you have many homogeneous resources and workflows. *Where* you have relatively stable surroundings.	[3] Scientific Management. [12] the approach called Engineering
Reengineering	Change is driven by fundamentally rethinking and redesigning the organization to achieve dramatic improvements	*Where* a need exists for major change, e.g. when the organization has ground to a halt. *Where* nothing new happens. *Where* decisions are made but not carried out. *Where* a crisis is eminent.	[2],[5],[8], [9],[10], [15],[16],[27]
Socializing	Change in organizational capabilities is driven by working through social relationships. Diffusion of innovations happens through personal contacts rather than through plans and dictates.	*Where* organizational skills and capabilities needs to be developed. *Where* no unhealthy power struggles occur (so people *can* talk). *Where* employees that can be exemplars are available.	[12] the approach called Socializing
Specialist driven	Change is driven by specialists, either with professional, technical, or domain knowledge.	*Where* work has vast complexity and variety so there really is a need for special knowledge. *Where* there is access to necessary specialists, eventually by in-sourcing them.	[7],[17] especially adhocracy, [22],[23]

And for the change approach called "Optionality," we formulated the assertions:

- Our employees are self-aware and always have an opinion
- We have very knowledgeable employees that know their areas well
- There are vast differences between the tasks of different employee

All of the assertions were formulated in a number of statements which represent expressions of the conditions for implementing change in relation to the organizational setting, the employees, the change ahead, and the current use of metrics. The statements were assembled into a query form where managers on a five level scale can express their degree of agreement or disagreement with the statements. When the query form is filled in by the management of an organization, the conditions for change in that organization can be compared to the conditions for each of the ten change strategies (Table 1). The fit of each is measured by the degree (0-100%) to which these conditions are present in the particular organization. A fit (score) calculated around 50% represents an indeterminate value. A fit calculated above 70% means that the corresponding change strategy fits the organization well (will be successful). On the other hand a score below 30% means that the corresponding change strategy doesn't fit the organization at all (should not be used).

5 Evaluation of the Framework and Tool

The framework for selecting change strategies was developed and evaluated within a field research study by a consortium (Talent@IT) involving two research institutions and four financial companies. When the parameters in the *ImprovAbility*™ model (Fig. 1) that promote or impede change had been extracted from interviews with the partners and literature, we were ready to evaluate the model and the *ImprovAbility*™ assessment method at the partner companies. The framework for selecting change strategies presented in this paper was included in two of these evaluations.

We asked the management group in the IT Division of the companies to fill out the query form. First they worked individually and afterwards we facilitated a discussion of any major differences in the individual assessments. For example, if one manager said "agree" to the assertion "In the past we have had successes in requiring or dictating change" while another manager said "partly disagree", then we brought out the difference in the discussion and facilitated the attainment of an agreement.

From the evaluations we obtained the following two list-of-fits (Table 2) detailing the degree of fit for each of the ten change strategies to the two organizations' vision or goals for change and the organizational setting. The application of the framework led in both companies to recommendations that combined the two best-fitting change strategies and strong advice against the least-fitting change strategy.

In both companies the management of the IT Division found the results quite positive and considered them very useful. In Company A the CIO called the results a major "Aha!" experience, and compared it to his wearisome exchanges with previous consultants who asked him to "run around with a box of matches" to establish a burning platform ("Reengineering"). The recommendations at Company B led to a discussion about whether the "Optionality" and "Commanding" approaches can coexist. The IT managers agreed that they would use the "Optionality" strategy on those many change initiatives which are driven by the individual's or group's need and motivation. They would use the "Commanding" strategy on only few (2-3) initiatives where they really needed to drive the change (e.g. because change was needed fast).

Table 2. The degree of fit for each of the ten change strategies in the evaluations

	Company A		Company B
60%	Socializing	71 %	Optionality
60%	Learning driven	65 %	Commanding
56%	Production organized	59 %	Socializing
55%	Employee driven	58 %	Production organized
54%	Optionality	56 %	Specialist driven
42%	Metrics driven	40 %	Metrics driven
37.5%	Specialist driven	34 %	Learning driven
35%	Exploration	29 %	Exploration
34,5%	Commanding	28 %	Reengineering
31%	Reengineering	18 %	Employee driven

6 Conclusion

In this paper we presented a framework and a tool to support the selection of an organizational change strategy. We developed a framework that binds together ten well-known organizational change strategies into a prescriptive recommendation for a cohesive and suitable change strategy for a particular organization's unique situation. The change strategies to be prescribed develop from a list-of-fit that indicates the relative suitability of each of the ten strategies to the organization's vision and setting.

The framework and tool was evaluated in two IT organizations in the Talent@IT consortium [26] (www.talent-it.dk). They considered the results quite positive and very useful. The framework evidently leads to operational management decisions about the selection of a suitable change strategy in a particular organizational setting.

References

1. Andersen, C.V., Krath, F., Krukow, L., Mathiasssen L., Pries-Heje, J.: The Grass Root Effort. In: Mathiassen et al. (eds.): Improving Software Organizations - From Principles to Practice, Addison-Wesley (2001)
2. Bashein, B.J., Markus, M.L., Riley, P.: Preconditions for BPR Success: And How to Prevent Failures. Information Systems Management (1994), 11(2), pp. 7-13
3. Benner, M., Tushman, M.: Exploitation, exploration, and process management: The productivity dilemma revisited. Academy of Management Review (2003), Vol. 28, No. 2, 238-256
4. Borum, F.: Strategier for organisationsændring (Strategies for organizational change). Handelshøjskolens Forlag, Copenhagen (1995)
5. Boudreau, M-C., Robey, D.: Coping with contradictions in business process reengineering. Information Technology & People (1996), Vol. 9 No. 4, pp. 40-57
6. Burnes, B.: Managing Change. 2nd Edition. Financial Times, Pitman Publishing (1996)

7. Ciborra, C.U. and Associates: From Control to Drift. The dynamics of cooporate information infrastructures. Oxford University Press, Oxford, UK (2000)
8. Davenport, T.H.: Process Innovation: Re-engineering Work through Information Technology. Harvard Business School Press (1993)
9. Hammer, M.: Reengineering Work: Don't Automate, Obliterate. Harvard Business Review, July-August 1990, pp. 104-112
10. Hammer, M., Champy, J.: Reengineering the Corporation; A Manifesto For Business Revolution. Harper Business (1993)
11. Handy, C.: Understanding Organizations. 4th Edition. Penguin Global (2005)
12. Huy, Q.N.: Time, temporal capability, and planned change. Academy of management Review (2001), vol. 26, no. 4, 601-623
13. Kensing, F.: Methods and Practices in Participatory Design. ITU Press, Copenhagen (2003)
14. Kensing, F., Blomberg, J.: Participatory Design: Issues and Concerns. Computer Supported Cooperative Work (1998), 7(3-4), 167-185
15. King, W.R.: Process Reengineering: The Strategic Dimensions. Information Systems Management (1994), 11(2), pp. 71-73
16. Malhotra, Y.: Business Process Redesign: An Overview. IEEE Engineering Management Review (1998), vol. 26, no. 3
17. Mintzberg, H.: Structure in Fives - designing effective organizations, Prentice-Hall (1983)
18. Oakland, J.S.: TQM – Text with Cases. 3rd edition. Butterworth-Heinemann (2003)
19. Pande, P.S., Holpp, L.: What is Six Sigma? McGraw Hill (2000)
20. Pries-Heje, J., Johansen, J.: AIM – Ability Improvement Model. EuroSPI 2005, Springer LNCS 3792 (2005)
21. Rogers, E.M.: Diffusion of Innovations. 5th Edition, Free Press (2003)
22. Simon, H.A.: The Structure of Ill Structured Problems. Artificial Intel. (1973), 4, 181-201
23. Simon, H.A.: Search and Reasoning in Problem Solving. Artificial Intel. (1983), 21, 7-29
24. Tingey, M.O.: Comparing ISO 9000, Malcolm Baldrige, and the SEI CMM for Software: A Reference and Selection Guide. Upper Saddle River, NJ: Prentice Hall PTR (1997)
25. Vinter, O.: A Framework for Classification of Change Approaches Based on a Comparison of Process Improvement Models. PROFES 2005, Springer LNCS 3547 (2005)
26. Vinter, O., Pries-Heje, J. (eds.): På vej mod at blive bedre til at blive bedre (On how to improve the ability to improve). DELTA Report D-266, Hørsholm, Denmark (2004)
27. Willcocks, L., Feeny, D., Islei, G.: Managing IT as a Strategic Resource. McGraw-Hill (1997). Chapter 10, pp. 238-273.

Building Software Process Line Architectures from Bottom Up

Hironori Washizaki

National Institute of Informatics,
2-1-2 Hitotsubashi, Chiyoda-ku, Tokyo 101-8430, Japan
washizaki@nii.ac.jp

Abstract. In this paper, we propose a technique for establishing process lines, which are sets of common processes in particular problem domains, and process line architectures that incorporate commonality and variability. Process line architectures are used as a basis for deriving process lines from the perspective of overall optimization. The proposed technique includes some extensions to the Software Process Engineering Metamodel for clearly expressing the commonality and variability in the process workflows described as UML activity diagrams. As a result of applying the proposed technique to hardware/software co-design processes in an embedded system domain, it is found that the proposed technique is useful for defining consistent and project-specific processes efficiently.

1 Introduction

Process tailoring is an approach for defining project-specific processes by adding, removing or modifying the activities and the required inputs/outputs of a base process model to develop high-quality system/software efficiently. Project-specific processes are a collection of interrelated, concrete activities along the time line of the project, which take into consideration the characteristics of the specific project. Conventional tailoring approaches can be divided into two major types[1]: component-based approaches and generator approaches. The former tries to build a project-specific process based on existing process parts, but it lacks a way to address the overall compatibility and consistency of the derived processes. The latter tries to build a project-specific process by instantiating a typical process architecture, but it lacks a way to reuse process fragments.

In this paper, we propose a new process-tailoring technique which solves the problems with component-based and generator approaches by building a *Process-Line Architecture* (hereafter *PLA*) and deriving project-specific processes from the PLA. A process line is a set of similar processes within a particular domain, and is an application of the idea of product lines to processes. Process lines were proposed by Romback[2] and Jaufman[1], but parts of the definition and technical system are still not well-defined, and not sufficient for creating a concrete framework. Other similar ideas have also been proposed, including process libraries[3] and families[4]; however, these are not always oriented toward overall optimization, and do not lead to generally-applicable process-model structures.

J. Münch and M. Vierimaa (Eds.): PROFES 2006, LNCS 4034, pp. 415–421, 2006.

2 Process Line Architecture

We define a *Process Line* as "a set of processes in a particular domain or for a particular purpose, having common characteristics and built based upon common, reusable process assets (such as PLAs, requirements)". The relationship between process lines and PLA is shown in Figure 1.

A PLA is "a process structure which reflects the commonality and variability in a collection of processes that make up a process line from the perspective of overall optimization". We mean "overall optimization" as preparing a PLA with general utility rather than defining separate but similar optimized processes. By deriving individual process from the PLA, the fixed amount of additional effort required in the future can be reduced, and timeliness of completion can be improved. Commonality in a PLA is represented by the core process, which is made up of the common parts of the set of processes. Variability is represented by the variation points and process variants. Variation points are activities (or the inputs/outputs or roles that effect activities) which can be changed according to the characteristics of a specific project. Process variants are the concrete candidate activities (or inputs/outputs, etc.) that are applied to the variation points. Processes that are specialized for a particular but similar project can be defined and applied effectively by combining, extending and reusing the core process and variants in a particular problem domain.

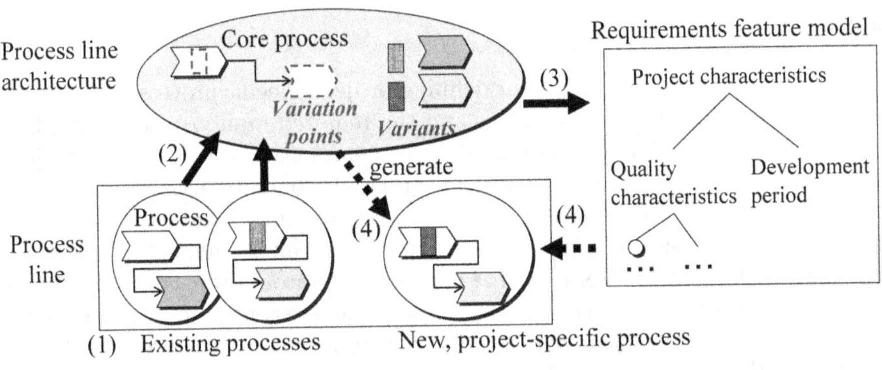

Fig. 1. Process line framework and bottom-up building activities

It is difficult to adequately analyze commonality and variability in a domain from scratch without missing anything; this is to say a "top-down" approach. So we propose the following "bottom-up" technique (shown in Figure 1) for building a PLA using existing knowledge on process definitions and applications in the well-known problem domain. We define *Process Line Engineering* as "a system of interrelated strategic and systematic approaches for building, applying and managing process lines". Based on this concept, the following activities (1)–(3) are in the domain engineering, and (4) is in the application engineering.

(1) Several existing processes in the selected problem domain are gathered together. These processes, sharing common parts, can be combined to form the process line P.

(2) Commonality of P (the gathered collection of process) is defined as the core process including variation points. Variability is defined as a set of variants defined for each variation point in the core process. In describing below how the PLA is built by our technique, we use some new, original extensions to the Software Process Engineering Metamodel (SPEM[5]) to clearly express the commonality and variability in the process workflows. These cannot be expressed with traditional SPEM. The procedure is described as follows:

(a) Make the smallest process in P a core process, p_c. Then apply (b) to all of the remaining processes in P ($p_i \in P - \{p_c\}$). We assume that p_c's workflow is composed of a set of interrelated activities and conditional branches along the time line, denoted as $p_c = e_{c1} \rightarrow ... \rightarrow e_{ck} \rightarrow ... \rightarrow e_{cm}$. Similarly, we denote the p_i's workflow as $p_i = e_{i1} \rightarrow ... \rightarrow e_{ij} \rightarrow ... \rightarrow e_{in}$.

(b) All activities and conditional branches e_{ij} in the p_i's workflow are compared with all elements in the p_c workflow, e_{ck}. If these elements are not the same, the following (c)–(g) are performed. The sameness, specialization and generalization relation between two process elements can be identified by comparing the activity details, pre/post-conditions, inputs/outputs, roles, and environments including tools. In our technique, the above-mentioned comparison is conducted manually. As our future work, we will try to use tool-supported techniques such as a technique proposed by Ocampo [6].

(c) If e_{ij} is a specialized element of e_{ck}, we create the generalization relationship denoted as $e_{ck} \triangleleft - e_{ij}$, label e_{ck} with a ≪`variationPoint`≫ stereotype, label e_{ij} with ≪`variant`≫, and add e_{ij} to p_c. Conversely, if e_{ck} is a specialized element of e_{ij}, exchange e_{ij} for e_{ck} in p_c and perform the same way.

(d) If there is no element which specializes or generalizes e_{ij}, and the element preceding e_{ij} (i.e. e_{ij-1}) on the p_i's workflow is equal to e_{cl} in p_c, set a transition from e_{cl} to e_{ij}. Label e_{ij} with an ≪`optional`≫ stereotype, and add e_{ij} to p_c. When actually defining a concrete process with a selection of the above-mentioned optional element, we will proceed the element e_{cl+1} after proceeding from e_{cl} to e_{ij}. In other words, the obtained process architecture with the optional element provides two different workflow definitions: $e_{cl} \rightarrow e_{cl+1}$ or $e_{cl} \rightarrow e_{ij} \rightarrow e_{cl+1}$.

(e) If there is no element which specializes or generalizes e_{ij}, and the element preceding e_{ij} (i.e. e_{ij-1}) already have the ≪`variant`≫ or ≪`optional`≫ stereotype, set a transition from e_{ij-1} to e_{ij} and add e_{ij} to p_c.

(f) If a ≪`variant`≫ or ≪`optional`≫ element was added in (c) or (d), add transitions to appropriate elements within p_c for each of that element's original transitions. When doing this, if there are two or more outgoing transitions for one element, not including conditional branch elements, draw a dashed line over these transitions and annotate the line with a constraint {xor} to show clearly that one transition must be selected when the concrete process is defined.

(g) If a ≪variant≫ or ≪optional≫ element e_x was added in (c) or (d), and e_x requires that other ≪variant≫/ ≪optional≫ elements (e_y) must be preceded, add a dependency relationship from e_x to e_y, denoted as $e_x \overset{\ll requires \gg}{\cdots>} e_y$. These dependency relationships and the exclusive selection relationships described above are important for maintaining process consistency.

(3) The project characteristics as predictable requirements for a process line are defined corresponding to the commonality and variability built into the PLA. Feature Diagram[7] can be used to define the requirements that accompany the commonality and variability. Feature diagrams are a way of expressing requirements having both variability/commonality and consistency, by allowing substitution and selection of logical units called features, which are functional or qualitative requirements.

(4) By reusing the PLA derived through the above procedure and the requirements including commonality/variability for the process line, project-specific processes that maintain consistency can be defined efficiently. For example, if the requirements on the process line are expressed by a feature diagram, and the part of the PLA which handles each feature is recorded (i.e. there is traceability between PLA and feature diagram), a customized consistent process can be derived easily by selecting features. Moreover, the PLA can be used as a basis for comparing similar processes.

3 Application to Hardware/Software Co-design

As an example, we consider building a process line for hardware/software co-design process in embedded system development. When defining this process, it is necessary to decide, on a per project basis, variations like when the hardware architecture specification will be decided, and whether the division and mapping of specifications will be iterated. As such, we tried building a PLA from the bottom up as described in the previous section.

(1) As representative but partially different processes for hardware/software co-design, we collected the Wolf process (denoted as p_W[8]), the Axlesson process (p_A[9]), and the process from the Kassners (p_K[10]). The workflow of each process is shown with an activity diagram based on SPEM in Figure 2. Due to space limitation, roles and inputs/outputs have been omitted from each diagram.

(2) The PLA workflow derived from the analysis for variability and commonality in these three processes is shown on the left side of Figure 3. Figure 3 clearly shows the core process with variation points, variants, optional elements, and exclusive transitions. For example, an activity ``Specification definition'' in the core process is labeled as a variation point, and can be substituted with a variant ``Executable behavior specification definition'' that

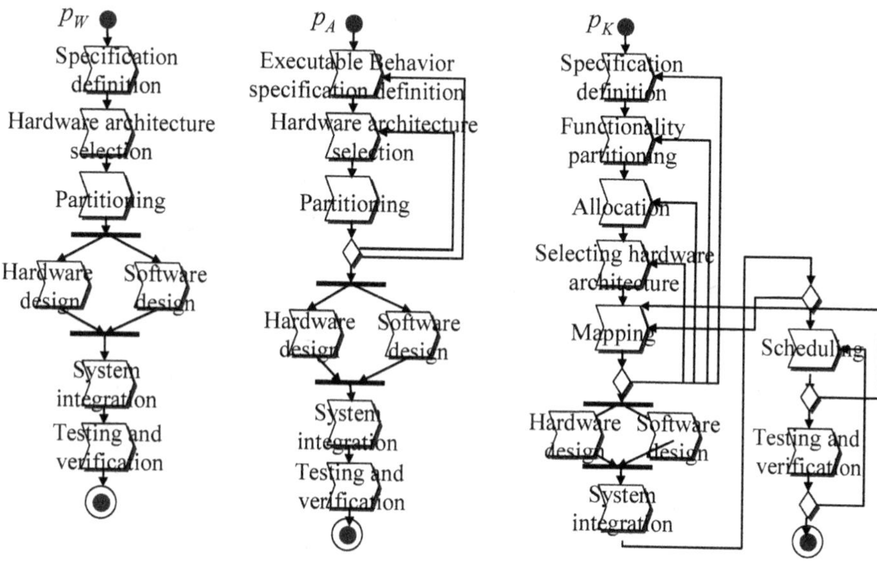

Fig. 2. Collected process workflows

expresses more detail. In addition, there are several conditional branches that implement iteration cycles in the process; these are optional elements.

(3) The project characteristics were analyzed as requirements corresponding to the variability/commonality in the PLA. A feature diagram on the right side in Figure 3 shows the result. We have related the optional and substitute features to the optional elements and variants in the PLA.

(4) Using the resulting PLA and feature diagram, various processes including the original three processes can be derived in a consistent and efficient way based on the requirements. For example, for a short-term project where the decision on hardware specifications is late, and performance and reliability might be sacrificed due to an extremely short development period, we will simply select the ``Late'' feature on the feature diagram. This defines a process where iteration cycles are excluded, and the ``Hardware architecture selection'' activity is done after ``Allocation''. This newly defined process is consistent; for example, ``Functional partitioningn'' will be included and located before ``Allocation'' according to the dependence relationship. Without using a PLA and feature diagram, it would not be easy to quickly define a similar, new and consistent process based on various project characteristics.

4 Conclusion and Future Work

In this paper, we have defined terminology and a framework for the development of process lines, and shown a technique for building practical process-line

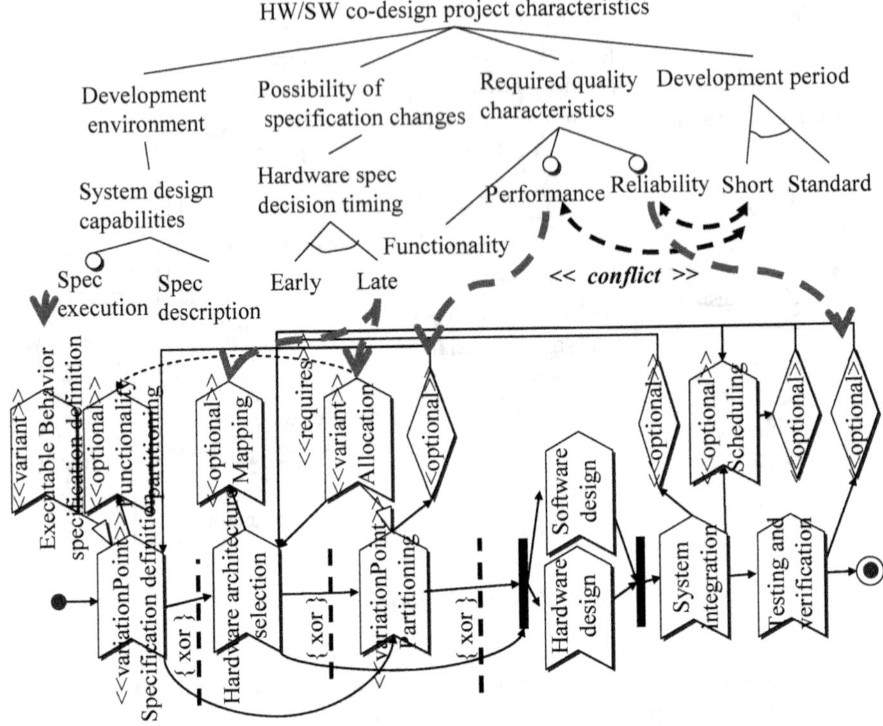

Fig. 3. Obtained co-design process line architecture and its feature diagram

architectures that allows consistent, project-specific processes in a given problem domain to be defined efficiently. Also, in order to express the commonality/variability in PLA workflows, we have proposed a notation which is an extension to SPEM. Finally, by building a PLA and feature diagram for hardware/software co-design process, we showed that consistent project-specific processes can be derived easily based on the proposed technique. In the future, we plan to explicitly handle factors such as resource limitations, inputs and outputs, and pre- and post-conditions in the proposed technique.

References

1. O. Jaufman and J. Munch: Acquisition of a Project-Specific Process, Proc. 6th International Conference on Product Focused Software Process Improvement, 2005.
2. D. Rombach: Integrated Software Process and Product Lines, Post-Proceedings of the Software Process Workshop 2005, LNCS Vol.3840, 2005.
3. P. Mi et al.: A Knowledge-based Software Process Library for Process-Driven Software Development, 7th Knowledge-Based Software Engineering Conference, 1992.
4. Y. Matsumoto: Japanese Software Factory, in Encyclopedia of Software Engineering, (ed.) J.J. Marciniak, John Wiley & Sons, 1994.

5. OMG: Software Process Engineering Metamodel Specification, Version 1.1, 2005.
6. A. Ocampo, R. Bella and J. Munch: Software Process Commonality Analysis, Software Process Improvement and Practice, Vol.10, No.3, 2005.
7. J.C. Trigaux and P. Heymans: Modelling variability requirements in Software Product Lines, Technical report PLENTY project, 2003.
8. W.H. Wolf: Computer as Components: Principles of Embedded Computing System Design, Morgan Kaufmann, 2001.
9. J. Axelsson: Hardware/Software Partitioning of Real-Time Systems, IEE Colloquium on Partitioning in Hardware-Software Codesigns, 1995.
10. K.C. Kassner and K.G. Ricks: Hardware/Software Co-Design of Embedded Real-Time Systems from an Undergraduate Perspective, Workshop on Computer Architecture Education, 2005.

Refinement of Software Architectures by Recursive Model Transformations*

Ricardo J. Machado[1], João M. Fernandes[2], Paula Monteiro[1], and Helena Rodrigues[1]

[1] Dept. of Information Systems
[2] Dept. of Informatics
University of Minho, Portugal

Abstract. The main aim of this paper is to present how to refine software logical architectures by application of a recursive model-based transformation approach called 4SRS (four step rule set). It is essentially based on the mapping of UML use case diagrams into UML object diagrams. The technique is based on a sequence of steps that are inscribed in a tabular representation that is used to derive the software architecture for a focused part of the global system.

1 Introduction

The most complex activity during development of software systems is probably the transformation of a requirement specification into an architectural design [1]. The other phases have also their challenges, but they are better understood and a variety of methods, languages and tools are available to support the software engineer.

The process of designing software architectures is, by far, less formalised and often is greatly an intuitive ad-hoc activity, poorly based on engineering principles. Since the architecture of a software system constrains the space solution, the design decisions taken during architectural design must be made with great care, since they typically have a large impact on the quality of the resulting system.

An architectural transformation approach, called 4SRS (four step rule set), is presented that employs successive transformations of the software architecture, in order to satisfy the elicited user requirements. It is essentially based on the mapping of UML use case diagrams into UML object diagrams. The iterative nature of the approach and the usage of graphical models are important issues to guarantee that the final architecture reflects the user requirements.

Fig. 1 illustrates the recursive application of the 4SRS technique. This paper addresses the problem of deriving the logic architecture of a given platform service (called service object diagram), from a functional refinement of the platform architectural model (called platform object diagram), by adopting a recursive version of the 4SRS technique. The first 4SRS execution supports the platform requirements analysis by generating one platform object diagram that corresponds to the logic architecture of the system (this first 4SRS execution is described in detail in [2]). The second

* This work has been supported by projects STACOS (FCT/POSI/CHS/48875/2002) and USE-ME.GOV (IST-2002-002294).

J. Münch and M. Vierimaa (Eds.): PROFES 2006, LNCS 4034, pp. 422 – 428, 2006.

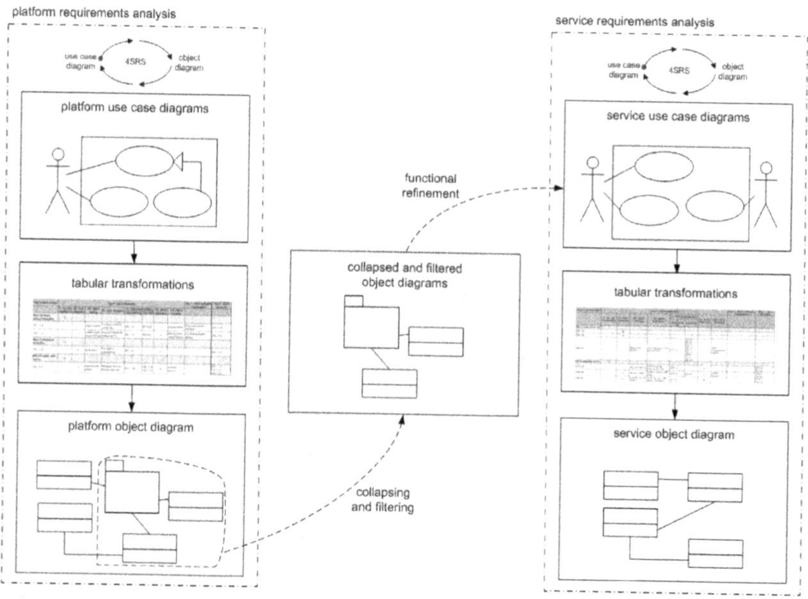

Fig. 1. Service specification with recursive 4SRS execution

4SRS execution supports the service requirements analysis by generating one service object diagram that corresponds to the logic architecture of the service to be specified (this second 4SRS execution is the aim of this paper).

The applicability of this technique is illustrated by presenting some results from a mobile application. For mobile applications, the definition of the underlying service oriented software architecture must consider as user requirements the services themselves, the mobile operators entry points and the final clients interfaces, and use them to characterize the platform. Within the presented demonstration case, the specification of one service of the mobile application was obtained by recursively applying the 4SRS technique.

2 Four Step Rule Set

4SRS is a technique proposed to transform users requirements into architectural models representing system requirements [3, 4]. It associates, to each object found during the analysis phase, a given category: interface, data, control. Each one of these categories is related to one of the three orthogonal dimensions, in which the analysis space can be divided (information, behaviour and presentation) [5].

For readability purposes, a brief description of the 4SRS technique is next presented. There is a complete description of its usage to obtain, in a non-recursive approach, the first logical architecture of the demonstration case used in this paper in [2]. In [6], an alternative version of the 4SRS technique is described for deriving the logical architecture for software product lines. This variant of the 4SRS technique deals with variability at functional and architectural levels; the IESE GoPhone demonstration case [7] was adopted to experiment the approach.

The 4SRS technique is organized as four steps to transform use cases into objects: (1) object creation, (2) object elimination, (3) object packaging & aggregation, and (4) object association. After the execution of the 4 steps of the 4SRS technique, we obtain the logic architecture for the system that captures all its functional and non-functional requirements. An object model shows how significant properties of a system are distributed across its parts.

Fig. 2 shows the filtered object diagram that was obtained by using collapsing and filtering techniques described in [2] by considering package *{P5}* as one sub-system for design. This diagram was included here as an example of how raw object diagrams can be used during the development process to stress parts of the system and allow sub-system specification and partition of sub-projects among various teams.

In this paper, we consider the refinement of package *{P5}* that has given origin to the *AVAccess* service (the *service object diagram* depicted in fig. 1).

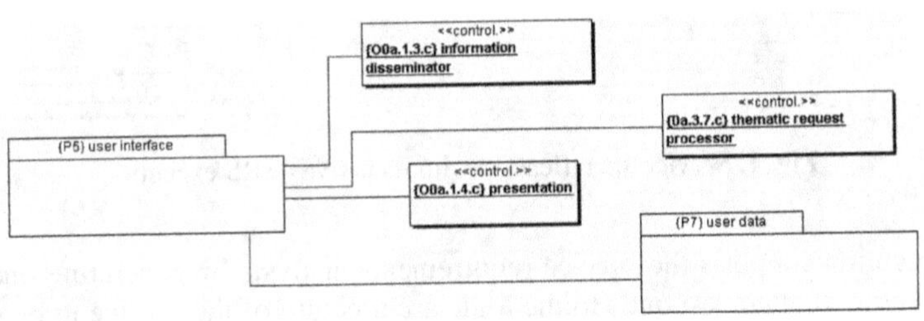

Fig. 2. Filtered object diagram for package {P5} service derivation

3 Recursive Architectural Refinement

{P5} can be considered as the system to be designed and apply, once more, the 4SRS technique to support its architectural refinement (within fig. 2). The recursive approach of the 4SRS technique suggests the construction of a new use case diagram (called *service use case diagram*, in fig. 1) that captures the users requirements of the new (sub-)system to refine. From this use case diagram the corresponding raw object diagram is derived (called *service object diagram*, in fig. 1). This proposed approach contrasts with the dominant one that suggests the application of design patterns to impose into the logical architecture a particular already proven reference architectural model [8, 9]. Our proposal does not reject this pattern-oriented view, only defers it into latter stages of development, allowing a previous functional refinement of requirements at architectural level, taking into account the specific aspects of the particular sub-system to be designed. The use case diagram depicted in fig. 3 was constructed for supporting the architectural refinement of *{P5}* to obtain the raw object diagram of the *AVAccess* service. This service constitutes the example considered in this paper to show the recursive application of the 4SRS technique. All the external entities (UML actors) existent in this diagram correspond to architectural elements connected to package *{P5}* in fig. 2. Object *{O0a.1.3.c}* in fig. 2 did not give origin to

any actor in fig. 3, because the architectural refinement of package *{P5}* did not consider the functionality that is associated with that object. The *user* actor is present in fig. 3, since it was already connected to the use cases that gave origin to the objects inside package *{P5}*, during the development process described in [2]. Actors in fig. 3 must be viewed as external sub-systems (components), from the point of view of the *AVAccess* service. To attain a better actor semantics within the associations with the obtained use cases, the actor *{O0a.3.7.c}* in fig. 3 was specialized into two different actors: *Application System Context Aggregation Service* and *Application System Service Repository*.

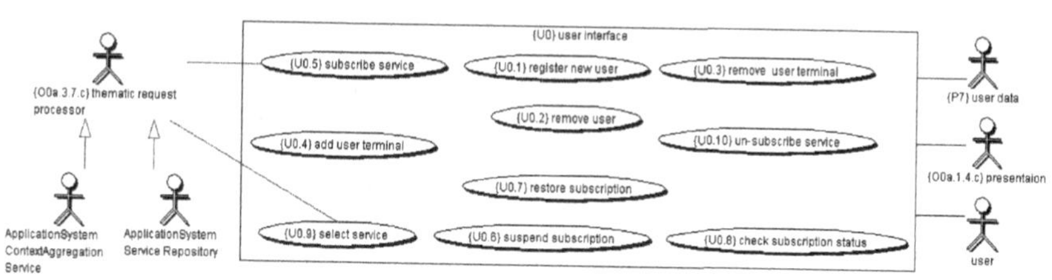

Fig. 3. Use case diagram for AVAccess service

4 Tabular Transformations

The execution of the 4SRS transformation steps can be supported in tabular representations. Moreover, the usage of tables permits a set of tools to be devised and built so that the transformations can be partially automated. These tabular representations constitute the main mechanism to automate a set of decision assisted model transformation steps. The 4SRS has been used both in academia and in industry [3, 4, 10] and has demonstrated to be agile in helping software engineers to find and refine architectural requirements, based on the elicited user requirements.

The table for the transformation steps is organized as follows: (1) each (micro-)step gives origin to one column; (2) each object gives origin to one row.

The 1st column corresponds to the execution of step 1. The first row allows the insertion of both the reference and the name of the use case. The next three rows allow the insertion of one interface, one data, and one control objects for the corresponding use case. For the demonstration case, there is no use case refinement, so step 1 is applicable to all (10) use cases in fig. 3, which gave origin to 30 objects. Fig. 4 depicts 4 different rows for each of the two previously exemplified use cases.

The 2nd column corresponds to the execution of micro-step 2i. In this micro-step, the software engineer classifies each use case as one of the 8 different combinations or patterns (Ø, i, c, d, ic, di, cd, icd). The idea behind this classification is to help on the transformation of each use case into objects. This classification would provide hints on which object categories to use and how to connect those objects. For the demonstration case, *{U0.1}* was classified as type "i", which means that only the interface object is kept (the control and data objects will be eliminated in micro-step 2ii), and *{U0.5}* was classified as type "icd", which means that all objects are kept.

The 3rd column corresponds to the execution of micro-step 2ii. The aim of this micro-step is to answer if each object created in step 1 makes sense in the problem domain, since the creation of objects in step 1 was blindly executed, not considering the system context for the object creation. Object that are to be eliminated are marked with "x" and objects that are to be kept are marked with "-". For the demonstration case, *{U0.1}* got two of its originated objects eliminated, since they do not make sense in the problem domain. *{U0.1}* is only responsible to send the new user information from the user to other sub-systems and vice-versa, which means that data and control dimensions are not within the scope of this use case.

Step 1 -object creation	Step 2 - object elimination								Step 3 - object packaging & aggregation	Step 4 - object association
	2i - use case classification	2ii - local elimination	2iii - object naming	2iv -object description	2v - object representation: is represented by	2v - object representation: represents	2vi - global elimination	2vii - object renaming		
{U0.1} register new user	i									
{O0.1.c}		x								
{O0.1.d}		x								
{O0.1.i}		-	register user interface	allows the parse of the user personal...	{O0.1.i}	{O0.2.i} {O0.3.i} {O0.4.i} {O0.5.i} {O0.6.i} {O0.7.i} {O0.8.i} {O0.9.i} {O0.10.i}	-	users managemment interface		
{U0.5} subscribe service	icd									
{O0.5.c}		-	subscribe service	will process the request subscribe...	{O0.5.c}		-			{O0.5.d} {O0.5.i}
{O0.5.d}		-	defined activities	interface with the data of the...	{O0.5.d}	{O0.9.d}	-	available activities		{O0.5.c} {O0.5.i}
{O0.5.i}		-	subscribe service interface	sends the subscribe service information...	{O0.1.i}		x			{O0.5.c} {O0.5.d}

Fig. 4. Table for 4SRS transformations

The 4th column corresponds to the execution of micro-step 2iii. In this micro-step, objects that have not been eliminated from the previous micro-step must receive a proper name that reflects both the use case from which it is originated and the specific role of the object, taking into account its main component. For the demonstration case, object *{O0.1.i}*, for instance, was named *register user interface.*

The 5th column corresponds to the execution of micro-step 2iv. Each named object resulting from the previous micro-step must be described, so that the system requirements they represent become included in the object model. These descriptions must be based on the original use case descriptions.

The 6th and 7th columns correspond to the execution of micro-step 2v. This is the most critical micro-step of the 4SRS technique, since it supports the elimination of redundancy in the user requirements elicitation, as well as the discovering of missing requirements. The "*is represented by*" column stores the reference of the object that will represent the object being analyzed. If the analyzed object will be represented by itself, the corresponding "*is represented by*" column must refer to itself. The "*represents*" column stores the references of the objects that the object analyzed will represent. *{O0.1.i}* does not delegate in other objects its representation (i.e. it is represented by itself) and it additionally represents a considerable list of other objects (each one of these objects must refer to *{O0.1.i}* in their columns "*is represented by*").

The 8th column corresponds to the execution of micro-step 2vi. This is a fully "automatic" micro-step, since it is based on the results of the previous one. The objects that are represented by other ones must be eliminated, since its system requirements no longer belong to them.

The 9th column corresponds to the execution of micro-step 2vii. Its purpose is to rename the objects that have not been eliminated in the previous micro-step and that represent additional objects. The new names must reflect the plenitude of system requirements. For the demonstration case, object *{O0.1.i}* was renamed *users management interface* to reflect the list of other objects that it additionally represents.

The 10th column corresponds to the execution of step 3. For the demonstration case, neither aggregations, nor packages were used, so column 10 remains unfilled.

The 11th column corresponds to the execution of step 4. For the demonstration case, the associations were solely derived from the use case classification executed in step 1. The classification of *{U0.5}* as type "icd" suggests the existence of three internal associations relative to the objects generated from the same use case. However, "id" association (between the interface and the data objects) was not allowed. Additionally, the following two tabular transformations imposed some constrictions to the object connectivity exercise: (1) in step 2v, it was decided that *{O0.5.i}* is represented by *{O0.1.i}*; (2) in step 2vi, {O0.5.i} was eliminated. These two decisions imply the existence of the following associations: (1) between *{O0.5.c}* and *{O0.5.d}*, suggested by the "icd" classification; (2) between *{O0.5.c}* and *{O0.1.i}*, due to the transitivity of the suggested association between *{O0.5.c}* and *{O0.5.i}* through the delegation executed by *{O0.5.i}* in *{O0.1.i}*.

5 Service Specification

Fig. 5 depicts the raw object diagram for the *AVAccess* service, obtained from the recursive application of the 4SRS technique.

The obtained raw object model (fig. 5) constitutes the canonical semantic reference for the service to be designed, since it has emerged from the software logical architecture of the platform by adopting a complementary functional refinement at architectural level. This architectural refinement has been explicitly executed within a component-based service development.

After obtaining this new architectural refined raw object model, the underlying service can be described through a set of diagrams as a means to specify the corresponding architectural component, namely, by designing a class diagram for the static characterization of the service component, a statechart for the life cycle characterization of the service, a set of activity diagrams for methods specification and a set of sequence diagrams for interface and protocol specification. These additional perspectives of the same service are not directly generated from the application of 4SRS technique, even though they are easier constructed after obtaining the raw object diagram of the service (fig. 5).

Fig. 5. Raw object diagram of the AVAccess service

6 Conclusions

The proposed recursive approach of the 4SRS technique suggests the construction of a new use case diagram that captures the users requirements of the new (sub-)system to refine a service. From this use case diagram the corresponding raw object diagram can be derive. This approach complements the usage of design patterns by allowing a previous functional refinement of requirements at architectural level, taking into account the specific aspects of the particular sub-system to be designed. This transformational approach shows that model continuity is a key issue and highlights the importance of having a well defined process to relate, map and transform requirements models. In the demonstration case, the 4SRS has allowed the specification of one particular service, taking into account all the architectural decisions previously taken to specify the platform where the service is intended to run, by assuring a continuous mapping between the platform and the service models.

References

1. J. Bosch, P. Molin. Software Architecture Design: Evaluation and Transformation. 7th IEEE Int. Conf. on the Engineering of Computer-Based Systems (ECBS'99), Nashville, Tennessee, U.S.A., pp. 4-10, IEEE CS Press, March, 1999.
2. R.J. Machado, J.M. Fernandes, P. Monteiro, H. Rodrigues. Transformation of UML Models for Service-Oriented Software Architectures. 12th IEEE Int. Conf. on the Engineering of Computer-Based Systems (ECBS 2005), Greenbelt, Maryland, U.S.A., pp. 173-182, IEEE CS Press, April, 2005.
3. J.M. Fernandes, R.J. Machado, H.D. Santos. Modeling Industrial Embedded Systems with UML. 8th IEEE/IFIP/ACM Int. Workshop on Hardware/Software Co-Design (CODES 2000), San Diego, California, U.S.A., pp. 18-22, ACM Press, May, 2000.
4. J.M. Fernandes, R.J. Machado. From Use Cases to Objects: An Industrial Information Systems. 7th Int. Conf. on Object-Oriented Information Systems (OOIS 2001), Calgary, Canada, pp. 319-328, Springer-Verlag, August, 2001.
5. I. Jacobson, M. Christerson, P. Jonsson, G. Övergaard. Object-Oriented Software Engineering: A Use Case Driven Approach. Addison-Wesley, 1992.
6. A. Bragança, R.J. Machado. Deriving Software Product Line's Architectural Requirements from Use Cases: An Experimental Approach. 2nd Int. Workshop on Model-Based Methodologies for Pervasive and Embedded Software (MOMPES 2005), Rennes, France, pp. 77-91, June, 2005.
7. D. Muthig, I. John, M. Anastasopoulos, T. Forster, J. Dörr, K. Schmid. GoPhone: A Software Product Line in the Mobile Phone Domain. IESE Technical Report no. 025.04/E, 2004.
8. F. Buschmann, R. Meunier, H. Rohnert, P. Sommerlad, M. Stal. Pattern-Oriented Software Architecture: A System of Patterns. John Wiley & Sons, 1996.
9. 9 R. Ahlgren, J. Markkula. Design Patterns and Organisational Memory in Mobile Application Development. 6th Int. Conf. on Product-Focused Software Process Improvement (PROFES2005),Oulu,Finland,pp.143-156,Springer-Verlag,June, 2005.
10. J.M. Fernandes, R.J. Machado. System-Level Object-Orientation in the Specification and Validation of Embedded Systems. 14th SBC/IFIP/ACM Symposium on Integrated Circuits and System Design (SBCCI 2001), Pirenópolis, Brazil, pp. 8-13, IEEE Computer Society Press, August, 2001.

A UML-Based Process Meta-model Integrating a Rigorous Process Patterns Definition

Hanh Nhi Tran[1], Bernard Coulette[1], and Bich Thuy Dong[2]

[1] University of Toulouse 2 -GRIMM
5 allées A. Machado F-31058 Toulouse, France
{tran, coulette}@univ-tlse2.fr
[2] University of Natural Sciences, VNUHCM
227 Nguyen Van Cu, Q5, HoChiMinh Ville, Vietnam
thuy@hcmuns.edu.vn

Abstract. Process Pattern is an emergent approach to reuse process knowledge. However, in practice this concept still remains difficult to be exploited due to the lack of formalization and supporting methodology. In this paper, we propose a way to formalize the process pattern concept by introducing it into a process meta-model. We provide a general definition to cover various kinds of process-related patterns in different domains. We define rigorously process concepts and their relations to allow representing processes based on process patterns and to facilitate the development of supporting tools. By distinguishing process patterns at different abstraction levels, we aim to develop a systematic approach to define and apply process patterns.

1 Introduction

Recently, process patterns approach has been adopted by process communities to capture and reuse proven processes. The expected interests of reduced development time and improved process quality make process patterns approach attractive. However, up to now works on process pattern have not been enough developed to permit applying this concept efficiently. Firstly, it lacks a definition that can cover the diversity of process patterns (c.f. [8][9] for more detailed discussions on process patterns definitions and taxonomy). Secondly, the representation of process patterns is not adequately formal to be directly reused in process modeling. Finally, a process patterns based methodology for developing processes is still needed to guide process designers applying process patterns systematically.

To cope with these issues, we believe that the first step is to formalize process patterns. This objective can be achieved by introducing the process pattern concept into a process meta-model. We present in this paper a UML-based meta-model integrating the concept of process pattern into the description of software processes. Our meta-model provides rigorous concepts to describe process patterns and processes based on process patterns. The meta-model will be presented in the following section and exemplified in section 3. Related works and contributions are summed up in the final section.

J. Münch and M. Vierimaa (Eds.): PROFES 2006, LNCS 4034, pp. 429 – 434, 2006.

2 A Meta-model for Representing Process Patterns

Our objective is to define process patterns as patterns for modeling processes. Thus, we provide a wide definition to cover all the related notions.

We introduce multi-abstraction levels[1] into process representation to promote process reuse. The relations between process models at different abstraction levels are defined in order to clarify the way of defining process models (and then process patterns which capture them). To allow process modeling based on patterns and facilitate patterns organization, we also define explicitly the aspects of process pattern concept as well as the relationships among patterns, between process patterns and process models. To attaint the requirement on standardization, initially we aimed at integrating the process pattern concept into the software process meta-model SPEM 1.1[4]. However, SPEM 1.1 has some deficiencies and is progressing towards a next version [5]. So, we decided to develop a meta-model which is strongly inspired by SPEM 1.1 for process description, but based directly on UML[2].

To present our meta-model, we use UML class diagrams[3] for the abstract syntax. The semantics is expressed in natural language and reinforced by OCL expressions[4].

2.1 ProcessModel

- This concept is used to describe (part of) a process. It is composed of process tasks (*Task*), the required products (*Product*) and the participating roles (*Role*) of these tasks (Figure 1a).

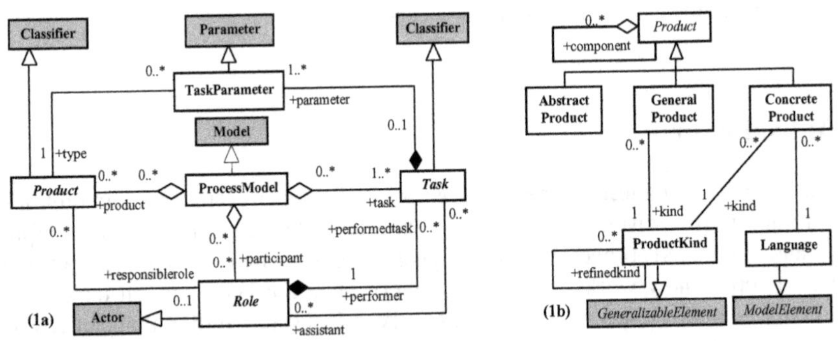

Fig. 1. Meta-model for *ProcessModel* and *Product*

Product is an artifact created, consumed or modified during the development. A *Task* is a unit of work realized to create or modify products. Necessary products for the execution of a task are described explicitly as its parameters (*TaskParameter*). A *Role*

---

1 The abstraction level of a process model reflects how detailed its content is described.

2 In our meta-model, the part describing processes (which is inspired by SPEM 1.1) is defined separately with the part introducing process patterns. Thus, in the future, we just need to change the first part to conform our meta-model to the stable version of SPEM.

3 Light grayed classes represent ones from UML; white classes represent new defined concepts.

4 Due to the space constraint, we cannot present here the OCL well-formedness rules.

is an abstract concept describing a set of competences of development using to realize or assist a task.

- **Typology of Products:** Products help to specify the precise meaning of a task. An *AbstractProduct* describes a certain product without any exact meaning. A *GeneralProduct* is specified by a product kind (*ProductKind*) which can be specialized further for more specific goals. A *Concrete Product* belongs to a product kind and is represented by a concrete formalism (*Language*) (Figure 1b).
- **Description of Tasks:** Figure 2 shows the detailed description of a task with the conditions to begin or finish (*PreCondition* and *PostCondition*) and sub-tasks.

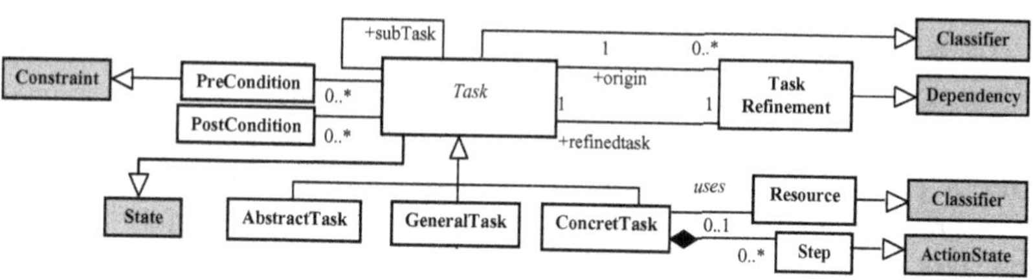

Fig. 2. Meta-model for *Task*

We propose a categorization of tasks abstraction levels based on abstraction levels of the products that they manipulate. An *Abstract Task* doesn't have any associated semantic action and is unexecutable. A *General Task* creates or modifies one or several general products. It has an associated semantic action but is not ready to be executed because the meaning of its actions depends on incompletely specified products. A *Concrete Task* creates or modifies concrete products. It can be decomposed into elementary actions (*Step*) that have a precise semantics. Actions of a concrete task are described completely in terms of resources (*Resource*) used to accomplish it. A concrete task is therefore ready to be executed.

If a task works on several products having different abstraction levels, the abstraction level of the task is deduced from the highest abstraction level of its products. The relation *«has subTask»* permits to decompose a task into sub-tasks which have to be realized together to accomplish the parent task. We also highlight the dependencies between tasks at different abstraction levels (*«TaskRefinement»*). This relation allows refining a task to obtain more specific tasks by specifying more details on its semantic action and its manipulated products.

2.2 ProcessPattern

A *Process Pattern* captures a *Process Model* that can be reused to resolve a recurrent process development *Problem* in a given *Context* (Figure 3). A *Problem* expresses the intention of a pattern and can be associated to a development task through the relation *«is applied for»*. It is possible to have several process patterns addressing the same problem. A *Process Model* represents the solution of a process pattern. A *Context* characterizes conditions in which a process pattern can be applied (*Initiation*), results that must be achieved after applying the pattern (*Resulting*) and situation recommended for reusing it (*Reuse Situation*).

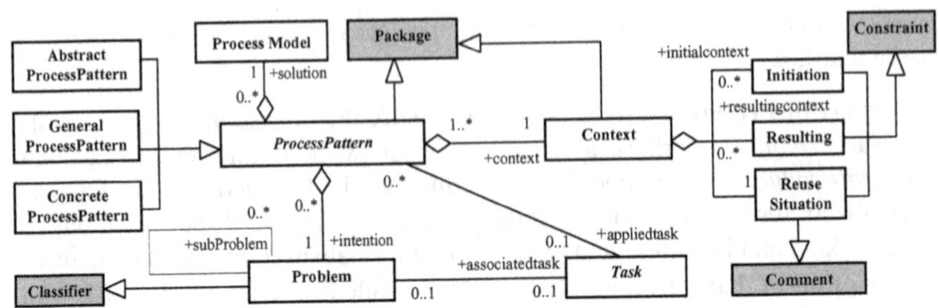

Fig. 3. Meta-model for *ProcessPattern*

We distinguish several types of process patterns according to abstraction level of their captured process model. An *AbstractProcessPattern* captures a recurrent generic structure for modeling or organizing processes. A *GeneralProcessPattern* captures a process model that can be applied to realize a general task and a *ConcreteProcessPattern* captures a process model that can be applied to realize a concrete task.

Our meta-model reflects four important relations between process patterns: *Sequence*, *Use*, *PatternRefinement* and *PatternAlternative* (Figure 4).

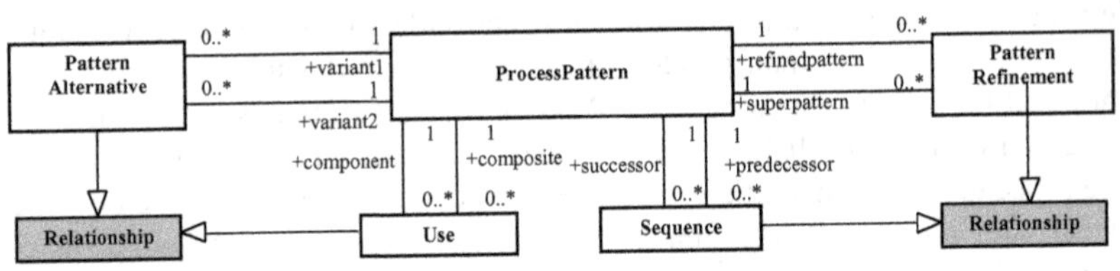

Fig. 4. Process Patterns Relationships

A *Sequence* relationship links two patterns if the predecessor produces all products required by the successor. A pattern "*uses*" another if the latter can be applied for one (or more) task in the solution of the composite pattern. A process pattern is "*refined*" from another if its associated task has the relation "*TaskRefinement*" with the associated task of the super pattern. Two process patterns are related by the relationship *PatternAlternative* if they solve the same problem with different solutions.

3 Example of Process Patterns

In this example, we will show how a process pattern is represented and how it can be applied in process modeling.

Fagan Inspection Process [1] is one of well-known processes used for detecting defects of software products. This process can be applied on different types of products (e.g. requirements, design, code test plans/cases and user documentation), therefore we define the general pattern "FaganInspectionPattern" to capture it[5] (Figure 5a).

[5] For the sake of simplicity, here we just represent the principal elements of this process.

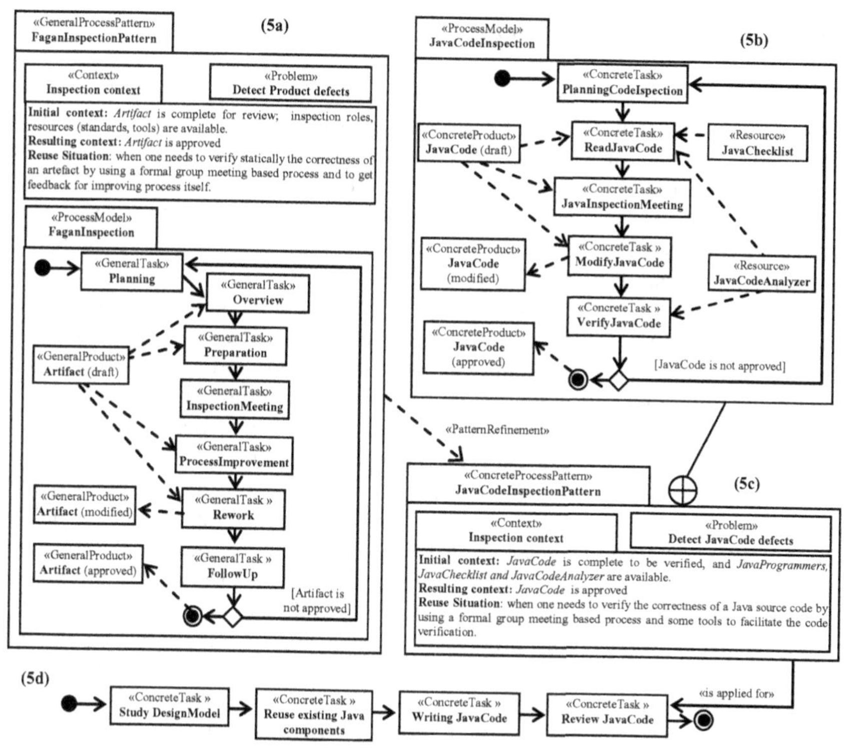

Fig. 5. Patterns for software artifacts inspection and their applications

When a process designer wants to define a group meeting-based process to review a Java source code, he can reuse the FaganInspection process by applying the pattern in Figure 5. To do so, he instantiates the captured process model of the pattern, then refines the general tasks by concrete tasks with their necessary resources (e.g. the concrete task *ReadJavaCode* which is refined from the general task *Preparation* uses the *JavaChecklist* and *JavaCodeAnalyser* as particular resources), and replaces general products by concrete products (e.g. the general product *Artifact* is replaced by the concrete product *JavaCode*). He can also modify the process model by choosing just the pertinent tasks to be refined (e.g. the task *Overview* and *ProcessImprovement* are omitted). Figure 5b shows the modified process model. After certain successfully applications of process described in Figure 5b, the process designer can capture this process model to define a new concrete process pattern "JavaCodeInspection" (Figure 5c). From now on, this concrete pattern can be applied over and over again in any process having a task of JavaCode verification. For example, Figure 5d shows a process for developing Java programs. In this process, the designer want to reuse exactly the process model captured in "JavaCodeInspectionPattern", thus he applies this concrete pattern directly for the task "ReviewJavaCode" by making a link from the task to the pattern. This reference mechanism is permitted in process modeling thanks to the relationship *"is applied for"* described in our meta-model (c.f. Figure 3).

4 Related Works and Conclusion

In regard to process patterns formalization, works are still modest. Gnatz et al. proposed a process framework[2] to describe software processes and introduced the notion of process pattern as a modular way for the documentation of development knowledge. Hagen et al. developed a the UML-based language PROPEL[3] to describe explicitly process patterns and their relationships. The process modeling language PROMENADE[7] defines the process pattern concept as a parameterized process template and proposes a set of high-operators for manipulating process models. In the field of method engineering, Rolland et al.[6] have developed a meta-model to capture "way of working" – a closed concept to process pattern. All of these meta-models are not based on a standardized process meta-model and just concentrate on general software process patterns, thus cannot cover other kinds and abstraction levels of process patterns. Compared with the above works, our approach aims at integrating process pattern to a widely accepted process meta-model, i.e. SPEM of OMG. We introduced a more general definition which covers a large variety of process patterns. Especially, our meta-model allows representing process models and process patterns at different abstraction levels. Furthermore, besides a semi-formal description, a set of OCL constraints are also defined to provide a more rigorous semantics for the proposed meta-model. In the first draft submission for SPEM 2.0[5], the process pattern concept is proposed as a Capability Pattern which describes reusable clusters of activities in common process areas. However, the internal structure of this concept as well as relationships between patterns is not defined. Moreover, in contrast to our approach, SPEM 2.0 does not pay attention to the different abstraction levels of patterns. Our work thus still will be useful on integrating and adapting to SPEM 2.0 when it is stabilized.

References

1. Fagan, M.E.: Advances in Software Inspections. IEEE Transactions on Software Engineering, Vol. SE-12, No. 7, Page 744-751(1986)
2. Gnatz, M. Marschall, F., Popp, G., Rausch, A., Schwerin, W.: The Living Software Development Process. Journal Software Quality Professional, Volume 5, Issue 3 (2003)
3. Hagen, M., Gruhn, V.: Process Patterns - a Means to Describe Processes in a Flexible Way. ProSim04, Edinburgh, United Kingdom (2004)
4. OMG: Software Process Engineering Metamodel (SPEM v1.1) Specification: OMG Document formal/05-01-06 (2005)
5. OMG: SPEM 2.0 Draft Adopted Specification. http://www.omg.org/docs/ad/05-06-05.pdf
6. Ralyté J., Rolland C.: An Assembly Process Model for Method Engineering. CAISE'01, Interlaken, Switzerland (2001)
7. Ribó J. M; Franch X.: Supporting Process Reuse in PROMENADE. Research Report LSI-02-14-R, Dept. LSI, Politechnical University of Catalonia (2002)
8. Tran H.N., Coulette B., Dong T.B.T. Towards a better understanding of Process Patterns. SERP 2005 (2005)
9. Tran H.N., Coulette B., Dong T.B.T. A Classification of Process Patterns. SWDC-REK 2005. Reykjavik, Island (2005)

Ad Hoc Versus Systematic Planning of Software Releases – A Three-Staged Experiment

Gengshen Du, Jim McElroy, and Guenther Ruhe

Laboratory for Software Engineering Decision Support, University of Calgary
2500 University Drive NW, Calgary, AB, T2N 1N4, Canada
{dug, mcelroy, ruhe}@cpsc.ucalgary.ca

Abstract. Release planning addresses the process of deciding which requirement of an evolving software system should be assigned to which release. We study two fundamentally different software release planning approaches: (i) ad hoc planning and (ii) systematic planning. Ad hoc planning is mainly based on human intuition, experience and communication. Systematic planning, based on formalization, assumes a quantitative description of the problem, and application of optimization algorithms for its solution.

We have performed a controlled experiment intended to investigate hypotheses related to confidence, understanding, and trust related to the two approaches. The stated hypotheses were based on an explorative pre-study and prior industrial release planning projects. Although limited in scope and size, the experiment provided interesting insight into the performance of the stated approaches. Overall, systematic planning based on tool support increased confidence into the solutions and was trusted more than ad hoc planning.

Keywords: Release Planning Process, Controlled Experiment, Decision Support tool, Confidence, Understanding, Trust.

1 Introduction

Requirements engineering is a decision-rich problem-solving activity [2]. Software release planning is an important part of that activity when incremental software development is considered. In its simplest description, release planning is the process of assigning features or requirements to releases of a product. The functionalities of the product are additive, but it is important to offer the right features at the right time. The overall goal of release planning is to find the most promising release plans such that some stated objective, such as the degree of satisfaction for all the stakeholders or the overall business value, is maximized and available resource constraints are met.

Release decisions are complex, especially when considering problems involving several hundred features and a large number of widely diversified stakeholders. It becomes an even harder problem when resource estimates, resource capacities, and dependencies between features are taken into account. For a more detailed description of the problems and existing solution algorithms, we refer to [11].

There is a lack of evidence in evaluation of technologies in general [8], and of release planning in particular [3]. Addressing trust in solutions generated by algorithms

J. Münch and M. Vierimaa (Eds.): PROFES 2006, LNCS 4034, pp. 435 – 440, 2006.

not easily understood by end-users, Lehtola et al. [7] conducted an empirical investigation to compare two well known methods of prioritizing requirements. The first one is based on pair-wise comparison of requirements, the other one is Wiegers' method [12] which is a cost-benefit method. One of the main findings was that participants mistrusted results they got from Wieger's method. So how can we achieve a higher degree of understanding, confidence and trust into proposed solutions on the user side?

We have performed a controlled experiment intended to investigate hypotheses related to confidence, understanding, and trust related to the two approaches. For that, we compared the (i) informal voting, manual and ad hoc generation of a release plans with (ii.1) the black box type of usage of an intelligent decision support (DSS-RP) system for release planning called ReleasePlanner to perform computer-based voting and generation of release plans. In addition, we have applied (ii.2) a white box usage of DSS-RP where the users were provided with both the results generated from the problem input and with further explanations and insights into the rationale of the proposed solutions resulting from performing two re-planning scenarios.

2 Software Release Planning in a Nutshell

Release planning in an ad hoc fashion focuses on human intuition, communication and human capabilities to decide which requirements should be selected to go into which releases. Physical meetings with stakeholders have to be arranged to elicit their priorities. Normally, this is hard to arrange. During the meetings, the expression of priorities is influenced by the persons attending. Based on that, a more or less accurate understanding of the real priorities is achieved. The actual planning using this understanding occurs on a manual basis, eventually including rounds of negotiations. This process can be supported by a list of the requirements to be released and/or story cards for a description of the requirements or use cases.

The systematic approach for release planning generates plans based on a formalization of the problem. This involves maximizing an objective function constituted from stakeholder ranking of the requirements based on urgency and/or value where different additional parameters for adaptation to the problem context are included. The actual optimization is further defined by a family of technological, resource and/or budget constraints. The result of this process is a set of five alternative solutions where each solution is at least 95% optimal. In addition, the solutions are maximally diversified among each other. For further details, we refer to [11].

ReleasePlanner is a decision support system (DSS-RP) that uses the above optimization approach as part of an evolutionary problem solving approach integrating human and computational intelligence. For industrial experience using the technology we refer to [1], [5], and [9].

3 Experimental Setup

The experiment was carried out at the University of Calgary, Canada. Nine Master's and PhD students majoring in software engineering participated. Further details can be found at http://sern.ucalgary.ca/~dug.

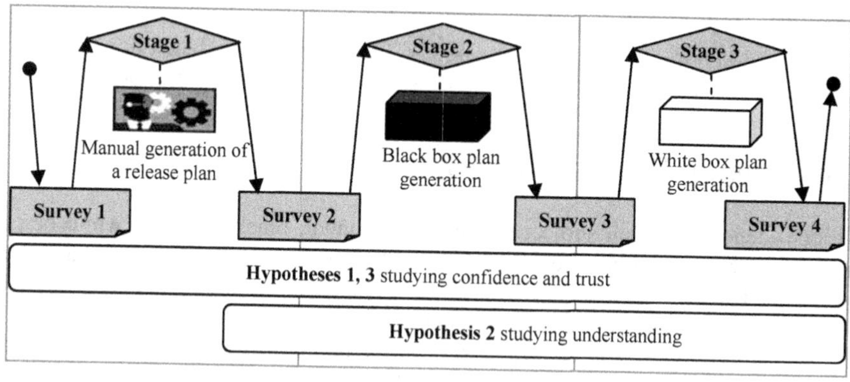

Fig. 1. Overview of the steps of the experiment

The individual steps of the experiment as shown in Figure 1 were performed in the following order:

(1) Survey 1 (Initial Survey): Subjects' background in software development and project management was surveyed.
(2) Stage 1 (Manual Release Plan Generation): Subjects were asked to manually generate one release plan.
(3) Survey 2 (Post Manual Plan Survey) focused on how long this task took, and the confidence the subjects had in their manual plans.
(4) Stage 2 (Black Box Plan Generation): Subjects were asked to take the same project data used in stage 1 to generate release plans using DSS-RP. Minimum instructions on using the tool or interpreting its results were provided.
(5) Survey 3 (Post Black Box Plan Survey) focused on the subjects' confidence in the automatically generated release plans, and their understanding of the results generated by DSS-RP, and their trust in the tool.
(6) Stage 3 (Black Box Plan Generation): Subjects used DSS-RP not only as a planning tool, but also performed prescribed re-planning steps. This was intended to provide a deeper understanding on the impact of parameter changes.
(7) Survey 4 (Post Black Box Plan Survey), filled out after Stage 3, again focused on the subjects' confidence, understanding, and trust.

Based on the findings in [4] and [6], and an explorative pre-study done at University of Sannio, we have stated three hypotheses to be investigated in this experiment.

Hypothesis 1 (Confidence)
(a) Confidence (ad hoc) = Confidence (systematic, black box)
(b) Confidence (systematic, black box) < Confidence (systematic, white box)

Hypothesis 2 (Understanding)
Understanding(systematic, black box) < Understanding (systematic, white box)

Hypothesis 3: (Trust)
(a) Trust (ad hoc) < Trust (systematic, black box)
(b) Trust (systematic, black box) < Trust (systematic, white box)

4 Experiment Results and Analysis

The confidence that each subject had in their manual, black box, and white box release plans was measured after each stage of experiment by surveys 2, 3, and 4 respectively. The average tendency of change in confidence and understanding between the three stages of the experiment was analyzed and is shown in Fig. 2. Seven out of nine subjects reported a moderate to significant increase in confidence in the plans that were generated by using DSS-RP in a black box mode, compared with that of manual generation. The remaining two subjects had no increase in confidence.

In stage 3 of the experiment (white box plan generation), we examined the effect of explaining the process of re-planning using DSS-RP on the understanding of results. As effective re-planning requires a thorough understanding of the original release plans, how these plans are generated, and how each element of release planning affects plan generation and regeneration, the re-planning exercise served as an effective vehicle for providing a thorough explanation of both ReleasePlanner and the plans it generates. Figure 2 shows that one subject actually reported a decrease in the understanding of the DSS-RP and its results after the white box explanation. One subject reported no increase in understanding, and seven subjects reported a moderate to significant increase in understanding of the DSS-RP and its results.

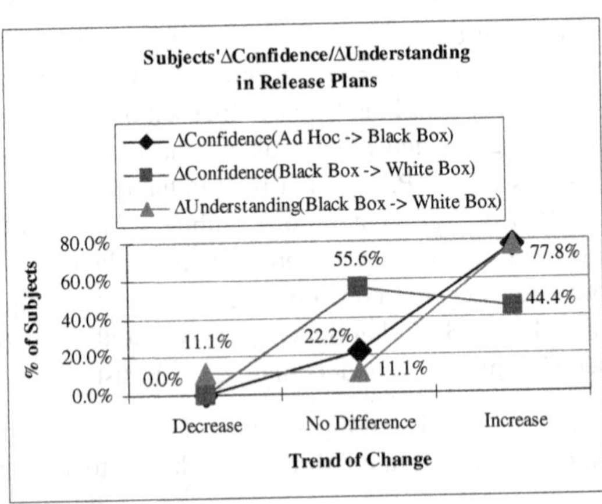

Fig. 2. Average degree's of change in confidence and understanding between the three stages of the experiment

The trust that each subject had in their black box and white box release plans was measured after each stage of experiment by surveys 3 and 4 respectively. The results are shown in Table 1.

Table 1. Subjects' trust on the method used

Subject	**Method Trusted**			
	Stage 2: Comparison between DSS-RP (Black box) and ad hoc		Stage 3: Comparison between DSS-RP (Black box vs white box)	
#	Preference	Degree	Preference	Degree
1	DSS-RP (Black box)	Strong	DSS-RP (White box)	Strong
2	DSS-RP (Black box)	Strong	DSS-RP (White box)	Strong
3	No preference	-	DSS-RP (White box)	Strong
4	DSS-RP (Black box)	Strong	DSS-RP (White box)	Strong
5	DSS-RP (Black box)	Strong	No preference	-
6	DSS-RP (Black box)	Weak	DSS-RP (White box)	Strong
7	Ad hoc	Weak	DSS-RP (White box)	Weak
8	No preference	-	No preference	-
9	DSS-RP (Black box)	Weak	DSS-RP (White box)	Weak

Because of the small sample size, we decided not apply any statistical tests. However, we formally analyzed the data of the experiment using rough set analysis [10]. Again, because of the small sample size, no clear patterns of behavior could be detected. The detailed experimental data relating to the three hypotheses is available at http://sern.ucalgary.ca/~dug.

5 Summary and Conclusions

In this paper, we have performed a three-staged experiment investigating research questions to evaluate the impact of decision support for software release planning. There are three kinds of results: (i) The actual findings of this experiment, (ii) lessons learned and suggestions for performing replications of the experiment, and (iii) suggestions how to further qualify decision support in software engineering.

For the actual findings, the experiment suggested that systematic planning based on tool support increases confidence into the solutions and is trusted more than ad hoc planning. White box usage of the used tool DSS-RP (ReleasePlanner) improved understanding and trust of the proposed solutions when compared to black box usage scenario, but did not appear to increase confidence into the generated solutions. This is the one potentially surprising finding, and warrants further investigation.

The results indicate the need for further research into providing explanation into proposed solution alternatives as part of the functionality of a decision support system [6]. The presentation of the computational results alone is often insufficient to establish enough confidence to actually implement the solution in the real-world. This is even true if very powerful (but hard to understand) computational methods such as specialized integer programming are applied.

There were some threats to the experiment. Specifically, these threats related to (1) Subjectivity of Data**:** A large number of the questions in the different questionnaires were asking for the subjects' judgments with respect to their confidence and understanding of the solutions. (2) Sample Size**:** The sample size for all performed analysis was only 9 data points. (3) Subjects' Experience: The subjects' experience (or lack of experience) in industry or academia related to release planning may have affected their answers to the surveys.

To achieve more confidence into the stated results, further empirical studies are necessary. To achieve higher confidence into the results, we plan two replications of the experiment in 2006 at the University of Calgary.

Acknowledgements

The authors would like to thank the Alberta Informatics Circle of Research Excellence (iCORE) for its financial support of this research. Many thanks are also due to the participants of the experiment for their participation.

References

[1] Amandeep, A., Ruhe, G., Stanford, M.: Intelligent Support for Software Release Planning. 5th Int'l Conference on Product Focused Software Process Improvement , April 5-8, Kansai Science City, Japan, LNCS Vol. 3009 (2004) 248-262

[2] Aurum, A., Wohlin, C.: The Fundamental Nature of Requirement Engineering Activities as a Decision- making Process. Information and Software Technology 45 (14) (2003) 945-954

[3] Carlshamre, P.: Release planning in Market-Driven Software Product Development: Provoking an Understanding. Requirements Engineering 7 (2002), 139-151

[4] Carlsson, C., Turban, E.: Decision Support Systems: Directions for the Next Decade. Decision Support Systems 33 (2002) 105-110

[5] Dantsigner, E.: Practical Release Planning and Management. University of Calgary, Laboratory for Software Engineering Decision Support, TR 006/04 (2004) 29p.

[6] Du, G., Richter, M. M., Ruhe, G.: An Explanation Oriented Dialogue Approach and its Application to Wicked Planning Problems. To appear in: Journal of Computing and Informatics (2006)

[7] Lethola, L., Kauppinen, M., Kujala, S.: Requirements Prioritization Challenges in Practice. Proceedings of 4th International Conference on Product Focused Software Process Improvement, Lecture Notes on Computer Science, Vol. 3009 (2004) 497-508

[8] Glass, R.L.: Matching Methodology to Problem Domain. Communications of the ACM, 47 (5) (2004) 19-21

[9] Momoh, J, Ruhe, G.: Release Planning Process Improvement – An Industrial Case Study. To appear in: Intl Journal of Software Process Improvement and Practice (2006)

[10] Pawlak, Z.: Rough Sets - Theoretical Aspects of Reasoning about Data. Kluwer Academic Publishers (1991)

[11] Saliu, O., Ruhe, G.: Supporting Software Release Planning Decisions for Evolving Systems. Proceedings of the 29th IEEE/NASA Software Engineering Workshop (2005)

[12] Wiegers, K.: Software Requirements. Microsoft Press, Redmont (1999)

A Software Process Tailoring System Focusing to Quantitative Management Plans

Kazumasa Hikichi*, Kyohei Fushida, Hajimu Iida, and Ken'ichi Matsumoto

Graduate School of Information Science, Nara Institute of Science and Technology
8916-5 Takayama-cho, Ikoma-shi, Nara, 630-0192 Japan
{kazuma-h, kyohei-f, matumoto}@is.naist.jp, iida@itc.naist.jp

Abstract. This paper presents a survey about use of quantitative management indicators in a Japanese software development organization. This survey is conducted in order to investigate possible criteria for selecting and customizing organizational standard indicators according to the context of each project. Based on results of the survey, we propose a process tailoring support system that is mainly focusing to quantitative management planning. The system EPDG+ (Electronic Process Data Guidebook Plus) helps project planners select / customize indicators to be employed in process control. Derived software project plans including measurement and analysis activities can be browsed in detail with this system.

1 Introduction

Quantitative management, i.e. the quantitative control in both of quality and schedule management is a key factor of the software processes. The quantitative management requires *indicators* based on quantitative data. Generally, we need to select indicators according to the context of each project, and then we also need to plan the activities for both of measurement and analysis of quantitative data that is required to derive the indicators. Organizations in a certain level of capabilities (e.g. CMMI-staged[1] level 3) usually define their own set of the project management indicators. Thus project planners must understand the purpose of each indicator, select/reject it according to the context of each project, so that activities for measurement and analysis are planned properly. This work is often very difficult for novice planners without sufficient knowledge of quantitative management.

In this paper, we report the survey about the use of indicators in a Japanese software development company (though we are not allowed to disclose the detail of the company, including its name, in this paper). This survey was conducted in questionnaire form in order to design the features of the process tailoring support system EPDG+ (Electronic Process Data Guidebook Plus) that is being developed by us. EPDG+ mainly focuses to the quantitative management, having features to expose appropriate indicators according to the context of each project based on the master list of organizationally standardized indicators. EPDG+ also supports to integrate the measurement and analysis activities required for selected indicators into an engineering process at project planning.

---

* Hitachi, Ltd. from April 2006.

J. Münch and M. Vierimaa (Eds.): PROFES 2006, LNCS 4034, pp. 441 – 446, 2006.

2 Related Work

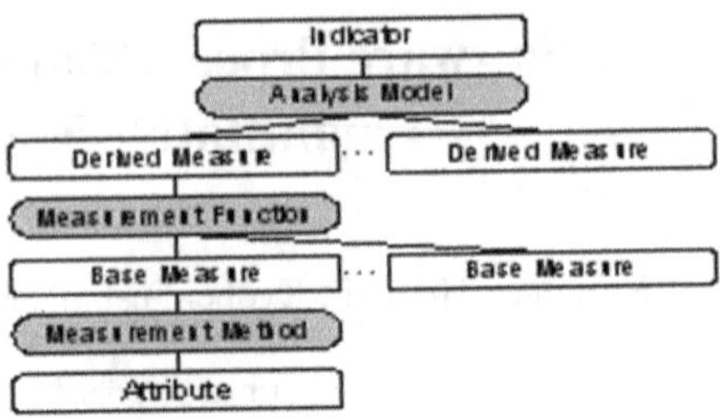

Fig. 1. Measurement information model in ISO/IEC15939

Many studies and standards related to quantitative management have been done since it has direct influence to the improvement of productivity and quality. ISO/IEC15939[2] shows the framework for software measurement, analysis, and construal to achieve various information needs, such as project management and quality assurance. Information structure handled in the measurement and analysis process is specified as a reference model as shown in Fig.1.

This model shows the way which eases objective decision-making based on quantitative information by associating well measurable attributes characteristic to process or product in a project, such as development scale, effort, and number of defects, with the indicator for decision making[3]. Thus, the primary data called *base measure* is collected by quantifying various attributes which exist in a project according to the defined measurement method. Then, the secondary data called *derived measure* is derived by assigning some base measures to measurement function. Finally, the indicator is obtained by analyzing these measures according to the defined analysis model. A project manager makes decision according to the finally derived information product with decision criteria. At the following discussions, we use this concept and the terms based on ISO measurement information model.

Meanwhile, several EPG (Electronic software Process Guidebook) systems are proposed in the past (e.g. [4]). Most of them mainly focus to support to understanding of the prescribed software process. Our approach is also capable of this field. though our current focus is how to utilize the information models, such as definition and flow of quantitative data, required by quantitative management. The ISO information models are useful and very important for the process tailoring.

3 Survey of the Current Status of Used Indicator

3.1 Background

In this study, we consider software development organizations, which perform following two practices, as targets of our approach to support quantitative management planning.

- Every project is planned and performed based on the development process which is defined as organizational standard, typically, in the form of WBS (Work Breakdown Structure).
- The indicator set for quantitative process management is prepared as an organization standard.

When quantitative management is to be planned, selecting appropriate indicators and integrating associated measurement and analysis activities into the project plans are to be performed. However, the definitions of standard indicators are shortly described in the natural language and almost none of formal explanation about an analysis model, function definition (i.e. calculation method), or a measurement method is provided in many organizations. Moreover, explicit tailoring guidelines are not provided. Inexperienced managers have great difficulty in selecting appropriate indicators for their project.

In order to develop the assistance system for novice managers to select and to customize standard indicators to fit their projects, we have conducted a survey to 17 projects in a Japanese software development company to see actual status of indicators selection and customization in industries at first.

3.2 Survey Outline

The survey was conducted by using the questionnaire for project managers who applied quantitative management in a software development (enterprise software system development section) with hundreds of employee. We sent the questionnaire to project managers in the company mainly asking about actual use of their organizational standard 45 management indicators. They are used for progress management, review tracking, testing, process quality assurance (PQA), requirement management, support process.

The first part of the questionnaire is questions about the profile of the project, such as project size, business area, and the profile of manager, e.g. months of experience as project manager and the number of project s/he ever managed.

The second part (main part) of the questionnaire is a list of indicators; for each indicator, questionee is requested to specify the extent of use. The extent of use is at first categorized into two answers, "Used" or "Unused". Then each answer is divided in to more detailed ones. "Used" is divided in 5 answers, and "Unused" is divided in 5 answers. The concrete reason why they used/unused the indicator is optionally provided.

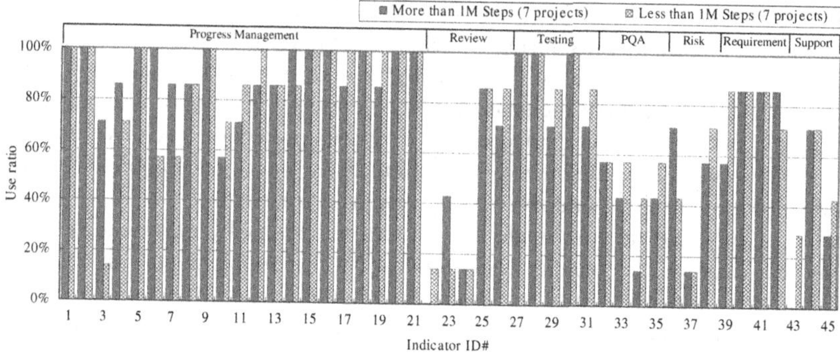

Fig. 2. Summary of the use ratio (used vs total) for each indicator

3.3 Results and Analysis

At first, we summarized usage data simply in two categories, "Used" or "Unused", to get rough trends of the answers according to product size (either less or more than 1 million steps) as shown in Fig.2. Then we proceed to detailed analysis regarding manager's experience (either less or more than 4 years) and also detailed level of indicator use. Since we had to exclude 4 samples without product scale information in program steps, 13 project samples are used in following analysis. This analysis is done because we assume novice managers of small projects would need systematic assist to selection and adaptation of standard indicators to fit the project size, meanwhile most indicators would be employed in large projects regardless of the experience of the managers.

As analysis results, we currently have following observations:

- Indicators for progress management, testing, and requirement management are used in most projects, except one indicator (#3 for tracking the delay of progress report meetings). Indicator #3 is employed in the large project group, but not employed in the small project group. We got a comment from a small project manager that there is little possibility of delay of meeting in small projects.
- Indicators for review tracking, for PQA, for risk management, and for support process showed low rate of use (reasons for these tendencies is not clear at this point).
- In the small project group, we found that experienced managers use many modified or alternative indicators, while novice managers seldom do such adaptation. We got a comment that experienced manager often use alternative information that is available with less cost, and omit some indicators according to their practical situations.
- In both of the small and large project groups, indicators #22~24 for tracking the effect of review are not employed by any projects. Furthermore, a few of experienced managers answered that they don't sufficiently understand the definition and usage of those indicators.

These observations just show trends of the indicator use in one organization "as-is", and we need to be careful to generalize it. However, we found those observations are actually valuable in considering systematic supports for selection and adaptation of indicators. We actually had following insights in designing the features of EPDG+:

As we observed, contexts of the project influence the use pattern of the indicators. By extracting influenced factors according to various project contexts, we will be able to provide indicator candidates to be employed. In order to accomplish this, further survey to more projects and more organizations are needed.

Alternation and modification made to standard indicators by experienced managers may be exposed to inexperienced managers as supplemental information of management planning. In order to accomplish this feature, functions to customize the standard indicators, to store them for future reuse, and to expose inherited indicator variations are needed.

Furthermore, by accumulating the such customization records, EPDG+ system itself will make this kind of survey quite easily and inexpensive.

4 Designing and Prototyping EPDG+

The EPDG+ system is an extended version of EPDG (Electronic Process Data Guidebook) system[5] which scopes to help to understand the process data definitions for analysis and measurement. EPDG+ extends its scope to project planning. It supports a tailoring in planning measurement and analysis activity depending on the characteristics of the project based on quantitative management.

Tailoring support is typically provided according to the following scenario. In this scenario, the work flow is assumed that the planner inputs a process description without management plan, integrates management plan based on quantitative management, and then outputs a process description with management plan.

1. A user inputs a process description, and specifies characteristics of the project to the system.
2. A user refers to the indicators that the system has exposed, and selects indicators.
3. A user browses the plan provided by the system in a graphical way (see Fig.3), and confirms excess and deficiency in the measurement and analysis activity.
4. If necessary, planner will return to step 2, and modifies indicator selections.
5. Once all indicators to be used were decided, project process with quantitative management plan is generated.

There are two major features of EPDG+ as follows:

- **Indicator recommendation:** Organizational standard indicators are listed with rating information based on various criteria. Rating based on records of indicator employment in the past projects with similar profile may be one useful criteria.
Browser of process with measurement and analysis activities integrated: In order to confirm measurement and analysis activities in the process while planning, this feature enables to browse planned processes with integrated measurement and analysis activities.

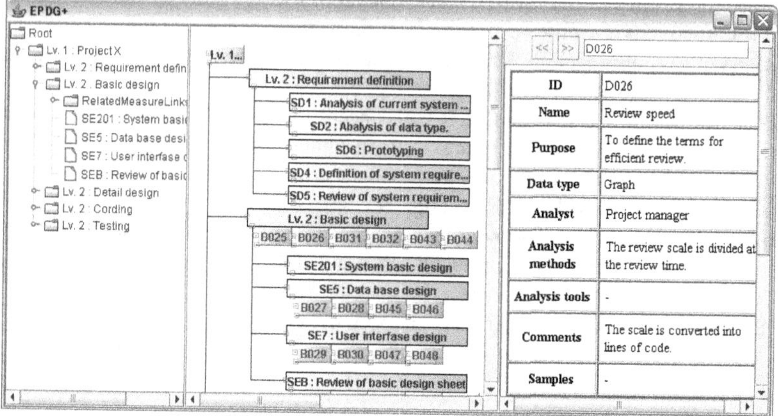

Fig. 3. A Screenshot of the EPDG+ prototype for WBS-style process descriptions

Fig. 2 shows a screenshot of the prototype system. The system window consists of three panes for process structure overview, zoomed detail of the process indicating measurement and analysis activities, and indicator explanations and examples.

5 Conclusion

This paper mainly presented a survey of organizational indicator use for the systematic support to process quantitative management. From the observations we confirmed that quantitative management indicators are actually selected and tuned in hand to fit to the characteristics of each project, and therefore systematic support to indicator selection and modification will be great help to efficient project management. Our EPDG+ is currently under development and it is planned to be integrated to the guideline system for a software company's managers.

Acknowledgements

We cordially thank the anonymous managers for their responses to our survey. We thank Mr. Yasutaka Kamei at NAIST in his help to EPDG+ prototyping. This research is partially supported by the Japan Ministry of Education, Culture, Sports, Science and Technology, Grant-in-Aid for Scientific Research (C) 17500024, and also by the EASE project[6] in Comprehensive Development of e-Society Foundation Software program of the Japan Ministry of Education, Culture, Sports, Science and Technology.

References

1. CMMI Product Team: Capability Maturity Model Integration for System Engineering / Software Engineering / Integrated Product and Process Development, Version 1.1. Software Engineering Institute, CMU/SEI-2002-TR-004 (2002).
2. ISO/IEC 15939:2002: Software engineering - Software measurement process (2002).
3. McGarry, J., et. al.: Practical Software Measurement: Objective Information for Decision Makers. Addison-Wesley Pub (2001).
4. Becker-Kornstaedt, U. and Reinert, R.: A concept to support process model maintenance through systematic experience capture. In Proceedings of the 14th International Conference on Software Engineering and Knowledge Engineering (Ischia, Italy, July 15 - 19, 2002). SEKE '02, vol. 27. ACM Press, New York, NY, 465-468.
5. Murakami, H., Iida, H., Matsumoto, K.: An Electronic Guidebook System for Support of Software Process Management Data Collection and Utilization. Technical Report on IEICE, SS2004-41 (2004) 43-48 in Japanese.
6. EASE Project, EASE Project homepage, http://www.empirical.jp/

An Extreme Approach to Automating Software Development with CBD, PLE and MDA Integrated*

Soo Dong Kim, Hyun Gi Min, Jin Sun Her, and Soo Ho Chang

Department of Computer Science
Soongsil University
511 Sangdo-Dong, Dongjak-Ku, Seoul, Korea 156-743
sdkim@ssu.ac.kr, {hgmin, jsher, shchang}@otlab.ssu.ac.kr

Abstract. Component based development (CBD), product line engineering (PLE), and model driven architecture (MDA) are representative approaches for software reuse. CBD and PLE focus on reusable assets of components and core assets, MDA focuses on transforming reusable models into implementation. Although these approaches are orthogonal, they can be integrated into a comprehensive and extremely effective framework for software development. In this paper, we first present our strategies of integrating CBD, PLE and MDA, and propose an integrated process that adopts reuse engineering and automation paradigm. By applying the proposed approach, it becomes feasible to semi-automatically develop a number of applications in a domain.

1 Introduction

Component based development (CBD), product line engineering (PLE), and model driven architecture (MDA) are representative approaches for software reuse [1][2][3]. CBD emphasizes engineering and reusing independent and customizable components. PLE focuses on modeling commonality and variability into a core asset and deriving applications by instantiating the asset. MDA centers on specifying platform independent model (PIM) and transforming the model into more concrete models and implementations. Although these approaches are orthogonal, we observe that they complement one another. Hence, they can be integrated into a single reuse framework for developing applications efficiently.

In this paper, we first present strategies of integrating CBD, PLE, and MDA to clarify rationales for the integration. Then, we propose an integrated methodology that adopts the components of CBD, the key activities of PLE, and model transformation feature of MDA. By applying the proposed methodology, it becomes feasible to semi-automatically develop a number of applications in a domain. As the result, we can achieve higher reusability and productivity for software development.

2 Strategies for Integrating CBD, PLE, and MDA

An ideal development methodology should have high levels of three quality criteria; *reusability, productivity,* and *standardization*, as shown in Fig. 1 The figure also shows

* This work was supported by grant No.(R01-2005-000-11215-0) from Korea Science and Engineering Foundation in Ministry of Science & Technology.

J. Münch and M. Vierimaa (Eds.): PROFES 2006, LNCS 4034, pp. 447 – 452, 2006.

what constructs/mechanisms of CBD, PLE and MDA potentially contribute to achieving the quality criteria. Based on this observation, we now present how each quality criterion can be achieved using the three technologies.

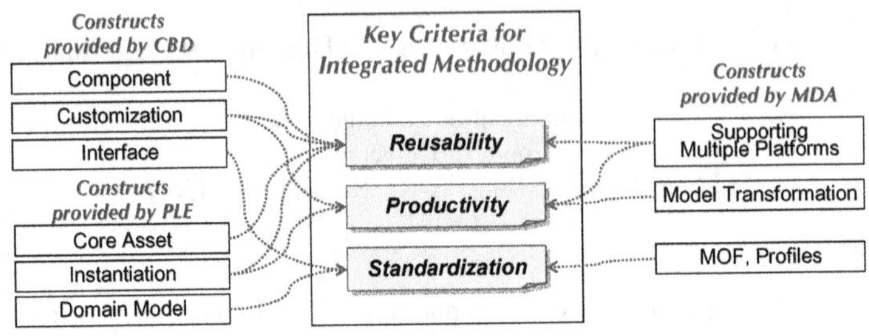

Fig. 1. Key Criteria for Integrated Methodology

Strategy for High Reusability: PLE emphasizes the reusability of core assets, i.e. domain level or architecture level reusability. However, current PLE processes do not address how the core asset can be implemented for specific programming language and platform. MDA can complement this with mechanisms to transform PIM to Platform Specific Model (PSM) which is a detailed design model for a particular platform such as Java, EJB, and .NET. By this, the scope of reusability is extended over different platforms as well as family applications in a domain.

Strategy for High Productivity: Current PLE application engineering includes a phase for core asset instantiation, but concrete instructions to instantiate the given core asset are not provided. The model transformation mechanism of MDA can be used to map core asset to instantiated core asset by specifying decision models and decision resolution models in MOF. By this transformation/automation, the productivity of development is greatly increased.

Strategy for High Standardization: PLE does not provide templates or standards for representing core assets but it provides domain commonality. The PIM, PSM and meta object facility (MOF) of MDA can be used to represent the generic architecture, components, and their interactions of core assets. Hence, this integration enforces standardization on the domain and artifact representations.

3 The Integrated Process

In this section, we present the overall process with instructions. Fig. 2 shows the 13 phases of the process, the associated artifacts in CBD and PLE, and representations in MDA. The phases of application specific design and component customization can be performed in parallel. If appropriate commercial-of-the-shelf (COTS) components are available, component customization activity can be performed with core asset instantiation.

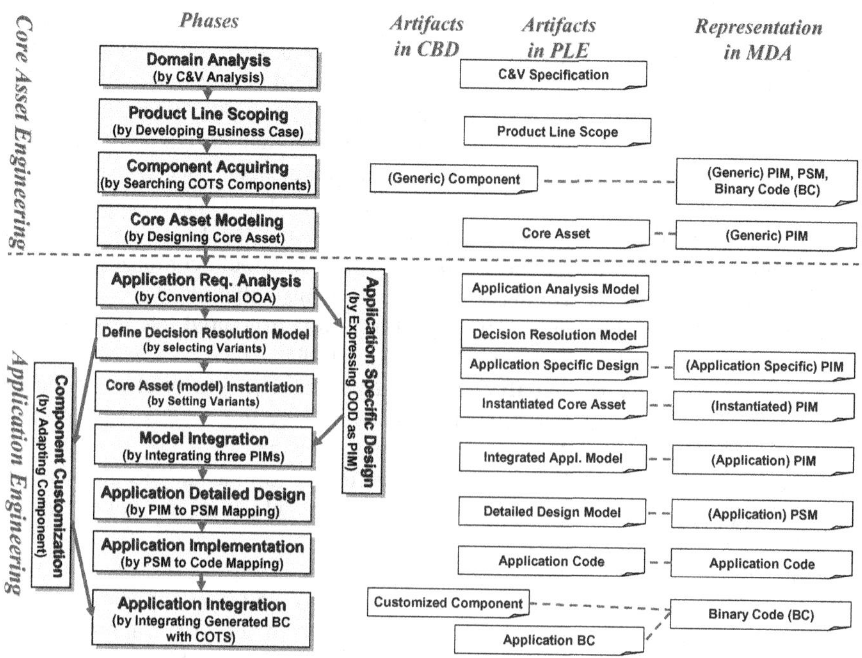

Fig. 2. The Integrated Process with Artifacts

Domain Analysis is to understand *features* of various members in a domain and to analyze their commonality and variability (C&V). Not only the commonality, but also the variability among members should be well-defined since the degree of variability modeling largely determines the applicability and customizability of reuse assets. A good source for the instruction of this phase is found in [4]. The identified C&V can be represented in any form like table and semi-formal. Variable features should be specified with variation points, possible variants for each variation point, variation type, scope of variation in terms of *open* or *close*, and default variant [5].

Product Line Scoping is to determine a set of potential products that can be constructed from a business case analysis on the core assets. Various metrics can be used to determine a product line scope which yields the most economical set. The scope of a product line is specified with descriptions on potential applications, features common, features uncommon, and functional/non-functional description of the common features.

Component Acquisition is to acquire components needed for a core asset by searching COTS components. First we locate a list of available COTS components, and then we identify candidate COTS components by matching feature list with the interfaces provided by COTS components and select the best one. When COTS components are first acquired, they are represented in the level of binary. To make use of the model transformation in generating applications, the acquired components should be represented in the level of PIM and PSM. Therefore, we acquire PIM and PSM representation of the interfaces provided by the COTS components through reverse engineering [6].

Core Asset Modeling is to realize the C&V into a core asset which consists of product line architecture, software components, and a decision model. Software components can be classified into two types; *COTS* and *newly designed model*. While the former, COTS, is acquired in the previous activity, the latter is designed in this activity. We first design the product line architecture, and then design components that all together can realize the required features. Finally, we specify decision models that describe the variability in terms of variation points, variants, related effects, and their attached task [7]. The core asset is represented as a PIM to utilize the model transformation scheme of MDA. Hence, the generic PIM should conform to the UML and MOF specifications. To automate the core asset instantiation in the later phase, the decision model should also be represented in a well structured form so that it can be effectively interpreted by core asset instantiation tool.

Application Requirement Analysis is to analyze the requirement of an application and to identify the application specific features which are not covered by core asset. Conventional OO analysis technique can be used for this phase.

Application analysis model can be represented in any form as long as the semantics of the model is well preserved. It is only an analysis model and so it is not represented as a PIM yet.

Define Decision Resolution Model is to define Decision Resolution Model (DRM) which contains the design decisions specific to the target application. Not all variation points in the decision model are applicable to the target application [7]. Therefore, we start by identifying variation points applicable for the target application. And then we select or define a variant for each variation point. Actual bindings of variant to each variation point are done at *Core Asset Instantiation* and *Component Customization* phases.

The representation of the DRM is same as the decision model except that only one variant is specified for each variation point.

Application Specific Design is to design the application specific features to be further developed and integrated. Note that we should refer parts of a core asset or COTS which may be interacted with the application specific features so that there wouldn't occur any collisions or conflicts.

The representation of application specific design is in the level of preliminary design model, i.e. PIM. This model should be consistent to instantiated PIM in terms of abstraction level.

Core Asset Instantiation is to instantiate the core asset for an application. Using the DRM, variants specific to the application are set into variation points. MDA transformation mechanism can be used to map core asset to instantiated core asset if decision models and application specific decisions are expressed in XMI. To automate the instantiation process, mapping rules that map elements of core asset to elements of instantiated core asset are required.

The representation of instantiated core asset will still be same as the core asset, i.e. generic PIM. Only the variable part of generic PIM is tailored for given variants of a specific application.

Model Integration is to integrate the interfaces of component, core asset model, and the application specific model into a complete application. This phase is to integrate these models and to produce a single coherent design model as shown in Fig. 3, so that, in later phases, it can be effectively implemented for a specific platform. Note that, it should be confirmed the application specific model can seamlessly interact with the interfaces of COTS and core asset model. While MDD focuses on transforming abstract model into more concrete model, model integration is not directly supported in MDD. Hence, it may not be done automatically by tools, but integrated by hand.

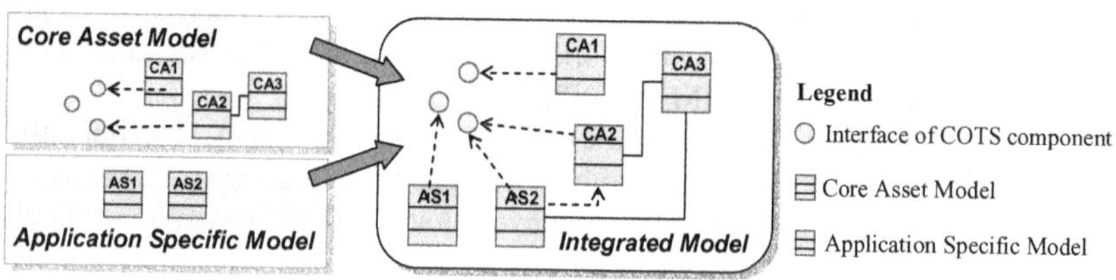

Fig. 3. Integrated Models

The representation of the integrated model will still be a conventional PIM. The scope of the integrated PIM is the entire application so that it can be transformed into a PSM in the next phase.

Application Detailed Design is to refine the integrated application design model for a specific implementation environment such as programming language, middleware and component platform. A key difficulty in this phase is to define a set of mapping rules that takes *integrated model* into *detailed design model.* Candidate techniques can be *marking*, *action semantics*, *UML profile* and *meta-model mapping*. The detailed design model can be represented as the conventional PSM which includes platform specific decisions.

Component Customization is to adapt generic components to satisfy the application requirements. COTS components have customization mechanisms [8] to solve variation points. Therefore, the components are customized by using variants via the customization strategy from the phase '*define decision resolution model*'. Eventually, the components are specialized for the application. This phase delivers customized components in a binary form.

Application Implementation is to take the *application PSM* and to produce executable application code and other associated implementations. This can be done by using the PSM to Code mapping facility of MDA. This phase delivers application code and associated implementations.

Application Integration is to integrate customized components and application binary code which are implemented from instantiated core assets and application specific design. Since COTS interoperate with application code, it is needed interoperability between COTS and application codes to be tested in this phase.

4 Concluding Remarks

CBD, PLE, and MDA are emerging as effective paradigms for building a family of applications in cost effective way. CBD supports this by assembling reusable components developed through component development process, PLE supports this by reusing common assets derived through core asset engineering, and MDA supports this by generating applications on diverse platforms through model transformation. These technologies can be integrated into a single reuse framework for developing applications efficiently.

In this paper, we presented strategies for integrating CBD, PLE, and MDA. Then, we proposed an integrated methodology that adopts the key activities of CBD and PLE and model transformation feature of MDA. The process consists of 13 phases, and each phase was specified with work instructions. We also specified how the artifacts can be represented as PIM and PSM of MDA.

By applying the proposed methodology, it becomes possible to efficiently and semi-automatically develop a large number of applications that vary on behavior and implementation platform. We also believe that the reusability, productivity, traceability, can be greatly increased.

References

1. Heineman, G. and Councill, W., *Component-Based Software Engineering*, Addison Wesley, 2001.
2. Clements, P., et al., *Software Product Lines: Practices and Patterns*, Addison-Wesley, 2002.
3. OMG, *Model Driven Architecture (MDA) Specification*, 2001.
4. Choi, S., et al., "A Systematic Methodology for Developing Component Core assets," *Lecture Notes in Computer Science Vol.2984, Proceedings of the FASE 2004*, 2004.
5. Kim, S., Her, J., and Chang, S., "A Formal View of Variability in Component-Based Development," *Information and Software Technology*, Vol.47, p.663-673, 2005.
6. Kang, K., Kim, M., Lee, J., and Kim, B., "Feature-Oriented Re-engineering of Legacy Systems into Product Line Assets - a Case Study", *Lecture Notes in Computer Science Vol.3714, Proceedings of the SPLC 2005*, pp. 45–56, 2005.
7. Kim, S., Chang, S., and Chang, C., "A Systematic Method to Instantiate Core Assets in Product Line Engineering," *Proceedings of APSEC 2004*, pp.92-98, Nov. 2004.
8. Kim, S., Min, H., and Rhew, S., "Variability Design and Customization Mechanisms for COTS Components," *Lecture Notes in Computer Science Vol.3480, Proceedings of the ICCSA 2005*, pp.57-66, May, 2005.

Experiences and Methods from Integrating Evidence-Based Software Engineering into Education

Andreas Jedlitschka and Markus Ciolkowski

Fraunhofer Institute for Experimental Software Engineering
Fraunhofer Platz 1, 67663 Kaiserslautern
Germany
jedl@iese.fraunhofer.de, markus.ciolkowski@iese.fraunhofer.de

Abstract. In today's software development organizations, methods and tools are employed that frequently lack sufficient evidence regarding their suitability, limits, qualities, costs, and associated risks. For example, in Communications of the ACM (Communications of the ACM May 2004/Vol. 47, No. 5) Robert L. Glass, taking the standpoint of practitioners, asks for help from research: "Here's a message from software practitioners to software researchers: We (practitioners) need your help. We need some better advice on how and when to use methodologies". Therefore, he demands:

- a taxonomy of available methodologies, based upon their strengths and weaknesses;
- a taxonomy of the spectrum of problem domains, in terms of what practitioners need;
- a mapping of the first taxonomy to the second (or the second to the first).

The evidence-based Software Engineering Paradigm promises to solve parts of these issues by providing a framework for goal-oriented research leading to a common body of knowledge and, based on that, comprehensive problem-oriented decision support regarding SE technology selection.

One issue that is becoming more and more important in the context of the evidence-based SE Paradigm is the teaching of evidence-based Software Engineering. A major discussion with regard to this issue revolves around the question of how to "grow the seeds"; that is, how can we teach evidence-based SE in a way that encourages students to practice paradigm in their professional life.

The goal of this workshop is to discuss issues related to fostering the evidence-based paradigm. The results from the workshop and especially from the working groups will be published in the "Workshop Series on Empirical Software Engineering", Vol.3.

The workshop itself is the fourth one in the workshop series on Empirical Software Engineering. The first one was held in conjunction with PROFES 2002 in Rovaniemi, the second one was held in conjunction with the Empirical Software Engineering International Week 2003 in Rome, and the third one was held in conjunction with PROFES 2005 in Oulu.

J. Münch and M. Vierimaa (Eds.): PROFES 2006, LNCS 4034, p. 453, 2006.

Workshop on Embedded Software Development in Collaboration

Pasi Kuvaja

University of Oulu, Finland
Department of Information Processing Science
PL 3000
90014 University of Oulu
pasi.kuvaja@oulu.fi

Abstract. The embedded systems industry is growing and getting a more dominant role in the markets. Due to tight time-to-market requirements and complexity of the systems, companies hardly ever develop embedded products on their own. In order to acquire the required expertise, efficiency and desired lead-time, embedded systems need to be developed globally in collaboration with subcontractors, third party developers and in-house development. Against this background, the workshop on Embedded Software Development In Collaboration addresses the increasing demand of the industry for finding and discovering new and more efficient ways to support collaborative embedded systems development. The short paper sessions provide an excellent forum and opportunity for industrial experts, scholars, and Ph.D. students to discuss their interests on collaborative (embedded) systems development.

J. Münch and M. Vierimaa (Eds.): PROFES 2006, LNCS 4034, p. 454, 2006.

Software Product Metrics – Goal-Oriented Software Product Measurement

Jürgen Münch and Dirk Hamann

Fraunhofer Institute For Experimental Software Engineering
Fraunhofer Platz 1, 67663 Kaiserslautern
Germany
muench@iese.fraunhofer.de,
hamann@iese.fraunhofer.de

Abstract. Quality is measurable – also in the case of software. Properly introduced metrics are the basis for efficient project- and quality management. This tutorial presents the basic concepts of measurement and gives guidelines on how to apply measurement in practice. Numerous examples included in the tutorial help quality managers, developers, and project leaders to understand the concepts presented and to select optimal metric sets for their specific organizational needs.

1 Introduction to Software Measurement

The tutorial starts with a short overview of measurement basics. It presents, for instance, different metrics classifications, measurement scales and their limitations, as well as quality models that use metrics as an input for the purpose of quality evaluation. This part of the tutorial also presents a measurement process, which consists of three major phases: definition, data collection, and data analysis. The structure of the concepts presented in this part of the tutorial is as follows:

- What are reasons for applying measurement and quantitative analysis of software processes und products?
- Basis of measurement and quantitative analysis
    - Types of metrics, scale
    - Measurement process
    - Metrics, context factors, influence factors
- Fixed quality models compared to self-defined quality models
    - The ISO 9126 quality model
    - Goal-Question-Metric (GQM) paradigm

2 Basic Metrics

The second part of the tutorial presents basic (core) metrics that have proven, in practice, to be good predictors of various software qualities. The metrics presented include example metrics of size, complexity, defect, and time. The structure of the concepts presented in this part of the tutorial is as follows:

J. Münch and M. Vierimaa (Eds.): PROFES 2006, LNCS 4034, pp. 455–457, 2006.

Metrics

- Size (Lines of Code, Function Points)
- Complexity (coupling, inheritance)
- Defects (defect metrics, defect classification)
- Time

3 Derived and Complex Metrics

The third part of the tutorial presents complex metrics derived from the basic metrics. Typical application scenarios of these metrics are also presented. The structure of concepts presented in this part of the tutorial is as follows:

- Maintainability
    - Indicators of maintainability (self-defined quality model)
    - Maintainability index (complex metrics)
- Reliability
    - Failures
    - Fault-proneness
    - Defect density
- Productivity

4 Data Analysis and Interpretation

The last part of the tutorial deals with the analysis of measurement. It presents an overview of the most common data analysis and visualization techniques. It also provides guidelines on how to choose appropriate techniques. Finally, examples of analysis and visualization tools are presented. The structure of concepts presented in this part of the tutorial is as follows:

- Data collection tools
- Data analysis techniques
- Data preprocessing
    - Data analysis (statistics, data mining)
    - Presentation of data and analysis results
- Tool support (data analysis and visualization)

5 Presenters´ Background

Jürgen Münch is Department Head for Processes and Measurement at the Fraunhofer Institute for Experimental Software Engineering (IESE) in Kaiserslautern, Germany. From November 2001 to December 2003, Dr. Münch was an executive board member of the temporary research institute SFB 501 "Development of Large Systems with Generic Methods" funded by the German Research Foundation (DFG). Dr.

Münch received his PhD degree (Dr. rer. nat.) in Computer Science from the University of Kaiserslautern, Germany. Dr. Münch's research interests in software engineering include: (1) modeling and measurement of software processes and resulting products, (2) software quality assurance and control, (3) technology evaluation through experimental means and simulation, (4) generic methods for the development of large systems, (5) technology transfer methods. He has been teaching and training in both university and industry environments, and also has significant R&D project management experience. Jürgen Münch is a member of IEEE, the IEEE Computer Society, and the German Computer Society (GI), a member of the program committee of various software engineering conferences, and has published more than 50 international publications.

Dirk Hamann did his study and PhD in the Computer Science department at the University of Kaiserslautern. He is working as project manager in national and international research projects in the area of software process definition, process deployment, process improvement as well as project and quality management at the Fraunhofer Institute for Experimental Software Engineering (IESE) in Kaiserslautern, Germany. In industrial technology transfer and consultancy projects, he has led numerous process assessment, process improvement and measurement projects, mainly in the automotive and banking/insurance sector. Since 2000, he is accredited by the QAI-USA as Competent SPICE Assessor, allowing him also to educate and train assessors according to ISO/IEC 15504.

References

1. Basili, V.; Weiss, D.: A Methodology for Collecting Valid Software Engineering Data, In: IEEE Transactions on Software Engineering, SE-10(6):728-738, 1984.
2. Birk, A.; Hamann, D.; Hartkopf, S.: A Framework for the Continuous Monitoring and Evaluation of Improvement Programmes. In: Oivo, Markku (Ed.) u.a.: Second International Conference on Product Focused Software Process Improvement. Profes'2000 - Proceedings. Berlin : Springer-Verlag, 2000, 20-35
3. Briand, Lionel C.; Differding, Christiane; Rombach, H. Dieter: Practical Guidelines for Measurement-Based Process Improvement. In: Software Process - Improvement and Practice 2 (1996), 4, 253-280
4. Münch, Jürgen; Heidrich, Jens, "Software Project Control Centers: Concepts and Approaches", International Journal of Systems and Software, vol. 70, issues 1-2, pp. 3-19, February 2004.
5. Münch, Jürgen; Heidrich, Jens„ "Tool-based Software Project Controlling", In: Handbook of Software Engineering and Knowledge Engineering, Vol. 3: Recent Advances", (S. K. Chang, ed.), World Scientific Publishing Company, pp. 477-512, August 2005.
6. Solingen, Rini van; Berghout, Egon: The Goal/ Question/ Metric Method. A Practical Guide for Quality Improvement of Software Development. London: McGraw-Hill, 1999

Art and Science of System Release Planning

Günther Ruhe and Omolade Saliu

Software Engineering Decision Support Lab
University of Calgary
2500 University Drive, NW
Calgary, AB T2N 1N4, Canada
ruhe@ucalgary.ca, saliu@cpsc.ucalgary.ca
http://sern.ucalgary.ca/~ruhe/,
http://cpsc.ucalgary.ca/~saliu/SEDS/Main.html

Abstract. Informed and qualified decisions are key factors for project failure or success. The idea of decision support always arises when timely decisions must be made in unstructured or semi-structured problem domains, where multiple stakeholders are involved, and when the information available is uncertain. Release planning (RP) addresses decisions related to the selection and assignment of features to a sequence of consecutive product releases such that the most important technical, resource, budget, and risk constraints are met. Release planning is an important and integral part of any type of incremental product development. The objective of this tutorial is to describe and position the 'art and science' of software release planning. The "art of release planning" refers to relying on human intuition, communication, and capabilities to negotiate between conflicting objectives and constraints. The "science of release planning" refers to emphasizing formalization of the problem and applying computational algorithms to generate best solutions. Both art and science are important for achieving meaningful release planning results. We investigate the release planning process and propose a hybrid planning approach that integrates the strength of computational intelligence with the knowledge and experience of human experts.

1 Presenters´ Background

Dr. Günther Ruhe is an iCORE (Informatics Circle of Research Excellence) professor and the Industrial Research Chair in Software Engineering at the University of Calgary. His research interests include software engineering decision support, software release planning, requirements and COTS selection, measurement, simulation, and empirical research. From 1996 until 2001 he was deputy director of the Fraunhofer Institute for Experimental Software Engineering in Kaiserslautern, Germany. He is the author of two books, several book chapters, and more than 140 publications. He is a member of the ACM, IEEE Computer Society, and German Computer Society GI. Dr. Ruhe has been PC member and/or PC chair of various conferences and workshops in many areas of software engineering and knowledge engineering. He has organized and chaired several workshops on software engineering decision support. He is a member of the Editorial Board of several international journals in the area of Knowledge Engineering, Software Engineering, Hybrid Intelligence, Cognitive Informatics, and Advanced Intelligence.

J. Münch and M. Vierimaa (Eds.): PROFES 2006, LNCS 4034, pp. 458–461, 2006.

Omolade Saliu is a PhD candidate and an iCORE (Informatics Circle of Research Excellence) scholar in the Computer Science Department at the University of Calgary, Canada. He has two years of industrial experience as a systems analyst. His research interests include software metrics and measurement, software engineering decision support, software process-related issues, and soft computing. He received his MS in computer science from King Fahd University of Petroleum & Minerals, Saudi Arabia. Omolade is a member of the IEEE and Computer Society. He is a PC member of the 2006 HICSS-39 workshop on Strategic Software Engineering. He is currently the vice President Operations of the Software Engineering Consulting Consortium (SECCO) at the University of Calgary, Canada.

2 Research Design

The main goal of the tutorial is to give a comprehensive overview of methods and techniques for performing release planning as part of incremental software development. The whole perspective here is on decisions to be made and how these decisions can be supported to make them more qualified.

What will the participants learn from the tutorial?

- The paradigm of software engineering decision support and its application to software release planning
- State-of-the art and state-of-the practice in software release planning
- The two fundamental approaches called art and science
- The synergy of art and science for release planning
- Case study project from Telecom
- Release planning for evolving systems

3 Scope

This tutorial is aimed at project managers who want to know about the possible support that they can get outside the existing state of practice. Also, it targets business customers who are interested in participating in the release planning process , while protecting their preferences without physical meetings. Software development professionals and academics would also benefit from the technical aspects of the discussion. No prior experience in performing release planning nor any background in computational algorithms is necessary.

4 Summary of Contents

4.1 Paradigm of Software Engineering Decision Support

The idea of decision support always arises when timely decisions must be made in unstructured or semi-structured problem domains, where multiple stakeholders are involved, and when the information available is uncertain. Decision support under these circumstances to us means all activities and techniques that would [1]:

- facilitate understanding and structuring of the problem under investigation
- help in understanding the information needed for making good decisions
- bring the concerns of relevant stakeholders to bear and allow them to contribute to the decision-making process
- generate, evaluate, and prioritize solution alternatives, and
- explain solution alternatives

4.2 Software Release Planning

The inability of humans to cope well with complex decisions involving competing and conflicting goals in software engineering suggests the need for supplementary decision support [1]. When considering problems involving several hundreds of features and large numbers of widely distributed stakeholders, it becomes very hard to find appropriate solutions without appropriate decision support. Instantiation of the release planning problem as a decision problem would be discussed in this tutorial.

4.3 Solution Approaches

This tutorial will present two approaches to release planning. First, the art of release planning approach, which relies on human intuition, communication, and capabilities to negotiate between conflicting objectives and constraints. Secondly, the science of release planning, which that formalizes the problem and applies computational algorithms to generate best solutions. The art-based approach has trouble coping with the RP problem's complexity as the number of factors grows. The science-based approach copes better with complexity but cannot evaluate the problem with the same analytical abilities as the human decision-maker. [2]

4.4 Release Planning for Evolving Systems

The tutorial would finally present an analysis of characteristics that constitute extra challenges for release planning of evolving software systems. As evolving systems demand the analysis of each feature in light of the components of existing system before feature selection and scheduling decisions, we will discuss an extended model of the marriage above that assists in integrating information and knowledge about existing system architecture into release planning decisions [4].

5 Structure of Contents

This tutorial discusses the following:

1. Introduce the paradigm of software engineering decision support
2. Discuss the release planning problem and characterize the difficulties involved
3. Release planning guidelines and process framework
4. Discusse the reasons for the pervasiveness of ad hoc planning strategies
5. Challenges involved in managing cognitive and computational complexities
6. The marriage of art and science of planning to provide appropriate decision support

7. Release planning with evolving systems dimension
8. Example projects, Case studies discussions, and Experience reports
9. Interactive session involving participants in the process
10. Summary and Conclusions

References

[1] Ruhe, G. Software Engineering Decision Support – Methodology and Applications. In: Tonfoni and Jain (Eds.) *Innovations in Decision Support Systems*, (2003), 143-174.

[2] Ruhe, G. and Saliu, O. The Art and Science of Software Release Planning. *IEEE Software*, 22, 6 (Nov/Dec 2005), In press.

[3] Ruhe, G. and Ngo-The, A. Hybrid Intelligence in Software Release Planning. International Journal of Hybrid Intelligence Systems, 1, 2, (2004), 99-110.

[4] Saliu, O. and Ruhe, G. Software Release Planning for Evolving Systems. *Innovations in Systems and Software Engineering: a NASA Journal,* 1, 2 (Sep. 2005), 189-204.

Multiple Risk Management Process Supported by Ontology

Cristine Martins Gomes de Gusmão[1,2] and Hermano Perrelli de Moura[1]

[1] Centro de Informática – Universidade Federal de Pernambuco (UFPE)
Caixa Postal 7851 – 50.732-970 – Recife – PE – Brazil
[2] Curso de Bacharelado em Sistemas de Informação – Faculdade Integrada do Recife (FIR)
Recife – PE – Brazil
{cmgg, hermano}@cin.ufpe.br
http://www.cin.ufpe.br/~hermano/gp2

Abstract. Multiple Projects Development Environments have evolved recently. However, most available environments do not provide risk management process support to the project manager's activities. This support could be provided through the analysis of the interactions between projects. One of the main weaknesses of the approaches up to now is that risk management process improvement based on the risks between ongoing projects and completed ones is being neglected. In this light, we propose the creation of a Risk Management Model for Multiple Project Environments to treat the risk interactions between projects.

1 Introduction

Software development projects, given their diverse and abstract nature, offer unique challenges and risks [Boehm and DeMarco 1997]. According to the Standish Group Report, "CHAOS: A Recipe for Success", only 28 percent of all software projects in 2000 were on time and within budget and had all planned features [Murthi 2002] – which means that the other 76 percent of projects failed or did not meet specified goals.

The increasing competition on the market and the challenging expectations of the clients´ requirements force the software developing organizations to closely manage their risks [Gusmão and Moura 2004]. Several risk management approaches [Charette 1990, Humphrey 1990, Boehm 1991, Higuera 1994, Chapman and Ward 1997, Kontio 1998, Jacobson 1999, Barros 2001] have been introduced during the past two decades. While some organizations defined their own risk management approaches, others do not manage their risks explicitly and systematically [Gusmão and Moura 2004]. Risk management based on intuition and individual efforts alone is rarely effective and consistent. Risk management is necessary during both project management and software development operations.

Whereas most research has focused on managing technical and project risks in software development projects, there are many other components of software development projects or multiple projects environments that are currently not being evaluated and managed effectively [Gusmão and Moura 2004]. Risk is always involved

J. Münch and M. Vierimaa (Eds.): PROFES 2006, LNCS 4034, pp. 462 – 465, 2006.

with loss, but also considers the possibility that the outcome of certain risks might be a gain.

In Multiple Projects Environments, the project manager has a particular challenge of balancing several projects with a seemingly limitless workload and limited resources, and doing it in a dramatically altered business environment [Dye and Pennypacker 2000]. This kind of difficulty is made worse by the fact that, the organizations managers need to make decisions that probably affect some projects with different lifetimes and resources. Every project decision involves risk because there is always uncertainty information [Moura et al. 2004].

Risk management is the heart of project management, and software product development inevitably requires project management. Risk management must be promoted via dynamic environments that support life cycle project processes based an organization issues. However, most organizations do not provide support to risk management processes, tools for communications, and neither to the project manager´s activities. In this light, this tutorial presents OntoPRIME – risk domain ontology – which supports multiple project environments helping managers to get project risk information in all phases of the software development process.

2 Overall and Detailed Objectives

Unfortunately, some project managers rely on a reactive risk management strategy, that is, merely reacting to risks as they occur. This is even worse in multiple projects environments. A more intelligent strategy is preventive risk management, which is a way to improve the organization´s knowledge about its projects.

Using software multiple projects environments concepts, this tutorial aims to present on Ontology for Project Risk Management to support a multiple project risk management process. Theoretically, the process is based on CMMI – Capability Maturity Model Integrated [SEI 2001], Software Engineering Institute Risk Model [Higuera 1994], Quantitative and Qualitative techniques in risk evaluation [Humphrey 1990], as a way to improve the risk management process in organizations. Using software multiple projects environments and ontologies concepts [Corcho et al. 2001] and based on Taxonomy -based Risk Identification [Carr et al. 1993], we developed the risk domain ontology – *Onto*PRIME.

*Onto*PRIME is an Artificial Intelligence component that helps software teams to evolve their project risk management. It is a part of the Multiple Project Risk Management Model, an artifact development in a doctorate study.

The methodological development is conducted in an action research manner within a real-life systems development project. *Onto*PRIME was modeled in a multidimensional structure to enrich and qualify the processes and stored knowledge.

Although many risk management approaches provide a process to support development software, what is really needed is a common vocabulary to improve and support all information resulting from this process in order to comfortably refer to it and add new contributions. The main idea is to facilitate risk analysis interaction between projects and communication as a way to provide access to the organization´s multitude of project information. Besides, it is a way to develop an organizational knowledge management [Falbo 2004].

2.1 Tutorial Learning Objectives

When completed, the attendee will be able to:

1. Understand the different kinds of risk within organizations.
2. Understand the importance of ontology, which includes the standardization and hierarchical arrangement of concepts.
3. Understand the importance and vantages of managing multiple project risks supported by ontologies as a way to increase knowledge and improve the risk management process.

3 Qualifications of the Instructors

Hermano Perrelli de Moura – Project Management Professional (PMP). PhD in Computing Science, University of Glasgow, Scotland. MSc in Computing Science, Federal University of Pernambuco, Brazil. Electronic Engineering, Pernambuco Federal University, Brazil. Professor of Project Management at Pernambuco Federal University, he has taught many courses on the subject and done consulting on project management for software development projects. Co-founder of Quality Software Processes, a company specialized in software process improvement.

Cristine Martins Gomes de Gusmão – PhD student in Computing Science Program, Risk Management research area, Federal University of Pernambuco. MSc in Computing Science, Federal University of Pernambuco, Brazil. Professor of Project Management and Software Engineering at Faculdade Integrada do Recife, she has taught many courses and presentations about project risk management and developing projects to support risk management processes based on intelligent components.

References

Boehm, B and De Marco, T. Software Risk Management. IEEE – Software. IEEE Computer Society Press. 1997.

Murthi, S. Preventive Risk Management for Software Projects. IEEE – Software. IEEE Computer Society Press. 2002.

Gusmão, C. M. G. e Moura, H. P. Gerência de Risco em Processos de Qualidade de Software: uma Análise Comparativa. Anais do III Simpósio Brasileiro de Qualidade de Software. Brasília – DF – Brasil. 2004.

SEI – Software Engineering Institute -CMMI -Capability Maturity Model Integration version 1.1 Pittsburgh, PA. Software Engineering Institute, Carnegie Mellon University. USA. 2001.

Jacobson, I. The Unified Software Development Process. Addison-Wesley Longman Publishing Co., Boston, MA, USA. 1999.

Corcho, O. et al. OntoWeb. Technical Roadmap v.1.0. Universidad Politécnica de Madrid. 2001.

Dye, L. D and Pennypacker, J. S. Project Portfolio Management and Managing Multiple Projects: Two Sides of the Same Coin? In: The Project Management Institute Annual Seminars & Symposium. Houston, Texas, USA. 2000.

Carr, M. J et al. Taxonomy -Based Risk Identification. Technical Report. Software Engineering Institute. Carnegie Mellon University. 1993

Humphrey, W.S. Managing The Software Process. Addison Wesley, 1990.

Boehm, B. Software Risk Management: principles and practices. In IEEE Software, Vol. 8. No.1, pp 32-41. 1991.

Charette, R. Application strategies for risk analysis. MultiScience Press, New York, USA. 1990.

Chapman, C. and Ward, S. Project Risk Management. John Wiley & Sons. Chichester, UK. 1997.

Higuera, R. P et al. An Introduction to Team Risk Management (version 1.0). Special Report CMU/SEI -94-SR-1, In Software Engineering Institute, Pittsburgh, Pennsylvania, USA. 1994.

Moura et al. Portfolio Management: A Critical View of Risk Factors Balancing. NORDNET - Proceedings of International PM Conference. Helsinki – Finland. 2004.

Falbo, R.A. et al. Learning How to Manage Risk using Organization Knowledge. Proceedings of the 6th International Workshop on Learning Software Organizations -LSO'2004, pp. 7-18. Canada, 2004.

Barros, M. O. Gerenciamento de Projetos baseado em Cenários: Uma Abordagem de Modelagem Dinâmica e Simulação. Doctorate Thesis. Federal University of Rio de Janeiro. 2001.

Kontio, J. et al. Experiences in improving risk management processes using the concepts of the Riskit method, In Proceedings of the Sixth International Symposium on the Foundations of Software Engineering (FSE-6) pp. 163-174. 1998.

Get Your Experience Factory Ready for the Next Decade: Ten Years After "How to Build and Run One"

Frank Bomarius[1] and Raimund L. Feldmann[2]

[1] Fraunhofer Institute for
Experimental Software Engineering (IESE),
Fraunhofer Platz 1,
67663 Kaiserslautern, Germany
Tel.: +49 631 6800 1201
frank.bomarius@iese.fraunhofer.de

[2] Fraunhofer Center for Experimental Software Engineering (CESE) 4321 Hartwick Rd - Suite
500 College Park, 20742 MD, USA
Tel.: +1 301 403 8933
rfeldmann@fc-md.umd.edu

Abstract. Ten years after the presentation of the tutorial "The Experience Factory: How to Build and Run One" at ICSE 17 in 1995 [4], the idea of building such a Learning Software Organization (LSO) is in wide spread use. Meanwhile, the Experience Factory (EF) concept [2], i.e., the systematic goal-oriented utilization of *experience*, is also being successfully applied outside the domain of Software Engineering [11], [12]. However, defining and implementing a successful Experience Factory is still a challenge [9]. In this tutorial we take a look at existing concepts on how to identify and structure the *content* of the experience base (EB), discuss solutions for how to *implement an* EB, and present *processes* on how to setup, run, evaluate, and maintain an EF in an organization. The tutorial is based on the authors' organizations' experiences with implementing EFs in research, industry, and government environments.

Keywords: Experience Factory, Experience Base, Knowledge & Experience Management, Experience-based process improvement.

1 Objectives

The general goal of this tutorial is to provide an overview on how to define and successfully implement a state-of-the-art Experience Factory (EF) infrastructure [2] and how to systematically build up and manage the experience of an organization. Based on our practical experiences (e.g., [5], [8], [11], [12]), we will discuss different aspects ranging from processes via tools and implementation techniques to different EF sizes and scalability. More specifically, the goals of this tutorial are:

- to provide participants with a method for setting the goals of an EF and identifying relevant content to be captured in the Experience Base (EB);
- to describe guidelines and principals on how to organize and structure an EB to effectively support the identified learning processes;

J. Münch and M. Vierimaa (Eds.): PROFES 2006, LNCS 4034, pp. 466–471, 2006.

- to discuss an approach for how participants can tailor EF requirements to their specific organizational needs (e.g., specific environment/domain, distribution, eBiz support);
- to give an overview of candidate implementation technologies and how to select the appropriate ones for incremental implementation of the EF;
- to guide participants in defining necessary processes for running, evaluating, and maintaining the EF;
- to present examples and lessons learned so as to help avoid common problems and pitfalls.

The material included in this tutorial is not limited to the authors' own experiences. Lessons learned and research results regarding EF installations such as [1], [3], [6], [7], [10] are integrated in the approach and presented as examples.

2 Scope

This tutorial aims at industry practitioners, managers, and developers alike, who want to learn more about how to successfully design, implement, and run an EF. Attending this tutorial will help the participants (not only from the software domain) to initially setup or to further develop and improve their organization's EF. Thereby, participants can effectively support improvement activities (such as TQM, ISO 9000, CMMI or SPICE, TSP) to gain competitive advantages. The tutorial will also provide practical guidance on how to evaluate the cost-benefit of an EF in an organization. .

3 Structure of Contents

I Introduction

The introduction sets the stage for understanding the EF concepts and its capabilities as well as its limitations. This includes:

- The "original" EF organization
- What can be expected from an EF
- Common misconceptions

II Example Applications of EF in Today's Organizations

Examples from different domains and of different sizes are presented, thus demonstrating the flexibility and scalability of the EF concept:

- Software engineering research support
- Software process improvement (SPI) support
- Knowledge intensive quality assurance support
- Knowledge portals

III Engineering an EF

This chapter covers all steps from the early identification of stakeholders down to the evolutionary enhancement of a running EF. Topics addressed include:

- Identification of stakeholders
- Assessment of existing processes and available knowledge
- Goal setting, technology selection, and introduction plan
- Techniques for knowledge structuring and representation
- Engineering the EF usage processes
- Prototyping and trial phase
- Incremental enhancement and continuous evaluation
- Deployment
- Planning the next increment

IV Technology

This chapter details a selection from the broad range of implementation techniques that can be successfully applied within an EF. The techniques will be classified regarding their purpose and applicability in different application contexts and organizational settings. Classification is based on issues such as:

- Scalability
- Ease of introduction
- Usability
- Distribution and replication
- Meantime to success
- Cost / benefit

V Additional Materials and References

Examples
- References

4 Presenter's Background

4.1 Prof. Dr. Frank Bomarius

Graduated from the University of Kaiserslautern, Germany, with a major in Computer Science and with a minor in Electrical Engineering in 1986 and received his Ph.D. (Dr. rer. nat.) in Computer Science in 1991. He then worked in an ESPRIT 2 project at the German Research Center for Artificial Intelligence in the area of Multi-Agent Systems. In 1993 he became a team leader and software developer at Tecmath GmbH. Since 1996, he has been head of the department "Competence Management" and since 2000, deputy director of the Fraunhofer Institute for Experimental Software Engineering (IESE). He holds a professorship at the University of Applied Sciences in Kaiserslautern and teaches computer science in the Department of Engineering.

At IESE, Bomarius is transferring continuous, goal-oriented software process improvement (SPI) programs to software organizations in different industrial sectors. He applies the Quality Improvement Paradigm (QIP), the Goal/Question/Metric (GQM), and the Experience Factory (EF) approach. He is doing applied research and technology transfer in the area of Learning Software Organizations (LSO) and introduces EF-based knowledge management into industrial engineering and production settings. His major focus is on the successful integration of knowledge management with existing organizational structures and work processes, alignment with ongoing improvement programs as well as the technical integration of experience bases with an organization's infrastructure.

Frank Bomarius has given numerous presentations at industrial as well as scientific workshops and seminars. He has 10 years of industrial experience and 20 years of experience in teaching and training of students as well as professionals.

He is serving as organizer, program chair and program committee member in national and international conferences and workshops in the area of software process improvement and knowledge management, such as SEKE, PROFES, CONQUEST, Net-ObjectDays, ICCBR and LSO.

Frank Bomarius is a member of the IEEE Computer Society, the German Computer Society (GI) and the Working Group for Artificial Intelligence of the GI, and a member of the board of the regional chapter of the GI.

You can contact him at:

Prof. Dr. Frank Bomarius
Deputy Director
Fraunhofer Institute for
Experimental Software Engineering, (IESE)
Fraunhofer Platz 1,
67663 Kaiserslautern, Germany

Phone +49 6301 6800 1201
Email frank.bomarius@iese.fraunhofer.de

Prof. Dr. Frank Bomarius
Department of Engineering
University of Applied Sciences
Morlauterer Straße 31
67657 Kaiserslautern, Germany

Phone +49 6301 3724 315
Email frank.bomarius@fh-kl.de

4.2 Raimund L. Feldmann

Received his M.S. degree (Diplom) in Computer Science with a minor in Economics from the University of Kaiserslautern, Germany in 1996. His research interests are focused on experience and knowledge repositories and Software Process Improvement (SPI). In 1997, Raimund joined the Software Engineering Research Group (AGSE) headed by Prof. Dr. H. D. Rombach at the University of Kaiserslautern, Germany, as an employee of the strategic grant project 501 "Development of Large Systems with Generic Methods" (SFB 501), funded by the German Science Foundation (DFG). As part of his work, Raimund established the central Experience Base in the SFB 501 Software Engineering Laboratory.

Currently, Raimund Feldmann is the technical lead for Knowledge & Experience Management at the Fraunhofer Center Maryland (CESE). He is actively involved in the definition and development of the US Department of Defense (DoD) Acquisition Best Practice Clearinghouse, a web-based EF for providing Software Engineering and System Engineering best practices for government employees and contractors. Before he joined CESE in 2004, Raimund participated in several technology transfer projects in Germany. Among others projects, he was responsible for the development of the underlying EB of the software-kompetenz.de portal (VSEK), funded by the Ministry of Education and Research (BMBF) of the German Federal Government, to offer up-to-date SE knowledge to Germany´s SMEs. As part of his employment at the University of Kaiserslautern, Raimund taught and organized practical courses and seminars on Software Engineering and Learning in Software Organizations.

Raimund Feldmann is a member of the IEEE Computer Society and of the steering committee for the international LSO (Learning Software Organizations) workshop series.

You can contact him at:
Raimund L. Feldmann
Fraunhofer Center for Experimental Software Engineering, Maryland (CESE)
4321 Hartwick Rd Suite
500 College Park,
MD 20742-3290, USA

Phone: +1 301 403 8933
Fax.: +1 301 403 8976
E-mail: r.feldmann@computer.org

Acknowledgments

This tutorial is based on the initial work of Victor R. Basili, H. Dieter Rombach and Frank McGarry, the fathers of the EF concept. Part of this work is based on previous tutorials by IESE and CESE. We appreciate the effort and support of our past and current colleagues from CESE and from IESE, who contributed to this and the previous tutorials.

References

[1] K. D. Althoff, K. U. Becker, B. Decker, A. Klotz, E. Leopold, J. Rech, and A. Voss: "The indiGo project: enhancement of experience management and process learning with moderated discourses," in Data Mining in Marketing and Medicine, vol. LNCS, P. Perner (Ed), Berlin, Germany, Springer Verlag, 2002, pp. 53-79.

[2] V.R. Basili, G. Caldiera, and H.D. Rombach: Experience Factory. In J.J. Marciniak, editor, Encyclopedia of Software Engineering, volume 1, pages 469–476. John Wiley & Sons, 1994.

[3] V.R. Basili, M. Lindvall, and P. Costa: Implementing the Experience Factory concepts as a set of Experience Bases. In Proceedings of the Thirteenth Conference on Software Engineering and Knowledge Engineering (SEKE), pages 102–109, Buenos Aires, Argentinia, June 2001.

[4] V.R. Basili and F.E. McGarry: The Experience Factory: How to Build and Run One. Tutorial given at the 17th International Conference on Software Engineering (ICSE17), Seattle, Washington, USA, April 1995.

[5] F. Bomarius and G. Ruhe: Learning Software Organization – Methodology and Applications. Lecture Notes in Computer Science # 1756, Springer Verlag, November 2000.
[6] K. Dangle, L. Dwinnell, J. Hickok, and R. Turner: Introducing the Department of Defense Acquisition Best Practices Clearinghouse. CrossTalk, May 2005, pp. 4.
[7] B. Decker, et al: A Framework for Agile Reuse in Software Engineering using Wiki Technology. KMDAP Workshop 2005: Knowledge Management for Distributed Agile Processes, Kaiserslautern, Germany, 2005.
[8] R.L. Feldmann and M. Pizka: An on-line software engineering repository for Germany's SME - an experience report. Advances in Learning Software Organizations. 4th International Workshop (LSO 2002), Chicago, IL, USA, 6 Aug. 2002.
[9] A. Koennecker, R. Jeffery, and G. Low: Lessons Learned from the Failure of an Experience Base Initiative Using Bottom-up Development Paradigm. In Proceedings of the 24th Annual Software Engineering Workshop (SWE24), Greenbelt, Maryland, USA, December 1999.
[10] C. Tautz: Customizing Software Engineering Experience Management Systems to Organizational Needs. PhD Thesis, Dept. of Computer Science, University of Kaiserslautern, Kaiserslautern, Germany, 2000. Published in 2001 by Fraunhofer IRB Verlag, Stuttgart, Germany, ISBN 3-8167-5881-9
[11] http://www.bridgeit.de/
[12] http://www.checkmate-online.de/

Author Index

Lecture Notes in Computer Science

For information about Vols. 1–3920

please contact your bookseller or Springer

Vol. 4039: M. Morisio (Ed.), Reuse of Off-the-Shelf Components. XIII, 444 pages. 2006.

Vol. 4034: J. Münch, M. Vierimaa (Eds.), Product-Focused Software Process Improvement. XVII, 474 pages. 2006.

Vol. 4027: H.L. Larsen, G. Pasi, D. Ortiz-Arroyo, T. Andreasen, H. Christiansen (Eds.), Flexible Query Answering Systems. XVIII, 714 pages. 2006. (Sublibrary LNAI).

Vol. 4024: S. Donatelli, P. S. Thiagarajan (Eds.), Petri Nets and Other Models of Concurrency - ICATPN 2006. XI, 441 pages. 2006.

Vol. 4021: E. André, L. Dybkjær, W. Minker, H. Neumann, M. Weber (Eds.), Perception and Interactive Technologies. XI, 217 pages. 2006. (Sublibrary LNAI).

Vol. 4011: Y. Sure, J. Domingue (Eds.), The Semantic Web: Research and Applications. XIX, 726 pages. 2006.

Vol. 4010: S. Dunne, B. Stoddart (Eds.), Unifying Theories of Programming. VIII, 257 pages. 2006.

Vol. 4007: C. Àlvarez, M. Serna (Eds.), Experimental Algorithms. XI, 329 pages. 2006.

Vol. 4006: L.M. Pinho, M. González Harbour (Eds.), Reliable Software Technologies – Ada-Europe 2006. XII, 241 pages. 2006.

Vol. 4004: S. Vaudenay (Ed.), Advances in Cryptology - EUROCRYPT 2006. XIV, 613 pages. 2006.

Vol. 4003: Y. Koucheryavy, J. Harju, V.B. Iversen (Eds.), Next Generation Teletraffic and Wired/Wireless Advanced Networking. XVI, 582 pages. 2006.

Vol. 4001: E. Dubois, K. Pohl (Eds.), Advanced Information Systems Engineering. XVI, 560 pages. 2006.

Vol. 3999: C. Kop, G. Fliedl, H.C. Mayr, E. Métais (Eds.), Natural Language Processing and Information Systems. XIII, 227 pages. 2006.

Vol. 3998: T. Calamoneri, I. Finocchi, G.F. Italiano (Eds.), Algorithms and Complexity. XII, 394 pages. 2006.

Vol. 3997: W. Grieskamp, C. Weise (Eds.), Formal Approaches to Software Testing. XII, 219 pages. 2006.

Vol. 3996: A. Keller, J.-P. Martin-Flatin (Eds.), Self-Managed Networks, Systems, and Services. X, 185 pages. 2006.

Vol. 3995: G. Müller (Ed.), Emerging Trends in Information and Communication Security. XX, 524 pages. 2006.

Vol. 3994: V.N. Alexandrov, G.D. van Albada, P.M.A. Sloot, J. Dongarra (Eds.), Computational Science – ICCS 2006, Part IV. XXXV, 1096 pages. 2006.

Vol. 3993: V.N. Alexandrov, G.D. van Albada, P.M.A. Sloot, J. Dongarra (Eds.), Computational Science – ICCS 2006, Part III. XXXVI, 1136 pages. 2006.

Vol. 3992: V.N. Alexandrov, G.D. van Albada, P.M.A. Sloot, J. Dongarra (Eds.), Computational Science – ICCS 2006, Part II. XXXV, 1122 pages. 2006.

Vol. 3991: V.N. Alexandrov, G.D. van Albada, P.M.A. Sloot, J. Dongarra (Eds.), Computational Science – ICCS 2006, Part I. LXXXI, 1096 pages. 2006.

Vol. 3990: J. C. Beck, B.M. Smith (Eds.), Integration of AI and OR Techniques in Constraint Programming for Combinatorial Optimization Problems. X, 301 pages. 2006.

Vol. 3989: J. Zhou, M. Yung, F. Bao, Applied Cryptography and Network Security. XIV, 488 pages. 2006.

Vol. 3987: M. Hazas, J. Krumm, T. Strang (Eds.), Location- and Context-Awareness. X, 289 pages. 2006.

Vol. 3986: K. Stølen, W.H. Winsborough, F. Martinelli, F. Massacci (Eds.), Trust Management. XIV, 474 pages. 2006.

Vol. 3984: M. Gavrilova, O. Gervasi, V. Kumar, C.J. K. Tan, D. Taniar, A. Laganà, Y. Mun, H. Choo (Eds.), Computational Science and Its Applications - ICCSA 2006, Part V. XXV, 1045 pages. 2006.

Vol. 3983: M. Gavrilova, O. Gervasi, V. Kumar, C.J. K. Tan, D. Taniar, A. Laganà, Y. Mun, H. Choo (Eds.), Computational Science and Its Applications - ICCSA 2006, Part IV. XXVI, 1191 pages. 2006.

Vol. 3982: M. Gavrilova, O. Gervasi, V. Kumar, C.J. K. Tan, D. Taniar, A. Laganà, Y. Mun, H. Choo (Eds.), Computational Science and Its Applications - ICCSA 2006, Part III. XXV, 1243 pages. 2006.

Vol. 3981: M. Gavrilova, O. Gervasi, V. Kumar, C.J. K. Tan, D. Taniar, A. Laganà, Y. Mun, H. Choo (Eds.), Computational Science and Its Applications - ICCSA 2006, Part II. XXVI, 1255 pages. 2006.

Vol. 3980: M. Gavrilova, O. Gervasi, V. Kumar, C.J. K. Tan, D. Taniar, A. Laganà, Y. Mun, H. Choo (Eds.), Computational Science and Its Applications - ICCSA 2006, Part I. LXXV, 1199 pages. 2006.

Vol. 3979: T.S. Huang, N. Sebe, M.S. Lew, V. Pavlović, M. Kölsch, A. Galata, B. Kisačanin (Eds.), Computer Vision in Human-Computer Interaction. XII, 121 pages. 2006.

Vol. 3978: B. Hnich, M. Carlsson, F. Fages, F. Rossi (Eds.), Recent Advances in Constraints. VIII, 179 pages. 2006. (Sublibrary LNAI).

Vol. 3976: F. Boavida, T. Plagemann, B. Stiller, C. Westphal, E. Monteiro (Eds.), Networking 2006. Networking Technologies, Services, and Protocols; Performance of Computer and Communication Networks; Mobile and Wireless Communications Systems. XXVI, 1276 pages. 2006.

Vol. 3975: S. Mehrotra, D.D. Zeng, H. Chen, B. Thuraisingham, F.-Y. Wang (Eds.), Intelligence and Security Informatics. XXII, 772 pages. 2006.

Vol. 3973: J. Wang, Z. Yi, J.M. Zurada, B.-L. Lu, H. Yin (Eds.), Advances in Neural Networks - ISNN 2006, Part III. XXIX, 1402 pages. 2006.

Vol. 3972: J. Wang, Z. Yi, J.M. Zurada, B.-L. Lu, H. Yin (Eds.), Advances in Neural Networks - ISNN 2006, Part II. XXVII, 1444 pages. 2006.

Vol. 3971: J. Wang, Z. Yi, J.M. Zurada, B.-L. Lu, H. Yin (Eds.), Advances in Neural Networks - ISNN 2006, Part I. LXVII, 1442 pages. 2006.

Vol. 3970: T. Braun, G. Carle, S. Fahmy, Y. Koucheryavy (Eds.), Wired/Wireless Internet Communications. XIV, 350 pages. 2006.

Vol. 3968: K.P. Fishkin, B. Schiele, P. Nixon, A. Quigley (Eds.), Pervasive Computing. XV, 402 pages. 2006.

Vol. 3967: D. Grigoriev, J. Harrison, E.A. Hirsch (Eds.), Computer Science – Theory and Applications. XVI, 684 pages. 2006.

Vol. 3966: Q. Wang, D. Pfahl, D.M. Raffo, P. Wernick (Eds.), Software Process Change. XIV, 356 pages. 2006.

Vol. 3965: M. Bernardo, A. Cimatti (Eds.), Formal Methods for Hardware Verification. VII, 243 pages. 2006.

Vol. 3964: M. Ü. Uyar, A.Y. Duale, M.A. Fecko (Eds.), Testing of Communicating Systems. XI, 373 pages. 2006.

Vol. 3963: O. Dikenelli, M.-P. Gleizes, A. Ricci (Eds.), Engineering Societies in the Agents World VI. X, 303 pages. 2006. (Sublibrary LNAI).

Vol. 3962: W. IJsselsteijn, Y. de Kort, C. Midden, B. Eggen, E. van den Hoven (Eds.), Persuasive Technology. XII, 216 pages. 2006.

Vol. 3960: R. Vieira, P. Quaresma, M.d.G.V. Nunes, N.J. Mamede, C. Oliveira, M.C. Dias (Eds.), Computational Processing of the Portuguese Language. XII, 274 pages. 2006. (Sublibrary LNAI).

Vol. 3959: J.-Y. Cai, S. B. Cooper, A. Li (Eds.), Theory and Applications of Models of Computation. XV, 794 pages. 2006.

Vol. 3958: M. Yung, Y. Dodis, A. Kiayias, T. Malkin (Eds.), Public Key Cryptography - PKC 2006. XIV, 543 pages. 2006.

Vol. 3956: G. Barthe, B. Grégoire, M. Huisman, J.-L. Lanet (Eds.), Construction and Analysis of Safe, Secure, and Interoperable Smart Devices. IX, 175 pages. 2006.

Vol. 3955: G. Antoniou, G. Potamias, C. Spyropoulos, D. Plexousakis (Eds.), Advances in Artificial Intelligence. XVII, 611 pages. 2006. (Sublibrary LNAI).

Vol. 3954: A. Leonardis, H. Bischof, A. Pinz (Eds.), Computer Vision – ECCV 2006, Part IV. XVII, 613 pages. 2006.

Vol. 3953: A. Leonardis, H. Bischof, A. Pinz (Eds.), Computer Vision – ECCV 2006, Part III. XVII, 649 pages. 2006.

Vol. 3952: A. Leonardis, H. Bischof, A. Pinz (Eds.), Computer Vision – ECCV 2006, Part II. XVII, 661 pages. 2006.

Vol. 3951: A. Leonardis, H. Bischof, A. Pinz (Eds.), Computer Vision – ECCV 2006, Part I. XXXV, 639 pages. 2006.

Vol. 3950: J.P. Müller, F. Zambonelli (Eds.), Agent-Oriented Software Engineering VI. XVI, 249 pages. 2006.

Vol. 3947: Y.-C. Chung, J.E. Moreira (Eds.), Advances in Grid and Pervasive Computing. XXI, 667 pages. 2006.

Vol. 3946: T.R. Roth-Berghofer, S. Schulz, D.B. Leake (Eds.), Modeling and Retrieval of Context. XI, 149 pages. 2006. (Sublibrary LNAI).

Vol. 3945: M. Hagiya, P. Wadler (Eds.), Functional and Logic Programming. X, 295 pages. 2006.

Vol. 3944: J. Quiñonero-Candela, I. Dagan, B. Magnini, F. d'Alché-Buc (Eds.), Machine Learning Challenges. XIII, 462 pages. 2006. (Sublibrary LNAI).

Vol. 3943: N. Guelfi, A. Savidis (Eds.), Rapid Integration of Software Engineering Techniques. X, 289 pages. 2006.

Vol. 3942: Z. Pan, R. Aylett, H. Diener, X. Jin, S. Göbel, L. Li (Eds.), Technologies for E-Learning and Digital Entertainment. XXV, 1396 pages. 2006.

Vol. 3941: S.W. Gilroy, M.D. Harrison (Eds.), Interactive Systems. XI, 267 pages. 2006.

Vol. 3940: C. Saunders, M. Grobelnik, S. Gunn, J. Shawe-Taylor (Eds.), Subspace, Latent Structure and Feature Selection. X, 209 pages. 2006.

Vol. 3939: C. Priami, L. Cardelli, S. Emmott (Eds.), Transactions on Computational Systems Biology IV. VII, 141 pages. 2006. (Sublibrary LNBI).

Vol. 3936: M. Lalmas, A. MacFarlane, S. Rüger, A. Tombros, T. Tsikrika, A. Yavlinsky (Eds.), Advances in Information Retrieval. XIX, 584 pages. 2006.

Vol. 3935: D. Won, S. Kim (Eds.), Information Security and Cryptology - ICISC 2005. XIV, 458 pages. 2006.

Vol. 3934: J.A. Clark, R.F. Paige, F.A. C. Polack, P.J. Brooke (Eds.), Security in Pervasive Computing. X, 243 pages. 2006.

Vol. 3933: F. Bonchi, J.-F. Boulicaut (Eds.), Knowledge Discovery in Inductive Databases. VIII, 251 pages. 2006.

Vol. 3931: B. Apolloni, M. Marinaro, G. Nicosia, R. Tagliaferri (Eds.), Neural Nets. XIII, 370 pages. 2006.

Vol. 3930: D.S. Yeung, Z.-Q. Liu, X.-Z. Wang, H. Yan (Eds.), Advances in Machine Learning and Cybernetics. XXI, 1110 pages. 2006. (Sublibrary LNAI).

Vol. 3929: W. MacCaull, M. Winter, I. Düntsch (Eds.), Relational Methods in Computer Science. VIII, 263 pages. 2006.

Vol. 3928: J. Domingo-Ferrer, J. Posegga, D. Schreckling (Eds.), Smart Card Research and Advanced Applications. XI, 359 pages. 2006.

Vol. 3927: J. Hespanha, A. Tiwari (Eds.), Hybrid Systems: Computation and Control. XII, 584 pages. 2006.

Vol. 3925: A. Valmari (Ed.), Model Checking Software. X, 307 pages. 2006.

Vol. 3924: P. Sestoft (Ed.), Programming Languages and Systems. XII, 343 pages. 2006.

Vol. 3923: A. Mycroft, A. Zeller (Eds.), Compiler Construction. XIII, 277 pages. 2006.

Vol. 3922: L. Baresi, R. Heckel (Eds.), Fundamental Approaches to Software Engineering. XIII, 427 pages. 2006.

Vol. 3921: L. Aceto, A. Ingólfsdóttir (Eds.), Foundations of Software Science and Computation Structures. XV, 447 pages. 2006.